Juvenile
Sexual Offenders

Juvenile
Sexual Offenders

A Comprehensive Guide
to Risk Evaluation

Phil Rich

WILEY

John Wiley & Sons, Inc.

Library of Congress Cataloging-in-Publication Data:

Rich, Phil.
    Juvenile sexual offenders: a comprehensive guide to risk evaluation/by Phil Rich.
        p.; cm.
    Includes bibliographical references and index.
    ISBN 978-0-470-20633-1 (cloth: alk. paper)
    1. Teenage sex offenders–Risk assessment. 2. Teenage sex offenders–Evaluation. I. Title.
    [DNLM: 1. Juvenile Delinquency–psychology. 2. Sex Offenses–psychology. 3. Adolescent.
    4. Child. 5. Models, Psychological. 6. Risk Assessment. WS 463 R499j 2009]
RJ506.S48R528 2009
364.15'30835–dc22   2008026323

Contents

Acknowledgments

T HANK YOU TO John Wiley & Sons for your continued support and confidence in my work. A special thanks to Deborah Schindlar, Senior Production Editor; Sweta Gupta, Editorial Program Coordinator; and Lisa Gebo, Senior Editor. Lisa worked hard to get the ball rolling with this particular book, and I very much enjoyed the afternoon we spent together in California discussing the book and getting to know one another.

As always, many thanks to Kathleen Lovenbury, executive director of Stetson School and Kerry-Ann Goldsmith, the former program director of Stetson School, for their unflagging support, confidence, opportunities provided, and, not least of all, their friendship and warmth. Thank you also to all of the many staff at Stetson School, across its entire operation, for their very hard work, their enthusiasm, their energy, and their commitment to working with sometimes enormously difficult children and adolescents, and for the great support, encouragement, and guidance they offer those children. A special thanks, of course, to all of our clinicians, those there now and those who have worked at Stetson over the years, and in light of this book a particular thanks to those Stetson School clinicians who have developed expertise in conducting comprehensive risk assessments, and in so doing have taught me a great deal about the process of risk assessment. Thank you so much.

Finally, as always I thank my very close friend, Bev Sevier, who also happens to be my wife, for always putting up with me and accepting the risks and hazards of living with me. And also, as always, a special acknowledgment to my daughter, Kaye Sevier, who in entering young adulthood has endured and weathered many of the risks that children and adolescents face in our world and who has come through these well, as a confident, bright, capable young adult ready to tackle the world, and a terrific musician on top of that!

Comprehensive Risk Evaluation of Juvenile Sexual Offenders: Understanding and Assessing Risk

I N PRACTICE, RISK assessment is neither straightforward nor easily under- stood. Neither is it necessarily accurate in terms of an assurance that the prognostication (or assignment) of risk is an iron clad and certain description of future behavior upon which we can depend. This is, of course, why it's called "risk," because the process of risk prediction always identifies concerns about what *might* happen, and conditions that create liability for harm, and not what *will* happen. This is of special importance because the very concept of risk implies the possibility that something harmful may occur at some point in the future, almost always involving consequences to people.

When we approach the question of whether someone may behave in a manner that places others at risk we should be aware of two special con- cerns. First, the possible harm that this individual may cause to others, and thus a concern for public safety and well-being. Furthermore, criminal harm to others has consequences far beyond the abuse perpetrated against one individual; it also often harms their families and their communities, as well as our social fabric, including our norms, culture, and values. In this regard, the aim of risk assessment is to ensure and protect public safety at both the level of the individual and at the macro level of social order and culture.

A second concern, which should also be of great, and perhaps equal, importance, is the well being of every individual in our society, including the individual whom we are assessing. This is no small matter. Indeed, with regard to this very point, the values of society are embodied within the

1

U.S. and British criminal justice systems. Named for William Blackstone, the 18th century English jurist, "Blackstone's ratio," as it is often known, is that it is better that 10 guilty persons escape than that one innocent person suffer. This idea, that it is more important to let a guilty party go free than condemn an innocent party, is central to the core of our social order and sense of justice, and central to tenets of due process in U.S. law.

There is, of course, great risk in letting a guilty person go free from several perspectives, including both the harm he or she may have already done in terms of both retributive and restorative justice and the harm he or she may yet do if not held accountable or separated from the community. However, Blackstone's ratio embraces the idea that by possibly convicting an innocent party we do even greater damage, both to the individual falsely convicted and condemned and also to the far larger social order. In our society, we have taken the position that it is better to protect the rights of all people than risk damaging a single individual who is actually innocent. A similar precept is also embedded into our medical system, including our model of mental health, which embraces the idea, *primum non nocere,* or "first, do no harm." The idea is similar to that expressed by Blackstone in that we recognize avoiding harm as a prime directive, even while attempting to correct a problem. In modern day medicine, we talk about iatrogenic injury, or an injury resulting from the diagnosis or the treatment of another injury.

We should be cautious, then, and recognize the possible injury to both the individual and society in assessing risk if we make an incorrect determination of risk in either direction. For instance, when we inaccurately estimate risk and assume all is well when, in fact, all is not well, we have produced a *false negative.* Imagine being told that you don't have a life-threatening cancer and no further treatment is needed when, actually, you have a serious medical condition that may cost your life if not treated. This is a false negative. On the other hand, we produce a *false positive* if we determine that a high risk exists (or any level of risk, for that matter) when there is actually no risk at all, or harm is quite unlikely. Returning to the cancer example, the risk here is to the individual who is provided invasive medical treatment when no treatment at all, or a much less intense level of treatment, is required. With respect to false negatives in assessing risk for a sexual reoffense, the risk is to the public. In the case of the false positive, the risk is to the individual who has been incorrectly assessed as being at high risk for continued sexually abusive behavior when he or she is actually at little to no risk at all. Here, we are reminded of the medical directive and keep in mind Hippocrates' admonition in his *Epidemics,* in which he wrote "As to diseases—make a habit of two things—to help, or at least to do no harm."

One idea, then, for the risk assessor to bear in mind is the sensitive nature and the possible damage that may be unintentionally done to the individual, the public, and the larger society in the process of risk assessment. This is especially likely if the process of risk assessment is not well informed. Thus, one goal of this book is to help clinicians assessing risk, as well as those who read and use risk assessments, to become more sensitive to these concerns and better informed in their understanding and their practice. This is equally relevant for both those who assess risk for sexually abusive behavior in children and adolescents and those who assess risk in adult sexual offenders.

However, despite the relevance of many of these ideas to the risk assessment process in general, this is a book about the assessment of risk in juveniles. Although there are many similarities to the assessment of adults, overall the assessment of risk in young people is very different. This is perhaps also true of the final purpose of the assessment, which is not simply about risk but, more to the point, and especially in juveniles, what to do about risk and how to reduce it. Risk in children and adolescents must be considered and practiced with the understanding that these are persons-in-development and in many respects a moving target, changing and with the potential to change from year to year in their capacities, attitudes, sense of self and others, and neurology. The child may well be the father of the man, as Wordsworth declared in his poem,[1] but nevertheless is not yet adult nor full grown, and, as we shall see, trajectory, context, and development are key in the assessment of juvenile sexual offenders. That is, if remaining on the same path, absent of change, who might the juvenile become and what might the juvenile do as he or she ages into adulthood? How can the juvenile's behavior be understood in the context of various shaping forces, both internal and social; who is the juvenile now, and what are the past and current influences on his or her development? What effects are physical and social developments likely to have on the juvenile as he or she continues to near and enter adulthood?

This book aims to describe our current thinking about and understanding of risk assessment for sexually abusive youth and to help further develop ideas and standards for the practice and administration of such assessments. It is written for professional clinicians and evaluators, focusing throughout on the need for comprehensive assessment at every level, and an integrated model of assessment that not only recognizes the

---

1. The poem is "My heart leaps up when I behold."

subtleties and nuances of the assessment process but also recognizes the whole child as the subject of the evaluation. Its goal, in part, is to provide a comprehensive overview of the process of evaluating juvenile sexual offenders. It focuses on the need for comprehensive assessment and describes in detail the theory, processes, and instrumentation of forensic risk assessment, as well providing clear guidance in how to approach and apply these ideas in the evaluation of risk for sexual reoffense.

The book introduces and describes the need for both theory and guidelines to inform and by which to structure the practice of assessment, and for that matter train and supervise evaluators, and helps further the development of practice standards. Chapter 1, for instance, starts by considering "why assessment?" and the need for those who conduct or read assessments to understand not just purpose of risk assessment, but also its nature, processes, and elements. Indeed, even in this Introduction I hope I have already begun to address this question.

The organization of the book moves from more theoretical and exploratory ideas to the practical application of these ideas through the use of explanation, principles, and guidelines, each of which are employed to bring ideas to life and blend and fold theory into application. Hence, where later chapters focus on practical explanation and application, earlier chapters consider and discuss the theory and practice of adult and juvenile risk assessment and its relationship to various and complex ideas about risk and what drives it. This includes risk and protective factors that both amplify and moderate the likelihood of harm; the social context within which risk develops and harm occurs, including social connection and social relatedness; and normative sexual, emotional, cognitive, and social development. Organizationally, loosely speaking, the first half of the book is about theory building and developing an in-depth understanding of the risk assessment concept and process, whereas the second half focuses on practical application of the ideas. Building on a broad understanding of assessment and, indeed a theory and model of assessment, later chapters focus on the application of theory and the actual processes of psychosocial and risk assessment, including a review of the materials and tools that both emerge from and define practice; the art, science, and methods of risk assessment; and the administration of the process, from information gathering to completion of the assessment report. If part one is about the "why" and "what" of juvenile risk assessment, part two is about how to conduct risk assessments.

Above all, the book aims at contributing to a greater understanding of risk assessment and the development of guidelines that can shape and guide the process of risk assessment. It also aims to help the practitioner become more sensitive to the ideas that underlie risk assessment and more critical and aware in his or her thinking about the task, and thus more highly skilled. An additional, and just as important, goal is that of assisting the sponsors and consumers of risk assessments to also think more critically and increase their awareness about the assessment process. They too should increase their expectations for what an assessment should look like in content and depth, as well as understanding the methods, elements, strengths, and weaknesses of the risk assessment process.

An important caveat, however, is that we simply do not know enough about the assessment of risk for sexually abusive behavior in girls and women to formulate clear ideas about such assessments. Certainly, females are not the only class of sexual offenders about whom we have limited ideas, experience, and research, although we are both discovering more female sexual offenders with every passing year and developing more research about and clinical experience with this population. To some degree, this is also true about children who engage in sexually abusive behavior, as well as those with intellectual impairments such as mental retardation. Nevertheless, even as we increasingly learn more about the sexually abusive behavior of girls and women, as well as other groups of offenders, most of our research with sexual offenders has been based on adult male offenders of average intellectual capacity and secondarily with adolescent boys. Further, despite an increasing level of specialization with female and cognitively impaired sexual offenders and sexually reactive children, our practical and clinical experience over the past 25 years or so has primarily been with both adult and adolescent males, again of average IQ.

It is not surprising that what we know about sexually abusive behavior is based on a male population, because, as is the case for criminal and aggressive behavior in general, most sexual abuse is perpetrated by males, both adolescent and adult. For instance, based on the results of nationwide survey of sexual offender treatment programs in the United States and Canada, in 1998 76 percent of treated sexual offenders were men and an additional 19 percent were adolescent boys, comprising 95 percent of the total (Burton & Smith-Darden, 2001). Among U.S. programs surveyed in 2001, 90 percent of the treated sexual offenders were male, among which 61 percent were adults and 25 percent adolescent boys (McGrath, Cummings, & Burchard, 2003). Similarly, the FBI Uniform Crime Report for 2006 (U.S. Department of Justice, 2007; Table 33) shows that 90 percent of arrests for sexual crimes in 2006 were of males (74 percent adult and 16 percent adolescent). The 2006 FBI report shows that juvenile females represented only 1.4 percent of sexual arrests, whereas the Office of Juvenile

Justice and Delinquency Prevention reports that juvenile males represented 99.9 percent of the total number of juveniles arrested for sexual crimes in 2004 (Snyder, 2006).

Accordingly, although many of the ideas in this book are applicable to understanding juvenile risk assessment in general and to the development of methods for such practice, the book is primarily and significantly aimed at the risk assessment of sexually abusive adolescent boys of average or higher intelligence. It is secondarily directed to the assessment of pre-pubescent boys with sexual behavior problems and male juvenile sexual offenders with impaired intellectual capacity. Nevertheless, I hope the book will be of use to all who engage in the assessment of sexually abusive youth, and that many of its ideas can be extended to our assessment of girls and young women. However, the reader must keep in mind that what we know and what is described and discussed in this book is most pertinent to males, and I must apologize for the necessary focus on juvenile males, rather than females.

A note, though, on the words "evaluation" and "assessment," which I use interchangeably. Even though they are sometimes described as two separate processes or connected aspects of a larger process, both words essentially have the same meaning. An evaluation involves assessing or establishing the meaning or value of something, and the same is true of assessment, which involves the act of appraisal or evaluation. It is therefore redundant to refer to "evaluation and assessment." They are essentially synonyms for the same process.

On a final note, even in the absence of efficacious risk assessment (that is, risk assessment that is consistently and reliably accurate in its predictions of future behavior), if comprehensive enough the study of risk and the enunciation of a theory about the development and projection of risk increases our awareness and understanding of the dynamics, development, and course of sexually abusive behavior, or its natural history. This alone makes it worth developing and articulating a risk assessment process. However, whereas it is the goal of this book to provide information and ideas, offer review and critique, and suggest structure and direction, the goal is not to be prescriptive or tell the reader how it *should* be done (or, for that matter, how it should not be done).

CHAPTER 1

The Concept of Risk in Adults and Adolescents

I N CONCEPTUALIZING RISK assessment, there are at least three questions intrinsic to the idea of not simply assessing risk, but understanding the risk assessment construct: at risk to whom, at risk for what, and at risk when or under what circumstances. In the first case, as risk implies harm to others it seems obvious that we are addressing the actual and potential victims of harmful behavior. It may also seem clear that in order to assess risk, or more accurately a level of risk (from, say, "none" to "high," or "immediate"), we don't actually need to have any sense of who the victim might be. That is, it's enough to know that the subject of the evaluation is at risk to cause harm to others, regardless of who the victim may be.

Nevertheless, in a well-informed model of risk assessment it is quite important to have a sense of against whom sexually abusive behaviors may be directed, or what class of person, and not simply whether the individual will (or will not), in the opinion of the evaluator, engage in sexually abusive behavior. As we are, in fact, trying to build a more sophisticated model of assessment than simply "Will he or won't he engage in sexually abusive behavior?" (noting that most sexual offenders are males, as highlighted in the introduction to this book), it seems quite relevant to build a more complex set of questions upon which to build an understanding and theory of risk assessment. On this note, the questions of risk to whom, risk for what, and risk under what circumstances are not three unrelated questions. They are clearly linked and should be recognized as such, unless we wish to adopt a single-minded and simplistic view of risk as strictly harm caused by one individual to another. That view can be most simply described as "Will he or won't he?"

Before exploring these questions, however, it is important to note that risk assessment always involves prognostication about the *recurrence* of a particular behavior in which the subject of the assessment has previously engaged at least one time. The prior behavior represents the static, or historical, basis for risk assessment. It follows, then, that assessment of risk can occur only after it has been determined that the behavior has *previously* occurred. Accordingly, although risk assessment is based upon a host of related factors, the primary and most central factor is the historical occurrence of the behavior of concern, without which risk assessment simply cannot move forward. In absence of certain knowledge that the risk behavior has already occurred at least once, we cannot assess the likelihood that it will recur. In the evaluation of sexual abuse, risk assessment therefore always involves predictions about the potential or likelihood for *re*-engagement in sexually abusive behavior, and not the possibility that a first-time sexual offense may occur.

RISK TO WHOM?

With respect to its actual application, it is obvious that in order to assess risk for harm we do not need to know who the actual or potential victim will be (and, in many cases, we are unlikely to know such specific details), but it is nevertheless important to have a clear sense of a likely victim "profile." Is the likely victim of a sexual assault a child, a family member, an acquaintance of some kind, a stranger, a male or a female, and so on, or some combination of the above? This helps point to the likelihood of a pattern of behavior in the offender, which in itself increases and makes more likely the possibility of predicting future behavior, and increases our capacity to make accurate assessments. Of perhaps equal importance, having a sense of "risk to whom" also points directly to the contextual nature of sexually abusive behavior and helps make it clear that sexual abuse occurs under specific conditions, as well as the fact that in absence of an "appropriate" or desired victim sexually abusive behavior is unlikely to occur. Asking about risk to whom, and thereby addressing risk as more than just a question of "will he or won't he," also connects to the other two questions that are conceptually present in risk assessment, even if they are not immediately recognized. That is, understanding the risk to a particular class of victim (risk to whom) is tied to risk for particular behavior on the part of the perpetrator (risk for what) and risk for the behavior being triggered under particular circumstances (risk when).

In a simplistic version of risk assessment, the assessed level of risk flags the possible recurrence of sexually abusive behavior, but tells us no more.

Although important in itself, the prediction of risk alone (even if accurate) is nonetheless an empty piece of information. The presence of a victim is, of course, presumed, independent of who the victim may actually be or the class of victim. In exploring risk, however, and attempting to predict the possible recurrence of harm, we are interested in understanding *who* is at risk. Understanding the nature of the possible victim may tell us a lot about the perpetrator as well, including preferences, patterns, motivations, access, and conditions under which risk factors may or are likely to be transformed into actual harm.

AT RISK FOR WHAT?

With regard to the second question (risk for what), risk assessment is obviously probing for the possibility of further sexually abusive behavior. However, at a deeper, more intrinsic, and frankly more meaningful level the question is about what *type* of sexually abusive behavior, and even whether the sexual behavior that may be manifested is actually abusive. To some degree the question is about not only the nature of sexually abusive behavior itself, but also the circumstances under which such sexual behavior becomes abusive and even changing standards by which sexual behavior is defined as abusive, as well as the intentions and knowledge of the sexual offender regarding the nature of behavior.

For instance, we have now adopted a standard of "no means no" when it comes to consent for sexual behaviors, which includes unwanted conjugal relationships and date rape as variants of unwanted, coerced, or forced sexual behavior. Nevertheless, before our sensibilities, awareness, and perspectives changed, in the twin contexts of the social consciousness of the time and the occurrence of the behavior within an existing intimate relationship, these behaviors were not necessarily considered to be sexually abusive. In fact, in many cases the perpetrator may have felt entitled to his behaviors and considered them appropriate, even if forceful, given the context of the relationship. In many cases, the same was true of the victim, who may have felt that she must succumb to and accept such behavior even if forced upon her and even if frightening. Our change in perspective, and the change in the perspectives of the perpetrators and victims of such situations, reflects a change in social understanding and acceptance and a new and evolving standard regarding what constitutes sexually abusive behavior.

To some degree, with respect to how we think of sexually abusive behavior in children and adolescents there are perhaps shifts in the other direction, in which we may be rethinking sexually abusive behavior, at least with the labeling of such behavior. Simply put, we see increasing changes in our terminology, in which the term "juvenile sexual offender," for instance, is being replaced by terms such as "sexually abusive youth" and "children (or adolescents) with sexual behavior problems." This change in terminology doesn't necessarily change our view of what constitutes sexually abusive behavior, but it does reflect changes in the way that we view and wish to treat those who engage in sexually abusive behavior, and perhaps especially children and adolescents.

In assessing sexually abusive behavior then, and especially in children and adolescents, we must be able to distinguish between sexual behavior that is clearly and incontrovertibly abusive, such as the rape of a 9-year-old child by a significantly older person or the rape of a stranger in an alleyway, and, at the other extreme, sexual behavior that is legally, and even socially, interpreted as abusive but may involve fully consensual sexual inter-course, or what Zimring (2004) refers to as "sexual status" offenders. For instance, despite being consensual, sex between an 18-year-old and his or her 16-year-old boy or girlfriend may nevertheless be prosecuted as a sexual crime. Sometimes referred to as a "Romeo and Juliet" crime, such behavior may result in imprisonment and/or lifetime registration on a state or national sexual offender registry for the older of the two. Between these two extremes of sexual behavior—that which is without question abusive and that which is perhaps more a legal or social artifice than an example of sexual abuse—lie many shades of sexual behavior ranging from sexually abusive to sexually inappropriate and sexually normative. The task of the risk assessment is to predict not just the recurrence of sexually abusive behavior, but what type of sexually abusive behavior is likely to recur. It also involves discerning between truly unwanted and abusive sexual behavior and sexual behavior that is considered abusive based on its legal definition or social implication rather than a lack of consent or the presence of abusive coercion.[1] Even within the realm of behavior that is clearly abusive by its very nature, rather than its social standing, there are clear distinctions. These include "hands off" and nonassaultive sexual behaviors, such as sexual expo-sure, public masturbation, voyeurism, and theft of items for sexual use (such as underwear), and "hands on" offenses that range from frottage to molestation, masturbation, oral sex, and penetration offenses.

Asking "at risk for what" then is not merely about semantics or hair splitting. By asking, we recognize that although the level of risk may be

---

1. Chapter 9 addresses the question of what constitutes sexually abusive behavior, and distinguishing sexually abusive from other sexualized behaviors.

high (that is, there is a high likelihood that the individual will reengage in similar behavior), the nature of the sexual behavior itself may range from behavior likely to be very harmful to others to behavior that is by comparison relatively low in impact and may cause little or no lasting harm or, in some cases, no harm at all if we are to judge harm by its effect on the victim.

For the sake of clarity, there is no assumption here that one form of sexually abusive or sexually inappropriate behavior is of greater or lesser harm than another. The relatively "mildest" and least invasive sexually inappropriate or abusive behaviors, such as frottage, exhibitionism, or voyeurism, may have devastating and/or long-lasting effects on the victim. The question posed here does not relate to nor judge the impact of the sexual behavior on the victim, but instead involves the nature of the behavior itself and the behavior that the juvenile sexual offender may be at risk to reenact.

The question of "at risk for what" is also quite relevant when the sexual behavior does not appear harmful to the immediate parties at all and even appears desirable, as in Romeo and Juliet romances. In this case, the sexual behavior is considered by law (and perhaps by the parents) to be abusive, but in reality it is likely normative and acceptable within the peer group, even if between an older and a younger teen. This is especially true in states where underage sex is itself illegal and, in effect, where *both* parties may technically be engaging in sexually abusive behavior by having a sexual relationship with one another if they are both underage. Knowing that sexual behavior among adolescents is common, and that close to half of all high school students have engaged in sexual intercourse, not only makes this point even clearer but also makes clear the normative nature of sexual behavior among adolescents, even if, in some cases, it is considered sexually abusive by law or social convention. According to the Youth Risk Behavior Survey (Eaton et al., 2006), in 2005 almost 47 percent of U.S. high school students experienced sexual intercourse, including 63 percent of high school seniors. The Kaiser Foundation's National survey of adolescents and young adults reported that 65 percent of high school students reported having been engaged in an intimate sexual relationship, including either sexual intercourse or oral sex, or both (Hoff, Greene, & Davis, 2003).

On a side note, but highly related to the subject of risk assessment, the normalcy of sexual behavior among adolescents may also serve as a motivating factor for children and adolescents to engage in sexual behavior, even if the behavior is non-consensual and therefore abusive. The pursuit of and engagement in sex as "normative" behavior is addressed later in the book,[2] but for now it is relevant with respect to the third question that underlies the risk assessment process, that of circumstance and context.

AT RISK WHEN?

From a public safety perspective, we may only be interested in the question of "will he or won't he," or, more realistically, "What are the chances that he will or won't?" However, even this essential and rudimentary (and rather simple-minded) question links to broader ideas about risk, and most specifically the connection between the emission of behavior and under what circumstances and in what conditions such behavior is likely to be emitted. That is, what stimulates a particular type of behavior in any particular individual? In this case, the question is under what circumstances or in what context is sexually abusive behavior likely to occur again, if it recurs at all.

One might easily argue that a dangerous person is dangerous all of the time. But, if we place latent potential (or the possibility that danger might explode at any moment) aside for one moment, we can also see that even the most dangerous individual is not likely to be dangerous all of the time, or even at any given moment, without the contexts in which dangerous or harmful behavior is embedded and the circumstances that trigger such behavior. With respect to the question of "at risk when," risk assessment is most concerned with both the potential for risk at any given time and the circumstances under which the risky behavior is most likely to emerge. Put another way, the essence of the question is this: When is the danger greatest that this individual might reengage in sexually abusive behavior? In turn, this reframes the risk assessment question as one that also asks about the circumstances that contribute to the greatest risk for this person. That is, although we might reasonably argue that "risk" is a latency, always present and waiting to emerge even if invisible, we must still recognize that circumstances must be favorable for the emergence of the latent condition. If this was not so, then the individual would be actively dangerous all of the time.

A wildly drunk individual poses a clear danger to self and others just by being drunk. Alcohol intoxication is clearly a condition that puts people at risk for any number of serious consequences, and especially when operating a vehicle. Yet although a heavily intoxicated individual behind the driving wheel poses a threat at every minute he or she is driving a vehicle,

---

2. See Chapter 9.

the risk that harm will actually occur exists only when the right (or wrong, if you prefer) circumstances come together to form the conditions from which harm actually emerges. Thus, even though being intoxicated is a clear risk factor for someone behind the wheel of a car, the same person, even if drunk, poses no risk at all for an automobile accident if he or she remains at home. Of course, driving while drunk is very risky, but it's not the being drunk part that's the real risk. Here, risk is found not so much in being intoxicated but in the context in which risk is played out—driving a car. Further, risk of harm is exponentially increased by adding other risk elements, such as nighttime driving, rainy and foggy road conditions, and other drunk drivers on the road. It is the combination of risk factors that turns *some* risk into *considerable* risk, and the more the risk factors and the greater their interaction, the greater the risk that harm will actually emerge out of risk.

When we are assessing risk we are assessing the likelihood of actual harm based upon the strength of individual factors. Of more significance, we are concerned with the *combination* of factors, which together increase the strength of risk beyond what any individual risk factor is likely to possess on its own. Using the intoxicated driver example, the condition of being drunk is a risk condition in its own right, but when added to driving a car risk is raised to a higher level, and to a still higher level when we add other factors such as nighttime driving or driving in the snow or fog. Assessment considers all of these risk factors in determining the level of risk, although there is obviously a point beyond which additional factors are unnecessary for us to declare a high-risk situation. In this case, risk is already high the moment the individual gets behind the wheel, and especially if he or she is very intoxicated.

Nevertheless, as we assess risk we also want to understand the elements that contribute to risk and elevate it, and in doing so also recognize the context in which risk develops and the circumstances under which it is most likely to turn into harmful behavior. Under what conditions is *some* risk amplified and transformed into *significant* risk? For instance, in the case of sexually abusive behavior, some risk in the form of sexual arousal to children and a history of child molestation is amplified to significant risk when the individual is subsequently left alone with a young child. The static risk factor carried within the individual himself (or herself), reflecting a history of perpetrating child sexual abuse, combines with a stable but dynamic risk factor that is also inherent in the individual, in this example being aroused by children. This factor is stable because the individual has long been aroused to children but, unlike historical risk, is also dynamic because of the possibility that this pattern of sexual arousal might change.

In the language of risk assessment, static factors are historical and therefore unchangeable, whereas dynamic factors are active at the present time and, if even stable over time, are therefore always subject to change (or at least the possibility of change).

In this simplistic example, the static and dynamic risk factors that reside within the individual combine to create a level of risk that increases significantly when the individual is exposed to an independent environmental risk factor (which is also dynamic as it is subject to change), which in this case is being left alone with a vulnerable child. Add another personal risk factor to the mix, such as the individual *wanting* to engage in sexual behavior with children, and yet another, such as his or her actively seeking out opportunity for such engagement, and still another, such as being intoxicated, and we can see how risk continues to increase, but only as risk factors combine and interact with one another. The same multiplying effect of combining risk factors is also true when the factors are external to the individual. For instance, rather than adding personal or internal factors (those residing within the individual) to the constellation of risk factors, add external factors (those residing in his environment) instead, such as recent separation from a spouse, loss of employment, or inability to find housing, and it is not difficult to see how external, as well as internal, factors can just as easily magnify risk, multiplying it from some to significant risk.

Understanding risk in this way increases our knowledge and understanding of the deeper factors that define, form, and grow risk, allowing us to see risk as more than a simple and unidimensional construct. This depth of understanding allows us to most realistically project risk in a way that can help guard the public and protect the rights of the individuals we are assessing by being aware of both false positives and false negatives. Asking "at risk when" allows us to picture risk in the context of the individual and the circumstances of his or her life. Indeed, Monahan (1995) noted that failing to incorporate situation or environmental information into risk assessment is one of the major blind spots in risk prediction.

TWO CONCEPTUALIZATIONS OF RISK

I referred to the idea that risk can be visualized as residing within the individual or within the environment. In fact, it may be quite reasonable to speculate that much risk is linked to the individual himself (or herself), in which risk factors are intrinsic to and held within the individual, perhaps the product of either shaping developmental experiences or biology, or both. However, it is also reasonable to consider that risk also resides in the environment outside and independent of the individual, within which he or she lives, functions, and interacts with others, and through which the individual comes to learn about him/herself and others through early and ongoing developmental experience.

Risk factors that are intrinsic to, or reside within, the individual may involve attitude, beliefs, sexual interests, poor self-regulation, self-right-eous anger, intellectual disability, or narcissism, for instance. They may also include limited capacity for social connection, empathy, remorse, or moral development that may be the product of either early developmental experiences or a biological condition, such as cognitive impairment or autism, or perhaps even sociopathy. Within the environment, risk factors that exist independently of the individual involve social attitudes and messages, family dysfunction or instability, exposure to violence and criminality, economic hardship, peer pressure and antisocial peer group values, and unstable or difficult living conditions. In fact, when we consider how internal risk factors *become* internalized, we recognize that in many, if not most, cases, it is through the interaction between the individual and the environment that personal attributes, including intrinsic risk factors, develop and take root. These can, in part, be considered the developmental vulnerabilities described by Marshall and Eccles (1993) by which susceptibility to a variety of later influences and events that would not otherwise significantly influence or affect other individuals results from developmental history. These vulnerabilities or susceptibilities can be considered to be risk factors carried by and within the individual, but nevertheless the product of external conditions.

That is, external conditions and risk factors often produce risk factors that come to reside within the individual rather than the environment, even if the environment is the source. Indeed, this is the very premise of attachment theory, in which the internalized world and perceptions of the external world stem from experiences and interactions with the environment (see, for instance, Rich, 2006). There is, then, a complex mix between the internal, endogenous world and the world that is external and exogenous to the individual. Thus, even in models in which risk is seen as largely or solely residing within the individual, we cannot fail to also see the power of the environment in either holding back or allowing risk to emerge as actual harm or as a shaper, or an actual element of, risk.

In a model in which risk is assumed to rest within the individual (in effect a latent trait carried around inside of him or her), external conditions merely serve to stimulate or allow the expression of risk. In this model, described by Epperson, Ralston, Fowers, DeWitt, and Gore (2006), risk is intrinsic to the risky individual, regardless of its origin (or how it got into

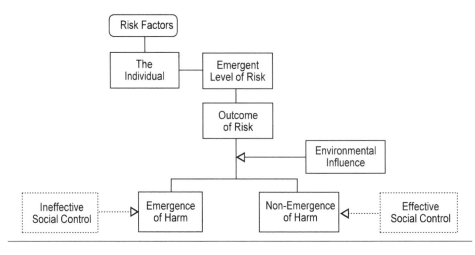

Figure 1.1 A model of risk in which risk resides within the individual and environmental conditions or social controls either restrict or allow the expression of risk.

the individual), and elements in the environment serve only to restrain or allow the expression of risk. In this conceptualization, risk is defined as the likelihood that the individual will engage in sexually abusive behavior in a community setting in which there are no external restraints to prevent the behavior. In Epperson's (2007) model, risk *indicators* represent the actual history of previous sexually abusive behavior (serving, in effect, as a historical marker of previous behavior that flags the possibility of further harm), whereas risk *factors* represent internal factors within the individual. In this model, although changes to the environment may restrict or even eliminate the possibility of actual harm (and may therefore neutralize the potential of risk), such changes do not eliminate, reduce, or alter risk factors, as risk exists elsewhere (i.e., in the individual). This model, shown in Figure 1.1, does not recognize a dynamic interplay between historical, internal, and environmental processes and forces, and this is a model of assessment that itself is static.

In a second model, shown in Figure 1.2, risk factors are considered to be both endogenous *and* exogenous in relationship to the individual, and come together in some combination to more fully define risk and the potential that risk will result in actual harm. Endogenous factors reside within the individual and include attitudes, sexual drive, capacity for empathy, sexual interests, and other elements that are the product of either biology or socio-developmental experience. Exogenous factors exist independently of the individual, reside in the environment, and include elements such as peer group, domestic violence, social messages, family

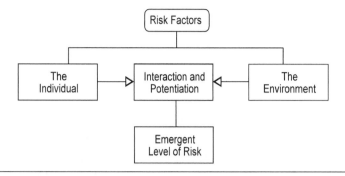

Figure 1.2   A model of risk in which risk resides within the individual and the environment, resulting in an emergent level of risk.

functioning, warmth and empathy experienced by the individual, and so on, but they are as much risk factors as personal characteristics that contribute to risk. Endogenous and exogenous risk factors mix and interact, each potentially catalyzing or amplifying the other and together bringing risk to the point of emerging or actual harm. In this model, neither risk factors that reside within the individual nor those that reside in the external environment are cause enough for harm to another person, in our case, represented by engagement in sexually abusive behavior. Boer, McVilly, and Lambrick (2007) for instance, advocate expanding assessment beyond risk factors solely related to the offender "to a broader framework in which environmental . . . variables are given equal consideration in a comprehensive appraisal of risk" (p. 3). Rather than being a model of static assessment, this is a more dynamic model of assessment, in which human behavior is recognized as a "joint function of characteristics of the person and characteristics of the environment with which he or she interacts" (Mohanan, 1995, p. 37).

Both of these models are mere constructs. Neither can be said to be an accurate depiction of the real world, and both represent ways by which we are able to understand the world around us—in this case, the relationship between driving (risk) factors and the emergence of sexually abusive behavior.

MODEL ONE

In the first conceptualization, the cause of harm is the direct result of risk factors that reside within the individual and are otherwise unfettered by environmental constraints. Internal risk factors can be inhibited and prevented from causing harm by external controls located in the environment. One obvious outcome of this model is the development of a theory of risk assessment that considers risk to reside only within the individual and therefore assesses risk only at the level of the individual. In terms of the treatment of risk, this model may also spawn methods for risk management, rather than risk elimination, or a containment and harm reduction model through environment control. Here, the goal is managing, reducing, or eliminating potential harm by controlling the individual within the environment, but not necessarily reducing risk itself as this exists within the individual. Risk is, in effect, neutralized through environmental controls. Nevertheless, risk containment and risk management are not the only possible products of a model in which risk is seen to exist only in the individual (rather than the environment). Such a model is also capable of recognizing that risk in the individual can be modified or eliminated by changing the person, and thus it allows for the treatment of risk within the person, as well as the external containment and management of risk. However, inherent in the model is the idea that risk can only be controlled, not changed, by environmental conditions. As risk is inherent in the individual, even though it can be contained by environmental control, it is "unchanged by external constraints in the environment" (Epperson et al., 2006, p. 120). This is effectively a model of social control, or one in which risk would always (or usually be) acted out in the absence of external control. From the perspective of social control theory, without external controls individuals are unrestrained from engaging in antisocial behaviors (Agnew & Passas, 1997; Hirschi, 2002).

MODEL TWO

The second model proposes not only that risk factors are inherent in both the individual and the environment, but that the transformation of risk into harmful behavior is the result of a multiplex relationship between and among risk factors found within the individual and the environment within which the individual lives and interacts. Here, the environment does not act as a simple container for or constrainer of risk, but itself is part of risk and must be considered an active element in the development and emergence of risk. Consequently, a model of risk assessment that results from this view of risk will seek out and evaluate risk factors within both the individual *and* the environment. In terms of treatment, although such a model may also lead to the development of techniques and methods for risk management and harm reduction, an attempt to eliminate risk itself will focus on treatment of the individual *and* the individual's environment, rather than just seeking to establish environmental control, as it believes that risk is derived from and is the interactive result of both sources.

THE TWO MODELS

The two models are different, not simply in how they define risk factors, where risk factors reside, and how risk factors interact with the environment to result in harm. In the first case, risk that is inherent within the individual is considered causative if powerful enough and either not restrained by the environment or eliminated or reduced in strength through treatment. On the other hand, the second model considers that, although playing a causative role, risk alone is not causative even when risk is high. This model recognizes the proximal cause of harm as the interaction between multiple risk factors in the individual and environment *and* environmental conditions that further fuel risk until it "tops over" and spills into antisocial behavior; such conditions either introduce the opportunity for harm or fail to prevent it. However, the second model considers the interplay between risk and harm as far more complex than simply the result of internal characteristics that are either restrained or unrestrained by environmental forces. Recognizing that risk exists in the environment itself, this model also recognizes the power of the social environment in still further amplifying risk or in reducing, inhibiting, or neutralizing it, often transmitted through interactions and relationships within that environment.

However, neither model of risk or risk assessment assumes that any single risk factor, no matter where it may reside or how potent, is powerful enough to cause criminal behavior, including sexually abusive behavior. And in the case of both models, regardless of how risk factors are defined, harmful behavior is contingent upon some variant of the interplay between risk factors and elements present in or absent from the environment. It is thus a combination of risk factors and environmental conditions that ultimately allows antisocial behavior to emerge from risk, and an assessment of risk must thus take context into account in order to both understand the development of risk and the likelihood that harm will actually take place.

TWO MODELS OF RISK ASSESSMENT

It is not surprising that these two models lead to very different models of risk assessment, one of which is largely static and the other substantially dynamic, although to some degree both may contain features of the other.

Out of the first model emerges a system of actuarial, mechanical, or statistical risk assessment in which risk is considered inherent in the individual, and a determination of risk is based entirely on a statistical comparison of the personal characteristics and past behavior of the individual to those of known recidivists. Things that have happened, such as prior criminal behavior, or existing characterological features, such as sexual arousal to children, provide the entire basis for the assessment of future antisocial behavior; as such the distinguishing feature of such assessments is the static, or unchanging and historical, quality of risk factors (or risk indicators, in Epperson's terms).

On the other hand, developing out of a more dynamic model in which risk exists within individuals and within their environment, and indeed within the interactions that link individuals to their environments, comes a risk assessment model that includes both static and dynamic, or changeable and changing, risk factors. In this model, risk is understood and ultimately assessed as the product of factors found within the individual, the social environment within which the individual develops and functions, and the social interactions and transactions that tie the individual to his or her environment. This is a more fluid and thus dynamic model. In the assessment world, this model is tied to models of clinical assessment, rather than actuarial assessment.

Stated briefly, an actuarial risk assessment is based on a statistical analysis of static risk factors and a resulting statistical projection of future behavioral trends. For now, clinical risk assessment can be simply defined as one in which risk estimates are based on observation, rather than statistical analysis, and the development of an understanding about the individual, risk factors at play within the individual and in the individual's environment, the relationship between the individual and defined risk factors, and, finally, factors that trigger or protect against the transformation of risk into actual harm. The clinical risk assessment does not preclude the use of actuarial or other psychometric data collection and evaluation, but builds these into a larger and more comprehensive model of assessment that ultimately rests on the skill of the clinical evaluator, rather than the statistical formulation and arithmetic process that is the heart of actuarial assessment. The key, or at least one key, to understanding clinical assessment is the addition of context, interpretation, and assignment of meaning to the examination and evaluation of both static and dynamic risk factors.

Although actuarial assessment can, and does, yield statistically meaningful predictions of risk (or actually of recidivism, which is the transformation of risk into actual harm), the theory behind the assessment is built on a rather mechanistic view of people and their behavior, and pays little attention to or fails to recognize that internal risk is related to external variables and not simply controlled by external forces. Accordingly actuarial assessment does not take into account environmental factors that may contribute to or produce risk, and in assessing risk considers only attributes related directly to the individual, treating these personal attributes as static and unchanging things from which future behavior can be statistically predicted. The model of actuarial assessment, in turn resulting from an underlying model in which risk is considered to be inherent in the individual, is unable to ascribe meaning to the behavior that is under assessment or to the individual emitting that behavior and, one might argue, does not care about or even recognize the person behind the behavior. And although it may be true that risk alone can be predicted through statistical methodology, the actuarial assessment process in effect concludes that it is enough to statistically project risk and that effective management can be based on social control alone, with little or no attention paid to changing the person.

Figure 1.3 illustrates a simplified view of both the actuarial and clinical process contrasted against one another. In fact, a model of risk that assumes that risk lies within the individual does not *necessarily* spawn an actuarial

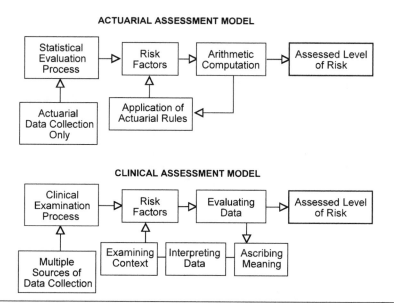

Figure 1.3 A brief and simplified comparison of actuarial and clinical assessment processes.

model of risk, and it is not necessarily the case that an actuarial method of assessment precludes the gathering of additional data or a treatment model that seeks change and rehabilitation in the individual. In fact, models of adult sexual offender risk assessment are expanding and evolving to include measures of dynamic (changing and changeable) risk and, to this degree, are moving towards clinical interpretations (and assignments) of risk (as discussed in Chapter 3). Neither is it necessarily true that clinical assessments examine, interpret, and ascribe meaning to risk factors and risky behavior or include multiple sources of data in the process. However, just as actuarial assessment is continually developing and even moving towards or incorporating a clinical model, so too is clinical assessment moving towards a more defined, structured, and empirically driven model.

Nevertheless, the two conceptualizations of risk described above are potentially distinctly different, not only in their view of where risk resides but also in the meaning of risk, how to recognize and where to look for it, the mechanisms by which risk is turned into or away from actual harm, and the nature of the person and/or the environment in which risk is found. The differences between these two models, then, is not just semantic; these really are two very different models, and they lead to different outcomes and possibilities, including how we assess risk and how we treat it.

THE CONCEPTUALIZATION OF PROTECTIVE FACTORS

Whereas the actuarial model of risk assessment focuses on elements of risk only, and particularly static risk (or risk indicators), a clinical model of risk recognizes a greater interaction between risk elements and other elements or conditions that serve to advance or inhibit the transformation of risk into actual harm.

Among these other elements are protective factors that, in effect, are conceptualized only in relation to risk factors. These exist independently of risk, can be conceived of in many different ways, and fill different roles in the life of each individual and the larger community. However, with respect to risk in particular, protective factors serve to inhibit or restrain the emergence of risk or protect against harm. Like risk factors, these can be found to reside within the individual and the external environment. Religious or spiritual beliefs, moral conviction, prosocial attitudes, secure attachment to others and social connectedness, and a well developed sense of empathy illustrate protective factors that are endogenous to the individual. Family support, prosocial peer group, positive role models, and a stable living environment are examples of protective factors that exist outside of the individual. High levels of supervision and control (such as probation, GPS monitoring,[3] and threat of incarceration) also represent exogenous protective factors, although these obviously belong to a class of factors that are not built upon the strength of the individual or community but are clearly aimed at decreasing risk through social control, and can be thought of as both protective factors (as they protect against harm) and environmental conditions that inhibit the expression of risk. Regardless, protective factors are characteristics or conditions that interact with risk factors to reduce their influence. In a dynamic, and typically clinical, assessment model, protective factors will be a consideration in evaluating risk and an element of the overall assessment process, with adjustments made in light of factors that inhibit, restrain, or protect against risk. Indeed, Monahan (1995) recommends that evaluators ask themselves whether they are giving consideration to factors indicating the absence of harmful behavior as well as those that suggest the possible recurrence of harm.[4]

IMPLICATIONS OF RISK ASSESSMENT FOR THE TREATMENT OF RISK

It is inevitable that our ideas about risk will be tied to our treatment of risk. It is likely, in all but a relatively few cases, that some form of activity will occur after risk assessment that is designed to curb risk and thus prevent harm, and this process constitutes treatment of some kind, however we may define treatment. Indeed, our very definition of treatment may itself be linked to concepts about risk, because treatment is about managing and eliminating the potential effects of risk.

An assessment of low risk may yield a limited response, and hence a more limited form of treatment; an assessment of high risk results in greater concern about the individual's potential to harm others and more intensive responses that are designed to protect against or eliminate harm. Treatment may be as basic as incarceration or heavy monitoring and supervision in the community, such as placement on a sexual offender registry, community notification, probation, or GPS monitoring, or, as shown in Figure 1.4, it may lay at the mental health end of the spectrum in which it is aimed at the psychological and emotional well-being of the individual.

The idea that risk is or should be linked to treatment has been much cited, especially in the work of Andrews, Bonta, and Hoge in their

---

3. Use of an ankle bracelet, for instance, that is tracked through a Global Positioning System.
4. Protective factors are discussed further in Chapter 8.

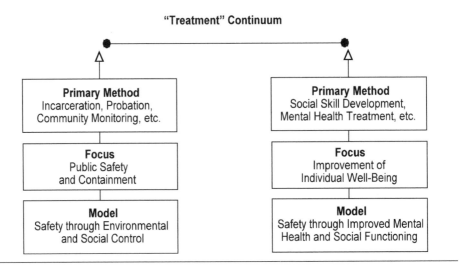

Figure 1.4 Simple illustration of a continuum of treatment options for sexual offenders.

Risk-Need-Responsivity (RNR) model (Andrews, Bonta, & Hoge, 1990; Andrews, Bonta, & Wormith, 2006; Hoge & Andrews, 2003), who reasonably argue that the level and intensity of treatment services provided to offenders (sexual and non-sexual) should be linked to the level of risk they pose for a reoffense, as well as their treatment needs and their likelihood of benefiting from treatment. The model itself describes risk in both the "risk" principle of the model, which includes both static and dynamic risk factors, and in the "need" principle, which focuses only on dynamic risk factors and clearly recognizes the assessment of dynamic risk factors as one important basis for the provision of treatment. The authors clearly correlate risk and needs as reflections of both static and dynamic risk factors (Bonta & Andrews, 2007, p. 5; Hoge & Andrews, 2003, p. 2), tying both types of risk factors to treatment, and especially the type and intensity of treatment provided. The "responsivity" principle is very much tied to treatment by recognizing that treatment effectiveness is in part tied to characteristics of the offender. In turn, it is obvious that in many cases both static and dynamic risk factors are directly related to the characteristics of the offender, and of course are the targets for treatment (in the case of dynamic factors, at least).

In earlier descriptions of the RNR model, a fourth principle of "professional override" was articulated. Postulating the necessity of clinical judgment, this principle asserted that final decisions about treatment must be guided by professional considerations regarding risk, need, and responsivity in the context of the individual situation and circumstances (Andrews, Bonta, & Hoge, 1990, p. 44): "having considered risk, need, and responsivity, decisions are made as appropriate under present conditions" (Hoge & Andrews, 1996, p. 10). Although professional override is no longer described as a fourth "principle" in consideration of case management and treatment, "professional discretion" (as it is now called) remains elemental in the application of the RNR model (Bonta & Andrews, 2007; Hannah-Moffat & Maurutto, 2003).

Not only do the ideas embodied in the Risk-Need-Responsivity model clearly link risk to treatment, but ideas about treatment are linked to essential ideas about risk. Hence, if risk resides solely within the individual and if treatment for sexual offenders is mostly about harm reduction through social control, then it need not be aimed at improving the mental health, social skills, and quality of life of sexual offenders. In this case, the intensity of treatment is merely about the level and degree of social control rather than the degree or type of mental health treatment.

The question of which end of the spectrum should treatment rest (social control or rehabilitation) is a facet of socio-political ideology and is for practitioners a question of personal choice, at least to some degree. However, if the primary goal is only for sexually abusive behavior to be managed and neutralized, then mental health and rehabilitation need not be a target. With such a basic goal the individual need not actually be a target for treatment or change, nor is it important to eliminate inherent risk factors that reside within the sexual offender; instead, we simply need to control for or neutralize risk factors. As risk remains largely static in this model (as it resides within the person, including the person's history), change in risk outcome can occur through social control alone. In fact, this is clearly one notable direction in which the social, political, and legal systems of the United States are moving. With the advent of the Adam Walsh Child Protection and Safety Act of 2006 comes the Sex Offender Registration and Notification Act (SORNA), which intends to create a national sex offender registry with lifetime registration for sexual offenders, including juvenile sexual offenders aged 14 and older who have committed certain sexual offenses (although the act allows the possibility of only 25 years registration for juvenile sexual offenders).

In truth, treatment ideas that are largely static in origin and seek public safety through social control do not *necessarily* result in a lack of treatment that also addresses the mental health and general well-being and rehabilitation of the sexual offender. Sex offender registration and GPS tracking, for instance, may be but one immediate and concrete step in the provision of a larger model of treatment that expands beyond social control alone to include a model of mental health treatment.[5] However, a treatment model that *depends* on containment and social control to maintain success is the very antithesis of a treatment model in which the greater good (e.g., public safety) may be served *and* the individual sexual offender may be rehabilitated and move towards meeting his or her goals in a prosocial and personally satisfying manner, improve in social skills and social functioning, increase mental health and well-being, and lead and experience a more satisfying life. In fact, the practices and outcomes of offender containment and management may even further marginalize sexual offenders and exacerbate some of the very conditions that contribute to sexually abusive behavior in the first place, at least in adults. The possibly unintended results of containment and social control may perhaps fuel the very fire we're trying to quell, in some cases increasing risk and therefore requiring even more social controls in a never-ending cycle.

Even if not within the general public and political world view, within the treatment field, ideas about treatment for adult sexual offenders are clearly moving towards the mental health treatment end of the spectrum. Ideas such as those proposed by Marshall (2005, 2006) and others (Craissati & Beech, 2003; Harkins & Beech, 2007a, 2007b) advocate a more psychologically minded and client-centered approach to treatment, which is more in line with our approach in other branches of mental health treatment. Perhaps best epitomized in the Good Lives model of Tony Ward and colleagues (Ward, Mann, & Gannon, 2007; Whitehead, Ward, & Collie, 2007), these models of treatment pay attention to changes within the person and the person's environment in order to reduce the chances of sexual offense recidivism without neglecting public safety. But, of particular note here, these changes in ideas about treatment for adult sexual offenders in turn reflect a change in our concept of risk.

The model of risk as static still holds great currency in the assessment of adult sexual offenders; however, shifting ideas about treatment also reflect a change in foundational ideas about risk conceptualization and assessment. This change recognizes not just static indicators of risk but also that dynamic risk variables are an important target in assessment, thus taking risk assessment beyond mechanical and statistically derived actuarial assessment. The extension of this thinking is that dynamic factors are also an important target for treatment, suggesting that risk is partly derived from current, and not simply historical, factors and experiences, and can

---

5. Indeed, the Comprehensive Assessment Protocol of the Center for Sex Offender Management (Bumby, Carter, Talbot, & Gilligan, 2007) asserts that treatment and registration are both integral to effective sexual offender management.

subsequently be reduced through mental health treatment and not simply controlled through containment.

Frankly, even if containment was a 100 percent fix for the problem of sexual abuse recidivism, there is also the question of what sort of society we wish to have, how we see individuals within our society, how we wish to treat and interact with individuals whom we have come to recognize as either dangerous or unwanted, and whether we believe that individual change is possible. All of these ideas are linked to our conceptualizations of risk, how we understand and assess risk, how we treat risk, and whether the goals of sex offender treatment are unidimensional (the prevention of recidivism) or multidimensional (the prevention of recidivism, the elimination of conditions that give rise to recidivism, and helping to improve the lives and mental well-being of those at risk for recidivism).

THE FOURTH QUESTION: AT RISK WHY?

Beyond the three questions already asked—at risk to whom, for what, and when—is a fourth related question: at risk why? That is, why is the individual likely to engage in sexually abusive behavior again? The question takes on importance if our intention is to understand not just the fundamental nature of risk assessment, but also the purpose that sexually abusive behavior fills for the offender, and even the meaning of the behavior to the perpetrator. More than the other three questions, this fourth question provides part of the foundation for treatment and, even if not immediately relevant to the assessment of risk, should be built into risk assessment if the assessment is to have meaning and serve as a basis for treatment.

Frankly, in a pure risk evaluation in which the sole question is one of will he or won't he, we wouldn't ask the question "why" or indeed any of the other three questions. In an ideal statistical model for risk prediction we wouldn't have to ask; even if we didn't fully understand the nature of risk and its causes, we would always spot risk and thus be able to control for it. With such a model, we might even imagine that the treatment we provide (from social control to mental health treatment) has nothing to do with our conceptualization or risk, how we assess it, or how we assign a level of risk. However, I've obviously argued that our treatment has everything to do with our conceptualization of risk and that our ideas about risk give birth to our ideas about treatment. Further, it is apparent that we lack an ideal assessment model, not just by the constant debate in the field about the best model (actuarial or clinical), but by the fact that assessment processes continue to evolve; clinical assessments are becoming more structured and, in some cases, actuarial assessments are being woven into larger assessment processes that are more dynamic and clinical.

Hence, understanding that treatment and risk are linked and without an ideal connecting model, a best practices model for assessment and treatment is built on our best understanding of the processes by which we understand risk and its development, rather than the simplistic question of "Will he or won't he?" I argue that in order to best answer that question, we must be able to explore important elements that give rise to risk.

Returning to the idea that risk assessment is always based upon a history of prior harmful behavior and is therefore an assessment for recidivism and not first-time behavior, the process of risk assessment always draws on the past in order to highlight possible future behavior. This is the static element of risk assessment, and there are two ways to use this slice of the assessment process. One is by statistical processes that may yield accurate results but fail to yield an understanding of the phenomenon we are observing and counting. In this case, we may come to recognize that certain historical events effectively predict the likelihood of a behavior occurring again, even if we don't know why or understand why these static factors are predictive for some but not others. A second way to use static data is from an observational and phenomenological perspective, not just through a process of counting how many times these factors appear in the histories of different recidivists.

In this case, in addition to spotting and counting, understanding an individual's past behaviors and experiences can lend itself to projections about future behavior based on an understanding of why (and under what circumstances) the prior behavior occurred. Recognizing and understanding the presence of past and current experiences and behaviors allows us to project a trend into the future which, if uninterrupted, may lead to a recurrence of the same behavior. In both cases, statistical or clinical, recognizing the occurrence of static events as predictive (even if not in every case) is an important link to predicting future behavior, and it embraces the idea that past behavior predicts (at least, in part) future behavior. However, only in the case of our clinical use of static data do we recognize that understanding the nature of past behavior, and not just counting its occurrence, provides us with the chance to not only interrupt future occurrences but also change and rehabilitate the conditions that gave rise to such behavior in the first place and that may do so again. We can best understand why a behavior may recur by understanding the reason for its past occurrence. Paraphrasing George Santayana: Those who cannot remember [or in this case, understand] the past, are condemned to repeat it.

RISK ASSESSMENT IN CHILDREN
AND ADOLESCENTS

The ideas presented in this chapter are generic in the sense that they apply to the assessment of risk of every sort for both adults and juveniles. Although addressed in detail in Chapter 4, questions about differences between adult sexual offenders and sexually abusive youth with respect to the meaning or risk and its assessment in these two populations is useful to at least consider before wrapping up the current chapter.

For now, it's important to say that we consider adolescents to not simply be smaller and less-experienced versions of adults, but qualitatively and quantitatively different in many facets of their lives, including their cognitive, emotional, behavioral, and neurological development. As such, we recognize that not only is risky behavior in adolescents different than similar behavior in adults but also that the causes, development, and further unfolding of risk over time is also different. Based on developmental difference between adolescents and adults, even if we understand risk in adolescents in the same way we understand it in adults, the way that risk operates in adolescents may be very different, as well as its effects on adolescent behavior. How we understand and view risk in children and adolescents, including how we visualize its developmental process, is quite different than how we view risk in adults.

Regardless of how we assess risk or the nature of risk factors believed pertinent to sexual recidivism in juveniles, unless we adopt a model of assessment in which the only or main question is "Will he or won't he?", the four questions asked in this chapter are of particular relevance to understanding risk for recidivism in sexually abusive youth. That is, who might be the target of future sexual harm, what is the nature of recurrent sexually harmful behavior likely to be, under what circumstances might the juvenile re-engage in harmful sexual behavior, and why did the sexually abusive behavior occur in the first place? These questions add substance to and structure the process of risk assessment and more clearly define what it is that we are seeking to discover, as well as adding both depth and context to the process of risk assessment and our understanding of the juvenile. Additionally, the fourth question, "Why?", not only adds increasing context, structure, and understanding, but it also sets the pace for the treatment that, in some form, will almost certainly follow assessment.

This book concludes with and is built upon the idea that assessments of risk in sexually abusive youth must always be drawn from and informed by a structured risk-assessment instrument. Nevertheless, notwithstanding the use of such an instrument, whether actuarial or clinical, risk assessment per se must be embedded within the larger and overarching framework of a more comprehensive assessment. From this perspective, which is the perspective adopted by this book, the process of risk assessment for adolescents should focus on developing a deep understanding of the juvenile and the context and circumstances of his or her life, as well as the context and circumstances under which sexually abusive behavior previously occurred (whether once or repeatedly).

The process of assessing risk, then, is based on understanding the youth in the context of his or her life and through the most detailed possible understanding of the individual. This represents a model of comprehensive assessment in which the juvenile is seen a whole person operating within the ecology of his or her whole life and environment,[6] and in which the assessment of risk is merely one slice of a larger assessment and, indeed, is derived from the larger comprehensive assessment.

---

6. The ecological environment is comprised of the interactions between individuals and the social systems in which they live and function. The social ecology is formed by the set of nested and interwoven structures that exist between social systems, starting with the individual, each one of which is subsumed within a larger and more encompassing social system that interact with and influence one another. From this perspective, individual development occurs within an ecological context which significantly influences the course of such development (Wiksröm & Sampson, 2003).

CHAPTER 2

The Fifth Question: Why Risk
Assessment?

I N ADDITION TO the four questions posed in Chapter 1, there is a fifth
question relevant to risk assessment: *Why* assess risk at all? Krueger
(2007, May) notes that one important step in determining what risk
assessment instrument and protocol to use has to do with the implications
of risk assessment and, in particular, the purpose for which the assessment
will be used, such as in decisions ranging from sentencing to case management to treatment. It seems imperative that we always consider these
questions in assessment, recognizing the different purposes for which
assessments may be used, as well as different circumstances under which
they may be used and different decisions that may flow from the process of
assigning risk for sexual recidivism. It seems especially important as we
consider the assessment of risk in children and adolescents.

Prescott (2006) describes risk assessments with sexually abusive youth as
problematic and offers a number of reasons to avoid such evaluations. He
writes that we do not fully understand which elements actually contribute
to risk in adolescents and notes that, although well developed, our risk
assessment methods are not well supported by empirical evidence. He
further points out that children and adolescents are not only in the process
of developmental change but actually do change over time, and that
sexually abusive youth are far less likely to recidivate sexually than
they are to engage in other forms of antisocial behavior. Additionally,
Prescott warns that the risk assessment process itself may be harmful to the
juveniles we are assessing, and may either reflect or contribute to poor
public policy. Nevertheless, whether actually advocating for the elimination of juvenile risk assessment or simply pointing out problems about
which we should be aware, Prescott's concerns are well noted. In either

case, however, risk assessment seems to me both an important and necessary process in our understanding of and work with sexually abusive youth, not only to expand our knowledge of risk itself but also to provide a foundation upon which to address and provide for public safety, understand the youths whom we are evaluating and almost certainly going to treat, and formulate and provide treatment. To these ends and in answer to the question "Why assess?", there are at least nine interrelated reasons to engage in risk assessment.

1. Risk assessment, or projection of potential dangerousness, is an important element in a forensic model, helping to ensure that we have a sense of what damage may be caused by an individual if things remain unchanged.
2. Risk assessment allows a common language and shorthand by which to identify those who may be at risk for harming members of the public.
3. Risk assessment allows a channel for clear communication and collaboration between systems that interact with and are affected by sexually abusive youth, including the public, the courts, and providers of services that range from community supervision to mental health treatment, as well as the family and victims of the sexually abusive youth.
4. Risk assessment can provide us with insight into the causes and nature of risk itself, as well as the natural history and trajectory of risk in each individual we assess and, by extension, the larger population that is comprised of those individuals.
5. Although individualized, risk assessment can nevertheless allow us a practical means for making comparisons within and among treatment groups.
6. Risk assessment is not only about predicting risk, but also about the development of means to diminish or protect against risk. The process of risk assessment can highlight and help us better understand the nature of protective factors that diminish the effects of risk and guard against harm.
7. Risk assessment can help us to meet the individualized demands required by an effective and efficient case management and treatment delivery model, such as that proposed by Andrews, Bonta, and Hoge (1990).
8. The process of risk assessment creates a practical link between research and clinical practice.
9. Risk assessment and the answers it potentially yields provide the foundation for the treatment that follows, as treatment without

assessment is either blind to individual differences in clients (one-size-fits-all) or uninformed and shooting in the dark and even potentially unethical. We have to know what we're treating if we are to stand a chance of treating it effectively, unless we believe that "sexually abusive behavior" is a unidimensional and undifferentiated single thing rather than a multi-faceted behavior with many elements and linkages.

To be sure, these nine reasons do not, and cannot, represent the be all and end all of assessment purpose. Indeed, for most reasons there is also a potential downside or pitfall, possibly reflecting our misunderstanding of the risk assessment process or misuse or misapplication of the ideas and process. Nevertheless, they provide a foundation and a rationale for risk assessment, and further drive the task for better understanding and creating better models for assessment.

FORENSIC EVALUATION

As the forensic purpose of risk assessment is described throughout the book, it is important to provide a definition. Most simply, Grisso (2006) has written that forensic evaluations are forensic because they are performed in order to inform court decisions. This is not always the case, however, and certainly the contexts in which juvenile forensic evaluations occur extend beyond the court, as not every child or adolescent engaging is sexually abusive behavior is legally prosecuted, even though the behavior itself invokes the law and the possibility of juvenile or criminal charges.

More broadly, forensics involves matters pertaining to the court and the systems of criminal and civil justice, or the law in general. This frequently involves any behavior that violates adult or juvenile criminal laws, and it also includes matters pertaining to civil law that require evaluation, assessment, or psychological input, such as child custody cases, adoption, or miscellaneous lawsuits. Practically, forensics applies to the investigation and assessment of facts and evidence in court or the application of scientific knowledge and technology to legal matters. The treatment of the juvenile sexual offender is a forensic speciality that crosses the lines between understanding criminal behavior, assisting the process of legal discrimination and decision making regarding the behavior, assessing the behavior for future occurrence, and treating the behavior. In working with juveniles, such work requires an additional understanding of the developmental and personal psychology of children and adolescents and surrounding social systems and social forces that shape and define the emotions, cognitions, and behaviors of the child.

Forensics includes science and art in covering matters of fact and legal jurisprudence, as well as causes and consequences of legal issues, whether in the courtroom or outside. Forensic psychiatry, psychology, and social work deal with the psychology of the individual as it pertains to criminal behavior and also broader aspects that involve sentencing recommendations, child custody, malpractice, and legal mediation.

PRACTICING RISK ASSESSMENT

Is it essential, or even necessary, for an evaluator of risk to think in the terms outlined in this chapter? The answer is no. When using an actuarial assessment, for instance, such thinking or knowledge is not only not required, but psychological insight has no bearing whatsoever on the outcome of the assessment. The same is far less true in the case of clinical assessment, but it is nonetheless also true that the evaluator only needs to grasp the basics in order to complete a risk assessment. In fact, a well-designed assessment process and instrument does not require insight or knowledge in the assessor beyond that necessary to use the instrument and complete the assessment. Nevertheless, if the goal of training is to produce sophisticated evaluators of risk—evaluators who understand the concepts behind risk assessment—then without question it becomes important to explore the ideas behind assessment and provide richness and depth to our understanding and our practice.

However, even if we can argue that risk evaluators technically don't *need* to be clinically sophisticated or conceptually aware and well trained, we can easily see that this is not a position supported by the field, and we can turn to the guidelines of the American Psychological Association to illustrate goals for risk evaluators (Turner, DeMers, Fox, & Reed, 2001). The APA Task Force on Test User Qualifications describes assessment as a complex activity that requires and combines knowledge of psychometric concepts with expertise in an area of professional practice or application. "Assessment is a conceptual, problem-solving process of gathering dependable, relevant information about an individual, group, or institution to make informed decisions" (p. 1100). The guidelines describe the evaluator's function in making meaningful interpretations of data, often collected from multiple sources, in which it is important that evaluators "be able to integrate knowledge of applicable psychometric and methodological principles, the theory behind the measured construct and related empirical literature, the characteristics of the particular tests used, and the relationship between the selected test and the particular testing purpose, the testing process, and, in some contexts, the individual test taker" (p. 1104). With regard to prediction in forensic and non-forensic settings, the guidelines stress that evaluators should be knowledgeable about the predictive capacity of assessment and understand how the characteristics and the social environment of the individual being assessed may influence prediction. Finally, the guidelines note that evaluators should understand the base rate of the behavior being assessed,[1] identify and evaluate critical factors that may influence outcome, and recognize the relevance or contribution of situation factors, or context and circumstance.

Evaluator sophistication aside, the question of whether actuarial or clinical assessment is the better method for evaluating risk is not only a very old debate, but also it cannot be resolved here. However, if the heart of risk assessment is about prediction alone, then why choose the clinical model over the actuarial? Even if the actuarial model is flawed, it has been strongly and repeatedly asserted that of the two models it is the more capable of accurate prediction (Hanson & Thornton, 2000; Harris & Rice, 2007; Meehl, 1996; Quinsey, Harris, Rice, & Cormier, 1998; Steadman, et al. 2000). On the other hand, there is far from complete agreement on the greater predictive power of actuarial over clinical risk assessment (Boer, Hart, Kropp, & Webster, 1997; Hanson & Morton-Bourgon, 2007; Hart, Michie, & Cooke, 2007; Litwack, 2001). Regardless, if it isn't already clear to the reader, my own perspective is that there are strong qualities and ideas to be found in both conceptualizations of risk described in the previous chapter (one of which fuels actuarial assessment and the other clinical assessment), but that the clinical and dynamic model is by far the stronger model, even though it lacks the specificity, structure, and certainly the relatively well-proven predictive power of the statistical model.

The actuarial/clinical assessment issue is further discussed in Chapters 3, 11, and 12. However, it is pointless, and even silly, to unequivocally state that one approach to assessment is the correct approach or even superior to another; approaches are ideological and are intrinsically social constructs often brought into operation or dominance through political and other social processes (Greenberg & Watson, 2005). Despite this, from a psychological perspective our field has generally come to recognize, and indeed insist, that children and adolescents are different than adults and that the person they will become is very much based upon their experiences in society, including our response to their experiences and their behaviors.

---

1. Base rate involves the frequency at which a particular behavior occurs, in this case sexual offense recidivism among sexual offenders.

From this perspective, this book addresses juvenile assessment as a qualitatively different process than that of adult assessment. Its goal is to help better define the concepts, tools, and methods of juvenile risk assessment, and an approach to assessment that is both helpful to the evaluator and at the same time helps to produce skilled and well-informed evaluators. Finally, in the choice of an assessment process and an approach to assessment, the evaluator should be aware of different orientations and approaches to risk assessment, even in the design of the assessment instrument and model, and in application should be aware of these different underlying concepts and constructs.

CHAPTER 3

A Theory of and Model for Risk Assessment

HAVING LAID DOWN a conceptual framework and understanding of both risk assessment and risk itself, and therefore the rudiments of a theory of risk assessment, this chapter further defines the ideas implicit in such a theory and represents a theory of professional practice. When it comes to models that describe deliberate human action (such as risk assessment), Argyris and Schön (1974) describe a theory of professional practice as a special case of an action theory that, like all theories, is generalizable, relevant, consistent, complete, and simple. A theory of practice consists of interrelated ideas and assumptions that are specific to the situations to which practice will be applied and will predict and help bring about the intended results. A theory of risk assessment, then, is both a theory of action and, more specifically, a theory of professional practice. It should therefore help the evaluator to grasp and better understand the process of risk assessment, enhance professional practice, and like all theories explain, describe, and guide.[1]

Accordingly, by theory I do not mean a model testable by experiment, but rather a model of reality that is capable of describing and offering a comprehensive view of a particular phenomenon (in this case, risk assessment), providing an explanation and definition of how the phenomenon operates and allowing a means by which to guide practice. To this end, theory should provide a self-contained, logical, and formal model or framework for describing the ideas and processes of practice. In this

---

1. In fact, one criticism of actuarial assessment is that it is atheoretical, and therefore functions without a guiding conceptual framework (Beech & Ward, 2006; Craig, Browne, Stringer, & Beech, 2004; Krueger, 2007, August).

case, theory does not refer to a conjecture, a hunch, or a hypothesis (all of which are ideas that can be tested). Instead it refers to a self-contained, logical, and formal model by which to understand, shape, and operationalize risk assessment, and thus provide a model for practice and a set of consistent rules that underlie such practice.

The testability of such a model lies in its generalizability (or capacity to make sense under all or most circumstances), its internal construction and consistency, its ability to hold up under scrutiny and in application, and its value as a working model by which to understand and guide practice. Accordingly, a theory of risk assessment begins by defining risk assessment, including its purpose, process, and elements.

A DEFINITION OF RISK ASSESSMENT

Risk assessment is the process of extrapolating and estimating the possibility of future harm, in which an assigned level of risk expresses the likelihood of or potential for future harmful behavior in an individual who has previously engaged in similar behaviors. The estimate of risk and assignment of risk level is derived from a review and analysis of a combination of elements known or believed to make this individual susceptible to engagement in harmful behavior under defined circumstances and when environmental conditions allow the expression of such behavior. Risk assessment is therefore the endeavor to project the likelihood of future harmful behavior on the basis of prior and current behaviors, social interactions and relationships, and mental processes.

This definition of risk assessment can be articulated in a series of 13 related propositions.

1. Assessment of risk for harmful behavior is based upon a history of at least one prior incident in which the individual being assessed engaged in similar harmful behavior.
2. Assessed risk reflects the potential for reengagement in future harmful behavior if conditions and risk factors present at the time of the assessment remain unchanged.
3. Risk for harm cannot be absolutely measured and neither can reengagement in harmful behavior be predicted with absolute accuracy; it can only be approximated.
4. Estimations of future harmful behavior are based on the presence of interpersonal and intrapersonal factors known or believed to be related to the risk for harm. These include static factors related to historical behaviors and experiences and dynamic factors related to current mental processes,

social interactions, behavior, and environmental conditions, all of which are subject to possible change.

5. Risk factors reside in both the individual, with respect to prior and current experiences and current mental processes and behaviors, and in the individual's environment, with respect to social experiences and interactions.

6. No single risk factor is likely to contain enough power to directly lead to harmful behavior when isolated from other risk factors, and the emission of harmful behavior is linked to combinations of risk factors that interact with, amplify, and catalyze one another.

7. Even if correlated with the enactment of harmful behavior, no postulated risk factor is absolutely known to clearly cause harm, and neither can any combination of risk factors be said to incontrovertibly cause or lead to harmful behavior.

8. Although risk factors are not solely responsible for the emission of harm, and no single risk factor can be considered to be causative, risk factors play a causative role in the emission of harmful behavior.

9. The presence of risk within the individual can be explained as a result of genetic predisposition or biological development; developmental learning experiences within the ecology of the social environment that are introjected into cognitive schema and emotional experience and organization; and interaction between biological and social experience.

10. Risk factors within the environment exist independently of the individual, although in some instances there is an interaction in which risk factors in one domain influence and catalyze, and perhaps create, risk factors in the other.

11. Environmental conditions are not causative, but they provide the conditions, and sometimes the stimulus, through which harmful behavior occurs. Environmental conditions thereby act as the medium through which risk is transformed into harm.

12. The potentiality of risk factors and the transformation of risk into harm is influenced and possibly mitigated by the presence of protective factors, which are also conjectured to reside both within the individual and the environment. In the assessment of risk, even if not overtly stated, the evaluation of protective factors is an additional target with particular regard to the interaction between risk and protective factors.

13. The assigned risk level always reflects the likelihood of a recurrence of harmful behavior when environmental conditions allow for such behavior. Such conditions include the presence of a potential victim and the absence of adequate restraining forces. Without favorable environmental conditions, harmful behavior will not recur and risk is low or non-existent.

A THEORY OF DYNAMIC RISK ASSESSMENT

Whereas the definition of risk assessment provided previously is general enough to cover both actuarial and clinical assessment, the inclusion of propositions that reflect dynamic and protective factors makes this a theory of dynamic assessment rather than a theory of actuarial or static assessment (which, in present practice, are generally the same thing). However the propositions of the theory, which operationalize its definition, allow the idea that actuarial assessment itself may be simply one element in a larger and more dynamic model of assessment. Indeed, it is already the case that the assessment of adult sexual offenders is extending beyond the narrow confines of actuarial assessment.

The Structured Risk Assessment process (SRA) (Thornton, 2002), the Structured Assessment of Risk and Need (SARN) (Webster et al., 2006), the Structured Anchored Clinical Judgment (SACJ) (Grubin, 1998), the Sex Offender Need Assessment Rating (SONAR) (Hanson & Harris, 2000a), and the Stable Dynamic Assessment (SDA) and its derivatives, the STA-BLE-2007 and ACUTE-2007 (Harris & Hanson, 2003; Harris & Hanson, 2007) are each built upon actuarial assessments but expand beyond the statistical assessment of static risk factors to incorporate dynamic risk factors. They each thus recognize the relationship between dynamic risk factors and recidivism in sexual offenders, and especially those in treatment or under supervision. In her development of the Inventory of Offender Risk, Needs, and Strengths (IORNS), for use in the assessment of a general criminal population, Miller (2006) is similarly developing a risk assessment measure that combines static and dynamic risk factors, as well as protective factors and strengths that can help in the risk assessment, treatment planning, and monitoring of offenders, "as well as providing a mechanism to explore the relationship between all three variables in combination with recidivism" (p. 779).

These are the third generation, and even fourth generation, assessment instruments described by Bonta and others.[2] They represent a risk assessment model that extends beyond the actuarially based model incorporating

---

2. First generation instruments were based largely on clinical judgment, whereas the second generation assessments that followed resulted in statistically derived and static actuarial assessment instruments. Third generation tools incorporate both the evidence base of the static assessment and the dynamic factors of the clinical assessment and fourth generation models integrate an even wider range of dynamic factors, incorporating factors relevant to treatment interventions and monitoring (Andrews, Bonta, & Wormith, 2006; Bonta & Andrews, 2007; Hannah-Moffat & Maurutto, 2003). Both third and fourth generation models thus represent the actuarially-based dynamic assessment model described in this chapter.

the evaluation of dynamic risk factors in an integrated and dynamic model, in which the inclusion of dynamic measures "can improve risk prediction beyond that achievable by static factors alone" (Allan, Grace, Rutherford, & Hudson, 2007, p. 348).

These instruments not only recognize the existence and utility of both static and dynamic risk factors, but also that "there is no reason to think that one type is superior to another when it comes to the predicting recidivism" (Bonta, 2002, p. 367). For instance, in their study of general criminal (non-sexual) recidivism Gendreau, Little, and Goggin's (1996) meta-analysis of 131 studies concluded that dynamic risk factors perform-ed at least as well as static risk factors in the prediction of general criminal recidivism, and they also concluded that different types of assessment procedures should be compared and combined. Mills (2005) similarly describes the "integrated method approach" (p. 238) that blends psycho-metric results and clinical data into risk assessment. Bonta writes that static factors not only have limited utility, but also that they may even be "somewhat redundant" as dynamic factors have comparable predictive value, and asserts that dependence "on static risk instruments may even be counterproductive" (p. 370). In their study of 60 adolescent sexual offenders, Martinez, Flores, and Rosenfeld (2007) found that the *dynamic* assessment scales of an empirically based risk assessment instrument (the Juvenile Sex Offender Assessment Protocol-II) showed the greatest accu-racy in predicting sexual recidivism; not only were the dynamic scales more effective than the static scales of the J-SOAP, but in this study the static scales were not associated with any of the outcome variables.

Indeed, Beech and Ward (2004) note several criticisms of solely actuarial assessments, including the invisibility of risk factors relevant to individ-ual cases and the exclusion of contextual risk factors that may signal increased risk. In fact, Martinez et al. conclude that one possible reason for the superior performance of the dynamic scales in their study was that the evaluating clinicians were familiar with and knowledgeable about the behavior and characteristics of the sexually abusive youth in their study (also making a strong argument for the effectiveness of clinical judgment in risk assessment, as the dynamic assessment usually invariably involves such judgment).

The idea that dynamic risk assessments may include and build upon actuarial assessments is welcome. It represents an acknowledgment and recognition that static actuarial assessment alone is not powerful enough to either clearly assess risk or assure that we avoid both false negatives (impinging on the safety of the public) and false positives (impinging on the well-being of the offender). Hence, we see two streams to dynamic assessment: (1) actuarially based dynamic assessments that include and incorporate a statistical level of risk (i.e., an actuarial assessment), and (2) clinically based dynamic assessments that do not contain a statistically derived base and are instead built upon a professional and literature-based understanding of risk (sometimes known as empirically guided or based). Developers of adult risk assessment processes already have the capacity and instruments by which to develop and continue to develop actuarially based dynamic risk assessments, and with the development of the Juvenile Sexual Offense Recidivism Risk Assessment Tool (Epperson, Ralston, Fowers, DeWitt, & Gore, 2006)[3] the same opportunities will be available in the evolution of adolescent risk assessment.

THE CLINICAL FOCUS OF DYNAMIC RISK ASSESSMENT

However, in the case of both actuarially and clinically based dynamic assessment streams, dynamic risk assessment is inherently *clinical* in its assessment of risk. Unless we get to the point where we can statistically predict the interaction between static and dynamic risk factors and the role that dynamic risk factors play in recidivism—especially *which* dynamic factors—it is unlikely that we will ever derive an actuarial assessment based upon the complexity or even a full understanding of dynamic risk and its variants. The moment that we include dynamic factors in our assessment of risk we also include a strong element of clinical judgment in our selection of dynamic risk factors, the way we evaluate their importance, and our beliefs about when the presence or absence of such factors maintains, increases, or decreases risk for sexual recidivism.

In the pure actuarial assessment, the application of judgment to determine final levels of risk is referred to as clinical adjustment or adjusted actuarial assessment and is considered by some to weaken, rather than strengthen, risk assessment. Campbell (2004) notes that clinical adjustment will invariably create inconsistency in the process of actuarial assessment and lead to increased errors in assessment. Harris and Rice (2007) write "the idea that actuarial methods can somehow be blended with clinical intuition is a logical non sequitur" (p. 1652). They advocate that "empiricism should replace clinical judgment wherever possible" (p. 1653). Quinsey, Harris, Rice, and Cormier (2006) assert their position clearly: "What we are advising is not the addition of actuarial methods to existing practice,

---

3. Although still in development, the JSORRAT is the first actuarial tool to be developed for risk assessment with juvenile sexual offenders, and is briefly discussed in Chapter 4 and in more detail in Chapters 12, 13, and 14.

but rather the complete replacement of existing practice with actuarial methods" (p. 197). However, despite the conclusion of Grove and Lloyd (2006) that there is no "true hybrid" of the clinical and statistical models of data collection and analysis, they recognize the clinical-mechanical interface in risk assessment and that subtypes of each method exist that contain elements of the other (p. 192).

Indeed, there is growing support for not only a model of actuarially based dynamic risk assessment, but also the relevance of clinical adjustment to actuarial assessment. Doren (2002) has written that no actuarial instrument can assess true reoffending risk because "existing actuarial instruments do not yet include enough of the relevant considerations to maximize our predictive effectiveness" (p. 113). Hence, Craig, Browne, Stringer, and Beech (2004) conclude that combining the predictive validity of actuarial methods with empirically guided clinical adjustments based on dynamic risk factors offers promise for the further development of risk assessment measures. Craig, Thornton, Beech, and Browne (2007) write "the measure and integration of psychological vulnerability factors [i.e., dynamic risk factors] . . . as additions to statistical systems of risk, are likely to further advance our understanding in predicting sexual reconviction" (p. 327).

The assessment models and instruments briefly described above, such as the SAJC, SARN, SONAR, STABLE-2007, and IORNS, attest to the development of actuarially based dynamic assessments. Mills (2005) writes that such an approach (which he calls dynamic actuarial) has all of the advantages of actuarial risk assessment while overcoming its reliance on unchangeable static risk indicators. He writes that the dynamic actuarial approach is especially of great value in indicating when risk has diminished and when, where, and how to intervene. Similarly, Gendreau et al. (1996) note that it is difficult to meaningfully reclassify an offender in absence of an assessment that recognizes and can measure dynamic change.

These models recognize that on its own actuarial assessment is not only based upon static variables but itself is static. Without the assessment of dynamic factors, risk level as assigned by the actuarial assessment alone must by definition remain unchanged for all time, or at least for the length of time covered by the statistical formulation upon which the actuarial assessment is based. Only by assessing other factors relevant to the individual, some of which change over time, is it possible to assess change, as static factors do not otherwise allow the possibility of change. In fact, only by applying a model of dynamic assessment can human beings be seen as capable of change and treatment be seen as a relevant model for introducing, inducing, and fostering change. It may be possible for relevant dynamic risk factors to be identified and selected through statistical analysis, and some determinations about change in dynamic areas of human functioning may be measured psychometrically. Nevertheless, in the main, the evaluation of dynamic factors is made through professional judgment, involving, as Gendreau et al. (1996) note, a degree of subjectivity.

Further, Witt (2000) and Campbell (2000, 2004) note that most actuarial risk assessment procedures or their supplementary assessment procedures in some way rely upon clinical processes and that actuarial procedures eventually fall back on clinical judgment. In fact, even the diagnosis of psychopathy, frequently an element in the actuarial risk assessment, is itself the outcome of a clinical process. Although the construct of psychopathy is most commonly derived through a statistical procedure, a determination that psychopathy is present is decidedly clinical, most commonly determined through the application of the Hare Psychopathy Checklist, which is itself a clinical instrument.

STABLE AND ACUTE DYNAMIC RISK FACTORS

In recognizing dynamic risk factors, we understand that they are comprised of many different types of complex factors and forces that are at work upon us, interacting with other elements in our lives to partially influence and shape our emotions, ideas, and behavior. Not only do these dynamic factors reside within the individual and within the individual's environment, but they also vary by their persistence and stability over time, as well as their relationship to sometimes fluctuating or temporary environmental conditions, described by Hanson and Harris (2000b) as stable and acute dynamic factors.

In the first instance, even though they may be amenable to change, dynamic risk factors may be stable in that they remain active and relatively unchanging for long periods of time and may even be relatively resistant to change, such as personality characteristics or patterns of social attachment. On the other hand, acute risk factors are brought into existence by unstable or impermanent conditions that may emerge relatively quickly or are temporary in nature. These too can be seen to exist within the individual, in terms of mood, cognition, and behaviors that disinhibit (such as intoxication), and within the environment, such as reduced family support, financial stress, decreased supervision, or increased opportunity to act out harmful behavior. Further, acute risk factors themselves may be transitory and passing, or they may be chronic with respect to their predictable reappearance in response to predictable personal, social, or other environmental conditions. Beech and Ward (2004, 2006) recognize these same factors but conceptualize them differently. They conceive of stable dynamic factors as relatively fixed characterological or psychological traits and acute factors as transitory state-like events that serve to amplify and trigger stable (or trait-like) risk factors.

Regardless of language, it is clear that dynamic factors are complex in their nature and interactions. It is easy to see that it is the constellation of dynamic factors, in concert with both static risk indicators and other risk factors, that makes it so difficult to fully understand them and predict their impact and the results of their influence.

PROTECTIVE FACTORS AND A THEORY OF ASSESSMENT

In his critique of forensic risk assessment, Rogers (2000) describes assessment as inherently flawed if it pays attention only to risk factors without consideration given to the presence, weight, and action of protective factors. Although not describing protective factors, per se, in his book on the clinical prediction of risk for violence, Monahan (1995) also notes the importance of giving balanced consideration to factors that indicate the absence of violent behavior, as well as factors that suggest the recurrence of violence. Regardless, despite the importance of recognizing and understanding the nature and strength of protective factors and factoring this into an assessment of risk, it is not clear that a theory of risk assessment must incorporate the function of protective elements. Similarly, without disregarding protective factors, it is not clear that a structured assessment instrument needs or can include a formal assessment of protective factors. Indeed, this would be a difficult task as it may be that assessing the role and weight of protective factors in predicting recidivism is an even more difficult task than understanding the action and assessing the impact of dynamic risk factors.

Protective factors and their role in risk assessment are discussed in detail in Chapter 8. However, for now, although protective factors may actually represent strengths independently found in the individual and his or her social environment,[4] for the purposes of risk assessment, protective factors are considered to exist only in relation to and as buffers against risk. Accordingly, a definition of dynamic risk assessment need not reference the nature, role, and power of protective factors, which can be thought of as current psychological and social elements and conditions that dampen the possibility of harm. The presence and action of protective factors must instead be inferred as either the absence of risk factors or as internalized or

---

4. Independent of risk, that is.

environmental conditions that inhibit the expression of harm. At the level of assessment in action, the presence of protective factors must be factored into risk evaluation at the intrapersonal, interpersonal, and impersonal levels of psychological functioning, social interaction, and environmental conditions.

A DEFINITION OF DYNAMIC RISK ASSESSMENT

Arriving now at a place where the description of risk assessment provided has been more fully explored and built on a conceptual framework, we are almost ready to further describe a theory of dynamic risk assessment.

Dynamic risk assessment integrates the evaluation of static risk indicators found in the behavioral and psychosocial history of the individual, dynamic markers of current psychological experience and functioning, and social forces to which the individual is currently exposed in his or her environment. Potential risk results from the interaction of static and dynamic risk factors and the further influence of current or possible environmental conditions that may amplify risk and allow its transformation into harmful behavior.

THEORY AS A MODEL OF REALITY

Figure 3.1 illustrates this formulation of dynamic risk assessment. As seen, static factors serve as both risk factors (and in the case of static behaviors, as risk indicators) and a mediating pathway by which dynamic personal factors (those risk factors that reside within the individual) develop over time.[5]

In fact, many dynamic, or current, psychological risk factors are the result of earlier (static) experience. This is because static and dynamic factors of human behavior, personality, and functioning are but reflections of one another. The roots of current psychological functioning are found in early developmental history, and early psychological experience and development sets the pace for and to some degree predicts the development of later psychological and behavioral development. That is, from the

---

5. Barr, Boyce, and Zeltzer (1996) describe variables (in this case, risk factors) as mediators if they influence or open a channel that links or even transforms stimulus to outcome. They describe variables as moderators if they increase or decrease the strength of the relationship between a stimulus and outcome, but do not alter the stimulus. Hence, mediators allow and influence transformation, whereas moderators act upon the transformational process to either strengthen or weaken it, thus influencing the likelihood of any particular outcome.

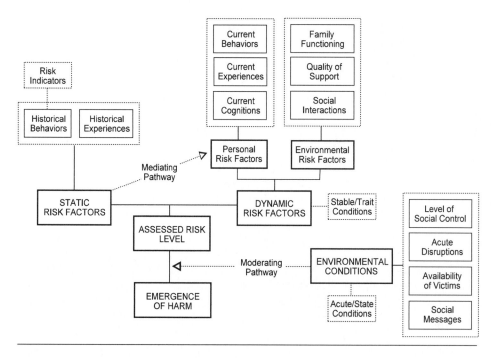

Figure 3.1 A formulation of risk assessment in which a combination of static and stable dynamic risk factors drive the assessed level of risk, and the emergence of harm is moderated by acute environmental conditions.

developmental and other conditions that give rise to risk grow the psychological schema and behavioral patterns that persist as ongoing and stable dynamic factors or, as Beech and Ward (2006) put it, behavioral risk traits. A strong example of this is described by attachment theory. The presence of a current insecure style of attachment, or even a disordered pattern of attachment, results from and may to some degree be predicted by attachment experiences occurring within the first two years of life. In this example, an earlier experience becomes a static element embedded within the developmental pathway that, if unchanged, leads to a later stable pattern of attachment that is present and active in, and therefore a dynamic aspect of, current psychological and social functioning.

Because static factors both contribute to risk directly and lead to the development of dynamic factors that reside within the individual, it is clear that each type of factor is linked to the other, which may help to explain why, as Bonta (2002) notes, dynamic and static risk factors have comparable predictive value, and risk may perhaps thus be predicted through either channel. Nevertheless, it is the combination of the two types of factors, including dynamic risk factors found in the environment (which are independent of the individual), that yield the greatest depth and breadth of understanding about the individual under assessment.

Whereas static risk is considered to partially mediate the development of dynamic risk (or serve as a link), in Figure 3.1 environmental conditions are shown as moderating risk. That is, the nature of environmental variables may serve to either restrict or neutralize risk or amplify risk and allow the emergence of harm. Thus, environmental conditions serve as moderators of risk. The figure also incorporates Hanson and Harris' depiction of stable and acute elements of risk, as well as Beech and Ward's conceptualization of these as traits and states. Dynamic risk factors are shown as stable, trait-like elements, whereas the environmental conditions that contribute to the emergence of harm are depicted as acute, state-like elements.

With regard to the elements shown in Figure 3.1 that contribute to static risk, dynamic risk, and environmental conditions, it is important to note that these are just examples and not intended to exhaustively represent such elements. Further, there is a complicated overlap between such elements, which often do not necessarily exclusively belong to one class of factor or condition. The point is that in any model we attempt to mirror reality in a way that can best explain it, but are unlikely to ever exactly duplicate or describe it fully. Hence, this model is simply that—a model designed to explain and illustrate a process rather than a exact reflection of reality.

Finally, although neither the definition of dynamic risk assessment nor the model depicted in Figure 3.1 make any specific reference to the role of protective factors, they should be inferred. Frankly, overtly including protective factors makes the model too complicated, in part because protective factors can be considered to operate at multiple points within the model. It is also true that in some cases protective factors can be inferred by their inverse relationship to risk factors or risky environmental conditions. In the case of environmental risk factors, for instance, where family instability and a lack of family support represents a risk factor, the converse—that is, the presence of family support—serves as a protective factor. With respect to environmental conditions, lack of social control amplifies a risk condition, but active monitoring and supervision, through probation for instance, represents protection. Hence, a definition that included protective factors would describe these as the presence or provision of conditions that serve to buffer against or neutralize the effects of risk factors, and in a diagram protective factors would be seen to function at various points throughout the illustration.

RISK ASSESSMENT AS A THEORY
OF PROFESSIONAL PRACTICE

As is always the case, theory offers an explanation rather than describing incontrovertible laws of nature. In this case, it offers a formal and systematic expression of ideas that explain and guide the process of risk assessment. It neither presents a series of facts or conjectures, but instead presents an organized and linked set of propositions that illuminate process and practice.

Of course, from a theory of risk can be extrapolated a theory about the conditions that create risk and, in our case, the emergence of sexually abusive behavior. However, a theory of risk assessment is not a theory about why certain elements create risk or how these elements came into being, and neither does it attempt to delineate the exact nature or content of risk factors. It is instead a theory about or a model of how risk factors are related to the expression of harm and how risk may be conceptualized and assessed.

APPLYING A THEORY OF RISK ASSESSMENT TO THE
ASSESSMENT OF JUVENILES

It may be true that risk can better be predicted through a statistical assessment of static risk factors or that risk can be inferred with equal validity from an assessment of the right dynamic factors. However, comprehensive assessment will take into account both types of factors, found within the environment as well as within the individual, and will further take stock of the environmental conditions under which assessed risk is most likely to emerge as harmful behavior and the protective factors most likely to inhibit risk.

Static assessment precludes, by design, the possibility of changing the assigned risk level. However, if we assume that treatment and other interventions can make a difference, and thus reduce risk, we have no choice but to adopt a model that, somewhere down the line, recognizes dynamic factors (which, after all, are the target of treatment). We must then select an assessment process that fits our philosophy of human behavior and engagement. In such a selection, we might bear in mind Bonta's (2002) guidelines for selection and use of risk assessments, and particularly guideline 10, which simply says "Be Nice" (p. 374). His perspective reflects a philosophy of assessment and intervention, walking a line between public safety and respect for the client, and the translation here is "be careful."

Nowhere is this philosophy of critical thinking and care (also reflecting Bonta's ninth guideline of exercising professional responsibility) more important than in our work with, and perhaps especially our forensic assessment of, young people, including those who engage in sexually abusive behavior. We must, then, remain aware of and cautious about the developmental status and changeability of children and adolescents. For this reason, virtually without exception all designers and students of juvenile risk assessment agree that such evaluation should be comprehensive in design, contextual in application, and not based solely on static factors. The principles of care for juvenile sexual offenders recently promulgated by the International Association for the Treatment of Sexual Offenders (Miner et al., 2006), for instance, notes that juveniles are best understood in the context of their families and social environments and that assessment of risk should be based on a developmental perspective and sensitive to the process of developmental change. That is, adolescent risk, per se, should be understood in a broader context than simply the trajectory that static factors point toward or initiate.

Hence, we move from this general and broad theory of risk assessment, and in particular the dynamic assessment of risk, to depth in our understanding of the children and adolescents we assess and the nature of risk and protective factors, which are picked up in the following chapters.

CHAPTER 4

Risk Assessment in Children and Adolescents

HEALTHY PEOPLE IN healthy families living in healthy communities engage in healthy behavior. This is the very crux of an ecological theory of prosocial behavior, which can be completed by the observation that healthy behavior fosters the development of healthy communities, healthy families, and healthy people.

In many respects when we discuss how to best understand and assess risk for continued sexually abusive behavior in children and adolescents, we can apply the very same concepts. When we consider assessment in this way, it provides an even richer contextual nature to the ideas of assessment already discussed in previous chapters. It means that we understand risk factors in light of developmental considerations regarding the biological and psychological growth and emergence of adolescence from childhood, and in turn adulthood from adolescence. It also means that we recognize risk factors emerging from and embedded within the deeply contextual and interwoven social environment and the systems and interactions therein.

However, adults are also influenced by, and are the products of, their environment, no less than adolescents. The difference is perhaps that, even if still developing, adults are far more formed than adolescents in every way: physically, neurologically, emotionally, cognitively, and behaviorally. Adult behaviors must also be understood contextually, but the contexts and circumstances under which adolescent behavior emerges are usually quite different than those that surround adult behavior, and adolescent behavior is far more sensitive to the background contexts and circumstances from which they emerge. That is, adolescent behavior, including sexually abusive behavior, is far more influenced by developing biological, emotional, cognitive, and social systems and the social environment in general, than adult behavior.

This view distinguishes adolescents from adults, not just by physical size or life experience, but by developmental stage and resulting differences in experiences of and responses to the social environment in which children and adolescents live, learn, and develop. Consequently, juvenile sexually abusive behavior must also be understood in a manner that is sensitive to physical (and especially neurological) and psychological development, circumstances present in the social environment that partially give rise to adolescent behavior, and the meaning of behavior in the context of the social environment. This exemplifies the view that endogenous and exogenous factors operate together and in mutual and reciprocal interaction with one another. Here, we no longer ask whether factors found within the individual or within the environment are more significant in shaping behavior or, more precisely, the individual behind the behavior. Instead, we have come to believe that there is no versus at all in the debate about nature or nurture; one invariably shapes the other so that, recognizing their reciprocal interactivity, nature cannot be separated from nurture (Shonkoff & Phillips, 2000). With respect to the assessment of risk, in order to understand risk, and therefore predict its possible consequences, we need to understand the interplay between nature and nurture (Rutter, 1997).

Accordingly, for most of us, it is the interaction between inherent individual characteristics and characteristics found in the environment that shapes behavior. Here, behavior is described by Monahan (1995) as a "joint function" of personal characteristics and the characteristics of the environment in which the person functions (p. 37). That is, our behavior in the present *and* in the future is not likely to be determined by purely internal or purely historical (or purely environmental) conditions, but by reciprocal and transformational transactions that bring about change in both the individual and his or her environment. Indeed, Monahan notes failure to take information about the individual's environment into account as a source of weakness in risk prediction. This idea about the ecological development of behavioral psychology is key, and it is reflected by Henry, Caspi, Moffitt, and Silva (1996), who write that children who become serious criminal offenders are characterized by features that consistently bring them into conflict with their surroundings.[1]

---

1. Henry et al. actually describe the fit between the child and environment "at a very early age" (p. 614), thus describing both the relationship between child and environment *and* the power of static variables.

Pless and Stein (1996) write that much of the research on stress, risk, protection against risk, and the development of resilience makes sense only when seen from a developmental point of view, in which a central feature of juvenile experience and behavior is "the dynamic background of developmental change" (p. 343). Similarly, LeDoux writes that "people don't come preassembled, but are glued together by life" (2002, p.3); the perspective taken here is that children and adolescents are still being glued together by life and, in reality, are very much in that process. This seems a reasonable starting point for this chapter, which is about assessing risk in children and adolescents who are still very much in the process of development and change and understanding that such development occurs not in isolation but within the social environment.

ASSESSMENT IN AN ECOLOGICAL CONTEXT

The developmental pathway of each individual cannot be separated from the social environment into which it is woven. An ecological perspective from this point of view relates to the interconnection between, and the mutual influence of, each part of the environment. Like general systems theory (Von Bertalanffy, 1976), an ecological model holds a view that individual elements are part of larger complex systems in which all elements interact with and influence one another. Systems theories of human behavior, including now standard models of family therapy, are based upon this perspective, in which individuals can only be fully understood in the context of the larger systems of which they are but one member (and in which whole systems are comprised of interacting individuals).

In the ecological environment described by Bronfenbrenner (1979), systems are contained within still larger systems, and interaction and communication occurs not only within systems but *across* systems as well. Without reference to the larger ecological system that surrounds the individual, Bronfenbrenner considers it impossible to fully understand human behavior or interaction. Similarly, Elliot, Williams, and Hamburg (1998) describe the ecological-developmental approach as a framework by which human development is understood as occurring through interactive social contexts that influence and shape behavior. Human development thus occurs within a complex and multiply nested, multiply interacting, and mutually transactional environment, depicted in Figure 4.1.

Our ability to understand human development and behavior thus requires an understanding of the individual affected by all levels of the ecological system. To a great degree, this becomes part of a guiding model

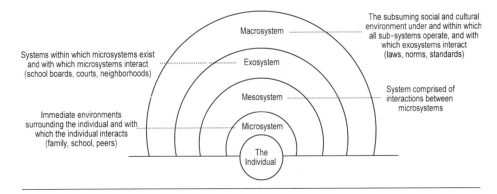

Figure 4.1   Bronfenbrenner's (1979) model of human ecology (Rich, 2006).

in risk assessment for sexually abusive youth, in which we understand risk in children and adolescents in the contexts of both their neurological and psychological development and their social learning environment.

THE BALANCE: SOCIAL DEVELOPMENT AND PERSONAL RESPONSIBILITY IN JUVENILE BEHAVIOR

By combining a view of juveniles in a developmental and social context, we thus recognize not only the effects of development on behavior but also psychological and behavioral development itself in the context of the developmental/learning environment in which children and adolescents exist. However, understanding children and adolescents partly as a product of physical development and partly the social environment is only a statement that we cannot reasonably or fully understand juveniles and their behavioral choices without understanding the larger contexts out of which behavior develops. It is not a way of saying that juveniles are not responsible for their choices, have no free will, do not understand or have no capacity to recognize the consequences of their behaviors, or are merely the products of physical and social developmental forces.

To some degree, all of these statements have some bearing and guide the choices that we make as a society about how to respond to juvenile behaviors. Nevertheless, as noted by Epstein (2007), adolescents are capable, and in many respects as capable as adults, of making choices informed by accurate perceptions of right and wrong. He argues that ideas by which adolescents are defined as less capable or less responsible than adults are a cultural artifact and not a reflection of their inherent inability. Hence, although we recognize juvenile behavior in the contexts of physical, psychological, and social development and the sociocultural environment, we also recognize that juveniles are not passive beings and do make volitional behavioral choices, including engaging in antisocial behaviors, for which, to varying degrees, they are responsible. Shoplifting, vandalism, breaking and entering, violence, and sexually abusive behavior are examples of antisocial behaviors in which some juveniles intentionally engage in the full knowledge that such behaviors are wrong,[2] have consequences to themselves if caught, and clearly have consequences to others.

Although varying forms of denial and cognitive distortions may shield the juvenile from thinking too deeply about the consequences to others or self (such as I'm not harming an individual by stealing things from the department store, or no-one will really get harmed, or I won't get caught), most juveniles nevertheless understand that the behavior is illegal and socially wrong. For instance, it's rare that a child will come home and tell his mother that he shoplifted earlier today and ask if she'd like some of the candy he stole, or tells his father, or his friend for that matter, that he's engaging in sexual behaviors with his 6-year-old sister and wants to make sure there's no danger of making her pregnant. This is because these juveniles know that the behaviors are wrong, even if they do not fully understand the seriousness of the behavior or the depth of possible consequences to others or self.

In these cases, despite limited depth of knowledge or insight, children and adolescents are capable of intentionally engaging in behaviors they know are wrong and, in some cases, clearly know will cause harm to others (such as beating up a younger child, stealing someone's bicycle, or breaking into a house). Understanding developmental learning and neurological development may help us understand the roots of the behavior, and understanding historical and current risk factors will help us project trajectory, but doesn't make the child less responsible or accountable for his or her behavior. Our decisions about how to respond may be altered, but we should not in most cases remove responsibility from the child engaging in the behaviors or assume the child is not responsible for intentional antisocial choices (and, in addition to projecting trajectory, assessment will help us to determine the level of comprehension, intentionality, and accountability that is relevant in each case).

Hence, as we move on to discuss assessment from the perspective that juvenile behavior of all sorts must be viewed and understood in the context of the environment, we also recognize that in most cases children and

---

2. I've intentionally left substance abuse off this short list as I want to ensure that we are addressing antisocial behavior in which there's little doubt that there are victims, with little moral greyness.

adolescents are responsible for their behavioral choices to varying degrees based, in part, upon their age, cognitive development, and cognitive skill. Here, we must recognize intentionality, even if not full comprehension of the consequences of behavior to self and others.

CHOOSING HOW TO ASSESS RISK
WITH SEXUALLY ABUSIVE YOUTH

Building on the ideas presented in Chapters 1, 2, and 3, if our sole goal is the most accurate prediction of risk for reengagement in sexually abusive behavior, then our choice should be the development and use of an assessment tool and process that is most geared to do this.

Presently, at least with respect to adult assessment tools, this seems to involve a statistically based actuarial instrument (although, as noted in Chapter 3 and also described in Chapter 12, the capacity of actuarial assessments to more accurately predict risk than dynamically oriented assessment processes is quite frequently and continually challenged). Regardless of its predictive validity[3] or predictive superiority over clinically adjusted or purely clinical assessment, actuarial assessment embraces a model in which judgment is based on simple arithmetic calculation alone rather than analysis and interpretation of data in order to produce meaning beyond the data itself. Actuarial assessment represents the sum of the parts, whereas clinical or dynamic assessment reflects conclusions and predictions that go beyond the sum total of arithmetic scores.

In fact, if our goal in the assessment of risk in sexually abusive youth is merely prediction, and we believe that history (i.e., static factors) is the best predictor of future behavior, then the use of an actuarial assessment tool may suffice. However, as has been made clear already, the position taken by virtually all evaluators of juvenile risk is that assessment must be made in a far broader manner. This clearly represents a model in which we believe that prediction alone, even if we were capable of making and proving accurate predictions of risk in children and adolescents, is inadequate, lacks substance, and fails to pay attention to the juvenile him or herself, who will undoubtedly in most cases be exposed to some form of treatment following assessment. Furthermore, even if an actuarial assessment is available, by design it cannot address or recognize gains or changes made in treatment that may reduce or otherwise change the assigned risk

---

3. The ability of a risk assessment instrument to actually predict recidivism and statistical proof that assigned levels of risk are accurately related to incidents of recidivism.

level. These ideas are of special note in the prediction of future behavior (including risky behavior) in children and adolescents who, to some degree, are a fluid moving target with respect to attitudes, beliefs, interests, ideas, and behaviors that change from year to year, accompanied or driven by still-developing cognitive capacity and skills and neural structure.

Actually, until very recently, the choice between actuarial or clinical risk assessment in the assessment of sexually abusive youth was moot, as we had no actuarial assessment instrument and, indeed, at this moment we technically still do not. However, this is about to change dramatically and already is changing with the advent of the Juvenile Sexual Offense Recidivism Risk Assessment Tool (JSORRAT-II), the first actuarial assessment instrument designed specifically for the assessment of juvenile sexual offenders. Although still in development and in a largely research form at the moment, it seems likely that the JSORRAT will be available for juvenile risk assessment within the foreseeable future, and it is already normed and available for use as a standardized risk assessment instrument in at least one state (Utah), with more standardized testing and norming of the instrument taking place at this time. The introduction of this new assessment tool not only offers an additional instrument for risk assessment, but also it brings the field of juvenile risk assessment closer to that of adult risk assessment and, accordingly, for the first time brings the same problems and controversies.[4]

That is, do we resort to and use only statistically derived assessments of risk to predict recidivism in adolescents (the JSORRAT is designed only for adolescents boys, and only those actually adjudicated on sexual charges) and make intervention decisions based on the results, or do we use a dynamic risk assessment to understand the juvenile and his or her behavior,[5] whether or not it includes an actuarial assessment? However, regardless of the capacity of an actuarial assessment to demonstrate strong predictive validity, it's clear that there's a great deal of support for dynamic assessment processes, whether they include an actuarial component or not, and the idea that actuarial assessment should simply be one part of a larger and more comprehensive assessment.

Certainly, the position taken in this book, and widely held in the field, is that juvenile risk assessment should and must be envisioned as part of and embedded within a larger and more comprehensive assessment. Whether

---

4. The JSORRAT is described in detail in Chapters 13 and 14.

5. At the moment, and for the foreseeable future, we only have dynamic clinical assessment tools available for use in assessing pre-pubescent children and adolescent girls.

an actuarial assessment or clinical assessment instrument is used as the primary vehicle for assessing risk, assignments of risk are derived from this larger evaluation. The difference here is that in the case of actuarial assessment the result generated by the risk instrument (i.e., the statistically derived level of risk) is fed into a larger, more dynamically oriented comprehensive assessment in which the assignment of risk level undergoes clinical adjustment in light of other information about the juvenile. In the case of the clinical assessment, there is no need for a "clinical" adjustment as the process itself is clinical, and the assessment of risk is derived from this process. The risk assessment tool is a clinical instrument in that, although it may (or may not) use validated risk factors, clinical judgment is required in every case to assign meaning and to a great degree in the selection of the risk factors that determine the structure of the instrument are derived through a clinical process.[6]

TAKING CARE

Only clinical evaluation can allow us to see the child or adolescent in the context of his or her life and development, whereas actuarial processes are inherently mechanistic and blind to the individual. In a nutshell, actuarial assessments are actuarial because they count up the number of statistically determined risk factors that appear in the history of the individual being assessed, and they then compare that individual against a class of other individuals who (a) also have a history of similar risk factors and (b) have recidivated. Thus, on the basis of his or her arithmetic score (based upon the number and intensity of historical risk factors), the individual being assessed is assigned a risk level based upon his or her similarity to recidivists. Actuarial assessment, then, judges individuals as members of a class and not as individuals. However, even in the insurance business, the home of the actuarial assessment (in determining risk for insurance policies and payouts on those policies), insurance adjustors are available to individualize the process, and frankly make it more human, in which insurance premiums and payouts can be modified to reflect actual experience rather than the statistical model of reality.

Returning to sexual offender risk assessment, only clinical assessments can gather the widest possible range of information from which to draw conclusions, including a wealth of information about the individual child

---

6. The JSORRAT is an example (and currently, our only example) of an actuarial assessment for juveniles, whereas the J-SOAP, J-RAT, and ERASOR are examples of structured clinical assessment instruments.

or adolescent. This is, of course, particularly important given the developmental contexts in which juvenile offenses occur.

In the risk assessment of juveniles we must take great care with respect to how we visualize children and adolescents and make sense of their behaviors, and we must recognize the consequences that our view of and interventions with them may have, both for each juvenile we assess and their families, communities, and our larger society. Differences between adults and juveniles should be reflected in the assessment of their behaviors and the possibility that in our response we may unintentionally place juvenile offenders on an adult criminal path by making ineffective, and even inhumane, treatment decisions. One of the primary and first considerations, then, is that juvenile sexual offenders are not merely younger and smaller versions of adult sexual offenders, although in relatively few cases some will go on to become adult sexual offenders. The goal in assessment, actually, is to spot those juveniles at increased risk for persisting in sexually abusive behavior and intercede in order to ensure that they don't develop into adult sexual offenders.

Further, if we believe that treatment interventions may work, or that juveniles can change even without treatment, we must have a means to reassess over time. This alone requires a dynamic process of assessment, at least for assessing change. Due to their nature, static assessments will *always* lead to exactly the same outcome, as though nothing has changed (which is why they're called static). That static model dooms the individual to pre-destiny; once something has occurred it can never be recognized as undone and stands forever. Even if we believe that risk in adolescents is inherent in the individual rather the environment, a reasonable question is whether factors or historical behaviors present at one point in child and adolescent development still represent and define risk for the juvenile one or two years later.

Although it certainly appears to be true that adverse circumstances in the early life of the child create risk for the development of later neurological, mood, and behavioral problems (Andersen & Teicher, 2004; Andersen et al, in press; Balbernie, 2001; Teicher et al., 1997; Teicher, Tomoda, & Andersen, 2006), it's equally true that risk factors operate in different ways and result in different outcomes at different points in child, adolescent, and adult development, and especially as they intersect and interact with stressful environmental conditions and protective factors (Haggerty & Sherrod, 1996, Lahey & Waldman, 2003; Moffit, 2003; Rutter, 1996; Rutter, Giller, & Hagell, 1998; Sroufe, Egeland, Carlson, & Collins, 2005). For instance, the report of the U. S. Surgeon General (U.S. Department of Health and Human Services, 2001) notes that risk factors are, in general, not static. Although we might draw a distinction here between risk factors and risk indicators in which indicators are historical markers, the Surgeon General's report refers to risk factors as active elements that are dynamic, interactive, and multi-layered, and found in multiple domains that include the individual, the environment, and the individual's ability to respond to the requirements and forces of the environment (or the influences of the multilevel environment described by Wachs, 1996). That is, different risk factors are at play and with more-or-less potency at different points in childhood and adolescent development; some risk factors are more significant and have greater impact during childhood, whereas other risk factors may not appear or fail to have significance until adolescence.

The Surgeon General's report notes that the meaning and predictive value of risk factors is dependent upon "when they occur in a young person's development, in what social context, and under what circumstances" (2001, p. 57). However, the static model, by definition, assumes the position that it is legitimate to regard indicators of risk as, in effect, permanent factors sealed in amber, simply because of their correlation with later recidivism regardless of the age of the individual in whose history risk factors are present. Even if this is a legitimate model by which to understand and assess adult risk for recidivism, given the nature of children and adolescents in development, it is a risky proposition (no pun intended) to assess future behavior solely upon past behavior or experience.

ADULT AND JUVENILE RISK ASSESSMENT IS DIFFERENT

In practice, in the relatively short history of specialized treatment for sexual offenders, we have increasingly come to believe that juvenile risk assessment (and treatment) is a different proposition than that of assessing risk in adult sexual offenders. In the 1997 statement of ethical standards and principles of the Association for the Treatment of Sexual Abusers (ATSA, 1997), comprehensive risk evaluation was stressed for all sexual offenders, whether adult or juvenile, with little consideration to differences in the approach to juvenile risk assessment. However, in a 2000 public policy statement, ATSA (2000) noted important distinctions between juvenile and adult sexual offenders and recommended that evaluation and treatment be provided by clinicians with specialized training; in their 2001 practice standards and guidelines, ATSA (2001) noted that evaluators must take age into account and recognize that less is known about the evaluation and treatment for juveniles than for adults. In its most recent edition of the practice standards and guidelines, ATSA (2005) now specifically notes that the standards and guidelines are intended for the evaluation, treatment, and management of adult male sexual abusers. ATSA (2005) refers readers to other ATSA publications regarding the evaluation and treatment of juvenile sexual offenders (p. v), and makes a complete distinction regarding the evaluation of pre-pubescent children in its recent Task Force Report on Children with Sexual Behavior Problems (Chaffin et al., 2006).

Regardless of its increasingly well-defined distinction between adult and juvenile sexual offenders, despite a focus on actuarial assessment, ATSA has long defined risk evaluation as a dynamic, comprehensive, and inclusive process designed to gather maximum information about the sexual offender, regardless of his or her age. Further, almost a decade ago the American Academy of Child and Adolescent Psychiatry (1999) published practice parameters for the assessment of sexually abusive children and adolescents, noting that the assessment of juvenile sexual abusers requires the same comprehensive evaluation as other children and adolescents.

Rasmussen (2004) writes that practitioners must conduct evaluations that take into account developmental distinctions between juveniles and adults (and, indeed, between children and adolescents for that matter). In fact, it's clear that we do not apply the same risk assessment protocols with juveniles and adults, and in actual practice the most commonly used juvenile risk assessment instruments are entirely designed for adolescents. We rarely use adult assessment tools in the evaluation of risk in adolescents; when we do, they are for use only with older adolescents, typically age 16 or older, and even then are not recommended for use without great care. The revised coding rules for the STATIC-99 (Harris, Phenix, Hanson, & Thornton, 2003), for instance, note that its use with juveniles should be interpreted with caution, "as there is a very real theoretical question about whether juvenile sex offending is the same phenomena as adult sex offending in terms of its underlying dynamics and our ability to affect change in the individual" (p. 5). Instead, the coding manual recommends the use of a risk assessment instrument designed for adolescent sexual offenders, and specifically names the ERASOR (Estimate of Risk of Adolescent Sexual Offence Recidivism).

The reasons for the use and design of separate tools are discussed later in the book, as well as the instruments themselves. However, the principles of design at work behind adult and juvenile assessment instruments are not different. For instance, the design and construction of the ERASOR, a clinical juvenile risk assessment instrument, is not particularly different than the design and construction of the SVR-20 (Sexual Violence Risk-20), an adult clinical risk assessment tool. Both instruments offer an approach that is structured around risk factors frequently cited in the literature as relevant to recidivism, with some level of available empirical support for included risk factors. The differences between the two instruments primarily lie in the fact that risk factors in either case are selected based upon their presumed relevance to either an adult or adolescent population of sexual offenders, as well as, to some degree, how they are actually used. However, both are structured, literature-based tools for the clinical assessment of risk. Similarly, design principles behind the development of the JSORRAT, the first and only current adolescent actuarial assessment tool (although still in development) are exactly the same as those behind the development of all adult actuarial instruments, although the included risk factors are different. In the development of the MEGA (Multiplex Empirically Guided Inventory of Ecological Aggregates for Assessing Sexually Abusive Adolescents and Children), Rasmussen and Miccio-Fonseca (2007a; 2007b) are critical of other juvenile risk assessment instruments for not being juvenile specific enough, and describe the MEGA as the only juvenile risk assessment tool that focuses only on research exclusive to sexually abusive youth (although this a questionable and even misleading assertion).

Thus, in contrasting adult and adolescents assessment it is not the design of the assessment process that is necessarily different, but the manner in which risk factors are selected and how they are understood in light of the individual juvenile being assessed, as well as how the juvenile sexual offender is conceptualized and the manner in which the assessment process is actually implemented.

ADULTS AND JUVENILES ARE DIFFERENT

Boer, McVilly, and Lambrick (2007) describe risk as "a complex interaction between psychological factors and an individual's history and current life transforming event circumstances" (p. 2). To this, I note that psychological factors are usually the result of each individual's history and both are thus intertwined and often inseparable, and I add environmental risk factors and conditions as essential elements in understanding risk. However, Boer and colleagues' description speaks well to the complexity of risk assessment, and the reader will by now recognize their conceptualization of risk as a dynamic process. All risk is defined by this combination of history, psychological and environmental risk factors, and social environmental conditions. It is especially important and noteworthy for the child or adolescent smack in the midst of formative cognitive, psychological, and social development, and very much caught up in and influenced by the social environment in which development and learning is occurring (hence, the "developmental-learning environment").

With respect to developmental differences, then, we understand that juveniles are very different than adults, not only at the psycho-socio-emotional level, but the neurological level as well. The emotions, relationships, attitudes and ideas, cognitive capacities, place and role in society and, not least of all, behaviors of adolescents are driven and motivated by very different experiences, forces, and factors than those of adults. Consequently, in juvenile and adult sexual offenders motivations, attitudes, ideas, and experiences related to sexually abusive behavior should not be considered the same in each population nor attributed to the same causes, despite the fact that both groups have engaged in similar behaviors. Even though adults and juveniles who sexually offend share behaviors and some characteristics, the pathways that lead to such behaviors should not be assumed to be the same nor each confused for the other, and juveniles who engage in sexually abusive behavior typically do so for entirely different reasons than their adult counterparts. Further, from all we know, the developmental pathways of sexually abusive youth do not necessarily lead juvenile sexual offenders into patterns of adult sexual offending, based on relatively low recidivism rates for juvenile sexual offenders.

As noted, ATSA's most recent practice standards and guidelines (2005) specifically distinguish between adult and juvenile sexual offenders. However, ATSA (2001) is not only clear that there are important differences between juvenile and adult sexual offenders but also asserts that "many juveniles who sexually abuse will cease this behavior by the time they reach adulthood, especially if they are provided with specialized treatment and supervision" (p. 1). With regard to recidivism, or continued engagement in sexually abusive behavior after apprehension (and usually treatment), statistics strongly suggest that relatively few adolescent sexual offenders develop into adult sexual offenders. Although rates have been reported as low as 0 percent and as high as 42 percent (Fortune & Lambie, 2006; Nisbett, Wilson, & Smallbone, 2004; Prentky, Pimental, Cavanaugh, & Righthand, in press), post-treatment recidivism is nevertheless typically reported as somewhere between 5–14 percent (for instance, Caldwell, 2007; Hunter, 2000; Kemper & Kistner, 2007; Parks & Bard, 2006; Waite et al., 2005; Weinrott, 1996; Worling & Curwen, 2000), with 10–13 percent representing the most recently robustly reported recidivism rates. In their thorough and excellent review of adolescent sexual recidivism studies and the methodologies of such studies, in which the authors offer a broad and detailed look of recidivism research, Fortune and Lambie (2006) described 10 percent as a typically reported recidivism rate. In their recent meta-analysis that included 2,986 juvenile sexual offenders, Reitzel and Carbonell (2006) found recidivism rates of 12.5 percent for sexual crimes, and Epperson, Ralston, Fowers, Dewitt, and Gore (2006) reported a 13.2 percent rate for sexual recidivism in one study of 636 juveniles, and 12.8 percent in a second study of 538 juvenile sexual offenders (Epperson, 2007).

The fact that juvenile sexual offending does not necessarily result in adult sexually abusive behavior tells us either that apprehension and treatment for sexually abusive youth is very effective (with somewhere between 86–95 percent of juvenile sexual offenders not reengaging in sexually abusive behavior), or that sexually abusive youth are not on a path that necessarily leads to adult sexually abusive behavior, or both. In either case, it tells us that many children and adolescents with sexual behavior problems are not yet "hardened" sexual offenders and may never become sexually abusive adults. Calder (2001) describes some of the significant differences between adult and juvenile sexual abusers, first and foremost with respect to differences between juveniles and adults. He writes that children and adolescents live in a world with different values, beliefs, and expectations than those of adults, in which they experience and expect a greater degree of external control over their behaviors and interactions, and in which the role of the family is more critical. However, he notes that juveniles have greater developmental flexibility than adults and are more open and used to education and the acquisition of new skills. In terms of sexual development, patterns of sexual interest and arousal are still developing and not yet fixed, and although engaging in or exposed to sexual behavior, adolescents have less-developed sexual knowledge than adults. Regarding sexually abusive behavior, Calder writes that perpetration behaviors are less consistent and sophisticated in adolescent sexual offenders, and situational and opportunity factors are more typical in juvenile sexual offenses, rather than the fixed internal cognitive factors often found in adult offenders.

Hence we see that the lives of children and adolescents are considerably different than those of adults, even young adults. They live and function within a substantially different family and community system, and they are subject to a different set of rules and obligations. They are, of course, also substantially different in their physical development, including their neurology, and in cognitive and personality development, the development of attitudes and beliefs, how they acquire information and the nature of that information, and in their emotional and behavioral maturity and type and level of social relatedness. "Children and adolescents are also more experimental, with fewer fixed ideas than adults and fewer fixed personality characteristics. Their interests are still developing, and ideas, attitudes, emotions, and behaviors that may be considered outlandish, inappropriate, hostile, antisocial, or even deviant in adults, may not represent any of these things in juveniles. In fact, many of these may be considered part of the normative development of older children and adolescents" (Rich, 2003, p. 104).

UNDERSTANDING AND ASSESSING JUVENILE BEHAVIOR

Given the physical, emotional, cognitive, social, and experiential differences between adults, children, and adolescents, it is clear that we have to apply a different lens through which to look at juvenile behavior and a different framework upon which to hang our understanding of their behavior, and perhaps of more importance their behavioral motivations. Whereas assessment may mean understanding the experiences that have brought the client to his or her present state (in which psychosocial assessment peers back into the past in order to explore and understand the individual through current and historical factors), risk assessment is not simply about understanding the individual but instead aims at behavioral prediction, using the past (static) and present (dynamic) to recognize and map trajectory. Where psychosocial assessment is diagnostic, risk assessment is prognostic.

In his critique (actually, criticism) of the manner in which juvenile sexual offenders have been perceived and treated in the United States, Zimring (2004) argues that social and legal policies regarding adult and juvenile sexual offenders are both based on broad stereotypes, but he also writes that these fail to take into account the developmental status of sexually abusive youth with respect to the moral significance of their behavior, predictions about future behavior, and implications for treatment. In this respect Zimring is, in effect, also tying risk to treatment and in this case is asserting that we have misunderstood and even overreacted to ideas about what constitutes risk in children and adolescents, have assumed that risk in juveniles is a mirror of risk in adults, and have made assumptions and built social responses and treatment programs on the basis of these faulty assumptions about risk in sexually abusive youth.

Zimring's points are well made, and the issues that he addresses are quite vast when it comes to adolescent development. In particular, his note about the moral significance of adolescent behaviors touches on substantial questions about what morality and its cousin, empathy, look like and how they are experienced in childhood and adolescence. This is of special importance given the clear relationship of both morality and empathy to cognitive and emotional maturation and development, in which neither should be judged in absence of an understanding of their nature and meaning in child and adolescent development.

For instance, in a study of empathy in both juvenile and adult sexual offenders, D'Orazio (2002) found no difference in measures of empathy between sexual offenders and non-offenders, but did find that juveniles are generally less empathic than adults, regardless of their status as sexual offenders or non-offenders. In other words, she found empathy to be developmentally age related, in which adolescents experience less empathy than adults in general, and limitations in empathy in adolescents are more normative than they are a feature of juvenile antisocial behavior. With respect to moral development, Stilwell and colleagues (Stillwell, Galvin, Kopta, & Padgett, 1998; Stilwell, Galvin, Kopta, Padgett, & Holt, 1997) describe moral development as a dynamic process that passes through five stages prior to age 18, with the development of an in-depth level of morality, or integrated conscience, developing sometime around age 16. Similarly, in Kohlberg's (1976) well-known model of moral development, Level II, or conventional morality, begins to develop only during adolescence and does not flower fully and into a higher stage of moral judgment until after age 20, if it develops at all. Consequently, as we consider the meaning and role of attitudes, concern for others, motivation, and social connectedness and their connection to risk, let's not judge and assess the role, function, and operation of morality and empathy too hastily when it comes to juveniles, and certainly not in terms of what we might expect to find in a well-adjusted adult. To do so might mean being extremely concerned at what we perceive as an absence of morality or a lack of empathy rather than a normative state of being for many children and adolescents. Our concern and assessment should be aimed at the *development* of empathic morality and the pathway that the juvenile seems to be on with respect to its trajectory. In keeping with a dynamic model, we not only understand morality and empathy as developmental constructs, but also that neither develops or operates in isolation and both grow within and are fostered by the social environment, both in the early child rearing/family environment and the larger social environment (Hoffman, 2000).[7]

Steinberg and Scott (2003) write that, even when the cognitive capacities of adolescents are close to those of adults, their judgment lags behind due to their psychosocial immaturity. In understanding differences between adult and adolescent decision making, in adolescents they point to greater susceptibility to peer influence, immature attitudes towards and perceptions of risk, a different and unformed orientation to the future, and a more limited capacity for self-management. Just as Zimring (2004) argues that

---

7. Chapter 20 takes another, deeper look at the development of both empathy and morality in the context of the social environment.

we must take into account the developmental status of youthful sexual offenders in our selection and inclusion of criteria for risk and culpability, Steinberg and Scott similarly highlight our need to recognize significant differences between adult and juvenile offenders in our understanding, evaluation, and decision making regarding adolescent antisocial behavior. Somewhat humorously, but with earnest seriousness, they describe young offenders (in general, rather than juvenile sexual offenders in particular) as "less guilty by reason of adolescence." They consider adolescents to be developmentally immature when compared to adults and, with particular respect to their decision-making capacity, note their increased vulnerability to social circumstances and their still forming character and personality, as well as brain maturation and general psychological development. Additionally, Steinberg (2003) warns of the "adultification" of juvenile offenders, cautioning against descriptions that sometimes label young offenders as "career criminals," "super predators," and "fledgling psychopaths." Like Zimring, Steinberg, and Scott urge us to recognize and respond to significant differences between juveniles and adults, essentially with respect to their developmental level and status, and develop models for intervention, including public policies, legal systems, and treatment mechanisms, that respond differently to juveniles than adults.

THE DEVELOPING BRAIN

Regarding neurological development in adolescents and differences between the adolescent and adult brain, we certainly have increasing evidence that neurobiology really is at work. Spear (2000) describes the adolescent brain in a transitional period, differing anatomically and neurochemically from the adult brain, and Giedd (2002, 2004) reports a wave of neural development somewhere around age 11 and 12 and continuing significant dynamic activity in brain biology until about age 16.

Spear (2000) describes cognitive and neurological development during adolescence in which, among other things, stress is experienced differently by adolescents and adults in part due to a greater neurological sensitivity to negative emotions and depressed mood (Spear, 2003). Similarly, Yurgelun-Todd (2002, 2007) reports that adolescents experience more emotional responses than adults, but have not yet developed the prefrontal capacity to accurately identify or process emotions. She describes adolescence as a critical period for maturation of neurobiological processes that underlie higher cognitive functions and social and emotional behavior, including changes in emotional capacity and self-regulation that, in part, contribute to adolescent behavior. Furthermore, Spear (2000) writes that greater sensitivity to stress and related neurochemical processes contributes to behavioral and mood problems in adolescents, and that adolescents are more susceptible than children or adults to neurological reward systems that drive and reward certain types of risk-taking and exploratory behavior. In a similar vein, Bjork et al. (2004) concluded that adolescents are neurologically less motivated than young adults to anticipate or actively seek rewards, but experience as much pleasure and are as motivated by the benefits of rewards. That is to say (in this study at least), adolescents are less anticipatory than adults but nevertheless experience just as much pleasure once rewarded.

These basic but essential ideas about adolescents and their motivations, driven partially by their level of neural development, highlight at least important and significant differences, not only between adolescents and adults, but also between juvenile and adult sexual offenders. Of most importance here, these ideas also help us to consider differences in how we recognize the course and meaning of prior sexually abusive behavior and how we recognize, understand, and evaluate risk for future sexually abusive behavior.

However, we should not be blinded by ideas of science about the developing adolescent brain. In our recent thinking Epstein (2007) notes the risk that we may remove responsibility from adolescents as though they are cognitively, emotionally, and neurologically incapable of behaving in a moral, accomplished, and sophisticated manner. He points to the many achievements of adolescents at virtually every level and in every field during the course of human history, and, as noted, asserts that it is culture rather than the inherent inability of adolescents that defines teenagers as less capable or less responsible than adults. With respect to the neurology of the brain, Epstein dispenses, perhaps carelessly, with many of the ideas about the "teen brain" but stresses that, regardless of differences in development, the teen brain neither "causes" adolescent behavior nor renders the adolescent incapable of significant cognitive and emotional decisions or accomplishment. In fact, Epstein describes the adolescent brain as in some ways more capable than the adult brain, and points to the work of Courchesne et al. (2000) who describe physical brain volume peaking at age 14, and declining in volume after that time. Epstein argues that modern society seeks to artificially extend childhood and asserts that "the teen years need to be what they used to be: a time not just of learning, but learning to be responsible" (p. 375).

Hence, it is not simply the adolescent brain, if you will, that creates and is responsible for problem behavior devoid of any judgment, decision making, or moral conviction on the part of the adolescent actor. As Rutter (1997) has written, "behavior has to have a biological basis, and it is necessary that we understand how the biology functions" (p. 396), but although biological and genetic factors are influential, "they do not cause antisocial behavior directly; rather they contribute one set of influences . . . as part of a multifactorial causation" (Rutter, Giller, & Hagell, 1998, p. 165).

Steinberg (2003) recognizes, of course, that adolescents have the capacity for abstract thought, understand the difference between right and wrong, and know what they're doing. Nevertheless, he emphasizes that differences in adolescent reasoning play out in action because adolescents differ from adults not only in brain development but also in psychosocial development, their capacity to consider the consequences of their behavior, the manner in which they weigh rewards and risks, in their ability to plan ahead, and in their ability to control their impulses.

UNDERSTANDING THE JUVENILE AS "IN DEVELOPMENT"

In his arguments for holding adolescents more accountable for their decisions and their behavior, and in order to not restrain adolescents from the accomplishments and reasonable choices of which they are capable, Epstein's (2007) work glosses over many of the complexities of adolescent development. However, his ideas illuminate a balance between recognizing the adolescent as a person-in-development and recognizing the need to also recognize that adolescents make choices and are capable of accepting responsibility for their choices. It is the balance that is so critical in how we understand adolescent behavior and how we treat the outcome of such behavior.

In fact, the United States has long recognized the different status of children and adolescents with respect to understanding and making decisions about their behavior. Nevertheless, elements of this philosophy that has understood and responded to juveniles differently than adults are significantly changing. For example, more adolescents are bound over to adult court at age 14 for specific types of criminal offenses and thus tried and held responsible as adults, and as noted in Chapter 1, the Sex Offender Registration and Notification Act (SORNA) provides for more-or-less lifetime national registration for juvenile sexual offenders aged 14 or older. Regardless, despite this swing of the proverbial pendulum, or perhaps because of it, it is important to recall the creation of the juvenile court in Illinois in 1899, with virtually every state following suit by 1925. The juvenile court provided treatment that was not adversarial, as in the adult court, and provided rehabilitation rather than punishment for juveniles, including sealed and expunged court records that did not follow adolescents into adulthood. Despite the serious nature of some juvenile crimes, including murder and rape, and understandable public concern about crimes of this sort, it is important for us to recognize that acts like SORNA and its provision for some youth are a step away from considering and treating juveniles as adults, despite the social and legal protections theoretically offered to youth adjudicated as delinquent.

In our understanding of risk and its development, its meaning, and its shaping role for future behavior in children and adolescents, it is all the more important that those who assess risk in sexually abusive youth be well informed about both juveniles themselves and their developmental process and its implication for the ideas and processes of risk assessment.

ASSESSING RISK IN CHILDREN AND ADOLESCENTS

Rasmussen and Miccio-Fonseca (2007a) stress the value of empirically guided clinical assessments in the assessment of sexually abusive youth. They further stress the importance of developing juvenile risk assessment instruments that are based on ideas and research that is child and adolescent specific, independent of research and ideas relevant to adult sexual offenders. Worling and Långström (2006) recognize an overlap between risk factors that pertain to both adult and adolescent sexual offenders, and argue that it is reasonable to assume a position that recognizes both distinctions and similarities between adult and juvenile risk assessment instruments. However, despite some overlap in risk factors as well as those that are unique to both groups of offenders, Worling and Långström assert that formats and processes used to assess risk in one group should not be used to assess risk in the other.

The idea that we require risk instruments specifically designed to better understand and project the sexual behavior of juveniles again speaks to a belief that children and adolescents are not merely smaller, less experienced, or less-developed adults. Although all of these descriptions are in some way true statements, they nonetheless each miss the essential developmental differences between adolescence and adulthood. Beyond the obvious absence of physical, neurological, and emotional experiences that come with adulthood, an understanding of juveniles as "in development" provides the contextual model of development described by Lewis (1997), which requires an understanding of not just the child but the environment in which the child grows and develops. Lewis argued against the idea that "development is a sequence of small progressions that are gradual but accumulative, that it has clear directionality, that it is causal" (p. 15), and that later events are necessarily the outcome of earlier events, thus making prediction possible. Instead, he proposed that it is the context in which lives are led, based on factors found in the present environment, that determines development through responsiveness and adaptation to current circumstances. This not only supports the need to assess current, or dynamic, factors, but asserts that it is not possible to predict the future with any certainty, other than to note developmental trends (or trajectory).

As life develops, some risk factors once dynamic during infancy and early childhood eventually harden to become static factors embedded in developmental history. Although others remain open to change, thus becoming stable but dynamic risk factors, these nevertheless also take on a static-like quality that makes them resistant (although not impervious) to change. In fact, in a model of actuarial assessment some of these stable dynamic factors are conceptualized as static factors, due to their believed historical significance, and are treated as such (that is, as unchanging). Examples include early experiences of abuse or other maltreatment, problematic behaviors, and attentional difficulties. Suboptimal attachment experiences offer an example of early experience that creates potential risk that may be considered either as a static factor given its role and development within the first two years of life or a dynamic but stable factor that takes on a static-like quality. For most attachment theorists early attachment experiences are considered to have an enduring and stable quality throughout the life span, and certainly into adulthood. In either case, early poor or adverse experiences become the static and stable risk factors that shape the development of cognitive and emotional schema, patterns of behavior, and the quality and experience of social interaction.

Hence, once formed, historical risk factors become static and impossible to change or lead to psychological and behavioral sequelae that are difficult to change (i.e., stable dynamic factors). With this mind, Ryan (2007) notes the importance of recognizing factors that may be static in adult sexual offenders but remain dynamic, even if stable, in juvenile offenders. She writes that immediate goals for juveniles include preventing the development of risk factors that may harden into static factors by the time children and adolescents reach adulthood, noting that "static risks can only be prevented before they occur," and that "history can only be changed prospectively, as it is created and experienced . . . despite the most rigorous treatment interventions" (p.169). Her argument is that static factors relevant to the child's risk of becoming abusive to themselves or others are best addressed preventively, in effect *before* they become static. This, of course, points to the need to recognize both "in development" risk factors, which are necessarily dynamic, and also the role and operation of risk factors at play during different developmental periods. This last point, most relevant to this chapter, involves the need to understand risk (and protective) factors in the context of juvenile development, and to thus understand that although juvenile and adult risk assessment tools follow the same ideas in their construction and use, and even consider and evaluate the same or similar risk factors, we understand the nature of risk and development, and thus behavioral trajectory, in a different way than we do adults.

THE CHANGEABILITY OF TRAJECTORY

Lewis (1997) comments that the nature of development is unclear, and cautions us to not believe that we can easily understand the conditions that give rise to the later behavior of children, adolescents, and adults. His model of "contextualism" focuses on current factors and conditions as major principles, and he writes that "how people act . . . is determined by their attempt to adapt to situations and problems as they find them" (p. 203).[8] To this I must add that the ability to accommodate, adapt, and respond to current circumstances is mediated and moderated by past experience and resulting psychological development, and thus Lewis' ideas about contextualism are linked to ideas about personal development. That is, the juvenile in the moment is subject to both historical experience and current forces, both internal and social, and future behavior is the product of both historical experience and current experience.

In their vast study of at-risk children, Sroufe, Egeland, Carlson, and Collins (2005) note that a "developmental transactional" view of the person and environment means more than simply recognizing the significance of both individual and environmental characteristics that shape development, or even the interaction between the individual and his or her environment. Such a view recognizes that the developing child and his or her environment are mutually transforming. That is, not only do environmental factors increase risk for and amplify risk within the individual, but the historical behavior of the individual in turn influences the very environment in which he or she exists and, in some cases, amplifies risk factors and conditions found in the environment. These "person effects on the environment" make it clear that "the experiences people bring about by their own behavior have important consequences for them" (Rutter, Giller, & Hagell, 1998, p. 173) and support the conclusion of Sroufe et al.

---

8. This mirrors the perspective of Henry et al. (1996) who assert that antisocial behavior is driven by the child's inability to successfully resolve issues that bring them into conflict with their environment.

that in a developmental approach to understanding human development the nature of cause is complex.

Garmezy (1996) points to the idea that although in some cases risk factors lead to disorders, in other individuals these very factors represent conditions which are overcome and to which a positive adaptation is made, which is also eloquently described by Werner and Smith (1992, 2001). They describe the capacity of some children born into high-risk environments to overcome challenge and adversity, reflecting the balance between risk and protective factors that operates during different developmental stages; whereas for some children this balance exacerbates risk and fails to protect against vulnerability, for others the balance develops resilience. Rutter, Giller, and Hagell (1998) note "turning point effects" that alter trajectory, in which, although experience is important, they emphasize that nothing is cast in stone: "Life events, turning points, and transition periods can all play a part in whether antisocial behavior continues or ceases" (p. 307).

To some degree, then, it is important that we recognize that future behavior is much like smoke; it is very and increasingly difficult to predict as it leaves its source, shaped by so many influences and forces that it becomes virtually impossible to know where it will end up or what it will look like as it spreads into and influences its environment. Nevertheless, our goal in the assessment of sexually abusive youth is not to define or describe the certain outcome of historical and current forces. It is, instead, to best estimate and approximate the likelihood of future sexually abusive behavior based upon risk factors present in both their histories and current psychological and social environment.

Because trajectory can change, the assessment of risk in children and adolescents itself should be not be static, one time events. This is true for all sexually abusive youth, and especially so for youth in treatment as treatment intends to change trajectory. Thus, risk for sexually abusive behavior should be assessed and reassessed in juveniles, and Worling and Långström (2006) recommend that evaluators stress that their estimates of risk are time limited and that risk assessments should be periodically repeated.

CORE COMPETENCIES FOR EVALUATOR OF SEXUALLY ABUSIVE YOUTH

Prescott (2006) warns that a sole focus on risk factors may lead us in the wrong direction in assessing sexually abusive youth, in that we may fail to recognize the entirety of the juvenile, assess other aspects of his or her functioning and needs, and fail to address larger treatment issues into which sexually abusive behavior is embedded. However, it's clear that practice guidelines and standards are beginning to emerge in the professional literature of juvenile sex offender treatment, as well as the further development of instruments that are increasingly used and accepted as state of the art for evaluating risk.

Gudas and Sattler (2006) have written that the forensic evaluation of children and adolescents is a task for clinicians with specialized training and experience in forensic work, pediatric mental health, and child development. In describing juvenile forensic evaluation in general, Grisso (1998) noted, in keeping with the message of this chapter, that "nothing about the behavior of adolescents can be understood without considering it in the context of youths' continued biological, psychological, and social development" (p. 27). Further, Grisso (2006) described at least three elements involved in the forensic assessment of juveniles that separate it from adult forensic evaluations: the law as it pertains to juveniles, the developmental process of childhood and adolescence, and the systemic perspective that both guides the juvenile evaluation and through which it must be interpreted into recommendations and interventions regarding the juvenile.

With regard to the law, Grisso (2006) notes that although forensic evaluations are always intended to inform the court, laws pertaining to juveniles are often quite different than those that relate to adults, and that child welfare and delinquency laws are not only changing more rapidly than their adult equivalent but have shorter "shelf life," requiring the juvenile evaluator to remain aware of changing laws as they pertain to juveniles and juvenile evaluation. In terms of development, Grisso highlights the rapidly moving development of juveniles, writing that "questions of growth and development are at the heart of all juvenile forensic evaluations," and suggests that it may be more relevant to refer to forensic evaluations for juveniles as "forensic developmental evaluations" (p. viii). Finally, Grisso describes the requirement that evaluators pay attention to the social environment and interactions of juveniles under evaluation, recognizing the juvenile in the context of the systems within which he or she lives, interacts, and functions, and that this systemic perspective is "essential in translating evaluation data into recommendations and actions in the youth's and society's interests" (p. ix).

Building on Grisso (1998, 2006), clinicians working with children and adolescents in forensic settings must demonstrate five core competencies developed during the course of their training and supervision (Rich 2003). This is no less true for evaluators as for clinicians. Used in conjunction with a defined risk-assessment process, these core competencies will come together to ensure an adequate and well-informed process that minimizes the concerns about risk assessment appropriately noted by Prescott (2006) and briefly described in Chapter 2.

Clinicians must have a strong understanding of (1) adolescent development, involving expected and normative attitudes, emotions, experiences, interactions, and behaviors of childhood and adolescent development; (2) juvenile antisocial behavior, or deviations in child and adolescent behavior that fall outside of age-appropriate and age-expected social norms, propelled by factors that drive the youth towards antisocial (or criminal) behaviors in an effort to meet personal needs; (3) adolescent psychopathology involving the nature and diagnosis of mental disorders; (4) adolescent assessment, requiring the capacity to evaluate, understand, and interpret behavior with a special emphasis in forensic work on projecting risk for future antisocial (in our case, sexually abusive) behavior; and (5) legal matters and processes that shape and affect evaluation and treatment, including issues of due process and legal rights, client confidentiality, client competence, and public safety.

For clinicians working with sexually abusive youth, it's important to add a sixth factor: knowledge of, or at least a strong theory about, the dynamics of sexually abusive behavior, including its development, onset, and maintenance (or further development) over time.

CONCLUSION: PRACTICING JUVENILE RISK ASSESSMENT

In juvenile risk assessment we recognize the importance of the developmental context within which history and current functioning is understood and against which trajectory is assessed. With this in mind, a question already asked and addressed to some degree is whether to apply to juveniles not just the same models of assessment we use to assess risk in adult sexual offenders, but the same ideas. Of course, we *can*, as shown by the development of the JSORRAT, but *should* we?

Another way to ask the question is whether we should apply the ideas about juvenile risk assessment described here and elsewhere to adult risk assessment? That is, a dynamic and clinically driven model of risk assessment is considered most appropriate for juveniles, whether or not an actuarial assessment is included in that process. Frankly, it's not that adult assessment can't or shouldn't follow the same process; it's just that it often doesn't. In fact, as noted, this is changing, and even in adult assessment we see a greater and increasing focus on the inclusion of dynamic risk factors, in which the sexual offender is understood as (a) more than the sum of past sexual behaviors and (b) capable of making change over time.

However, in understanding the nature of risk and harm, we lack a clear understanding of how risk factors operate together, across, and within lines that demarcate different types of risk factors; how risk factors operate in different environments, under different conditions, and when present at different points in child and adolescent (and indeed adult) development; and how risk factors interact with protective factors. Nevertheless, although many questions about risk and protection remain, we know enough about risk in children and adolescents to understand that a relationship exists between prior and current behaviors and experiences, biological and genetic development, individual psychology, and social interactions, as well as a relationship between risk, protection, and harm. We lack many of the details to make perfect predictions, or even assess the validity of our predictions over time, but we know enough already to make informed predictions about risk and harm if trajectories remain unchanged, at the same time knowing that the expected course of events can change.

Building further on the idea that professional standards are beginning to emerge that define and shape juvenile risk assessment, it's also increasingly clear that training and informed practice are key in the administration of juvenile sexual offender evaluations. In the next two chapters we will explore and discuss heterogeneity among juvenile sexual offenders, and in Chapter 7 further explore the nature of risk and protective factors in juveniles and continue moving toward a clearer understanding of how to apply these ideas.

CHAPTER 5

Distinctions and Heterogeneity among Juvenile Sexual Offenders

AMONG ADULT SEXUAL offenders we note distinctions in criminal behavior. We recognize "specialists" and "criminally versatile" sexual offenders, or those who sexually abuse but seem to engage in no other criminal behavior, and those who engage in a range of criminal behavior that includes, but is not limited to, sexual abuse (Kemper & Kistner, 2007; Polaschek, Ward, & Hudson, 1997; Smallbone, Wheaton, & Hourigan, 2003; Thornton, 2006). The former are most typically child molesters, whereas the latter, or those engaging in more general criminality, are frequently rapists in which we recognize typical targets as older adolescents or adults rather than children.

To some degree, the dichotomy between those who primarily sexually abuse children and those who abuse adults appears to hold true for juvenile sexual offenders as well. That is, it seems that we can recognize juvenile sexual offenders who typically and most often target child victims and those who sexually victimize adolescents or adults, although there is a smaller group (as is true for adult sexual offenders as well) of those who victimize both. However, unlike adult sexual offenders, it seems apparent from many sources that most juvenile sexual offenders are child molesters, rather than sexual abusers of peers or adults. Statistics are notoriously misleading (not to mention difficult to consume) and can vary from statistical analysis to analysis. Nonetheless, in reviewing crime victimization and perpetration statistics, it seems clear that the targets of juvenile sexual offenders are typically children below the age of 12, rather than adolescents or adults.

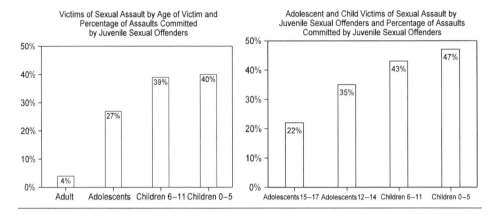

Figure 5.1   Victims of juvenile sexual assaults, by age of victim and percentages of total offenses. (Based on Snyder, 2000; Snyder & Sickmund, 2006).

WHOM DO JUVENILE SEXUAL OFFENDERS VICTIMIZE?

Data gathered through the National Incident-Based Reporting System (NIBRS) suggests that most juvenile sexual offenders victimize younger children, rather than peers or adults. Based on 1991–1996 data (Snyder, 2000), only 4 percent of all sexual assaults against adults were perpetrated by juveniles, whereas juvenile sexual offenders perpetrated 33 percent of all sexual offenses against children and adolescents (aged 0–17). Although juveniles were responsible for 27 percent of all sexual assaults against adolescents, they perpetrated 39 percent of assaults against children aged 6–11 and 40 percent of assaults against children below the age of 6. NIBRS data for 2000–2001 shows similar, and even higher, figures (Snyder & Sickmund, 2006). Whereas juvenile sexual offenders were responsible for 37 percent of all sexual assaults against all minors, they were responsible for 47 percent and 43 percent of sexually assaults against children aged 0–5 and 6–11, respectively, and on average 29 percent against adolescents (35 percent against adolescents aged 12–14 and 22 percent against adolescents aged 15–17). These statistics are more simply shown in Figure 5.1.

This view of juvenile sexual offenders targeting children rather than peers is a consistent finding in studies. Of the 156 juvenile sexual offenders (average age 15) in their study, Miner, Berg, and Robinson (2007) categorized 69 percent as child molesters with victims with an average age of 6. Similarly, of the 296 sexually abusive youth in their study, Kemper and Kistner (2007) classified 67 percent as child molesters, compared to 26 percent peer offenders and only 7 percent as mixed child and peer offenders. Parks and Bard's (2006) study also showed the same sort of weighting, with 47 percent of the 156 juvenile sexual offenders categorized as child offenders, 33 percent as peer/adult offenders, and 20 percent mixed. However, the authors selected age 10 or below as the age at which victims were considered children; had they selected age 11 as the age at which victims were considered children (rather than peers), the number of child molesters in the study would have been greater, further supporting the proposition that the majority of juvenile sexual offenders select child victims.

Further, although one can only extrapolate from arrest reports, the annual FBI Uniform Crime Report (UCR) suggests that juvenile sexual offenders target children far more than they do peers or adults. Including only rape of a female in the "forcible rape" category, the FBI report lumps all other sexual crimes[1] under the broader label of "sexual offense." Hence, as this category includes arrests for less invasive sexual abuse of females and all sexual abuse of males, we can reasonably conclude that this class of sexual crime substantially involves the sexual abuse of children. With this in mind, consistent with UCRs of previous years, the 2006 FBI Crime Report shows that juvenile arrests for sexual offenses were 357 percent more frequent than those for "forcible rape" (U.S. Department of Justice, 2007), offering further evidence that children are most frequently the targets of adolescent sexual offenders.

This suggests, then, that most juvenile sexual offenders are what we might call child molesters, rather than rapists of peers or adults, in that their victims are typically less than age 12. This also suggests that different motivational forces are at play in adolescents who sexually abuse children than in those who sexually assault peers or adults. Ideas about purpose, motivators, and driving forces are important to bear in mind in the assessment of juvenile sexual offenders, to which we will return shortly.

The dichotomy between chid molesters as "specialists" and rapists (those who sexually abuse peers/adults) as criminal "generalists" will further hold true if juvenile sexual offenders who molest children are less criminally versatile than those who victimize adolescents and adults. That is, are *all* juvenile sexual offenders criminally versatile and can they all be said to be conduct disordered (which implies at least some form of criminal versatility), or are there important variants that exist across the range of juvenile sexual offenders and between child molesters and peer/adult victimizers?

---

1. Excluding prostitution.

SEXUAL AND NON-SEXUAL CRIMINAL RECIDIVISM

It's widely reported that recidivism for adult and juvenile sexual offenders is significantly higher for non-sexual offenses than criminal offenses. Although varying from study to study, the rate of various forms of non-sexual criminal recidivism for adult sexual offenders always falls higher than their rate of sexual recidivism (for instance, Hanson & Bussière, 1998; Hanson & Morton-Bourgon, 2007; Proulx et al., 1997).

Similarly, the idea that juvenile sexual offenders are at greater risk for reengaging in non-sexual criminal behavior than a sexual offense is commonly noted (Caldwell, 2002, 2007; Fortune & Lambie, 2006; Hagan & Gust-Brey, 1999; Reitzel & Carbonell, 2006; Waite et al., 2005; Weinrott, 1996), a finding reported by Letourneau and Miner (2005) as consistent across nearly all studies of juvenile sexual offender recidivism. For instance, in his study of recidivism in 249 juvenile sexual offenders and 1,780 non-sexual juvenile offenders, Caldwell (2007) noted that the juvenile sexual offenders were nearly ten times more likely to recidivate non-sexually than sexually. Nevertheless, when comparing non-sexual recidivism, he found that the sexual offenders were significantly less likely to be charged with a non-sexual offense than the non-sexual offenders. This suggests that the nature of non-sexual offenses by juvenile sexual offenders may be different than non-sexual offenses committed by non-sexual juvenile offenders, a point to be further explored as we think about sexually abusive youth.

When comparing adult child molesters with adult rapists, it is also usually the case that the rate of non-sexual recidivism is significantly higher for rapists. This provides support for the idea that rapists are generally more "criminally versatile" than child molesters, and child molesters are more typically "specialists" who are not more widely criminal in their behavior. The same seems to be true for sexually abusive youth as well, which brings us back to the point about antisocial and conduct-disordered behavior in juvenile sexual offenders. That is, although by definition one may rightly refer to sexually abusive behavior as a variant of a conduct disorder, this term simply homogenizes the behavior and, as we understand the term and meaning of "conduct disorder," fails to recognize that different dynamics are at play in different variants of the behavior. That is, based on both the *DSM-IV* description of conduct disorder and antisocial personality disorder (American Psychiatric Association, 2000) and concepts of psychopathy that are clearly related to conduct disordered behavior in children and adolescents, conduct disorder represents more than troubling or antisocial behavior. The diagnosis requires a persistent, pervasive, and repetitive pattern of behavior which violates social norms or the rights of others in at least three distinct domains.

SEXUALLY ABUSIVE BEHAVIOR, CONDUCT DISORDER, AND ADOLESCENT PSYCHOPATHY

Of course, sexually abusive behavior in children and adolescents is a form of conduct disorder. In adults, we might more appropriately and more simply describe conduct disorder as a variant of criminal behavior and be done with it. However, children and adolescents are not adults, and, in most cases, juvenile delinquents are not hardened criminals. Hence, in juveniles the distinction between troubling and antisocial behavior in general and conduct disorder in particular has a clear role to play in our ability to understand juvenile sexual offenders, and thus help assess the possibility of future sexually abusive behavior.

However, conduct disorder itself is not a homogenous construct, and it varies both dimensionally from mild to severe and with respect to child-hood or adolescent onset, in which earlier onset predicts a more enduring pattern of antisocial behavior lasting through adolescence and into adult-hood, and therefore carries with it a prognosis of greater concern (American Psychiatric Association, 2000; Frick, 2002; Gore & Eckenrode, 1996; Loeber et al., 2005; Moffitt, 2003; Rutter, Giller, & Hagell, 1998). It is this more significant form of conduct disorder that is most closely and necessarily linked to the *DSM* diagnosis of antisocial personality disorder, which may only be made at age 18. Involving the hallmark features of callousness, lack of empathy, social disconnection, and lack of regard for others, antisocial personality disorder requires a diagnosis of conduct disorder to be in place since at least age 15, reflecting not only its developmental nature but also our capacity to observe serious antisociality in adolescents.[2]

More than simply troubling and disturbed behavior, serious conduct disordered attitudes and behaviors in children and adolescents are clearly linked to concerns we have for continuing sociopathic behavior. Further, in adult sexual offenders, whether called antisocial personality disorder or

---

2. Although *DSM-IV* does not allow the diagnosis of antisocial personality disorder before age 18, in its equivalent diagnosis of dissocial personality disorder, the European ICD-10 (World Health Organization, 2004) does not specify a lower age limit, although it notes that personality disorder diagnoses are not appropriate before the age of 16 or 17. Further ICD-10 recommends, but does not require, a diagnosis of conduct disorder prior to diagnosing dissocial personality disorder.

psychopathy,[3] the diagnosis is frequently linked to the risk for sexual reoffense in adult sexual offenders (Hanson & Morton-Bourgon, 2007; Olver & Wong, 2006). In keeping with the idea that adult sociopathic behavior is necessarily linked to adolescent, and even childhood, behavior, Hare and others point to developmental predictors of adult psychopathy (Frick, 2002; Hare, 1999; Lynam, 2002). Forth, Kosson, and Hare (2003) describe psychopathy as a stable personality disorder that is first evident in childhood and conclude that psychopathic traits are observable in adolescents and children, and Frick et al. (2003a, 2003b) also believe that evidence of later psychopathy can be found in pre-adolescent children, and especially those who exhibit severe forms of impulsivity and conduct disorder. However, Seagrave and Grisso (2002) urge against assessing juveniles as psychopaths, and describe the risks and possible mistakes inherent in diagnosing adolescents in this manner. Hart, Watt, and Vincent (2002) echo this perspective and express their concerns about the implications of diagnosing psychopathy in children and adolescents, writing that "the assessment of juvenile psychopathy is like an Impressionist painting: fine from a distance; but the closer you get, the messier it looks" (p. 241).

In fact, shallow and superficial affect, inconsideration for others, lack of empathy, and risky lifestyle—all considered elements of psychopathy—are normative behaviors in many adolescents. D'Orazio (2002), for example, found empathy in adolescents to be underdeveloped when compared to empathy in adults, and neurologically Bjork et al. (2004) report that compared to adults adolescents are less motivated to anticipate or intentionally engage in reward-seeking behavior. Further, in troubled children elements considered psychopathic in adults may reflect difficulties with attachment and social connection, the results of early or ongoing attachment experiences, rather than psychopathy (Rich, 2006).

Nevertheless, it is clear that Frick and Forth correctly identify a subset of troubled children and adolescents who demonstrate unusually severe behavior and social disconnection, which, if unresolved, signals and may develop into antisocial personality disorder and/or psychopathy as these individuals approach and enter adulthood. However, these adolescents represent only a small subset of conduct disordered children and adolescents, as shown in the study by Forth et al. (2003) in which the Hare Psychopathy Checklist-Youth Version (PCL-YV) was administered to more

---

3. Although Robert Hare (1999) considers psychopathy to be a limited and more serious subset of antisocial personality disorder, the psychopath label bears many resemblances to the diagnosis of antisocial personality disorder.

than 2,400 conduct disordered juveniles. With a cut score[4] of 30, about 70 percent of the sample scored less than 4, less than 20 percent scored between 28–32, and only 9 percent scored higher than 36.

In other words, although a diagnosis of conduct disorder is a necessary precursor to a later diagnosis of antisocial personality disorder (or psychopathy), the diagnosis of conduct disorder is nevertheless insufficient for us to conclude that it signals adult psychopathy. Even though the conduct disorder diagnosis may predict behavioral problems in later adulthood, and is therefore a concern in its own right, most forms of conduct disorder will not evolve into psychopathy. Hence, even if, with the advent of the PCL-YV, it is possible to diagnosis psychopathy or antisocial personality disorder in minors, most sexually abusive youth do not meet the diagnostic criteria for psychopathy, despite their troubled thinking and behavior.

CONDUCT DISORDER OR DISORDERED CONDUCT?

In fact, many juvenile sexual offenders do not even meet the criteria for the *DSM* diagnosis of conduct disorder. That is, although many juvenile sexual offenders do have a history of non-sexual conduct disordered behaviors (Efta-Breitbach & Freeman, 2004; O'Reilly & Carr, 2006; Worling & Långström, 2006), and are far more likely to get into future trouble for non-sexual rather than sexual behaviors, in many cases the behaviors don't add up to a diagnosis of conduct disorder.

From France and Hudson's (1993) assertion that approximately 50 percent of juvenile sexual offenders may be diagnosed with a conduct disorder, it may also be implied that approximately 50 percent may not be conduct disordered. However, Seto and Lalumière (2006) give far more thought to the question of conduct disorder in juvenile sexual offenders than most who have written on the subject. Recognizing a high incidence of conduct-disordered behaviors in sexually abusive youth, they nonetheless note the possibility that it is only among a *subset* of juvenile sexual offenders that highly antisocial behavior is found, and they describe the additional possibility that a further subset of sexually abusive youth may not be broadly criminal or antisocial but instead restrict their antisocial conduct to sexually abusive behavior. Of their meta-analysis of 24 studies that included more than 1,600 juvenile sexual offenders and 8,000

---

4. A cut score represents the score that divides test subjects into different groups, and beyond which, in psychological testing, a clinical condition may be said to be present.

non-sexual juvenile delinquents, Seto and Lalumière wrote, "we expect that juvenile sexual offenders will show substantial conduct problems, but it is unclear how they will compare with juveniles who have engaged in nonsexual offenses only" (p. 168).

Seto and Lalumière concluded that although many juvenile sexual offenders are conduct disordered, they generally score lower in conduct-disordered behavioral problems than non-sexual juvenile delinquents. "As a group they had less extensive criminal history than non-sex-offenders. . . . Many juvenile sexual offenders showed evidence of conduct problems, but juvenile non-sex offenders had even more conduct problems" (p. 181). This was especially true of juvenile sexual offenders who abused children, who, as noted, appear to represent the majority of sexually abusive youth and who demonstrated less conduct problems relative to both non-sexual juvenile offenders and juvenile sexual offenders who offended peers or adults. Seto and Lalumière suggest that it is in the lack or reduced level of conduct-disordered behavior that we see a substantial difference between juvenile sexual offenders and non-sexual juvenile delinquents. Their conclusion is that factors relevant to the development of juvenile delinquency have relevance to understanding the development of sexually abusive behavior in juveniles. However, because juvenile sexual offenders score lower in conduct problems than non-sexual juvenile offenders, they are, as a group, quite different in some respects, and Seto and Lalumière accordingly suggest that juvenile sexual offending may have unique causes.

In practical terms, despite its diagnostic simplicity and utility, conduct disorder is not a unitary or categorical construct in which behavior is either categorized as conduct disordered or not. It is instead better understood and applied as a dimensional construct that takes variation into account in the nature, quantity, intensity, shape, and context of the behavior. This is what Seto and Lalumière are addressing in their work. And, without recognizing conduct-disordered behaviors as multidimensional, we risk having the label mislead us into homogenizing sexually abusive youth into a single group, rather than recognizing subtleties and variations in the social experiences, behaviors, skill sets, motivations, and, above all, the underlying dynamics of juvenile sexual offenders. In our search for commonalities among juvenile sexual offenders, it is important that we avoid simplifications and do not mistake all behaviors that look alike as the *same* behavior. We must instead seek the nuances that will help us to distinguish juvenile sexual offenders from one another and thus allow greater depth in our insight and capacity to understand the children and adolescents we are assessing and treating.

CONDUCT DISORDERED AND SEXUALLY ABUSIVE CRIME

We can further recognize the antisocial behavior of juvenile sexual offenders as different than "classic" conduct-disordered behavior by reviewing arrest statistics as reported in the FBI annual Uniform Crime Report. For instance, as simply shown in Figure 5.2, although by 2006 there was a reduction of 3.9 percent in juvenile arrests for all crimes in the United States as a percentage of all arrests over a 10-year period (1997–2006), there was a reduction of only 1 percent in juvenile arrests for sexual crimes when compared against all arrests for sexual crimes during the same decade (U.S. Department of Justice, 2007; Table 32). In fact, this was an improvement over the FBI reported arrest rates for 2005, which actually showed an increase of approximately 0.6 percent in the percentage of juvenile arrest for all sexual crimes over a 10-year period. (U.S. Department of Justice, 2006; Table 32). According to a bulletin of the Office for Juvenile Justice (Snyder, 2006), despite an decrease of 22 percent in overall juvenile arrests for all crimes committed between 1996 and 2004, during the same 10-year period there was an increase of 12 percent in juvenile arrests for non-rape sexual offenses committed by juveniles, also briefly illustrated in Figure 5.2.

Developing an accurate picture of crime in the United States, including juvenile crime, is difficult and complex. However, based on arrest statistics such as these, we can at least form an approximate and working view, and can see that juvenile sexual crime activity is not a direct correlate of general juvenile delinquency. As a percentage of the whole, sexual crime arrests are not only higher than non-sexual arrests, but are dropping far less dramatically. Given this admittedly simplistic statistical view of the juvenile sexual offender, we can nevertheless recognize sexually troubled behavior among

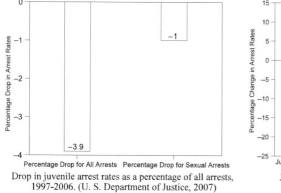

Drop in juvenile arrest rates as a percentage of all arrests, 1997-2006. (U. S. Department of Justice, 2007)

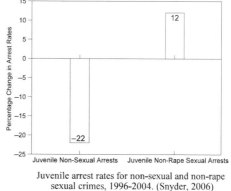

Juvenile arrest rates for non-sexual and non-rape sexual crimes, 1996-2004. (Snyder, 2006)

Figure 5.2 Overview of juvenile sexual and non-sexual arrest rates.

adolescents as different than that of general adolescent conduct-disordered behavior.

Further, arrest statistics for juvenile sexual offending make it appear a different crime than generally violent crime in terms of racial group. Whereas 51 percent of juvenile arrests for violent crime and 67 percent for robbery in 2006 were of black juveniles, 70 percent of juvenile arrests for sexual crimes were of white juveniles (U.S. Department of Justice, 2006; Table 43). A simplistic and perhaps skewed picture, these figures none-theless again suggest that juvenile sexual offending represents a different type of crime than other forms of conduct disorder, and certainly violent and aggressive crime.

If we follow this general line of reasoning, we see that significant elements of conduct disorder, including high levels of antisociality and general criminal behavior, are limited to a *subset* of sexually abusive youth. Many, and quite likely most, juvenile sexual offenders engage in a different variant of conduct disordered behavior, reflected to some degree in arrest rates that do not follow the same trends as arrest rates for crimes of general juvenile delinquency. We recognize, then, that it is the *non*-conduct dis-ordered behaviors and causes in which we should be equally interested. These are more likely to help us distinguish between juvenile sexual offenders and other children and adolescents, including other conduct disordered juveniles, and better define treatment interventions.

JUVENILE SEXUAL OFFENDERS: GENERAL DELINQUENTS OR SPECIAL CASES?

Caldwell (2002) notes that high levels of non-sexual recidivism among juvenile sexual offenders lend support to those who ask whether juvenile sexual offenders constitute a distinct group separate from other juvenile delinquents. Although research is inconsistent and provides quite mixed results depending on the study, those who assume this position conclude that juvenile sexual offenders are essentially much like other juvenile delinquents, in demographics, characteristics, and general behavior, and much the same in their rate of non-sexual recidivism. This perspective on sexually abusive youth is quite different from that of others who recognize a difference, not only between sexually abusive youth and non-sexual juvenile offenders but also, to a great degree, between *types* of sexually abusive youth.

THE FIRST POSITION: JUVENILE SEXUAL OFFENDERS AS GENERALLY DELINQUENT

The former point of view in effect argues that sexually abusive youth are conduct disordered, to some degree proven by a higher rate of non-sexual recidivism than sexual recidivism, as well as historical, psychological, and behavioral aspects shared in common with non-sexual juvenile offenders. This leads to the position that juvenile sexual offenders should be more-or-less understood and treated in much the same way as other juvenile delinquents, even if as a subset. Letourneau and Miner (2005), for instance, conclude that "juvenile sex offenders are similar to other juvenile delinquents, and most would benefit from similar legal and clinical interventions" (p. 307). Similarly, in comparing juvenile sexual offenders to both non-sexual juvenile offenders and a group of juvenile non-offenders, Ronis and Borduin (2007) reported few differences between juvenile sexual offenders and non-sexual juvenile offenders, or between types of juvenile sexual offenders (i.e., those with child victims and those with peer/adult victims). Hence, their study did not support distinguishing between sexually abusive youth and juvenile delinquents, asserting that "the reality is that juvenile sexual offending is often part of a broader pattern of serious antisocial behavior" (p, 161). The authors ask whether the developmental pathways for sexual offending are identical to those for non-sexual offending, and their position is essentially that the same treatment model can be applied to sexually abusive youth and juvenile delinquents, namely multisystemic therapy (their own treatment model).[5]

Hagan, Gust-Brey, Cho, and Dow (2001) compared three groups of juvenile offenders (sexual offenders of children, sexual offenders of peers or adults, and non-sexual juvenile offenders) and found no significant difference between any group (although, not surprisingly, found that the sexual offenders were at greater risk for committing future sexual offenses than the non-sexual offenders). The authors concluded that delinquency is a general risk factor for sexually abusive behavior, and that conduct-disordered behavior in those who have already engaged in sexually abusive behavior serves as an additional risk factor. Milloy (1998) argues that, as most juvenile sexual offenders do not sexually recidivate and many are at greater risk for non-sexual recidivism, they should be considered as "generalists" (in effect, criminally versatile) and treated as delinquents and not sexual offenders, per se.

Lewis, Shankok, and Pincus (1979, 1981) also concluded that juvenile sexual offenders are similar to non-sexual juvenile offenders and experience the same psychological, neurological, and behavioral problems. Going further, based on a small sample size of 17 incarcerated sexually abusive youths, they argued that juvenile sexual offenders are similar to non-sexual violent offenders, and that the development of sexually abusive behavior

---

5. Letourneau, cited above, is also a strong proponent for multisystemic therapy (MST).

and generally violent behavior has the same etiology. They found that the 17 sexually abusive youths and 61 violent youths were more like one another than they were the 19 non-sexual non-violent adolescents included in the study. A similar position was more recently taken by Jacobs, Kennedy, and Meyer (1997) in their study of 156 incarcerated juvenile sexual and juvenile non-sexual offenders. Unlike Ronis and Borduin or Hagan et al., they examined only differences and similarities between juvenile sexual and juvenile non-sexual offenders, and did not further explore differences within either group. However, Jacob et al. found no meaningful differences between the sexual and non-sexual groups, and concluded that sexually abusive behavior by the subjects in their study was "likely to be but one expression of antisocial, violent behavior" (p. 201). Nevertheless, despite their clearly stated position that juvenile sexual offenders do not represent a group that is distinct from other "violent delinquents" (p. 216), Jacobs et al. also provided support for the position that sexually abusive youths are not merely a variant of general delinquents. They noted that the sexual offenders in their study had fewer state commitments than did the non-sexual offenders and "were a less chronic, less versatile, and in some ways more benign group than the non-sexual offenders" (p. 314).

The Second Position: Juvenile Sexual Offenders as Special Variants of Delinquency

Despite his observation that juvenile sexual offenders may be generally indistinguishable from non-sexual juvenile offenders, Caldwell (2002) takes the position that juvenile sexual offenders represent a different group, and within the population of juvenile sexual offenders they may be further sub-typed. This represents a second and more finely grained position that recognizes, as do Seto and Lalumière (2006), that although sexually abusive youth engage in juvenile delinquency by definition, their antisocial behaviors are often different than those of non-sexual offenders. Indeed, drawn from their literature review, Varker, Devilly, Ward, and Beech (2008) assert that "adolescent sexual offenders are a distinct group from juvenile delinquents" (p. 258). Based on their literature review, van Wijk, Vermeiren, Loeber, Hart-kerkhoffs, and Bullens (2006) reach a similar conclusion. Although noting that the current literature does not support clear or consistent conclusions regarding similarities or differences between juvenile sexual offenders and juvenile non-sexual offenders, van Wijk et al. nonetheless write that the literature supports differences between the two groups, writing that "it is likely that sex offenders are different from non-sex offenders in specific ways"(p. 237).

Those taking this second position clearly recognize heterogeneity among types of juvenile sexual offenders and therefore, by extension, between sexual and non-sexual juvenile offenders. In recognizing sub-groups within the population of juvenile sexual offenders, such as those with child victims and those with peer/adult victims, it is also implicitly implied that sexually abusive youth are a special subset of the larger population of juvenile delinquents. From this perspective, sexually abusive youth are not seen as simply "garden variety" juvenile delinquents, as some assert. Instead, the etiology, dynamics, social skills, and social orientation of sexually abusive youth, not to mention their sexually abusive behaviors, are recognized as a unique and special strain of juvenile delinquency that is significantly different in many respects and driven by different risk factors and motivations. In their study of risk assessment instruments, for example, Viljoen et al. (2008) concluded that among sexually abusive youth a different set of risk factors may be relevant to their sexual and non-sexual offending antisocial behaviors, recognizing differences between the development and dynamics of sexually abusive behavior and those of non-sexual conduct disordered behavior.

The position taken here is that juvenile sexual offenders do represent a significant variant of juvenile delinquency, falling into two basic groups: (1) those who are actively and broadly antisocial, but who represent a relative minority of sexually abusive youth, and (2) those whose accompanying antisocial behaviors do not significantly match those of criminally conduct-disordered youth and who represent the relative majority of sexually abusive youth. In either case, despite sharing common features, behaviors, and needs with non-sexual juvenile delinquents, sexually abusive youth represent a significantly different group of children and adolescents.

WITHIN-GROUP AND ACROSS-GROUP HETEROGENEITY: SEXUAL OFFENDERS AND DELINQUENTS

A number of studies yield data to support the perspective that juvenile sexual offenders are not only different from one another, but as a group are generally different from non-sexual juvenile delinquents. These studies reach similar conclusions in which general and non-sexual antisocial behavior is prevalent among juvenile sexual offenders, but it is more commonly found, and more intense and broad in nature, among juveniles who sexually assault peers or adults compared to those who sexually assault children. These adolescents more closely resemble non-sexual juvenile offenders in this regard. They more typically engage in a range of antisocial or criminal behaviors, not only in addition to their sexually abusive behavior but also in or connected to the commission of sexual offenses.

Beyond this, however, despite the prevalence of antisocial and troubled behavior in the sexually abusive youth included in these studies, there are generally clear differences in the type and intensity of antisocial behaviors they display, which is often of a less-criminal nature than the antisocial behaviors exhibited by non-sexual juvenile delinquents. Even among juvenile peer and adult offenders who engage in more intense conduct-disordered behaviors than child molesters, there are differences that distinguish them from non-sexual juvenile offenders. In general, there are clear differences between juvenile sexual offenders and non-sexual juvenile offenders, not only in terms of the type of non-sexual antisocial behavior, but also in personality traits, social skill development, and social connection and experience.

A Review of Studies Supporting In-Group and Across-Group Differences

Hunter and colleagues (Hunter, Hazelwood, & Slesinger, 2000; Hunter, Figueredo, Malamuth, & Becker, 2003) assert that juvenile sexual offenders represent a diverse population in both their crimes and psychological makeup and that juvenile child molesters and those who sexually abuse peers/adults differ significantly along a number of dimensions. They conclude that juvenile sexual offenders of peers or adults primarily target non-family member females, rather than males or family members. Compared with juvenile child molesters, these youth more typically commit their crimes in a public location, are more likely to engage in other types of criminal behavior in association with the sexual assault, such as burglary, substance abuse, or use of threats or a weapon, and are generally more broadly aggressive, violent, and criminally oriented. Comparatively, Hunter and colleagues describe juveniles who sexually abuse children as less psychosocially skilled and less outward going; more likely to target boys or girls, often in their families or extended group of acquaintances; and less likely to use serious aggression or force in the commission of sexual abuse.

Parks and Bard (2006) compared juvenile child molesters, peer/adult offenders, and those with mixed-age victims. Although all groups scored high in measures of antisocial behavior, with respect to sexual recidivism child molesters showed a 4 percent recidivism rate compared to 6.5 percent sexual recidivism among mixed victim offenders, and 10 percent among peer/adult offenders. Consistent with Hunter et al. (2000, 2003), Parks and Bard concluded that peer/adult offenders are more opportunistic and less sexually preoccupied than child offenders, more typically target females, and combine their sexual offenses with other non-sexual delinquent behavior. Similarly grouping sexually abusive youth into three groups based on victim age, Kemper and Kistner (2007) reported antisocial behavior among all three groups. Like Parks and Bard, they too found that the rate of sexual offense recidivism differed significantly between groups, ranging from 1 to 8 percent, thus supporting a difference among types of juvenile offenders. Richardson, Kelly, Bhate, and Graham (1997), using a four-group model also based on victim age, again noted antisocial behavior across all groups. However, like Hunter et al., Richardson and colleagues concluded that juvenile peer/adult offenders were the most frequently and most widely antisocial across the spectrum of antisocial behaviors, whereas those engaging in child molestation within their own families were the least generally antisocial in frequency, aggression, or association with an antisocial peer group.

Ford and Linney (1995) compared juvenile child molesters, juvenile peer/adult sexual offenders, violent juvenile non-sexual offenders, and non-violent juvenile non-sexual offenders, and found both similarities and differences in the histories of each subject. However, child molesters experienced more family dysfunction, personal abuse, and greater exposure to sex at a younger age than other groups, whereas juveniles peer/adult offenders were more similar to non-sexual offenders in these areas. Compared to juvenile child molesters, the juvenile rapists were more socially detached, although not to the same degree as the violent non-sexual offenders. Hsu and Starzynski (1990) also studied differences and similarities between a group of juvenile child molesters and juvenile peer/adult offenders. Unlike Ford and Linney, they found no essential differences in family history or history of personal abuse, but they did find that the peer/adult offender group was substantially and clearly more aggressive in their offenses. As Hunter et al. found, these juveniles selected female targets, as well as strangers or acquaintances rather than family members, and their sexual assaults also involved the incidence of non-sexual offenses, including substance abuse, burglary, the use of violence, and sexual assaults in outdoor public environments.

Carpenter, Peed, and Eastman (1995) similarly compared a group of adolescent child molesters and peer offenders. They too found that adolescents in both groups engaged in antisocial behaviors, but they also found that the child molesters were frequently submissively dependent upon others, non-competitive, experienced low self-efficacy, withdrew from social relationships, and experienced loneliness and isolation. However, like other study authors, Carpenter at el. treat antisocial and conduct disordered behavior as a categorical construct, failing to describe the nature of the antisocial behavior, or later non-sexual convictions, or distinguish between the type and intensity of antisocial behavior. This is not so in the 10-year follow-up study conducted by Waite et al. (2005), who found and identified significant differences in antisociality in their comparison of juvenile sexual offenders in specialized sex offender treatment and juvenile sexual offenders in a more generalized treatment program.

Consistent with virtually all studies, Waite et al. found a significantly higher re-arrest rate for non-sexual offenses (almost 59 percent) compared to the re-arrest rate for sexual offenses (4.7 percent). However, although there was barely any difference in the sexual recidivism rates between the two groups, there was a significant difference in non-sexual recidivism, with a 47 percent non-sexual recidivism rate for the specialized treatment group compared to 70.5 percent non-sexual recidivism among the more generalized group of juvenile sexual offenders. Further, juveniles in the specialized treatment group had a history of greater child molestation, were more likely to have been sexually victimized themselves, had significantly fewer prior criminal offenses, and engaged in fewer types of offenses, supporting the premise that not all juvenile sexual offenders are equally conduct disordered, or conduct disordered at all, despite having more non-sexual than sexual behavior problems.

Waite and colleagues also found that more impulsive and antisocial juveniles within either group were more likely to recidivate than those who were less impulsive and antisocial (64 percent compared to 52 percent), and they were likely to recidivate far more quickly (within 48 months compared to 65 months). Moreover, highly impulsive and antisocial juveniles in the generalized group had a higher rate of recidivism and a shorter time to re-arrest than impulsive and antisocial juveniles in the specialized group. These findings are again consistent with the idea of heterogeneity among sexually abusive youth and even within types of juvenile sexual offenders. They also support the idea that levels and types of antisocial and criminal behavior vary significantly, and criminally conduct-disordered behavior is most prevalent among juveniles who sexually abuse peers and adults.

Unlike studies that group classify juveniles based upon the type or age of the victim or the nature of the offense behavior, Worling (2001) grouped juvenile sexual offenders along the four dimensions of *antisocial-impulsive, unusual-isolated, overcontrolled-reserved*, and *confident-aggressive*. Consistent with other research, all groups showed a higher rate of recidivism for any type of reoffense (46 percent) than for sexual reoffense (11 percent). However, the more behaviorally disturbed and pathological antisocial-impulsive and unusual-isolated groups showed higher reoffense rates for both sexual and non-sexual offenses, again supporting the idea that antisocial behavior is both multidimensional and that different subgroups of sexually abusive youth engage in different types of antisocial behavior, at different rates, in different ways, and for different reasons.

Almond and colleagues also employed different means to group and compare sexually abusive youth with one another, conducting two studies with adolescents who sexually assaulted children. In one study (Almond & Canter, 2007), sexually abusive youth were classified into one of three groups based on their implied view of their victims.[6] Each of these groups experienced different levels of social relatedness with their victims and engaged in different levels and types of antisocial behavior. Sexually abusive youth in the largest group (41 percent) saw their victims as people, experiencing some form of reciprocal relationship with their victims, using relational methods to induce compliance, and demonstrating little anti-social behavior in their offenses other than the offense itself. In their second study (Almond, Canter, & Salfati, 2006), the sexually abusive youth were grouped as either impaired, abused, or delinquent,[7] based on personal characteristics. Of these groups, impaired or abused youth comprised 57 percent of the total and delinquent youth were 14 percent (other juveniles were represented by hybrid combinations of the classification), and only the delinquent youth engaged in a wide range of delinquent behaviors in addition to the sexually abusive behavior.

Both of Almond's studies demonstrate not only the heterogeneity of sexually abusive youth, but also that the same group of sexually abusive youth may be understood and classified in different ways, making rigid or comprehensive typologies inadequate and unrealistic. Further, in both types of grouping most sexually abusive youth were not primarily delin-quent, again supporting the idea, as I have contended here and elsewhere (Rich, 2006; in press), that most juvenile sexual offenders represent a

---

6. Those who experienced their *victim as a person* (41 percent) in which a relationship was implied and no physical coercion occurred, those who experienced their *victim as a vehicle* (30 percent) against whom to vent anger and frustration, and those who experienced their *victim as an object* (15 percent) to be used for personal gratification, including aggression and control, and often including other crimes at the time of the abuses (per Hunter et al., 2003).

7. *Impaired* youth experience a wide range of emotional, psychological, physical or other difficulties. *Abused* youth are characterized by a background of physical or sexual abuse. *Delinquent* youth do not "specialize" in sexual offenses, but engage in a wide range of delinquent behaviors in which sexually abusive behavior is embedded.

special class within a larger model of juvenile delinquency, and that in most cases we will find that the victims of sexually abusive youth are children (the average age of the victims in Almond's studies ranged between 8 and 10, in which 70 percent of the victims were two or more years younger than the offenders).

SOCIAL COMPETENCE AND SOCIAL ORIENTATION

In their ongoing work on social connection, attachment, and juvenile sexual offending, Miner and colleagues also recognize subtypes of juvenile sexual offenders, and in particular describe juvenile sexual offenders who offend children and those who offend peers and adults.

Miner and Swinburne-Romine (2004) found that sexually abusive youth who molest children have fewer friends, feel more isolated, associate with younger children, and have more concerns about masculinity than juvenile sexual offenders who target peers or adults, or non-sexual juvenile offenders. Although juvenile sexual offenders do not differ significantly from non-sexual juvenile offenders in either attitude or behavior, they are significantly more isolated from family and more socially isolated from peers than violent delinquents and non-offenders (Miner & Crimmins, 1997). In comparing differences in attitudes, normlessness, and social isolation among juvenile sexual offenders, non-sexual juvenile delinquents, and non-delinquent adolescents, Miner and Munns (2005) found that juvenile sexual offenders experienced more social isolation in school and in their families than non-sexual offenders, and were more isolated from their peers than non-sexual juvenile delinquents.

Berg (2007) found partial support for the hypothesis that juvenile sexual offenders with child victims feel socially disconnected and isolated from peers, and Miner points to the possibility that juvenile sexual offenders expect adult and peer rejection. In general, Miner proposes that juvenile sexual abuse is driven by socially isolated and normless behaviors rather than by aggression, at least in those who molest children, echoing Hudson and Ward's (2000) conjecture that adult sexually abusive behavior among adults is often more connected to the need for social connection and the acquisition of social goals than deviant sexuality. Miner concludes that juvenile sexual offenders experience a deeper level of social isolation than non-sexual juvenile delinquents and non-offenders, and suggests that the inability to experience satisfaction in social relationships may turn some adolescents to younger children to meet sexual and social needs. This is, of course, of special importance as it appears that most juvenile sexual offenders offend children rather than peers, which suggests that most juvenile sexual offenders experience social isolation and lack important social skills and that this is an avenue to sexually abusive relationships with children.

Miner (2004) also expects to find evidence that a high level of hostile masculinity is linked to juvenile sexual abuse of peers and adults, whereas low masculine adequacy will be linked to juveniles who sexually abuse children. Hostile masculinity, as defined by Malamuth (2003), involves a hostile narcissistic orientation to women, which Malamuth proposes is one important facet that contributes to sexual aggression towards women. Whereas the idea that juvenile child molesters experience a poor sense of masculine adequacy, the idea that adolescents who sexually offend peers and adults experience a hostile masculinity, or hyper-masculinity, fits with a description of this type of juvenile sexual offender as more generally aggressive and antisocial in orientation and more classically conduct disordered.

Daversa and Knight's (2007) study of adolescent child sexual abusers supports the position that juveniles who sexually assault children experience social isolation and experience themselves as inadequate. The study, which statistically hypothesized four pathways by which adolescent males sexualize and sexually abuse children, supported early developmental and maltreatment experiences as contributing factors to such behavior, as well as the interplay of personality traits that included dislike of, hostility towards, or aversion to adults and peers. Their study supports prior research that suggests that adolescent child molesters are submissive, dependent, and socially isolated and that such adolescents may also experience feelings of sexual inadequacy, as well as feelings of social inadequacy, anxiety, and rejection. Daversa and Knight suggested that adolescent sexual offenders who struggle with the challenges of adolescent masculinity, are embarrassed by their physical appearance, and are worried about their appeal to peer-aged girls may choose younger victims as a way of compensating for their inability to compete with other young males in the adolescent world. However, the authors also identified a subgroup of adolescent child molesters who shared many of these elements, but also were impulsive and aggressive in their offense planning, sadistic, and sexually aroused by young children, once again supporting the idea of heterogeneity and diversity even within subgroups.

JUVENILE SEXUAL OFFENDING AS A SPECIAL FORM OF DELINQUENT BEHAVIOR

Caldwell (2002) describes the heterogeneity of sexually abusive youth as "one of the most resilient findings in the research on juvenile sexual offenders" (p. 296). He notes the importance of distinguishing between types of juvenile sexual offenders, lending support to the idea that not only are sexually abusive youth different from one another, but they are not simply cut from the same cloth of juvenile delinquency, even if a special variant. Nevertheless, as the reader you must decide for yourself whether juvenile sexual offenders are essentially a variant of general juvenile delinquency or whether they represent a special case of troubled behavior.

However, as described, the perspective adopted in this book is that the phenomenon of juvenile sexually abusive behavior represents a special pathway. This pathway is subtly, but quite distinct from the pathway that leads to non-sexually abusive juvenile delinquency, even if the ideation and behavior of both juvenile sexual offenders and non-sexual juvenile offenders share similarities and even common roots.

This is important because as we further discuss risk factors that contribute to reengagement in sexually abusive behavior we will not be looking at sexually abusive behavior as just another form of juvenile delinquency. Although many of the risk factors will be the same or similar to those we might look at in assessing general delinquency, a substantial number will be quite different, and we will not be asking the same questions of the juveniles we assess, their families, or other informants. In other words, in understanding sexually abusive behavior in children and adolescents and assessing the risk for sexual reoffense we are exploring a different behavior than that involved in general delinquency, despite commonalities in some instances.

The review of research that explores the heterogeneity of juvenile sexual offenders by type or groups should make it clear that, in a very simple model, some forms of sexually abusive behavior, and particularly those that involve adolescent sexual assault of peers or adults, resemble generally conduct-disordered and criminal behavior. On the other hand, the sexual abuse of children appears to be a very different variant of sexually abusive behavior, involving not only different behavior but a different route of development that is quite unlike general juvenile delinquency. Further, as sexual abuse reporting and arrest statistics seem to indicate that most juvenile sexual offenders engage in child molestation rather than rape of peers or adults, this suggests a more complex pathway for most sexually abusive youth than simply understanding them as antisocial and conduct-disordered juvenile delinquents.

The work of Miner and his colleagues adds depth to ideas about juvenile sexual offenders already identified by other researchers. It adds to and confirms the value of recognizing at least two different types of juvenile sexual offenders—those who sexually abuse children and those who assault peers or adults—and the different pathways, motivations, and behaviors that exist for each type. Understanding sexually abusive youth from the perspective of social connection, social skill, self-perception, and perception of others gives us greater insight into the sexually abusive and related behaviors of individual juvenile sexual offenders, and the different risk and protective factors that may be at work in general and in each individual case.

However, whereas Miner is largely describing the social disconnection and social inadequacy experienced by the juvenile sexual offender of children, Hunter et al. (2000, 2003) describe the more criminally versatile juvenile sexual offender as sexually assaulting female peers and women, and thus resembling adult rapists. Unlike Miner's prototype juvenile child molester, Hunter's prototype is clearly conduct disordered in the classic sense, and engaged in a wider variety of antisocial and criminal behavior than sexual abuse alone, including a more significant level of general aggression and violence, both within and separate from their sexually abusive behavior. Nevertheless, as described, sexual abuse reporting and arrest statistics indicate that most juvenile sexual offenders engage in child molestation rather than rape of peers or adults; in turn, this suggests that most sexually abusive youth are more appropriately characterized as socially troubled and socially inept than antisocial and criminally oriented. Regardless, both types of juvenile sexual offenders exist, and both must be assessed in ways that will help us to best understand them as individuals, and not simply members of a class of sexual offenders.

HETEROGENEITY IN JUVENILE SEXUAL OFFENDING

Just as there are distinctions between types of offenders with regard to their victim selection, their level of conduct disorder and type of antisocial behavior, their criminal versatility, and even their personality type, so too must there be distinctions *within* each of these subgroups. For instance, within the group of juveniles who sexually abuse children there are no doubt highly conduct-disordered and criminally versatile youths, as well as socially inept youth who lack social connection and self-confidence. Similarly, among juvenile sexual offenders who are socially awkward and lack socially competence, there are certainly children and adolescents who also engage in highly conduct-disordered behavior, including aggression and violence, such as the subgroup identified by Daversa and Knight (2007) in their study.

Then there are those offenders who, regardless of the presence or absence of persistent conduct-disordered behavior or their level of social skill or competence, are motivated by anger, by curious experimentation, by lack of self-confidence in their sexual abilities with peers, or by a perseverative interest in sex that may reflect a psychiatric disturbance. Additionally, even though *DSM-IV* does not allow the diagnosis of pedophilia until at least age 16, there are also those adolescent offenders who are actually attracted to and sexually aroused by children and those who engage in sexual behaviors with children because the children are, in effect, available to them but not because they are sexually aroused to children per se.

In fact, there are almost unlimited variations, including combinations of the possibilities just described, not to mention the additional variables of intellectual capacity, offender gender (as we know, girls sexually offend as well as boys, although at a much lesser rate), and age of the offender (i.e., pre-pubescent, young adolescent, or older adolescent). These each add further variety and heterogeneity to the mix of possible types of juvenile sexual offenders, as well as types of motivations for and drives behind the perpetration of sexually abusive behavior. It is not only pointless to talk about juvenile (or adult) sexual offenders as a single group, but almost as pointless to talk about types of juvenile sexual offenders as there are so many variants and possible combinations of human personality, motivation, and behavior.

This is precisely why typologies have only a limited utility. They can be, and are, helpful in drawing simple distinctions and defining population characteristics typologies; typing individuals into categorical groups can help us to recognize not only similarities between individuals within groups, but also, of equal importance, differences between people and classes of people. However, typologies are always necessarily artificial in nature, and themselves are merely artifacts of statistical analyses or subjective interpretations of research or clinical observation. To some degree this was made clear in the studies conducted by Almond et al. (Almond, Canter, & Salfati, 2006; Almond & Canter, 2007) in which the same group of sexually abusive youth was classified into two completely different typologies.

Without overlooking the value of typologies, then, we also should not make the mistake of thinking of them as mirrors of reality, as they can never hope to capture the complexity of the human psyche or resultant behavior. Even if they share commonalities or can be statistically clustered into groups, and even if typologies can help us in our research and development of treatment interventions and in our assignments of risk for re-offense, it is important for us to recognize, treat, and, for the purpose of this book, assess sexually abusive youths as *individuals*. To this degree, there is little value in assigning juvenile sexual offenders to groups which must, necessarily, overlook their essential heterogeneity. Although juvenile sexual offenders may be broken into general groups or types, they nevertheless vary by individual and by individual life story.

HETEROGENEITY AND THE "OTHER" JUVENILE SEXUAL OFFENDERS

Even as we recognize the utility of creating subgroups or types of juvenile sexual offenders, it is important to also recognize that most of the research on sexual offenders has primarily been conducted with adult men, and secondarily with adolescent males, with IQs that typically fall somewhere between the low average to high average range of intellectual functioning. Therefore, as we discuss sexual offenders, as individuals or as types, whether adult or adolescent, we are most typically exploring the behavior of average IQ male sexual offenders, even if we adopt a personality-based approach like Worling's (2001).

This view of sexual offenders, of course, necessarily excludes and almost treats as invisible, female, cognitively impaired, psychiatrically disordered, and pre-pubescent sexual abusers, as well as sexual offenders from significantly different cultural and ethnic backgrounds. Our general research and ideas about adult and juvenile sexual offenders fail to inform us about these other sexual offenders unless we assume that the same factors and dynamics are at play for them as those that shape the psychologies of adolescent and adult male sexual offenders in Western cultures. Frankly, even understanding ideas like antisociality in these other groups can be quite challenging if we see members of these populations through the same lenses through which we observe Western males.

CONCLUSION: HETEROGENEITY AND RISK ASSESSMENT

It is quite likely that a risk profile on each youth will yield a very different portrait of each child. However, this does not mean that it is not possible to describe factors that place children and adolescents at general risk, and in the case of sexually abusive youth, at risk for sexual reoffense. Instead, it means that from the same list of risk factors we are likely to recognize that different risk factors are at play for different individuals, and perhaps even at different times in their development or based upon differences in their cognitive capacity. We will find that from a single list of risk factors different permutations or combinations will spell out risk for different individuals.

All of this is by way of saying that juvenile sexually abusive behavior is not a cut-and-dried or well-understood phenomenon, although we are learning more about differences between juvenile sexual offenders and non-sexual juvenile offenders, as well as differences between juvenile sexual offenders who typically sexually abuse children and those who target peers or adults. As we continue into the next chapters and a further description of the risk assessment process, it is, once again, important to bear in mind that this book essentially addresses the assessment of risk in male adolescent sexual offenders with IQs broadly falling within the low to high average range. Many of the ideas will be and are applicable to cognitively impaired juvenile sexual offenders, as well as sexually abusive children and even female juvenile sexual offenders, but these groups are still not well understood and represent populations that are even less understood than adolescent male sexual offenders.

CHAPTER 6

Case Studies in Heterogeneity

THIS BRIEF CHAPTER picks up on where Chapter 5 left off regarding heterogeneity and illustrates differences, not only between sexually abusive youth and non-sexual juvenile offenders, but among adolescent sexual offenders. Case studies can be tedious to read, but I hope that these are sufficiently short to not bore, but detailed enough to highlight differences in not only the sexually abusive behavior, but also in the individuals perpetrating the behaviors; one highlights a case that is probably not abusive at all, even if disturbed in origin and practice. You will also, no doubt, recognize similarities in each case, with particular respect to elements, at least, of early and social development.

PAUL

Now aged 18, at age 13, Paul was accused by a 10-year-old girl of sexually molesting her at a local youth center by touching her breasts and putting his hands up her skirt to touch her vagina. One year later, at age 14, Paul was accused of similar behaviors with a 14-year-old girl at a local library, and shortly after this the first girl further claimed that Paul has had actually raped her vaginally. Two other young teenage girls came forth and alleged that Paul had similarly sexually molested them, but they declined to press charges, and one actually later recanted. However, on the basis of the reports of the first two girls, Paul was adjudicated on several counts of sexual assault, including rape in the second degree. In addition to sexually abusive behavior, Paul has exhibited a range of conduct disordered behavior, including alcohol and marijuana abuse, aggressive behavior including fighting in school and in the community, angry and oppositional outbursts, and other general behavioral problems. However, Paul has friends, who are also somewhat conduct disordered in orientation, and a range of social skills, at least on the surface, and he can be a loyal and supportive friend and supporter of others.

Paul was retained in first grade, diagnosed with attention deficit/hyperactivity disorder and a learning disorder at age 8, and has been a special education student since age 11. Despite this, and significant problems with writing and reading, Paul is of average intelligence, bright and competent, a very capable thinker and, although reserved at times, he can be quite eloquent and insightful. Paul grew up in a chaotic and dysfunctional household and was exposed to domestic violence and drug addicted parents. His father has been out of his life with no further contact since Paul was 6, and Paul's mother was only sporadically involved in his life from age 8 on, by which point Paul was being raised by his grandparents. His mother died of a drug overdose when Paul was age 15, and this continues to be a source of great difficulty for him.

JON

Jon has been engaging in sexual behaviors with younger children, same age and slightly older peers, and older adolescents and adults since he was age 11 or 12. At 13, he was adjudicated on multiple counts of sexual abuse against an 11-year-old boy, including fellatio and masturbation, and at 15 he was further adjudicated on similar charges of sexually abusing a 10-year-old boy. Jon was also actively engaged in consensual fellatio and masturbation with same-age peers, and also made himself sexually available to older adolescent boys and adult men, who, of course, were the sexual perpetrators in this case, even though Jon was a willing and active participant and sought out such contact, including through the Internet. In treatment, Jon reported ongoing sexual interest in pre-pubescent and adolescent boys and young adults, and acknowledged several additional sexual behaviors (i.e., offenses) against younger children, as well as performing fellatio on two of his father's friends after they had passed out following intoxication at a party at his father's home. At age 16, given his description of continued sexual arousal to children, as well as his history of child sexual abuse, Jon was provisionally diagnosed with pedophilia.

Jon is of above-average intelligence and does not otherwise have a history of general conduct-disordered behavior. However, Jon has no friends and has never been part of a social group. He reports that the only person with whom he has ever felt close was an adult male he met through an Internet sex chat room, although they never actually met in person despite a plan to meet for a sexual encounter. Jon is not liked by peers in treatment, and he does not feel close to anyone, including his parents. Throughout treatment in a residential facility, Jon continued to try to engage peers of varying ages in sexual contact.

MARVIN

Marvin is a 15-year-old boy who was adopted at age 5, along with his 14-month younger sister. He was significantly affected by his adopted parents' divorce at age 11, and has a significant history of engaging in sexually inappropriate behaviors from this time on. From age 11 to 14, Marvin engaged in sexualized behaviors with his younger sister, including oral sex and vaginal penetration. At age 13, he was involved in consensual oral sex with a 12-year-old boy, witnessed by Marvin's 11-year-old adopted brother. At age 13, Marvin exposed himself to his brother, sister, and his brother's friends by running around the house naked after drinking alcohol, as, at the time, he thought it would be funny. However, Marvin does not have a significant history of alcohol abuse and no known history of drug use. There were a series of other sexualized behaviors and relationships, all involving consensual sexual relationships with same-age male and female adolescents, within 1–2 years of Marvin's age. At 14, Marvin met a 29-year-old man through the Internet, ran away with him, and reported being later raped by the man. While being pursued by the police with Marvin in the car, the perpetrator had a car accident in which he died and his legs were severed, in Marvin's presence, and Marvin's neck was broken, although he recovered.

Marvin is a bright, capable, and affable adolescent of slightly above average intelligence who easily makes friends and has always had friends, although reports never feeling very close to anyone. He has current symptoms of depression and anxiety and a history of mild self-injurious behavior, dating back several years. Although he has an IQ of 115, Marvin has been a special education student since age 9. Marvin was admitted to treatment for sexually abusing his sister, although never charged with any sexual crime, and he has never been charged with any other crime, nor generally engaged in any significantly troubled behavior, other than the sexual behaviors described. His sister does not have any significant psychological or intellectual deficits, does not appear to have been significantly bullied or coerced into sexual activity, and is only 14 months younger than Marvin. She reported that the sexual behavior, which continued for three years, was consensual. Certainly, the sexual behavior with his sister is incestuous and of great concern, but given the similarity in age and her own report that the behavior was consensual, did Marvin engage in sexually abusive behavior?

JUAN

Juan was diagnosed with Asperger's Disorder, although nevertheless has an average IQ.[1] He was adjudicated on charges of sexually abusing a 7-year-old boy over a period of two years, when Juan was aged 13–15. Following adjudication and while on probation, Juan demonstrated evidence of sexual preoccupation and lack of sexual self-control, including several instances of masturbation on a school bus, masturbating in the school gym showers, obvious erections while in school classrooms, allowing his penis to be seen while wearing shorts, and downloading pornography on school computers. Similar behaviors continued even after Juan was admitted to treatment in a group home. Even at age 17, Juan continued to be sexually aroused by thoughts of the young boy he had victimized. Even though he likes people and seeks social approval, Juan is socially isolated and awkward, and unusual in physical appearance with daytime enuresis and obviously poor hygiene. For the first 10 years of his life, Juan lived in an unstable single-parent family environment, with a mother who had a history significant of substance abuse and mental illness and several older brothers with a history of violence and one with a history of sexual offending. Juan has not seen his mother or brothers since age 10, when his father obtained custody, and since that time Juan has been part of a healthy family system. Nevertheless, Juan began to engage in sexually abusive behavior after being placed with his father, and his sexually preoccupied behaviors continued throughout his adolescence, even after being placed in a group home treatment program.

HUGH, ADRIAN, AND CLIVE

Here are three more brief cases. *Hugh* is a 17-year-old mildly retarded male with some additional neurological damage. As well as engaging in persistent sexually inappropriate behavior throughout his late childhood and adolescence, at age 15 he sexually molested his 4-year-old male cousin in the garden of the family home. Although eventually admitted to a residential facility for treatment, Hugh was discharged by his adopted

---

1. Individuals with Asperger's Disorder often have higher than average or superior IQs, especially in their verbal skills.

mother against the recommendation of the program, and within three months he sexually molested his 5-year-old male cousin in a room in the family home immediately adjacent to a room in which other adult family members were present, including the child's mother.

Adrian was raised in an Eastern European orphanage for the first eight years of his life, at which time he was adopted and brought to the United States. Beginning at age 15, for 18 months he repeatedly vaginally penetrated his 4-year-old adopted sister. He reported feeling close to his adopted family. However, he also reported feeling little remorse for his behavior at the time or since, and he experienced little empathy for his sister or other family members, although he was sorry that this had led to disconnection from his adopted family who essentially refused to allow him to re-enter the family after the discovery of his behavior. Now 17, Adrian is a very likeable boy of average intelligence who gets along with peers and adults and has never been in any other serious trouble. He reports not really knowing how to get close to people and having always worried that he would be rejected by family and others.

Clive is a 15-year-old with a history of seriously conduct-disordered behavior dating back to childhood. He has been raised by an uncle and aunt since age 7, and has engaged in many forms of troubled behavior since and prior to that time. Behaviors have included drug abuse and drug trafficking, physical assault, shoplifting, theft in school and from peers, frequent school truancy, and ongoing oppositional behavior and angry and violent episodes in the home, school, and community. Clive has been arrested several times, and is on probation until age 18. Clive was accused of raping a same-age girl in the hallway of her apartment building. Two weeks prior to this, as part of a pattern of persistent conduct disorder, Clive shot this girl in the leg with a BB gun on a dare from a friend. Although he initially denied raping the girl, claiming that she had been his girlfriend and the act was consensual, Clive later acknowledged that, although they had engaged in consensual sex, on this occasion she did not want to have sex and he forced her against her will. He also later admitted that he had vaginally penetrated her against her will on at least three other occasions.

CONCLUSION

These cases I hope illuminate difference. The thread, of course, is sexually abusive behavior, although the connection with Marvin is more likely sexually inappropriate behavior of a serious nature, rather than abusive behavior. Some of the ideas illustrated in these cases are picked up in later chapters, for instance regarding social connection and attachment (Chapter 20) and recognizing assessment differences between sexually normative, sexually inappropriate, and sexually abusive behavior (Chapter 9).

Wrapping up this short chapter, however, although we can see some similarities in each case (and a more detailed analysis would reveal even more similarities and commonalities), we also see vast differences. These differences figure prominently in prosocial and antisocial behavior and the relationship between sexual behaviors and other behaviors; the sexual behaviors themselves, as well as the targets of sexual abuse; motivation and drive, and even intention; sexually normative interests and sexual deviance; and the role filled by, and perhaps purpose of, sexual behaviors for each of these individuals. Significant differences are also revealed in the nature, psychology, cognitive capacity, and level of social skill and comfort of the adolescents in each case.

In the process and practice of risk assessment, recognizing and understanding these differences as best we can is a central task.

CHAPTER 7

Risk Factors for Juvenile Sexual Abuse

T HERE IS A fairly extensive body of literature on stress, risk, protection, and resilience in children and adolescents. In this larger context, "risk" involves the potential for a wide range of personal problems and problematic behavior, including educational failure, physical and mental health concerns, economic hardship, teen pregnancy, substance abuse, and violent and non-violent crime. These each represent variants of failure to achieve personal success or optimal functioning, or perhaps the development of self-destructive or more generally antisocial behaviors. As risk is tied to both individual factors and factors found in the environment, and ultimately the interaction between the two, failure to accomplish personal success also represents failure for our social order.

Synder, Reid, and Patterson (2003) describe antisocial behavior occurring "in social interaction," rather than being carried as an "in the person" trait. From this perspective, it is the relationship between individual dispositions and environmental factors that influences and shapes development, and not the separate influence of either in isolation from the other (Wachs, 1996). In an ecological model, failure at the social level signals the failure of social structure to protect individuals and enhance and foster their well-being. In an ecosystem, social-level failures also mean the secondary creation of effects that act reciprocally upon the ecosystem to permeate and shape the social structure itself, thus creating still more risk for individuals and structures within society. In fact, it is likely that individuals at risk for any one problem are almost certainly at risk for, and experiencing, more problems than those limited to that risk condition alone. This helps to explain why juvenile sexual offenders tend to experience more difficulty in their behaviors and social functioning than that demonstrated by their sexually abusive behavior alone, and are at greater risk for recidivating in non-sexual ways.

The same is true for protection and protective factors.[1] It is likely that children and adolescents experiencing the buffering against risk offered by one protective factor have more than one protective factor at work in their lives. Hence, juvenile sexual offender treatment that strengthens existing and builds new protective factors is likely to help mitigate the effects of risk and promote well-being and success in many areas of life, and not just that in which sexually abusive behavior resides.

FORENSIC RISK ASSESSMENT

When we discuss risk in relationship to forensic assessment, although clearly related to larger risk concepts, "risk" is clearly and necessarily more limited in scope than risk for a broad range of social failures. Pointed towards the development of antisocial and criminal behavior, in forensic assessment, and of course risk for continued sexually abusive behavior, analysis of risk is focused specifically upon risk factors believed related to risk for re-engagement in criminal behavior. Nevertheless, although more limited and more pointed, a significant and broad range of psychosocial variables have been associated with risk for conduct disordered behavior (Rutter, 1994), and even a cursory review of risk factors makes it clear that forensic risk (i.e., risk for criminal behavior) is linked to, and in some ways a subset of, an understanding of more global risk.

Hence, many of the essential risk factors for crime are identical to those for other personal or social problems, as is true for the presence of protective factors. This again reflects a holistic, or ecological, approach to understanding the development of risky and dangerous behavior, highlighting the fact that such behavior emerges from the same social conditions that give rise to other troubling conditions.

Despite this, to be more precise and to aim at predicting trends for future criminal behavior, the development of a risk assessment process must focus primarily on those risk factors considered relevant to criminal recidivism. This has led to the development of risk assessment instruments aimed at specific behaviors, including general criminal and sexually abusive behavior. The Violence Risk Assessment Guide (VRAG), for instance, is an actuarial assessment instrument aimed at statistically classifying adults into risk categories for general violent crime, and the Structured Assessment of Violence in Youth (SAVRY) is a clinical assessment instrument intended

---

1. Protective factors are discussed in Chapter 8.

to predict risk for violence in juveniles. Both are based on the presence of risk factors believed related to the occurrence or possibility of violence, in which risk factors are selected on the basis of their hypothesized link to prior aggressive behavior and presumptive ability to predict or point to the likelihood of similar future behavior.

With reference to instruments aimed at assessing risk for sexual abuse recidivism, these fall into the categories of adult or juvenile instruments and also actuarial and clinical assessment instruments. As described in previous chapters, in adult sexual offender risk assessment both types of assessment tools are available, whereas for juvenile assessment we have until recently had only clinical assessments available. However, with the introduction of the JSORRAT-II, we now have a prototype adolescent actuarial assessment as well. Regardless, whether adult or juvenile, actuarial or clinical, risk assessment tools are built from those risk factors believed specifically relevant to sexually abusive behavior.

RISK FACTORS AND TREATMENT

In developing assessment instruments that attempt to predict future behavior based on existing risk factors, we intrinsically recognize that factors linked to prior sexually abusive behavior also serve as risk factors for future sexually abusive behavior unless they are eliminated or in some way mitigated. That is, as long as risk factors remain in play, unless buffered they act as predictors for re-engagement in the same behavior.

For this reason, the identification of risk factors not only serves to predict, but also to direct treatment aimed at the elimination or reduction of risk factors, or the internal or external factors that contribute to risk. This may mean reducing risk through effective anger management, increasing empathy, eliminating sexually deviant thoughts, psychiatrically managing emotional conditions that may contribute to sexual risk, building closer family relationships, providing more opportunities for social success, and stabilizing environmental conditions that contribute to decisions to engage in sexually abusive behavior. Buffering against risk, on the other hand, is another way to describe the role of protective factors such as increasing family support, building social networks, supervision and monitoring, and removing opportunities for sexually abusive behavior. This brief list highlights the similarities between reducing risk and increasing protective factors, particularly when it comes to environmental variables. Improving social networks, for instance, both reduces risk through enhancing the chances for prosocial success and serves to protect against the risk for acting upon antisocial urges.

THE STRENGTH OF STATIC RISK FACTORS: THE EARLY DEVELOPMENT OF RISK

The reason that static risk factors offer so much to risk prediction is because history counts, not just as a predictor but as a foundation upon which present ideation and behavior is built and as the basis for continued trajectory. Just as resiliency against adversity and stress is laid down in early positive development (Sroufe, Egeland, Carlson, & Collins, 2005), so too is the foundation for antisocial behavior, as well as many other kinds of risk, laid in early life. This is easily seen by the number of general risk factors that make their appearance in childhood, before age 12. For this reason, these risk factors may be better called risk indicators, as Epperson (2007) and Rutter (1994, 2003) have noted.

Just as Marshall and Eccles (1993) describe early developmental vulnerabilities that establish the potential for a developmentally troubled path, Henry, Caspi, Moffitt, and Silva (1996) note that children who become serious criminal offenders are characterized by features that consistently bring them into conflict with their surroundings during early childhood. Individual characteristics that make individuals susceptible to risk are perhaps at their greatest during early childhood as they come into contact and interplay with environmental conditions that may catalyze risk or build a backdrop out of which antisocial behavior may later emerge (Rutter, Giller, & Hagell, 1998). However, rather than risk factors unexpectedly emerging at a later point in adolescent or adult development, Loeber et al. (2005) write that risk factors for serious crime can be observed in earlier childhood, and later antisocial behavior is often based on processes that accumulate over many years, associated with multiple risk factors in multiple domains.

At the same time, it's important that we recognize the difference between what Moffitt (2003) calls life-course persistent and adolescence-limited antisocial behavior. She describes persistent antisocial behavior clearly originating in childhood when the troubled behaviors of the high-risk young child are acted out in and amplified by a high-risk social environment, whereas the adolescence-limited variant is a more transient form of antisocial behavior that first appears during adolescence. The assertion, of course, is very much in keeping with the *DSM* model of childhood onset conduct disorder (American Psychiatric Association, 2000). It does not mean, however, that we should not be concerned about antisocial and conduct-disordered behaviors that first appear during adolescence or that antisociality in children inevitably means a lifetime of antisocial behavior. Nevertheless, early experience and behavior defines but doesn't set in stone the foundations of personality, and life circumstances of all kinds can alter trajectory as pointed out by Belsky and Nezworski (1988) and Rutter, Giller, and Hagell (1998), who write, "experiences continue to be important . . . Life events, turning points, and transition periods can all play a part in whether antisocial continues or ceases" (p. 307).

This also doesn't mean that we should consider the prognosis for sexually abusive behavior that begins in childhood as worse than sexually abusive behavior first perpetrated during adolescence, or assume that the latter simply represents a "passing phase" in adolescent development. However, it does mean that in assessing risk for sexual reoffense we should bear in mind many factors, including the juvenile's history as well as current behaviors, and bear in mind that even behaviors that look alike may have very different causes and have different trajectories. One important key to risk assessment with juvenile sexual offenders lies in recognizing the presence and action of multiple risk factors and predicting risk based upon a detailed understanding of those factors.

THE OPERATION OF MULTIPLE RISK DOMAINS DURING CHILDHOOD AND ADOLESCENCE

In focusing on risk factors for serious delinquency or violence, Lipsey and Derzon (1998) identified risk residing within and spread through five essential domains: individual, family, school, peer group, and community. Although none of the risk factors show a high effect size,[2] with most falling into the low range, the most significant early risk factors in childhood development (ages 6–11) included low family socioeconomic status and antisocial parents. These were followed by factors that while less statistically significant were nonetheless meaningful, including poor parent-child relationships, harsh or lax parental discipline, broken homes, poor attitude towards or performance in school, and exposure to television violence, as well as weak social ties.

Of the 23 childhood risk factors identified in the U.S. Surgeon General's report on youth violence (U.S. Department of Health and Human Services, 2001, largely based on the work of Lipsey and Derzon, 1998), none showed a strong effect size; only six fell into the moderate range, and of these only two fell towards the higher end of moderate. However, this does not mean

---

2. Effect size in statistical analysis indicates the strength of relationship between two variables and, in particular, the impact (or effect) of one thing (the independent variable) on another (the dependent variable). In this case, each individual risk factor represents an independent variable, whereas the dependent variable is serious or violent offending by mid-adolescence.

that these risk factors are inconsequential. Instead, it suggests, as previously described, that it is a *combination* of risk factors, and no single factor alone, that best predicts risk, as also noted by Hanson and Bussière (1998) in their meta-analysis of sexual offender recidivism. That is, although some risk factors are stronger in effect than others, and are therefore better predictors of later antisocial behavior, no single factor is itself necessary for nor sufficient enough to predict or produce antisocial behavior. In addition, not only is risk best predicted by multiple risk factors, but the likelihood that an individual will engage in antisocial behaviors is greatly increased by the number of risk factors to which the individual is exposed (Farrington, 1997; Garmezy, 1987; Hawkins et al., 2000). Further, risk that produces antisocial behavior is driven not just by multiple risk factors but, as noted, interactions among risk factors across multiple domains (Haggerty & Sherrod, 1996; Loeber et al., 2005).

However, many of the childhood risk factors identified by Lipsey and Derzon take on a greater role during adolescence whereas others drop in significance, reflecting the idea that the same risk factors operate differently at different points during childhood and adolescent development and have more or less impact. Of note here, the influence of risk factors associated with social connection increases in strength during early adolescence (ages 12–14), such as weak social ties that increase considerably in effect size and by adolescence become the strongest indicator in Lipsey and Derzon's inventory of risk factors, as well as an increase in the risk power of poor child-parental relationships. During adolescence, other factors not especially prominent during childhood take on more significance; in the case of serious and violent criminal behavior, these especially include association with antisocial peers, which is a factor that may be less relevant when we consider risk for sexual reoffense and especially among those who sexually abuse children. Nevertheless, the point here is that important seeds of risk are often sown early in childhood development and take greater root in adolescence, along with other risk factors that may have held less importance at an earlier point in development. As attachment patterns are considered to develop early in childhood, setting the pace for later social connections (Rich, 2006), it is not surprising that the effect size of weak social ties as a predictor of risk in Lipsey and Derzon's model increases by 160 percent during early adolescence.

With respect to risk factors for general youth violence, Hawkins et al. (2000) followed the same model as Lipsey and Derzon in recognizing risk factors within the five discrete domains of individual, family, school, peer-related, and community risk. In their catalogue of 27 primary risk factors they include aggressiveness, early violent behavior, and antisocial attitudes and behavior (individual risk factors); parent criminality, child maltreatment, poor family bonding, family conflict, low parental involvement, antisocial parent attitudes, and parent-child separation (family risk factors); academic failure, poor school bonding, frequent school changes, and school truancy and drop out (school risk factors); delinquent siblings and delinquent peers (peer-related risk factors); and poverty, community disorganization, crime ridden neighborhoods, and exposure to violence and prejudice (community risk factors).

The National Council on Crime and Delinquency (Howell, 1995) adopts a similar analysis of risk factors for behavioral problems, again recognizing that risk factors reside in different domains and not simply within the individual. The National Council defines only four risk domains, incorporating individual and peer group risk factors into a single group, and provides a similar inventory of 19 risk factors across the domains. However, its analysis assumes that the greatest number of risk factors exists in the community, including community norms favorable to antisociality, media portrayals of antisocial behavior, community stability, community socioeconomic status, and community attachment and organization. To better understand this, we can best consider the trajectory of antisocial behavior in relationship to the social environment in which it travels. As described, according to Synder, Reid, and Patterson (2003) antisocial behavior is better understood as the result of social interaction in which the environmental context is catalytic rather than simply a trait carried within the person. Here, studying development *in context* is the operative strategy (Wiksröm & Sampson, 2003).

PASSIVE, REACTIVE, AND ACTIVE RISK CO-VARIANCE

Regardless of their location, risk factors do not merely act upon children or adolescents as though they are simply corks bobbing on an ocean of life and experiences over which they have no control. That is, juveniles themselves, and not simply events in their past or present, have influence over their behaviors and their ability to gravitate towards or resist risky behavior.

Hence, although many of the environmental risk factors that surround the individual are independent of his or her history, the development of many of these factors for any given individual are, in actuality, influenced or mediated by his or her own history. As Anthony (1987) writes, development is an interactive process and individuals are not merely passive receptacles for external stimulation that simply writes upon and shapes them. He describes the child, from the start, as not a bucket waiting to be filled with experience but a searchlight exploring the horizon, and the child as "not a simple tape recorder on whom experiences are registered like sounds, but a busy painter" who creates and shapes his or her own world (p. 33). Similarly, Rutter (1994) notes that individuals are not passive recipients of experience, but actively interact with their environment and actively process experience. With particular regard to the interaction of risk factors that reside within the individual and those that reside in his or her environment, juveniles have agency. That is, children and adolescents make decisions about the behaviors in which they choose to engage, even if their decision-making process is different than that of adults, and different again based on their age and cognitive development or capacity. When high-risk juveniles are drawn to and actively seek out environments, peers, or conditions that allow or promote the expression of antisocial behavior, they themselves directly influence and increase the number or risk factors present in their lives, and thus the chances that antisocial behavior will actually occur. Wachs (1996) refers to this as "active" co-variance[3] in which the child or adolescent is an active player in the confluence and interaction of otherwise separate risk factors, as opposed to risk factors that naturally co-occur ("passive" co-variance) or are the result of environmental response to the juvenile's behavior ("reactive" co-variance).

These forms of risk co-variance, in which the incidence of risk factors are more-or-less affected directly by the juvenile sexual offender him or herself, should be an additional concern for us in risk assessment. A focus in this case is on whether reoffense might, in part, result from passive influences that are to some degree outside of the youth's control (family factors, for instance), the influence of social reaction to the youth's behavior (in which a socially inept youth, for example, faces rejection or social failure), or active choices that the youth might make in selecting behaviors, peers, and situations that only increase risk.

Although a bit of stretch, a parallel to this idea can be found in the self-regulation model proposed by Ward et al. (2004), which describes four pathways to sexual recidivism in adult sexual offenders. The authors refer to the first two pathways in the model as *avoidant-passive* and *avoidant-active* in which the offender wishes to avoid further sexual offenses but makes no effort to cope with difficulties or create plans for relapse prevention, or builds and engages in ineffective relapse prevention plans. The third and fourth pathways are described as *approach-automatic* and *approach-explicit* as the offender actively seeks out and engages in risky behaviors that increase

---

3. Co-variance refers to the degree to which two variables move in tandem with one another, in which a change in one variable mirrors or implies a change in the other.

the chances that a reoffense will occur. Although the model is not a risk-prediction model, it nicely illustrates the idea that people can be, and are, either more or less passive or active in the way that they recognize and manage risk and in the choices they make about their behavior. In the case of the self-regulation model, Ward et al. propose that for some adult sexual offenders risk is inherent in their environment and they are passive recipients of its effects, whereas others actively and, in some cases, intentionally increase risk. In the case of the self-regulation model, recidivism occurs, whether by passive or active means, pointing to the fact that risk factors may influence reoffense, even in the case of passive co-variance.

RISK FACTORS AS INDICATORS, NOT CAUSES

We should remain aware that risk factors found within the individual and the environment (whether the family, school, peer, or community environment) are indicators or predictors of risk and not causes of risk. That is, risk factors represent items believed to contribute to harm, but in most cases they are not direct causes of harm even if they correlate strongly, and we should bear in mind the adage that correlation is not cause.

For example, the Surgeon General's report (U.S. Department of Health and Human Services, 2001) notes that being a male is itself a risk factor. This doesn't mean that being male is the cause of antisocial behavior, however, or at least we hope not. It simply means that a statistical correlation exists between being male and serious and violent criminal behavior. The correlation itself may reflect other factors, including a biological predisposition towards aggressive and risky behavior (O'Connor and Rutter, 1996, describe a genetic level of risk factor) or perhaps a social construct in which, as Hayslett-McCall and Bernard (2002) assert, male aggressiveness in the United States is facet of the way in which male children are reared. Perhaps the correlation results from a combination of both biology and child rearing (nature and nurture), or perhaps still more risk factors come together to produce more antisocial behavior in males than females. The same is true for IQ and low socioeconomic status, both of which Lipsey and Derzon (1998) identify as risk factors. We can assume that neither cognitive limitations nor poverty is a cause of antisocial behavior, even if correlated with general crime.

The idea that risk factors act as indicators but not necessarily causes of antisocial behavior highlights the fact that, although we can recognize and catalog risk and protective factors, this does not equal understanding them or their course, why some high-risk individuals engage in seriously troubled behavior while other do not, or understanding "the course of maladjustment"

(O'Connor & Rutter, 1996, p. 788). Here we can turn to the work of Werner and Smith (1992, 2001), who demonstrated that by late adolescence and into adulthood many individuals born into high-risk environments were able to lead relatively risk-free lives, attributed by the authors to the presence of some degree of protective factors in their lives. Rutter (1994, 2003) hence distinguishes between risk *indicators* and risk *mechanisms* by which risk is transformed into actual troubled behavior. The difference is perfectly well illustrated in the examples of the correlation between committing a serious crime and being a male, low socioeconomic status, or having limited intellectual capacity. Rutter (2003) writes that variables like these may be associated with risk for antisocial behavior, but "on their own are completely uninformative about the nature of the risk process" (p. 3).

Hence, a theory about risk assessment, or a description of the risk assessment process, is not a theory of causality. It simply identifies and addresses the correlates that indicate risk and point towards the development of and future engagement in antisocial behavior. At the same time, risk indicators tell us something about the pathway that leads to antisocial behavior. Despite not postulating how risk turns into antisocial behavior (risk as mechanism instead of a pointer), risk factors to some degree do help us recognize cause, as long as we understand that just as risk is multidimensional and resides in different domains, so too is "cause" actually the product of a multifactorial and multidimensional process, and not a discrete event. That is, risk factors point towards the future, suggesting the recurrence of troubled behavior, and point back at the past, suggesting a causal process. However, "cause" represents the process by which risk is *actually* transformed into troubled behavior.

DEFINING RISK FACTORS FOR SEXUALLY ABUSIVE BEHAVIOR

Regarding the specific development of sexually abusive behavior, Knight and Sims-Knight (2003, 2004) consider three childhood risk factors as early physical or emotional abuse, early antisocial personality and behavioral traits, and early antisocial attitudes and ideas. In particular, they argue that antisocial and aggressive behavior that begins in early childhood and continues through adolescence is a risk factor when combined with early childhood sexual abuse and the development of a callousness unemotionality that results from early physical and emotional abuse. Similarly, Malamuth (2003) considers early abusive home life as a risk factor for the later development of sexually abusive behavior.

However, a cursory review of the literature on juvenile sexual offending of the past decade finds it full of risk factors, with more than 130 factors proposed as associated with or partially responsible for sexually abusive behavior or important to note in assessing the offender (Rich, 2003). Including only those that seem unique and not replicated among the other identified factors, as shown in Figure 7.1, 101 factors can be roughly broken into six categories: (1) characteristics related to the sexually abusive behavior, (2) characteristics related to the victim or the offender's relationship to the victim, (3) characteristics of the juvenile offender, (4) the offender's psychosocial and developmental history, (5) the offender's social connection, and (6) the offender's history of general antisocial behavior.

The literature identifies still more variables believed related to juvenile sexual offending, many of which are poorly defined and others that have even less validity than some of those included in Figure 7.1. Bearing in mind the vast quantity of ideas out there, a primary task in developing a clinical risk assessment tool is deciding which factors to include in assessment. The large number of risk factors reflects Rutter's (2003) observation regarding general (non-sexual) juvenile delinquency, in which the "huge" number of risk factors identified represents a problem in which we can "explain everything but predict nothing" (p. 11). On a similar note, Farrington (2000) notes that research has failed to detail the causal mechanisms that link risk to actual criminal behavior, leading to an inability to distinguish between causative risk factors and those that are merely correlated with cause or indicators of risk for future criminal behavior.

Indeed, in trying to distinguish between a multitude of risk factors, in their three-factor etiological model, Knight and Sims-Knight (2003) propose that sexual aggression in adult men can be statistically understood through the presence of just three primary elements: early childhood sexual abuse, childhood onset aggressive antisocial behavior, and the presence of callous unemotionality. Similarly, in his model Malamuth (2003) statistically links adult male sexual aggression to just two primary risk factors: early abusive home life that contributes to the development of impersonal and promiscuous sexuality and the presence of hostile masculinity.

Instruments designed to predict risk for reoffense in juvenile sexual offenders also condense risk factors, both by reducing the number of included factors or by grouping them into discrete groupings of similar factors. In the Juvenile Sex Offender Assessment Protocol (J-SOAP), Prentky and Righthand (2003) propose 28 essential risk factors grouped into four scales, and in the Estimate of Risk of Adolescent Sexual Offence Recidivism (ERASOR.V2) Worling and Curwen (2001) group 25 risk factors into five domains (with a 26th factor in an "Other" domain). Rich (2007b) proposes

101 Factors Associated with Risk Grouped into Six Categories

Characteristics of Sexually Abusive Behavior (21)
Affect states related to offense
Degree of aggression or force in offense
Degree of planning
Deviant sexual arousal and interests
Duration of offense history
Engaged in offense even after apprehension
Evidence of sexual preoccupation
Frequency of offenses
History of male victim
History of predatory behavior
Intent and motivation
Nature and extent of the offending behavior
Number of offenses
Number of victims
Power and control
Precipitating factors to offense
Prior charged sex offenses
Progressive aspects of sexual offenses
Sexual arousal preference
Use of deception/grooming in sex offenses
Victim access

Victim Characteristics and Relationship (10)
Age difference between abuser and victim
Age of victim
Attitude towards victim
Characteristics of victim that attracted offender
Degree of access to victims
Male child
Preferred victim
Relationship between offender and victim
Verbal interchange with the victim
Victim characteristics

Offender Characteristics (32)
Anger management problems
Attitudes
Denial
Cognitive distortions
Cognitive problems
Cooperation with evaluation process
Coping ability
Degree of accepted responsibility
Degree of remorse and regret
Depression and suicidal ideation
Empathy
External motivation for treatment
Honesty and forthrightness
Hyper-masculinity
Impulsivity
Insight into morality of sexual offending
Intellectual capacity
Internal motivation for treatment
Internal motivation for change
Locus of control: internal or external
Medical/neurological issues
Psychiatric problems
Response to confrontation
Self-concept
Self-expression
Social competence
Social skills deficits
Temperament
Understands effects on victim
Understands consequences of behavior
Understands relapse prevention
Worldview and perspective

Offender Social Connection (3)
Attachment bonds
Quality of peer relationship
Social relationships

Offender General Antisocial Behavior (11)
Aggression and violence level
Alcohol abuse
Attempts to avoid detection
Arrests prior to age 16
Behavioral problems
Criminal arrests, convictions, or incarceration
Drug abuse
Sexual and nonsexual offenses
Other exploitive or addictive behaviors
School behavior problems
School suspensions or expulsions

Offender Psychosocial History (24)
Caregiver stability
Cultural and ethnic background
Developmental history
Educational history
Exposure to domestic violence
Developmental history
Family background
Family relationships and structure
Family system functioning
Medical history
Parental alcohol abuse
Psychiatric history
Past victimization
Peer relationship history
School achievement
Sexual history and adjustment
Social development
Social learning experiences
Stability of school/employment
Stability of current living situation
Stability of historical living conditions
Support systems
Trauma history
Treatment history

Figure 7.1   Risk factors identified in the juvenile sexual offender literature grouped into six primary domains.

12 broad and overarching risk factors in the Juvenile Risk Assessment Tool (J-RAT.V3), within which individual elements of risk are subsumed, adding further depth and clarity to each broad risk factor domain. In the Juvenile Sexual Offense Recidivism Risk Assessment Tool (JSORRAT-II), Epperson et al. (2006) identify 12 essential risk factors that are statistically related to the recidivism among convicted juvenile sexual offenders. However, only the JSORRAT clearly derives its risk factors from a statistical analysis of juvenile sexual offender recidivists thus yielding a level of predictive validity.[4] Risk factors for the J-SOAP, J-RAT, and ERASOR were developed chiefly through review and analysis of the literature and are thus clinically derived and lack predictive validity.

In fact, Worling and Långström (2003, 2006) write that most identified risk factors for juvenile sexual offending lack empirical validation. Describing 21 commonly cited risk factors, they write that only five are empirically supported through at least two published independent research studies, with an additional two "promising" factors that have empirical support in at least one study. The remaining 14 factors they describe as either third-tier "possible" risk factors, based on general clinical support, or fourth-tier "unlikely" risk factors that either lack empirical support or are contradicted by empirically derived evidence. Their typology, including details of identified factors, is shown in Figure 7.2.

Although Worling and Långström's perspective illustrates the difficulties inherent in understanding and identifying risk factors, it nevertheless does little to illuminate any underlying truth about which risk factors are, or are not, valid predictors of risk. In fact, they go on to conclude that "there is support for a number of risk factors such that evaluators can make empirically based . . . and defensible judgements (sic)" (2003, p. 359), even though only five of the variables they examined had such empirical support, and they report that 14 lack any kind of empirical support at all and are supported largely only by their inclusion in the literature. Their conclusion is surprising, then, in light of their own estimate that most risk factors have little to no empirical support.

In fact, Worling is one of the two coauthors of the ERASOR, a risk assessment instrument that itself uses only four of the five factors reported by Worling and Långström as empirically supported, nine factors that fall into the third tier of not empirically supported but possible, and 10 factors which are not among the 21 factors described by Worling and Långström.

---

4. Predictive validity is a statistical measure of how well variables predict the occurrence of a phenomenon. In the case of risk assessment instruments, this means that risk factors have statistical evidence that they actually predict recidivism.

Worling and Långström's Typology of
Validated Risk Factors for Juvenile Sexual Reoffense

Empirically Supported	1. Deviant sexual arousal 2. Prior convicted sexual offenses 3. Multiple victims 4. Social isolation 5. Incomplete sexual offender treatment
Promising	1. Problematic parent-child relationships 2. Attitudes supportive of sexually abusive behavior
Possible	1. Impulsivity 2. Antisocial orientation 3. Aggression 4. Negative peer group association 5. Sexual preoccupation 6. Sexual offense of a male 7. Sexual offense of a child 8. Use of violence, force, threats, or weapons in sexual offense 9. Environmental support for reoffense
Unlikely	1. History of sexual victimization 2. History of non-sexual offending 3. Sexual offenses involving penetration 4. Denial of sexual offending 5. Low victim empathy

Figure 7.2 Worling and Långström's typology of risk factors for juvenile sexual reoffense, ranging from empirically validated to unlikely risk factors (based upon Worling & Långström, 2003, 2006).

THE EMPIRICAL BASIS OF RISK FACTORS

Prentky, Pimental, Cavanaugh, and Righthand (in press) provide a thorough overview and review of risk factors associated with juvenile sexual recidivism, and they conclude that the vast majority are only weakly, if at all, related to sexual reoffense and note that most have never been examined empirically. Frankly, although Worling and Långström describe two risk factors as promising, there is little support for the idea that they are much more supported than any of the third-tier "possible" factors. Not only are both of the second-tier risk factors empirically supported by only a single study, but also each study itself offers weak support. "Attitudes supportive of sexual offending" as a promising risk factor is thinly supported by Kahn and Chambers' 1991 study of 221 juvenile sexual offenders, which found a sexual recidivism rate of only 7.5 percent among which offenders who blamed their victims had a slightly higher sexual recidivism rate.[5] Worling and Curwen's 2000 study of 58 juvenile sexual offenders offered equally weak support for "problematic parent-child relationships" as a promising risk factor, as it found only a small correlation (0.22)[6] between experiences of parental rejection and sexual recidivism among the 5 percent who recidivated.

As we discuss and come to understand risk factors for juvenile sexual re-offense, it becomes clear that we have no strong basis upon which to judge the efficacy or validity of any of the risk factors we select as predictive. Further, there is a question of whether a risk factor should be considered valid based only on our capacity to statistically measure its correlation with sexual offense recidivism. That is, if we cannot establish empirical proof should we reject a risk factor as a valid or useful predictor of future risk behavior? It is true, of course, that empirical evidence offers us far more than clinical judgment that is absent of any empirical evidence. However, this raises two points about the nature of supporting evidence.

The first point addresses an assumption that clinical observations cannot be considered valid without accompanying statistical evidence. This point is illustrated by two articles published in the *British Journal of Medicine*, reminding us that "absence of evidence is not evidence of absence." In their evocation of that adage, Altman and Bland (1995) further remind us of the "non-equivalence of statistical significance and clinical importance" (p. 485); put another way, statistical results do not necessarily match clinical observations and judgments. The authors write that failure to establish a statistically significant relationship between two variables reflects an absence of empirical evidence, but it is not evidence per se that a relationship does not exist. It simply means that no correlation was found. Thus, Altman and Bland describe the risk, in single study research as well as meta-analyses, of misinterpreting nonsignificant results as evidence that a relationship between variables does not exist: "usually all that has been shown is absence of evidence" (p. 485).

In fact, taking the same position, Alderson (2004) argues that is it never reasonable to claim that a study has definitively proved that a relationship does or does not exist between two variables, because uncertainty will

---

5. Kahn and Chambers (1991) do not further define the slightly higher recidivism rate, and the data are no longer available (T. J. Kahn, personal communication, January 21, 2008).

6. Correlations of between 0.3 and 0.49 are considered moderate, and 0.5 to 1.0 high.

always exist. In medicine at least, he presents the view that when it comes to differences between clinical judgment and statistical proof we must be comfortable estimating and continuing to discuss uncertainty or the absence of empirical evidence in light of clinical observation. Nevertheless, Greenberg and Watson (2005) argue that the dominant view in psychology at the moment is that absence of evidence does mean evidence of absence (p. 113).

In their very amusing article that makes a serious point, Smith and Pell (2003) wrote about the lack of statistical evidence in establishing parachutes as effective in preventing death. They write that as no randomized controlled trials of parachute use have been undertaken, the basis for the efficacy of parachute use in overcoming "major trauma related to gravitational challenge" (i.e., death upon impact) is "purely observational" (p. 1460). They suggest that the "quest for the holy grail of exclusively evidence based" practice (p. 1460) may create dependency on such research, precluding clinical expertise and judgment.

THE FALLIBILITY AND CHANGEABILITY
OF STATISTICAL RESEARCH

The second point about evidence is more down-to-earth and less ideological. It involves the accuracy and meaning of statistical measurement in light of and in the context of the research designs from which such statistics emerge. For example, we have seen already that "empirical evidence" can be thin indeed, as in the case of the two promising risk factors described by Worling and Långström, in which although their ideas about these risk factors may be correct there is nevertheless slim empirical proof. There is also a question of research that is sometimes contradicted by other research and even reversed by later study.

We can explore this point by examining the role of denial as a factor that can help predict sexual recidivism. Returning to the Worling and Långström (2003, 2006) typology of empirically supported risk factors, as shown in Figure 7.2, they describe denial of sexual offending as an unlikely risk factor. They write that, despite its obvious appeal, there is no empirical evidence to support denial as a predictor or indicator of risk. So far, this is no different than third-tier factors that Worling and Långström describe as possible risk factors based on the frequent support they receive in the literature. However, they also argue that in the case of denial and other fourth-tier (unlikely) risk factors empirical evidence exists to contradict their validity as risk factors.

Nevertheless, Worling and Långström are not discussing evidence that disproves denial as a risk factor; they are simply discussing a failure to find a significant statistical correlation between denial and sexual recidivism.

As Altman and Bland (1995) wrote, "these are quite different statements" (p. 485). A quick look back at Altman and Bland will remind us that absence of statistical evidence is not proof that a relationship does not exist or a phenomenon does not occur.

The conjecture that denial is not a risk factor is largely drawn from the literature of adult sexual offending. In particular it is derived from the meta-analyses of Hanson and Bussière (1998) and Hanson and Morton-Bourgon (2005), which found no significant correlation between denial and sexual offense recidivism. However, the role of denial is neither resolved nor closed to further inquiry, and the lack of support for denial as a risk factor in the Hanson meta-analyses is questionable and was challenged by Lund (2000). Further, there now exists empirical evidence that denial is or may be a risk factor.

In contrast to studies that fail to show evidence of correlation (absence of proof), we now have studies that provide statistical evidence that denial is linked, in some cases, to sexual recidivism and may therefore be considered a risk factor. In a recent article, "Denial predicts recidivism for some sexual offenders," Nunes et al. (2007), with Hanson as second author, described two studies that included 1,000 adult sexual offenders in which, "contrary to expectations," denial was associated with increased sexual recidivism among both low-risk offenders and incest offenders, and replicated in two independent samples. The authors conclude "that denial merits further consideration for researchers as well as those involved in applied risk assessment of sexual offenders" (p. 92), and now concur with Lund's (2000) speculation that "denial could be a real . . . risk factor" (p. 102). In an even more recent article, Langton et al. (2008) described both minimization and denial in adult sexual offenders as significant predictors of sexual recidivism, with minimization as a significant predictor among high-risk offenders (in contrast to the finding of Nunes et al.). In their study of 436 sexual offenders, they report that denial was associated with serious (including sexual) recidivism and conclude that it is reasonable to postulate that the presence of denial and minimization, specifically during and at the conclusion of treatment, represents "an increased risk among higher risk offenders for sexual recidivism" (p. 91).

Lund challenged Hanson and Bussière's (1998) conclusion that denial was not a risk factor through a careful analysis of the seven studies included in the meta-analysis that addressed the relationship between denial and treatment. He noted a broad range in the definition of denial and how and when it was measured in assessment and treatment, and that those who completely denied offending were frequently excluded from treatment and were therefore absent in the meta-analysis. Further he speculated that heterogeneity among sexual offenders may result in differences in strength of denial as a risk factor for different offenders. Lund thereby foreshadowed the suggestion of Nunes et al. (2007) that denial might have a differential effect on recidivism for low- and high-risk offenders, and also that the influence of denial on higher-risk offenders might be made invisible by the presence of other high-risk factors. Overall, Lund concluded that the Hanson and Bussière meta-analysis did not clarify the relevance of denial in predicting recidivism, and wrote that "the failure of meta-analysis to clarify the relevance of denial should not be construed as indicating support for the opposite conclusion that denial is a risk factor" (p 285), mirroring the admonishment of Altman and Bland (1995).

There is further support that denial has relevance to risk prediction. In their study of adult sexual offenders, Levenson and Macgowan (2004) found that treatment progress was correlated with lower levels of denial, and that engagement in treatment and denial were negatively associated with one other. In their work on stable and acute risk factors, Hanson and Harris (2000b) similarly observed that failure to engage in treatment and denial (in this case of future risk to reoffend) was a significant predictor of sexual recidivism. As completion of treatment supports reduced risk for recidivism (Marques et al., 2005; Seager, Jellicoe, & Dhaliwal, 2004; Worling & Curwen, 2000), or conversely failure to complete treatment is a risk factor for sexual recidivism (Hanson & Bussière, 1998; Hanson & Morton-Bourgon, 2005; Worling & Långström, 2006), it is reasonable to conclude that denial is also linked to treatment outcome or recidivism rates.

That is, if low denial is related to engagement in treatment which, in turn, is related to lowered recidivism, then level of denial must also be related to treatment outcome (i.e., the presence or absence of recidivism). This represents a logical inference drawn from information that has empirical support. On the basis of its relationship with treatment engagement, even without direct empirical evidence, we can conclude that denial must be a risk factor if failure to complete treatment presents risk for recidivism.

On a final note regarding both the uncertain and changing nature of research, the Juvenile Sexual Offense Recidivism Risk Assessment Tool (Epperson et al., 2006) offers empirical support for both a history of sexual victimization and a history of non-sexual offending as actuarially based risk factors, both of which are described as unlikely risk factors by Worling and Långström (2006).

The point here is not to lambast Worling and Långström's typology or perspective, both of which are of great value and add much to our work. Instead, as we discuss the search for risk factors that hold meaning, it is important that we recognize no single point of view as the sole or unchallenged source of legitimacy, and that we do not hold all of the answers, although we may have some. In understanding the art and science of predicting future behavior, we also understand the fallibility of human judgment and scientific prescription. To adopt the scientific method as the only source of our knowledge is to accept the idea that the methods of quantitative science are applicable to all spheres of life and experience and that which cannot be measured lacks legitimacy.[7]

RISK FACTORS FOR SEXUAL REOFFENSE

Having said a lot about risk factors both for general juvenile delinquency and sexually abusive behavior, let's simplify things by noting that, despite a great deal of variation in risk factors and their selection, among the risk assessment tools in use or development there is a great deal of overlap. That is, despite some significant differences in risk factors selected and differences in how similar risk factors are described, similar groupings of risk factors are found in juvenile risk assessment tools.

Currently, the two instruments most commonly used in the United States are the J-SOAP-II (Juvenile Sex Offender Assessment Protocol) and the ERASOR (Estimate of Risk of Adolescent Sexual Offence Recidivism); the J-RAT (Juvenile Risk Assessment Tool) is also widely used, although to a far lesser extent. Although not well known or in wide use, the JRAS (Juvenile Risk Assessment Scale) was recently developed and adopted by the New Jersey court system to be used in classifying juvenile sexual offenders into sexual offender registry tiers (Hiscox, Witt, & Haran, 2007). In development is the MEGA (Multiplex Empirically Guided Inventory of Ecological Aggregates for Assessing Sexually Abusive Adolescents), as well as the RSBP<12 (Risk for Sexual Behavior Perpetration) for risk assessment in pre-adolescent children (less than age 12). Although these are described in more detail in Chapter 14, for now it's most pertinent to describe the similarities between these instruments; in fact, despite differences between each instrument, they are more similar than they are different. Of importance, their selection of risk factors represents those predictors of risk that are both drawn from the professional literature and are the most typically considered in considering the risk for sexual reoffense.

---

7. i.e., Scientism.

Each of these instruments is a clinical assessment tool, often described as empirically based in reference to their clear relationship to factors frequently described by the professional literature as relevant to risk for juvenile sexual reoffense. However, as we've seen, very few of these risk factors actually have any empirical support. It's thus more accurate to describe these instruments as structured and literature-based clinical tools, rather than empirically grounded.

In addition to being grounded in or guided by the professional literature, each instrument provides a structure for clinical assessment by its inclusion of defined risk factors and a means by which to evaluate the relevance of each risk factor in the overall assessment of risk. They are thus of enormous importance in assisting trained[8] clinicians as they assess risk in sexually abusive youth, providing the evaluator with a structured assessment format based upon factors most commonly supported by the literature. However, none of these instruments are statistically based, nor do they have any significant psychometric properties with respect to predictive validity (or the capacity to statistically prove they actually predict risk).

The introduction of the JSORRAT-II (Juvenile Sexual Offense Recidivism Risk Assessment Tool) adds a significant new dimension to juvenile risk assessment by adding the first actuarial assessment in which risk factors are truly founded in empirical evidence and thus statistically derived. Nevertheless, despite major differences in how risk level is determined, risk factors included in the JSORRAT significantly mirror the risk factors that commonly show up in the clinical tools briefly described above. The JSORRAT thus provides an additional level of empirical support for at least some risk factors and generally reflects and supports commonly held beliefs about the sort of factors that are predictive of sexual recidivism.

Regardless of their source, then, the same sort of risk factors appear in these assessment instruments. Despite clear differences among instruments and their inclusion of risk factors, across the instruments described above risk factors commonly appearing can essentially be grouped into 10 categories (even though not every individual risk factor or risk domain appears in every risk assessment instrument). Given the content of this chapter, none of these categories come as a surprise. Predictable also is the split between factors specific to sexually abusive behavior and those

---

8. "Trained" is a key word here, as even the best assessment instruments should not be used by those unfamiliar with or untrained in the process of risk assessment, unless supervised. This harkens back to ideas presented in Chapter 2 regarding standards and expectations for those engaging in evaluation.

relevant to antisocial and troubled behavior in general. Here we recognize juvenile sexual offending as a special class of juvenile delinquency, sharing some qualities common to all behaviorally troubled youth and others that diverge from the course of non-sexual juvenile offending. These common risk factor categories are briefly described below, and more detail regarding specific risk factors commonly included within each domain is provided in Figure 7.3.

1. *Sexual Beliefs, Attitudes, and Drive* includes those factors most relevant to the youth's experience of sexuality, nature of sexual ideation, level of preoccupation, and drive to engage in sexual behavior.

2. *History of Sexually Abusive Behavior*, which includes severity and type of behavior, duration and number of incidents, progression of sexually abusive behavior over time and range of sexually abusive behavior, number and gender of victims, victim age in relationship to the offender, victim relationship to the offender, the use of violence or aggression, the role of planning and intentionality, and continued sexually abusive behavior after apprehension.

3. *History of Personal Victimization* essentially involving a history of physical or sexual abuse and details related to that history, including both past and current responses to these experiences.

4. *History of General Antisocial Behavior*. Not surprisingly, this domain includes general behavioral problems in the community and school and age of onset, aggression, the seriousness and range of antisocial behaviors, substance abuse, and antisocial attitudes, including peer group association.

5. *Social Relationships and Connection* primarily involving a lack of close peer relationships and deficits in social relationships in general.

6. *Personal Characteristics* includes a wide range of characterological features, including motivation for change, deficits in empathy and remorse, denial and lack of responsibility, denial of behaviors, and deficits in cognitive ability and insight.

7. *General Psychosocial Functioning* is a broad category, but it includes poor self-regulation and impulse control, poor anger management, deficits in social skills and social competency, and overall difficulties in social functioning.

8. *Family Relationships and Functioning* pertains, of course, to the family environment past and present. It includes generally stressful family life, general family functioning, the consistency of parental figures and parent figure functioning, history of and exposure to family violence, internal

Common Risk Factors for Sexually Abuse Recidivism Grouped by Risk Category	
Risk Factor Category	Commonly Included Risk Factors
1. Sexual Beliefs, Attitudes, and Drive	• Deviant sexual interest • Sexual preoccupation • Attitude and beliefs that support sexually abusive or inappropriate behavior • Desire to continue behaviors that may be sexually abusive or inappropriate
2. History of Sexually Abusive Behavior	• Multiple victims • Use of violence, force, or threats • Level of coercion involved • Age difference between perpetrator and victim • Victims of both genders • Stranger victims • Multiple types of sexually abusive behavior • Prior history of sexually abusive behavior • Continued sexually abusive behavior after prior apprehension • Duration of sexual abuse history • Progression and development of sexually abusive behavior over time • Use of planning • Severity of sexually abusive behavior
3. History of Personal Victimization	• Victim of prior sexual or physical abuse • Current response to prior victimization
4. History of General Antisocial Behavior	• Aggression • Behavior problems in community and school • Non-sexual arrests • Early onset behavioral problems • Range of antisocial behavior; multiple types of behavioral problems • Substance abuse • Antisocial peer group

Category	Risk Factors
5. Social Relationships and Connection	• Lack of close peer relationships • General deficits in social relationships
6. Personal Characteristics	• Motivation for change • Deficits in empathy • Deficits in remorse • Denial of behaviors, and lack of responsibility • Deficits in cognitive ability and insight
7. General Psychosocial Functioning	• Poor self-regulation • Impulsivity • Poor anger management • Deficits in social skills and social competency • Overall difficulties in social functioning
8. Family Relationships and Functioning	• Stressful family environment and general family functioning • Stability and consistency of parental figures and relationships • Parents uninvolved with or unsupportive of treatment • History of and exposure to family violence • Psychosocial functioning of parent figures • Family physical and sexual boundaries • Weak parent-child relationships
9. General Environmental Conditions	• Stability of living situation • Stability of school situation • Nature and quality of support system • General environmental conditions • Opportunities for sexual reoffense
10. Response to Treatment	• Failure to complete treatment • Grasp of and response to treatment ideas

Figure 7.3 Risk factors commonly found in juvenile sexual risk assessment instruments, grouped by category.

family boundaries, the quality of parent-child relationships, and the attitude of parent figures towards and involvement in treatment.

9. *General Environmental Conditions* incorporates the general stability of the youth's living situation, the stability of school, the nature and quality of support systems, general environmental conditions, and opportunities for sexual reoffense.

10. *Response to Treatment*, includes both the youth's response to and success in prior treatment and in current treatment, if the youth is presently in treatment. It especially includes failure to complete treatment, as well as grasp of and response to treatment ideas.

The general list of factors categorized into these 10 domains and presented in Figure 7.3 is drawn from those factors that most commonly appear, although with some variation, in the J-SOAP, ERASOR, and J-RAT, as well as the lesser developed JRAS and the current iterations of the still developing MEGA, JSORRAT, and RSBP<12. Also included are those factors included in the Risk Assessment Matrix (Christodoulides, Richardson, Graham, Kennedy, & Kelly, 2005), a U.K. risk assessment instrument that has since been modified and renamed the SHARP (Sexually Harmful Adolescent Risk Protocol), a clinical assessment instrument that includes 46 risk factors (Richardson, in press). However, the RAM/SHARP is in limited use and appears currently quite weak, but it is nevertheless worth noting here in terms of the commonality of risk factors across the range of juvenile risk assessment instruments. Similarly, virtually all of the 51 risk factors (including both static and dynamic concerns) incorporated into the AIM2 (Print et al., 2007), another U.K. literature-based structured instrument used to clinically assess risk in sexually abusive adolescent boys, can be categorized under one of these 10 domains.[9]

Indeed these are the risk factors that we generally believe represent the greatest risk to reoffend. An essential difference in how each of these assessment tools presents and uses these factors is found, not only in their specific wording and description, but in the numbers of factors believed necessary to assess and assign risk. The JSORRAT, the only actuarial assessment in the pack, requires only 12 entirely static risk factors, largely centered around the history and details of prior sexually abusive behavior

---

9. The AIM2, described in Chapters 8 and 14, offers a different approach to risk assessment than the other instruments described. It defines outcome in terms of the level of supervision required by the adolescent, rather than risk, and describes risk factors as "concerns" rather than "risks," and embeds the assessment of risk (or concern) into a larger assessment that helps determine the level of supervision and support required by each adolescent.

coupled with a history of non-sexual criminal behavior. At the other extreme lies the J-RAT. Although it requires an assessment of only 12 risk domains, each domain is further broken into individual elements of risk that together form the basis of the level of risk assigned to each domain, for a total of 117 elements spread throughout the 12 domains. The J-SOAP and ERASOR respectively require an evaluation of 28 and 25 risk factors.

Although basing his perspective on risk assessment in general, rather than the actual risk factors that appear in our risk assessment instruments, Prescott (2007) also suggests that risk factors for juvenile sexual offense recidivism can be grouped into five general categories. He describes these as factors related to sexual arousal, attitudes that contribute to sexually abusive behavior, self-evaluation and social functioning, self-regulation and personal management, and relationships with significant others. Although general, Prescott's categories indeed reflect those risk factors commonly used to assess risk, and again point to those risk factors (or in this case, categories of risk factors) most commonly believed relevant to the assessment of risk in sexually abusive youth.

CONCLUSION: RECOGNIZING THE PRESENCE AND ACTION OF RISK

It bears repeating that a theory of risk assessment is neither a theory of causality nor a description of the mechanisms that transform risky conditions into behavior that is harmful to self or others. Some set of forces independent of risk itself act upon risk factors, both internal and external, in some cases to mediate the further development of risky behavior and eventual harm and in others to moderate that development and dampen the chances of harm. That much is obvious, or everyone who experienced the same set of risky conditions would end up in the same place. In fact, similar points of origin lead to different outcomes for different people.

However, regardless of whether we can distinguish between risk as indicator, causal mechanism, or contributor to developmental vulnerability, risk factors can nevertheless serve as predictors of future behavior. Whereas no single risk factor alone has the strength to produce or predict the occurrence or recurrence of harmful behavior, the presence and interaction of multiple risks has an additive and potentiating effect that reasonably allows for prediction. To put it another way, the additive presence of risk factors allows us to consider the potential for and probability of future behavior based upon the presence and interaction of those factors. It is the role and function of the risk assessment instrument to create a structure and form by which to recognize, tally, and assess the presence and strength of risk factors and thus assign a level of risk.

Like all statistical analyses, the actuarial assessment attempts to provide an absolute estimate of risk in numerical terms (for example, 98 percent chance of an occurrence), whereas the clinical assessment must use relative and non-numerical terms like "low," "moderate," and "high" risk (Harris & Rice, 2007; Hilton, Carter, Harris, & Sharpe, 2008) to characterize the risk of an occurrence. However, regardless of whether we assess risk in terms of numerical probability (assuming we can truly measure human behavior this way) or by contrasting the likelihood of something occurring (high risk) against it not occurring (low risk), in either case the risk assessment process produces a cumulative index of risk factors by which to make well-calculated judgments about the possibility of future behavior. This index is built on the historical presence of risk factors (static), their continuation into the present day (stable dynamic), and the presence of other factors that may either serve to amplify static and stable risk or fail to restrain it (acute dynamic). It is the presence and combination of these static and dynamic factors and their combined strength that we are assessing regardless of what method we employ to conduct the assessment.

Recognizing and understanding risk factors and their multiplicative operation, and subsequently understanding how to evaluate what behavior they may foreshadow, is the essence of the risk assessment process. To this end, we must identify and assess risk factors not only by their presence but by their strength and level of interaction as well. Statistical analysis recognizes only presence, in which strength is but a quantitative offshoot of presence (strength is measured by the number occurrences, for instance, rather than the quality of the occurrence or its impact on others). However, in the real world, and perhaps especially the world inhabited by children and adolescents, presence (often quantitative) and strength (often qualitative) come together and must be understood in quite different ways than that allowed by the mechanistic process of actuarial assessment.

CHAPTER 8

The Power of Protection: Protective Factors and Risk

UTTER (1994) ASKS what is it about adolescence that constitutes "the risk factor." Of course, Rutter, who has written extensively on risk, resilience, and protection, knows that there is no "Factor X"—no single risk factor, but that risk is multivariate and multidimensional.

In the real world, risk is a complex phenomenon. It represents the possibility that something harmful will occur or our exposure to something that represents the possibility of harm. "Risk" thus represent jeopardy, and in this context risk factors allow us to further understand the essence of risk. That is, what it is that makes risk "risky."[1] However, the presence of risk factors alone doesn't automatically tell us that harm will actually occur, or that risky situations and circumstances will lead to or be transformed into actual harm. As noted in Chapter 3, we can recognize that some elements of risk mediate a path that takes us further towards actual harm; in this case, risk factors, and especially static risk factors, act as *mediators* that help to transform the original condition into actual harm (Figure 3.1). Other factors, some of which reside within the individual and others within the environment, act as *moderators*. These variables in effect act upon the relationship between forces that stimulate or propel (in our case, risk factors) and actual outcome (i.e., harm or no harm), and they serve to increase or decrease the chances of a particular outcome (Barr, Boyce, & Zeltzer, 1996). Whereas to some degree mediators are transformative, moderators serve to amplify or diminish the strength of the stimulus condition, and thus have a significant role to play in actual outcome.

---

1. We can simply define "essence" as that thing without which that thing would not be that thing. In this context, risk factors represent those things that actually form risk.

THE MODERATING ROLE OF PROTECTIVE FACTORS
IN THE ASSESSMENT OF RISK

Risk factors beget risk factors, and risk factors tend to both create and potentiate (increase the strength of) other risk factors. Protective factors, on the other hand, serve only to decrease the potency of risk factors and thus diminish the chance of harm. Unlike risk factors, then, which can act as mediators or moderators, protective factors function only as moderators. As we consider the relationship between risk and harm, clearly we must consider the combined power of multiple risk factors and in treatment directly take aim at reducing the number and strength of risk factors. However, it's also clear that we must pay close attention to the presence and strength of protective factors as well. To this end, Rogers (2000) writes that risk assessment is flawed if it pays attention *only* to risk factors without also considering protective factors; similarly, Monahan (1995) notes the importance of balancing factors that suggest the *absence* of problem behavior against those that suggest recurrence.

However, I argued in Chapter 3 that, despite Rogers' admonition, it is difficult to build into risk assessment a means for clearly recognizing and assessing protective factors, at least in the process of assessing the strength of individual risk factors and using this as the basis of assigned risk. In both actuarial and clinical risk assessment, projections of risk are based entirely on the presence and assumed action of evaluated risk factors and not the presence and possible effect of variables that may neutralize risk. That is, risk assessment assesses risk, and not protection, and in that process the assessment of protection is secondary. This is because protection is necessary *only* when risk is present.

I don't need protection against the weather if the weather is good. Using this example, the absence of bad weather does not represent a protective condition; it means that there is no risk. Protection is necessary only under conditions of risk—that's when I need an umbrella or warm jacket. Likewise, if lack of family support is a risk factor for harmful behavior, then the presence of family support does not represent protection per se; it merely denotes that this risk factor does not exist (and therefore protection against the condition is not required). In other words, absence of risk does not automatically equal protection.

However, life, and risk assessment, is far more complex. Although the presence of family support does not represent a protective factor in and of itself, it may well represent a protective factor in relationship to *another* risk factor. For instance, strong family support may serve as protection against a history of behavioral problems in the community or association with a delinquent peer group, both of which are risk factors. So, even if lack of a particular risk factor does not in itself equate with protection, given the complex and interactive nature of risk the absence of a risk factor in one area may indeed signify the presence of protection against a completely separate risk factor. In the multiplex[2] manner by which risk functions, any given risk factor, although having a independent life, is linked to all other risk factors. Thus, the absence of risk in one domain may well represent a protective factor against a risk factor in another domain. To this degree, even though they exist only in relation to risk, protective factors have a important life of their own as Rogers (2000) clearly observes when he rhetorically asks whether protective factors merely reflect the absence of risk.

UNDERSTANDING PROTECTIVE FACTORS

Rutter (2003) writes that "it seems obvious that attention must be paid to the possibility of factors that protect against antisocial behavior as well as to those that predispose to it" (p. 10). But he also points out that if protection exists in an inverse (opposite) relationship to risk, there is little to be gained by simply focusing on the harmful effects of one condition (family harmony) or the beneficial effects of the opposite condition (family discord) as "in essence, the two are providing the same message" (p. 10). Indeed, Jessor, Van Den Bos, Vanderryn, Costa, and Turbin (1995) describe risk and protection as opposite ends of the same variable and thus highly correlated, making it difficult to fully understand the role of protection. Protection, then, has meaning only in the presence of risk and not simply as its polar opposite.

Further, protective factors must be considered not only in the presence of risk, but also in relationship to risk that lies in another region of the individual's life. That is, protection against family discord is not family harmony, as these both occupy exactly the same region and are simply the same condition reversed. On the other hand, family harmony may offer protection against risk located in another region, such as a dangerous community environment or academic failure. Similarly, a strong peer support system or a mentoring relationship with an adult outside of the family may help protect against family disharmony.

---

2. In a multiplex process different elements are combined and operate simultaneously along the same channel, even though each has a separate and independent existence and can be experienced or observed individually.

Accordingly, the action and effect of protective factors can only be understood when compared against the "wall" of risk factors that may exist. Nevertheless, even then the power and mechanism of protection is unclear. In fact, although we have concluded that it is a combination of risk factors that leads to the likelihood of harm, it seems possible that just a *single* protective factor might alter this outcome. Despite this, it is equally clear that although the presence and action of protective factors may divert the possibility of harm, even multiple protective factors are often not powerful enough to change outcome. This begs the question of what constitutes protective factors, and how they act to both protect against harm and/or alter an otherwise likely trajectory. It is thus difficult to estimate the role of protective factors in the assessment of risk, even though the process of risk assessment must somehow take into account the absence or presence of protective factors.

Just as risk resides in different locations—within the individual, in his or her social relationships, and in the surrounding environment—protective factors also reside within these same domains. Residing within the individual, at the intrapersonal level, protective factors may include a well-developed moral code, religious beliefs that prohibit certain behaviors, or a fear of getting caught and punished. Protective factors that reside within the interpersonal social environment include family support, for example, and positive peer relationships and friendships. In the impersonal domain of the environment within which the individual lives and functions, protection may include prosocial media messages, strong school or community values and support, or a strong community response to antisocial behavior.

Indeed, several studies recognize protective factors residing within the same realms of human experience in which risk factors are found, including the domains of individual, family, school, peer group, and community functioning (Hawkins et al., 2000; Howell, 1995; U.S. Department of Health and Human Services, 2001). In turn, this means that protective factors operate differently, depending on the key attributes of the domain in which they exist and with which they interact. This leads to conceptualizations of protection essentially involving the strengths of the individual, the support provided by the family, and resources offered by the community, and it includes the process of attachment and commitment to prosocial people, institutions, and values, as well as clear family, school, and community standards for prosocial behavior (Consortium on the School-based Promotion of Social Competence, 1996; Gore & Eckenrode, 1996; Howell, 1995).

Not only found in different domains, protective factors also vary in terms of when they are developmentally most instrumental, as well as by their action or type. It is clear that, like risk factors, the strength and relevance of protective factors is linked to social, emotional, cognitive, and behavioral characteristics that emerge during different developmental periods (Jessor et al., 1995), in which some protective factors are active only at specific stages in development but inactive or insignificant at others (Salekin & Lochman, 2008). It is thus possible to understand the actions and effects of both risk and protection only within the developmental context in which they appear, and factors highly influential with one age group may have little influence with another (Pless & Stein, 1996). Additionally, independent of developmental level, both risk and protective factors are most relevant at what Rutter (1987) describes as key turning points in life, because the power of each is most critical at these junctures. Here, "life events, turning points, and transition periods can all play a part in whether antisocial continues or ceases" (Rutter, Giller, & Hagell, 1998, p. 307).

WHAT ARE THE PROTECTIVE FACTORS?

Just as one risk factor is likely to signal the presence of other, often related, risk factors, it is similarly likely that the presence of a single protective factor is linked to the co-occurrence of other protective factors (Gore & Eckenrode, 1996). It seems equally likely that the presence of multiple protective factors have an additive effect in helping to protect against harm, whereas in reality a single protective factor has probably only a small effect (Howell, 1995). Nevertheless, it is clear that even multiple protective factors may not prevent harm from occurring and, equally, even a single protective factor, despite small effect size, may serve to help alter trajectory. For instance, in their description of high-risk children who avoided serious problems, Werner and Smith (1992) noted the presence of "at least one person in their lives who accepted them unconditionally" (p. 205).

Werner and Smith (1992, 2001) discuss the balance that exists at each developmental stage between risk factors that exacerbate vulnerability and protective factors that enhance resilience. They describe parental competence and warm and supportive parenting as protective buffers in the lives of high-risk children, as well as temperamental attributes that solicit positive response from adults, affectionate ties with parents and other family members, and an external, non-family support system. As noted, they also highlight the importance of positive and supportive adults in the lives of high-risk children, and the development of self-esteem and self-efficacy, mediated through supportive adult relationships. Similarly, Salekin and Lochman (2008) note the effect of parental warmth during pre-adolescence in protecting against the development of highly antisocial traits in adolescents, and especially during the first five years of life. Protective factors of this sort are described over and over in the literature on risk and resilience, in which resilience, a subject far beyond the scope of this chapter, is invariably linked to protective factors that buffer against adversity.

With respect to the applicability of these commonly described protective factors to the assessment of sexually abusive youth, there is no reason to believe that any significantly different factors are at play. Bremer (2006a) writes that, as many of the risks involved in sexually abusive behavior are the same as those that lead to more general antisocial behavior, the same factors that protect against general risk will apply to sexually abusive youth. Drawn from the work of multiple authors (Catalano, Haggerty, Oesterle, Fleming, & Hawkins, 2004; Hawkins et al., 2000; Howell, 1995; Libbey, 2004; Luthar, Cicchetti, & Becker, 2000; Rutter, Giller, & Hagell, 1998; U.S. Department of Health and Human Services, 2001; Werner & Smith, 1992, 2001); typically described themes related to protection against general delinquency include:

- a stable and warm relationship with at least one parent, closely related to secure parental attachment,
- parental supervision,
- close connections with other supportive, competent, and prosocial adults in the wider community,
- the development of an autonomous self,
- self-esteem and self-efficacy enhancing experiences, positive school experiences, effective and safe school environments, academic success, and positive relationships with teachers and peers,
- prosocial peer groups,
- experiences that open new opportunities, and
- emotional and behavioral self-regulation and a positive approach to planning and problem solving.

Figure 8.1 depicts the most commonly described protective factors, grouping them into the domains described by the Office for Juvenile Justice and Delinquency Prevention (Hawkins et al., 2000; Howell, 1995) and the Surgeon General's Office (U.S. Department of Health and Human Services, 2001). However, it is important to note that distinctions between groups are somewhat artificial, as it is clear that a number of protective factors could easily be placed in more than one domain.

It is clear by now that, like risk, protective factors are distributed throughout multiple domains, including the biological domain, reflected

Domain	Protective Factor
Individual	• Intolerance for social inappropriate behavior • High IQ • Being female • Prosocial social orientation • Expectation that antisocial behavior will receive sanctions • Interest and involvement in conventional activities • Temperamental resilience
Family	• Warm, supportive relationships with parents or other adults • Parental interest* • Supportive family relationships • Prosocial parental values • Stable parental care • Parent self-regulation • Parental monitoring • Appropriate sanctions for poor behaviors • Stable care with stable care giver • Parental positive evaluation of peers *or alternate significant caregivers, if more appropriate*
School	• Commitment to school • Recognition for achievement • Involvement in conventional school activities • Relative academic success • Prosocial school environment • Positive relationships with staff, faculty, and peers
Peer Group	• Positive peer relationship • Close friendships • Friends who engage in prosocial and conventional behavior
Community	• Positive relationship with prosocial adult • Positive adult role models • Engagement in prosocial community activities • Connection to community based organization • Modeling of prosocial behaviors, attitudes, and values • Appropriate community sanctions for antisocial behavior or values

Figure 8.1 Commonly cited protective factors roughly grouped by domain.

in temperament, IQ, and gender, as shown in Figure 8.1. Protection against risk, then, is multidimensional, but it is also clear from a glance at Figure 8.1 that far more protective factors are found within the social environment than within the individual, pointing to the largely dynamic, interactive, and social operation of protection.

Beyond having supportive family relationships, the youth's experience in the community is paramount. Libbey (2004), for instance, examined the experience of adolescents with respect to their sense of attachment to their school, and found that school success was often related to a sense of belonging, having a voice, positive peer relationships, engagement in school activities, teacher support, and a sense of safety. Similarly, Catalano et al. (2004) described a relationship between academic success, social competence, and school bonding, which they define as emotionally attached relationships with peers and faculty and an investment in the school environment. Consistent with the reciprocal quality of protective factors in other social domains, they report that these bonds result from opportunities for involvement, recognition of effort and success, and the teaching of social, emotional, and cognitive competencies. Once strongly established, Catalano and colleagues report that school bonding inhibits behavior that is inconsistent with the norms and values of the school and reduces antisocial behavior. Conversely, Hawkins et al. (2000) identified low bonding to school as a predictor of risk, along with low levels of parental involvement and poor family bonding.

This concept of an attached or bonded emotional relationship between youths and their schools speaks to the general nature of protective factors—that is, they are most typically of a reciprocal nature, involving interactions and transactions between individuals and their environments, including the people and institutions in those environments. Accordingly, although many of the protective factors are drawn from the youth's social environment, the process is not simply one way; that is, it is not simply a matter of social forces lending support to the individual youth. There is a two-way interaction in which available social support, resources, and response are often a measure of the child's behavior and presentation in the social environment. Recall from Chapter 7 Anthony's (1987) description of the child as a "busy painter" who acts upon the canvas of his or her world, in part shaping the world in which he or she lives and in which others engage with the child. Pardini and Loeber (2008) note, for instance, the possibility that dysfunctional parent-child relationships contribute significantly to the development of interpersonal callousness in the developing child and adolescent, but also that the behavior problems of children "may negatively influence parenting behavior over time" (p. 192). Here, the behavioral difficulties of children in turn directly influence dys-functional parenting and elicit greater levels of verbal conflict with and less warmth from parents, an effect described by Larsson, Viding, and Plomin (2008) as child-driven (rather than parent-driven). Larsson et al. do not discount the effects of parenting on the behavior of their children, but note the bidirectional and reciprocal relationship between parenting and childhood antisocial behavior. Accordingly, a central protective factor is the youth's ability to engage with others, speaking to the complexity and linked nature of different types of protective factors.

We must also bear in mind the admonishment of Luthar et al. (2000) to remain aware that protective factors at work in one domain should not cloud our ability to recognize the possibility of significant problems and risk at work in other spheres.

A NOTE ON SECURE ATTACHMENT AS PROTECTIVE

Like resilience, a discussion of attachment and its secure and insecure variants, is beyond the scope of this book.[3] However, whereas insecure attachment, as the product of suboptimal or disrupted early experience, may be considered a general risk factor for many difficulties (but not for mental health issues or juvenile delinquency in particular), secure attach-ment almost certainly serves as a protective factor.

In a nutshell, the attachment model proposes that early and ongoing attachment experiences provide a foundation upon which identity is built and internalized. These experiences either contribute to secure attachment and resiliency, serving as a protective factor against negative or hostile life circumstances or as a developmental vulnerability in which insecure attachment not only fails to protect but under adverse conditions, and particularly when combined with other risk factors, is quite possibly a risk factor in its own right. On the other hand, secure attachment strengthens the individual, buffering against adverse social conditions and helps neutralize and weaken both internal and external risk factors that may otherwise increase risk (Rich, 2006, 2007a). Atkinson and Goldberg (2004) describe secure attachment serving a protective function because, through-out life, under adverse or anxiety-provoking circumstances, it triggers distress-regulating and support-seeking behaviors.

Simply speaking, secure attachment as a protective factor has already been noted, and security of attachment is implied in the capacity for close

---

3. See Rich (2006) for a detailed description of attachment theory, as well as the implications of attachment theory in the treatment of sexual offenders.

and connected relationships to parents, and other adults, and further in the capacity to form bonded relationships to community organizations like schools, accept and connect with prosocial norms and values, demonstrate self-regulation, and experience self-efficacy. Secure attachment thus serves more as a rubric, or a class of protective factors, under which these other protective factors may be included. However, as secure attachment cannot be simply conferred upon an individual who is insecurely attached, it is important to note that it is a far more theoretical construct and far less operational than the individual protective factors that may be considered the outcome of security in attached relationships.

THE ACTION OF PROTECTIVE FACTORS BY TYPE

As well as defining protective factors, we have also described domains in which protective factors may be found, resources upon which protective factors draw for their strength, and the relevance and power of protective factors at different developmental and key moments. Additionally, Rutter et al. (1998) describe several mechanisms by which protective factors work to buffer the individual from risk or assist the individual in dealing with the consequences of exposure to risk. Although Rutter and colleagues described eight such mechanisms, they are condensed here to five main protective processes:

1. Those that reduce sensitivity to risk through previous successful experience.
2. Those that reduce the impact of risk through supportive relationships and avoidance of further difficulties.
3. Those that promote self-esteem and self-efficacy.
4. Those that open up new positive opportunities and experiences.
5. Those that build strengths and coping skills following exposure to risk and cognitive processing of negative experiences.

However, despite our general understanding of what we mean by "protective factor," including differences in their location and action, Luthar and colleagues (2000) report a lack of clarity and inconsistent use of the term. They note that in some cases protective factors are described as having an ameliorative or corrective effect, and in others merely refer to variables that distinguish between children who are able to overcome adversity and those who are not (as in Werner and Smith's [1992] research, for instance, or Anthony's [1987] "invulnerable" child). To resolve the inconsistency and uncertainty of meaning, Luthar et al. suggest subtypes of protective factors, recognizing that some protective factors build upon and enhance existing personal competencies, some stabilize the individual at times of stress, and others ameliorate (or directly protect against) risk in the environment.

Missing from this trichotomy (ameliorative, stabilizing, or enhancing) are those protective factors that act directly upon the individual by restraining him or her from directly engaging in harmful behavior, perhaps through electronic monitoring or other close supervision, for example, or threat of incarceration. Even though it seems clear that protective factors typically protect the individual from risk, in risk assessment we are concerned about the risk that the individual represents to others. If we are to consider protective factors as mitigating risk potential, then we must consider all classes, including those that build upon and increase the strengths of the individual, thus reducing the potential for harm, and those that serve to restrain the individual from succumbing to risk and causing harm.

Drawn from the processes described by Luthar et al. (2000) and Rutter et al. (1998), and building on classes of protective factors identified by Nettles and Plack (1996) and Rutter (1987), we can further recognize four classes, or types, of protective factors and the processes by which they may reduce the strength of risk. In each of these classes, we can also recognize the presence of protective factors as either personal competencies within the individual or sources of support found within the environment, or both, and how they may be expressed in these domains.

1. Exposure limiting: Those protective factors that limit exposure to high-risk situations. These fall into both the individual or environmental domains, including a personal conviction to avoid risky situations and environmental circumstances under which the individual is highly supervised or kept away from such situations.

2. Post-exposure regulating: Protective factors that reduce the likelihood of uncontained reactions that result from exposure to risk. Again, these may reside within the individual or the individual's environment, and they may be demonstrated by his or her use of a relapse prevention or safety plan following exposure to a risky situation or the response of the family or community to contain and control for poor self-regulation.

3. Socially connecting and esteem building: Rutter (1987) describes this type of protective factor as increasing self-efficacy through the development of secure relationships. This class clearly involves the interpersonal and social realm and the capacity of both the individual to form meaningful relationships and the capacity and availability of people in his or her

social environment to similarly form attached relationships with the individual.

4. Success building: Protective factors that provide opportunities for success and achievement largely fall within the individual's social environment, and they may involve emotional support and recognition, as well as resources that contribute to social and personal accomplishment.

In reviewing these four classes, also evident is the dynamic quality of protective factors, which you'll recall play a moderating, rather than a mediating, role. That is, although protection may be considered static if embedded in developmental history, our interest is essentially limited to those protective factors that exist in the present moment or can be built. The dynamic quality of protection is captured by Werner and Smith (1992), who describe the opportunity at every developmental stage for protective factors to offset the negative effects of adverse experience. Similarly, Garmezy (1990) and Luthar et al. (2000) note that resilience can be achieved at any point in the life cycle, including the capacity for positive outcomes even in later life.

RECOGNIZING PROTECTIVE FACTORS IN RISK ASSESSMENT

With respect to the treatment process that usually follows juvenile risk assessment, given the powerful role of protective factors we can see that treatment should be aimed at strengthening existing protective factors and building new ones, and not simply aimed at the reduction of risk factors. Nevertheless, this perspective is largely reserved for treatment, as the goals of assessment are not the same as the goals of treatment. At the level of risk assessment, the goal is to establish the likelihood of or potential for sexual reoffense, and to some degree serves to define the type and focus of treatment that will usually follow.

Risk assessment, as we have described it and in its practice, is for the most part not a strength-based process. To a significant degree the process of risk assessment is based on the presence of vulnerabilities, especially in the first stage of risk assessment with respect to the application of a risk assessment instrument. At this level, assessment of risk is built on a review and analysis of risk factors, rather than ameliorative strengths and resources found in the individual or his or her environment. This stands in contrast to the strength-based focus that has entered the arena of sex offender specific treatment, in which we recognize and consider the strengths and capacity for growth that juvenile and adult sexual offenders bring to their treatment.

Nevertheless, even in the objective and dispassionate process of risk assessment we can recognize the function, presence, strength, and impact of protective factors in our projections of future risk, and to some degree incorporate these into a global assessment of risk. Here, in considering the role of protective factors in assessment we think not only in terms of deficits and vulnerabilities that influence the likelihood of reoffense, but also strengths and supports that may diminish such risk. Further, if we recognize the likelihood that, for most juvenile sexual offenders, treatment will follow assessment, we are in a position to identify both risk and protective factors that are targets for treatment. However, despite their significance, incorporating protective factors into the risk assessment process without significantly adjusting scores derived from risk assessment instruments is not a simple task, and it may to some degree weaken the assessment process.

ASSESSING FOR PROTECTIVE FACTORS
IN THE EVALUATION OF RISK

With the exception of the J-RAT, none of the currently available juvenile sexual offender risk assessment instruments consider the presence of protective factors in their assessment of risk. However, even though the J-RAT makes specific reference to and defines protective factors and allows protective factors to influence the final assessment of risk,[4] it makes no clear provision for considering protective factors in the body of the assessment instrument. Neither of the two most commonly used clinical instruments, the J-SOAP and ERASOR, recognize or take protective factors into consideration. This is not the case for the currently in development MEGA (Rasmussen & Miccio-Fonseca, 2007b), which both recognizes protective factors and includes a protective factors scale in its construction. Comprised of seven chief domains, risk and protective factors residing within each domain are considered in the evaluation.[5]

---

4. The J-RAT notes that "protective factors represent relationships, attitudes, beliefs, skills, and other factors at play in the life of the juvenile that may help mitigate the level of risk in any given domain, or the overall level of risk. Although the J-RAT does not assess protective elements, these should be considered and taken into account by the clinician in evaluating risk. In some cases, a low or no level of concern or risk in any individual risk element or risk domain may also represent a protective factor" (Rich, 2007b, p. 2).

5. As the MEGA is not yet available, at this time it has not been possible to review the actual instrument or better understand how it may function, and thus how risk factors and protective factors are assessed or incorporated into the overall assessment of risk.

Despite the goals of the MEGA, although we have a fairly clear sense of the nature of protective factors and how and in what domains they function, we have no clear way to measure them or their influence on risk factors. Accordingly, although risk assessment instruments may be able to better recognize the contribution of protective factors to the final assessment of risk, they largely focus on the presence and assessed strength of risk factors. Frankly, at this time, it is not clear how it could be otherwise, although this does not mean that later adjustments to risk level are not possible within a larger model of risk assessment in which the completion of a formal assessment instrument is just the first step. That is, in the process of clinical assessment it is possible to adjust for the presence of protective factors in the assessment itself, if the design of the assessment instrument allows for it (as in the case of the J-RAT, for instance, and the MEGA, which contains a specific protective factors scale).

However, in the case of all actuarial assessments, and in the case of clinical assessment tools that don't provide for the mitigating effects of protective factors, adjustments must follow the final assessment of risk. For actuarial assessments this process is referred to as clinical adjustment, a process frowned upon by some as described in Chapter 3. However, in their discussion of the Iterative Classification Tree, an actuarially based assessment instrument developed to predict risk for violence in mentally disordered patients, Monahan et al. (2001) specifically address protective factors. They recommend that actuarial instruments be best viewed as "tools that support, rather than replace, the exercise of clinical judgment" (p. 134), and hence support clinical revisions to actuarial assessment in order to account for protective factors and other factors that may otherwise be unaccounted for in the assignment of risk. Nevertheless, other than the exercise of clinical judgment in some variant, there is no clear means by which to methodically assess the weight or influence of protective factors in offsetting the cumulative assessment of individual risk factors.

Further, all actuarial assessments, including the JSORRAT, and almost all of the currently available clinical assessment instruments are essentially categorical in their measurements, including juvenile and adult clinical instruments aimed at sexual recidivism or risk for general violence. That is, each risk factor is assigned to some version of an "either-or" condition, either by classifying them as present, not present, or partially present, or by assigning a numerical score based on quantity, frequency, or severity. By design, such scoring systems disallow adjustment as, in one form or another, a condition is either present or it is not. For example, if the strength of a particular risk factor is based on the number of sexual offenses, then there is no way to adjust the score or assignment without ignoring the data on which the factor is scored (i.e, the number of offenses). Similarly, if a risk factor is based on the presence of family violence, then there is no way to adjust the score, even if protective factors are present. In this case, there either is family violence or there isn't. Such categorical scoring doesn't easily allow for adjustment, as opposed to dimensional scoring, which assesses risk factors as a "more-or-less," rather than an "either-or," condition.

Risk instruments that assign risk factors to "either-or" conditions are therefore not easily able to make adjustments to risk; despite the fact that clinical risk tools by design allow for judgment, "either-or" assignments often preclude such judgments. This alone makes it difficult to recognize and build in the risk-diluting effects of protective factors. Of the current risk assessment instruments, only the J-RAT uses a dimensional scale that measures risk items as more-or-less present. Based on the level of their *significance* as concerns (rather than *presence*), individual elements of risk are assessed along a four-point scale that ranges from "not significant" to "significant." However, a dimensional scale provides a less clear-cut means for assessing risk factors than does a categorical scale. Nevertheless, dimensional scales allow a far greater degree of clinical judgment than categorical scales, and thus they more easily allow the presence of protective factors to influence and weight judgment.

Nevertheless, in the final analysis, whether assessed as present or as significant, and whether more dimensional or more categorical, risk factors are ultimately classified categorically (low, moderate, or high, or some variant) and risk assessment instruments focus on the presence of risk factors, almost to the exclusion of protective factors. It is thus important for the evaluator to understand the nature and function of protective factors, recognize and estimate the strength of their presence and action in each evaluation, and consider their impact on the final assessment of risk.

THE BALANCE BETWEEN PROTECTION AND RISK: UNDERSTANDING THE EQUATION

In essence, despite perhaps overly complicated descriptions, the role of protective factors and the ways in which protection operates is somewhat obvious and not especially complex. Nevertheless, as described, it's difficult to know exactly how to apply ideas about protection in the assessment of sexual risk, and thus balance the presence and strength of protective factors against the presence and strength of risk factors in predictions of future behavior. In other words, it's the balance between risk and protection that is complicated and subtle.

Despite previously considering several classes, types, and actions of protective factors, we can simplify this by considering just two essential classes of protective factors, both of which serve to restrain harmful behavior.

Protection as Absence of Risk

The first class involves protective factors in an inverse relationship with risk factors. Here, protection is the polar opposite of risk, although we can just as easily picture this as the absence of risk rather than the presence of protection. However, absence has special relevance if the behavior that is now absent was once quite active, and in which it is important to understand the reason for the current absence.

In the case of sexual acting out that has now diminished, for example, we can understand the subsidence of the sexual behavior as the result of a reduction in the risk factors that drove the former behavior or the presence of protective elements that have served to restrain the behavior. In fact, in this case it may be impossible to tell the difference between the effects of the two conditions (which may be closely related) as either condition may lead to an identical outcome. In either case, however, it may not matter. In the assessment of risk it is enough to simply note the reduction in risk regardless of its cause and without reference to the action of protective factors.

Protection in the Presence of Continued Risk

The second class of protective factor represents, not the absence of a behavior or risk factor, but the presence of something that acts upon the individual to protect him or her against risk that continues to be present (as opposed to the previous class, in which the presence of protection equals the absence of risk). An example of a protective factor in this class is the presence of strong and prosocial family support that serve to buffer the individual from the effects of risk present in other domains of his or her life. Another example, at the other extreme, is the threat of incarceration, which may serve to restrain the individual from succumbing to risk. It is far easier to see direct evidence of this class of protective factor because it is made visible by the presence of some condition in the life of the individual (such as family support or threat to imprison), rather than being inferred by the absence of a condition.

Returning to the weather example I used earlier in this chapter, the role, action, and presence of a protective factor is clear when I use an umbrella in a rainstorm. This is not only because it is the concrete presence of the umbrella that is protecting me, but also because regardless of protection the risk is still there. That is, it is still raining. To use another example, if I wear a radiation suit in a radiation filled room I remain perfectly safe, even though the room is still radiation filled and the risk therefore remains high; it is the radiation suit that is clearly protecting me, not the absence of risk. Thinking of protective factors, and this class of protective factors, in this way makes their action very clear. Although risk remains, protection renders it harmless.

THE RELATIONSHIP AND BALANCE BETWEEN THE TWO CLASSES

If I decontaminate the radiation-filled room, the risk is gone, and there is no more need for a radiation suit. This new condition places protection into the first class: Protection results from the absence of risk. Further, one can clearly argue that absence or risk means that there is no need for protection. Moreover, if we are strictly assessing risk for harm and nothing more, we really do not need to know the cause of reduction. In this case, it is enough to simply note that the risk condition has vanished and risk has therefore dropped to zero.

On the other hand, if we wish to know the *cause* of the reduction in order to ensure the risk condition does not recur, we would be wise to assess the conditions that led or contributed to the drop to zero risk (or the factors that protect against a recurrence of risk). However, in the example of the radiation-filled room, based on outcome condition alone it is difficult to distinguish between a reduction in risk and the presence of protection. But what if the only reason I drained the room of radiation was because I feared being heavily fined by the Nuclear Regulatory Agency and losing my license to operate a nuclear reactor? In this case, the absence of risk (the now decontaminated room) is actually the result of a protective factor at work (my fear of high fines and loss of license). Here, there is a strong convergence between reduction in risk and the action of protection. In this case, the absence of risk (a class one protective factor) is the direct result of a protective factor at work (a class two protective factor).

It is not always the case that a relationship exists between the two classes of protection. However, in some cases there is a relationship, even though it may not be obvious at first, illustrated I hope by the example just given. From a risk assessment perspective, particularly as we want to understand factors that contribute to risk, it will be important to recognize not only those factors that drive risk but also those that reduce and inhibit it. In the balance between risk and protection, in some cases the insertion of protective factors serves to buffer the impact of risk factors that remain active despite an increase in protection; in other cases, an increase in protection equals a reduction in the power of risk. In other cases still, the presence of protective factors that restrain influences a condition in which risk disappears completely, and the absence of risk can now be considered to be a protective factor.

INCORPORATING THE EVALUATION OF PROTECTIVE FACTORS INTO RISK ASSESSMENT

As we near the end of the chapter, I hope that we're clearer about the nature of protective factors and the balance and interaction between risk and protection. Nevertheless, questions about how to weigh protective factors against risk factors, and even the relevance of protection to risk assessment (rather than its obvious relevance to the treatment process that follows), make it difficult to build ideas about protection into an instrument primarily designed to assess risk. This is partly because we better understand how the presence of risk factors influences trajectory than we understand how the presence of protective factors may alter this trajectory. A risk assessment instrument, in effect, views trajectory based on the presence of past (static) and present (dynamic) risk factors. Ideas about how protective factors offset or eliminate risk currently have a far stronger theoretical basis than they do empirical validity, and these ideas have only recently begun to appear in the professional literature and are not well understood.

For instance, Salekin and Lochman (2008) note that considerable work lies ahead in recognizing protective factors that guard against psychopathy in youth and understanding how they work, and they identify the need for more powerful statistical means for recognizing and detecting protective factors. In their study on the development of psychopathic traits from adolescence into early adulthood, Lynam, Loeber, and Stouthamer-Loeber (2008) note the disappointing failure of what they describe as "classic protective factors" to reduce future psychopathy in at-risk adolescents, noting that the success of these moderating protective factors would have suggested potential targets for treatment.

Nevertheless, it's certainly possible, and even desirable, to review and incorporate the strengths conferred by protective factors into a more comprehensive and global clinical assessment of the youth,[6] in which the outcome of a formal risk assessment instrument is merely one element

---

6. Without empirical evidence, however, the process of including and weighing protective factors can only be theoretical and clinical.

in a larger multistep assessment process. As an example, the Structured Assessment for Violence Risk in Youth (SAVRY), a clinical instrument used to estimate risk for general (not sexual) violence, does build in a review of six protective factors, permitting the assessment of risk to be made "as a professional judgment, including consideration of . . . SAVRY risk and protective factors" (Borum, Bartel, & Forth, 2002, p. 17). In effect, this allows the evaluator to weigh and consider the balance of protective factors against the balance of risk factors and accordingly make a clinical decision about the likelihood of violence based on this. However, the relationship between risk and protective factors is complex, and the concept that there is a simple balance between the two types of factors is somewhat rudimentary. Hence, it is not clear that the presence of six protective factors can or does outweigh the presence of the 24 or more risk factors included in the SAVRY.

Indeed, the very idea that there is a simple balance appears to oversimplify the relationship and interaction between protective and risk factors, and even more so when one considers that SAVRY protective factors are scored categorically as either present or absent, whereas risk factors are rated as low, moderate, or high in valence. Other than simply balancing protective factors against risk factors, then, as in the case of the SAVRY, it's unlikely, at least at this time, that the assessment of protection can be easily or meaningfully incorporated into a risk assessment instrument. That is, although the findings of a risk assessment instrument may represent only one step in a multilayered set of decisions about risk, the risk instrument itself is nonetheless most likely to focus on risk alone, and not on the presence or strength of protective factors. The MEGA is moving in a different direction, as briefly described above, but it is not yet available for review and so it is not clear how or how meaningfully protective factors will be built into the instrument or weighed in the balance against risk factors.

However, the inclusion of protective factors addresses the idea of risk being determined through a risk assessment process, rather than a risk assessment instrument. In this case, the assessment of risk provided by the instrument represents only one slice of a larger assessment. The initial assessment of risk, whether derived from an actuarial or clinical instrument, is later adjusted following the inclusion of other elements into the assessment process, resulting in a necessarily clinical adjustment to and final assessment of risk. Here, the risk assessment instrument is used as a jumping off point, expanded upon as the assessment process continues beyond the completion of the instrument and the level of risk it supports.

In the world of risk assessment for adult sexual offenders, both the Structured Risk Assessment (Thornton, 2002) and Structured Anchored

Clinical Judgement (Grubin, 1998) models offer examples of this process. Both use a static actuarial assessment as the first step in a three- or four-stage model of risk assessment, in which the final assessment of risk is adjusted to accommodate the inclusion of dynamic risk factors, a decidedly clinical process. Hanson (2002) describes models like these challenging current risk assessment processes and shaping the direction for future assessment. However, he is describing only actuarial models because clinical assessment instruments in adult assessment already include processes that involve clinical judgment; in fact, Thornton writes that the SRA model is designed in a similar manner to the HCR-20[7] (Webster, Douglas, Eaves, & Hart, 1997), a structured clinical assessment instrument for assessing risk for general violence.

Regardless, in adjusted actuarial assessments or the dynamic risk assessment process in general, multiple other sources of information can be included that may reflect upon risk for or protection against sexual reoffense. For instance, psychometric testing may be used to reveal psychological functioning and personality facets (helping to assess the psychosocial factors assessed by the SRA), and inventories may be used to explore and establish attitudes, beliefs, and perspectives that may support or diminish further sexually abusive behavior. It is at this level of overall assessment that protective factors can probably be most effectively and easily applied, and thus incorporated into the assessment process. In this case, an instrument may be administered that can help the evaluator recognize and assess protective strengths, assets, and resources present in the juvenile's life.

INSTRUMENTS FOR THE ASSESSMENT OF PROTECTIVE FACTORS

Among instruments designed to consider and assess resilience in children and adolescents, the Protective Factors Scale (Bremer, 2006b) and the Clinical Assessment Package for Client Risks and Strengths (Gilgun, 1999; Gilgun, Klein, & Pranis, 2000) are both well suited to the evaluation of adolescents with sexual behavior problems, in part because they both measure strengths (and vulnerabilities) associated with sexual behaviors and interests in their sexuality scales. The PFS in particular was developed specifically for work with sexually abusive youth, and its sexuality scale reviews three elements specifically related to problematic sexual behavior.

Although neither the PFS or CASPARS are particularly strong instruments, both are nonetheless useful in helping point to strengths and assets,

---

7. Historical, Clinical, Risk-20.

and therefore protective factors, and thus helping to guide and structure the evaluator's thinking. Furthermore, both recognize the inverse relationship between strength and vulnerability, and particularly the CASPARS, as vulnerability and protection lie at opposite ends of the individual scales. Therefore, in the case of both instruments, a high level of vulnerability (or a score of no strength) represents risk, even though in the case of the PFS this does not seem to be the intention. Instruments like the PFS and the CASPARS can help to better recognize and understand the nature of protective factors in children and adolescents, and also recognize that quite often there is an inverse relationship between protection/strength and risk/vulnerability.

As described, although used to clinically assess risk for general violence, the SAVRY also includes an index of protective factors to be applied against the estimate of risk, albeit in a rather simplistic manner. It is nonetheless useful in pointing to a simple list of protective factors to consider in risk evaluation. In specifically assessing risk for sexual recidivism, rather than general violence, the MEGA also plans to provide a means by which to assess protective factor and balances these against risk. However, it is currently not available other than in its research form, where it is being used in studies that will help validation for its construction, and is not therefore available for further examination or critique at this time. Hence, it's not clear how or how successfully the MEGA will be able to incorporate or balance protective factors against risk, and whether or not its process will be any more complex or meaningful than that offered by the SAVRY. One instrument that has managed to incorporate both risk and protective factors into a multistep assessment instrument is the AIM2 (named for the treatment program out of which it first developed) briefly mentioned in Chapter 7.

The AIM2 (Print et al., 2007) is not defined by the authors as a risk assessment instrument, but instead a process by which to determine the level of supervision required by adolescent sexual offenders. However, the AIM2 assesses both risk and protective factors, although describes risk factors as "concerns" (and not risks) and protective factors as "strengths," and assesses static and dynamic variants of both risk and protection. Assessing 51 risk factors/concerns (26 static and 25 dynamic) and 22 protective factors/strengths (6 static and 16 dynamic), the AIM2 yields scored profiles for both concerns and strengths and combines these into a matrix that results in an assessed level of required supervision. One might argue that the AIM2 is a risk assessment instrument, at least at the level of assessing what it refers to as concerns. In fact, at that stage of assessment it appears virtually indistinguishable from a literature-based, structured clinical risk assessment tool other than by its own definition and the fact that, in its design, the instrument is incomplete at that stage. Its inclusion of a second step in which strengths are assessed and a third step by which scores are combined provides an example of a multistep assessment process rather than a single-step assessment instrument, and it illustrates how risk assessment and strength assessment may proceed as separate entities in which the assessment of protective factors later serves to adjust assigned risk. The only difference in the case of the AIM2 is that its authors don't describe it as a risk assessment instrument and it doesn't assign a level of risk that is later adjusted by an assessment of protection, but instead produces a single assessed level of required supervision.

The AIM2 confirms the difficulty of combining protective factors directly into a risk assessment instrument, but it also makes clear that consideration of protective factors can be built into the risk assessment process at a stage following the assessment of risk. It is also clear that, even if not included in the formal risk assessment tool, the idea of protective factors should and can remain within the thinking and notice of the evaluator. If the use of a risk assessment instrument is embedded within a larger clinical and more comprehensive assessment, as it should be from the point of view of this book, then multiple sources of information will be used to understand and evaluate the child behind the sexually abusive behavior. These will include case records, psychological and other testing results, and face-to-face interviews, and this is the point at which protective factors can probably be most easily recognized, assessed, and built into the assessment process. This is, in effect, how the AIM2 works.

In fact, many of the data derived from these various sources will be required in order to complete an instrument such as the J-SOAP, ERASOR, or J-RAT. In the case of the J-RAT, because of its dimensional scoring, protective factors can be included in the evaluator's scoring of each element of risk.

CONCLUSION: THE ROLE OF PROTECTION IN TREATMENT AND REASSESSMENT

Do these descriptions of protective factors or the equation between risk and protection make it easier to balance risk against protection, or inject protection into the assessment of risk at the level of the risk assessment instrument? Probably not, in large part because risk assessment instruments focus on the presence and strength of risk factors, regardless of how they're assessed (i.e., statistically or clinically), with little to no regard paid to protection. Indeed, for the reasons described this may always be the case.

It's therefore likely that any consideration of protective factors will follow the completion of a risk assessment instrument, rather than during this stage of the risk assessment process. Moreover, it's likely that in practice the most powerful role for an assessment of and focus on protective factors lies in the treatment process that will typically follow assessment. In the treatment environment, with respect to their role and influence, protective and dynamic risk factors are probably two ends of the same process, or close cousins, and their effect will emerge in the next assessment (that is, reassessment) of risk, as long as that next assessment focuses on dynamic rather than static factors alone.

Ultimately, without disregarding the significance and power of protective factors, for now at least it may be best and simplest for risk assessment to focus primarily on the assessment of risk factors. However, regardless of whether protective factors are somehow injected into the risk assessment process (as in the case of the AIM2 or MEGA) or remain only in the background, it is in treatment that a focus on protective factors must rise fully to the surface and come into play. Treatment will thus focus on both reducing the strength and presence of risk factors and enhancing and building protective factors as steps toward decreasing the possibility of sexual recidivism, an idea inferred in the concept of strength-based treatment. In such a case, if treatment is successful, later reassessment will reflect a reduction in risk factors in part because of the presence of increased protective factors that, in part, are the business of treatment.

CHAPTER 9

Distinguishing Sexually Abusive
Behavior from Other
Sexualized Behaviors

I N EVALUATING SEXUALLY abusive behavior, it perhaps goes without saying
that we must distinguish between behavior that is sexually abusive,
sexual behavior that may be inappropriate in any number of possible
variants but is not necessarily abusive, and sexual behavior that is behaviorally and culturally normative for the children or adolescents engaging in
that behavior. Take the example of Marvin, given in Chapter 6.

Although entering treatment for the sexual abuse of his 14-month-
younger sister and other troubling sexual activity, the initial comprehensive risk assessment raised the question of whether any "abuse" had
occurred at all, as the index behavior appeared to be consensual incest
between two similarly aged siblings. Certainly, compounded further by
Marvin's other sexually troubling behaviors, this pointed to the need for
treatment of his sexual behaviors and other emotional difficulties (as well
as flagging his sister's probable treatment needs), but it also raised a serious
concern about how to view the behavior and how to assess it. Should we
assess for the risk of continued sexual abuse in this case, and can we
reassess for a reoffense if no sexual abuse has occurred in the first place?
Even though the sexual behavior for both siblings is without question an
offense as it almost certainly violates sexual laws in almost every jurisdiction, should we designate Marvin as a "sexual offender" in this case? In
treatment, should we ask him about his victim and how he victimized her,
assess his risk for a sexual reoffense (which implies future victims, rather
than consensual partners, no matter how inappropriate or troubled the
partnership), and even require him to register as a sexual offender if the

degree of sexual activity was significant enough? Furthermore, if the behavior was consensual between similarly aged siblings, should we also haul Marvin's sister in for sex offender assessment and sexual offender treatment?

This is perhaps an extreme case in which the line between sexually abusive behavior and sexually troubled behavior is quite blurred. However, it nicely illustrates that there is not always a sharply demarcated line between sexually troubled and sexually abusive behavior. The line between sexual behavior that is normative but inappropriate is also sometimes blurred, often based on where, when, and how often it occurs rather than the nature of the behavior itself. This is true of sexual intercourse between two consenting teenagers, for instance, whose sexual behavior is clearly inappropriate, and even troubled, if it takes place in an alcove in a school hallway during the school day. The act of masturbating is another example of normative sexual behavior, but (aside from religious conventions or beliefs) the appropriateness of masturbation is based upon where, when, and how often it occurs, as well as with whom. Focusing on the sexual behavior of prepubescent children offers another instance where we must be cognizant of normative psychosexual development and troubled or reactive sexual behavior in children.[1]

As evaluators, it is probable that we will most often be called upon to assess risk in cases where sexually abusive behavior is quite evident (to us, even if not the juvenile offender) and there has been a clear violation of sexual and physical boundaries. However, there will also be many instances where the case is not so clear, as briefly described above or in other cases where the nature of the behavior as sexually abusive is unclear. Uncertainty in these cases not only raises the question of whether it is appropriate or possible to assess risk for reoffense, but also the possibility that the results of an improper risk assessment[2] will be extremely damaging to the juvenile being assessed.

Many people have concerns about labeling sexually abusive youth as juvenile sexual offenders even under circumstances when a clear offense or pattern of offenses has occurred. However, labeling a juvenile as a juvenile sexual offender, a sexually abusive youth, or a youth with harmful sexual behaviors (pick your preferred term) when no offense has actually occurred burdens that youth with a label that is not only grossly inaccurate but is also highly stigmatizing and carries with it the increasing possibility

---

1. The sexual behavior of pre-adolescent children is addressed in the next chapter.
2. That is, when an assessment has been administered in a case absent of any prior sexual offense.

of lifetime legal implications. Accordingly, we must be vigilant in ensuring that we are assessing sexual behavior that is, in fact, abusive, and especially under conditions when the lines between sexually abusive and other sexual behavior is uncertain.

CONSENT, INEQUALITY, AND COERCION: THE DYNAMICS OF SEXUAL ABUSE

A first step is to be sure that we understand the nature of sexually abusive behavior, as best as we can. However, in 1993 the National Task Force on Juvenile Sexual Offending noted the difficulty in clarifying the exact nature of sexually abusive behavior, writing that in some cases sexual behaviors that are not abusive are nevertheless prohibited by law, and thus considered to be sexual offenses. Rather than turning to the law for further clarity, the task force instead framed sexual behavior as abusive or nonabusive based upon a number of interacting and overlapping elements within the relationship, including the presence and nature of consent, the equality of participants, and the use of force, deception, manipulation, or coercion in inducing participants to engage and remain engaged in sexual behavior. The task force therefore concluded that sexually abusive behavior is best represented by a continuum of behaviors, which contain some or all of these and related elements.

The three key elements that emerged from the report define sexual abuse as any sexual behavior that occurs without consent, without equality, and/or as a result of coercion. This model offers a useful platform upon which to understand the nature of sexual behavior that is truly abusive as opposed to sexual behavior that is inappropriate but not abusive, or sexual behavior that is appropriate but nevertheless outlawed in some fashion. However, although this model provides an important basis for understanding and discerning the elements of sexual abuse, the presence and nature of these elements is not always clear when applied to the sexual behavior of children and adolescents.

CONSENT

The strongest and clearest characteristic of sexual abuse is lack of consent, regardless of lack of equality or method of compliance. Here, sexual contact is unwanted to one degree or another, falling along a continuum. At one end it is experienced as a boundary violation that otherwise presents no great risk of harm; at the other end, sexual contact represents an extreme violation of boundaries in which consent is neither given nor sought and the victim experiences great fear and harm. Both ends constitute sexual crimes, but it is in the latter case that consent is most clearly lacking.

There is an additional variation on consent, however, which can be quite confusing in some cases. This involves sexual contact with a minor, and it is most clear when the minor is younger than age 14. In this case, minors are generally considered incapable of giving consent for sexual contact, but the rule varies by jurisdiction and circumstances. Hence, in some states, the age a child may give consent for sexual contact typically ranges between 16 and 17, and as young as age 14 in some states, as well as other countries. Nevertheless, the principle here is that juveniles, and young adolescents and children in particular, are unable to give consent by virtue of their young age and experience, and also because as a society we do not allow them the option of voluntarily engaging in sexual activity (even if they choose to do so). Thus, even if a child or young adolescent gives consent or doesn't actually deny consent for sexual contact, their actual or implied consent is not considered an expression of true or informed consent.

The element of consent is in sexual relationships with juveniles, at least young adolescents and children, overlaps with the idea of equality in relationships if the party initiating sexual contact is significantly older than the juvenile, or is in a clear position of authority. Consent and equality also overlap with ideas about coercion when the sexual initiator exercises some form of pressure by which to gain consent, an idea to which we'll return.

Regardless of these variants, there are easily recognized circumstances when sexual contact is clearly made against the stated or unstated wishes of the victim or involves an older adolescent or adult engaging in sexual contact with a young adolescent or child with or without the stated or implied consent of the child. In these cases, we need look no further than the absence of consent to declare contact as sexually abusive. The obvious lack of consent eliminates the need to consider the presence of inequality or coercion as factors that determine the behavior to be abusive, although it is likely that or one or both of these elements served as the conduit through which the sexually abusive behavior was enacted. However, in the case of juvenile sexual behavior there is sometimes lack of clarity about consent or lack of consent.

Take the Marvin example again. His sister was 14 months younger than him. He should have known better and is the older sibling, but based on the case history the sexual behavior was mutual. In this situation, did Marvin sexually abuse his sister or was consent given between two adolescents close in age (even though they are siblings)? There are numerous examples of sexually abusive youths who honestly report that their younger victim, often a sibling or other family member and sometimes a neighbor, did not stop them, call out, or tell anyone about the sexual behavior, and in some cases seemed to seek out the behavior at times, even if they denied consent at other times. Is the question of consent completely clear in a case where the perpetrator is 13 and the victim 10 or 11, and when consent was never denied and the victim sometimes appeared to readily engage in the behavior? In many cases, we have resolved the difficulty that arises when the behaviors appear to be consensual and even mutual, by imposing an absolute age difference between the parties. Typically, in adolescents and children we consider the behavior abusive if one party is older than the other by three or more years, although the law in many jurisdictions considers a four-year age difference as the line of demarcation. In either case, however, these standards allow us to judge sexual behavior between a 13-year-old and a 9-year-old as abusive, although not necessarily between a 13-year-old and an 11-year-old.

Hence, when there is no clear lack of consent and the age difference is not a significant factor, as in the case of Marvin, we must turn to the elements of equality and coercion to discover whether consent is actually the product of other forces or influences on the possible victim.

INEQUALITY AND COERCION

Clear and unmistakable lack of consent[3] eclipses the need to assess for the presence of inequality or coercion as factors that define a sexual behavior as abusive. Even so, as mentioned, the presence and role of these elements will be important to assess as risk factors because they tell us a great deal about the history and course of sexually abusive behavior, and how the perpetrator gained compliance and cooperation. For instance, the use of force and restraint is an extreme form of coercion that tells us something about the nature of the perpetrator, contrasted against the coercive use of bribes and promises to gain compliance, which tells us something different about the offender. In one case, physical force is used to gain compliance, in the other psychological strategies are used, and perhaps in another a relationship approach is taken (e.g., "if you don't, I won't be your friend").

However, in defining sexual behavior as abusive, even when consent appears to be given, or was at least not overtly denied, we may also look to the nature of equality and free choice (the opposites of inequality and

---

3. For instance, the victim asked for the sexual behavior to stop, or never willingly engaged in such behavior; the victim was a 2-year-old child; the victim was severely retarded; the victim was unconscious.

coercion) in the relationship. Here, in seeking evidence that the behavior was abusive, we're seeking to understand the role played by the juvenile's physical size, authority or power, relationship, or mental capacity in gaining compliance and, perhaps as important, the juvenile's knowledge that he or she was in a more powerful position and could thus exert influence as a result.

Coercion is a close cousin to inequality as it implies power or control of some kind, and it is the level and type of coercion that helps point to a sexual behavior as abusive. Extreme forms of coercion such as threats, actual use of force, blackmail, and extortion make it clear that the behavior was unwanted and thus make it equally clear that there was no consent. Milder forms of coercion are commonplace in juvenile sexual offending and include promises or actual rewards of various kinds or forms of manipulation or exploitation by which consent for sexual behavior was freely given, or at least implied. The elements of inequality and coercion are closely intertwined and, as described above, sometimes overlap with the presence of consent. For example, in some cases, although consent is given, it is not freely given and is actually the result of a misuse of authority or prestige (inequality) or promises, rewards, intimidation, threats, or actual harm (coercion).

Thus, although they operate independently of one another, inequality and coercion in their various forms often operate together and are difficult to tease apart. Having power over someone and convincing or requiring him or her to engage in sexual behavior, for instance, involves both inequality and coercion as one person is more powerful than another or has a greater level of control and is thus able to gain the compliance of the less powerful party through some means. Inequality can mean being a beloved older sibling whose very presence induces compliance, which is furthered strengthened by the promise of spending more time together, or a feared older sibling who coerces compliance with a threat of some consequence.

However, in any relationship between an older and younger sibling or person, or a smarter and less smart, a bigger and smaller, or more powerful and less powerful person, inequality is present in the very fabric of the relationship; thus inequality itself cannot serve at face value as *the* factor that is the agent of coercion or induces consent. It is the quality of the difference, how the juvenile uses it to gain advantage, and the juvenile's knowledge of the inequality that moves it toward being an element of abusive behavior, and not the inequality itself. Similarly, it is the type, intensity, and purpose of coercion that identifies its role as a conduit for abuse. The clearest variant of coercion as a force for harm is that which uses threats of or actual harm of some kind to gain compliance. However, coercion at the other end of the scale is a regular feature of many relationships in which one person wants another to do something, and it can be considered as normative behavior in many cases. Older siblings frequently coerce their younger siblings to do something, and it is not unusual for adolescents in romantic relationships to attempt to coerce their partner into sexual activity. The classic behavior of the adolescent boy who attempts to get his girlfriend to engage in sexual behavior through cajoling her, threats to leave, sweet talking, alcohol use, expressions of love, and so on are all forms of coercion that tie it directly to sexual behavior that is otherwise unwanted and not necessarily in the best interests of the girlfriend. If the behavior becomes sexual against the stated wishes of the partner, then it can be considered as abusive and classified as rape if it includes unwanted sexual intercourse.

However, even though we can point to sexual behavior as abusive in the absence of true consent and in the presence of inequality and coercion, it's also clear that it's the particular combination of circumstances and one or more of these elements that come together to produce abuse. It's equally clear that in some cases sexual behavior is not necessarily abusive, even when consent is not freely given and there is a level of inequality and coercion, as in the prior boyfriend/girlfriend example.

THE DYNAMICS OF SEXUAL ABUSE

In the final analysis and to paraphrase Ryan (1999), in distinguishing between sexually abusive and sexually nonabusive behaviors, it is the nature of the interaction and the relationship that defines a behavior as abusive, and not the sexual behavior itself. To this I add that it is the quality and nature of consent, including the age and cognitive capacity of the person giving consent, and how and under what conditions consent is gained that helps us to clearly recognize sexual behavior as abusive or nonabusive, as well as the context in which sexual behavior develops and occurs.

Rasmussen and Miccio-Fonseca (2007b) describe these particulars as "sexually abusive dynamics" or the set of characteristics unique to each sexual offender in his or her history of sexually abusive behavior. They are thus more properly describing the dynamics of the sexual abuser than they are the dynamics of sexual abuse. However, as used here, these dynamics reflect those general characteristics, conditions, and elements that point to sexual behavior as abusive, and they apply equally to the behavior of the juvenile engaging in the behavior, the nature of the relationship within which sexual behavior unfolds, and the context in which the sexual behavior occurs.

It is these dynamics that we should bear in mind, perhaps most simply described in terms of consent, inequality, and coercion, as we strive to ensure that we fully understand the sexual behavior driving risk assessment as abusive. Referring one last time to Marvin's case, in applying these ideas what do you conclude? It was our position that the sexual behaviors with his sister, and indeed Marvin's entire history of troubled sexual behavior, did not constitute sexually abusive behavior and therefore could not provide a basis or rationale for an assessment of risk for sexual reoffense.

RECOGNIZING SEXUAL BEHAVIOR AS ABUSIVE

Sometimes the picture is clear and there is no question about the sexually abusive nature of the behavior. Moreover, in most cases referred for assessment and treatment sexually abusive behavior is clearly apparent. This doesn't necessarily make it any easier to assess risk of the possibility of reoffense, but it allows us a solid footing upon which to build the assessment and apply the process. Nevertheless, it is not always going to be the case that every referral will involve a clear-cut case of sexual abuse. It is with respect to these less frequent cases that the evaluator must be aware that, even when sexual behavior is clearly sexually inappropriate or troubling, there may no history of actual abuse and therefore no basis for an assessment of risk for sexual reoffense.

It goes without saying that not every act of inappropriate, irresponsible, or troubled sexual behavior should be treated as abusive. Similarly, it's important to recognize that not every sexual act in which a juvenile sexual offender engages is necessarily, or likely to be, abusive or even problematic. However, it is easy to depict all sexual behaviors in juvenile sexual offenders as troubled and further evidence of a sexual problem, and therefore pathologize otherwise normative behaviors and interests. I have seen many instances, for example, where an evaluator or treating clinician identifies every sexual contact between a sexually abusive youth and a partner as an "offense" and every partner as a "victim." In some cases, the behaviors may in fact be inappropriate or represent a concern, such as having sexual contact with another youth while in residential treatment, but the issue is not one that directly involves sexually abusive behavior. On the other hand, the behavior may well reflect a disregard for sexual boundaries or a sexual preoccupation and, in either case, represent an inability to contain sexual behaviors, even while in treatment. Under such circumstances, the sexual behavior may well be considered to be a dynamic risk factor given the conditions under which it emerged.

Either way, it is once again not the sexual behavior per se that identifies it as problematic, nor the fact that a juvenile with a history of sexually abusive behavior is engaging in sexual behaviors. It is instead the particulars of the sexual behavior and the circumstances under which it is appears that flag it as problematic or not, such as the nature and quality, time and place, and frequency of the sexual behavior. Sexual interest, sexual arousal, and sexual behavior are normal and expected elements of human existence, perhaps especially for adolescents. It is the context and meaning of the sexual behavior with which we should be concerned as evaluators, including the possibility that the behavior is related to risk for continued sexually abusive behavior.

Early in the Chapter I noted the importance of vigilance when administering risk assessment in cases where it is not clear whether sexually abusive behavior has actually occurred. Here is one more brief case example, then, to illustrate the importance of how we make sense of sexual behavior that is not necessarily abusive, and in this case involved current sexual preoccupation and ideation rather than actual behavior. However, a juvenile sexual offense had occurred several years prior to assessment and treatment, which to some degree justified an assessment of risk in this case.

At age 17, Carey entered sexual offender treatment for a single mild sexual offense that he had committed at age 12, but for which he never received treatment. However, although Carey had not engaged in any other known or suspected sexually abusive or sexually inappropriate behavior in the years since, he had continually demonstrated a sexual preoccupation and recently an increasingly odd and worrisome sexual ideation. A decision was made to accept Carey into sexual offender treatment on the basis that he had continued to engage in troubled sexual ideation and had a history of engaging in sexually abusive behavior, albeit only once several years earlier. At the completion of 16 months of treatment, Carey, now age 18, was denied entry into a public high school and described by the school as a high-risk offender even though at the completion of treatment he was deemed at low risk for a sexual reoffense.

Should the evaluator have administered a sexual offender risk assessment for Carey for a sexual offense he committed five years prior to the assessment, and thus unintentionally supporting the use of a label that may be wholly inappropriate at this point in Carey's life? Should the evaluator have instead declined to administer a risk assessment on the basis that such an assessment was both unnecessary and inappropriate given the lapse of so many years free of further sexually abusive or inappropriate behavior?

Consider these to be rhetorical questions with no real answers. However, as should be clear by now, risk assessment is complex, difficult, and uncertain under the best of circumstances, and it is an art and craft as much as, and perhaps more than, it is a science. The Carey example in this case is intended only to illustrate the still further difficulties of risk assessment under circumstances where it is not clear how a risk assessment process may be best applied or whether it should be applied at all.

It is clearly not the role of the forensic evaluator to undertake an investigation of the circumstances that led to an allegation of sexually abusive behavior. However, based on information available the evaluator will have to make a determination of whether or not the sexual behavior can be assessed as abusive, sometimes regardless of an adjudication on sexual offense charges. If a risk assessment moves forward, it may in some cases conclude that risk for reoffense is uncertain based on a lack of information, and in other cases the evaluator may decline to assess for risk of sexual reoffense at all on the basis that the prior behaviors don't appear to constitute behaviors that were sexually abusive in nature.

THE PRIME TARGET IN RISK ASSESSMENT: BEHAVIOR THAT IS SEXUALLY ABUSIVE

We can recognize three classes of sexual behaviors, only two of which are of concern to us as evaluators of troubled behaviors. These are (1) appropriate sexual behaviors between consenting and equal partners who have reached the age of consent, (2) sexual behaviors that are considered to be inappropriate or troubled for any number of reasons, and (3) sexually abusive behavior.

In the first case, we can certainly imagine objections raised to certain sexual behaviors as appropriate, even if they are consensual, such as sexual relationships between adolescents of any age, sexual relationships between unmarried individuals or adulterous sexual relationships, or sexual relationships between persons of the same gender. Nevertheless, despite the many objections and concerns that may be raised by different social groups, here we note these relationships as appropriate on the basis of mutual agreement between partners, in which all partners are old enough to give consent and are more-or-less equal. The second class is far more broad and indistinct, however, as sexual behavior may be considered inappropriate for any number of reasons. These may include the circumstances surrounding the sexual behaviors even if the behaviors involve consensual partners (such as sexual intercourse in a public environment) or sexual behavior that is inappropriate because it is unwanted by the target of the sexual behavior even though no actual physical contact has occurred (sexual comments, remarks, and gestures that may constitute sexual harassment). Sexual behaviors considered to be inappropriate may also include sexual overtures or sexual relations that involve an abuse of power but no actual criminal behavior (such as sexual interactions between a teacher and older adolescent student, a therapist and client, or an employer and employee). We have already discussed the third class, sexual abuse, which is, of course, the prime and sole class of sexual behaviors that is our target in risk assessment.

However, the lines that demarcate sexually inappropriate behavior are blurry at both ends. On one end sexual behaviors may be inappropriate because of the circumstances under which they occur, such as in the park, or in the downstairs living room while there are children in the home. At this end, inappropriate sexual behaviors differ from appropriate[4] sexual behaviors only because of their context and circumstances, and not the nature of the behavior itself or the relationship between sexual partners. At the other end of the sexually inappropriate spectrum, these behaviors border on the abusive, sometimes differing from abusive behaviors by a hair. In some circumstances, it is difficult to tell significantly inappropriate sexual behavior from mildly abusive sexual behavior (such as slapping someone on their buttocks), and such behavior may be prosecutable. In other cases, socially reprehensible sexual behavior at this end of the spectrum also borders on the abusive, but has a different complexion, such as a sexual relationship between a 30-year-old teacher and a consenting 17-year-old student. Clearly inappropriate, this behavior may not be abusive from a legal standpoint (even if resulting in loss of a teaching license), and it certainly may not be experienced by the student as abusive.

It is, nevertheless, perfectly clear that in the assessment of risk for sexual reoffense it is sexually abusive behavior with which we are concerned, and not sexually inappropriate or appropriate behavior, other than in an examination of the broader range of sexual behaviors which may surround or accompany sexually abusive behavior. That is, as evaluators of sexual risk we are concerned with the assessment of risk in cases where there has been an occurrence of sexually abusive behavior on at least one occasion. In this case, where sexually abusive behavior has occurred, our interest in sexually inappropriate behavior has a double focus. In the first instance, in our evaluation we want to understand the interplay between sexually abusive and sexually inappropriate behavior in the event that there is a

---

4. Note that we are not discussing "healthy" sexual relationships, just appropriate sexual relationships on the basis of consent and equality. Many appropriate sexual relationships may, in fact, be quite emotionally or physically unhealthy or unsafe.

wider display of sexual behavior than just the abusive behavior. What is the juvenile's full range of sexual experience, including non-abusive sexual experiences, and how do they interact with or even give rise to or fuel sexually abusive behavior?

However, and especially given the theme of this chapter, the other pressing concern, and perhaps of prime importance, is to ensure that we are not confusing sexually inappropriate behavior (or sexually appropriate behavior for that matter) for sexually abusive behavior and therefore assessing risk on the basis of troubled sexual behavior in absence (or instead) of sexually abusive behavior. Although we will be interested in understanding sexually inappropriate behavior as part of a pattern in which sexually abusive behavior may be embedded, it is *only* sexually abusive behavior that gives rise to the appropriateness and capacity to assess risk for continued sexually abusive behavior or sexual recidivism.

Accordingly, although it is not our role as evaluators to establish whether or not a sexual offense has occurred (that is the role of the police or other authorities), it may well be the role of the evaluator to tease out and understand differences between sexually abusive and inappropriate behavior, and to discover whether some alleged sexually abusive behavior is better understood as sexually troubled but nonabusive and even whether sexually inappropriate behavior is actually sexually abusive in nature.

CONCLUSION: RECOGNIZING SEXUALLY ABUSIVE BEHAVIOR

It's perfectly clear that when we discuss risk we're talking about risk for sexual behavior that is abusive to others, and we've already discussed the dynamics of consent, equality, and free choice that separate nonabusive from abusive sexual behavior. The mere presence of these three elements, however, doesn't necessarily signal healthy sexual behavior; they just eliminate the behavior as abusive. In fact, there are many types of behaviors, sexual and otherwise, in which people can freely and mutually engage with others that are neither healthy or socially appropriate, such as shared drug abuse or alcoholism, theft, or harm to others. Hence, people can be engaged in sexual relationships that are mutual in every way, but not necessarily healthy with respect to what they bring to the personal growth or the self-esteem of each individual.

I hope this chapter has not only helped further clarify those dynamics that come together to produce and exemplify sexually abusive behavior, but also defined the differences between troubled but nonabusive sexual behavior and sexual behavior that is abusive, and especially the evaluator's role in not confusing the two or mistaking one for the other.

Even in evaluating sexually inappropriate and other sexual behaviors in the context of sexually abusive behavior, it remains important for the evaluator to distinguish between abusive and inappropriate sexual behavior. Hence, even if promiscuous or inappropriate, it is important that not all inappropriate sexual behaviors simply be lumped in with and treated as sexually abusive. For example, if a juvenile sexual offender in residential treatment engages in consensual sexual activity with a peer equal in both age and in other respects, even if inappropriate (given the circumstances and context) the behavior is clearly not abusive. Yet, it is not uncommon to hear behavior of this type described as a "sexual offense." The behavior is of concern given the context of treatment and the youth's poor containment of sexual urges, assuming the treatment program prohibits sexual relationships between peers; it constitutes poor judgment given the fact that the youth is in treatment for sexual behavior problems. The issue in this example, then, is not that the behavior is not inappropriate or troubled, but that it should not be confused for and defined as sexually abusive.

In point of fact, I suggest that the very act of engaging in sexual behavior under the circumstances described may even elevate or maintain concerns about sexual recidivism at a later point, but not because the sexual behavior was abusive. Instead, engagement in the behavior may be diagnostic of poor self-regulation and sexual containment, inadequate judgment and poor problem-solving skills, lack of regard for authority, failure to recognize consequences, and perhaps even an assumption that it is okay to engage in the behavior as long as one doesn't get caught.

However, beyond the need to carefully understand the nature of abusive and non-abusive sexual behaviors, and the differences and relationship between the two, there are still other special circumstances in risk assessment to which we must pay attention. One of these involves the assessment of risk in pre-adolescent children who engage in sexual and sexually abusive behavior, the subject of the next chapter.

CHAPTER 10

Assessing Risk in Children with Sexual Behavior Problems

ADOLESCENTS ENGAGE IN sexual behavior with one another, some of which represents significant sexual activity, up to and including sexual intercourse. Recall from Chapter 1 that in 2005 almost 47 percent of U.S. high school students experienced sexual intercourse (Eaton et al., 2006), and 65 percent reported having been engaged in intimate sexual activity including either sexual intercourse or oral sex, or both (Hoff, Greene, & Davis, 2003). In 2006, about 750,000 teenage girls and young women ages 15–19 became pregnant (Guttmacher Institute, 2006), or a little over 8 percent of that population (Ryan, Franzetta, & Manlove, 2005), and in 2006 about 2 percent of teenage women aged 15–17 gave birth (Hamilton, Martin, & Ventura, 2007). So we can be fairly certain that sexual behavior among teenagers is relatively commonplace, even if we disagree with the idea of adolescents having serious sexual relationships of any kind. But, even for those who don't object to this relatively normative behavior, what is the lower acceptable age at which adolescents or children may engage in sexual behavior, ranging from intercourse to oral sex to sexual fondling and heavy petting? Is it okay, emotionally healthy, physically safe, or socially appropriate for 14 year olds to be engaged in sexual intercourse or oral sex? How about age 12? Even though it's possible that we're seeing the earlier onset of puberty in both girls and boys (Parent et al., 2003), and hence with it an earlier onset of sexual drive, can we approve of sexual behavior in children aged 9, 10, or 11?

UNDERSTANDING CHILDHOOD SEXUAL BEHAVIOR

Of course, like all other areas of growth, sexual behavior develops over time, from childhood through adolescence and into adulthood. This means that, to some degree at least, the roots of sexual behavior, and certainly sexual development itself, are found in childhood. This includes the initiation and presence of various forms of sexual play and activity, many of which are appropriate, healthy, and normal for children at certain ages.

However, as Cantwell (1995) points out, there's little agreement regarding normative and expected sexual behavior in children versus troubled sexual behavior, and sexual behavior in young children is not well tolerated by adults. This is quite understandable, even though it has been long recognized that childhood sexuality and sexual behavior is for many children a normal and expected aspect of childhood development, even if not all children display or engage in such behaviors. With the increased exposure of children and adolescents to sexual material, ranging from general and vague to quite explicit and detailed, through the general media[1] in all of its forms, it is also no surprise that childhood interest in sexual information and behavior may be more significant and definite now than it was a decade ago, as well as better informed (for a more detailed review of the role of the media in childhood and adolescent sexuality, see Rich, 2003). The more pertinent question, though, is not about the why of childhood sexual behavior or its appearance, but how such behavior is manifested. As with adolescent sexual behavior, the question relates to the line between normative childhood sexual behavior and childhood sexual behavior of concern and, included within that category, childhood sexual behavior that is abusive or harmful to others (usually other children).

The questions of consent, equality, and coercion are still plainly evident in childhood sexual behaviors but they certainly carry less weight, partly due to the presence of other elements related to childhood behavior of any kind, and especially behaviors of concern. That is, even if lack of consent, equality, and free choice are evident in the behavior of one child toward another (in instances of bullying, for example), the picture is far more complicated when we add the further elements of reason and judgment, intentionality, moral understanding, and the effects of social messages and the social pressure it may bring with it. These are among the very same elements that we consider in adolescent assessment for sexual risk, but they take on a very different meaning and significance in evaluating the behavior of children. Children may be keenly aware that they are more

---

1. Not including the Internet and its easy access to explicit and pornographic sexual images and content.

powerful than another child (a 7-year-old is considerably more powerful than a 5-year-old, for instance, despite an age difference of only two years) and unquestionably know that they are engaging in forceful or other coercive behavior, and in fact may be intending to do so (again, bullying as a clear example). However, depending on age and cognitive development, in children higher levels of judgment, moral reasoning, and empathic understanding are not yet significantly in play and therefore cannot act as brakes on decision making and action, nor as filters through which social messages are interpreted that guide and control behavior.

DEVELOPMENTAL CONSIDERATIONS IN UNDERSTANDING CHILDHOOD BEHAVIORS

We recognize from the outset, then, that children require outside external guidance, structure, and control in order to teach them the rules of social behavior, the effects of behavior on others, and a moral code, because in childhood the capacity to spontaneously generate or understand these ideas is not sufficiently well formed. In this respect, morality is induced (Hoffman, 2000) in children by their parents and other social agents who act as the child's teachers, not just of facts but of social intercourse as well. The premises of moral thinking and behavior are taught and expressed through socially institutionalized values and behaviors; societies with contradictory or confused moral values or practices are likely to contribute to an arrested moral development, confused or inconsistent morality, or amorality in their children (Shweder, Mahapatra, & Miller, 1987). Thus, even though children are developing agency,[2] they are thus not yet their own agents and have not yet developed the "agentive mind," (Bruner, 1996; Fonagy, 2004) or the self-reflective mind that is aware of itself, its actions, and its responsibilities, and thus also aware of its interactions with others and, indeed, the minds of others.

Other elements are thus very much embedded into the social behavior of children, including behavior that harms others. Aspects of cognitive and social development, such as moral behavior, awareness and judgment, empathy, and social understanding, have each been explored and discussed, by Piaget for instance (1932, 1937), in how children adjust, adapt, and accommodate to their world, and in the development of who they are to become as they enter adolescence. Stilwell and colleagues (Stilwell et al.,

---

2. The experience of the self as the initiator or the cause of action, or a recognition of self-will and self-determination in causing and being responsible for personal behaviors and their effects. Compare this to an internal locus of control.

1994, 1997, 1998) have also discussed the development of morality but from a perspective that wraps ideas about attachment, social development, and moral development together into the development of conscience, or what Stilwell refers to as the "moralization of attachment" as she ties these ideas together.

However, there is no intention here to launch into a further or more detailed discussion about moral judgment, decision making, and cognitive and social capacity in children other than to note that these are some of the considerations that we must take on board when we think about any harmful behaviors displayed by children, including those that are sexually harmful. Keeping development in mind as we discuss the sexual behaviors of children allows us to keep a perspective that recognizes that, just as adolescents are not simply smaller and younger versions of adults, children are not just smaller versions of adolescents. Just as adolescents are developmentally different than adults, children are developmentally different than adolescents, and the developmental gap between children and adolescents is even greater than that between adolescents and adults.

CHILDHOOD SEXUAL BEHAVIOR: FROM NORMATIVE TO ABUSIVE

Despite the normalcy of childhood sexual behaviors, it is clear that some are of concern and some may be harmful to the child and others. Toni Cavanagh Johnson's work on sexual behaviors in children has been illuminating. In particular, she has defined what is, in effect, a four-group typology of sexual behavior in children aged 12 and younger (2002), ranging from normative sexual behavior in group one to increasingly more troubled behavior in the other three groups, in which Johnson believes most or all children have themselves been sexually or physically victimized or exposed to sexually explicit materials or environments (2000, 2001).[3]

- *Natural and Healthy,* in which children engage in healthy, appropriate, and natural sexual experiences.

---

3. However, despite Johnson's assertion that all or most of these children have experienced some form of victimization or maltreatment, in their study of 201 children with sexual behavior problems Bonner, Walker, and Berliner (1999) found only 59 percent of the sample had experienced at least one form of abuse or neglect, and only 48 percent had a history of being sexually victimized. In their study sample of 127 children, Pithers, Gray, Busconi, and Houchens (1998) reported that 86 percent had experienced sexual maltreatment, 43 percent physical abuse, and 33 percent emotional maltreatment.

- *Sexually-Reactive* in which children engage in more sexual behaviors than their peers.
- *Children Engaged in Extensive Mutual Sexual Behaviors*, including children engaged in frequent and precocious sexual behavior with a consensual peer.
- *Children Who Molest* includes children who coerce or force other children into sexual acts, often aggressively.

Others have created similar groupings for children aged 6–12. Describing three groups of sexually troubled behavior, Bonner, Walker, and Berliner (1999) classified children as either sexually inappropriate, sexually intrusive, or sexually aggressive. Pithers, Gray, Busconi, and Houchens (1998) described a similar range of sexually problematic behavior in 127 children, describing five groupings as sexually aggressive, abuse reactive, highly traumatized, rule-breaking, and non-symptomatic (other than the sexual behavior). Working with children aged 3–7, Hall, Matthews, and Pearce initially grouped these very young children into three groups (1998), but later (2002) into five groups: unproblematic developmentally expected sexual behavior, problematic self-focused sexual behavior, problematic unplanned sexual behavior involving others, problematic planned but non-coercive sexual behavior with others, and problematic planned and coercive sexual behavior with others.

These studies and groupings of children with sexual behavior problems all point to the range of sexual behavior that runs the gamut of expected to abusive. Clearly, some cases, such as the self-focused group of Hall et al., involve sexual behavior that does not include others, but for the most part these groups represent sexual behavior problems that differ by quantity, intensity, and severity, as well as by differences in the quality of sexual relationships with other children, ranging from consensual to coercive, in which Chaffin et al. (2006) describe children with more severe sexual behavior problems experiencing a broader set of mental health, social, and family problems.

The recent report of the ATSA task force on children with sexual behavior problems (Chaffin et al., 2006) describes the importance of distinguishing sexual behavior problems from normative childhood sexual play and exploration, which is described as occurring spontaneously, intermittently, and non-coercively, and does not cause emotional distress. They report that although sometimes including sexual curiosity, interest in sexual body parts, and sexual stimulation, normative sexual behavior in children does not involve preoccupation or include advanced and adult-like sexual behaviors. In assessing whether the sexual behavior is inappropriate, the task force notes the importance of considering the behavior in the context of the child's developmental level and age, as well as the child's culture; the frequency, extent, and form of the sexual behavior, and the degree to which it has become a focal point for the child; and whether the child responds to adult direction to stop the behavior. With regard to childhood sexual behavior as potentially or actually harmful to others, the task force points to several distinguishing features, including age and developmental differences between the child and other children involved in the behavior, emotional distress in other children or problems in social functioning as result of the behavior; and any use of force, intimidation, or coercion to gain compliance.

As a member of the ATSA task force, Johnson (1999, 2001) has previously developed a checklist of sexual behaviors or attitudes in children that signal concerns, including the presence of sexually abusive behavior, the main aspects of which can be consolidated here in nine points:

1. Sexual play should not be the only kind of play in which children engage.
2. Children should not sexualize relationships or see other children or adults as objects for sexual interactions.
3. Children should not be engaged in sexual play with children much younger or much older than themselves, or direct sexual behaviors toward adolescents or adults.
4. Children should not be preoccupied with and driven to engage in sexual play and behaviors, and stop when told to by an adult.
5. Children should not have unusual or precocious knowledge of sex beyond their age, or behave in a sexual manner that is more like an adult than a child; children's sexual behaviors and interests should be similar to the sexual behaviors and interests of other same-age children, and should not become more intrusive and more noticeable over time.
6. Children's sexual behaviors should not lead to complaints from or have a negative effect on other children; should not be connected to bribery, threats, or manipulation; and should not cause physical or emotional pain or discomfort to themselves or others.
7. Children aged 4 and older should understand the rights and boundaries of other children in sexual play; children should not use distorted logic to justify their sexual play.
8. Children should not experience fear, shame, or guilt in their sexual play; sexual behaviors shouldn't follow or be followed by expressions of anger or other negative feelings.
9. Children should not engage in sexual relationships or activities with animals.

Although the elements of consent, equality, and coercion are embedded within both the ATSA task force description of inappropriate sexual behavior and the nine points drawn from Johnson's work, it is also apparent that they incorporate ideas about childhood sexual behaviors that go beyond the three elements alone. This helps us to recognize that these elements alone cannot necessarily help us to pinpoint sexually abusive behavior in children, partly because the nature of these qualities are not always so clear in childhood and adolescent relationships. There are different forms of consent, different forms of equality, and different forms of coercion that come into play and particularly when it comes to young children, none of whom have the capacity to make highly reasoned decisions by virtue of their cognitive, social, and neural development.

SEXUALLY TROUBLED CHILDREN AS "SEXUALLY REACTIVE"

Just as there is no distinct profile for adolescent sexual offenders, neither does such a profile exist for sexually troubled children, nor is there a "clear pattern of demographic, psychological, or social factors that distinguish children with sexual behavior problems from other groups of children" (Carpentier, Silovsky, and Chaffin, 2006b, p. 3).

Also like adolescent sexual offenders, there is a significant level of adversity and maltreatment in the background of children with sexual behavior problems. Although it not necessarily true that every child exhibiting troubled sexual behavior has a definite history of being maltreated, as Johnson (2000, 2001) asserts, it is nevertheless clear that a history of victimization or maltreatment is common in the population: As noted, Bonner et al. (1999) reported that 59 percent of the children they studied had experienced at least one form of abuse or neglect, and Pithers et al. (1998) reported that 86 percent of their sample had experienced sexual maltreatment and 43 percent physical abuse. Nevertheless, despite similarities in the experience of adversity and maltreatment, one significant difference lies in the fact that such history may be relatively static in the lives of adolescents, whereas these experiences are likely more recent, and even current, in the lives of sexually troubled children and therefore active dynamic and developmental features.

In fact, although sexually troubled and sexually abusive behavior in children can look remarkably like its adolescent counterpart, the developmental differences suggests major distinctions between the age groups, even if the behaviors and dynamics of sexually abusive and/or inappropriate behavior and the personal histories of both groups are similar. To this end, Carpentier et al. (2006b) write that studies and experience "support conceptualizing children with sexual behavior problems as qualitatively different from adolescent and adult sexual offenders" (p. 2). It is precisely the presence of so many developmental factors that contribute to troubled childhood sexual behaviors that leads to the idea of the "sexually reactive" child in which there is a far lower level of culpability for the perpetration of sexually abusive behavior than would be the case for an adolescent.[4]

The term sexually reactive, typically applied to children aged 12 or younger (to a great degree pinned to the age at which adolescence begins, the general onset of more defined puberty, and the development of a higher level of cognitive development), is used here in a broader manner than that used by Johnson, who uses this term to describe just one particular group of children with sexual behavior problems. As used here, however, the term includes all three of Johnson's groups of sexually troubled children, and it describes any child with inappropriate or unhealthy sexual behavior as reactive. As noted, Johnson (2001) considers that all, or most, children in these three groups have been sexually or physically victimized or exposed to explicit sexual experiences; the idea behind the descriptive label of sexually reactivity, then, is that prepubescent children who engage in troubled sexual behaviors do so as an expression of, and in reaction to, earlier or concurrent exposure to inappropriate sexual experiences.

Such exposure may vary from the child's own sexual victimization to his or her exposure to developmentally and age-inappropriate sexual materials or behavior (viewing pornography, for example, witnessing another family member engaged in sexual behavior, or witnessing the sexual abuse of another individual). Similarly, so too may sexual acting lie somewhere along a spectrum that ranges from extensive sexual interest or frequent sexual play at one end to the sexual molestation of children at the other. This moves from potentially troubling sexual play to increasingly more precocious and advanced sexual behavior, including behavior that is sexually abusive, as the behavior advances along the continuum, covering the entire range of sexually troubled behaviors described by Bonner et al. (1999), Hall et al. (1998, 2002), Johnson (1999, 2001), and Pithers et al. (1998).

However, the sexually reactive label has been defined inconsistently and often differently, as in the case of its use here compared to Johnson's more narrow use of the term, and labels such as "trauma reactive" and "abuse

---

4. This assumes adolescents with average or higher or relatively unimpaired cognitive functioning. Behavior may also be more reactive and culpability reduced in the case of adolescents whose cognitive capacity is limited by mental retardation, neurological deficits, or a significant psychiatric disorder.

reactive" have also been used to describe essentially the same behavior. Children in this category have also been described more simply as "children with sexual behavior problems." The term is simple and clear in its meaning and requires little further explanation of the behavior in question. Although the CSBP label doesn't provide an explanation for the problem (contrasted to the term "sexually reactive," which describes both the behavior and its putative cause), it is more eloquent in its clear description, allowing us to recognize and respond to the same range of problematic sexual behavior in children described as sexually reactive.

THE SIGNIFICANCE OF CHILDHOOD SEXUALLY ABUSIVE BEHAVIOR

Regardless of which term we use, the idea of the sexually reactive child should not suggest for a moment that the nature of the abusive behavior perpetrated by children is substantially different in its effects on the victims of abuse than the effects of sexual abuse perpetrated by an adolescent or adult. It may have just as profound an effect, or little effect. Neither should the term be taken to imply that children, even children in mid-childhood or younger, do not know the difference between right or wrong, even though their moral compass is quite different and far more limited than that of the older child and adolescent.

However, the term "sexually reactive" recognizes that, compared to adolescent sexual behavior, there is a different quality to the cognitive understanding, emotional motivation, and physical drive behind the sexual behaviors of prepubescent children. It presumes to some degree not just that troubled sexual behavior is a reaction to prior sexual experiences, but also that the expression of significant sexual behavior in prepubescent children has its basis in prior experience, and not sexual drive, arousal, or libido.[5] Nevertheless, we should not dismiss troubled sexual behavior in children as a passing phase, or as less important than troubled sexual behavior in adolescents, especially because, as Bancroft (2006) notes, the prepubertal sexual experience is intrinsically about normal sexual development that sets the pace for and reaches into adolescence.

Even though for some children, sexually reactive behavior can be easily managed and treated, we should not presume such behavior to be less significant because it is most likely a developmental response to personal experience, environmental stimulation, or both, rather than a product of

---

5. Bancroft (2006) describes pre-pubertal sexual arousal occurring around age 9, but sexual attraction first developing at age 11 for boys and age 13 for girls.

sexual drive and motivation. Indeed, even among adolescent sexual offenders, it is quite frequently the case that sexually abusive behavior serves emotional and social needs more than sexual needs, as described in Chapter 5. This may also be the case for many adult sexual offenders, for whom sexually abusive behavior may meet social, rather than sexual, needs (Hudson & Ward, 2000). If, in fact, sexually troubled and abusive behavior for many adolescent and adult sexual offenders can be considered the product of poor early social experiences, deficits in social skills, and the struggle for social connection, then it is surely all the more important and relevant to recognize the same forces at work in children who are in the midst of the very developmental experiences and social conditions that will shape their future behavior, perhaps even as sexually abusive adolescents or adults. Indeed, one significant goal in the assessment of sexually troubled behavior in children is to understand the nature and strength of the behavior, forces that drive the behavior and protect against it, and the possible trajectory of the behavior into later childhood and adolescence.

ASSESSING SEXUAL BEHAVIOR IN CHILDREN

Despite the many developmental differences that are important in understanding and assessing childhood sexual behaviors, as we distinguish between normative sexual behavior in children, sexual behaviors that are troubling but non-abusive, and those that are abusive (both classes of which constitute sexual behavior problems or, as defined here, sexual reactivity), we also recognize emotional and broad behavioral patterns attached to the sexual behaviors. Indeed, these are the elements that distinguish among the groups of normative, inappropriate, and abusive sexual behavior. Just as they do among adolescent sexual offenders, these patterns range from non-symptomatic, as described by Pithers et al. (1998) in which there were relatively few symptoms of co-occurring mental health disorders, to sexually aggressive children who, in Pithers' study, showed the greatest and most significant level of sexual abuse and the most significant level of childhood onset conduct disorder.

Given the sometimes blurry distinction between normative and troubled childhood sexual behaviors, Araji (2004) notes that grouping children who engage in sexual behaviors not only provides a clear view of the range of behaviors, but also allows evaluators to identify the behavioral, social, psychological, and environmental factors that point to such behavior as abusive or otherwise, and the trajectory along which sexual behavior may be traveling. The goal of the evaluator in assessing childhood sexual behavior, then, is in part to first distinguish among these types of behavior and, with respect to sexually troubled behavior, distinguish between sexual behavior that is non-abusive and that which is abusive. Only after those distinctions are made can the evaluator assess for risk. In this case, we can conceptualize risk in terms of projection for continued troubled non-abusive sexual behavior and, in line with risk assessment for adolescents and adults, risk for continued sexually abusive behavior. It's taken a long time to reach this point in the chapter, and I hope not too long, as, just as we have to take care to not confuse adolescent sexually inappropriate behavior with sexually abusive behavior, it's equally important to do the same in the case of children, but perhaps more difficult at times.

Making things even more difficult in the case of children, is the fact that it's not clear what childhood sexually abusive behavior may mean in terms of its continuation into adolescence, although it seems likely that the more significant and severe the sexually abusive behavior, in conjunction with early onset, the greater its likelihood of persisting into adolescence if not interrupted and treated. Just as early onset conduct disorder is considered a more serious prognosticator for future behavior than adolescent onset conduct disorder,[6] it is likely also the case that sexually abusive behavior that has its onset in childhood and persists into adolescence is a greater indicator of later risk for sexual recidivism. The first iteration of the JSORRAT (Epperson, Ralston, Fowers, & DeWitt, 2004), for instance, showed a statistical link between sexual recidivism and a history of sexually abusive behavior dating back more than three years; this takes the 12-15-year-old adolescents included in the study back to age 9–12 in terms of their offense history.[7] At any rate, the key here may not be whether sexually abusive behavior begins in childhood, but whether it continues uninterrupted into adolescence.

However, Chaffin, Letourneau, and Silovsky (2002) report the likelihood of multiple trajectories of sexual behavior problems in children, with persistent sexually abusive behaviors as the exception rather than the rule. The ATSA Task Force report (Chaffin et al., 2006) similarly concludes that few children continue to demonstrate sexual behavior problems into late adolescence and early adulthood. However, the conclusions of the ATSA task force and the work of Chaffin and colleagues are closely tied. In

6. This has already been described in Chapter 5, and *DSM-IV* (American Psychiatric Association, 2004) notes that early onset conduct disorder predicts a worse prognosis and an increased risk in adults for antisocial personality disorder and substance-related disorders.

7. The current version of the instrument (JSORRAT-II) no longer shows a sexual offender duration of three plus years as significant, but instead focuses on a history of 12 months or more as a risk factor.

fact, the task force conclusion is based substantially on the results of a 10-year follow-up study of children with sexual behavior problems conducted by Carpentier, Silovsky, and Chaffin (2006a), in which there was a recidivism rate of between 2 and 10 percent depending on the type of treatment provided. However, Bonner, Walker, and Berliner (1999) reported a recidivism rate of 15 and 17 percent in their study of sexually troubled children over a two-year follow-up period, also depending on treatment type. More recently, Prentky, Pimental, Cavanaugh, and Righthand (in press) reported a sexual recidivism rate of almost 31 percent among the 123 sexually troubled behavior preadolescent boys in their study, extending over a 67-month follow-up period, compared to a 23 percent recidivism rate among adolescent sexual offenders in the study.

Frankly, these recidivism rates don't support the conclusions of the ATSA task force that sexual behavior problems in children are, in effect, of less concern and more easily treated than sexual behavior problems in adolescents (Chapter 4). The recidivism rates in these few studies approximate the range of recidivism rates found among adolescent sexual offenders, and in the Prentky et al. study actually exceed the recidivism rate of adolescents in the same study. Indeed, based on his study of 331 children with sexual behavior problems, with a 24 percent sexual recidivism rate, Prentky (2006) concluded, "it certainly appears from the present findings that early onset of sexually inappropriate and coercive behaviors is associated with the persistence of sexual offending" (p. 40). Similarly, Prentky et al. (in press) write that the higher sexual recidivism rate of preadolescent boys compared with adolescent sexual offenders "may lend some support for heightened risk associated with earlier onset."

Further, it is likely that a substantial number of adolescent and adult sexual offenders began to engage in sexually abusive behavior or had sexual behavior problems prior to age 12, and as young as age 9 (Burton, 2000; Zolondek, Abel, Northey, & Jordan, 2001). It is clear that without intervention some sexually troubled children will continue to engage in troubled sexual behaviors into adolescence, including sexually abusive behavior if this is part of their history. Even without a history of sexually abusive behavior, it is quite possible that for some children sexual behaviors will progress to more significant and intrusive behaviors, in which sexually troubled behavior develops and progresses into sexually abusive behavior over time.

The key to assessment in children involves a detailed and thorough understanding of the sexual behavior, first distinguishing between normative and troubled sexual behavior and then between sexually inappropriate and sexually abusive behavior. "Obtaining a clear, behavioral description of the sexual behaviors involved, when they began, how frequently they occur, and how and whether they have progressed or changed over time is a core assessment component" (Chaffin et al., 2006, p. 9). It is thus important to understand the nature of the actual sexual behaviors and if and in what manner they involved others, as well as the development, sequence, and progression of sexual behavior over time and its relationship to significant events and circumstances in the child's life.

THE EMPIRICAL RECORD

There is little published research regarding sexually troubled children, and therefore little to draw upon in reaching either well-formed or well-informed conclusions built upon a well-defined empirical base. As it pertains to sexually abusive behavior, much of what we do have is retrospective, as in the studies of Burton (2000) and Zolondek et al. (2001), who reviewed the histories of juvenile sexual offenders. Similarly, Laumann's (1996) description of a strong relationship between childhood sexual abuse and elevated rates of sexual activity, sexual dysfunction, and sexual discomfort in adults is based entirely on retrospective data.

In contrast, prospective studies start at the beginning and work forward. That is, they follow the case as it unfolds from point A to point B and then C, and are longitudinal in design. They thus provide a far more certain sense of the relationship between stimulus and outcome, and avoid the inherent weakness found in retrospective studies. However, there is a paucity of such studies regarding the outcome of childhood sexual behavior problems. The empirically derived conclusions of the recent ATSA Task Force report (Chaffin et al., 2006), for instance, focused on treatment rather than assessment and conclusions about treatment requirements and effectiveness were largely built upon only two studies (Carpentier, Silovsky, & Chaffin, 2006a, and Pithers et al., 1998). Alternatively, although well defined and of great value, conclusions about the assessment of sexually troubled children were almost completely drawn from the clinical literature.

Absent of strong, broad, and independently replicated[8] empirical data, much of our conclusions are thus necessarily heavily weighted by clinical experience and perspectives. Based, then, on descriptions in the clinical literature and a limited empirical base, caution is thus required lest we overgeneralize in one direction or the other. In one direction we may

---

8. Robust and dependable support for empirical conclusions is always based on more than one study, and studies replicated by research teams independent of the original researchers.

conclude that all inappropriate, and especially abusive, sexual behavior in children represents a five-alarm fire. In the other direction, we may conclude that even inappropriate or abusive sexual behavior is merely an extension of normative sexual development and play and can, in most cases, be corrected easily. Nevertheless, in our estimates about childhood sexual behavior, and especially lacking strong or even moderate empirical support, we should be guided by our experience, as long as this is well grounded in the clinical literature and, in the process of assessment, guided by structured and literature based instruments.

INSTRUMENTS FOR ASSESSMENT

In actual practice, then, most of what we know is guided by clinical experience combined with empirically derived ideas about childhood sexuality. We are thus most likely far off from being able to develop a meaningful actuarial assessment by which to understand and evaluate the risks associated with sexually abusive children. Hence, regardless of our preferred choice of assessment process or type of instrument, clinical assessment is the only process available to us in the assessment of childhood sexual behavior problems, guided by the use of structured assessment instruments that are informed by the literature on childhood sexuality and childhood sexual behavior problems.

Structured clinical assessment will examine the many factors in the child's life, and especially those that we believe are related to sexual behavior problems. These are not especially different than those that influence general and sexual behavior problems in adolescents. This is not a surprise as we have noted already (in Chapters 7 and 8) that risk factors, as well as protective factors, are in many ways developmental and first appear in early childhood.

In fact, there are several tools available to help evaluators explore and examine childhood sexual behavior. The Child Behavior Checklist (CBCL) provides a broad overview of behaviors of concern in children ages $1^1/_2$–5 and children and adolescents ages 6–18 (there are two separate instruments); nevertheless, although the CBCL includes several items that address sexual behaviors of concern, the instrument addresses far broader and more general behavioral concerns and is not designed to specifically address and help assess sexual behavior in children. However, the Child Sexual Behavior Inventory (CSBI) is designed specifically to evaluate sexual behaviors in children, and it focuses entirely on the presence and nature of current sexual behavior in children aged 2–12 who have or may have been sexually abused. Neither the more general CBCL nor CSBI are risk assessment instruments, nor should they be used as such, but they identify and help evaluate the seriousness of behavioral and, especially in the case of the CSBI, sexual behavioral problems.

With specific regard to risk for continued sexually abusive or inappropriate behavior, the Latency Age-Sexual Adjustment and Assessment Tool (Rich, 2007c) is a structured and literature-based clinical assessment instrument designed to help assess future possible sexual acting out or continued sexualized behavior in boys age 8–13 who have previously engaged in sexual behavior that appears inappropriate due to age or the nature and/or extent of the sexual behavior. For children who have behaved in a sexually aggressive manner or perpetrated sexual abuse against others, the LA-SAAT is designed to help evaluators assess the risk for future sexually abusive behavior (sexual reoffending). Mentioned in Chapter 7, the RSBP<12 (Risk for Sexual Behavior Perpetration for children below the age of 12) is currently being developed by Tracey Curwen (Curwen, 2006, 2007; Curwen & Costin, 2007), one of the two coauthors of the ERASOR. It is also intended as a literature- and empirically based and structured risk assessment instrument for clinically assessing risk for continued sexually abusive behavior in preadolescent boys and girls. The MEGA (Multiplex Empirically Guided Inventory of Ecological Aggregates for Assessing Sexually Abusive Adolescents and Children), also in development, is designed for the clinical assessment of sexual risk in boy and girls aged 5–18. The LA-SAAT, RSBP, and MEGA are each described in more detail in Chapter 14, along with other risk assessment instruments for adolescents.

In many instances, risk factors for adolescent and adult behavioral problems are the very same factors that drive childhood behavior problems, and many of the risk and protective factors that drive later behavioral and emotional problems are significant and active during childhood. It is therefore not unreasonable to conclude that we can modify and extend adolescent risk assessment instruments downwards to the assessment of children, as long as adjustments are made to recognize and accommodate the differences between children and adolescents. In part, these differences must not only take into account elements related to childhood, as opposed to adolescent, development but also ensure the exclusion of elements common to adolescent and adults, such as sexual arousal to children and other forms of deviant arousal. Similarly, although concepts of arrested moral development and poorly developed empathic connection to others may be relevant in the assessment of adults and, to some degree, adolescents, these are far less relevant in the assessment of children. Consequently, as noted by the

ATSA task force, "assessors should guard against projecting adult constructs onto children"(Chaffin et al., 2006, p. 11).

ASSESSMENT AND TREATMENT

With respect to our response to childhood sexual behavior problems, it's likely that children who do not display a vast complex of emotional and behavioral disorders beyond their sexual behavior problems may respond well and easily to an outpatient model of psychoeducational treatment such as that proposed by the ATSA task force. This may include, for instance, the nonsymptomatic group proposed by Pithers et al. (1998) or the self-focused and unplanned sexual behavior groups described by Hall et al. (2002). On the other hand, children with a myriad of complicated problems, among which sexual behavior is but one aspect, may need a more intense, structured, and contained level of treatment than that provided by out-patient psychoeducational treatment. Hence, Pithers et al. noted that children in their sexually aggressive grouping were the most difficult to treat, continuing to demonstrate sexual behavior problems even after treatment, and Hall et al. similarly found the worse treatment outcome among children who had engaged in planned and coercive sexual behaviors with others.

Children in these more sexually aggressive groups more typically engage in behaviors that we would consider to be sexually abusive, regardless of their developmental level and related culpability, and also tend to appear the most uncontained and globally troubled. Their sexually troubled behavior cannot be easily separated from these other aspects of their psychological and social functioning and, indeed, are almost certainly part and parcel of the same underlying problem. That is, the conditions are probably not co-occurring at all, but simply manifestations of the same condition that, in turn, is the result of multiple shaping forces.

Compared to children in less coercive, aggressive, and/or troubled groups, these children may require a more comprehensive and intensive treatment that address problems permeating their entire life, rather than the single domain of sexual behavior. Indeed, beyond projecting a level of risk for continued sexual behavior problems, one of the goals of comprehensive assessment is to help determine the nature and level of required treatment.

CONCLUSION

In assessing children with sexual behavior problems, and in using a structured assessment instrument, it's important to know that there's little empirical support for any risk factors and therefore a tool can be, at best, informed broadly by the literature of childhood sexual development and behavior. The tool and process we select should therefore be useful to the evaluator in helping to examine some of the factors that may be related to childhood risk in general, and sexual behavior in particular, and thus help the evaluator make sense of the behaviors and predict the trajectory along which the behaviors may be traveling. Therefore a tool sensitive to general childhood problem behavior and childhood sexual behavior is required.

The next chapter returns to the more global assessment of juvenile sexual offenders, as opposed to children with sexual behavior problems, examining and describing the comprehensive evaluation process through which the assessment of risk is both made and explained. Rather than being understood as a stand-alone tool, the use of the structured risk assessment instrument is applied within the larger comprehensive assessment, which itself provides the data by which the assessment instrument is completed. I end this chapter, then, with a final word from the ATSA task force, which both sums up the assessment of sexually troubled children and sets the pace for an understanding of the comprehensive assessment process within which assessment of sexual risk is embedded: "Good assessment of children with sexual behavior problems includes a broad assessment of general behavior and psychological functioning, as well as a specific assessment of problematic sexual behavior" (Chaffin et al., 2006, p. 8).

CHAPTER 11

The Comprehensive Assessment of Risk

B Y NOW, WE'VE described two aspects of risk assessment that may be described as either static or dynamic, statistical or clinical, or, for the purpose of this chapter, as limited or comprehensive.

In one case, the goal of risk assessment is a straightforward prediction that yields no information other than a statement that risk for sexual reoffense exists at one level or another, ranging from low[1] to high, or perhaps even uncertain or impossible to assess. Here, risk is a label devoid of any other information about the individual under assessment.[2] If correct, it simply tells us that the individual is more-or-less likely to reoffend, but it does not indicate against whom, under what circumstances, or in what way. In this case, the assignment of a risk level doesn't distinguish among types of offenses (from, say, hands-off offenses to forced sexual intercourse), types of victims (children, peers, or adults), the circumstances under which reoffense is most likely to recur or risk is highest, or any of the myriad pieces of information about risk in any individual case. This model excludes and treats as unimportant information that might help us to better understand the nature of risk and the at-risk individual (such as how, where, and when risk might be transformed into actual harm, and why), reporting instead only the likelihood that a reoffense may occur. This

---

1. It's unlikely that risk for a recurrence of dangerous behavior would ever be assessed as "none," and "low risk" does not equal "no risk."

2. In an actuarial analysis of risk, the individual is recognized only by group characteristics in which he or she is statistically similar or dissimilar to other individuals previously designated at a level of risk. Individual characteristics are relevant only to the degree that they match those of individuals who fall within statistically designated risk groups.

narrow description of risk is relatively uninformative about risk itself and also with respect to whether or how to provide treatment and what to target in the content of treatment.

In the other case, the assessment of risk is a prediction of future behavior based upon the gathering of a wide range of information about the individual and his or her prior and current behavior, in which risk emerges as a property of the person within his or her environment. Assessed risk, in this case, is neither absolute, as in its more narrow counterpart, nor is it assessed or understood in absence of a deep understanding of the individual and his or her circumstances. Information about risk is gathered through a broad process of exploration and examination, and the individual's assessed level of risk both emerges from and is understood in context of the larger assessment process. Rather than yielding only a categorical description of risk (as low or high, for instance) in a more comprehensive variant of risk assessment, the assignment of risk represents the application of a risk assessment instrument embedded within and as part of a larger process. In fact, in this case it is not possible to assess risk independent of a larger process, as it is from the process itself that the information necessary for the completion of the risk assessment instrument is provided. Hence, the assessment of risk both emerges from the application of a comprehensive process and is comprehensively understood within the context of the individual and his or her life.

As we consider the assessment of risk in children and adolescents—developmentally "moving targets" as we have already described them in previous chapters—it is difficult to imagine that we could easily predict their future behavior. It is equally difficult to imagine that we would want to, given their emotional, biological and neurological, cognitive, and behavioral development and our role as adults in shaping their futures and the persons they are yet to become.

This chapter approaches and describes risk assessment from this latter point of view: as a comprehensive process, even though the use of a structured and focused risk assessment instrument is integral to the process. Further, the perspective clearly held by this book is that only a comprehensive evaluation can produce assessments of risk most appropriate to the changing nature of sexually abusive youth. From this perspective, risk is considered a dynamic element of behavior and the environment in which it develops and unfolds, and the discovery and exploration of risk yields valuable information about the individual being assessed, the circumstances of his or her life, and how to proceed with treatment. Indeed, the risk, need, and responsivity model described in Chapter 1 (Andrews, Bonta, & Hoge, 1990) requires a comprehensive assessment in order to operationalize the model. Whereas risk may be derived through the narrow description of static risk, need and responsivity can only be explored and understood through the comprehensive assessment of dynamic factors.

THE NARROW ASSESSMENT OF RISK

The most likely source for the more narrowly defined form of risk assessment is the actuarial assessment. However, a theoretically derived checklist of risk factors could just as easily produce a narrow assessment if it too depended only on easily ascertainable facts (such as number of adjudicated offenses, number of victims, history of other antisocial behavior, etc.) and did not seek further information or clarification from other sources or other information that might yield additional insight into the individual being assessed. Nevertheless, the theoretical assessment instrument, even if it followed an actuarial model in appearance and structure, could clearly not provide anywhere near the level of predictive validity that is key to the actuarial assessment.

The difference is that in actuarial assessment the inclusion of risk factors and the computation of risk is based on a complex statistical process that has a series of psychometric properties and takes into account the base rate,[3] whereas the theoretical prediction model does not. Instead, the checklist it produces has a strictly theoretical basis, although may be designed very much like an actuarial assessment in that it may assign numerical ratings for each included risk factor that can be totaled to produce a designated level of risk (in which 0–2, for instance, equal low risk, and 10–15 equal high risk, thus eliminating a clinical decision-making process in assigning risk). However, in the case of the actuarial assessment, risk based on the numerical total is defined in absolute arithmetic terms of probability (for example, individuals in this risk group have an 86 percent chance of sexually reoffending within five years),[4] rather than in terms of relative risk, such as *low, moderate,* or *high* risk, that both lack absolute meaning and may also lack consensual meaning among evaluators (Harris & Rice, 2007).

Nevertheless, even if capable of drawing from strictly empirical data that are less available for clinical assessments (or not available at all), actuarial assessments and simple theoretically derived assessment checklists yield a

---

3. A base rate involves the rate at which a behavior occurs, in this case recidivism.
4. Only a statistical tool, and not a theoretical checklist, can produce an arithmetic number like this with any level of certainty.

narrow view of risk, and lack any view of the person who is considered to be at risk. This is of special significance as we evaluate and attempt to predict the future behavior of children and adolescents based on their past behaviors. Illustrating this point, even with the advent of the JSORRAT-II,[5] the first actuarial assessment for adolescent (male) sexual offenders, there is no presumption that the assessment of risk produced by the mechanical application of the instrument[6] is enough to either accurately predict the sexual future of the adolescent or to guide treatment, and there is no assumption that risk cannot change over time. In fact, the authors of the JSORRAT-II note that their own results "call into question the possibility of making lifelong predictions based on risk assessments of juveniles" (Epperson et al., 2006, p. 163), and that the JSORRAT must be limited to initial risk assessment only and cannot be used as a measure of treatment outcome, and hopefully a resulting reduction in risk.

Indeed, Epperson et al. describe the requirement for a "second level of assessment" that can result in a modified level of risk (2006, p. 123). Epperson's admonition itself speaks not only to the fact that actuarial assessment is of limited value for still changing and changeable adolescents, but that a narrow assessment of risk has limited utility. In the case of child and adolescent assessment, narrow actuarial assessments are not only "passive predictions of limited practical use" (Boer et al., 1997, p. 4), but also may be extremely damaging. One of the risks of using actuarial assessment instruments with juveniles is not only the narrow interpretation they yield, but also that the risk level is itself static and unchangeable (other than by a process of clinical judgment, eschewed by actuarial purists) and therefore potentially permanent.[7] Harris and Rice (2007) have recently written that the results of actuarial assessments should not be tempered by clinical judgment under any conditions. This simply does not make sense in the assessment of adolescents (or worse, children).

Further, the assessment of risk is derived through a process that is itself narrow. The actuarial instrument is completed, and its statistically powerful and static description of risk is derived absent of any comprehensive process or awareness of the individual. Even in the case of adolescent actuarial assessment, there is no need to ever meet the adolescent as the

---

5. Described in Chapters 12, 13 and 14.

6. That is, risk level is strictly derived from the total numerical score, absent of clinical judgment.

7. The assessment of risk derived from a static actuarial assessment is unchanging regardless of the passage of time; the same static data will always yield the same level of risk, despite any dynamic changes.

JSORRAT can (and should) be completed entirely from a record review. Even a brief description of actuarial assessment, including the JSORRAT, makes clear the difference between a narrow process of risk assessment and the stark description of risk it yields independent of the individual being assessed and the broader and more comprehensive process that is required to complete a clinical risk assessment.

However, even if it is enough to assess risk by narrow means and in a narrow manner, detached from context and circumstances, as Harris and Rice (2007) write, "knowing the probability of something is only the first part of making a competent decision," in which decision making involves a policy or method of practice. In the simplest of terms, they recognize the narrow assessment of risk yielded by the narrow process of actuarial assessment as merely the most effective basis for a proficient decision policy, which itself "requires many pieces of data" (p. 1653). This idea, that many pieces of data are required, provides the basis for the comprehensive assessment of risk in which risk is both part of the larger evaluation and the product of that larger assessment.

THE COMPREHENSIVE ASSESSMENT OF RISK

In a comprehensive assessment, the assessment of risk is both a statement of assessed risk that emerges from the use of a risk assessment instrument (as it is in the more narrow variety of risk assessment) and the result of a broad process in which risk emerges as a characteristic of the individual being assessed in the context of the myriad of forces at work upon him or her. To this end, Prentky and Burgess (2000) have written that sexual offender treatment "cannot, or at least should not, proceed without the benefit of an informed, comprehensive sex offender specific assessment" (p. 97), which, they write, will include a series of assessments subsumed within the larger assessment and may include both observational and statistical assessments.

Similarly, Hanson (1997, 2000) notes that although actuarial assessment instruments are effective screening measures they have limited overall utility, and does not recommend their use in isolation. Alone, a narrow assessment (actuarial or otherwise) cannot be used to select treatment targets, measure change, evaluate treatment benefit, or predict when or under what circumstances sexual offenders are likely to recidivate (Hanson & Thornton, 2000), whereas a multistep assessment of risk takes into account "the complexity of the real situations in which risk assessments take place" (Hanson & Thornton, 1999, p. 17). Similarly, Hudson and Ward (2001) write that risk assessment should reflect the development and etiology of the sexually abusive behavior, at least with respect to its immediate and direct antecedents and causes. Hence, in describing comprehensive assessment, it is perhaps more relevant to say that in addition to ascribing a risk level it is also how risk comes to be understood that has meaning, as well as the context within which risk is embedded.

Unless we wish to adopt a unidimensional and categorical view of individuals in which they are simply assigned to one category or another, we recognize that in the real world people are more complex, as well as being multidimensional. This is precisely why it is so difficult to create typologies by which human behavior can be easily or exhaustively categorized, including sexually abusive behavior. In the world in which people actually live, they carry within themselves complexities and engage in complex interactions with their environments that make it difficult to easily predict behavior, and especially in those who are in the process of developmental change at every level. Hence, Hannah-Moffat and Maurutto (2003) note that even risk instruments that demonstrate predictive validity cannot identify with certainty whether individuals will actually reoffend, but rather those individuals who are more likely to reoffend than others. This process of assessing probability involves assessing both the history of each individual and a comparison of that individual against risk factors that suggest susceptibility for reoffense.

Comprehensive risk assessment simply means that the use of a risk assessment instrument, even if it provides the basis for the formal assessment of a risk level, is built into and is itself but a slice of a larger assessment process. In this context, the assessment process seeks as much breadth and depth as possible in providing the data that inform the evaluation risk and add meaning to the assessment of risk in the life of each individual under assessment. Whereas it is possible and perhaps even desirable to complete an actuarial assessment from file review only, it is impossible to complete the ERASOR, J-SOAP, or J-RAT from a review of records or even from direct interviews with the juvenile alone, absent of access to many sources of information. These clinical instruments explore multiple aspects of the juvenile's life and require multiple sources from which to gather the necessary information, and they are thus designed to both stimulate and be part of a comprehensive assessment.

Almost a decade ago the American Academy of Child and Adolescent Psychiatry (1999) published practice parameters for the assessment of sexually abusive children and adolescents, noting that the assessment of juvenile sexual abusers requires the same comprehensive evaluation as other children and adolescents. As we consider the assessment of sexual risk with juvenile sexual offenders, then, it appears clear that our best and perhaps *only* real recourse is to ensure that assessed risk is the product of a broad and comprehensive assessment of the child or adolescent, and not the outcome of a narrow window that views merely one, often static, element in the life of the juvenile.

THE EXPANSION OF EMPIRICALLY BASED EVALUATION TO COMPREHENSIVE ASSESSMENT

One of the key differences between actuarial assessment and clinical assessment lies in how individuals are evaluated for risk. Actuarial assessments statistically compare the individual to a pool of sexual offender recidivists in which there is both a known base rate of sexual recidivism in that pool and a high enough rate of recidivism so that the comparison is statistically meaningful. Hence characteristics of the individual sexual offender (that is, the static risk factors that constitute the assessment) are compared against the same characteristics in the pool of recidivists, and the level of assessed risk is derived from the statistical similarity. However, in clinical assessment the evaluation of the individual is based on that individual's behavior and the circumstances in his or her life, measured against a series of risk factors believed relevant to sexually abusive behavior. The greater the match between that individual's behaviors and life circumstances and the risk factors assumed relevant to risk for sexual reoffense, the greater the possibility of sexual reoffense. In this respect, the key difference lies in the evaluation of the individual as a person in the context of his or her actual life, rather than as a member of a statistical class.

The assessment of psychopathy in adults and adolescents offers an example of both the clinical assessment process and the process of comprehensive clinical assessment. The Hare Psychopathy Checklist (PCL) is an empirically derived clinical assessment instrument; the factors drawn upon in order to assess and identify psychopathy have been statistically derived, but a determination of psychopathy itself is made clinically. That is, even though the risk factors and structure of the instrument have been empirically developed, the diagnosis of psychopathy is based upon the judgment of the evaluator. Nevertheless, it's possible to complete the Hare PCL without ever meeting the subject, although this is not recommended by the instrument manual. That is, the PCL can be completed entirely from a record review in which case the judgment of the evaluator is based upon evaluating the quality of the information presented in the written record. However, when the component of an interview or multiple interviews is added the assessment becomes richer in its clinical underpinning and process. In either case, whether based on record review alone or record review plus interview, completion of the PCL and determining the presence of psychopathy is a clinical process.

If the evaluator moves beyond file review (as recommended by the PCL manual) *and* subject interviews, and additionally interviews other collateral sources, we'd see the clinical process expanding outwards and becoming more complex, specifically in order to better understand the individual who is being evaluated, to better understand how the individual is experienced by and interacts with others, and to better interpret the nature of data available about that individual. If the evaluator goes still further, going beyond interviewing collateral informants and also delving into his or her background and psychosocial functioning, the evaluation becomes increasingly broader and provides more depth and detail upon which to understand the subject and base an evaluation of psychopathy. And if, in addition, the evaluator applies other testing in order to get a still better sense of psychological functioning, then the evaluation becomes still broader. This process of increasing levels of data collection and data inclusion is simply illustrated in Figure 11.1, in which more basic processes are nested within the larger and more comprehensive assessment.

Hopefully, it has become clear already that we can move from a very narrow assessment based on file review to an increasingly broad clinical assessment that becomes more and more comprehensive until, by embracing all the elements noted, it becomes a truly comprehensive

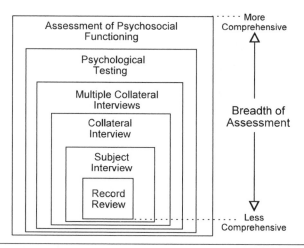

Figure 11.1   The expansion of the assessment process from a basic assessment to a more in-depth, inclusive, and comprehensive process.

psychosocial assessment with both breadth and depth, in part based on psychosocial history and in part, if we include such testing, psychometric evaluation. Given the weight of the psychopathic label, it seems important to not only have evaluators who are well trained in the concept and the evaluation of psychopathy, but also who base their ultimate diagnosis on as broad a range of details, facts, assessments, and impressions as possible. This, then, is the comprehensive clinical assessment in a nutshell. And, in the case of the PCL, we can clearly see how it is possible for an empirically derived instrument to serve as the foundation for either an actuarial or clinical assessment, and upon which comprehensive assessment may be built. In fact, because the PCL-Youth Version is a clinical tool, Forth, Kosson, and Hare (2003) recommend that whenever possible the scores of two independent raters be used and later consolidated. Further, they recommend that evaluators be familiar with the general clinical and research literature that pertains to psychopathy in adults and adolescents and that they not complete the instrument without access to collateral information. The PCL-YV manual recommends a two-hour interview that may be spread over several sessions and the use of a semistructured interview format.

In describing the skills of the clinical evaluator, Morrison (1995) writes that subjects can be viewed in "an astonishing variety of ways," and that all clinicians must be able to view each individual from interactive dynamic, behavioral, social, and biological perspectives. He notes that it is only through comprehensive assessment that these multiple perspectives can be introduced and folded into the assessment outcome and treatment plan, if one follows.

THE GOAL OF THE COMPREHENSIVE PSYCHOSOCIAL ASSESSMENT

Epps (1997) describes the target of juvenile risk assessment as the synthesis of psychosocial, statistical, factual, and environmental information, thus allowing defensible clinical decisions to be made about matters of management, treatment, and placement. Describing the elements of this process, Will (1999) describes three broad purposes of sexual offender evaluation as the assessment of risk (the likelihood of ongoing dangerous behavior), the development of a clinical formulation upon which treatment can be based and developed, and assessment of the juvenile's motivation to accept and engage in treatment. Also adopting a more global view of juvenile risk assessment, Graham, Richardson, and Bhate (1997) describe six overarching and interactive goals: (1) identifying troubled patterns of thoughts, feelings, and behavior, (2) recognizing and understanding learned experiences and processes contributing to the development and maintenance of juvenile sexually abusive behavior, (3) identifying situational contexts and correlates of sexually abusive behavior, (4) evaluating the probability of sexual recidivism, (5) assessing the juvenile's motivation to engage in treatment aimed at emotional and behavioral regulation, and (6) gathering the information required to develop interventions and treatment.

Each of these authors adopts a definition of risk assessment that implicitly recognizes that the goals of a comprehensive risk assessment process extend beyond the concrete assessment of risk per se (that is low, moderate, or high). In each case, the formal assessment of risk (that is, the application of a risk assessment instrument) is but one part of a larger process of assessment and embedded within that larger process. There's clearly a purpose, then, to the larger and more complete assessment and that is to understand as fully and deeply as possible the subject of the evaluation to the degree that we can make reasonable inferences about how he or she came to be, how he or she functions in his or her life now, and how, if things remain unchanged, he or she may function in the future and, indeed, what interventions might be provided if current or future functioning are considered to be problematic. Indeed, without applying such a model it is difficult to imagine how we can apply the risk, need, and responsivity model that itself recognizes the need to gather a wide variety of information about the individual being assessed.

In this vein, Prentky and Burgess (2000) write that treatment for sexually abusive youth should not (indeed, cannot) proceed absent of an informed and comprehensive assessment; Prentky, the primary author of the Juvenile Sex Offender Assessment Protocol, notes that decisions about risk for reoffense should not be based exclusively on the results of the J-SOAP-II, which "should always be used as part of a comprehensive risk assessment" (Prentky & Righthand, 2003, p.1). Recommendations for the comprehensive assessment of sexually abusive youth are not new. The 1993 report of the National Task Force on Juvenile Sexual Offending highlighted the need for comprehensive assessment, including record review and multiple interviews with all relevant informants, and, as noted, in 1999 the American Academy of Child and Adolescent Psychiatry wrote that the assessment of juvenile sexual abusers requires the same comprehensive evaluation as other children and adolescents. Similarly, the Office for Juvenile Justice and Delinquency Prevention (Righthand & Welch, 2001) noted that comprehensive clinical assessment of juvenile sexual offenders is required both in order to assess risk and facilitate treatment, emphasizing that any attempt to explain or treat juvenile sexual offenders must be based on the specific factors pertinent to that juvenile's offenses and individual psychology.

Even with adult sexual offenders, comprehensive assessment serves a critical role, providing important information that cannot be discovered or examined through limited static actuarial assessments, which, although effective as screening measures, have limited utility and are not recommended for use in isolation (Hanson, 1997, 2000). Hanson and Thornton (2000) note that actuarial assessments cannot be used to select treatment targets, measure change, evaluate treatment benefit, or predict when or under what circumstances sexual offenders are likely to recidivate, and they write (1999) that a multistep risk assessment process takes into account "the complexity of the real situations in which risk assessments take place" (p. 17). Similarly, Hudson and Ward (2001) write that assessment should reflect the development history of sexually abusive behavior, and not simply risk alone.

Hence, the goal of comprehensive assessment is to explore and evaluate the risk for sexual reoffense in the context of the cognitive, emotional, social, and transactional ecological environments in which behavior develops and unfurls, reaching deeply into the individual's history, social environment, thinking, and behaviors. Comprehensive assessment reveals details about the juvenile's personal characteristics, skills, and abilities, including his or her capacity for honesty, self-disclosure, motivation, and responsibility; the youth's developmental and social history, and experience of social attachment and relatedness to others; and the social and personal circumstances out of which his or her behavior, including sexually abusive behavior, developed and continues to be prompted. The goal of comprehensive assessment is not that of exacting the truth about the sexually abusive behavior, even if this is a desirable and ideal goal; the purpose is instead to understand the youth and his or her behaviors, and the development and natural history of those behaviors, in the full context of the youth's life.

It is from this information that risk factors included in the risk assessment instrument are understood and evaluated, and it is from this data set that the evaluator learns about the individual behind the behavior. The comprehensive assessment provides the evaluator with maximum information upon which to draw with respect to risk for future sexually abusive behavior and the capacity to make informed decisions and recommendations about treatment needs and interventions.

Simplistically, then, comprehensive risk assessment is a process designed to: (1) understand the development and type of sexually abusive behavior, (2) understand the nature of risk in the life of the individual and the circumstances that allowed risk to be transformed into actual harm, (3) predict the likelihood that sexually abusive behavior will continue if untreated, and (4) make recommendations regarding treatment.

THE RELATIONSHIP OF THE RISK ASSESSMENT INSTRUMENT TO THE COMPREHENSIVE ASSESSMENT

Despite the broad goals of comprehensive assessment, if we adopt a point of view in which it is both possible and legitimate to assess risk devoid of the context in which it has developed and may continue to operate, we are able to complete the risk assessment based entirely on file material without gathering any additional material, and without considering context and circumstance. In such a model, the assessment of risk can be adequately derived from just the static risk factors that comprise the actuarial assessment instrument, without the necessity of further information, and certainly absent of clinical interpretation or judgment (which is disallowed by the actuarial process, unless the evaluator subscribes to the idea of clinical adjustment). This process represents the antithesis of comprehensive risk assessment if risk is determined solely through the application of the instrument. However, the moment that the process extends beyond the actuarial assessment of static factors, and especially if it includes consideration of dynamic factors, a clinical perspective is introduced into clinical judgment and required at some level, even to the degree of deciding what dynamic factors to include or how to interpret them.

Further, if the assessment goes beyond assessing static items, the assessment increasingly becomes more clinical and more comprehensive, depending on what sort of additional information is sought, as well as the quantity and source of additional information. In part, this is because the inclusion and assessment of dynamic factors *requires* gathering information that is possibly and likely not in the file, as well as qualitative judgments about the information gathered. The focus is thus placed on the expansion of the risk assessment process beyond the simple and stand-alone use of a structured assessment (whether actuarial or clinical), and how to best recognize and use the instrument as an element in a larger assessment. In this case, the assessment instrument is both fed by the larger and more comprehensive assessment process in terms of the information required to complete the instrument, as well as folded within the comprehensive assessment process.

If the risk assessment instrument is clinical and dynamic, as is the case for most juvenile instruments, it is necessarily fed by the comprehensive assessment because it is from the larger assessment that the data are gathered that allow the assessment of individual risk factors; this is especially true if the instrument includes questions about dynamic risk factors. Conversely, the risk assessment instrument is folded within the larger assessment because its results are best understood against the backdrop of the larger assessment and the information it reveals about the individual being assessed and the factors, forces, relationships at work and play within that individual's life, and his or her overall psychosocial functioning. In the context of comprehensive assessment, then, risk assessment is itself a process, an element within the process, and a product of the entire assessment.

In a model of dynamic clinical assessment, risk assessment, even though administered through the use of an assessment instrument, is not a separate event disconnected from a larger assessment. It is instead an integral part of a comprehensive clinical assessment that incorporates the risk assessment instrument and its assignment of risk into a larger and more in-depth evaluation of the individual that integrates large quantities of information that add depth (detail) and breadth (range) to the assessment.

THE PROCESS AND SEQUENCE OF COMPREHENSIVE RISK ASSESSMENT

I have several times described comprehensive assessment in terms of psychosocial assessment. In fact, it is the target of the assessment that makes it psychosocial, in that the goal is to evaluate and understand the psychosocial capacity and functioning of the individual or the individual's psychological and social functioning in which both forms of functioning represent facets of and influences on the other. The comprehensive assessment, on the other hand, reflects the breadth and depth of the psychosocial assessment and how deeply and how broadly the evaluation explores psychosocial functioning and capacity. A broad psychosocial assessment is thus comprehensive because it explores many areas of the individual's life and functioning, and a comprehensive evaluation is, by necessity, psychosocial as it too explores many areas of the individual's life and functioning. Comprehensive assessments are thus psychosocial in that they examine and understand the individual in the context of his or her psychological and social development, or view psychological and behavioral development and functioning within and in interaction with the social environment. Long, Higgins, and Brady (1988) describe the psychosocial assessment in terms we have already described: as the gathering of data about emotional, behavioral, mental, environmental, and interactional processes, and the goal of integrating those data with other information, some of which is factual or suspected (such as the history of sexually abusive behavior), in order to obtain as complete and as multidimensional a description and understanding of the individual as possible. The more complete term is really "comprehensive psychosocial assessment."

Thus, comprehensive assessment quite appropriately uses the perspective of psychosocial history as the means by which to recognize the development of psychosocial functioning, both historically and in the present. Its inclusion of sexual development and behavior, including troubled sexual behavior, creates a form of psychosocial assessment that is sometimes known as "psychosexual" assessment. By further focusing the assessment on the possibility of continued sexually abusive behavior, the comprehensive assessment seeks to understand risk and project its trajectory by understanding the individual from a holistic developmental perspective, and thus becomes an instrument for comprehensive risk assessment. However, whereas *psychosocial* assessment starts in the present and peers back in time in order to understand the development of psychosocial functioning, *risk* assessment gazes into the future by projecting the trajectory of past and current trends if otherwise uninterrupted. Thus, psychosocial evaluation both offers a theory of etiology and is diagnostic, whereas risk assessment is prognostic and offers best-guess estimates of outcome based on present conditions.

However, Long et al. (1988) describe psychosocial assessment as much more than a series of questions used to collect information. They also describe it as a *process* by which the evaluator comes to understand the individual through the multiple domains in which he or she has developed and currently lives; thus, understanding the individual's psychosocial functioning "requires multiple observations of the client and his or her life for it to be as complete as possible" (p. xiii). Regardless of how we conceptualize and operationalize it, then, comprehensive assessment involves a series of steps, from questioning and information collection to case formulation and prognosis. These steps necessarily involve a sequence of activities that both describe and structure the entire process, as shown in Figure 11.2.

The obvious first step of data gathering is followed by the organization of that information so that it can be analyzed and interpreted in order to yield meaning. This spans a sequence of three steps, or phases, in the process: data collection, data structuring, and data analysis. Hence, once collected, information is subsequently consolidated and synthesized so that it is both manageable and concrete enough to provide a means for analysis and interpretation. This represents the purposeful, organized, and logical collection of data, followed by the assignment of meaning to those data in which diagnosis can be made only after sufficient data have been collected (Long et al., 1988). Information has thus been transformed, if you will, from raw data to a more refined and smoothed data set through which developmental history and the interconnection of life domains is recognized and an understanding of the individual can be derived in the

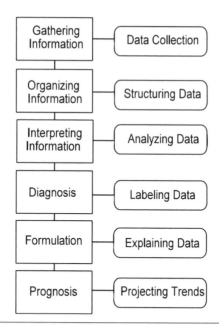

Figure 11.2   Sequential steps in the assessment process.

context of his or her life. This allows for the further refinement of information about the individual into diagnoses, or essentially the shorthand description of conditions best reflected by the difficulties in psychosocial functioning.

In turn, as information is further refined and synthesized, case formulation provides a more concise summary and overview, offering a conceptualization and understanding of the case. Formulation, in effect, provides a clinical theory about the development of the individual, an explanation for past and current psychosocial functioning, and the basis for prediction of future behavior if things remain unchanged and current trajectory persists, thus flowing seamlessly into prognosis and from which recommendations for interventions can be made. There is, to a great degree, a funneling and synthesis of information from the first step to the last, as shown in Figure 11.3, which also offers an overview of the tasks associated with each step in the assessment process.

ELEMENTS AND TOOLS OF COMPREHENSIVE ASSESSMENT

Clearly, then, the assessment process involves much more than asking questions, and it is thus a mistake to imagine that completing the step of data collection completes or represents the assessment. Nevertheless, the

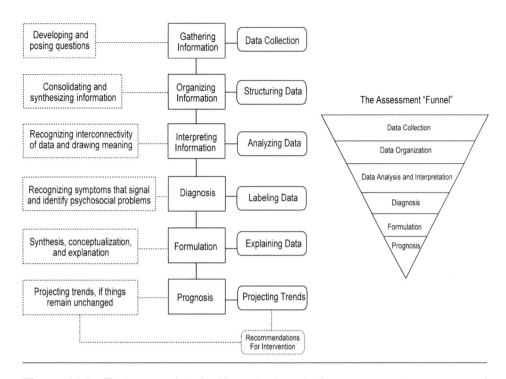

Figure 11.3 Tasks associated with each steps in the assessment process, and the "funneling" of the assessment process.

first step is data collection, and this means having questions that must be answered and, of more importance, knowing which questions to ask. This can be facilitated by a formal or semiformal process in which questions to be asked are framed or actually defined by a format of some kind, such as an interview schedule, which offers predetermined questions as well as a sequence by which questions are to be asked.

Instruments such as the Structured Clinical Interview for *DSM* Disorders and the Children's Interview for Psychiatric Syndromes are examples of structured interviews used to help form a diagnosis. In the case of risk assessment, the risk assessment instrument itself provides the basis and structure for questions to be asked that are specific to the assignment of risk. However, in both cases these instruments serve to focus on only part of the comprehensive assessment (i.e., diagnosis of risk level). They do not address the larger questions posed by the comprehensive assessment, such as developmental history, family functioning, social relationships and interactions, and so on, although there are any number of tools and instruments that can be used to address each element of a comprehensive assessment, or a question guide can be developed to help the evaluator know what questions to ask. The content of and format for comprehensive assessment is described in more detail in Chapters 15 and 19, and examples of questionnaire guides are provided in the Appendix. Nevertheless, the goal here is not to define the questions to be asked or format for a psychosocial assessment. It is, instead, to describe the process itself and create in the reader an understanding such that it is unnecessary to define for the evaluator what questions to ask or how to ask them. This book is intended to be informative, but not *prescriptive*. That is, the goal is not to *tell* evaluators how to evaluate but help them to understand the process in detail and through training, supervision, and experience best define the methods, means, and approaches to assessment for themselves.

Regardless of approach and content, however, it is clear that comprehensive assessment is neither limited to the type of material gathered, nor to a single means for gathering or analyzing data. It must not only recognize and understand the development of emotion, cognition, and behavior in the individual, but also the multiple domains in which emotional, cognitive development occurs at the individual, family, and social level. In so doing, the comprehensive assessment will call upon different sources of information, from the juvenile to his or her family and other informants, prior written records, and current formal evaluations of various forms of social adjustment, psychological functioning, behavioral self-regulation, and cognitive processes and capacities, and it must take into account information that ranges from facts to impressions. The comprehensive assessment thus must not only approach different sources of information, but must also utilize different means for gathering such information. Accordingly, a comprehensive assessment of risk will minimally include record review, direct clinical interviews, and the use of a structured risk assessment instrument as primary methods for gathering and exploring information, but it may also include many assessment tools and measures that extend the reach of the assessment.

Figure 11.4 provides an overview of the possible elements of comprehensive assessment grouped into the general subcategories of psychosocial assessment, psychological evaluation, risk assessment, physiological measurement, and psychiatric evaluation, each of which act as feeders to the overarching comprehensive assessment. As noted, the use of a formal risk assessment instrument represents only one aspect of this larger assessment.

Although in the brief description that follows, I depict psychosocial assessment as an aspect or component of the overall assessment separate from other components, this is merely to break the process of assessment

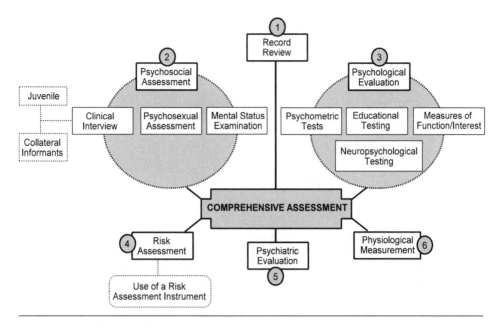

Figure 11.4 Elements that may be found within the larger comprehensive assessment, in which the use of a risk assessment instrument represents just one aspect of the overall assessment process.

into parts and allow us to review individual elements. In action, the entire assessment is actually psychosocial given its purpose of understanding the individual in terms of his or her psychological and social history, development, functioning, and capacities. Each of the components identified below, then, can be considered to be aspects of and folded into the larger, and comprehensive, psychosocial assessment, even though they can, in other cases, be used as stand-alone assessment measures, intended for purposes other than comprehensive psychosocial assessment.

1. *Record Review* is that component of assessment that involves gathering and carefully reviewing all records pertinent to the case, from police, court, and social service records that address sexually abusive behavior to prior evaluation, treatment, social service, educational, and medical records that describe the individual and his or her history, including early developmental history.
2. *Psychosocial Assessment* represents the gathering of information about the developmental, psychological, and social history of individuals (often known as the psychosocial history), with the emphasis on

gathering information about and understanding the individual in the context of his or her life. Psychosocial assessment includes at least three elements:

- *The clinical interview*, which involves the process of meeting face-to-face with the juvenile and in person or by phone with other individuals who will serve as informants to the assessment. The specific purpose of the interview involves gathering information about events that occurred, the juvenile being assessed, the juvenile's history, and sometimes about the person providing information (such as a parent). In conducting the clinical interview, the evaluator is able to make assessments about the quality and meaning of that information and the source of the information.
- *Psychosexual assessment* involves the specific part of the assessment focused on exploring and understanding the development of sexual knowledge, sexual interests, and sexual behaviors.
- *Mental status examination*, which is most typically a brief and basic screening assessment used to evaluate the general mental clarity and condition of an individual at the time of the assessment.

3. *Psychological Evaluation* is a general term that includes standardized methods and measurements of psychological states and traits, including feelings and thoughts, attitudes and values, behaviors, intellectual functioning, and cognitive and thought processes.

- *Psychometric tests* include psychological, neuropsychological, and educational tests that are based on statistical concepts and quantitative measures that allow meaningful comparison between the individual tested and other individuals in the general or specific population, and allow comparison among psychological test measures (not all evaluations are psychometric in nature).
- *Educational testing* measures academic achievement, the acquisition of information, and cognitive states and intellectual functioning, as well as other measures related to learning, cognitive processing, and retention of learned information.
- *Neuropsychological tests* examine and screen for the possibility of neurological problems that may have an impact on psychological (cognitive, emotional, and/or behavioral) functioning.
- *Measures of function and interest* are typically non-psychometric questionnaires and scales that identify and measure interests, attitudes, functioning, and so forth.

4. *Risk Assessment* is intended to predict future dangerous behavior or related conditions if the current condition goes untreated, and as

noted should be based on the application of a structured and well-defined assessment instrument.

5. *Psychiatric Evaluation* is conducted by a psychiatrist, and often focuses on, but is not limited to, assessment of disturbances in emotions, behaviors, or thinking that may be helped through the prescription of psychiatric medication, but also may include a wide-ranging psycho-social assessment that follows a medical perspective.

6. *Physiological Measures* involve attempts to measure honesty, sexual arousal, sexual interests, and other psychological conditions through physical correlates such as changes in blood pressure, galvanic skin response, respiration, physical (including visual) reaction time to stimuli, and changes in penile tumescence. These measures most typically involve either polygraph examination (also known as psy-chophysiological detection of deception, or PDD) that attempts to measure honesty and detect evidence of deceit; the use of the ple-thysmograph to detect sexual arousal through penile erection (also known as phallometric assessment); and the use of visual reaction tests that assess sexual interest based on how long the subject views images that have sexual content.[8]

The fact that any and all of these measures and sources of information may be included in a comprehensive assessment of risk does not mean that they will all be included. In fact, it's unlikely for any number of reasons that all possible sources of information will or should be included, including availability, cost, time restraints, and, in some cases, intrusiveness (with special reference to physiological measures). The purpose here is simply to describe the range of informational sources and methods that together contribute to comprehensive assessment. It is, of course, possible, feasible, and commonplace to engage in comprehensive assessment without the full inclusion of all sources. Furthermore, it's possible to complete an assessment without having all of the relevant information or "true" facts, and there is always a point at which the data collection process must end and the assessment be completed, with or without all of the pertinent information. However, the primary focus must be on ensuring that meaning, diagnosis, formulation, and prognosis is based upon the acquisition of data that are both sufficient and accurate. As Long et al. (1988) note, we must "guard against assignment of meaning or conclusions based upon insufficient [and I would add, inaccurate] evidence" (p. 9).

---

8. Physiological measures are described in a little more detail in Chapter 16.

FOCUSING COMPREHENSIVE ASSESSMENT ON RISK

As described, comprehensive assessment can expand outwards to include many sources and types of information. However, regardless of its breadth or depth, comprehensive assessment must, at a minimum, review and explore broad details of the juvenile's life gathered through record review, direct interviews with the juvenile and other important informants in his or her life, and perhaps other sources of information, as well as a formal risk assessment instrument.

Above all, however, we must keep in mind that, although comprehensive, the heart and purpose of the evaluation rests in the assessment of risk. That is, regardless of approach, methods and sources of data collection, or the breadth and depth of the evaluation, a comprehensive risk assessment must ultimately identify and understand those risk factors that were present at the time of the sexually abusive behavior and those that continue to serve as indicators of current risk and the possibility of future sexually abusive behavior. Although to a great degree many of these broad indicators of risk, illustrated in Figure 11.5, are built into formal risk assessment instruments, they also help to orient the comprehensive assessment towards those risk factors that have become intertwined with the developmental and social experiences of sexually troubled children and adolescents. Focusing assessment on the presence of risk factors and thinking of these as indicators of current and future risk helps us to understand their role in shaping the development of sexually abusive behavior and, as we consider case formulation and explanation, their influence as causative agents, at least in part.

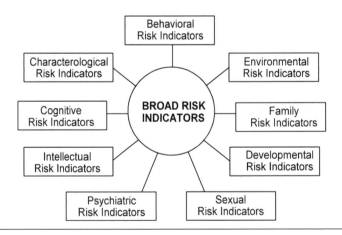

Figure 11.5   The constellation of risk indicators.

- *Characterological risk indicators* are those already, or becoming, incorporated into the juvenile's personality.
- *Behavioral risk indicators* are reflected in the juvenile's general behavior, and with particular regard to antisocial behaviors and attitudes and relationships that go hand in hand with such behavior.
- *Cognitive risk indicators* reflect ideas, attitudes, beliefs, and other patterns of thinking that influence and shape the juvenile's behavior and capacity and motivation to engage in sexually abusive behavior.
- *Developmental risk indicators* contributed to and shaped problematic aspects of personality development, patterns of behavior, and responses to stimuli.
- *Sexual risk indicators* include sexual experiences and interests that contribute to engagement in sexually troubled and/or abusive behavior.
- *Psychiatric (or comorbid) risk indicators* involve co-occurring mental health disorders that may both drive troubled behavior and also hinder the ability to participate in, or benefit from, sex offender specific treatment.
- *Intellectual risk indicators* reflect cognitive deficits and intellectual disabilities that interfere with the development of social understanding, executive functioning skills, self-regulation, moral development, and insight and judgment.
- *Family risk indicators* include those conditions within the family structure that have helped define and shape the juvenile's behavior and may continue to serve as risk factors.
- *Environmental risk indicators* include those that lie outside of the juvenile and reside in his or her larger social world, but which affect and influence thinking and behavior.

CONCLUSION: COMPREHENSIVE ASSESSMENT AND THE EVALUATION OF RISK

Thomas and Viar (2001) described the major goal of assessment as developing the most complete understanding of the circumstances surrounding the problem, and Welldon (1997) noted the requirement for a broad understanding of all factors concerning the individual, including psychological development, family history, and life circumstances. Others, too, have described multiple goals and purposes for the assessment (Graham et al., 1997; Houston, 1998; Perry & Orchard, 1992; Will, 1999). However, the essential functions of the comprehensive assessment are those of data collection, analysis, and synthesis, thus allowing it to serve as the keystone upon which insight into the case may be developed and decisions rendered regarding treatment and intervention. Minimally, then, the comprehensive assessment provides a means by which to:

1. Explore and understand the nature, development, and trajectory of sexually abusive behavior, as well as targets of sexual interest, sources of sexual arousal, and patterns of sexual behavior.
2. Estimate the risk for continued sexually abusive behavior, including the presence and influence of factors that may increase or decrease the chances for reoffense.
3. Recognize the presence and influence of historical and current environmental, social, and personal factors in the juvenile's life, including learned social experiences that have influenced and shaped his or her thinking and behavior.
4. Assess motivation and capacity for treatment.
5. Build a formulation and understanding of the case from which to develop and launch interventions for management and treatment.

In meeting these goals, in addition to establishing a sound and well-described basis for risk assessment, the evaluation also meets the goals of the risk, need, and responsivity model. It provides an estimate of risk for recidivism based on static and dynamic factors, establishes an understanding of the dynamic and current treatment needs of the juvenile,[9] and assesses the likely responsiveness and engagement of the juvenile to and with treatment interventions. Further, the process of comprehensive assessment avoids the piecemeal approach to understanding the individual described by Long et al. (1988), and it allows the evaluator to view the juvenile as a whole person functioning in a complex ecological environment whose behavior is the result of a complex set of psychosocial interactions.

Nevertheless, conducting a broad assessment is a complex and complicated task. Although we can structure and define an approach to such assessment, as well as the focus and contents of the evaluation, only the evaluator can render meaning from the data. We should thus remain aware that psychological evaluations, risk assessment instruments, inventories, and questionnaires of every sort are passive instruments that can yield information but not meaning. Indeed, Prentky and Burgess (2000) have noted that risk assessment studies have generally found that psychometric

---

9. Or the "criminogenic" needs, as defined by the RNR model.

evaluations are not particularly useful in predicting sexual recidivism. Structured tools, then, provide a means for organizing, examining, and piecing together complex and multifaceted pieces of information, but only the clinician can recognize the patterns, connections, and circumstances that lend themselves to an understanding of the case. In the final analysis, assessment implies not simply gathering information, but the development of insight and understanding in the clinician. This requires a process that allows the evaluator to gather, organize, and integrate sufficient information in a manner that allows the pieces to fit together to reveal meaning and provide explanation.

In the assessment of sexually abusive youth, comprehensive assessment and the evaluation of risk are intertwined. The broader assessment fuels and directs the process of risk assessment, and the risk assessment instrument offers structure, method, and purpose to the larger evaluation. However, it is only by blending the two processes into one that we can arrive at the most meaningful assessment of risk. That is, the assessment of risk in children and adolescents can be most meaningfully and sensitively made by recognizing and understanding the psychosocial history of the individual, guided by an examination and understanding of risk factors that contribute and point to further sexually abusive behavior.

CHAPTER 12

Projecting Risk: Tools for Risk Assessment

B EFORE FURTHER DESCRIBING and discussing the larger assessment process, we return to the formal risk assessment instrument, its construction, and use. As you are aware, these instruments are designed specifically to address and assess risk for sexual reoffense, and for the most part are either actuarial or clinical in their construction and theory. Both types of assessment instruments have already been discussed extensively in previous chapters, but prior to describing those instruments in use or development for the assessment of sexually abusive youth it's useful to provide an overview of these two types of instruments, as well as their underlying construction and theory.

Part of the reason for this further explanation is that evaluators should know their tools; unlike the qualified use of psychometric testing, which usually requires advanced graduate training, risk assessment instruments may be used by anyone. Hence, they may be used by individuals who have little understanding of the principles behind their design, and they may be administered without a clear understanding of their inherent weaknesses, the differences between instruments, and the need to embed the instrument within a larger, more comprehensive assessment process. In particular, the goal of utilizing a risk instrument as one element within a larger assessment, as described in Chapter 11, highlights the need to view the results of risk assessment from a larger perspective. Nowhere is this clearer than in the use of a *clinical* risk assessment instrument, which intends only to shape and guide clinical judgment and not make the assignment of risk for the evaluator.

Although the actuarial assessment defines the assigned risk level, which it does through the numerical scoring of risk factors, the clinical assessment merely points towards approximate risk and does so without the statistical certainty implied or claimed by the actuarial assessment. Consequently, where the actuarial assessment can be rightly considered an instrument built on firm psychometric principles and a statistical base rate against which to compare the individuals it assesses, the clinical assessment instrument can at best be considered a guide for making informed decisions about risk for recidivism. To this degree, the clinical tool serves as an organized checklist formed from the professional literature and shaped by theory by which the clinical evaluator may reasonably make predictions of risk. Clinical assessment instruments thus represent an assessment method "rather than a test or scale" (Boer et al., 1997, p. 25).

The need to carefully understand how risk assessment instruments are constructed and work is central to professional practice, and of special importance in the use of clinical tools, as these can serve only as organized and structured guides. However, it is equally true that in the use of actuarial assessment the evaluator must be aware of the limitations of an assessment process built essentially on static history, and perhaps especially so in the developmental and developing world of the sexually troubled child and sexually abusive adolescent.

In this chapter, we explore and outline the principles behind instruments that define, guide, and add both consistency (reliability) and empirical relevance (validity) to the clinical assessment of risk in the juvenile sexual offender.

TWO CAMPS: ACTUARIAL AND CLINICAL ASSESSMENT

Despite the fact that we can most easily define risk assessment instruments as either actuarial or clinical, the field of risk assessment is changing, moving perhaps towards the center. On the one hand, in the Juvenile Sexual Offense Recidivism Risk Assessment Tool (JSORRAT-II-II) we now have the first actuarial assessment for adolescent male sexual offenders, thus allowing the evaluation of sexually abusive youth to include an actuarial component if we so choose, albeit under limited conditions at this time.[1]

On the other hand, with respect to adult assessment for sexual recidivism, we have seen already (Chapter 3) that the field is moving toward greater use of multistep assessments that build upon actuarial assessment

---

1. As described in Chapter 4, and again later in the current chapter, at the time of this writing the JSORRAT is normed only for use in Utah (with Idaho pending), and is for use only with adolescent boys who have been adjudicated (convicted) on sexual charges.

to include second- and even third-step clinical evaluations of dynamic risk factors. This has led to the development of third and fourth generation adult assessment instruments and processes that extend assessment beyond static actuarial assessment (Andrews, Bonta, & Wormith, 2006; Bonta & Andrews, 2007; Hannah-Moffat & Maurutto, 2003), built in part on the premise that static factors not only have limited and passive value, but, when used in isolation, may be counterproductive (Boer at al., 1997; Bonta, 2002).

Thus, with the likely capacity to include actuarial assessment in otherwise clinical evaluations of juvenile sexual offenders and the inclusion of the clinical process of including and assessing dynamic factors into the evaluation of risk in adult sexual offenders, we see the field moving toward the center. This represents a position in which actuarial and clinical processes are not seen as mutually exclusive or incompatible but may be blended, not only into a multilayered assessment of risk itself, but into a larger and more comprehensive assessment as described in Chapter 11 and again in Chapter 15. Hence, even advocates of clinical assessment, such as Thomas Litwack (2001), write that good clinical practice should include the results of actuarial assessments when available, and Robert Prentky, who has long strived towards the development of actuarial assessment instruments for adolescents, writes that treatment of sexually abusive youth should not proceed without the completion of a comprehensive assessment that includes both clinical and actuarial assessment, describing clinical work as a critical component of all assessments (Prentky & Burgess, 2000).

Nevertheless, despite a move towards the center and the development of more comprehensive assessment processes, two distinct camps remain in which the clinical vs. actuarial prediction debate is described by Douglas, Cox, and Webster (1999) as one of the "persisting controversies in the risk assessment field" (p. 154). In the actuarial camp, writers such as Quinsey, Harris, Rice, and Cormier (2006) continue to advocate for a strictly actuarial approach. In the most recent edition of their book, they support the complete elimination of clinical practice in forensic risk assessment, writing "what we are advising is not the addition of actuarial methods to existing practice, but rather the replacement of existing practice with actuarial methods" (p. 197).

Harris and Rice (2007) describe the idea of blending actuarial and clinical assessment as an illogicality, asserting that forensic decision makers must inevitably choose between the two methods, and that "empiricism should replace clinical judgment wherever possible" (pp. 1652–1653). However, not all actuarial specialists share this view, a position characterized by Sjöstedt and Grann (2002) as "extreme," and who describe "the implications of the pure actuarial stand taken by Quinsey et al. (as) extremely problematic" (p. 182). For instance, Monahan et al. (2001) describe their belief that actuarial instruments should be used as tools for clinical assessment, used to "support, rather than replace, the exercise of clinical judgment" (p. 134).

Squarely in the clinical camp, Litwack (2001) argues that actuarial assessments of risk have not been proven superior to clinical assessment and that the picture emerging from research is complex with little empirical support for the greater effectiveness of actuarial assessment of risk. He concludes that "it is premature to substitute actuarial for clinical assessments of dangerousness" (p. 410), and in advocating for the use of clinical assessment Boer et al. (1997) write that actuarial assessment instruments are passive tools that disengage professionals from the evaluation process because, by design, they require minimal professional intervention and judgment.

Nevertheless, in their metaanalysis of 67 studies, stretching back over a 56-year period, that compared clinical and actuarial methods of assessment, Ægisdóttir et al. (2006) concluded that, in general, methods for statistical prediction were 13 percent more accurate than clinical methods, and that virtually all statistical types did better than clinical types. Even in exceptional cases, clinical methods were able to only draw with statistical methods and in no cases did better.

In fact, the debate about the better, more accurate, or more rational method for predicting risk has been continuous since the early 1940s. Although these arguments were aimed at prognosis in general rather than the prediction of risk, as early as 1941 Stouffer was describing and favoring the attributes of the clinical approach to assessment (the "case study" approach) compared to statistical techniques in which information about the individual is lost to the statistical procedure. Alternatively, Lundberg (1941) was arguing that in making clinical predictions evaluators were actually drawing on the same essential material employed by the statistician, albeit in a cruder and more intuitive fashion, and that we should thus use clinical assessment only when more refined and formal statistical procedures do not exist. Similarly, Sarbin (1943, 1944) was defending the actuarial position over the then more popular clinical method for prediction. He refuted the then relatively common claim that "the clinical or individual method of predicting behavior is superior to the actuarial or statistical method" (1943, p. 593), asserting that clinical methods for predication were not more accurate, and argued that clinical methods should neither be substituted for nor do they add anything to actuarial prediction. He declared that on the basis of efficiency and economy, actuarial assessment was the preferred method over the intuitive method of clinical prediction (1944, p. 226).

In 1954, Paul Meehl asserted that prediction made by statistical assessment needed no further clinical judgment or inference, in which the prediction itself could be made by a clerical worker. Like Lundberg and Sarbin, Meehl considered clinical prediction to be actually based upon empirically known factors, including estimated or expected frequencies among a similar population. That is, clinicians form opinions and render decisions about individuals based on their experience of other individuals who have engaged in similar behaviors or exhibit similar symptoms; they thus compare the current individual against professionally or empirically known factors and the expected base rate among a similar population, and make decisions built upon this information. In this regard, Meehl asserted that clinicians, in effect, already act as naive actuaries and creating and using an actuarial table is an obvious advancement and more accurate version of this system.

Noting that both the clinical and actuarial method must be assessed by their success in accurately predicting risk (predictive validity), Meehl (1954) asserted that the statistical method was superior, and that with few exceptions the question of whether to "use our heads instead of the formula" should only be decided in favor of the clinical method when there is no adequate statistical method available (1957). Nonetheless, Meehl did not completely disregard the clinical method or that the predictive power of the two methods remained steady under all conditions (1956), and even argued that he did not claim that objective psychological tests necessarily predict better than clinical processes: "not only did I *not* say that psychometric tests always predict better, in fact . . . I do not believe they do" (1996, p. vi). Nevertheless, Meehl makes it quite clear that the "the mechanical method is almost invariably equal to or superior to the clinical method" (Grove & Meehl, 1996, p. 293). Built significantly on Meehl's work, as noted in Chapter 3, advocates of actuarial assessment argue that there is no true hybrid of clinical and statistical methods of prediction and the two methods are incompatible (Grove & Lloyd, 2006; Harris & Rice, 2007).

Nevertheless, Witt (2000) has written that few actuarial risk assessment instruments are truly actuarial, and Campbell (2000) observes that most actuarial risk assessment procedures eventually fall back onto clinical judgment. Grisso (2000) similarly notes that many of the present actuarial assessment instruments require some degree of clinical judgment, such as the assessment of psychopathy on the Sexual Offender Risk Assessment Guide (SORAG), a diagnosis itself derived through a clinical process, as described in Chapter 11.

ACTUARIAL OR CLINICAL: THE DEBATE CONTINUES

Although it is often stated that actuarial assessments are more accurate and more predictive than unstructured[2] clinical assessments (for instance, Ægisdóttir et al., 2006; Hanson & Thornton, 2000; Steadman et al., 2000), the debate is nonetheless far from resolved or stagnant.

Boer (2006) describes the risk prediction literature as fragmented and oppositional, in which neither the authors of actuarial or structured clinical instruments acknowledge the effectiveness of instruments in the opposing camp. In their 1999 paper, Douglas, Cox, and Webster concluded that both actuarial and clinical assessments have clearly identified different strengths, and are critical of the "gap" between the practitioners of actuarial and clinical evaluation in which neither method could be said to be intrinsically more effective than the other. Despite the contention of Grove, Zald, Lebow, Snitz, and Nelson (2000) that actuarial assessment proved to be superior to clinical assessment in 33–47 percent of the 136 studies examined in their meta analysis, they also noted that actuarial assessments were only substantially more accurate in about 10 percent of the studies, and that clinical predictions were "often as accurate as mechanical predictions" (p. 19), noting also that many of the studies included in their meta analysis were "methodologically unsound" (p. 25). However, in their review of the Grove et al. meta analysis, Hart et al. (2003) pointed out that in about 40 percent of the cases the two approaches to prediction were equal, and in about 20 percent of the cases the clinical method was more effective. They concluded that "although it is correct to conclude from this that the actuarial approach was equal or superior 80 percent of the time, it is equally correct to conclude that the clinical approach was equal or superior 60 percent of the time" (p. 11).

Further, Boer er al. (1997) assert that there are no well-validated actuarial scales of risk for sexual violence, and Melton, Petrila, Poythress, and Slobogin (1997) write that "the bottom line is that the research has not delivered an actuarial equation suitable for clinical application in the area of violence prediction" (p. 285). Similarly, Doren (2002) has written that no actuarial instrument can assess true reoffending risk because current actuarial instruments do not yet "include enough of the relevant considerations to maximize our predictive effectiveness" (p. 113). Summarizing this position, Hart et al. (2003) write that no methods currently exist for making precise estimates of future risk with any degree of certainty, and that the "superiority of actuarial

---

2. The comparison has been most often made between actuarial and *unstructured*, or unaided, clinical assessment. These are clinical assessments that are not structured or guided by a structured or assessment instrument or process, and are discussed later in this chapter.

decision-making is an article of faith. Any claim of actuarial superiority is an inference" based on questionable evidence (p. 11).

Nevertheless, in an unpublished presentation that addressed ethical issues in adult sexual offender risk assessment, Grisso (2000) expressed concern that the results of actuarial assessment instruments are given far more weight than the instruments can actually support. In his address, Grisso concluded that the process of actuarial assessment in predicting sexual offense recidivism is in its infancy, and that questions about construction, standardization, inter-rater reliability, and ambiguous base rates raise questions about the capacity of such instruments to meet legal standards for scientific evidence. Just as Hart et al. (2003) describe "pseudo-precision" in actuarial assessments, he pointed out that the base rates upon which actuarial assessments are necessarily built are not really known with respect to the various populations with whom the instruments may be applied, and highlighted other difficulties and concerns about the psychometric validity of the instruments. Illustrating this point, describing current adult actuarial risk instruments as immature in their development, Grisso noted that none have yet appeared in the catalogs of any test publisher because of their lack of robust and proven psychometric properties.

Further, Grisso (2000) commented that in some cases actuarial assessment instruments have been placed into use absent of any kind of manual to guide their standardized application, and in other cases manuals or guides that have been made available by test authors lack information on reliability, standard errors of measurement, or evidence of validity. His comments and observations are mirrored by Hart el al. (2003), who similarly note the absence of published manuals by which to ensure the correct administration, scoring, or interpretation of current actuarial assessment instruments, and assert that such tools have not yet achieved the level of psychometric rigor to meet publication standards. Further, Grisso observed that many evaluators who use the instruments are not specialized in the evaluation of sex offenders and may thus use the tools blindly, making them subject to misuse and misinterpretation. Grisso finally points to the ethical guidelines of the American Psychological Association that render it improper to presume that a score on a test of any kind means the same thing in all cases, noting that scores of any kind must be interpreted because the value of a score in any given situation is dependent on many variables.

THE FLAWS OF BOTH METHODS

Campbell (2004) argues strongly that both clinical and actuarial risk assessment instruments are significantly flawed. He argues that the "elasticity of clinical judgment allows stretching it to conform with the *a priori* expectations of an evaluator" (p. 35), and that actuarial assessments are "systematically biased in the direction of ruling-in recidivism risk" (p. 67). He further asserts that neither method stands up to rigorous scientific scrutiny, characterizing all current actuarial and clinical risk assessment processes as inadequate. Campbell asserts that all current evaluation instruments are insufficiently standardized, lack inter-rater reliability, are absent of adequate operational manuals, and generally fail to satisfy significant scientific standards. Campbell argues that current instruments are capable of maintaining scientific credibility in light of full disclosure of their limitations and create an appearance of precision that exceeds their actual accuracy. With respect to actuarial assessment, Campbell (personal communication, September 21, 2004) describes predictive accuracy as not exceeding chance if classification accuracy is obtained by relying on the recidivism base rate.

Hart et al. (2003) write that all forms of risk assessment share problems and deficiencies, including their focus on risk factors, rather than those associated with strengths, resources, and protective factors (described in Chapter 8, for instance). They describe a second problem as the failure of risk assessment instruments to address intervention strategies, and yet a third as a lack of quality assurance, in which they recognize that it is naive to assume that all professionals will function similarly in their work.

Douglas, Cox, and Webster (1999) take the approach that both assessment approaches have clear strengths but are both flawed, perhaps less by their intrinsic operational methods than by the global manner in which they are carried into practice by evaluators. They hold the view that actuarial prediction is generally superior to clinical prediction in terms of predictive validity, but nevertheless inapplicable and inappropriately used when the goals of risk assessment include management, prevention, and treatment. Their view is that risk assessments should "reach into the future" and specify the level of risk as a function of various possible conditions so that treatment and management can be organized to reduce risk for recidivism. Their position is that "something more than mere prediction is normally needed" and that actuarial instruments are appropriate and important only as part of a larger assessment process (p. 157). Douglas et al. believe that each method must inform the other in order to attain a level of sophistication in both science and application. Their focus, then, is on narrowing the wide gap they describe between researchers and practitioners, and thus significantly on training, noting the need for clinical risk assessment to be informed by research, and actuarial research to be informed by and responsive to the realities of clinical practice.

Sjöstedt and Grann (2002) agree that both actuarial and clinical risk assessment processes have strengths and weaknesses. In their study, actuarial assessment instruments worked well under certain conditions but were less accurate in discriminating among types of sexual reoffenses, and they were of little value in distinguishing between types of sexual offenders. Hence, they are in agreement with Douglas et al. (1999), as well as Hart (1998), in conceptualizing the scope of risk assessment as the management, treatment, and prevention of sexually abusive behavior and not simply prediction, writing that prediction alone provides so narrow a focus as to become meaningless. They relegate the role of actuarial assessment, therefore, to "rough screening and pretreatment assessments" (p. 312), in keeping with Hanson and Thornton's (2000) observation that when used in isolation actuarial assessment cannot be used to plan for or implement treatment, recognize or assess change, or predict when or under what circumstances sexual recidivism is most likely to occur. Sjöstedt and Grann recommend that actuarial instruments be used cautiously, knowing that whereas they may predict well under some circumstances they may go "far off target" in other cases (p. 183).

STRUCTURED AND LITERATURE-BASED CLINICAL ASSESSMENT

Most of the comparisons between actuarial and clinical assessment, and indeed most of the criticism aimed at clinical assessment, have been based on unguided or unstructured clinical judgment. On the other hand, virtually all of the support and advocacy for clinical risk assessment has been directed toward those assessments guided by a structured instrument, the design of which is, in turn, anchored in the professional and empirical literature. As described in Chapters 4 and 7, the literature-based clinical assessment instrument represents the heart of this aspect of risk assessment, often referred to as structured and empirically guided risk assessment. Nevertheless, given the lack of strong empirical support for many of the risk factors such tools are better described as literature based.[3]

Whereas unstructured risk assessment is based entirely on the evaluator's experience, training, orientation, and approach, structured risk assessment is shaped by a highly defined instrument that both determines and limits the type and range of information to be gathered and the specific nature of those factors considered to represent risk. Moving from unaided clinical judgment or unstructured professional judgment, the structured

---

3. See Chapter 7 for a review and discussion of the empirical and professional basis for the inclusion of risk factors into structured clinical risk assessment instruments.

clinical assessment instrument guides the evaluation process through its inclusion of defined risk factors, allowing the evaluator to estimate the chances of sexual recidivism by, simply put and in effect, matching the individual against the risk factors. The way in which a match is made varies from assessment instrument to assessment instrument, but essentially it involves the presence of risk factors along some form of continuum that ranges from absent to present.

In an actuarial assessment, which is always structured and defined completely by the rules, a numerical score is given to each risk factor based on the level of its presence. For instance, zero sexual offense adjudications may result in a score of zero whereas adjudication/conviction on one, two, or more sexual offenses may each result in an increasingly higher score (depending on the design of the particular actuarial instrument). However, the final assignment of risk is entirely the result of the summed risk factor scores. The higher the score, the greater the risk level. The same process is practiced in clinical risk assessment instruments as well, but in matching the individual against each risk factor (again, depending on the design of the particular instrument) it is the clinical evaluator who determines the weight given to each factor. For instance, it is the evaluator who may determine the severity of the sexual offense or the significance of a particular personal characteristic in assessing risk, rather than a rigidly or even clearly defined criteria. Despite clear problems with such a model, it is precisely this level of judgment that makes the process clinical. Indeed, Doren (2002) has written that one of the strengths of the structured and empirically guided approach to risk assessment is that "evaluators can give weight to the different risk considerations based on the case dynamics" (p. 108).

Even though structured clinical instruments have no psychometric attributes, in order to have at least face validity, as well as content validity,[4] the instrument must be built around risk factors that are known or believed to be related to the risk for sexual recidivism, which is where literature-based or empirically guided assessment comes into play. Beyond this, given the level of clinical judgment required in assessing when a risk factor is in play and to what extent, two things are required to ensure the integrity of the risk assessment process. One is a high level of structure and definition, both in order to clearly define each risk factor and to provide

---

4. Content validity requires that a measure represent all facets of the construct being examined, whereas face validity refers to the measure's appearance of measuring the "right" variables, rather than variables that are irrelevant to the construct—in this case, the assessment of sexual risk.

clear instruction on how the instrument should be used and completed; the second involves the supervision and training of the evaluator in risk assessment in general and the use of the specific risk instrument.

Together, these two requirements help ensure not just the integrity and strength of each use of the instrument, but an increased likelihood that (1) the same evaluator will conduct the evaluation in the same manner each time, and (2) different evaluators will recognize and assess the same risk factors as other evaluators and in the same manner each time they engage in the use of the same risk instrument. This builds consistency both in use and interrater agreement, both important facets of reliability. Thus, a structured clinical instrument can demonstrate qualities of both validity and reliability, even though it is far short of the statistically designed psychometric instrument.

Describing this model as "structured professional judgment," Hart et al. (2003) write that structured professional guidelines help improve the consistency and usefulness of decisions and improve the transparency of decision making, important in the absence of a method for making scientifically precise estimates of risk. In clinical assessment, one way to do this is to build the evaluation process and method on sound underlying theory, and shape the evaluation through a defined structure, embodied by the structured, literature-based and empirically guided clinical assessment instrument.

THE CONSTRUCTION OF THE STRUCTURED CLINICAL INSTRUMENT

Clinical assessment instruments that are both structured and informed by the professional literature will to the greatest degree possible involve empirically based ideas. How they are organized and designed, including the selection of risk factors, the inclusion of other content, and the method by which risk is evaluated and a risk level assigned, remains entirely within the domain of the author. Although a well-designed and careful instrument will be based on the literature and research, the ideas and information selected and presented are nevertheless eventually based upon the selection and choice of the author. This means that, to some degree, theory and personal sensibility shape the instrument. Just as clinical processes, by definition, ultimately define the assessment of risk in a clinical assessment, so too do clinical processes partly shape the design of the clinical instrument. This explains, of course, why there is more than one clinical instrument and the likelihood that more will be developed. If this were not so, we would have but a single clinical risk assessment instrument, and it would be the correct version. The same, of course, to some degree is true of actuarial assessment instruments, which also explains why more than one is available and why they are each different from one another.

THE FRAMEWORK PROVIDED BY A STRUCTURED INSTRUMENT

Although I am reluctant to say this, there is no great science involved in the creation of a clinical risk assessment instrument. Anyone can make one. However, without care, depth of knowledge, breadth of experience, clear organization, and strong design, the resulting instrument is not likely to have much value; in fact, given its purpose it may cause actual harm rather than simply failing to meet a need. Consequently, building a useful, meaningful, and sensitive risk assessment instrument requires a significant understanding of the mechanics of such tools, as well as a commitment to thoroughly understanding the directly and indirectly related research and professional literature that must be incorporated into the design and application of the instrument. It is the author's responsibility to ensure the quality of the instrument and that instructions for its use are available and clear. As a user of such an instrument, it is the consumer's responsibility to ensure that the instrument meets an acceptable professional standard, as well as knowing how to use it.

However, without understating the skills, knowledge, effort, and energy required to create a meaningful and useful clinical assessment tool, no matter how much the tool is based on research and literature, it is not a psychometric tool or a psychological test instrument statistically designed and tested with proven statistical validity. Although statistical procedures of test construction may go into the development of the instrument, such as construct, content, and criterion validity and content analysis, structured risk assessment instruments are not psychometric tools; they are simply organized and informative checklists designed for the purposes of risk assessment. In fact, the structured assessment instrument is little more than a well-developed, well-informed, and well-organized checklist of ideas and information against which risk assessment can be professionally implemented.

The instrument is the *aide-mémoire* described by Webster et al. (1997) or the structured professional guidelines described by Hart et al. (2003). It's an organized aid to the systematic risk assessment process described by Borum, Bartel, and Forth (2002), providing reference to a checklist of risk factors that have a demonstrated or believed relationship to recidivism, based on the literature. The clinical risk assessment instrument, then, is a synthetic instrument derived from the research and literature, incorporating ideas believed to be important and valid into a formal, organized, and coherent instrument for use in a defined and organized assessment. When the assessment process becomes organized and shaped by the instrument, it becomes a structured assessment and thus assumes the same format as every other clinical assessment organized by the guide (helping to ensure reliability).

THE ESSENCE OF THE CLINICAL INSTRUMENT

Frankly, the construction of clinical instruments does not require the energy, time, and resources that go into the research, development, testing, validation, and analysis required for the creation of an actuarial instrument. Although guided and shaped by both the literature and empirical evidence whenever possible, as well as principles of test construction, clinical assessment tools need not have any statistical properties whatsoever, and are generally not psychometric tools. Further, without evidence that they actually predict risk, they cannot even be said to be accurate. Neither can clinical assessment instruments claim to accurately or definitely compare the individual under assessment against other individuals who have sexually recidivated, without specific reference to the base rate for sexual recidivism or the known and validated characteristics of sexual recidivists. Clinical risk assessment instruments simply provide estimates of risk, based essentially on a comparison of that individual against risk factors known or believed related to risk for sexual recidivism.

In fact, the three features that most distinguish the clinical risk instrument from the actuarial instrument are (1) its lack of predictive validity, (2) its inability to compare the individual against other individuals known to have sexually recidivated, and (3) its assignment of risk based upon the judgment of the evaluator rather than a statistically derived and defined set of rules and scoring system. By contrast, the actuarial assessment is defined by (1) its capacity to make estimates of risk based on its predictive validity or proof of accuracy in predicting risk, (2) comparison of the individual against known sexual recidivists, including predicted rates of recidivism based on group data, and (3) assignment of risk based entirely on a set arithmetical score that does not involve or require professional judgment. Indeed, the lack of psychometric properties and statistical rigor are weaknesses of a clinical tool and may limit the willingness of others in the field to use the instrument or accept its findings, thus limiting its use in research and as expert evidence in criminal or civil proceedings. A poorly developed tool may also (and probably will) fail to do the job it sets out to accomplish (i.e., the assessment of risk for a sexual reoffense) and may even cause potential harm and lead to false positives or false negatives.

Assessment instruments must first and foremost be well tuned to the literature of the field, and especially empirical evidence, that supports the selection of risk factors. There must then be a process of evaluating and culling risk factors in order to determine those factors that will be included in the assessment. After this comes the process of designing and organizing the instrument, including developing a scoring system and writing operational definitions and instructions that allow clarity and consistency in administration and use. Despite the fact that there are different methods to achieve these goals, the development of the instrument is nonetheless driven and defined by a process of professional expertise and judgment.

In the development of the MEGA (Multiplex Empirically Guided Inventory of Ecological Aggregates for Assessing Sexually Abusive Adolescents and Children),[5] Rasmussen and Miccio-Fonseca essentially describe this process. They describe first reviewing the specific literature and empirical research, then reviewing current risk assessment instruments, and then applying their clinical expertise by "drawing upon our almost half a century of combined clinical and research experience" (2007a, p. 188). Their description nicely summarizes the process, but it is their reference to clinical experience that perhaps most reflects the influence of personal expertise, theory, and sensibility that offers the last word in determining the final shape of clinical instruments.

ENSURING QUALITY IN CLINICAL ASSESSMENT: WEAKNESSES AND REQUIREMENTS

To some the fact that the clinical instrument is not objective, but has a subjective quality to it, is a downside. As a clinical tool, however, it is not only a necessary feature, but also a defining quality, just as subjectivity defines the clinical work of psychotherapy. If one sees subjectivity and clinical judgment as a downside and impairment to the process of risk assessment, then one may just as well see the process of psychotherapy as an impairment to the evaluation and treatment of mental health disorders. It is training and its practical and hands-on correlate, supervision, that makes the difference in clinical work, and not the subjective process itself. Hence, the subjectivity inherent in a clinical assessment instrument is not an inherent weakness. The more knowledgeable the author and the better the instrument design, the greater the strength of the instrument. Conversely, poorly designed instruments are highly subjective and are neither well informed nor supported by the literature.

---

5. In development, as described in earlier chapters, and later in this chapter.

In fact, the strengths of the clinical assessment instrument, and indeed the larger clinical assessment process, are also its weaknesses. For instance, the ability to exercise professional judgment and make decisions based on such judgment leads to the possibility of ill-informed opinions and poorly made decisions. Accordingly, clinical assessment instruments can be narrow in focus, poorly designed and organized, lacking in clear explanation, and poorly informed in their selection of risk factors. Beyond the instrument itself, Monahan (1995) described four general weaknesses in the practice of clinical prediction: (1) lack of specificity in clearly defining exactly what is being assessed and predicted, (2) identifying and relying on misleading, or "illusory" correlations, (3) not being aware of or ignoring the statistical base rate of the behavior being predicted, and (4) failing to incorporate situational or environmental information into assessment.

Nevertheless, a combination of well-developed clinical instruments and well-trained clinical evaluators will correct these problems, and with respect to the instruments we can set criteria against which such tools can be compared and themselves evaluated. That is, we can establish some objective markers, or markers of quality assurance, by which to guide the construction of state of the art instruments and by which to evaluate them. This can help define the sort of content that should be included in the instrument, as well as the conditions it should meet in order to be capable of reasonably estimating risk. Accordingly, to be considered well developed, well organized, and well informed, a clinical risk assessment instrument should meet at least these 14 criteria, each one of which is of importance, not least of all criteria number 14.

1. Comprehensive in depth and breadth of included content.
2. Rationally and logically organized.
3. Clear explanation of design, intent, and limitations.
4. Clear instructions for use.
5. Inclusion of static and dynamic risk factors supported by professional literature.
6. Sufficient range of dynamic risk factors.
7. Clear definition of each risk factor.
8. Covers multiple aspects of risk in multiple life domains.
9. Rational and clearly defined scoring system.
10. Allows weighting of different risk factors.
11. Allows consolidation of data.
12. Yields transparent results, obvious to the reader.
13. Clearly oriented towards specific population for whom intended.
14. Allows re-evaluation of risk based upon dynamic risk factors.

THE CONSTRUCTION OF THE ACTUARIAL INSTRUMENT

Despite describing the construction of actuarial instruments in a few paragraphs, it's not my intention to suggest a simplicity to the process. On the contrary, these are complex instruments that are the result of complex data gathering and statistical analyses. As Grisso (2000) notes, in the broader field of general violence risk assessment, acceptable actuarial tools are just beginning to be developed after more than 20 years of work, and with the support of several millions of dollars. In part, this is because, unlike clinical instruments, actuarial assessment instruments do require a comparison group, and a large one at that, and do require defined and coded means of measuring standardized bits of information against that base population, and in addition must know and be built upon the base rate at which the risk behavior occurs—in this case, sexual recidivism.

Unlike clinical instruments, which compare the individual against a set of risk factors (and perhaps protective factors, as well) but not against anyone else, actuarial instruments compare the individual against a pool of other individuals. In actuarial assessments, evaluation based on the presence and quantity of risk factors serves as a means by which to build a group portrait of the individual being assessed, in which he or she resembles others in a risk pool who have previously been classified as either low, moderate, or high risk (or some variant) based on their actual recidivism. Thus, the individual is not being truly assessed as an individual, but as a member of a group in terms of his or her resemblance to or membership in a class, in our case, sexual recidivists. The actuarial assessment thus throws a net out and captures individuals within that net. The narrower the net, the greater chance that it will catch those most likely to recidivate (reduce false positives) but also lose many others who may also be at risk for recidivism (allow false negatives). The broader the net, however, the less the false negatives but the greater the chance of creating false positives (that is incorrectly identifying individuals at a higher risk).

There are other elements to be considered also, including the selection of risk factors and the process through which they are selected, the weighting of scores (for example, the weight given to three sexual offense convictions, compared to one or six; personal or social factors believed related to sexual recidivism; or scores on a psychopathy scale), and decisions about cut-off scores that determine the differences, for instance, between low-, moderate- and high-risk offenders. Adding more complexity, cut-off scores can also be used to determine a far greater level of specificity, such as a 30 percent, 50 percent, or 90 percent chance of sexual recidivism, as well as determining the period of time during which risk for recidivism is the greatest; for instance, a 30 percent chance of reoffending within three years, or a 55 percent chance of reoffending between years 7 and 10.

The grouping of individuals is one of the strengths of statistical prediction, but it also has downsides. For one thing, the assessment cannot be specific to the individual in the way allowed by a clinical assessment, and aimed at group data it inevitably creates false positives or negatives. In providing a lecture to a large audience for whom lunch is provided free, the conference organizers must determine how many people will eat lunch. Based on their experience with similar events and audience demographics, the organizers have a clear sense of how many people usually eat lunch (the base rate) and furthermore how many will want a vegetarian lunch. They can thus say with reasonable certainty that 85 percent of the audience will eat lunch, of whom 12 percent will require a vegetarian meal. And, because of their experience they're more or less correct in their estimate, and if they have enough base rate data and demographics on the past and current audience (and the time on their hands), they may even be able to state with some authority and precision the type of person most likely to eat lunch. Nevertheless, even though they may be able to create a statistical profile of the individual lunch eater, it's unlikely that the organizers can name the specific individuals who will actually eat lunch.

Nevertheless, the profile of the low, moderate, and likely lunch eater would be enough to classify individuals within the audience into one of these groups, or even into the vegetarian subgroup. The clinical assessment instrument does not have this capacity, and neither does it attempt to classify the individual by direct (or indirect statistical) comparison to a group. Instead, it attempts to identify who is more-or-less likely to eat lunch by examining each audience member as an individual. This is clearly a lot less economical and efficient than the process of actuarial assessment, which in addition, once developed, offers a straightforward and simple process with, most likely, a higher hit rate (that is, higher level of predictive accuracy).

Essentially, however, to build an actuarial instrument one must have a known and large enough base rate, that is a substantial pool of known sexual recidivists. As we want to know about sexual recidivism, we have to know what it is about sexual recidivists that makes them alike and yet distinguishes them from those sexual offenders who don't recidivate. That's why there must be a large enough base rate of sexual recidivism from which to draw meaningful data and statistical conclusions, and why the instrument must be validated and revalidated on different populations of sexual offenders so that we can be sure that the data were not simply idiosyncratic to the sample we happened to study.

To use two adolescent risk assessment instruments as an example, of the 96 adolescent sexual offenders comprising the original sample for the J-SOAP (Juvenile Sex Offender Assessment Protocol), follow-up data were obtained on only 75 youth of whom only three recidivated, for a base rate of only 4 percent of the 75 youth (Prentky & Righthand, 2003). This provides no basis for actuarial assessment, even though it was, and remains, the goal of the J-SOAP to become an actuarial instrument. In the development of the JSORRAT-II (Juvenile Sexual Offense Recidivism Risk Assessment Tool), presently the only actuarial assessment instrument for adolescent sexual offenders, among the original sample population of 636 juvenile sexual offenders 84 sexually reoffended before their 18th birthday, for a recidivism base rate of 13.2 percent. This provides a clear basis for the development of an actuarial tool (Epperson et al., 2006), which presented itself as just one early step in the development of the instrument, although it has been fully validated in only one state at the time of this writing. Epperson and colleagues worked through the data and their statistical analysis, eventually arriving at the current instrument and the 12 risk factors of which it is statistically comprised (described in Chapter 14). At the time of this writing, the instrument is being validated in a second location, with plans to continue validation in different parts of the United States (that is, testing for the same results with the same cohort but in different locales). In fact, in the second validation study, there was a recidivism rate of 12.8 percent among a sample of 538 adjudicated juvenile sexual offenders, again enough of a base rate from which to draw meaningful data in terms of recidivism.

WEAKNESSES OF ACTUARIAL ASSESSMENT

Actuarial assessments have clear and inherent weaknesses, many of which have already been described, including and perhaps especially their reliance upon static risk factors and what Grisso (2000) has therefore referred to as the "tyranny of static variables," given their unchanging nature and their complete independence from life as it unfolds and develops. These weaknesses are even more amplified when we consider their use with still-developing children, assuming that is even really feasible to meaningfully apply an actuarial assessment for children and adolescents (including the JSORRAT).

In addition to limitations already noted:

1. Although mostly based upon objective facts, actuarial assessments in construction or application often depend upon clinical judgment or

interpretation to either produce risk factors, interpret situations under which risk occurs, or assess behaviors or relationships.

2. Actuarial assessments are limited in scope to facts or pseudo-facts, and are unable to infer or search out important data that do not fit into the structure of the assessment or do not take the form of fact.
3. Actuarial assessments are rigid and lack the ability to provide meaning or render judgments about data.
4. Actuarial assessments lack the ability to formulate, and are thus able to present only a simple picture without any explanation.
5. Actuarial assessments are static and do not allow the possibility for re-evaluation or the re-assignment of risk over time.
6. Actuarial assessments for sexual recidivism are not based upon truly valid variables as there is no clear or definite set of risk factors or combination of risk factors that unequivocally contribute or lead to sexually abusive behavior, resulting in the selection of variables that, in themselves, are the product of judgment or other processes subject to error, and not fact.
7. Actuarial assessments fail to incorporate situational or environmental variables.
8. The ability to determine the effectiveness and utility of an actuarial assessment is based entirely on its predictive power, which cannot be fully evaluated without adequate and meaningful recidivism studies.
9. Actuarial assessments do not take the age of the offender into consideration, except in a very general manner, and thus do not address or recognize developmental issues related to childhood and adolescence.

THE ITERATIVE CLASSIFICATION TREE APPROACH TO RISK ASSESSMENT

There is currently no Iterative Classification Tree (ICT) approach to assessing risk for a sexual reoffense. In fact, the approach was developed by Monahan et al. (2001) to assess risk for violence in hospitalized mental health patients and is currently available for this purpose as a software assessment package called the Classification of Violence Risk. It has not been used for risk assessment outside of this use, but may at some point be a tool developed to assess other forms of risk, referred to as "an exceedingly important methodology" by Campbell (2004), who virtually dismisses every form of sexual offender risk assessment methodology (as described above).

The model is based on a "classification tree" that is algorithmic, in that of an entire set of questions the actual questions selected are contingent upon the subject's answer to the previous question. In this way, although based on an set of questions that may be empirically derived, the assessment is decidedly individualized and aimed at only those questions (or, in the case of risk assessment, risk factors) that apply to the individual being assessed, a process to which Monahan et al. refer as "customizing risk assessment."

The ICT model, however, builds and uses several classification tree variants, each of which is comprised of different risk factors believed related to violence in hospitalized mental health patients. Every individual is assessed through the "parent" classification tree. Upon completion of the classification tree (the actual application of which is customized) individuals are assessed as either low or high risk, but individuals who cannot be classified into one of these two groups pass into a second classification tree process, or a second iteration. Those not assessed at a low or high risk are considered to be at an average level of risk compared to the entire population being assessed. The ICT assessment continues with classification tree iterations until all individuals have been classified as low, high, or average risk. However, it is also possible to pass individuals assessed at high or low risk through multiple iterations, thus confirming or disconfirming their assessment of risk; Monahan et al. found that this strengthened the risk assessment process significantly, increasing the certainty of assessed risk levels.

The methodology is frankly too complex to easily explain here, and it is not currently applicable in the risk assessment of adult (and certainly not juvenile) sexual offenders. However, it offers a glance into a different means for assessing risk also built on known base rates and actuarial procedures. The entire MacArthur Study on Mental Disorder and Violence, including the Iterative Classification Tree assessment process, is described in Monahan et al. (2001), and the ICT process alone is described in Monahan et al. (2000), both of which are worth reading.

Of special importance, Monahan and colleagues describe this tool as having practical value to clinicians. Further, they describe their belief that actuarial tools, including the ICT, are best viewed and used as tools for clinical assessment, used to "support, rather than replace, the exercise of clinical judgment. This reliance on clinical judgment—aided by an empirical understanding of risk factors for violence and their interactions—reflects, and in our view should reflect, the standard of care at this juncture in the field's development" (Monahan et al., 2001, pp. 134–135).

THE BALANCE BETWEEN STRUCTURE, CONTENT, AND PROCESS

Whether actuarial or clinical, the structured assessment instrument directly defines the risk factors to be reviewed and assessed. In so doing, it also indirectly defines the information that must be collected in order to assess each risk factor. For instance, in defining as a risk factor the age difference between the sexually abusive youth and the victim, the assessment instrument makes clear the definition of the factor and its parameters. However, in doing so, it also makes it clear that the evaluator has to gather the specific information that is required to actually address the question. That is, what is the age difference? Likewise, if the instrument additionally defines general antisocial behavior as a risk factor, it must directly define what is meant by antisocial behavior (its nature and delimiters), thus ensuring clarity and consistency in assessing for the presence of the factor. In doing so, it also necessarily, but indirectly, requires that the evaluator gather whatever information is required to assess for the presence of the factor. Thus, the assessment format defines both the risk factor content and creates a structure by which information must be gathered in order to address each individual risk factor.

However, although the assessment instrument defines content and, albeit indirectly, what information must be gathered to address required content, the instrument does not necessarily define how the information is to be gathered. In fact, all of the current assessment instruments define the risk factors and thereby tell the evaluator what information is required, but none instruct the evaluator on how to get the required information. The manner in which the information is gathered, how it is interpreted, and the formulation derived from the gathered information is determined by the evaluator, based upon the parameters and rules of the assessment instrument. There is thus a balance between *what* is gathered (determined by the instrument), *how* it is gathered, and *how* it is interpreted (both determined by the evaluator). The risk instrument therefore provides content and structure, but not an approach to the process.

The same is true for both actuarial and clinical instruments, in that both define the included risk factors and both therefore require the evaluator to gather the necessary material, but neither tells the evaluator how to gather the information. However, in the case of the necessarily cut-and-dried actuarial assessment the required information is all static, and although it can be gathered from different sources it need only be gathered from file material if the evaluator so chooses. This is not the case for the clinical assessment instrument, although some information may and should be gathered through file material. For the most part, though, the clinical assessment will require multiple types of information to be gathered from multiple sources, and is thus necessarily part of a larger assessment process, moving at least partially in the direction of comprehensive assessment.

CONCLUSION: THE CHOICE OF RISK ASSESSMENT INSTRUMENTS

Finally, in the choice of assessment tools, the evaluator should be aware of different orientations and approaches in the underlying model, and even in the design, focus, and scope of the assessment instrument, and in application should be aware of these different underlying concepts and constructs. This is certainly true, and perhaps most obviously so, when it comes to differences between actuarial and clinical assessment instruments, but it is also true to some degree when it comes to the things and the ideas that distinguish clinical assessment instruments from one another.

However, the differences between instruments within the same class (that is, actuarial or clinical) can frankly be difficult to fully discern, and differences often seem more a matter of degree than substance with respect to selected risk factors, scope, design, and wording. That is, actuarial assessment instruments appear similar to one another, and the same is true of clinical instruments and their similarities. Within their class (actuarial or clinical), these instruments generally espouse the same ideas and principles and advocate for the same processes in understanding the sexual offender and his or her risk for sexual reoffense. Nevertheless, there are, of course, significant differences or there would be but one instrument in either class.

Two adult clinical assessment instruments illustrate this point nicely. The Sexual Violence Risk-20 (Boer, Hart, Kropp, & Webster, 1997) and the Risk for Sexual Violence Protocol (Hart et al., 2003) not only share similar risk items and a virtually identical scoring system, but also share two of the same authors (even the name of the two tools is similar). Although the SVR-20 is built on 20 risk factors[6] grouped in three domains and the RSVP on 22 factors in five domains, of these risk factors 20 are virtually identical (albeit with slightly different wording and descriptions in a number of case), with only two risk factors clearly distinguishing the RSVP as a different tool. The most significant difference is perhaps in how the risk tools are presented, in which the SVR-20 provides a format, explanation, and structure for assessment, but the RSVP presents a six-stage model by which to implement and complete the risk assessment process from the gathering of case

---

6. Hence, the designation "20" in the name of the instrument.

information (step 1), to assessing the presence and relevance of risk factors (steps 2 and 3, which are actually a single step), the description of possible risk scenarios (step 4), the description of case management needs (step 5), and evaluation outcomes and recommendations (step 6).

The essential difference, then, between these two instruments lies less in their selection and definition of risk factors than in their approach to the risk assessment process, in which the RSVP provides a structured means for implementing and recording the process from the first to last step, whereas the SVR-20 does not. This represents a matter of greater specificity, organization, and practicality, then, more than a significantly different perspective or approach to risk assessment, or a different view of risk and how to recognize and measure it. Indeed, the two instruments are otherwise so similar that it is not clear what the other differences are, other than two additional risk factors in the RSVP. As the SVR-20 is currently being revised, it will be interesting to see if further differences emerge.

There is a greater degree of difference among the few clinical instruments available for the assessment of juvenile sexual offenders, however, partly because there are clearly different authors and designs behind each instrument. With respect to the actuarial-clinical instrument split, there is only one current choice for actuarial assessment, the Juvenile Sexual Offense Recidivism Risk Assessment Tool-II, and so there is no means for comparison with other tools in its class. However, it looks very much like the Minnesota Sex Offender Screening Tool—Revised, a frequently used adult actuarial assessment instrument, which is no surprise as Douglas Epperson is the primary author in both cases. With regard to clinical assessment instruments, which, until the advent of the JSORRAT, were the only available means for assessing sexually abusive youth, despite differences these each embody the same ideas, methods, mechanisms, and processes as one another; each describes the need to understand the sexually abusive youth as a young person first and foremost, as well as the need for the assessment to be part of a larger and more comprehensive assessment process, rather than the final word.

Examined in more detail in Chapter 14, these instruments have clear differences from one another, but despite differences in their appearance, inclusion of risk factors, and depth and breadth, are more alike than different. This is perhaps the way it should be, as they advocate for and embrace the same ideas: that risk is a multidimensional construct best and only thoroughly understood when examined globally, and that measuring risk in juveniles is like shooting at a moving target. No matter which of the clinical assessment instruments the evaluator chooses to use, and some evaluators choose to use more than one even within the same case (in effect, for cross-validation), they each thus take us to more-or-less the same place.

I conclude the chapter with 10 questions that Hart et al. (2003) suggest are important for the evaluator to consider in selecting a risk assessment instrument. These questions, paraphrased by me, summarize much of what has been said in this chapter and to some degree mirror the 14 quality assurance markers described earlier, and they clearly reflect the role of the risk assessment instrument as part of a larger process, and not necessarily the process itself. Consider these questions not only in the selection of an evaluation tool, but also as criteria to consider in the development of instruments and the philosophy and ideas embedded within their structure and content.

1. Does the evaluation gather information concerning multiple domains of the individual's functioning?
2. Does the evaluation use multiple methods to gather information?
3. Does the evaluation gather information from multiple sources?
4. Does the evaluation allow users to evaluate the accuracy of relevant information?
5. Does the evaluation involve both static and dynamic risk factors?
6. Does the evaluation allow reassessment, to evaluate change in risk over time?
7. Is the evaluation comprehensive?
8. Is the evaluation comprehensible and acceptable to those who will use its results?
9. Can evaluators be trained to use the evaluation in a consistent manner?
10. Does the evaluation process result in information, ideas, and recommendations that can reduce sexual risk?

CHAPTER 13

Using the Instruments

CONSIDER THIS PERSPECTIVE drawn from the standards and guidelines for the evaluation, treatment, and supervision of sexually abusive youth, developed by the Colorado Sex Offender Management Board (Colorado Department of Public Safety, 2002). The Board asserts that a juvenile's level of risk should not be based solely on the sexual offense, and it requires that a complete knowledge of the history, extent, type of sexual offending, and other factors is needed before a risk of reoffense and risk to community safety can be adequately determined. The standards note also that the evaluation of sexually abusive youth must be comprehensive and in estimating risk for reoffense include assessment of cognitive functioning, personality, mental health, social history, behavioral issues, family functioning, risk and protective factors, awareness of victim impact, and amenability to treatment, in addition to an evaluation of sexual behavior.

These ideas are certainly not new to you, as the same ideas have been expressed repeatedly in previous chapters, but they are worth repeating now, from yet one more source, as we consider the application of the risk assessment process at the level of the risk assessment tool.

ATTRIBUTES OF A CLINICAL ASSESSMENT INSTRUMENT

It's also clear by now that, unlike the actuarial assessment instrument, the clinical assessment tool is merely a shell used to organize and record information and reflect on and assign a level of risk. The data that inform and activate the assessment risk tool are collected through the psychosocial assessment, and, as previously described, the tool itself is really no more than a sophisticated checklist that allows the evaluator to cover a great deal of territory, assess multiple specified risk areas, and organize data in a prescribed manner. The use of such a tool ensures that the assessment of risk is comprehensive, follows a clearly defined model, and provides a consistent means for arriving at a clinically defined assessment of risk for sexual reoffense. The organized aspect of the instrument keeps the evaluator focused on literature or empirically based risk factors that apply to *all* risk assessments, whereas the clinical aspect allows the evaluator to consider and weigh the many factors that impinge upon the life and behavior of the particular individual being assessed.

Despite the fact that clinically assessing risk is neither simple nor cut-and-dried, the clinical assessment tool has the capacity to go beyond the function of *only* assigning a risk level. A well-developed clinical assessment instrument can also elicit additional information that not only helps explain and justify the level of risk assigned, but also identifies and highlights: (1) characteristics of prior sexual offenses, such as types of victims and elements present in prior offenses, (2) likely scenarios and conditions under which risk is highest, as well as possible victim types in the event that the juvenile does reoffend, and (3) possible motivators for the offense and extenuating circumstances. In addition, a thorough risk assessment instrument will include a written formulation that summarizes and explains the risk assessment level assigned and also present a perspective about the sexually troubled youth that helps explain his or her behavior, describes personal development and characterological and psychological traits, central issues and problems for the youth, and the prognosis if things go unchanged. Finally, the risk assessment instrument can highlight or suggest recommendations for placement, treatment, and supervision that will be useful in the process of disposition and treatment planning.

In terms of its utility as both a tool by which to assess risk and assign a risk level and a step in a larger risk assessment process, risk assessment instruments may be considered in terms of the 14 quality assurance markers that address the design of the instrument itself, or the 10 questions posed by Hart et al. (2003) that describe the role of the instrument in the larger risk assessment process, both of which were described in Chapter 12. Alternatively, culled in part from these combined 24 factors, risk instruments can be compared against 10 simple points that address attributes of utility and design.

1. *Relevancy:* How well suited is the instrument for the population it is intended to evaluate?
2. *Scope and range:* How broadly does the instrument allow the gathering of information from domains across the youth's life, in order to

gather an expansive view of his or her past and current psychosocial functioning and capacities; developmental experiences and processes; and family, social, and environmental supports, challenges, and experiences?

3. *Depth:* How deeply does the instrument penetrate *within* (rather than *across*) separate domains and engage the information necessary to form a broad picture and understanding of the youth's psychological, emotional, social, and behavioral functioning?

4. *Range of data type:* Does the instrument rely on one type of data, or does it allow for or require multiple types of data?

5. *Range of data sources:* Does the instrument rely on one means for gathering data, or does it allow for, and in its design require, multiple sources for data acquisition?

6. *Utility:* How practical is the instrument in helping to achieve the goal of risk assessment and in defining, structuring, and directing the process?

7. *Clarity:* How clear and adequate are the instructions for use and the methods for assessment?

8. *Ease of use:* How easy is the instrument to use?

9. *Transparency:* How apparent to the reader is the process and reasons by which the evaluator arrived at the formal assignment of risk?

10. *Capacity for reassessment:* How well does the instrument lend itself to re-evaluation over time?

ORGANIZATION OF THE RISK INSTRUMENT

Risk assessment must consider multiple aspects of risk, and the final assignment of risk is based upon the interrelationship among all of the individual factors, or groups of factors. In a statistical model scores are assigned to each factor (according to scoring rules), adding to a total score that assigns the level of risk. However, in a clinical model, the evaluator examines each risk factor as an *element* of risk, taking into account the actual history of sexually abusive behavior and related static factors, the relationship among all factors, and the personal and contextual factors that lend themselves to a more complete understanding of the youth and the circumstances that shaped, contributed, or led to the sexually abusive behavior.

Recognizing that there are multiple risk factors and that they must be examined and pieced together, it is useful to create categories of risk that incorporate and contain these multiple factors and allow the assessment to remain highly organized and coherent. Hence, similar elements of risk are grouped together into larger risk categories or domains and within each individual risk elements are assessed. This is not the case for most actuarial assessment instruments, including the JSORRAT, which typically assesses and assigns points to each risk factor separately and then totals the points, thus consolidating and combining risk factors into a single outcome score. However, in the case of existing clinical instruments, individual risk factors are always grouped into larger categories, and in effect assessed category by category, rather than as individual elements. This ranges from the four risk groupings of the J-SOAP to the 12 risk domains of the J-RAT.

Beyond the selection of risk factors and how they are presented or grouped, risk instruments have varying utilities, involving how risk factors are explained or defined, how much information is gathered about each risk domain or grouping, and how much they move beyond a strict focus on risk factors alone. For instance, do they allow the consolidation of information about protective factors (as described in Chapter 8), do they offer an opportunity for or require written explanation, do they consolidate data, or do they offer information that goes beyond risk assessment per se. Chapter 12 illustrated this process at work by describing the RSVP, a clinical instrument used to assess adult sexual offenders, which provides a six-stage process for assessment that moves past the assignment of risk level alone to describing possible risk scenarios, case management needs, and final evaluations and recommendations. The J-RAT similarly moves beyond risk assignment alone, and additionally describes characteristics of the juvenile's sexually abusive behavior, future possible risk scenarios, and primary motivators and factors that may help better understand the individual and his or her risk for sexual reoffense.

One consideration, therefore, is how the instrument is organized and how much information it yields, and, frankly, ease of use without sacrificing detail and the value of the material that the instrument yields. Using the RSVP and SVR-20 examples again (Chapter 12), the additional organization and information provided by the RSVP may be considered unnecessary by some evaluators, and the shorter SVR-20 may yield just the right amount of information needed by the evaluator to make an assessment or risk. Less experienced evaluators may prefer the more focused RSVP, whereas more experienced evaluators require less of the bells and whistles. On the other hand, one might argue that less experienced evaluators may prefer the SVR because it is briefer and they lack the experience to recognize and appreciate the value added by the RSVP, and experienced clinicians may therefore favor the longer and more complex instrument as it adds far more to their assessments and yields more detailed information. The same is thus true for evaluators using the J-RAT, which is far more detailed and complex than other adolescent risk assessment instruments. Some evaluators may feel that the far shorter 25-factor ERASOR (26 actually, as it allows for an additional "other factor" score), broken into five scales, yields adequate information from which to make clinical assessment of risk, as opposed to the 117 risk elements of the J-RAT grouped into 12 risk domains. On the other hand, the J-RAT is designed to gather, and requires far more information, and thus offers greater depth and breadth, and accordingly both gathers and yields more information about the individual being assessed from which to form an estimate of risk.

To some degree, then, organization allows a logic and ease of use to instruments, but it is the evaluator's needs and experience that will, to some degree, at least, determine the value of a particular instrument in terms of its content, breadth, and depth. In the final analysis, evaluators must find risk assessment instruments both user friendly and valuable in content and utility.

SCORING AND GIVING WEIGHT TO RISK FACTORS

Each instrument, of course, allows some form of scoring, described in Chapter 8, that allows each risk factor to be assessed across a range from not present to highly present, although how this range is described varies by instrument. The ERASOR, for instance, ranges from unknown, to not present, partially or possibly present, or present, whereas the J-SOAP assigns from 0–2 points per factor (in effect, from not relevant to very relevant). On the other hand, the J-RAT uses a more dimensional rating scale, moving from no concern to significant concern per risk element, and includes a rating for not applicable and another for unknown. The actuarial JSORRAT assigns points (as do all actuarial instruments) that start at 0 for least concern and range upwards to denote statistically greater concern.

One of the main differences, of course, between the actuarial method and the clinical approach is that in the former case the risk assignment process is entirely mechanical and is simply the statistically determined product of the summed total of numerical scores. However, for clinical assessments, although the evaluator may be reasonably sure that a behavior exists (i.e., is present) or does not (is not present), determining or weighting the importance of that particular risk factor is up to the evaluator. In the case of the actuarial assessment, the weights for individual risk factors have already been determined statistically, usually through the process of multiple linear regression. For instance, the importance of (or weight given to) unrelated, stranger, or male victims, and the number of victims in any of these categories[1] is the result of a prior statistical process, and the job of the evaluator is to simply assign a point score based on the actual presence of the behavior; no further weighting, and certainly no clinical judgment, is necessary. The chief problem here comes only when the evaluator is uncertain of the answer or has additional information that is not formally recorded in documents. In either case, however, if the conditions that define the presence or absence of a risk factor are not met then a zero score must be given (absent of clinical adjustment).

However, unlike the actuarial evaluator, the clinical evaluator usually must decide how to balance any given piece of information against the totality of gathered information. For example, even though the individual being assessed engaged in only one sexual offense it was particularly heinous, or alternatively even if the single offense was quite severe it seemed to represent an anomaly for this individual. How does this one risk factor then stand up against the other 27 risk factors included in the J-SOAP or the other 116 risk elements that comprise the J-RAT, many of which perhaps suggest the individual is at either high or low risk in other significant social, psychological, or behavioral areas of his or her life? Weighting thus requires the clinical evaluator to decide upon the relative importance or strength of each risk factor when compared against and added into the aggregated whole. Accordingly, recognizing that "some items simply are more important than others when it comes to predicting outcome" (Prentky & Righthand, 2003, p. 8), through the process of discovery embodied by the assessment procedure, the evaluator may choose to place emphasis (weight) on one specific risk category, or even a specific single risk factor within that domain. Hence despite the evaluator's assessment of low concern for many risk factors, she or he may still decide to assign a final level of high risk due to the presence of a single high-risk factor or category that, in the evaluator's judgment, is critical and elevates risk.

Among the adult and adolescent clinical instruments, the J-SOAP handles this aspect of risk assessment and the weighting of individual items differently because, as noted, it assigns numerical scores rather than nominal or descriptive labels (such as "present" or "not present"). Accordingly, the authors of the tool have already weighted each risk factor, much as in the design of actuarial scales, which is why the J-SOAP is often described as an "actuarial-like" instrument (and sometimes mistakenly described as an actuarial assessment). The J-SOAP weights its risk factors through the process of "unit item weighting," which the authors consider

---

1. Three items from the 10-item STATIC-99, an adult actuarial assessment instrument.

superior to "clinically derived" item weights in which the evaluator decides the importance of each factor and its resulting weight compared to other factors in the instrument. However, unit item weighting represents little more than assigning a ratio-based higher score[2] to risk factors that are more severe or more significant in their presence (such as more sexual offense charges or greater parental instability). In the absence of empirical data supporting weighting in one direction or another, this represents little more than a safe approach to determining one item to be of greater importance than another, and strips the clinical evaluator of the capacity to make decisions about the comparative importance of risk factors. In itself, a decision to go with unit weighting rather than clinical weighting represents a clinical decision made by the instrument author about how to assess and score items. Nevertheless, for the evaluator it also offers a safer and easier route to weighting as decisions about weighting have effectively already been made by the author of the instrument.

Nevertheless, the J-SOAP itself, of course, is a clinical instrument. Although it requires that evaluators do not make adjustments to the risk factor score, it allows the idea of clinical adjustment in drawing conclusions about risk, "based on risk-relevant information that the J-SOAP-II did not take into consideration" (Prentky & Righthand, 2003, p. 9). In fact, the J-SOAP specifically does not assign a risk level and yields only a total score that the evaluator must interpret, and evaluators are specifically instructed to not make decisions about risk based exclusively on the results of the J-SOAP, which "should always be used as part of a comprehensive risk assessment" (p. 1).

In describing a scoring system that uses descriptive, or nominal, labels that reflect the absence or presence of a risk factor (or the quantity of presence, such as partially or fully present), Boer et al. (1997) write that "although admittedly crude, such simple coding is readily comprehended by other decision-makers and easily translated into action" (p. 34). They also write "it is not possible to specify a method for reaching a summary or final decision that is appropriate for all situations. . . . For clinical purposes, it makes little sense to sum the number of risk factors present in a given case and then use fixed, arbitrary cutoffs to classify the individual as low, moderate, or high risk. It is both possible and reasonable for an evaluator to conclude that the individual is at high risk for violence based on the presence of a single factor." However, in the absence of single highly weighted factors, "it is reasonable for assessors to conclude that the more

---

2. That is, a score than moves up in equal increments from a lower to higher number, from a zero score baseline.

factors present in a given case, the higher the risk for violence. Even here, though, assessors must be cautious" (p. 36).

The evaluator faces a choice, then, in deciding upon a clinical instrument in which the weighting has already been taken care of by the instrument designer, as in the case of the J-SOAP, or an instrument that places far more in the hands of the assessor. In the latter case, the process is admittedly and clearly a lot cruder and fraught with difficulty and the possibility of inconsistency, and requires a higher level of trust in the evaluator. This is not reason to discard such a process; indeed, these are statements that can be made about all clinical work. However, it is a reason to recognize the possibility of poor clinical practice, build clinical tools that are as clear and structured as possible, and ensure adequate training and supervision of clinicians and clinical evaluators.

TAKING STOCK OF RISK FACTORS

The actuarial evaluator may only take stock of and include in the assessment information that is in the written record or other form of documentation allowed by the assessment instrument.[3] In the absence of information approved in this manner, data may not otherwise be recognized or admitted into the assessment. For instance, again referring to the STATIC-99, points are assigned for the number of sexual criminal charges or convictions. However, in reality, charges are often pleaded down to a lower charge, such as a non-sexual charge, or are dismissed, or a sexual offense is not charged at all even though it has occurred. In each of these cases, the evaluator must score a zero, even though the evaluator may know that one or more sexual offenses actually occurred. Nevertheless, the evaluator may not add points, even if there is certain knowledge of a history of sexual offenses, unless prepared to make a clinical adjustment to the actuarial assessment. Hence,

---

3. Indeed, one may say the "instrument rules" in actuarial assessment, whereas in clinical evaluation, the "evaluator rules." This is the very crux, perhaps, of the actuarial-clinical debate. From the perspective of arithmetical and positivist science, actuarial decisions are sharp, dependable, unequivocal, and unbiased, and professional judgment is viewed as suspect, biased, and crude (unless supported by empirical evidence, in which case the judgment is no longer clinically based, but is empirical instead). Conversely, the science of statistical assessment is viewed from the clinical perspective as rigid, unrealistic, and uninformed by and inapplicable under field conditions, in which a sterile and single minded view is imposed upon practitioners. From this perspective, a trained clinician must trust his or her training, experience, and judgment in making decisions that affect and shape the lives of other human beings, informed by and drawing upon empirically driven science that instructs but does determine clinical practice.

242 JUVENILE SEXUAL OFFENDERS

in an actuarial assessment, this may mean ignoring a sexual offense because it has not been charged. In the case of the JSORRAT, there is an even higher standard as adjudication (i.e., conviction) is required, and not just a criminal charge. The same is true for every risk factor in which the factor may be included in the assessment only by meeting the defined rules of the instrument, and not the judgment of the evaluator.

The clinical evaluator does not face the same problem as the actuarial evaluator in recognizing and including known information that is provided through a source other than the file record. Here, even though there may be no sexual offenses with criminal charges for example, it may be perfectly clear that the individual has engaged in one or more incidents of sexually abusive behavior. It may even be that the information was learned through or substantiated by the offender himself, who honestly reported his history of sexually abusive behavior, even though not charged or convicted. The clinical evaluator has the capacity to include this information in his or her evaluation of the juvenile, whereas the actuarial evaluator does not have this option, absent of the process of clinical adjustment. Hence, without clinical adjustment to the actuarial assessment, important information pertaining to risk for reoffense is nullified and may not be considered in an assessment for sexual reoffense. It may also be that the reverse is true; that the individual was charged or convicted inaccurately or even unfairly, as in the case, perhaps, of a Romeo and Juliet conviction (Chapter 1) involving 19-year-old and 16-year-old consensual partners. There may even be several charges related to the same Romeo and Juliet romance, elevating actuarial risk even further. The problem in either example (more offenses than criminally charged or criminal convictions that don't reflect a real sexual offense) cannot be addressed or resolved without the application of clinical judgment.

The problems are frankly even clearer and far more pertinent in the world of juvenile sexually abusive behavior where such behavior is quite frequently never criminally prosecuted. In these cases there are no charges, let alone adjudications, and the court system is never brought into play. Instead, the case is handled by social services, even under circumstances of substantiated sexually abusive behavior. In other cases, even when criminal charges are filed, both juvenile and adult courts prosecuting the cases may lower the charges to non-sexual charges, or quite frequently continue the case throughout treatment. In any of these situations, evaluations for sexual reoffense must be made absent of the sort of highly defined circumstances (such as number of adjudicated sexual offenses, or even nonsexual offenses) that make up the body of the actuarial assessment. In fact, of the 12 risk factors that comprise the Juvenile Sexual Offense Recidivism Risk Assessment Tool-II, seven pertain to actual adjudications[4] or criminal charges. For this reason, the JSORRAT may only be administered to adjudicated sexual offenders as that is the population upon which the instrument was built and standardized, thus making it a tool of choice only in certain conditions. If used with uncharged or unadjudicated juvenile sexual offenders, the instrument will necessarily reflect low risk for sexual recidivism. Hence, when it comes to youths receiving evaluation and treatment through the social service system, only clinical evaluation can address the population.

Depending on the clinical assessment instrument, the clinical evaluator may decide, not just on how to weight risk factors, but also on how and even what information to include in the assessment in order to most meaningfully explore and assess the risk factors named and described by the instrument. Regardless of the instrument itself, the evaluator is empowered by the clinical assessment process to gather, use and, frankly, interpret information from multiple sources, and therefore must apply professional judgment in order to consolidate complex data. Unless one doubts clinical judgment under any circumstances, this is a strength and defining feature of the clinical assessment instrument, which although not replacing clinical judgment nevertheless provides structure and shape to otherwise unaided clinical judgment.

THE GUIDING LIGHT

In taking stock of risk factors, then, the structured assessment instrument adds guidance and organization to the process, and anchors clinical judgment to the professional literature and, whenever available, an empirical base. Indeed, the limitations of clinical judgment require strongly designed and well-organized risk assessment instruments, as well as instruments that allow for transparency, so that the reader of the final evaluation may see how the evaluator arrived at the final destination.

It is true that clinical practice is flawed and imperfect; the same, of course, is true of actuarial and research-driven practice in general. Risk assessment instruments create a more level and even map from which to observe the territory, take stock, and approach and complete the journey.

CLINICALLY ASSIGNING RISK

In the actuarial assessment, risk is assigned entirely from the total risk factor score. However, despite the fact that information for a clinical assessment of risk is obtained from the psychosocial assessment and other

---

4. Adjudication is the juvenile court equivalent of a conviction.

means, the evaluator is still faced with the task of actually assigning a level of risk, most often rendered as low, moderate, or high risk, or with in-between categories such as low-moderate and moderate-high for greater distinction and nuance.

In the most straightforward description, unless assessed by point score as in an actuarial assessment, the risk level is based upon the more-or-less confluence of a pattern of high-, moderate-, or low-risk items. In fact, determinations that risk factors are "present," "partially or possibly present," or "not present" is simply another way of saying that an individual risk factor is assessed as high, moderate, or low risk. This is not true in the case of the J-RAT, which uses a more dimensional scoring system, and assigns a specific risk level to each of 12 risk domains (in effect, "super" risk factors) that, in turn, determine the overall level of risk.

Regardless, in the simple scoring models employed by clinical risk assessment instruments, the greater the number of risk factors or domains assessed at high risk, the greater the likelihood that overall risk will be assigned as high, as noted by Boer et al. (1997). Conversely, the fewer the number of risk factors assessed as present (in effect, designating them as low-risk factors), the lower the overall assigned level of risk. However, unless all of the risk factors are assessed as high or low, which makes the final assignment of risk level relatively easy, the trick here (when using nominal designations, not numerical scores) is figuring out what counts as moderate risk, or, if "in-between" labels are used, what constitutes moderate-high or moderate-low risk. Even if weighting risk factors did not come into play earlier in the process, it certainly does here. Do equally balanced numbers of high- and low-risk factors, for instance, neutralize one another and equal moderate risk? When the well-defined instrument is used by a well-trained and experienced evaluator, informed and guided judgment come into play.

Even in the case of the J-SOAP's numerical scoring system, clinical judgment comes into play, and must. However, in the point scored system of the J-SOAP, the evaluator applies clinical judgment *after* the total score is derived. At that point the evaluator must weigh the point score[5] against other variables and information noted by the evaluator but not included in the J-SOAP assessment. In fact, this may mean the contribution or neutralizing effects of protective factors results in an assigned risk level lower than the J-SOAP point score may indicate; equally, it may mean that having

---

5. Although the J-SOAP doesn't render a risk level based on the point score, the meaning of the point score is perfectly clear; simply put, high point score equals high risk.

access to and interpreting additional information elevates the risk level to beyond that indicated by the J-SOAP point score. In the nominally (rather than numerically) scored assessment instrument, clinical judgment is embedded *within* the actual assigned risk level, although its flexibility is decided by the tool design.

In the ERASOR, for instance, the evaluator must simply scrutinize the overall confluence or pattern of risk factors and decide whether they add up to high, moderate, or low risk for sexual reoffense. Unlike the J-SOAP (which never formally assigns a risk level), any adjustment to risk level must come after a risk level has first been determined by the ERASOR. The J-RAT is a little different as patterns of risk elements within larger risk domains are examined and then clustered into a level of risk for that particular risk domain, at which point additional information, such as that considered by the J-SOAP, can influence and shape the level or risk assigned at the risk domain (or super risk factor) level. This may involve the weighting of items within each domain, and almost certainly deciding how best to interpret the aggregate of risk elements within the domain, as well as the possibility of protective factors coming into play. As described below, unlike other assessment instruments, the J-RAT assesses risk elements within domains not as present, partially present, or absent, but in terms of the level of concern about an item, ranging from none to significant concern.

STATISTICAL SUPPORT AND PREDICTIVE CAPACITY OF CURRENT RISK ASSESSMENT INSTRUMENTS

Regardless of the instrument used, if well designed and embodying the quality assurance criteria described in Chapter 12, the current risk assessment instruments are likely to lead to the same or similar conclusions regarding risk. The same is true of well-developed instruments used to assess anxiety, depression, and self-esteem, for instance. In part, this is because similar instruments measure similar constructs and, if well informed and well developed, they are likely to embrace and build upon the same ideas, and if they seek to establish concurrent validity[6] they are likely to use other similar instruments as a measure of their own effectiveness.

---

6. Concurrent validity reflects either the degree of similarity when two different ways of measuring something produce similar results, or how well one test matches another in measuring the same phenomenon (especially when one test has already demonstrated validity).

In selecting a clinical assessment instrument, then, the issue for the evaluator is more likely to be one of practicality and comfort, and less one of greater or lesser confidence in the instrument. If solid psychometrics and statistical method are key, then the evaluator is likely to seek an actuarial assessment, and now has one available in the JSORRAT, although as noted it can presently be used only with adjudicated adolescent male sexual offenders. If more interested in the flexibility and comprehensiveness of an instrument, then a clinical instrument will be the choice, and for evaluators seeking as much empirical validation as possible the choice will be either the ERASOR or the J-SOAP as they have had the most research applied to them, whereas the J-RAT has been exposed to no testing at all.

Statistical work on the J-SOAP and ERASOR have for the most part focused on the internal construction and reliability of the instruments, as well as correlations with delinquent behaviors in general, including sexually abusive behavior, rather than on predictive validity (the essential key to the effectiveness and accuracy of risk assessment instruments). Various studies show general support for the manner in which these instruments are constructed, including inter-rater reliability[7] and their capacity to differentiate between nondelinquents and nonsexual juvenile offenders, and perhaps among types of juvenile sexual offenders. Worling (2004), for instance, described studies that offer support for measures of reliability (such as internal construction and inter-rater reliability) in the ERASOR and mild "tentative support" (p. 250) for the capacity of the ERASOR to distinguish between first-time juvenile sexual offenders and those who have previously recidivated. Nevertheless, Worling (2004), Worling and Långström (2006), and Viljoen et al. (2008) each note the absence of prospective data regarding predictive validity for either the J-SOAP and ERASOR (or the JSORRAT), and Prentky and Righthand (Righthand et al., 2005), the authors of the J-SOAP, also note that regarding the J-SOAP "we can provide no definitive feedback regarding the critical question of predictive validity" (p. 25). Viljoen and colleagues additionally describe a general absence of well-validated assessment instruments to assist in the prediction of sexual recidivism for juvenile sexual offenders.

In their study of risk instruments in the assessment of sexual recidivism in juvenile sexual offenders, Viljoen and colleagues (2008) applied and contrasted the J-SOAP-II and the JSORRAT-II, both of which are designed to assess risk for recidivism in juvenile sexual offenders (the former is a

---

7. Inter-rater reliability reflects the level of consistency by which different evaluators yield similar results when independently using the same instrument to assess the same case.

clinical instrument and the latter, actuarial), and the Structured Assessment of Violence Risk in Youth (SAVRY). The SAVRY (Borum, Bartel, & Forth, 2002) is a 30-item clinical assessment instrument designed to assess and predict general (nonsexual) violence in adolescents, including 24 specific risk factors and six protective factors (described briefly in Chapter 8). The three instruments were used to examine and predict sexual recidivism in 169 adolescent (male) sexual offenders both while in treatment and following discharge from treatment over a follow-up period of $6\frac{1}{2}$ years. Consistent with other recidivism studies (Chapter 5), there was a low recidivism rate for sexual reoffense (8.3 percent) compared to a recidivism rate of 42.8 percent for any reoffense (including sexual and nonsexual violent and nonviolent offenses). However, none of the three instruments predicted sexual recidivism (note that the SAVRY is not intended for this purpose). Neither the J-SORRAT or J-SOAP total scores predicted reoffending of any type (sexual or nonsexual), although J-SOAP scores "nearly reached significance" (p. 14) and the SAVRY was *somewhat* effective at predicting nonsexual violent offenses (as designed); however, both the J-SOAP and SAVRY were more effective in predicting nonsexual violent reoffending in adolescents age 16 and older than in younger adolescents. Viljoen et al. concluded by noting the limited ability of either the J-SOAP-II or J-SORRAT-II to predict sexual recidivism in their study.

In their study of 60 adolescent sexual offenders, Martinez, Flores, and Rosenfeld (2007) showed low to mild predictive validity for the J-SOAP with respect to a sample of adolescent male sexual offenders. The total J-SOAP score showed a correlation of .34[8] with any reoffense and .31 with sexual recidivism in the follow-up period (which is unfortunately not specific in the article, nor was the identified contact author able to provide this information, although nonsexual recidivism is cited as 20 percent and sexual recidivism at 13.3 percent). The J-SOAP is composed of two scales (with two subscales within each), one of which assesses static scale risk factors and the other dynamic factors. However, although the dynamic scale was somewhat modestly associated with sexual reoffense at .41, the static scale was not (correlation $r = .13$). The authors note though "the superior performance of the dynamic items" might have been partially influenced by the fact that evaluators completing the J-SOAP in this study were also the clinicians treating the adolescents who were thus "quite

---

8. Correlations between 0.3 and 0.49 are often considered in the low-moderate range, and 0.5 to 1.0 high.

familiar with the adolescent offenders" (p. 1293), possibly pointing to the far greater influence of professional judgment when guided by a structured clinical instrument than the instrument itself.[9]

However, Prentky's (2006) study involving 667 male juvenile sexual offenders, showed moderate support for the J-SOAP's capacity to correctly classify risk into the three categories of low, moderate, and high, and especially supported the idea that a prediction of low risk is likely to be the most robust. In this study, among boys classified by the J-SOAP as low risk there was 6.1 percent sexual recidivism, compared to a recidivism rate of 15.8 percent for boys assessed at moderate risk, and 56 percent recidivism for those assessed at high risk. The study supported a .50 correlation between J-SOAP assignment and reoffense for pre-adolescent boys and a .43 correlation for adolescents, both falling into the high end of moderate correlation. In a more recent study drawn from the same sample of sexually abusive youth, Prentky, Pimental, Cavanaugh, and Righthand (in press) found a 30.7 percent sexual recidivism rate among 123 preadolescent boys and 23 percent recidivism among the 69 adolescent boys, for a 27.6 percent overall recidivism rate. In this study, the J-SOAP total score accurately predicted recidivism in 47.3 percent of the cases and accurately predicted low risk in 88.6 percent of the cases, again showing greater accuracy, or predictive validity, in estimates of low risk.[10]

One study has been completed on the Juvenile Risk Assessment Scale (JRAS) by its authors (Hiscox, Witt, & Haran, 2007). The study followed 231 adjudicated male adolescent sexual offenders for an average follow-up period of $8\frac{1}{2}$ years, and found a 16 percent sexual recidivism rate and a nonsexual recidivism rate of 52 percent. Fifty-one percent of the sample was rated low risk for a sexual reoffense, 42 percent at moderate risk, and 7 percent at high risk. Of the three primary factors of the JRAS, the "antisocial" factor was moderately predictive of nonsexual recidivism and mildly predictive of sexual recidivism (ROC scores of .70 and .67

---

9. However, the conclusion that evaluators fared better in their risk assessments because of their familiarity with the subjects of the assessment also points to the inconsistencies between clinical practice and statistical research. Ægisdóttir et al. (2006) assert that evaluators should be skeptical about the relative accuracy of their clinical judgments, even when they are working with familiar cases in familiar contexts, as "studies show that clinical predictions were worse than statistical predictions in these conditions" (p. 371). That does not seem to be the case in the Martinez et al. (2007) study.

10. R. A. Prentky, personal communication, April 15, 2008.

respectively[11]), whereas the "sexual deviance" factor proved to not be predictive of either. In fact, regarding predictive validity in terms of true positives and true negatives, that is the number of youths assessed at a risk level that correctly matched actual recidivism, 42 percent of youth assessed at low risk did not sexually reoffend (compared to only 11 percent of low-risk youth who did reoffend). However, only 19 percent of youths assessed at moderate risk and 25 percent of youths assessed at high risk actually sexually recidivated, suggesting a false positive—or incorrect—rate of 81 percent and 75 percent for youth assessed at moderate and high risk. Again, it appears clear that it is far easier for a risk assessment instrument to accurately assess low risk than moderate or high risk.

Other than the Viljoen et al. (2008) study that compared the J-SOAP, JSORRAT, and SAVRY, the only research involving the JSORRAT is being administered by the primary authors of the instrument. It is still undergoing validation studies, with its focus on both internal construction and especially predictive validity, and at the time of this writing it has thus far been fully validated in Utah and tentatively validated in Iowa, with additional studies planned for California and Georgia. In the meantime, again at the time of writing, the California State Authorized Risk Assessment Tool for Sex Offenders (SARATSO) Review Committee has adopted the JSORRAT as the instrument to be used in that state for the risk assessment of juvenile sexual offenders (California Department of Mental Health, 2008).

THE PREDICTIVE POWER OF NONSEXUAL RISK ASSESSMENT INSTRUMENTS

It is worth noting that assessment instruments that attempt to predict risk for general criminal or violent recidivism show the same weaknesses as assessment instruments that attempt to correctly flag sexual risk.

The SAVRY, for instance, already discussed, shows significant weaknesses regarding predictive validity, and its weaknesses illustrate the difficulty in accurately predicting risk. Catchpole and Gretton (2003) describe limited data available on the SAVRY's psychometric properties; nevertheless, data that are available suggest the instrument's greater capacity to distinguish between low- and high-risk juvenile offenders than accurately predict risk for a violent reoffense. That is, the SAVRY

---

11. A receiver operating characteristic (ROC), or area under the curve (AUC), score of .50 is considered to equal chance only. Scores of .70 and above offer moderate support for accuracy in correctly assigning risk, whereas a score of .85 and above represents moderate to high accuracy in terms of true positives and true negatives.

appears relatively accurate in assessing nonsexual juvenile offenders at low risk for violence, but less accurate in its assessment of high-risk offending. In their study, Catchpole and Gretton noted that the SAVRY correctly classified 40 percent of youth classified as high risk and 96 percent of youth as low risk (based upon actual recidivism rates for violent behavior within the following year). However, whereas the SAVRY correctly assessed 94 percent of youth as low risk, it incorrectly assessed 60 percent of youth as high risk (thus creating a substantial number of false positives, or youth assessed at high risk whose follow-up behavior did not support this risk level). Similarly, Meyers and Schmidt (2008) found the SAVRY accurately assessed low-risk juvenile violent offenders in 97 percent of the cases studied over a three-year follow-up period, whereas 74 percent of the adolescents assessed at moderate risk and 44 percent assessed at high risk did not violently reoffend during the follow-up period. The SAVRY performed similarly in a study of 169 male adolescents conducted by Viljoen et al., 2008), in which it had an accuracy rate of 93 percent in correctly predicting low risk, but an error rate of 90.3 percent among adolescents assessed as moderate risk (only 9.7 percent committed a violent offense), and an 84 percent error rate among adolescents assessed at high risk for violence, among whom only 16 percent actually committed a violent offense during the follow-up period (J. L. Viljoen, personal communication, March 17, 2008). Hence, an adolescent assessed at low risk by the SAVRY will most likely not reoffend, whereas the "picture is less clear for youth who receive ratings of moderate or high" (Meyers & Schmidt 2008, p. 351).

The Youth Level of Service/Case Management Inventory (YLS/CMI) is the very instrument designed to embody the principles of the risk, needs, and responsivity model, and was developed by Hoge and Andrews (2003), two of the authors of the RNR model. However, designed to assess risk for general (nonsexual) criminal recidivism in adolescent offenders, it too has difficulty in accurately predicting risk for reoffense. Although in wide use as a risk assessment and case management instrument, Onifade et al. (2008) point out that there are few studies that demonstrate the validity of the instrument, other than those conducted by its proponents. In their study of 328 adolescent offenders (age 10–16), Onifade et al. found that the YLS/ CMI performed only slightly better than chance in distinguishing between recidivists and nonrecidivists (59 percent accuracy in discrimination). Like the SAVRY, the YLS/CMI was far more effective in correctly identifying low-risk offenders than it was moderate- or high-risk offenders, in which its predictive validity "seems to drop off as the juvenile increases in risk score" (p. 481), and in which 90 percent of the variance in recidivism rate was unexplained by the instrument. They conclude that the predictive validity of the YLS/CMI is small, and is accurate in prediction of recidivism by only 11 percent over chance. Similarly, Catchpole and Gretton (2003) noted that the YLS/CMI demonstrated a 94 percent accuracy rate in correctly identifying low- and moderate-risk offenders in their study of 74 juveniles, but inaccurately assessed high-risk offenders in 70 percent of the cases. In a still earlier study, Jung and Rawana (1999) found that the YLS/CMI (or the Ministry Risk/Need Assessment Form, as it was then called) was able to distinguish between recidivists and nonrecidivists, but again was far more effective in accurately predicting low rather than moderate- or high-risk offenders. With a false positive rate of only 15 percent, the MRNAF accurately assessed low risk in over 85 percent of the cases, but showed a 36 percent false positive rate among high-risk offenders, incorrectly predicting recidivism in almost 58 percent of cases assessed at moderate risk and over 44 percent of cases assessed at high risk.

Thus, it is difficult to accurately assess risk for reoffense, whether for a sexual or nonsexual offense, and predictive validity is difficult to come by. Even though risk assessment instruments seem able to discriminate between recidivists and nonrecidivists, among offenders it is far easier to assess low risk than it is moderate or high risk. This does not mean that we should stop using these instruments. It does, however, mean that we must recognize serious limitations in such instrumentation, and therefore both exercise caution and demonstrate good judgment in using the tools, and wrap them within a larger and more comprehensive risk assessment process.

TO WHAT CONDITIONS DO PREDICTIONS OF RISK APPLY?

Before wrapping up this chapter and moving on to review currently available and in development risk assessment instruments, there is an additional question to be addressed. When we assign a level of risk, under what circumstances are we asserting that the risk level applies?

Risk assessment depicts risk as the product of static and dynamic factors and influences that may allow harm to emerge under certain conditions. "Risk" is therefore greatest, or most active, under conditions when harm can actually occur. Typically, this involves a situation or circumstance where the risky individual is placed into a generally unsupervised setting where he or she can engage in harmful behaviors. However, this is only generally true and may not always be the case, and it is quite possible to imagine that someone may re-engage in harmful behavior even under high-security conditions or under close scrutiny or supervision. So, perhaps a better way of putting this is that risk level is most pertinent under conditions that fail to restrain the individual from causing harm. Consequently, in assessment it's most pertinent to consider risk under circumstances when the individual is placed in an at-risk situation (which will be different for different individuals).

It's not likely, for instance, that a juvenile sexual offender will engage in a sexual offense of a child while in residential treatment.[12] Hence, as we assess risk there's little point in describing the juvenile at a "moderate" level of risk for child molestation while in residential care and under staff supervision 24 hours a day, but at "high" risk if released into the community at this time. If we are to meaningfully assess and describe risk for harm, we are *only* interested in risk when in a situation that may fail to otherwise restrain harm. Hence, the juvenile either is or is not at high risk, because we are only interested in knowing about his or her risk level under conditions where the youth is unrestrained, and not conditions where conditions prevent the emergence of harm. There is, thus, no dual level of risk (one while in custody, for instance, and another when out of custody), and no risk assessment instrument provides the means for providing more than one assigned level of risk, although an instrument may provide a means for describing circumstances when the individual is at the greatest level of risk. In fact, it is precisely when the sexual offender is unsupervised or under conditions that fail to restrain him or her, and therefore capable of harm, in which we are interested in assigning risk.

Hence, we assign risk based on conditions under which harm may emerge, not under conditions that are likely to restrain harm. To use another example, we may be very worried about the level of risk a rapist poses when he is in the community, but while he's in jail we're generally not worried about his risk as he is contained. If we believed him at high risk for rape upon release, we would be unlikely to say he's low risk at the moment (i.e., while in jail); we'd simply note that he's at high risk for a sexual reoffense.

CAN RISK FOR REOFFENSE ALWAYS BE ASSESSED?

Finally, what if you cannot assess risk? The capacity to do so requires that you have adequate information upon which to base an estimate of the probability that a sexual reoffense may occur. This information may range from adequate forensic or other definite evidence that a previous sexual

---

12. Although the juvenile sexual offender certainly could sexually abuse a child while on a home pass or while unsupervised *if* a child is available.

offense has occurred, including prior adjudication or a history of sexually abusive behavior substantiated through social services and/or the acknowledgment of the youth that he or she engaged in prior sexually abusive behavior. This is the starting point, of course—that is, the certainty that prior sexually abusive behavior has in fact occurred. Beyond this, the evaluator needs adequate information about the behavior itself and its circumstances, the juvenile and his or her history, and all the other information pertaining to risk (and protective) factors and related material that has been liberally described throughout the book.

Without such information, however, although it is quite possible to conduct a comprehensive psychosocial evaluation, with all of its related components, and arrive at a mental health diagnosis (if that's part of the evaluation), it is not possible to evaluate risk for reoffense. To do so, you must know that a previous offense has occurred (hence, risk for *re*offense). As it is not likely that the evaluator was present at the time of the known or alleged offense, he or she depends on the information provided. Although the evaluator may unearth more relevant information during the assessment of risk, perhaps including the juvenile's acknowledgment that an offense occurred or disclosure of further details of prior sexually abusive behavior (including perhaps more victims than were previously known, or more severe sexually abusive behavior), it is nonetheless not the evaluator's job to investigate whether an offense occurred or not. That is the job of either law enforcement or social services, which in turn provide such information to the evaluator upon which to build assessment.

For instance, in a case where there is no substantiated evidence that an offense occurred—the previously alleged victim recants and now reports that no sexual abuse occurred, and the juvenile denies engaging in any sexually inappropriate behavior—there is no basis for an estimate for reoffense. This doesn't mean that the evaluator will not try to engage the alleged offender and get past what may be denial on his or her part, or perhaps recommend to social services or the police that a further investigation be initiated. It certainly doesn't mean that the evaluator should question the previously alleged victim, as it's unlikely that the evaluator will or should be in direct contact with the alleged victim, although they may have contact with the alleged victim's parents or (with consent from the legal guardian) the alleged victim's therapist if he or she is in treatment of some kind. And it certainly doesn't mean that the evaluator or any one else necessarily believes that an offense did not occur (in fact, people may be sure that an offense has occurred). It simply means that there's no basis for evaluating risk for reoffense. Based on this description, in fact, it's likely that there wouldn't be grounds for prosecuting the case, assuming prosecution was sought.

This is a clear example of a circumstance where assessment for further risk is not professionally or ethically possible. In order to assess risk for reoffense, an index offense must have occurred and be known to have occurred, at least to the point where there is strong and supported evidence of the alleged offense. Under those circumstances, if the juvenile (or adult, for that matter) continues to report that he or she did not engage in the offense, we would consider this a possible case of denial, and risk assessment could proceed, although with some caution. However, without definite proof we cannot say the offense occurred as alleged and perhaps it didn't occur at all, or at least as described. That is, perhaps the alleged offender is telling the truth, or some variant of the truth.[13] Accordingly, the risk assessment instrument selected must allow the evaluator to note uncertainty, and the risk assessment process must therefore allow for an exploration and description of such uncertainty. The process itself should also allow for the possibility of an "uncertain" risk assessment, or even a conclusion that it is not possible to assess risk at all given the uncertainties of the case.

However, if risk level for reoffense is assessed as uncertain or not possible to assess, it may nevertheless be both possible and acceptable to reflect on what the risk level might be if the offense occurred as alleged, so long as it is clear that this is completely conjecture and if the risk assessment instrument or larger risk assessment process allows for such speculation and formulation (which it should). An assessment of uncertain or not possible to assess, frankly, may not be a popular decision to make in terms of whoever has made the referral to the evaluator, but nonetheless it may be the only appropriate and ethically proper outcome. One way or another, a well-designed risk assessment instrument will lead the evaluator through the process and help point to the outcome, including the level of the risk. In the case of an actuarial assessment, such as the JSORRAT, without facts it either will not be possible to conduct the assessment at all or it will produce a low (or no) assignment of risk.

There is also the scenario in which the adolescent did previously engage in sexually abusive behavior, but several years before he or she entered treatment. For adolescents, several years could mean that their prior offense occurred at age 8 or 9 and they are now 12, 13, 14, or older. In Chapter 9, I described the case of Cary who entered sexual offender treatment at age 17 for a single and mild sexual offense that he had committed at age 12, but for which he never received treatment, although

---

13. Under these circumstances, "alleged" is certainly the term to use in describing all aspects of the situation.

he had engaged in continued sexually troubled (but non-abusive) behavior during his adolescence. Let's now quickly look at the case of Ramon, however, who engaged in three incidents of sexually abusive behavior with a younger child when he was 8, for which Ramon was never treated and is now age 13. Although he has continued to act out in a behaviorally troubled manner, and unquestionably needs treatment (probably in a contained residential setting), there have nevertheless been no further incidents or allegations of sexually abusive, or even sexually troubled, behavior since he was age 8. Is it possible, then, to ethically assess Ramon for the possibility of a sexual reoffense when his last known or alleged offense was five years ago when he was age 8, and he is now age 13?

Not only may it not be possible to meaningfully reassess risk in Ramon's case, but in cases like Ramon and Carey's the consequences of assessing risk (and therefore applying the concept of "juvenile sexual offender," or its less harsh sounding counterpart, "sexually abusive youth") may be significant, unnecessarily punitive and stigmatizing, and have very direct consequences on the life of the adolescent. Further, as Calder (2001) notes, risk assessment is not about determining guilt or innocence: "We do not have sufficiently accurate instruments to know who is guilty or not guilty. It is the task of the court to decide who is guilty"(p. 12).

Addressed again in Chapter 15, as we look clearly at principles and guidelines upon which to base the risk assessment process, it may be enough for now to say that it will not always be possible to assess risk for sexual reoffense. The evaluator should thus be prepared, and know how to handle this eventuality.

THE DESIGNER-USER COVENANT

I've spent two chapters covering the nature and use of risk assessment instruments without yet reviewing the instruments themselves. The fact that there is so much to say about such instruments speaks to our need for a broad understanding of and knowledge about the use of risk assessment tools, as well as the sometimes hidden complexities that lie in the process of applying a risk assessment instrument. Actually, difficulties and complexities are less hidden than they are not obvious until one uses risk assessment instruments and discovers that they are not cut-and-dried, even if they are the best we have available to us. This is, of course, because the process of risk assessment and determination of risk level is itself complex and not easy. To expect tools to do anymore than guide the process is asking for a great deal. The promise of actuarial instruments is that, through statistical means, assessment can be made straightforward and easy, perhaps even removing any responsibility for outcome (i.e., assignment of risk level) from the shoulders of the evaluator. Clinical assessment instruments, on the other hand, at least those currently available, neither make nor imply such a promise. They merely pledge to provide a well-informed, well-structured, and well-defined set of guidelines by which to assist trained evaluators to engage in evaluation.

The covenant, however, that must exist between instrument authors and instrument users is this. The author will provide a meaningful method and tool for engaging in a thorough assessment of risk upon which the user can depend for its foundation in the theoretical and empirical literature. In turn, the user will develop the professional knowledge and expertise required to use the instrument in a well-informed manner and allow it to guide but not determine the assignment of risk level.

Highlighting the responsibility of the instrument "end user," Ward, Gannon, and Birgden (2007) write that "practitioners have obligations to always use such measures appropriately, ensure they are trained in their administration, and most importantly, make sure that the assessment process culminates in an etiological formulation that is based around the individual's features alongside those they share with other offenders" (p. 207). Given the developmental "moving target" element of juvenile risk assessment, the issues and stakes are higher still than they are for adult sexual offenders, and perhaps even more so in light of national sexual offender registry laws that pull sexually abusive youth into their net as well as adult sexual offenders.

CHAPTER 14

Reviewing Available and In Development Instruments

T HIS CHAPTER REVIEWS and provides a summary and overview of risk assessment instruments in current use or development, although some instruments require a little more explanation and description than others.

The most commonly used instruments have already been described in previous chapters, and as you know by now the JSORRAT is presently the only actuarial assessment, even though not fully validated. In terms of clinical assessment instruments, the ERASOR and J-SOAP are the most commonly used and cited clinical tools, with the J-RAT used far less frequently, but nevertheless also in common use. Each of these instruments is available at no cost and is available either through the Internet or through the authors.

The JRAS was developed as an empirically guided clinical instrument in order to meet the needs of the New Jersey court system to assess and classify juvenile sexual offenders into a low-, moderate-, and high-risk tiering system for the New Jersey sexual offender registry tier system, and was adopted for use by the New Jersey juvenile court system in 2006 (Hiscox, Witt, & Haran, 2007). The MEGA and RSBP<12 also represent clinical assessment instruments, although both are in development. The SHARP, based upon and replacing the earlier Risk Assessment Matrix (Chapter 7), is also in development as a clinical risk assessment instrument, although not as far along in its development and not easily accessible. However, its inclusion is notable as it represents the same model and philosophy followed by each of the other clinical instruments, and like the AIM2 risk assessment process, also noted in this chapter, is an assessment instrument developed in the United Kingdom, rather than North America.

This chapter also briefly describes instruments like the Sexual Adjustment Inventory-Juvenile (SAI-J), Multiphasic Sex Inventory (MSI), and Multi-dimensional Inventory of Development, Sex, and Aggression (MIDSA), each of which may contribute significantly to the risk assessment process, although none are risk assessment instruments (although the SAI-J is described by its authors as a risk instrument). I also describe the Treatment Progress Inventory for Adolescents who Sexually Abuse (TPI-ASA) and Juvenile Sex Offense Specific Treatment Needs & Progress Scale, both instruments that, while not intended for risk assessment, may be useful in reassessment over time.

As we review the risk assessment instruments, we note the similarities as well as the differences. However, in many ways the evaluator's choice may be based upon the design of the instrument, its applicability and ease of use, and its familiarity to the evaluator, as well as the method, philosophy, or ideology behind the design. This may be particularly true when selecting between an actuarial or clinical instrument. However, the evaluator may also choose to use and combine more than one instrument, whether actuarial or clinical, within the same assessment. Further, regardless of differences in conceptualization there are mostly similarities among instruments, especially, of course, among the clinical instruments. That is, although a wide range of risk factors is included across the span of available assessment instruments, as described in Chapter 7, these most commonly fall into 10 types: (1) sexual beliefs, attitudes, and drive, (2) sexually abusive behavior, (3) personal victimization, (4) general antisocial behavior, (5) social relationships and connection, (6) personal characteristics, (7) psychosocial functioning, (8) family relationships and functioning, (9) general environmental conditions, and (10) response to treatment.

CULTURE, GENDER, AND ASSESSMENT INSTRUMENTS

In the case of the AIM2 and the SHARP, it is not at all clear that their origins in the United Kingdom makes any difference in their construction or application. Their construction, model, underlying premises, and selection of risk factors do not appear in any way to reflect a different culture or set of risk factors or appear specific to a population of sexually abusive youth found in the United Kingdom as opposed to the United States or Canada. They thus appear, for the most part, very similar to and almost in-distinguishable from North American clinical instruments (the J-SOAP, J-RAT, and ERASOR). Likewise, the North American tools do not appear any less relevant to assessments in the United Kingdom than they do assessments in Canada or the United States. We can extend this to assessments in other parts of the world, as well, including Europe, Asia, Australia, and New Zealand, where these instruments are also used.

We can thus either conclude that juvenile sexual offenders and the conditions that give rise to the development of juvenile sexual offending are the same the world over, or these instruments are far more culture bound than we have considered or realized. In fact, they may not be appropriate for use in countries and cultures for which they were developed, and the evaluator should be aware of this possibility in reviewing the instruments. Frankly, even in translating the instruments from one language to another (in these cases, always from English), significant and unintended changes may be made to the intention or meaning of items included in the instrument.

The exception to this is the JSORRAT, and the same will (or should) be true for any actuarial assessment instrument given its dependence on a validated base rate bound to a specified geographic location. Actuarial instruments, therefore, always start out as geographically, and possibly culturally, bound due to their process of construction and validation.

So, evaluators, be aware of cultural biases built into the development of risk assessment instruments, and be equally aware that most risk assessment instruments have been developed for use with adolescent boys of more-or-less average intelligence. Even those tools that specify they may be used for girls or lower functioning adolescents may be wandering outside of the parameters within which they were developed and the empirical or literature base from which their ideas were drawn.

THE RISK ASSESSMENT INSTRUMENTS

For the remainder of the chapter I provide relatively brief summaries of currently available or in development instruments designed and intended specifically for the assessment of sexual recidivism in sexually abusive youth. These overviews are necessarily brief, although some offer more detail than others, but to some degree the length and detail of the description is related to the complexity of, or special issues related to, the instrument or its design. It is, of course, not possible to provide copies of actual assessment instruments, or include these in an Appendix. However, I have included details[1] of how to obtain copies of each tool, some of which are available at no cost, or how to gather more information about instruments still in development.

---

1. Acquisition and contact details are accurate at the time of writing.

Juvenile Risk Assessment Tool (J-RAT)

The J-RAT is available at www.stetsonschool.org/Clinical_Materials/Assessment_Tools/assessment_tools.html

The J-RAT (version 3) is a literature/empirically based instrument designed for the structured clinical assessment of adolescent males, ages 12–18, who have or are alleged to have engaged in sexually abusive behavior. The J-RAT may also be used to more generally assess individuals reported to have engaged in sexually inappropriate behavior that may not be defined as sexually abusive. However, in this case, the J-RAT will not yield an assessment of risk for sexual reoffense, due to the absence of a history of sexually abusive behavior.

The J-RAT is composed of 117 individual risk elements grouped into 12 logically derived risk domains:

- Responsibility (8 risk elements)
- Relationships (10 risk elements)
- Cognitive Abilities, Skills, and Insight (4 risk elements)
- Social Skills (7 risk elements)
- Response to Past Trauma (6 risk elements)
- Personal Characteristics (14 risk elements)
- Psychiatric Comorbidity and Prior Treatment (6 risk elements)
- Substance Abuse (4 risk elements)
- Nonsexual Antisocial Behaviors (13 risk elements)
- History of Sexually Abusive Behavior (22 risk elements)
- Family Factors (18 risk elements)
- Environmental Conditions (5 risk elements)

Each risk domain represents an area of activity, attitude, skill, behavior, personality, history, or environment relevant to the development of a complete picture of the individual youth and identified as an area of possible risk. Included within each domain are risk elements (in effect, risk factors themselves), which together provide a sense of the risk for reoffense attached to that domain. Accordingly, each risk domain is, in effect, a super-risk factor, consolidating and representing individual risk elements within the domain. Risk elements within each domain (ranging, as shown, from 4 to 22 risk elements within any particular risk domain) are fully described in the instrument to ensure consistency in interpretation and scoring among evaluators, and each element is assessed with respect to the level of concern associated with it, ranging from none or not applicable to mild, moderate, and significant concern, as well as allowing a "not known" choice. Each superordinate risk domain is assessed from no risk to high risk (with increments of low, low-moderate, moderate, moderate-high, and high), also providing an option of "uncertain."

Once risk domains are used to group and organize similar factors (i.e., risk elements), the evaluator is able to assess each individual risk element with relative ease, leading to a complete assessment of risk in each given risk domain. Such a model allows the evaluator to concentrate on many individual areas of possible risk without becoming overwhelmed or disorganized by the sheer amount of information that must be examined, and it creates a series of smaller assessments within and across each risk domain which together add up to the complete assessment of risk. As a result, the final assessment of risk is actually the outcome of a series of smaller assessments in distinct risk domains. The advantage of subsuming individual elements of risk under larger risk domains is that it allows the evaluator to examine many individual potential risk factors before rendering a clinical judgment about risk in any given risk domain. That is, *macro* decisions about risk are always informed by *micro* decisions at a lower level, adding up to the overall assessment of risk as the assessment is completed, illustrated in Figure 14.1.

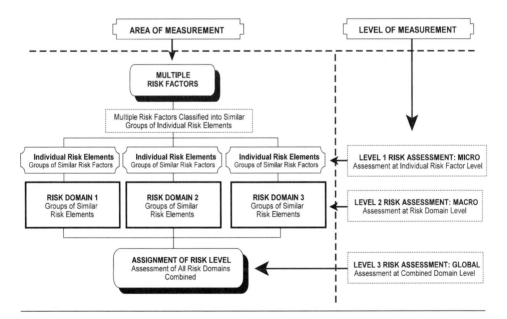

Figure 14.1   Assessment of risk factors and domains at micro, macro, and global levels.

The J-RAT requires written comments that explain assigned risk in each domain, as well as requiring a written concluding narrative that explains the overall assigned risk level. Although not factoring protective factors directly into the assignment of risk, the J-RAT directly addresses protective factors and allows the evaluator to reflect upon and include a review of protective factors in the assessment. The dimensional nature of assessing individual risk elements along a continuum of significance allows protective factors to be considered at that level, and the instrument further requires the evaluator to describe protective factors that may contribute to a reduction in assigned risk level. Following the assignment of a risk level, the instrument also defines characteristics specifically related to the adolescent's sexually abusive behavior, possible risk scenarios, and factors that may have motivated or contributed to the juvenile's history of sexually abusive behavior.

Reassessment over Time   The J-RAT can be used for re-evaluation, and each domain includes a section that allows for the evaluator's assessment of recent changes (within the past six months) in each risk element. However, although the J-RAT may be used for reassessment over time, it has a companion instrument specifically designed for reassessment of risk, with a focus on dynamic risk factors and, in effect, response to treatment. The Interim Modified Risk Assessment Tool (IM-RAT) measures 110 individual risk elements folded into 13 risk domains, all which assess dynamic risk factors or those associated with, and the targets for, treatment, as well as four additional factors linked to static assessment, and 20 that directly assess the youth's progress in treatment for sexually abusive behavior (for a total of 134 factors in 16 risk domains).

J-RAT Variants   The J-RAT may be used to assess risk in cognitively lower functioning adolescents, but its variant, the Cognitively Impaired/Juvenile Risk Assessment Tool (CI/J-RAT), is designed for risk assessment in lower functioning adolescents. For children age 12 or younger, the Latency Age-Sexual Adjustment and Assessment Tool (LA-SAAT) is an additional variant of the J-RAT intended for the assessment of sexual behavior problems and sexually abusive behavior in younger children. However, both the CI/J-RAT and LA-SAAT are derivatives of the J-RAT. Although both are structured and literature-based instruments like the parent J-RAT, in absence of much literature addressing cognitively impaired juvenile sexual offenders or children with sexual behavior problems (see Chapter 10), these instruments are far more theoretical in design and orientation than fully informed by empirical literature as little literature exists. Like the

J-RAT, although both the CI/J-RAT and LA-SAAT may be used for reassessment, they both have companion interim assessment instruments designed specifically for reassessment with a focus on dynamic risk factors.

ESTIMATE OF RISK OF ADOLESCENT SEXUAL OFFENCE RECIDIVISM (ERASOR)

The ERASOR is available at www.forensicare.org/images/ERASOR2.0.pdf, or through the lead author, James Worling at jworling@ican.net

The ERASOR (version 2.0) is an empirically guided checklist developed to assist clinicians in estimating the short-term risk of a sexual reoffense for youth aged 12–18, and can be used to assess both males and females. It is composed of 25 risk factors falling into five categories:

- Sexual Interests, Attitudes, and Behaviors *(4 risk factors)*
- Historical Sexual Assaults *(9 risk factors)*
- Psychosocial Functioning *(6 risk factors)*
- Family/Environmental Functioning *(4 risk factors)*
- Treatment *(2 risk factors)*
- The ERASOR additionally allows an "Other Factor" category

Each risk factor is coded as either present, possibly or partially present, not present, or unknown, and the instrument provides an overall risk assessment rating of low, moderate, or high. The ERASOR does not describe nor provide any means for considering protective factors in the assignment of a risk level.

The ERASOR is a briefer and far less complex tool than the J-RAT, and thus far simpler to use and complete. Nevertheless, like all risk assessment instruments, using the ERASOR carefully and sensitively requires clinical experience. In addition to the instrument itself, a coding manual is also available (Worling, 2006b), which offers examples of how to assess each risk factor and provides further instruction on how to use and score the ERASOR.

JUVENILE SEX OFFENDER ASSESSMENT PROTOCOL-II (J-SOAP-II)

The J-SOAP is available at www.csom.org/pubs/jsoap.pdf or www.ncjrs.gov/pdffiles1/ojjdp/202316.pdf

The J-SOAP-II is an empirically guided checklist used to aid in the systematic review of risk factors that have been identified in professional literature as being associated with sexual and criminal offending. It is designed to be used with 12–18-year-old males who have been adjudicated for sexual offenses, as well as nonadjudicated youths with a history of sexually coercive behavior. The J-SOAP-II is composed of four scales that include 28 risk factors, two of which measure static risk factors and two of which measure dynamic factors, and are thus of particular importance in reassessment over time.

1. Static Scale:
   I. Sexual Drive/Preoccupation (8 risk factors)
   II. Impulsive/Antisocial Behavior (8 risk factors)
2. Dynamic Scale
   I. Intervention (7 risk factors)
   II. Community Stability/Adjustment (5 risk factors)

The J-SOAP rates each factor from 0–2 (0 = absence of factor, 2 = clear presence of factor), but it does not assign risk ratings. The J-SOAP manual notes that assessments of risk should not be assigned based on J-SOAP scores alone, and that the instrument should be used as part of a larger and more comprehensive assessment of risk.

Although the J-SOAP is very straightforward and simple to use, it is nevertheless worth noting one more time that a significant ingredient in the use of the instrument is clinical insight and expertise.

THE JUVENILE RISK ASSESSMENT SCALE (JRAS)

The JRAS manual is available at www.state.nj.us/lps/dcj/megan/jras_manual_scale_ 606.pdf

The JRAS was adopted by the New Jersey court system in June 2008 to classify juvenile sexual offenders into low-, moderate-, and high-risk tiers for the New Jersey sexual offender registry system. It is an empirically guided clinical instrument designed to assess male and female juvenile sexual offenders, although only adolescent males, aged 11–19, were included in the single validation study (Hiscox, Witt, & Haran, 2007); the JRAS is used to assess juveniles aged 18 and younger, with no lower age cutoff (P. H. Witt, personal communication, May 15, 2008). The instrument uses a point-based scoring system, and combines fact-based data (such as age of victim) with clinical judgment and evaluation (such as response to treatment and residential support).

Although a manual is available, offering examples of how to score each risk factor, neither the instrument nor manual are especially well defined. The instrument itself does not describe nor allow for the incorporation of protective factors, and its use with boys and girls of all ages is questionable as it does not reflect any differences between male and female juvenile sexual offenders or recognize or take into account developmental differences with regard to younger children.

The JRAS groups 14 risk factors into three categories (sex offense history, antisocial behavior, and environment characteristics), scoring each item from 0–2 points, for a total possible score of 28, in which a score of 0–9 equals low risk, 10–19 moderate risk, and 20 or above high risk. Each risk factor is assessed as low risk (0 points), moderate risk (1 point), or high risk (2 points).

Sex Offense History
- Degree of Force
- Degree of Contact
- Age of Victim
- Victim Selection
- Number of Offenses/Victims
- Duration of Offensive Behavior
- Length of Time Since Last Offense
- Victim Gender

Antisocial Behavior
- History of Antisocial Acts
- Substance Abuse

Environment Characteristics
- Response to Sex Offender Treatment
- Sex Offender Specific Therapy
- Residential Support
- Residential/Educational Stability

JUVENILE SEXUAL OFFENSE RECIDIVISM RISK ASSESSMENT TOOL-II (JSORRAT-II)

The JSORRAT-II is presently available through its primary author, Douglas Epperson at dle@iastate.edu or Epperson et al. (2006).

The JSORRAT-II stands alone as the only actuarial risk assessment instrument. It is designed to statistically assess the likelihood of a sexual reoffense prior to age 18 in male adolescents aged 12–18, with a history of at least one prior adjudicated sexual offense committed between the ages of 12–17. At the time of writing, the instrument technically remains a research tool only in most applications, but it has been validated for use in Utah and is close to validation for use in Iowa, and, as described, has been adopted by the state of California as the instrument of choice in the assessment of juvenile sexual offenders. Despite the fact that it has not been fully validated, its adoption by California virtually ensures its current and immediate use. Nevertheless, the JSORRAT continues to undergo validation and possible revision.

The current prototype was initially normed on 636 male juveniles, age 12–17, adjudicated for a sexual offenses (Utah) between 1990–1992. Based on that sample, the JSORRAT-II is comprised of 12 items or risk factors:

- Number of actual adjudications for sex offenses
- Number of different victims in charged sex offenses
- Length of sex offending history *(charged or adjudicated)*
- Under supervision when any charged or adjudicated sex offenses occurred
- Felony level *(charged or adjudicated)* sex offense committed in public
- Use of deception/grooming in charged or adjudicated sex offenses
- Prior sex offender treatment status
- Number of incidents of hands-on sexual offenses in which the offender was the victim
- Number of incidents of physical abuse in which the offender was the victim
- Any placement in special education
- Number of educational time periods with discipline problems *(elementary through high school)*
- Number of adjudications for non-sexual offenses.

Each risk factor is scored between 0–3 points per item, with a highest possible score of 21. Based on the Utah development sample, for which the JSORRAT-II was tailor made, a total score of 12 or more is considered high risk: 0–2 = low risk (*1 percent recidivism in the original sample*), 3–4 = moderate-low risk. (*6.6 percent recidivism in original sample*), 5–7 = moderate risk (*24.3 percent recidivism in original sample*), 8–11 = moderate-high risk (*43.1 percent recidivism in original sample*), and a score of 12 or more = high risk (*81.8 percent recidivism in original sample*). However, predicted possibilities for reoffense has varied in validation samples in which the JSORRAT-II is being tested elsewhere, and the instrument is thus not only still being validated in other states, but also undergoing continued development and will perhaps result in revisions and, hence, possibly the JSORRAT-III.

However, even in the case of the JSORRAT, evaluators will quite often find that clinical expertise and professional judgment is required. A glance at the risk items that comprise the JSORRAT, for instance, will demonstrate that judgment will sometimes have to be applied in determining if and how conditions related to any particular item are actually met. Further, as the JSORRAT assumes and, in fact, depends upon, adjudications or charges for sexual crimes, the evaluator will have to contend with and decide how to handle plea bargains, charges or adjudications reduced to alternative nonsexual charges by prosecutors or the court in order to avoid stigmatizing youth or the sexual offender registry, and of course cases that never get to court and are handled instead by state social service departments.

THE MULTIPLEX EMPIRICALLY GUIDED INVENTORY OF ECOLOGICAL AGGREGATES FOR ASSESSING SEXUALLY ABUSIVE ADOLESCENTS AND CHILDREN (MEGA)

The MEGA is not available at time of writing. Contact author for further information: L. C. Miccio-Fonseca at lcmf@cox.net.

As noted several times, the MEGA is still in development and is not available for review at this time. It is presently undergoing validation studies, although these seem to be focused on establishing internal construction and reliability rather than predictive validity. Despite several chapters or articles that describe the MEGA (Miccio-Fonseca & Rasmussen, 2006; Rasmussen & Miccio-Fonseca, 2007a, 2007b) it is not clear how the validation studies are designed or what is being validated. In any case, at this time, the MEGA is not yet available.

In its current description, the authors describe the MEGA as a clinical instrument designed to assess potential risk for sexually abusive behaviors and/or sexual improprieties for all youth through age 19,[2] male and female, and at all levels of developmental and cognitive ability. It is intended for use by clinicians and nonclinicians in order to define sexually abusive youth, assess and estimate risk for sexually abusive behavior, guide treatment planning, and evaluate youth over time for improvement.

The MEGA consolidates 76 assessment items into seven broad "ecological aggregates," or superordinate categories by which to assess both risk and protective factors:

- Neuropsychological aggregate (including intellectual functioning, attention problems/deficits, special education)

---

2. The MEGA is designed for youth through age 19, even though if has been described as applicable for all youth *below* age 19 (Rasmussen & Miccio-Fonseca, 2007a, p. 177, p. 195) as well as youth through age 19 (Rasmussen & Miccio-Fonseca, 2007b, p. 85, p. 86, p. 101). The author confirms that the correct cut off age is the 20th birthday, or actually 19 years, 11 months, and 29 days (L. C. Miccio-Fonseca, personal communication, March 17, 2008).

- Family lovemap aggregate (family history, including family history of sexual and general abuse and maltreatment)
- Antisocial aggregate (history of nonsexual criminal offenses and other antisocial behavior)
- Sexual incident aggregate (history of nonconsensual sexual behavior)
- Coercion aggregate (the degree of coercive behavior in sexual behavior)
- Stratagem aggregate (behaviors that suggest intent and motivation for engaging in the sexual behavior)
- Relationship aggregate (the nature of the relationship with the victim, and differences in age, mental capacity, and physical capacity)

It is difficult to address the MEGA in any more detail or further address its strengths or weaknesses, not simply because it is not yet fully developed or available, but because it has not been made available for review at this time.

RISK FOR SEXUAL BEHAVIOR PERPETRATION – BELOW 12 (RSBP<12)

The RSBP<12 is in development. For availability contact author, Tracey Curwen at traceyc@nipissingu.ca

The RSBP<12 is being developed by Tracy Curwen (Curwen, 2006; Curwen, 2007; Curwen & Costin, 2007), one of the two authors of the ERASOR. It is a literature- and empirically based and structured risk assessment instrument for clinically assessing risk for continued sexually abusive behavior in preadolescent boys and girls age 11 and younger. Because it is still in development, the RSBP<12 is currently available only through the author. It is composed of 34 total risk factors identified as either static or dynamic, classified into nine categories.

- Static Characteristics of Sexual Behaviors *(8 risk factors)*
- Static Victimization History *(4 risk factors)*
- Static Family and Environment *(1 risk factor)*
- Dynamic Characteristics of Sexual Behaviors *(5 risk factors)*
- Dynamic Victimization History *(3 risk factors)*
- Dynamic Family and Environment *(4 risk factors)*
- Dynamic Violence and Control *(4 risk factors)*
- Dynamic Personal and Interpersonal Characteristics *(3 risk factors)*
- Dynamic Intervention *(2 risk factors).*

LATENCY AGE-SEXUAL ADJUSTMENT AND ASSESSMENT TOOL (LA-SAAT)

The LA-SAAT is available at www.stetsonschool.org/Clinical_Materials/Assessment_ Tools/assessment_tools.html

As described, the LA-SAAT (version 3) is a variant of the Juvenile Risk Assessment Tool, designed for the structured clinical assessment of pre-adolescent boys, ages 8–13, who have or are alleged to have engaged in sexually inappropriate behavior and/or sexually abusive behavior. The LA-SAAT may be used to assess children reported to have engaged in sexually inappropriate behavior who may not be defined as sexually abusive, as well as children who have engaged in behavior that is sexually aggressive or otherwise sexually abusive. All children assessed by the LA-SAAT are considered to be sexually reactive (Chapter 10), and assesses sexually reactive behavior as abusive to others, exhibitionist, consensual, sexual seeking/consensual, or not possible to assess.

The LA-SAAT contains 19 Domains of Concern that incorporate 160 different elements of risk or concern. These domains contain information and risk elements for both sexual acting out and sexually aggressive behavior. Each domain represents an area of activity, attitude, skill, behavior, personality, history, or environment relevant to the development of a complete picture of the child and his risk to continue in age-in-appropriate and sexualized behaviors (or to sexually reoffend in the case of children who have been sexually abusive to others). Domains are further categorized into four primary areas:

- Personal, Nonsexual Factors
- Sexual History
- Environmental Factors
- Current Status of Sexually Abusive Behaviors.

The scoring scheme and rudiments of the LA-SAAT are essentially the same as the J-RAT, described previously.

AIM2 MODEL OF INITIAL ASSESSMENT (NOT AN ACRONYM)

The AIM2 manual and model is available for purchase through The AIM Project, Quays Reach, 14 Carolina Way, Salford, M50 2ZY, United Kingdom.

Described in Chapters 7 and 8, the AIM2 model of initial assessment is defined by its authors as a risk assessment process by which to determine the level of supervision required by adolescent sexual offenders. However, the AIM2 is virtually indistinguishable from a formal risk assessment instrument, although it provides more extensive process and organizational structure for risk assessment than available formal instruments. The AIM2 model assesses 51 risk factors/concerns (26 static and 25 dynamic) and 22 protective factors/strengths (6 static and 16 dynamic), and yields scored profiles for both concerns and strengths, combining these into a matrix that results in an assessed level of required supervision. The AIM2 doesn't assign a level of risk that is later adjusted by an assessment of protection, but instead it produces a single assessed level of required supervision.

SEXUALLY HARMFUL ADOLESCENT RISK ASSESSMENT PROTOCOL (SHARP)

The SHARP is in development only and not currently available. For more information contact its author Graeme Richardson at Graeme.Richardson@ntw .nhs.uk.

The SHARP (Richardson, in press) is another clinical instrument in development, and it is not clear what it may look like in its final version or even whether it will be further developed and distributed for use. However, I include it here because it offers an additional example of a clinical risk assessment instrument, and further demonstrates the common ground upon which such instruments are built and stand.

Although described as a case management system to address the risk and needs of sexually abusive youth, in its current form the SHARP nonetheless appears very much like a risk assessment instrument rather than an instrument for case management. Intended for the assessment of adolescent males aged 12 through 18, like other clinical instruments the SHARP provides a structured and literature-based approach to the evaluation of sexual recidivism. It is a further development of the Risk Assessment Matrix (Christodoulides, Richardson, Graham, Kennedy, & Kelly, 2005), a literature-based two-stage risk assessment instrument that consisted of 26 risk factors. However, the RAM has since been further developed and renamed the SHARP. In its current form the instrument is comprised of 46 risk factors grouped into 12 domains:

- Sexually Harmful Behavior *(10 risk factors)*
- Antisocial Behavior *(3 risk factors)*
- Adverse Life Experiences *(4 risk factors)*
- Sexual Development and Adjustment *(12 risk factors)*
- Social Development and Adjustment *(2 risk factors)*
- Emotional Development and Adjustment *(2 risk factors)*
- Personality Development and Adjustment *(2 risk factors)*
- Mental Health Development and Adjustment *(2 risk factors)*
- Cognitive Development and Adjustment *(2 risk factors)*
- General Self Regulation and Level of Independence *(2 risk factors)*

- Environmental Risk *(3 risk factors)*
- Motivation and Compliance *(2 risk factors)*.

The SHARP follows the same guiding principles as other described clinical assessment instruments, and it is intended to follow the principles of the risk, need, and responsivity model in helping to structure both case formulation and case management interventions, yielding an overall risk level of low, moderate, or high. Nevertheless, the instrument presently requires continued work to refine and better operationalize and organize its content, structure, terms, definitions, and clarity. For instance, in defining risk factors the SHARP is often vague and in some instances lumps together and consolidates different aspects of risk into single categories, thus treating disparate risk elements as though they were elements of a single taxonomic item. This makes it difficult to clearly understand the conceptual root of the risk factor or how to assess it. Similarly, in some cases it is not clear that the labels assigned to different risk factors correctly identify the type of risk actually addressed by the risk factor.

As noted, it is not clear whether the SHARP will get to the point of development where it is a more practical and defined instrument, or will even be released as a working tool. However, the fact that it is a UK-based instrument rather than North American may also make it more appealing to evaluators in the United Kingdom and Europe if it undergoes further refinement and development. Even so, like the AIM2, the fact that it is a UK instrument does not seem to make a difference in its approach to assessment or its selection of risk factors. One thing, however, that does jump out about the SHARP in its present form is its inclusion of psychopathy as a risk factor included in the personality development and adjustment domain, a concept not included in other risk assessment instruments used to assess juvenile sexual offenders.

The assessment of this particular risk factor requires the additional use of either the Antisocial Process Screening Device (ASPD) or the Hare Psychopathy Checklist-Youth Version (PCL-YV), both instruments that assess for the presence of psychopathic traits in children and adolescents (ages 6–13 and 12–18, respectively). The risk factor therefore buys into the idea that both children and adolescents may exhibit psychopathic traits,[3] and indeed

---

3. The PCL-YV (Forth, Kosson, & Hare, 2003) specifically notes that it is used to assess the presence of psychopathic traits in adolescents, but also that adolescents may *not* be assessed as psychopaths. Nevertheless, this is merely hair splitting as the instrument itself is named the Psychopathy Checklist, and is clearly built on the premise that psychopathy exists in adolescence (and in childhood), even if it is cautious about using the term to define such adolescents.

may be considered psychopaths (or psychopaths in the making), following the lead of the SAVRY (Chapters 7, 8, and 13), a clinical instrument used to assess risk of (nonsexual) violence in adolescents.[4] However, although the presence of serious antisocial behavior is recognized in children and adolescents, there is controversy about defining children and adolescents in such terms (Hart, Watt, & Vincent, 2002; Seagrave & Grisso, 2002; Vitacco, Rogers, & Neumann, 2003), and the evaluator should be aware of such ideas in selecting and using an instrument that extends ideas about antisocial behavior in juveniles to the concept of childhood and adolescent psychopathy. In the SHARP, in particular, there is also a double whammy, just as there is in the SAVRY, because the sort of antisocial behavior that contributes to an assessment of psychopathic traits on the PCL-YV is also assessed elsewhere in the instrument (domain 2: antisocial behavior). This means that the same risk factors are, in effect, measured twice and are therefore bound to increase assessed risk in juveniles assessed by the SHARP or SAVRY as having psychopathic personality traits (as noted in Chapter 13, the SAVRY overestimates moderate and high levels of risk).

The inclusion of the SHARP here, then, not only reflects a clinical risk assessment instrument in the making, but also demonstrates many of the requirements and difficulties in developing a strong and well-designed instrument.

INSTRUMENTS RELATED TO RISK ASSESSMENT

The following five instruments are not risk assessment instruments (although the SAI-J, as previously noted, is described by its authors as a risk instrument). Nevertheless, each contains information relevant to sexual offender risk assessment and may be included in either an initial comprehensive risk assessment or the ongoing assessment of progress in treatment over time. They each are closely related to risk assessment instruments in their structure and content.

MULTIDIMENSIONAL INVENTORY OF DEVELOPMENT, SEX, AND AGGRESSION (MIDSA)

The MIDSA is not currently available as a risk assessment instrument. In its present form it provides a vehicle for gathering psychosocial data and generating comprehensive assessment materials. It can be purchased through www.midsa.us

---

4. Of note, Adele Forth is the lead author of the PCL-YV and is also an author of the SAVRY.

The MIDSA is presently not a risk assessment instrument, and was instead designed to identify important targets for assessment and therapeutic intervention. However, it is likely to be further developed at some point into an empirically validated risk assessment tool for both juvenile and adult sexual offenders. The MIDSA was built from its earlier prototype, the Multidimensional Assessment of Sex and Aggression (MASA), and was designed to produce report material that can be meaningfully used in the comprehensive assessment of juvenile and adult sexual offenders based on 54 empirically validated scales relevant to the development and maintenance of sexually abusive behavior.

The MIDSA is actually not an instrument, but instead a software package administered by computer. It is designed to gather information by self-report and compare this against an empirically validated database in order to provide clinical reports about juveniles and adults entering assessment or treatment for sexually abusive behavior. Substantial data have been gathered in the development of the MIDSA, and in its current use as an inventory of sexual and other development it is consequently able to compare individual (adult and juvenile) sexual offenders against a normed database of other sexual offenders in the generation of clinical psychosocial and psychosexual reports. The MIDSA gathers data on social, academic, sexual, and antisocial histories and assesses a large number of domains related to sexual coercion, including behavior-management problems, impulsive acting out, substance abuse, and sexual behaviors that range widely from normal to troubled deviant sexual behaviors. Despite its treatment focus, MIDSA scales thus measure domains believed important in predicting sexual recidivism in juvenile and adult sexual offenders.

However, because follow-up data have not yet been gathered to determine the predictive validity of its scales, the MIDSA cannot presently serve as a risk assessment instrument. Nevertheless, it is expected that risk scales will be developed from the MIDSA scales when follow-up recidivism data are available. Accordingly, although probably some time away, the MIDSA is likely to serve this role at some point in the future, in risk assessment for both juveniles and adults.

Multiphasic Sex Inventory-II Adolescent Version (MSI-II A)

The MSI is available for purchase through Nichols and Molinder Assessments at www.nicholsandmolinder.com.

The MSI-II A is not a risk assessment instrument. It is instead designed to measure and assess the characteristics, attitudes, ideation, and behaviors of known or alleged adolescent male sexual offenders, ages 12–18 (14–18 for adolescents who deny any sexually abusive behavior). There is also a female adolescent version of the MSI, but this has such a limited database that the authors consider this version to be a research instrument only.

The adolescent version of the MSI is a refinement of the adult instrument, and it is an empirically based self-report instrument comprised of 559 questions. Almost all of the scales of the adult version are included in the adolescent version, which also includes scales to assess attentional and behavioral problems, as well as social adjustment and history of personal victimization. Like the MIDSA, the MSI essentially compares the answers of the juvenile being assessed against answers to the same questions given by other sexual offenders. However, most of the current database is made up of adult sexual offenders, with a far smaller sample of adolescent sexual offenders included. The MSI thus arrives at descriptions of the juvenile being assessed based upon both juvenile and adult sexual offenders, but mostly adults. In particular, the MSI classifies the juvenile along the four "core paraphilia" scales of Child Molestation, Rape, Exhibitionism, and Voyeurism, and along six others indices: (1) Additional Sexual Deviance-Paraphilia, (2) Sexual Functioning/Body Image, (3) Psychosexual, (4) Behavioral, (5) Accountability, and (6) Adolescent/Gender Development. It also includes six reliability and validity scales to assess the juvenile's consistency, attitude, and approach in completing the instrument.

The MSI is a useful addition to a comprehensive assessment, but it provides interesting and useful information more than it does critical and essential information, and adds value to the assessment as an inventory of attitudes and behaviors compared to the database of juvenile and adult sexual offenders. However, composed of 559 questions, it's quite a grueling task for many adolescents to complete the self-report and certainly requires average reading and comprehension skills. Moreover, as noted, the database presently consists of mostly adults, against whom the juvenile is being compared. At the time of writing, the normed database included 460 adolescent child molesters compared to 1,200 adult child molesters, with no adolescent rapists, voyeurs, or exhibitionists included in the database. However, the MSI developers are continuing to develop the database to include more adolescent and adult sexual offenders, and this will change over time. Most recently, MSI norms have been expanded to include 1,696 adolescent (age 12–20 in their samples) child molesters, 462 adolescent rapists, 89 exhibitionists, and 77 voyeurs (Ilene Molinder, personal communication, March 26, 2008), hence MSI comparisons will, in the future, have a far wider and more relevant database upon which to draw. However, in the meantime, the evaluator must remain aware that

MSI scales that classify juveniles do so mostly compared against adult sexual offenders, and must therefore exercise caution both in interpreting and using the results of the MSI.

SEXUAL ADJUSTMENT INVENTORY-JUVENILE (SAI-J)

The SAI-J is available for purchase through Behavior Data Systems, Phoenix, Arizona 85064, or bds@bdsltd.com

Like the MIDSA and MSI, the Sexual Adjustment Inventory-Juvenile is an empirically based, self-report instrument used to identify sexual and nonsexual concerns in male and female adolescent sexual offenders, aged 14–18. The instrument is computer-scored, and comprised of 195 items broken into 13 scales, five scales of which assess sexual concerns and six scales that assess general risk, such as substance abuse, antisocial behavior, and depression. The SAI-J also includes two "lie" scales that offer an assessment of the subject's truthfulness in completing the assessment.

However, unlike the MIDSA and MSI, which are not risk assessment instruments, the SAI-J is described by its publisher as a risk assessment instrument (Behavior Data Systems, 1997; Lindemann, 2005). Nevertheless, it is not a risk assessment instrument in the same way as other risk assessment instruments described here. In fact, like the MSI and MIDSA, rather than making predictions about sexual recidivism, the SAI-J is actually offering a comparison between the adolescent completing the SAI-J and other juvenile sexual offenders in the computerized database. That is, it is measuring and comparing the self-reported answers of the assessment subject against how other juvenile sexual offenders (in the database) previously answered the same questions. Hence, in its assessment of the adolescent at low, medium, problem, or severe risk along each of the five sexual scales and six nonsexual scales (there is no global, or overall, level of risk assigned), the instrument is providing an assessment of concern about the adolescent's self-reported attitude, ideation, or actual behavior on each scale, compared to other similar adolescents. Thus, an assessment of "problem" risk, for example, is based upon the manner in which the assessment subject answered items compared to peers in the database, not on actual data concerning recidivism.

Although Lindemann (2005) describes predictive validity for the SAI-J, he is actually describing the similarity between the adolescent being assessed and cohorts in the database who have known histories of sexually abusive and other troubled behavior, rather than the percentage of assessed juvenile sexual offenders who have actually recidivated (which, as noted, is the true hallmark of a risk assessment instrument). In fact, although based on empirical data (i.e., the computerized database), like clinical risk assessment instruments, the SAI-J is unable to assign a risk level based on a known base rate of sexual recidivism or similarities between the adolescent being assessed and known adolescent sexual recidivists.

In addition, there are problems with the construction and clarity of the instrument that weaken the instrument and its computer-generated conclusions. For instance, in asking questions such as "I have had sex with my brother or sister," or "I am sexually active," the instrument never makes clear what is meant by "sex." In these cases, what constitutes "sex": intercourse, fellatio or cunnilingus, masturbation, molestation, and so on? It is not that I mean to be picayune, but the way that instruments are designed and questions are phrased has everything to do with the results they produce. Whereas the SAI-J can help to both "assess attitudes and behaviors that contribute to meaningful sex offender" assessments and "collect a vast amount of information that is important in sex offender evaluation" (Lindemann, 2005, p. 7.18), as a risk assessment instrument it is specious and leaves much to be desired. As an assessment of sexual ideation and behavior contrasted against that of other sexually abusive youth, it appears weaker than either the MSI or MIDSA, although it is far easier to apply and score.

Treatment Progress Inventory for Adolescents who Sexually Abuse (TPI-ASA)

The TPI-ASA is currently in development, and available through the primary author, BJ Oneal at bjoneal@u.washington.edu

The TPI-ASA (Oneal, Burns, Kahn, Rich, & Worling, 2008) is not a risk assessment instrument, but nevertheless it is worth noting as a tool in development designed to help clinicians track progress in treatment for sexually abusive behavior. It is thus significantly informed and to some degree shaped by the risk assessment literature.

The instrument is intended as a treatment planning and progress inventory for sexually abusive adolescents during the 12-month (for initial progress assessment) or three-month (for re-evaluation of progress over time) period immediately prior to the use of the instrument. It is designed to monitor and measure 64 elements common and relevant to the evaluation and treatment of juvenile male sexual offenders, classified into nine dimensions: (1) Inappropriate Sexual Behavior (9 elements), (2) Healthy Sexuality (10 elements), (3) Social Competency (8 elements), (4) Cognitions Supportive of Sexual Abuse (6 elements), (5) Attitudes Supportive of Sexual Abuse (6 elements), (6) Victim Awareness (4 elements), (7) Affective and Behavioral Regulation (8 elements), (8) Risk Prevention Awareness (7 elements), and (9) Positive Family Caregiver Dynamics (6 elements).

The dimensions (and the elements included within each) were selected on the basis of empirically and consensus-based research, as well as their relevancy to both treatment planning and monitoring progress in treatment. The instrument was also designed so that it could be administered as part of a comprehensive risk evaluation. In a study that involved a sample of 90 sexually abusive adolescents, support was provided for internal consistency and convergent and discriminant validity of the nine dimensions (Oneal et al. 2008). Whereas the TPI-ASA is clearly not, nor intended to be, a risk assessment instrument, it may nevertheless be a useful instrument to be applied in the reassessment of risk over time, as well as helping to provide a useful guide in the process of comprehensive risk assessment.

JUVENILE SEX OFFENSE SPECIFIC TREATMENT NEEDS & PROGRESS SCALE

The Needs & Progress Scale is available online at www.csom.org/ref/ JSOProgressScale.pdf

Like the TPI-ASA, the Needs & Progress Scale (Righthand, 2005) is not a risk assessment instrument. Developed by Sue Righthand, one of the authors of the J-SOAP, the scale is a means by which to conceptualize and measure factors specifically related to sex offender specific treatment. Accordingly, like the TPI-ASA, the 14 items that comprise the scale are also closely related to the sort of risk factors or domains of risk factors found in risk assessment instruments: (1) Motivation to Change, (2) Sexual Interests, (3) Sexual Drive, (4) Social Skills, (5) Personal Maltreatment History, (6) Victim Impact/Empathy, (7) Attitudes/Beliefs, (8) Emotion/Impulse Management, (9) Positive/Stable Self-Image, (10) Responsible Behavior, (11) Family Relationships/Support, (12) Peer Relationships/Support, (13) Community Supports, and (14) Risk Management.

The Needs & Progress Scale (NPS) is far less detailed, less comprehensive, and less well developed than the TPI-ASA. Accordingly, although of some value to the clinician in considering elements of sex offender specific treatment and the progress of the client in treatment, the NPS offers only a cursory look at progress. Each item on the scale is presented as unidimensional, rather than as a domain within which treatment progress can be examined and assessed in more detail and with more discrimination. The NPS thus offers a quicker look at progress in sex offender specific treatment than the TPI-ASA, but it has less value and meaning, provides a more superficial view of treatment progress, and overlooks the complexities and depth of treatment.

THE CAPACITY AND LIMITATIONS OF ASSESSED RISK

It is clear that the developmental nature of childhood and adolescence requires that risk estimates remain relatively fluid, subject to change, and short-term, and not be confused or taken for estimates of lifetime risk for sexual reoffense. Hence, both the ERASOR and J-RAT, for instance, describe risk estimates as relevant for only one year before the need to reassess risk.

This may not be entirely true for actuarial assessments of risk, however, given their statistical consideration of base rates of sexual recidivism over given and extended periods of time. Hence, it is possible that actuarial assessments may be more capable of long-term risk assessment than clinical assessments of risk. However, the actuarial assessment of adolescents is still very much in its infancy, having just moved out of prenatal care, and developmental considerations may still be highly significant in the long-term accuracy of juvenile risk assessment. Epperson et al. (2006), the developers of the JSORRAT, note that the instrument is significantly more accurate in predicting juvenile sexual recidivism prior to age 18 than sexual recidivism that occurs only after age 18, and thus lifetime sexual recidivism. They describe the JSORRAT-II as less predictive of sexual recidivism during young adulthood than during adolescence, and suggest several possible reasons for the "substantially lower" level of accuracy of prediction into young adulthood. These include both a significantly different set of variables at play (in adulthood versus adolescence) and the alternative explanation that "it simply may not be possible to achieve greater accuracy in predictions of adult sexual offending based on adolescent behavior based on the complexity and magnitude of development changes occurring during adolescence" (p. 157).

Regardless of whether risk assessment instruments can generate estimates of risk into the far future, or whether clinical or actuarial in design, it seems evident that risk assessments have a great deal to offer with regard to informing us about the likelihood or potential for reoffense within the next year of the youth's life, and probably even two to three years. They thus provide a reasonable basis for decision making regarding management and intervention in the immediate and near future. On the other hand, it is frankly pointless, and perhaps unreasonable, to assess the meaning and value of clinical risk assessment instruments over the long run as they are not intended to assess juvenile risk far into the future and neither do they purport to.

Furthermore, if the assessments of risk generated by such instruments are treated as relevant, and management and intervention decisions are thus based upon their recommendations, then we may not actually witness a reoffense in the next year or two because of the intervention response. For instance, if an assessment of high risk is treated seriously it is likely that the juvenile will be highly supervised and monitored, and may even be housed in a residential treatment program. In either case, a sexual reoffense is unlikely. That is, the very assessment of risk and the treatment that follows may create a situation in which the predicted behaviors do not occur *because* of the assessment of risk. The high-risk situation is, in effect, dissolved and the likelihood of harm diminishes greatly or vanishes entirely. Under such circumstances, the fact that a juvenile does or does not reoffend is surely a measure of the effectiveness or ineffectiveness of treatment, rather than the capacity of the risk assessment instrument to accurately predict risk over an extended period of time.

CONCLUSION: THE CLINICAL BASIS FOR RISK ASSESSMENT

We've now spent considerable time reviewing risk assessment instruments, how they work and how to score and best use them, and what individual instruments look like, how they are constructed, what they contain, and how they are similar and different from one another.

However, at the conclusion of Chapter 13, I described the covenant between the instrument designed and the evaluator, highlighting the requirement for well-designed and meaningful tools and the need for the evaluator to acquire the training and supervised experience necessary for well-informed professional practice. In the case of every clinical instrument, the assessment of risk ultimately lies in the domain of the evaluator and his or her judgment.

The exception to clinical judgment may be found in the practice of actuarial assessment, in which the user, in theory, merely has to follow the data collection and scoring system. However, as described, even in the case of actuarial processes, evaluators will quite often be called upon to exercise judgment and make decisions about how to interpret a behavior or situation in order to score a risk factor, or even make sense of what circumstances meet the conditions of any particular risk factor. For instance, item 5 of the JSORRAT-II describes the occurrence of a sexual offense in a public environment, and gives clear examples of such locations which are clearly community areas "open to the scrutiny of others." However, what happens if the sexual offense occurred in a private home (clearly not a public environment) but during a party, for instance, when many people were present? Would the home count as a public environment in that case (as it may now temporarily meet the criteria of being open to public scrutiny)? In this case, then, does the evaluator mark the factor as "present" or "not present" (the only choices in the case of this item)? Either way, some form of judgment may be required to score the item. Although questions like this may seem trivial to some, they are not. In fact, as no scoring manual can describe every possible situation when more than plain fact is in question, it is virtually certain that evaluators will have to exercise judgment, and this is even more the case if the evaluator considers it acceptable to make clinical adjustments to an actuarial assessment.

Despite the fact, then, that a well-designed assessment tool will guide and shape clinical judgment, competent evaluation is not merely a technical skill. As noted in Chapter 2, good evaluation requires well-trained evaluators who don't simply score, add up, total, and make interpretations of psychological tests or make important and sometimes life-changing decisions based simply upon those scores. They instead, as described in the psychological evaluation guidelines of the American Psychological Association (Turner, DeMers, Fox, & Reed, 2001), use their advanced training and knowledge of psychology, human behavior, and social interactions, to draw clinical conclusions. Even when using an actuarial assessment tool it will be important to apply clinical judgment under circumstances where so much is at stake.

Finally, it is good news that there are increasing numbers and types of risk assessment instruments currently available or in development, as well as other instruments and tools related to risk assessment. This speaks to the further refinement of our knowledge base and our ideas and methods for juvenile risk assessment, as well a strengthening of practice methods, guidelines, and expectations. However, regardless of the empirical base and our developing field, risk assessment remains as much, or more, art and craft as science or technical method. Effective risk assessment is guided by, and depends upon, structured risk assessment instruments, but it remains very much a clinical process that requires a great deal from the practitioner.

CHAPTER 15

Practice Guidelines and Processes for Comprehensive Risk Assessment

C HAPTER 11 DESCRIBED the nature and steps of assessment, highlighting the capacity of the comprehensive evaluation to: (1) explore and understand the nature, development, and trajectory of sexually abusive behavior, (2) assess risk for sexual reoffense recidivism and the impact of risk and protective factors, (3) explore and describe psychosocial history, and particularly those elements that have shaped current thinking and behavior, (4) assess motivation for treatment, and (5) build a case formulation from which to develop treatment plans, activities and interventions, and assessment.

This chapter picks up from Chapter 11 by describing the stages and elements involved in organizing and conducting a comprehensive assessment. It thus addresses the operationalization of the assessment process, including principles and guidelines upon which to build the comprehensive evaluation. However, these principles have already been described adequately in previous chapters, and they essentially involve understanding the individual being assessed as a whole person and in the broadest possible manner, regardless of the purpose or type of assessment. That is to say, the goal of the comprehensive assessment is to understand the depth and complexity of who's arrived at our door. Even though this book is aimed directly at the assessment of juveniles, these ideas apply equally to the assessment of children, adolescents, and adults; nevertheless, they are especially pertinent to juvenile assessment given the very active physical, emotional, cognitive, and social developmental process experienced by children and adolescents. In addition, juveniles function within a social system that is quite different than that experienced by adults, including the influence of family and adult authority subsystems, as well as the increasing power of the peer group as children age that, by adolescence, has a greater influence on the teenager than the parental system (Hawkins et al., 2000; Lipsey & Derzon, 1998).

We have already discussed in detail the developmental process through which children and adolescents pass, the need to recognize the holistic nature of the child and the environment in which he or she learns and functions, and the ecological systems through which individuals are intertwined and engaged in mutual influence with their environment. There is no need, then, to further highlight these ideas as we move into practical application of the process of psychosocial assessment; these ideas are, thus, a given as we move into the chapter.

Returning to a point made in the introductory chapter, evaluation and assessment both represent the same process and goal. There is nothing substantially different about either term or what each implies conceptually or in operation, and it is redundant therefore to refer to evaluation and assessment as separate practices.

COMPREHENSIVE EVALUATION: INTEGRATING PSYCHOSOCIAL AND RISK ASSESSMENT

As noted in Chapter 11, psychosocial assessment describes both the target of the assessment (the psychological and social functioning, or the interaction between and integration of the two spheres) and a process by which information about the individual is gathered and understood. Comprehensive assessment, in turn, refers to the breadth and depth of such an evaluation, and incorporates and consolidates different types of evaluation procedures into a single evaluation with the function of evaluating psychosocial functioning and, in particular, the assessment of risk within the context of psychosocial functioning. Typically, however, when we discuss psychosocial assessment we are also describing a *method* by which information is collected for the larger assessment. This method, of course, is very different than the methods of psychological testing, physiological examination, or the identification and evaluation of risk factors (i.e., the use of the risk assessment instrument), all of which also gather and provide data for and may be included in the comprehensive assessment. Although each of these evaluation types and methods may be used as standalone evaluation tools and may be used for purposes other than psychosocial or comprehensive assessment, in a comprehensive assessment of risk they are all blended into the overall assessment, often under the general heading of comprehensive psychosocial assessment.

Hence, the psychosocial label appropriately describes and is synonymous with the overall evaluation process, in which the individual is understood in terms of his or her psychosocial functioning, assessed in different ways. It is the psychosocial aspect of the assessment that most provides insight and meaning to an assessment process in which other elements, such as psychological testing or the use of a risk assessment instrument, are incorporated into the assessment. To this end, Long, Higgins, and Brady (1988) describe the psychosocial assessment as the gathering of data about the individual's emotional, behavioral, mental, environmental, and interactional processes, with the goal of integrating those data with other information in order to obtain the most complete and multidimensional description and understanding of the individual possible.

However, whereas psychosocial assessment looks backwards, seeking an explanation and context by which the development and meaning of present behavior can be explained, risk assessment looks ahead and projects estimates about future behavior. In a comprehensive assessment of risk, then, psychosocial assessment and risk assessment are folded together (and especially in the case in which risk is assessed clinically). The structured risk assessment instrument provides a formal, and literature/empirically guided means by which to address, consider, and assign a risk level, and the larger assessment provides the material that populates, fuels, and informs the clinical risk assessment instrument. By integrating the two processes, we provide an assessment of risk that is comprehensive and well-informed. Given the difficulty in adequately or reliably projecting risk, the perspective here is that comprehensive assessment offers not only the best means for evaluating and estimating risk, but also the most well informed.

Frankly, as the review of the predictive ability of risk assessment instruments shows (Chapter 13), it far easier to assess who is not likely to engage in antisocial, general delinquent or criminal, or sexually abusive behavior than who is. This both helps to explain the effectiveness of the SAVRY in distinguishing between low- and high-risk youth and its capacity to predict who is not likely to reoffend violently, and its limited ability to accurately identify moderate- or high-risk offenders and its subsequent overestimation of moderate- and high-risk adolescents (Chapter 13). Even so, it is almost certainly easier to assess risk for continued general delinquency or continued violent behavior than continued sexually abusive behavior, which is a far more complex and less understood behavior (which also explains the capacity of instruments like the J-SOAP and SAVRY to do a better job of assessing nonsexual risk than sexual risk).

ASSESSMENT AND CASE FORMULATION:
CLINICAL THEORIZATION

In a standard mental health assessment, there are three basic elements: etiology (past), diagnosis (present), and prognosis (future). Whereas etiology reflects what has occurred and how it has led to the current circumstances, and diagnosis reflects present symptoms, prognosis predicts likely or possible trends if symptoms remain unchecked. It is, however, etiology that provides the historical foundation for both diagnosis and prognosis. Hence, in a comprehensive assessment of any kind, past, present, and future are inextricably intertwined. Without understanding history, it is difficult to do any more than comment on the present or render an explanation for current circumstances and foolish to predict future behavior. In fact, static actuarial procedures base their projections of the future entirely on the past, bypassing the present all together.

With respect to comprehensive evaluation, it is through the process of psychosocial assessment that etiology is discovered, and through which foundation and depth add richness and meaning. However, case formulation adds another level of richness to the assessment. Case formulation involves the capacity to reduce and synthesize information to a more precise form that expresses broad ideas concisely. It represents a visualization of the case, and reduces history, facts, symptoms, and circumstances into a brief summary that provides meaning, conjectures causes, outlines current issues, and informs prognosis. To some degree, the formulation puts forth a clinical theory about the case, providing explanatory information, identifying hypothesized cause, and suggesting meaning and future action. It thus allows the basis for understanding the case, both historically and dynamically, and its likely trajectory, as well as interventions that may interrupt trajectory and create a new prognosis.

In this sense, case formulation follows a model of theory construction covering the elements of *description, explanation, prediction,* and ultimately *control or intervention.* Theory provides a description of and explanation for observed behavior, and in so doing must necessarily review prior events and forces that contribute to explanation and thus describes current behavior as an outcome of prior forces. Theory also projects trends based on historical and current events, and thus makes predictions about trajectory or what can be expected if things remain unchanged. The final element is that of control, or the means by which theoretically understood ideas lead to the ability to intervene and thus possibly change trajectory. Theories of climate or weather forecasting offer a good example of a theory. Current weather conditions are understood by means of historical data that explain current conditions, and from which forecasts (predictions) are made of expected trends and a means is provided for control (e.g., take an umbrella with you when you go out). It also offers an excellent example of how difficult it can be to make adequate or accurate predictions, regardless of a vast knowledge of historical, or even dynamic, data because of the complexity and changeability of dynamic conditions. Interestingly, Monahan et al. (2000) note that in weather prediction, clinical involvement and interpretation improves the accuracy of prediction, and is "consistently more valid" than an unrevised actuarial forecast (p. 134).

However, formulation is an individualized approach to recognizing the idiosyncratic particulars of each case and understanding each case as unique, and it does not equal a formulaic approach to, or interpretation of, cases. To this end, Drake and Ward (2003) write that formulation-based approaches to treatment require that evaluators understand psychological problems and vulnerabilities for individual clients, rather than utilizing a manualized or cookbook approach to understanding behavior. In formulation, treatment interventions are individualized and emerge from different case formulations. Despite the perspective that sexual offenders share common dysfunctions and can thus be treated through prescribed and manualized treatment, Drake and Ward argue that this position is limited and results in weak and poorly targeted treatment that fails to meet individual needs. Although it is reasonable to assume that sexual offenders share common problems, difficulties, and dysfunctions, individualized case formulation is nevertheless likely to improve understanding and lead to more finely tuned and precise assessment and treatment. They write that case formulation highlights specific developmental factors for each individual that made that specific individual vulnerable to engaging in sexually abusive behavior. This, in many ways, lies at the heart of comprehensive risk assessment, at least with respect to understanding the pathway to sexually abusive behavior and the risk factors that must be recognized and addressed for each individual if treatment is to be individualized and geared towards the needs of that individual (the "needs" element of the risk, needs, and responsivity model).

A COMPREHENSIVE VIEW OF THE INDIVIDUAL OFFENDER: A CHANGING SENSIBILITY

The idea that the evaluator should understand the individual being assessed, and not simply the individual's behavior, broadens the assessment of risk to an assessment of the circumstances of every type that contributed, or even led directly, to the sexually abusive behavior. Comprehensive assessment, then, is always dynamic. Nevertheless, we may ask whether we really require a dynamic and comprehensive assessment if we have a good enough risk assessment instrument, that is a risk assessment instrument that can accurately predict risk.

The answer is clearly yes, as I hope I have argued clearly throughout, and particularly in the case of children and adolescents. One need only turn to the practice standards and guidelines of the Association for the Treatment of Sexual Abusers (2005) to see that evaluation of sexual offenders, including adult sexual offenders, is expected to go beyond the use of a risk assessment instrument alone, whether actuarial or clinical. The ATSA standards note that psychosexual evaluation is required to determine not just risk for sexual reoffense, but also to clearly describe dynamic risk factors, specific treatment needs, the strengths of the offender and his or her amenability to treatment, and recommendations regarding the intensity and type of required intervention and risk management strategies. In general, the standards follow the principles of the risk, need, and responsivity model, including elements and factors that may affect the individual's response to treatment such as culture, ethnicity, age, IQ, neuropsychological disorders, personality, mental health, physical disabilities, medication, and motivation. Ideas like this, then, make it clear that assessment is a *comprehensive* process, including and going beyond available psychometric data, including actuarial information, by which to further strengthen and add even more meaning to the overall assessment.

With a strengthened expectation for comprehensive assessment, we're seeing changes in the way that evaluators view and conduct the assessment of risk, not just in the case of sexually abusive youth but also in the case of adult sexual offenders. These changes, which now reflect a far broader view of both the assessment process itself and the individual offender, show not only in the ATSA practice standards, for instance, but are also reflected in a recent article by Ward et al. (2007), published in the ATSA journal. The article addresses the human rights of adult sexual offenders, including the idea that "any intervention has to be consistent with the rights of other people without losing sight of the fact that it is the offender's life that is [also] of concern" (p. 207). This is a brave new world in sexual offender assessment and treatment; we have not only moved from a concrete view of risk assessment in adults to the need for a more comprehensive assessment for sexually abusive youth, but also onto the idea that risk in adult sexual offenders also needs to be understood comprehensively and in the context of their whole lives.

SEXUALLY ABUSIVE BEHAVIOR IN CONTEXT

In Chapter 1, in outlining keys concepts about risk assessment, I noted four key questions to be asked and answered in the risk assessment process: (1) Who are the possible or likely victims (risk to whom); (2) what is the nature of the anticipated or likely sexually abusive behavior (at risk for what); (3) under what circumstances is the offender at increased likelihood for re-engaging in sexually abusive behavior (at risk when); and (4) what are the driving elements and forces that increase potential for or drive risk to sexual reoffend (at risk why)?

These four questions are not unlike the five questions that Cummings and McGrath (2005) describe as critical in risk assessment: what is the probability of an offense, what degree of harm may result from a reoffense, under what conditions might an offense recur, who will be the likely victim of a reoffense, and when is a reoffense most likely to occur? Written primarily for probation and parole officers, Cummings and McGrath nevertheless ask their questions for the same reasons that they were posed in Chapter 1: In order to allow for a broad analysis of risk by which to yield an in-depth understanding of and maximum information about the individual being assessed. Only comprehensive assessment can help to answer such questions, as well as provide clear guidance for case management and treatment interventions.

If we wish to know more than just the likelihood or possibility of sexual recidivism, then, as described by Wiksröm and Sampson (2003), we must ask and learn about the causal mechanisms that push individuals to consider and choose to act upon options that constitute acts of crime, in which "studying development *in context* is the operative strategy" (p. 140). Similarly, with respect to the assessment of sexually abusive youth, Caldwell (2002) writes that meaningful risk assessments require a precise understanding of the patterns of sexually abusive behavior. Calder (2001) takes comprehensive assessment one step further in writing "whatever route a juvenile has taken into offending, it is important that the sexual offending is seen in the context of the life experience of the juvenile" (p. 51).

THE NEED FOR PRACTICE GUIDELINES
FOR COMPREHENSIVE ASSESSMENT

Prentky and Burgess (2000) describe a central task of assessment as accurately identifying the most critical factors that contributed to the offense, and write that sex offender specific treatment should not proceed without the benefit of an informed and comprehensive assessment. They also write that "unfortunately, there are no standardized or even commonly accepted models for conducting such an assessment" (p. 98). Nevertheless, in addition to clearly identifying the elements that should be included in a comprehensive assessment we can also focus on guidelines that not only define the content of the assessment but also the approach to, method of, and principles that lie behind the comprehensive assessment of risk.

However, because the clinical assessment is not a defined psychometric evaluation with required, prescribed, or sequential steps that must be followed, the informed and effective clinician may proceed in the manner that most suits the situation and the clinician's own preferred style, rather than follow a prescribed format that limits flexibility, does not take *in vivo* interactions into account, and is rigid and shallow. Houston (1998) describes this process as *idiographic*, meaning that the focus is on the individual, framed within a *nomothetic* process, or the larger framework that governs the way that all assessments are designed and carried out. Nevertheless, there are a number of sources from which underlying principles and guidelines can be drawn. The 2005 ATSA practice standards and guidelines, for instance, offer a well-defined description of the evaluation process, establishing the goal of an "objective, fair, and impartial assessment" (p. 12). The standards identify the expected content of the evaluation and the need to use multiple sources of information. They also provide a clear framework by which to guide the administration of the evaluation, including the use of appropriate risk assessment instruments and the need for evaluators to be fully informed about the strengths and limitations of such instruments, as well the limitations of the assessment process itself. Standards also ensure that individuals being assessed clearly have explained to them the purpose of the evaluation process and its possible outcome and, particularly with special populations, the meaning of the assigned risk level and the nature of any related recommendations.

The ATSA description of the evaluation process is quite thorough and detailed and, although the practice standards are written with adult male sexual offenders in mind (p. 5), they are certainly applicable to the comprehensive assessment of sexually abusive youth. Others, too, have provided overviews and guidelines for the comprehensive assessment of juvenile sexual offenders, including the American Academy of Child and Adolescent Psychiatry (1999), the American Psychiatric Association (1999), the National Task Force on Juvenile Sexual Offending (1993), and the Colorado Sex Offender Management Board (Colorado Department of Public Safety, 2002). Drawn from these and other sources (for instance, Calder, 2001; Monahan, 1995; O'Reilly & Carr, 2004; Righthand & Welch, 2001; Rich, 2003), it is possible to both broadly define the risk assessment process and synthesize a set of 29 principles and guidelines by which to further define and shape the practice of comprehensive risk assessment.

A DEFINITION OF COMPREHENSIVE RISK ASSESSMENT

Comprehensive risk assessment for sexually abusive youth is aimed at estimating and defining the likelihood of a sexual reoffense. This is based on an understanding of the juvenile's prior sexually abusive behavior, the circumstances and context under which such behavior developed and occurred, and the presence of current risk and protective factors that may contribute to or diminish the possibility of sexual reoffense. Comprehensive assessment also includes a detailed understanding of the juvenile's developmental experiences and the interactive (ecological) social environment in which he or she has lived and learned, the personal capacities of the juvenile, and the shaping forces that have significantly shaped and defined his or her psychology and behavior.

Inherent in such a definition are ideas that have already been discussed, which recognize the interaction between types of risk factors and between risk and protective factors, the interactive nature of the social environment and the individual who lives and grows up in that environment, the whole nature of the juvenile that extends far beyond his or her sexually abusive behavior, and the need to gather a broad and detailed range of information that serve both to help understand the sexually abusive youth and to make projections about the likelihood of sexual recidivism.

PRACTICE GUIDELINES

Moving from a broad definition to specific guidelines that define expectations and highlight content, method, and approach, as well as the outcomes of comprehensive risk assessment, from the literature we can derive at least 29 principles and guidelines[1] by which to further operationalize and guide the administration of the comprehensive assessment. These can be categorized into four areas: (1) Underlying Principles, (2) Application and Practice, (3) Content, and (4) Outcome.

UNDERLYING PRINCIPLES

1. The assessment of juvenile sexual abusers requires the same level of comprehensiveness required of all clinical evaluations of children and adolescents.

---

1. These are based upon and further developed from the 21 practice guidelines described in Rich (2003).

2. The evaluator must ensure that questions raised by the evaluation fall within his or her level of expertise.
3. The evaluation or risk for sexual recidivism should involve the use of an assessment instrument specifically designed for the purpose of risk assessment, and the evaluator should be aware of the strengths and limitations of such instruments and have the skills, experience, or supervision required to professionally and ethically utilize such instruments.
4. In addition to the prediction of risk for sexual recidivism, the focus of the assessment is on understanding the behaviors of the juvenile and the development and causation of his or her behaviors, the juvenile's motivation for treatment and required level of care, and the development of treatment plans.
5. The assessment should assume a broad and holistic view of the juvenile in which it is impossible to fully understand or interpret the juvenile's behavior without understanding the ecological environment in which he or she was raised and currently lives.
6. There is no known profile or set of characteristics that differentiate juvenile sexual offenders from nonoffending juveniles.
7. The assessment process is not a process by which to determine guilt or innocence.

APPLICATION AND PRACTICE

8. The evaluator should adopt a nonjudgmental and patient stance in the evaluation, remaining persistent and focused.
9. The evaluator must be aware of the individual's cognitive functioning, including reading, writing, and comprehension skills and abilities, and provide alternative means for gathering information directly from the juvenile if cognitive, intellectual, and/or language skills are poor.
10. Informed consent for the assessment is required, which in the case of a juvenile must include consent of legal guardians.
11. The purpose, use, and possible outcome of the evaluation should be described to the juvenile and the juvenile's legal guardians.
12. All parties must be aware of any limits to confidentiality, especially if there is any possibility or likelihood that evaluation results will be shared with external agencies such as police, court, or social services.
13. Record or chart review provides the background information that serves as the basis for the evaluation, and provides historical and

other pertinent data about the juvenile. The evaluator must be prepared for the evaluation and ensure a thorough review of existing documentation prior to the assessment, including police reports, victim statements, reports of social service and child protection agencies, mental health assessments, treatment progress reports, psychological tests, and so forth.

14. The evaluator must be aware that information available in prior reports may be incomplete, incorrect, or not fully understood, and take care to not simply pass along inaccurate or poorly understood information.

15. Clinical interviews are used to gather specific data and also to observe, supplement, question, review, and clarify information obtained from other sources. Interviews should include meetings with the juvenile as well as in-person or phone interviews with collateral informants such as parents, therapists, social service workers, other prior treatment providers, and probation or parole officers.

16. The evaluator should be aware that information provided directly by the juvenile may not be true, complete, or sufficiently detailed, and recognize the possibility that the juvenile may lie, deny, distort, or minimize, and that the same may be true of informants in the juvenile's family.

17. Psychological, physiological, and other objective and subjective measures, such as psychometric testing, polygraph or phallometric (plethysmograph) examination, or self-report inventories and questionnaires, are used to gather additional information outside of the process of record review and psychosocial assessment.

18. Neither psychological nor physiological testing can be used to prove or disprove that an individual will engage or re-engage in sexual offending behavior.

CONTENT

19. Information should be gathered from multiple sources, including family members, probation and parole officers, current or former treatment practitioners such as therapists and psychiatrists, teachers, and treatment staff in former treatment programs or hospitals.

20. The assessment should employ multiple evaluation methods, if available and appropriate, including clinical interviews, psychological and educational testing, and physiological testing.

21. The evaluator should seek multiple types of information, including, but not limited to, early developmental history, intellectual and

cognitive skills, social functioning and relationships, development and acquisition of social skills, psychiatric disorders and mental status, behavioral history, history of substance use, history of trauma and/or victimization, history of sexual development, attitudes and beliefs, personal characteristics, level of denial or acceptance of responsibility, family structure and current relationships, family history, and history of sexually abusive behavior.

22. If possible, the evaluator should assess sexual interests and patterns of arousal in the juvenile, recognizing that such assessment does not necessarily indicate the presence of sexual deviance or prove that the juvenile will engage in future sexual offenses.

Outcome

23. Assessment of treatment needs and the development of treatment goals should be based on an understanding of the juvenile's needs, including both strengths and weaknesses, as well as an assessment of risk based on the juvenile's history and current level of functioning.

24. The evaluator must recognize that evaluations without broad and supporting collateral information should be interpreted with caution, and such caution should be noted in the written evaluation report if the assessment was conducted and completed in the absence of such information.

25. An assessment of risk should not be made in the event that adequate information is not available from which to draw such estimates.

26. Placement and/or treatment recommendations must be based on the assessment of risk and public safety, the treatment needs of the juvenile, and the juvenile's motivation to engage in treatment, and should not be made on the basis of whatever treatment services and resources are actually available, or drop below or rise above the level of treatment that the evaluator believes is required.

27. The written report must be accurate, complete, transparent, and free of speculation and judgment.

28. The evaluation report should: (a) note all records reviewed and informants interviewed; (b) note any limitations on the assessment, including lack of collateral or supporting information that may affect the ability to make informed judgments about the juvenile, the reported offenses, or the risk for future sexual offending; (c) describe that consent was given for the evaluation, and any limits to confidentiality explained to the juvenile and legal guardian; (d) ensure a nonjudgmental and impartial style, and that all data presented are

both objective and accurate; (e) avoid making speculative statements, except when stating clinical formulations and when ample evidence exists to adequately support the hypotheses of the formulation; (f) document any denial of offenses that the juvenile may make, as well as his or her explanation, if any, for inaccurate or false allegations; and (g) provide a clear explanation in the event that it is not possible to make an assessment of future risk.

29. Neither written nor verbal results of the assessment should be released to anyone without the express written consent of the appropriate party, which in the case of juveniles will be the legal guardian, other than when a report is legally required to be released.

These 29 practice guidelines cannot possibly be all-inclusive, but they represent a means for conceptualizing, organizing, and ensuring a risk assessment process that reflects our current knowledge base, embraces our current ideas, meets our current expectations, and is cognizant of essential ideas about not only the risk assessment process, but the children and adolescents with whom we work.

REQUIRED CONTENT

We've addressed the sort of material that should be included in the comprehensive assessment, which is essentially material that provides both depth and breadth. The assessment, then, illuminates the contextual setting and circumstances of psychological, social, and behavioral development and thus helps reveal and explain the course and development of present day behavior, including the pathway leading to sexually abusive behavior. In turn, our understanding of the past and its relationship to the present can help us to estimate likely trajectory into the future if things remain unchanged, and thus to make reasonable and well-informed assessments of risk.

In addition to learning about the developmental circumstances of the juvenile's life, comprehensive assessment also delves into and reveals details about the juvenile, including personal characteristics, skills, abilities, vulnerabilities, and deficits, including level of honesty, self-disclosure, motivation, responsibility, and attachment and relatedness to others. In this way, we can discover and understand the child and the mind behind the behavior, in the context of his or her whole life, and not simply see the behavior itself.

The ATSA Task Force Report on Children with Sexual Behavior Problems (Chaffin et al., 2006) defined several key components required in the assessment of risk in sexually reactive children, which are useful to describe here as they are pertinent to the assessment of any juvenile, regardless of age, whether child or adolescent. The task force notes the requirement for multiple sources of information and a comprehensive process by which to develop a broad view of the child, including assessment of three distinct elements: family and social ecological environment, general psychological and behavioral functioning, and, of course, sexual behavior and contributing factors, including situations or circumstances under which sexual behavior problems have occurred. Among the 29 practice guidelines described above, guideline 21 describes the need for multiple types of information, and generally describes the sort of information required, which sets the pace for the content to be included in the assessment. Content is described in more detail in Chapter 19, with specific reference to the preparation and completion of the written assessment report, but in reality there is no definitive and exhaustive description that marks the complete and proper assessment. However, it is instead possible to describe the sort of content that should be included in a comprehensive assessment and, indeed, this mirrors the sort of content found in any comprehensive psychosocial assessment. It is the focus on sexual development and sexually abusive behavior that transforms a standard comprehensive psychosocial assessment into a comprehensive psychosexual assessment.

A review of existing guidelines for both standard psychosocial and psychosexual assessments (cf. ATSA, 2005; Coffey, 2006; Colorado Department of Public Safety, 2002; Morrison, 1995; Rich, 2003; Shea, 1988) illustrates the sort of information or content that should be included in a comprehensive assessment of risk. Grouped into distinct and overarching categories, or content regions (Shea), the assessment should include material in at least 20 domains that, together, subsume relevant, detailed, and specific content.

- Relevant background and identifying information
- Cognitive functioning and intellectual capacity
- Social, developmental, and medical history
- Educational history
- Trauma history
- Mental health history and general psychological functioning
- Personality characteristics
- Social relationships and social functioning
- Family history
- Current family functioning

- History of nonsexual problem behavior
- History of substance abuse
- Sexual development and sexual interests
- History of sexually abusive behavior
- Details of index and related sexual offenses
- Offender's description of index and related sexual offenses
- Assessment of risk factors and assignment of risk for reoffense
- Environmental concerns
- Availability of environmental support
- Amenability to treatment

Together, these content areas provide definition for the sort of material that adds up to a broad psychosocial assessment. Chapter 16 describes the structure and methods of the assessment process, Chapters 17 and 18 discusses the nature and content of assessment interviews, and Chapter 19 addresses the written assessment report. Together, these chapters more thoroughly explore content areas and how to gather and interpret information, and included in the Appendix is a guide to content area, including the sort of information to include within each of the content areas noted above. However, these 20 content areas for now offer a general overview; in some cases, areas such as family history, for instance, will include still more subcategories of content, such as family mental health, substance abuse, and family stability. Furthermore, there are still other content areas that may be included that will depend upon the specific form of the evaluation, and may, for instance, include a mental status exam and diagnostic history for the juvenile being assessed.

In fact, the individual evaluator, or the agency or program for whom the evaluator is producing the evaluation, must decide what information should or must be included and presented in a comprehensive assessment, in what order, and in how much depth. There is no hard-and-fast rule, no defined musts, and no set model, as noted by Calder (2000), who has written that there "is no ideal risk assessment method or framework"(p. 27).

RISK ASSESSMENT AND DISCLOSURES OF SEXUALLY ABUSIVE BEHAVIOR

In discussing content, it is clear by now that comprehensive assessment is focused on developing a detailed understanding of the juvenile in order to both estimate future behavior and establish a means by which to decide upon or recommend treatment interventions. As noted, the assessment is not intended to pursue questions of guilt, even if the subject arises during the course of the assessment; the assessment process is therefore not intended for the purpose of disclosure or an admission of sexual offenses, although this may well be an ideal state. The purpose, instead, is to make sense of the sexually abusive youth and his or her behaviors, and to make an estimate of risk based on that understanding. The rest—acknowledgment of responsibility, disclosures of sexually abusive behavior, developing empathy, improving social connectedness, developing self-regulation, and the like—follow initial assessment and mark the course of treatment at whatever level and however and wherever it is provided.

Thus, disclosure, or the youth's willingness or ability to fully describe, admit to, and take responsibility for sexually abusive behavior, typically follows assessment and is a matter for treatment, even if addressed in the process of evaluation. It is clear, in fact, that many things that remain undisclosed during the initial risk assessment may emerge later in treatment. Baker, Tabacoff, Tornusciolo, and Eisenstadt (2001) note that sexually abusive youth and their families may deny, minimize, or hide sexually abusive behavior for any number of reasons, and they warn clinicians that they may not gather a full picture of the youth, including his or history of sexually abusive behavior, until a therapeutic alliance is formed through the treatment process that (usually) follows assessment. Mussack and Carich (2001) have similarly noted that it is unreasonable to expect a sexual abuser to make a full disclosure during an initial assessment, and "are likely during the course of therapy if intervention is at all effective" (p. 12).

THE ROLE AND NATURE OF THE FORENSIC EVALUATOR

Coffey (2006) asserts that the forensic evaluator is objective and does not have a treatment relationship with the juvenile being assessed. This is a common position to take in reference to the differences between forensic evaluation and clinical health treatment, and it assumes not only that the differences are irreconcilable but also that forensic work applied to children and adolescents is the equivalent of forensic work with adults.

Practically, forensic work involves the investigation and assessment of facts and evidence in court, and forensic work as it pertain to behavioral health (i.e, mental health) involves the application of ideas about psychology to legal matters, and vice versa. However, with reference to child and adolescent offenders, at least, forensic work extends past evaluation to treatment. As assessment for sexual recidivism is likely to continue throughout treatment, and not merely at its outset, such evaluations are always forensic in nature and principle and the line between evaluation and treatment is further blurred, especially if treating clinicians also administer reassessments for risk (which is likely).

In the forensic mental health evaluation, clinicians assess the individual in a manner relevant to both the legal and the mental health system, communicating ideas and outcomes in ways that are understandable and meaningful to both systems, and in a manner that allows the legal system to act upon and apply the results of the evaluation (Grisso, 1998). All evaluations are thus forensic if intended for direct use or to assist decision making in a legal environment, and Grisso notes that they require a different way of thinking than nonforensic evaluations, which are typically applied in a purely clinical context. He writes that "clinicians can never merely transport their clinical skills to the juvenile court and carry out their evaluations as though they were in a clinical setting" (p. 24). Similarly, McCann (1998) has written that the role of the mental health practitioner in the forensic setting is distinctly different from the role played by the clinician in the nonforensic treatment setting, and warns that failure to recognize or acknowledge the difference can be "disastrous for anyone who applies the values and roles of one to the other" (p. 181). Like Coffey and Grisso, McCann sees the roles of forensic evaluator and mental health clinician as mutually exclusive and wonders if the two roles can cross, recommending that clinicians avoid engaging in the dual roles of therapist and forensic evaluator. Greenberg and Shuman (1999) also consider the two roles to be inherently different, incapable of being filled by the same individual. They write that by failing to recognize inherent conflicts and a dual relationship, clinicians who practice as forensic evaluators and therapists in the same case risk harm to their profession, their clients, and the legal process.

Grisso (2006) identifies an additional bifurcation in juvenile forensic evaluation, noting differences between evaluations of children and adolescents who have been harmed and those who have harmed others, the latter of which, of course, relates to the forensic evaluation of sexually abusive youth. He writes that these two subspecialities often clash with one another, given their nature, purpose and sometimes the age of the child, and require a different mindset and set of interviewing skills, and that it is rare that a juvenile evaluator can practice competently in both subspecialities.

These writers highlight that forensic and mental health practice are driven by different sets of needs, ideas, and end purposes. Nevertheless, recognizing and acknowledging the differences between serving and informing the legal system and serving and treating the client, Bluglass (1990) writes that it is the task of the forensic practitioner to reconcile these differences in order to be effective in both arenas. Indeed, in the treatment of sexually abusive youth both roles must be consolidated, unless we are to separate the functions of evaluation and treatment completely, from the initial assessment of risk through all subsequent risk evaluations. Further, risk evaluations for juveniles take place in a variety of settings, sometimes involving the court and the legal process and sometimes through social services. The world in which sexually abusive juveniles live is very different from that of adult sexual offenders. Hence, assessments of juveniles are likely to take place under different circumstances than for their adult counterparts, and there may be a crossover between social services and the juvenile court or between the juvenile and adult courts. Further, juveniles may receive a comprehensive risk assessment at various points in their treatment, as described below, whether serving to provide preadjudication information to the court, making recommendations to social services for management and treatment, or upon admission to a treatment program.

Welldon (1997) describes the blending of forensic and clinical work as an integration of both orientations and the subsequent transformation of the treatment relationship in the forensic treatment environment into a triangular one that represents the goals of and relationship between clinician, client, and society. Accordingly, the work of both the forensic evaluator and the forensic clinician must be synthesized into an overarching model of forensic mental health, encompassing both components if we are to ensure an assessment and treatment model that embraces the principles of risk, need, and responsivity, provides effective management for and treatment to sexually abusive youth, and serves the public good.

Under any circumstances, McCann (1998) comments that the use of mental health evaluations in forensic settings requires an objective and neutral stance. Regardless of your particular position on whether the role of forensic evaluator and forensic clinician can be taken by the same practitioner, the need for objectivity and neutrality should serve as a guiding principle throughout both assessment and treatment.

ASSESSMENT VENUE AND THE PURPOSE OF ASSESSMENT

As briefly mentioned, it is clear that, whether a basic risk assessment or comprehensive assessment of risk, such evaluations may and are likely to occur at various points in the juvenile's journey from being discovered engaging in sexually abusive behavior to completing treatment and beyond.

We thus make a mistake if we describe risk assessment as a one-time event or a cut-and-dried process that is equally well understood by all parties, always serves the same purpose, and itself is a static and un-changing process over time or venue. In reality, not only will the assessment assume a different form based on the methods and approaches of the evaluator, but it will serve a different purpose and perhaps be structured differently depending on the point at which the assessment is applied in the life of the sexually abusive youth and its purpose. The National Task Force on Juvenile Sexual Offending (1993), for instance, described risk assessment as an ongoing process that may by applied at six distinct points in the process of intervention, treatment, and management, including (1) pretrial; (2) presentencing; (3) postadjudication and disposition; (4) needs identification, treatment planning, and treatment evaluation; (5) predis-charge and release; and (6) monitoring and follow-up. Hoge and Andrews (1996) similarly describe the administration of a risk assessment at several key points in the decision-making process.

In fact, the point in the process of intervention at which an assessment is administered may have significant effects upon the evaluation and how and why it is administered, and even whether an evaluation should or can be administered. As shown in Figure 15.1, there are multiple points at which an assessment may be conducted, both pretreatment and

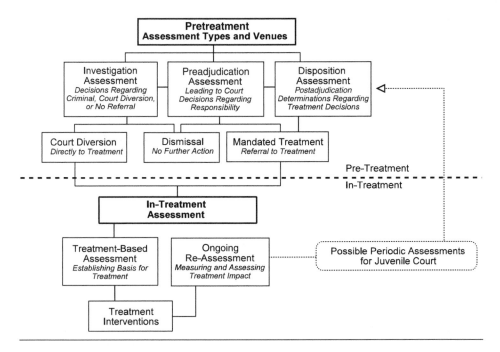

Figure 15.1 Assessment types and venues

in-treatment, and in some cases in-treatment evaluations may result in further prosecution if new information emerges that the legal system decides is prosecutable. Accordingly, there may be different outcomes for assessments administered at different points, as well as different purposes for the assessment.

As part of the pretreatment process, assessments can be used as an investigative tool that helps inform and guide authorities, such as social services or the police, as to the appropriate course of action. In some cases, the assessment may lead to all further action being dropped, but in others it may result in a referral to either the legal system or to social services, in which case the referral may completely bypass the juvenile court (court diversion), and lead directly to treatment. In the event of an arrest, assessments may also be used at the preadjudication level, assisting the court in learning about the juvenile before a decision is made as to guilt (or responsibility) or innocence. Still at a pretreatment stage, assessment may also be used to guide a postadjudication disposition, helping the court decide where to proceed following adjudication as responsible or guilty.

On the in-treatment side of the line, risk assessment is typically intended to gather further information in order to further understand the sexually abusive behavior and the juvenile, set a baseline assignment of risk (against which the goal of treatment is to presumably lead to a lower risk level), and establish and begin treatment, during the course of which periodic re-evaluations of risk will be administered. As noted, however, in the event that in-treatment evaluations highlight evidence of previously undisclosed sexually abusive behavior, they may lead to further prosecution for those juveniles who have already been through a court process and have been adjudicated or a new prosecution for those juveniles not previously charged with or adjudicated on a sexual offense charge. In either case, however, whether administered at the pretreatment or in-treatment level, the goal of the assessment is to estimate the possibility or likelihood of a sexual reoffense. It is not to determine guilt, although a byproduct of the assessment (and, indeed, treatment) process may result in the establishment of guilt.

A particularly difficult and touchy question arises when an evaluator is asked to assess risk with a juvenile who is being prosecuted for a sexual offense but has not yet been adjudicated on the charges. The juvenile is thus innocent of the charge until proven guilty. However, the evaluator will find that it is common for children and adolescents charged with sexual misconduct to be referred for either risk assessment or treatment prior to adjudication. In either case, this means that a risk assessment must be administered prior to the completion of court proceedings as treatment hinges on comprehensive risk assessment and should not proceed until an assessment has been completed.

In some cases, even prior to adjudication the juvenile acknowledges sexually abusive behavior and evaluation and treatment proceeds accordingly, even absent of closure to the case, and the court case is continued without a finding, pending the juvenile's progress in treatment. In other cases, the prosecution decides to declare "nolle prosequi," in which a decision is made to not prosecute the case *at this time*, and evaluation and treatment may follow if the juvenile makes an admission of responsibility, even though the possibility remains that prosecution may still follow. In still other cases, presenting the most difficult of conditions, an assessment of risk is sought when the juvenile denies the charges, or at least refuses (often under counsel from his or attorney) to discuss the allegations or acknowledge responsibility. When an evaluator conducts a risk assessment under such circumstances, the assessment must result in an inability to assign risk for reoffense on the basis that the charge is merely an unproven allegation (as described in Chapter 13). An assignment of risk would otherwise imply or declare that the charge is legitimate and that the juvenile engaged in the behavior as charged.

In still other cases, sexual offense charges are reduced to nonsexual charges, such as risk of injury to a minor or simple assault. Under such circumstances, the judge may have decided to accept a plea for a lower charge in order for the juvenile to get sex offender specific treatment but avoid the stigma of more serious sexual charges or the requirement to register on a state sexual offender registry. Nevertheless, assessing for risk and subsequently assigning a risk level clearly assumes guilt for a sexual (and not a nonsexual) offense.

To a significant degree, each of these variants reflects significant differences in the structure, mission, and approach of the juvenile court compared to the adult court system. Nevertheless, they create significant problems for the evaluator and the process of risk assessment. Although Letourneau (2003) has written that conducting risk assessments for clients charged with, but unadjudicated on, sexual offense charges contains the potential for benefit as well as harm, standard 16.03 of the 2005 ATSA practice standards and guidelines now clearly note, under "professional conduct," that ATSA members "do not provide expert testimony during the guilt phase of a criminal trial from which a reasonable person would draw inferences about whether an individual did or did not commit a specific sexual act" (p.10). Bear in mind the important caveat that these are clearly stated by ATSA as standards and guidelines to be used in the evaluation, treatment, and management of adult male sexual abusers, and the standards also note that "Juveniles . . . who have committed sexual offenses are in many ways distinct populations with distinct needs. Practitioners are urged to use caution and professional discretion if applying these standards to populations other than adult males" (p. v).

An additional practice guideline, then, is to remain aware of potential differences in the application of the risk assessment process when conducted under different circumstances, at different points in the process of juvenile apprehension and intervention, in different venues (pre- and in-treatment, for instance), and for different purposes. Of special importance is the capacity to assess a juvenile who is in a preadjudication stage of prosecution, or the prudence of conducting such an assessment. Here, aside from the impression that guilt may have been prejudged, bear in mind that in absence of an adjudication and in light of the juvenile's denial of the charges, or that the charges occurred as alleged, it is not possible to fully assess risk or assign a level of risk for a sexual reoffense. In this case, an assignment of a risk level necessarily requires at least one adjudicated or otherwise substantiated prior sexual offense.

CONCLUSION: THE RAISON D'ÊTRE

The Office for Juvenile Justice and Delinquency Prevention (Righthand & Welch, 2001) has described comprehensive clinical assessment as required in the evaluation of risk for sexually abusive youth and emphasized that any attempt to explain or treat juvenile sexual offenders must be based on the specific factors pertinent to that juvenile's offenses and individual psychology. Even though there is no clearly defined or unequivocally correct means by which to define, or single method by which to complete, such an assessment, we can nonetheless clearly describe practice guidelines, standards, and expectations by which to define an approach to a comprehensive assessment, as well its requisite components.

However, regardless of the comprehensive nature of the process and guidelines by which to shape it, given the essential purpose of a sexual offender assessment the central question to be addressed and answered revolves around the assessment of risk and an estimate of the potential for sexual recidivism. The rest of the assessment is merely a means by which to form such an opinion and provide the data set that is most likely to best contribute to a sensitive, meaningful, and well-informed assessment of risk. Of course, I do not mean to casually dismiss the rest of the comprehensive assessment; having spent so much time describing and having repeatedly discussed the importance of comprehensive assessment, I assume the reader by now recognizes the value this book places on the process. Nevertheless, I do want us to keep in mind that the comprehensive assessment of risk is designed not simply to learn about the juvenile, but also to learn about the juvenile specifically in order to assess risk, and thus provide the basis for decisions about treatment and management interventions if trajectory appears to be moving in the direction of a reoffense.

As the entire reason for the comprehensive assessment is the estimate of risk, we might well conclude by paraphrasing four important questions posed by Monahan (1995, pp. 115–116), who was addressing clinical risk assessment for violence:

1. Can I be sure that the information I have obtained is accurate?
2. Am I giving adequate attention to what I estimate the base rate of sexually abusive behavior to be among persons similarly situated to the person being examined?
3. What evidence do I have that the particular factors I have relied upon as predictors are in fact predictive of sexually abusive behavior?
4. Am I giving a balanced consideration to factors indicating the absence of sexually abusive behavior, as well as to factors indicating its occurrence?

CHAPTER 16

Approaching and Conducting the Assessment

W E HAVE BY now fully outlined the comprehensive assessment in terms of purpose and form, and to some degree content has also been addressed. Chapter 11 provided an overview of the materials and evaluation processes that might be included in a comprehensive assessment, and Chapter 14 reviewed currently available and in-development risk assessment instruments and related supplemental tools instruments or processes. Building on the guidelines presented in Chapter 15, by which the assessment may be conceptualized and itself evaluated, this chapter more fully discusses an approach to the assessment process, including its structure and organization and the means by which information is gathered and incorporated into the assessment.

We start by reiterating that comprehensive assessment is essentially psychosocial in nature, even though it may include valuable contributions from nonpsychosocial sources, such as psychological tests, inventories, and scales, and physiological examinations. In addition, the process of psychosocial investigation itself is for the most part clinical in method and application. That is, it is dependent upon the evaluator's direct interaction with and observations of the subject(s) of the evaluation, the evaluator's subjective review of case-related records and materials, the evaluator's interpretation and inclusion of information, and, ultimately, the evaluator's capacity to form judgments, draw conclusions, and make decisions based upon these processes. It is also multidimensional in design. Interpretation and understanding is based upon a complex and multipoint view of the individual, at the intrapersonal, interpersonal, and ecological levels, as well as in emotional, behavioral, and cognitive domains. Additionally, assessments gather information from multiple sources and through multiple means. Information is thus gathered from the youth, family members, probation officers, social workers, teachers, and attorneys, and through written records, interviews, observations, and potentially other sources, such as psychological, educational, and psychiatric evaluation and self-report.

Comprehensive assessment thus attempts to fully understand the individual and place his or her behavior in the context of his or her whole life. With respect to the particular goal of estimating risk, the comprehensive assessment provides a formulation about the circumstances of the sexually abusive behavior, its natural history, and its likely prognosis if things remain unchanged, as well as recommendations for treatment and management.

However, just as there is no single method by which to complete an assessment, there is no universal structure by which to understand and organize the assessment process, nor a uniform format or content by which the assessment is defined, physically organized, or made complete. Nevertheless, just as we can provide guidelines and describe an approach to assessment, we can also describe ideas about the assessment process so that it may be more easily conceptualized in terms of structure, method, and content. In providing a framework for assessment and a means by which to consider the assessment process, and even in establishing guidelines by which to conduct and complete risk assessments and criteria against which assessment may be judged, it is nonetheless up to the reader to decide how best to apply these ideas, or indeed whether to apply them at all. That said, we begin by taking a look at the structure or organization of the assessment process.

THE COMPLETE ASSESSMENT

How long does it take to complete a comprehensive assessment of risk? To a great extent this depends on the degree of comprehensiveness, including how long it takes to get signed releases, gather the necessary records, and contact the appropriate informants; how many records are read and how many are sought; how many informants are interviewed and how many interviews are conducted; and how much additional testing or evaluation is administered outside of the risk assessment itself. The amount of time required to conduct and complete the evaluation will vary widely, depending on factors that include the specific questions to be asked and answered, how much is already known about the case, the clinical complexity of the case, the availability of and need for corroborating information, and the youth's amenability to being interviewed and participation in the process (Medoff & Kinscherff, 2006). Of course, the length of time available to complete the assessment is also determined by the requirements of the referral source. However, it takes more than a day to complete such an assessment; between even minimal record review and minimal interviews, completing a risk assessment instrument, and writing the assessment report, absent of any other form of testing, the evaluation takes a minimum of 12-plus hours, spread over at least several days. Minimally, then, a comprehensive assessment that is rather basic is a five-day proposition, from start to finish. I would call this a hurried assessment, however, and two weeks (10 working days) is a more reasonable length of time to start and complete the assessment, and perhaps longer if the evaluator has the luxury of time and the youth is in an environment where he or she is safe from potential harm and from potentially causing harm to others during the assessment period.

Unlike psychological testing or psychiatric interviews that can be completed in a single step or two and involve little coordination or integration with other assessment methods, comprehensive assessment is a multidimensional process, requiring multiple steps and involving multiple sources of information that must be seamlessly consolidated.

However, as with all things, there is a beginning, middle, and end to assessment, regardless of how long it takes to complete. As such we can structure and sequence the process, and at the same time understand what tasks are most closely associated with different points in the assessment sequence. Most typically, the process of evaluation begins with a review of all prior records and concludes with the establishment of a diagnosis (if this is part of the evaluation format), an assignment of risk level, a summary (and, ideally, formulation) of the case, and recommendations regarding management and treatment individualized to the specific needs of the juvenile being assessed.

As shown in Figure 16.1, when conceptualized this way the assessment can be seen to not just have a beginning and end, but particular elements, tasks, and outcomes associated with different aspects of the sequence that not only build upon earlier elements but also contribute to later elements and conclusions. Thus, we can see that the psychosocial element of the comprehensive assessment allows the acquisition of information that can help both understand and subsequently assess risk for reoffense, and in turn is followed by a case formulation that helps summarize the case and put it into perspective and finally leads to recommendations related to the decision-making process.

PHASES OF THE ASSESSMENT

The assessment process has more than just a vague beginning, middle, and end; it can instead be broken down into three distinct phases by which its general tasks can be clearly seen and organized, as shown in Figure 16.2.

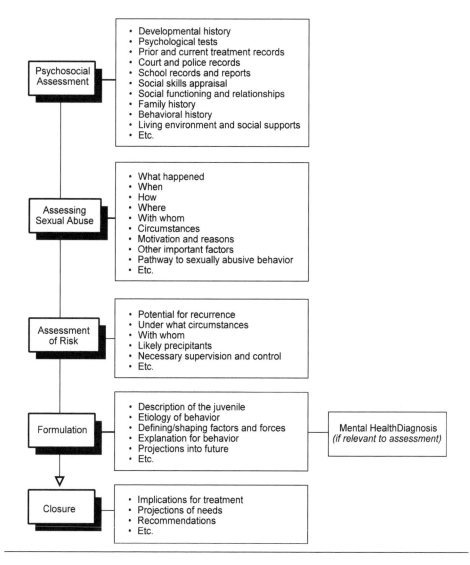

Figure 16.1   Process and associated outcomes at each stage of comprehensive assessment.

1. *Preassessment,* during which the evaluator develops a rudimentary understanding of the case by reviewing all available materials, requests additionally needed case records for review, identifies informants with whom to speak, and distributes and collects necessary release of information consent forms.

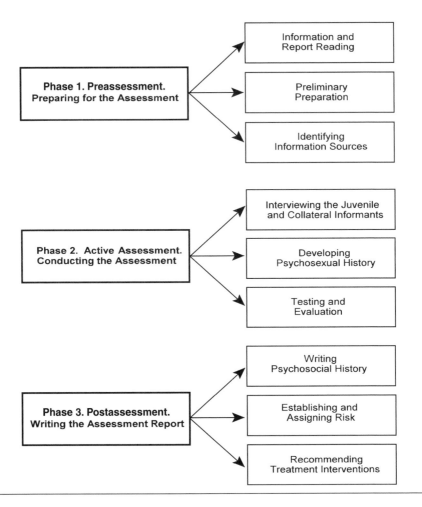

Figure 16.2   Overview of the psychosocial and risk assessment process.

2. *Active Assessment*, or the process of engaging fully with the juvenile and other related informants and parties, as well as remaining cognizant of the behaviors of the juvenile or important events that may be occurring during this phase of the assessment and that may have a bearing on the assessment process. This phase sees the active gathering of information that will be used to fuel and complete the risk assessment instrument. This includes not only information gathering through the interview process, but also observing the juvenile during the assessment period, if possible, in the home, school, or residential

treatment setting, adding to the depth and complexity of gathered information.

3. *Concluding the Assessment*, which essentially involves tying the assessment process together, assigning risk, and preparing the written assessment report.

Thinking of the assessment in this way helps to further organize and structure the thinking and planning of the evaluator, and clearly assigns the primary tasks of assessment into a sequential order, even though there may be overlap between phases in some cases.

PHASE 1. PREASSESSMENT: PREPARING FOR THE EVALUATION

Preassessment simply refers to the idea that the evaluator is preparing for the active process of meeting with the juvenile and other informants, or that part of the process during which information is directly gathered through interviews, discussion, clinical contact, and observation.

The preassessment phase therefore provides the groundwork during which the evaluator:

- Conducts a record review.
- Reads all pertinent information: *victim reports; witness reports; court and probation reports; inpatient, or residential, day treatment, and outpatient treatment summaries; court and psychological evaluations; police reports; state/referral agency reports and evaluations; and so on.*
- Identifies gaps in the record and requests and gathers additional records or information missing from the current record.
- Identifies important collateral informants: *parents (or parent figures), foster parents, prior therapist(s), teachers, probation officer, and so on.*
- Gathers signed release of information consent forms, allowing discussion with informants and the gathering of additional records.

PHASE 2. ACTIVE ASSESSMENT: CONDUCTING THE EVALUATION

During this phase, the evaluator engages directly with live informants from whom information will be gathered, including direct interviews, conversations, and meetings with relevant informants (i.e., those people who can provide a perspective or information about the juvenile that is relevant to the assessment). During this phase, the evaluator:

- Informs informants of confidentiality limits and the purpose of the evaluation.

- Ensures that release of information forms are signed by the legal guardian and juvenile, if necessary.
- Interviews the juvenile, preferably multiple times depending on availability and need.
- Interviews collateral informants (i.e., people other than the juvenile).
- Provides or arranges for additional testing that falls outside of record review, interviews, and observation.
- If able, remains aware of the youth's daily interactions and functioning, including patterns of behavior, mood, thinking, or interactions that develop or emerge during the course of the assessment period.

PHASE 3. CONCLUDING THE ASSESSMENT: WRITING THE EVALUATION REPORT

This final aspect involves the consolidation of information gathered through record review, interviews, additional testing, and observation and the synthesis of ideas into a case formulation. The assessment is concluded by the written report that:

- Summarizes pertinent historical and current data.
- Formulates hypotheses about the development of sexually abusive behavior.
- Formulates a description of the psychological profile of the juvenile.
- Formulates a description of the environment that shaped and influenced the juvenile's emotions, behavior, and ideation, and in which sexually abusive behavior developed and eventually occurred.
- If relevant to the particular assessment format, identifies diagnoses that address co-occurring psychiatric or substance abuse disorders.
- Assigns a level of risk for sexual reoffense.
- Proposes treatment needs and identifies suggested treatment goals.

Like all phases these may overlap with another; thus, although the evaluator may be well into the active phase of the assessment he or she may also be engaging in aspects more closely related to the first phase, such as collecting and reviewing additional case records or identifying additional informants who should be contacted. Similarly, even though in the middle, or active, phase of the assessment, the evaluator may start to write the assessment report even though it cannot be completed until the final phase of the process. And, even during the third and final phase, the evaluator may find it necessary to return to the active phase and reinterview the juvenile or another informant or to the first phase in order to reread records.

CONFIDENTIALITY AND CONSENT TO RELEASE INFORMATION

Before discussing how information is gathered, and from what sources, it is important to discuss confidentiality. Always a prime concern in any form of treatment, it is of special and heightened concern when attached to behavior so potentially stigmatizing as sexually abusive behavior, and also so potentially damaging to others and society as whole. Even the label "juvenile sexual offender" raises flags, and with the very real possibility of social judgment, ostracism, segregation, and rejection, issues of confidentiality loom large.

CONFIDENTIALITY

Some issues around confidentiality are not left up to the client-clinician relationship. Mandated reporting, for instance, requires professionals to report situations involving the abuse or neglect of a minor, even if they themselves cannot substantiate an allegation of abuse or neglect. In such cases, the professional is responsible only for reporting, and it is up to a state or regional social service agency (usually) to actually investigate and substantiate the report. In fact, failure to report alleged or possible abuse or neglect may result in civil penalties being levied against the professional. In some localities, mandated reporting also applies to the abuse or neglect of elders, and in some cases the disabled as well. In other cases, whereas the clinical licensing of some professionals (such as social workers and psychologists) provides for privileged communication, in which confidentiality is legally protected, this may not be true for other licensed clinicians. Mental health counselors or practitioners, for instance, may not have the same level of protection attached to their communication with clients, and in some cases may additionally be required to report certain acts, even if not covered by mandatory reporting laws.[1]

Under any circumstances, regardless of license or clinical discipline, legal precedents such as the Tarasoff case have resulted in the civil and often legal requirement for clinicians to report any knowledge of certain or likely harm to a known (and sometimes even an unknown) victim, to the potential victim, family members, or law enforcement. The death of Tatiana Tarasoff in 1969 at the hands of a therapy client who revealed his plans to

---

1. Licensing requirements, standards, privileges, and expectations not only vary from discipline to discipline, but also from one state or locale to another. Licensed clinicians should be aware of the requirements and privileges of their particular license, whereas unlicensed practitioners (and, of greater importance, their clients) may have no protections at all.

his therapist resulted in the Tarasoff warning, or the clinician's duty to warn a potential victim of harm that may be caused by a therapy client.

Further, if an evaluation is being administered under the auspices of or directly for the court, the results of the assessment are going to be released to the court, for the specific purpose of prosecution. In these cases, although varying from jurisdiction to jurisdiction, it is most likely that the evaluator is required to inform the juvenile and legal guardian, prior to the evaluation, of the purpose of the evaluation and its role in possible prosecution. In circumstances where the court has ordered an evaluation, the subject must be notified that communication between the evaluator and subject is not privileged, as in the Massachusetts "Lamb Warning."[2]

Aside from circumstances such as these, many clinicians and programs that treat sex offenders adopt a *no confidentiality* protocol in treating sexual offenders, whether adult or juvenile, in which disclosures, including disclosures of formerly unknown sexually abusive behavior or victims, will be reported to some version of the authorities. This, of course, may place the sexual offender in legal jeopardy if a new disclosure is made, as it may result in further or new criminal charges and/or prosecution. For juveniles, aside from the possibility of legal prosecution, there is also the possibility of removal from home or a lengthier separation from home if already in residential treatment, for instance, or the requirement for lengthier, more intense, and more intrusive restrictions on their independence and freedom. In turn, knowledge that a disclosure or acknowledgment of sexually abusive behavior may place an offender in jeopardy may dampen or shut down honesty and full engagement in treatment. Nevertheless, better that the individual refuses to engage in treatment or accept responsibility than reveals information under the belief that it will be held confidential only to discover that the clinician subsequently shared this information with others, including the authorities. Hence, if such information must be shared, due to mandatory reporting or duty to warn, or it is the clinician's or agency's policy to share such information, this must be disclosed in advance to individuals entering the evaluation process, and in the case of juveniles to their legal guardians. Under such conditions, the confidentiality policy and its limits on confidentiality should be presented in writing and explained to the offender and/or legal guardian, and they in turn should sign a statement acknowledging that they understand the policy, its limitations on confidentiality, and circumstances under which information will be shared with authorities. Under these circumstances,

---

2. *Commonwealth vs. Charles E. Lamb*, 365 Mass. 265, 1974.

clinicians or agencies should further consider having a signed "waiver of confidentiality" agreement.

Descriptions of confidentiality and its limitations, as well as waivers of confidentiality, protect the individual (i.e., the sexual offender), the individual's family if he or she is a minor, and the clinical and treatment agency, and certainly ensure that the individual (and his or her family, if a juvenile) is fully informed about the goals of evaluation (and treatment) and disclosures of information. As the privilege of confidentiality lies with the client, and not with the clinician,[3] it is entirely within the client's purview (or the client's legal guardian, if a juvenile) to waive confidentiality. Waivers of confidentiality also level the playing field among different clinical professions and licenses, as they provide for no privileged communication when it comes to acknowledgments and disclosures of sexual offenses, regardless of clinical discipline. They thus allow the evaluator and clinician to act in the best interests of both client and society, offering informed practice for the individual being assessed and protection for the community.

Issues of confidentiality, then, should be fully explained to the juvenile sexual offender and his or her legal guardian, and furthermore they should continue to be explained as a reminder to the youth during the evaluation process. One clear step that can be taken is to remind the youth of the limits of confidentiality at the beginning of every interview or meeting during the evaluation process. Without going overboard, the evaluator may also want to remind the youth about confidentiality limits when being directly asked about his or her history of or allegations about sexually abusive behavior or when it appears likely that the youth is going to acknowledge or report a sexual offense. It is also critical that the legal guardian is aware of limits on confidentiality and understands possible consequences.

INFORMED CONSENT

Before engaging in evaluation, and before gathering information about the sexually abusive youth or sharing information with others during the assessment process, informed consent is required from the juvenile and/or

---

3. The right to confidentiality is the client's, although it is the clinician's responsibility to maintain confidentiality. Clinicians may ask clients to waive confidentiality in which case the client may decline treatment with that clinician, but equally clinicians may not hold treatment matters as confidential if the client says that they must release the information. Confidentiality is the client's right, and not the clinician's.

the juvenile's legal guardian. In the case of minors, with some exceptions,[4] such consents do not hold water without the consent of the legal guardian. In these cases, the consent of the juvenile is not actually necessary, other than as a pro forma courtesy to the juvenile.

However, the evaluator should ensure that he or she has determined who is actually the legal guardian, as only the legal guardian may sign any consent documents, including consents for release of information. In the case of juveniles entering evaluation or treatment legal custody may rest with a parent or may have been temporarily or permanently transferred to another person or entity, such as the state. Sometimes, for instance, the state holds *physical* but not legal custody (and therefore does not hold guardianship), and other times it has both. Regardless, only the legal guardian can sign consent, so it is important for the evaluator to be fully and accurately aware of the identity and nature of the legal guardian. In some cases, the evaluator should be aware that legal guardianship for an individual over the age of 18 may also rest with someone other than the individual, on the grounds of some form of personal incompetence due to a serious mental health condition or significant mental retardation, for instance.

Consents for release of information allow the evaluator to gather relevant treatment and developmental information about the juvenile from others who, without permission, would not be otherwise entitled to share such information, either verbally or by passing along records. However, in order to protect the individual, and those who share information, consents should be *informed*. That is, they should very specifically state the name of the individual or agency from whom information is being requested, whether information can be shared with that entity as well as being collected, and the type of information being requested and for what purpose.

Releases should be dated, signed by the legal guardian, and countersigned by a witness (preferably with printed names, as well, for readability), and they should also be time limited so that they do not extend the right to gather or share information forever. In the United States, the release of information form should be in accordance with HIPAA, or the Health Insurance Portability and Accountability Act of 1996, which is designed to protect the privacy and confidentiality of medical records.

Regardless, informed consent requires that consent for information is given by the individual signing the consent with a full understanding of

---

4. In some states, for instance, juveniles may give consent themselves for certain medical or treatment procedures and the related sharing of relevant information, without the consent or even knowledge of their legal guardians.

the information being gathered, from whom, and for what purpose. Combined with an understanding of the possible outcomes of the evaluation process, as described previously (under confidentiality), the individual's permission to gather and share case-related information is thus informed.

THE FAILURE OF CONSENT FORMS: INABILITY TO GATHER NECESSARY INFORMATION

As confidentiality is the privilege of the client (and not the treating entity), with an appropriately signed release the informant is not only permitted to share information (and thus protected), but also compelled to provide the information. Nevertheless, a signed release does not mean that the evaluator will always get cooperation from the former provider or informant, and in reality it is often quite difficult to get such information.

Sometimes the release of information form itself is poorly developed or not in compliance with HIPAA. In other cases, a lack of cooperation from an informant or informing agency is simply a matter of poor organization and even ineptitude on the part of the entity from whom information is being requested. Law enforcement and agencies related to the court may also refuse to disclose information, even with a signed consent, and sometimes records are sealed by the court. This may include material directly related to the evaluation of sexually abusive behavior, such as victim and witness statements, police reports, and statements and testimony given by the juvenile. Sometimes social service agencies themselves, including the very agency that has referred the juvenile for the assessment, will not share information about the individual. In many cases, the reluctance or refusal of a court system or social service agency to share such information makes no sense and is self-defeating, even if intended to protect the juvenile's rights, in the face of the forensic evaluation that has been requested, usually by a state social service agency or court system.

However, whether the result of a zealous protection of individual rights, agency ineptitude, organizational bureaucracy, suspicion of the evaluation process, poorly designed or technically inaccurate consent forms, informant disorganization or laziness, or any number of other reasons, the reality is that even a signed release of information form may not get the evaluator the requested information, or it is received in an untimely manner (after the evaluation is completed, for instance). As described in Chapter 19, failure to get requested information should itself be documented in the written evaluation report, especially as the absence of such information may affect the overall quality or accuracy of the evaluation.

These are the just the realities with which the evaluator will have to contend in gathering, or trying to gather, information. Nevertheless, information should not be sought or shared without signed informed consent.

SOURCES OF AND MEANS FOR INFORMATION GATHERING

Beyond its focus on guidelines and principles by which the process of comprehensive assessment may be operationalized, Chapter 15 also provided a cursory look at content regions to be included in the assessment, and these are fleshed out in more detail in Chapter 19, which addresses the writing of the assessment report. However, without reviewing these content areas in further detail at this time, it's important to note for now that the psychosocial assessment is essentially defined by these areas of content, and these content areas are, in turn, filled in, developed, and defined by the process of psychosocial assessment. This process is inclusive of the various sources of information from record review to clinical interviews, objective testing, and self-report inventories that together constitute a broad, multidimensional, and multiple-source process of information gathering.

Aside from bringing in more than one point of view about the case and understanding different facets of the individual and his or her behaviors, a multidimensional/multisource approach also minimizes the possibility of error in data collection and formulation. Paraphrasing Grisso (2000), as there is likely an error of some sort in every assessment method we apply, whether clinical or statistical, an obvious means to reduce such mistakes is to adopt a multimethod approach to assessment and thus ensure that our conclusions are supported by data drawn from more than one method and more than one source. These methods include the clinical processes of record review, interview, and observation, as well as the use of non-psychosocial and sometimes standardized sources of information, such as psychological tests, inventories, and scales, and physiological examination.

Generally speaking, the application of clinical processes for gathering and interpreting information largely revolves around the professional judgment and experience of the evaluator, in which the psychosocial process depends on the evaluator's capacity to form judgments, draw conclusions, and make decisions. Conversely, nonclinical methods for acquiring data involve questionnaires, testing, and other processes that are specifically or generally free of the approach, judgment, and interpretation of the evaluator.

RECORD REVIEW

The goal of record review, of course, is to gather important information about the juvenile. The process involves the examination of all relevant material in the record and requesting other material that may be missing from the record (although in many cases you will never actually get some of the requested records).

DEPTH AND BREADTH OF RECORDS

The information is used to inform the evaluator about the individual being assessed[5] and includes records of every kind, including prior treatment records, records of early development, parental and family history, behavioral history, medical history, educational records, social service studies and reports, prior forensic evaluations and sexual risk assessments, and criminal records, including arrest, police, and investigation reports, victim and witness statements, and any statements made by the youth being assessed. Even though it will not always be possible to acquire all relevant documents, records should also be sought and reviewed that date back to birth and thus document the juvenile's earliest experiences, and even prenatal history in terms of parent and other family history.

Knowing about the family history, even before the juvenile's birth, may yield a great deal of information about the family and environment in which the juvenile was raised. Similarly, knowing about the child's emotional, behavioral, cognitive, and medical development from birth and through his or her early years may also yield much information, not only about the development of behavior but the possibility of an autistic or early developing psychiatric disorder, for instance, as well as pathogenic child rearing and other environmental conditions.

History is important, then, not simply to reflect back on the past but to understand the direct and continuous etiological (ontogenetic) connection from the child's birth to the present day. Knowing about the juvenile's social and school interactions and environments, and his or her behavior and interactions throughout early and middle school, provides not just important background but the very information that is relevant to the development of past and current behavior, including sexual behavior, and current attitudes, ideas and beliefs, behaviors, self-regulation, and social functioning. Record review, then, is an enormously important aspect of the comprehensive assessment.

---

5. Of course, exactly the same applies to records for adult clients; it's just that the record is longer, extending past childhood or adolescence and into adulthood.

APPROACHES TO RECORD REVIEW:
PSYCHOMETRIC AND CLINICAL

Whereas the face-to-face interview is intrinsically clinical in nature, the process of record review is intrinsically clerical. However, the data collected through the record review may serve a technical (nonclinical) or a clinical purpose; further the process of record review itself may be more clinical or more clerical/technical, depending on both its ultimate purpose and how it is conducted.

TECHNICAL/PSYCHOMETRIC RECORD REVIEW

Record review can be highly structured and guided by a defined set of questions or data that the record reviewer has been instructed to focus upon. Such a protocol both defines and restricts data collection in terms of what information is to be gathered for the assessment. In this case, the review can be conducted by anyone and not necessarily the evaluator or a clinician.

In a technical record review, not only can the type of desired information be guided by a defined protocol, but the information itself can be quantified and coded. This usually involves noting and labeling the presence or occurrence of specified historical events, such as arrests, history of sexual maltreatment, school suspensions, parental marriages and divorces, for example, as well the quantity, frequency, or intensity of types of events (number of arrests, level of previous treatment, number of school suspensions, etc.). This information is labeled according to a predefined coding system and transferring to a code book where it can later be counted. In this model, only specific information is sought, coded, and recorded, and other historical information is ignored or discarded if it fails to meet the definition assigned by the code book, thus becoming invisible.

When information from the juvenile's record is collected and coded in this manner, the specified information of interest has been, in some way, previously selected as having specific value to a database, which itself is based on the parameters of a research model or study of some kind. Record review in this case is statistically driven in some way, rather than clinically driven. The record reviewer will seek and gather only the information defined as important by the code book, and not the judgment of the data collector. Additionally, some sort of statistical process will later be applied in order to quantify and make sense of collected data, rather than the application of a clinical process that involves the judgment, insight, and interpretation of the evaluator. Whereas the clinical process depends on professional, but nevertheless subjective, experience and expertise to select and make sense of the data, the psychometric process instead depends upon objective statistical formula.

CLINICALLY-ORIENTED RECORD REVIEW

In considering differences between a technically and clinically driven approach to record review, we see a difference between the clinical process of formulation and the formulaic application of a statistical or technical process. This is certainly the case when record data is used to develop or score an actuarial procedure, in which record review is used to pick out only certain and specific data and the rest is essentially ignored as irrelevant to the purpose. There is no clinical application for the information and no exercise of clinical judgment in selecting and interpreting the information, or putting one bit of information together with another bit, in order to make judgments, form conclusions, or be evaluative.

In a psychosocial assessment, however, record review is decidedly clinical in practice, in the manner in which records are reviewed, information is selected and gleaned, and judgments formed. In this case, record review is not a technical process conducted by a clerk or technician, but it is instead a clinical process conducted by the evaluator. Here, the evaluator is seeking a wide range of information that, based on his or her judgment, is useful and can be pieced together with other information in the record to form a whole that is larger than any individual bit of information.

Based on this review, the evaluator gathers knowledge, develops direction, establishes ideas, develops a rudimentary understanding of the individual, and interprets and evaluates. This is the clinical process, and it is dependent upon the skill and experience of the clinical evaluator. This is not to say that clinical record review cannot be aided by structured tools that may allow the evaluator to make decisions about what sort of information to seek and to find ways to record, quantify, and reflect upon certain pieces of information. However, the structure merely helps define, guide, and perhaps streamline record review, rather than replacing the clinical process.

THOROUGH AND ACCURATE RECORD REVIEW

Regardless of how record review is conducted, it should not be taken for granted. Records will be missing and should be sought, but, like gathering information through signed releases, despite the evaluator's best efforts some will remain missing and simply not be available or made available to the evaluator. Again, in the final assessment report, missing records should be documented as requested but not available. Furthermore, the evaluator will not only find that records are often incomplete, but also that available and existing records are sometimes inconsistent with one another (and sometimes even within the same report or record) or inaccurate.

Despite the importance of records, depending on them as either a complete, consistent, or accurate record of the juvenile's life is a serious error. Assuming the infallibility and accuracy of the record may not only result in a poor and sloppy evaluation, but also in an inaccurate evaluation in which conclusions about the juvenile and his or her level of risk have been made without sufficient or adequate information or are made in error. It is the evaluator's responsibility, then, to check the accuracy of prior records, whenever possible and certainly when gaps in the record are present, as well as inconsistencies, inaccuracies, or questionable information, and not simply pass on such information as accurate. In such an instance, the evaluator is not only passing along weak or inaccurate information, but he or she is actively contributing to a record that is weak and inaccurate. And, just as missing records should be noted in the written assessment report, if prior records contain inaccurate, inconsistent, vague, confusing, or questionable data, this too should be documented in the final assessment report.

THE INTERVIEW

Interviews are central to any form of comprehensive assessment and are discussed and described in detail in the following two chapters. Accordingly, a brief discussion at this point will suffice to outline the general nature, process, and role of the interview in risk assessment.

Unlike the record review, interviews are inherently clinical in nature. That is, they always require some form of direct contact between the interviewer and the subject. However, like the record review, interviews can be used for nonclinical purposes, such as gathering information for a statistical study (such as polling America voters). Interviews can also be administered in a nonclinical fashion, in which the interviewer closely or completely follows a prescripted questionnaire in interacting with the interviewee. Here, the clinical nature of the interview is determined to a great degree by how tightly the interview is scripted and defined by an interview guide and how much free rein is given to the evaluator in deciding how to conduct and engage in the interview and what questions are asked.

Although always involving direct contact between the interviewer and subject, it is the function and intended purpose of the interview, how interview data are to be used, and the format of the interview that defines the interview as clinical or non-clinical. Even if relatively clinical in application, if the interview is guided by a structured and coded interview format, such as the Adult Attachment Inventory,[6] for example, interviews can nevertheless serve a completely nonclinical purpose. In such a case, the interview follows a structured or semistructured guideline that may require some clinical skill on the part of the interviewer. Nevertheless, the interview, which is often audio or video recorded, is later nonclinically microanalyzed and coded based upon the presence of specific bits of information or behavior, and, as in the coded use of record reviews, other data are discarded or not held relevant for the purposes for which the interview is being used.

However, although interviews can be either clinical or nonclinical in administration, purpose, and analysis, in the psychosocial assessment they are *always* clinical in purpose, design, and process, and are described in detail in Chapters 17 and 18.

NON-CLINICAL DATA COLLECTION

As described in Chapter 11, other than record review and informant interviews, assessment information can also be collected through objective psychological and physiological tests and various forms of attitude and inventory scales that identify and measure interests, attitudes, functioning, and so forth.

However, it is important to reiterate that neither psychological nor physiological testing can be used to establish whether or not a juvenile sexual offender will re-engage in sexually abusive behavior, and this is equally true for subjective self-report measures. Neither can these instruments form a profile of the average juvenile sexual offender nor should they be used for this purpose. Nevertheless, they each can gather useful information and thus be used effectively as tools in comprehensive assessment.

PHYSIOLOGICAL TESTS

Physiological tests are essentially limited to the polygraph (sometimes referred to as PDD, or psychophysiological detection of deceit), penile

---

6. A semi-structured assessment instrument used to assess the experience of childhood attachment in adults.

plethysmography (PPG), or tests of visual reaction time.[7] The polygraph examination is most likely to be used in treatment rather than evaluation; its only likely use in evaluation is to help establish how honest the juvenile is with regard to sexually abusive behavior. However, given that the ultimate purpose of the evaluation is to assess risk for a sexual reoffense and not establish guilt or innocence, evaluators should think twice about seeking a polygraph examination as part of the assessment, although it is perfectly reasonable to include the results of prior polygraph exams in the assessment. Typically, the greatest value of a polygraph examination is testing for honesty and deception, although the polygraph cannot determine whether the individual is actually being honest or not, which is why the results of polygraphy are most often not accepted as evidence in court proceedings. As Becker and Harris (2004) have noted, there is general controversy in the field regarding the validity and reliability of the polygraph, and especially in forensic use. Further, in addition to general questions about the use of polygraph examinations, questions persist about the appropriateness and value of the process with adolescents (Craig, 1998; Emerick & Dutton, 1993; Craig, 1998).

Penile plethysmography, or phallometric examination, is not popular with adolescents as it is so intrusive, although it is an effective means for establishing sexual arousal. The PPG measures tumescence, or growth, of the penis when the individual is exposed to sexual materials or ideas, and hence measures sexual arousal and interests, including deviant sexual arousal (for example, arousal to prepubescent children, sexual sadism, or animals).[8] However, deviant sexual arousal is not considered an easily operationalized construct in juveniles under 16. Further, Hunter and Lexier (1998) have pointed out that the reliability and validity of plethysmograph assessment has not yet been established and also have questioned the wisdom of exposing juveniles to sexual stimuli.

Nevertheless, Seto, Lalumière, and Blanchard (2000) found phallometric testing relevant to the assessment of sexual deviance in adolescent boys aged 14 and older who had previously sexually abused younger boys (but not younger girls). On the other hand, Fanniff and Becker (2006) note both limited research on the reliability and validity of plethysmography for adolescent sexual offenders, as well as ethical concerns associated with

---

7. Detailed descriptions of phallometric, visual reaction time, and polygraph examination can be found in the appendices of the ATSA Practice Standards and Guidelines (Association for the Treatment of Sexual Abusers, 2005).

8. Female vaginal plethysmography is also available, but is less reliable, and obviously functions differently.

using an invasive procedure with adolescents. They write that while the plethysmograph offers promise, it is premature to consider it a valid measure of deviant sexual arousal in all juveniles, and they suggest that it is most appropriate with only a limited population of juvenile sexual offenders. Specifically, Hunter and Lexier (1998) and Becker and Harris (2004) suggest its use is most appropriate with older adolescent boys who have sexually abused younger boys and acknowledged their sexually abusive behavior. Fanniff and Becker conclude that until further evidence of its utility is provided, the plethysmograph does not presently seem to be an appropriate instrument to use routinely in assessing juvenile assessments.

Tests of visual reaction time (VRT) chiefly include the Abel Assessment of Sexual Interest (AASI)[9] and the Affinity Measure of Sexual Interest, both of which can be used with adolescent boys and girls. These assess sexual interest (rather than arousal) based on the length of time, in milliseconds (thousandths of a second), the test subject spends viewing images that either have direct sexual content or represent sexual imagery. Although the plethysmograph is probably the strongest physical measure of sexual interest, in that it seems to unmistakably measure sexual arousal,[10] VRT measures are far less intrusive and therefore ethically more acceptable in use with adolescents. Nevertheless, Worling (2006a) has noted that there have been few published studies that support the validity of VRT with adolescents.

The Affinity VRT assessment is too new and untested of a process to be fully evaluated, and its accompanying manual notes its use with adolescents is for research use only, since evidence has not fully emerged that indicates legitimate value (Glasgow, 2003). The AASI is far more well known and well used, but it has mixed reviews, and its utility in assessing sexual interests in adolescents has been questioned. Although Becker and Harris (2004) describe the AASI as a promising instrument, they also note that there are few available studies on its use and validity with adolescents. Although Abel et al. (2004) argue that the AASI is able to discriminate between adolescent child molesters and non-molesters, Smith and Fischer (1999) concluded that, in their study, the AASI failed to prove either reliable or valid in assessing deviant sexual interest among adolescent sexual offenders. Additionally, the

---

9. The recently developed Abel-Blasingame Sexual Interest Assessment for Individuals with Intellectual Disabilities (ABID) is designed for VRT assessment with lower functioning individuals.

10. Nevertheless, there are any number of factors that may influence plethysmograph testing, and especially in adolescents in whom sexual interest and development may be peaking, and hence may be easily aroused.

AASI is currently unable to fully describe the age ranges of the targets of sexual interest, which to some degree limits its utility.[11]

Becker and Harris (2004) have written that, despite shortcomings, VRT, phallometric testing, and polygraph examination each offer some potential benefit to the clinician in treatment planning and risk management. Nevertheless, under any circumstances, none of these tools are risk assessment instruments. As such, they should not be used either as a means to identify sexual offenders or to predict risk for sexual reoffense, although they may point toward serious concerns that, in turn, may be described and highlighted in the comprehensive assessment report. For example, phallometric or VRT testing may point toward significant sexual interest in young children, which may signal concern in the case of an adult or adolescent who has previously engaged in the sexual abuse of a child. Equally, polygraph examinations may suggest deceit in self-reports about alleged or substantiated sexually abusive behavior. In such cases, results may not only be included in the written assessment, but also inform the risk assessment instrument, support the presence of relevant risk factors for possible re-engagement in sexual abuse, and be reflected in the assignment of a risk level.

Psychological Evaluation

Psychological evaluation can establish a means for gathering and developing important psychological data and help us learn about the psychological makeup of an individual compared to a larger population. Such testing is usually psychometric in design, meaning that the test is constructed in order to objectively and statistically compare data gathered from the tested individual against other similar individuals (in terms of age or gender, for instance).

A psychological evaluation is intended to tell us something significant about an individual, reflecting mood or emotion, intellect and related cognitive processes, attitudes or beliefs, interests, functioning, mentation and thinking processes, self-perceptions and perceptions about others, character traits, or other aspects of personal psychology and behavioral functioning.

Such tests attempt to tell us something about the way an individual functions at the time of the test. In the case of psychometrically based

---

11. The AASI assesses the sexual interest of the subject in children, adolescents, and adults ages 2-4, 8-10, 14-17, and age 22 and older. For statistical design and practical purposes, it is unable to assess sexual interest in the missing age ranges.

testing, we can draw conclusions about current behaviors and make reasonable inferences about future behaviors if things remain unchanged. However, like physiological tests, psychological tests often provide important information about the individual, but are not and may not be used to either determine risk for a sexual reoffense or assess the individual as a sexual offender.

Although psychological testing plays an important role in the comprehensive assessment of risk, it is also important to note the nature and limitations of such testing. In fact, even the best psychological tests are flawed, and regardless of how well a test may work statistically, we can never be sure of how accurate it may be with any particular individual. The best developed tests are designed to recognize and adjust for the manner in which the test taker responds to test items, and often include scales that measure things like intentional deceit, inconsistency in how questions are answered, or a pattern of socially desirable answers or intentionally understating (fake good) or overstating (fake bad) symptoms. Nonetheless, in some cases psychological tests may be manipulated by the individual being assessed, and particularly vulnerable are those tests that are so transparent that it is easy for subjects to understand their goal and answer in a particular direction. In other cases, tests are so poorly designed and convoluted that subjects may not fully understand questions and unintentionally provide inaccurate answers. In either case, responses to test items may not be true representations of the items we're attempting to measure. Further, although testing infers that future behaviors are built on current psychological functioning, for the most part the primary function of such testing is to describe the psychology of the individual at the time of the assessment.

Hence, whether determining the adequacy of testing, the manner in which the subject approached and accurately responded to test items, or projections about the individual's current or future functioning, clinical judgment is eventually required in order to interpret the results of psychological testing. That is, although test scores may be summed up by a technician, test results must always be interpreted by a clinician, ideally an evaluator who knows the subject and the subject's history. Thus, although statistically possible trajectories may be identified, test results serve to fuel and inform, but not define, the outcome of psychological testing in terms of diagnosis, prognosis, and recommendations.

For these reasons, the results of psychological testing should not necessarily be taken at face value and should be carefully folded into the larger comprehensive assessment in a sensitive and well-informed manner, using reason and judgment to add to a larger picture of the sexually abusive youth and help assess risk.

OTHER MEASURES

Although completed by self-report, the MSI, MIDSA, and SAI-J, described in Chapter 14, each provide objectively assessed information about sexual (and other) interests and history. These, again, are not risk assessment instruments,[12] but they may provide useful supplemental information to be incorporated into a comprehensive assessment of risk. In addition to these tools there are numerous instruments that provide useful information about the individual being assessed, including both evaluator-generated and self-report measures and inventories of attitudes, beliefs, and ideas related to virtually every facet of human experience, including sexual behavior, motivation, interest, and knowledge.

However, not all psychologically oriented evaluation instruments are psychometric or objective in construction. In fact, many (if not most) of these instruments, whether completed by self-report or by the evaluator, consist of theoretical scales that possess no psychometric properties. These generally consist of attitude and inventory scales that identify and measure interests, attitudes, functioning, empathy, remorse, and other aspects of human interest, beliefs, behavior, and experience. Although many of these may be of value to the evaluator, inventories and scales of perhaps greatest interest are those that pertain to sexual beliefs and behaviors. These are frankly too numerous to mention. However, Prentky and Edmunds (1997) and Calder (2001) describe multiple inventories, self-reports, and other resources that may be used as part of the assessment process, and in many cases they reproduce various instruments for use. The reader should be aware that some of these materials may now be outdated, and also that any selected materials must be appropriate for the age, intellectual capacity, and gender of the juvenile under assessment. Hence, materials developed for adults should not be used in juvenile assessment, and the same is true in the assessment of girls with respect to material developed for use with boys. In the assessment of preadolescents, material developed for adolescents should not be used and, similarly, materials developed for use with juveniles with IQs in the average range are possibly not appropriate for juveniles with cognitive impairments.

Further, the reader should be aware that in almost every case materials available in the form of inventories are not normed and have no statistical validity or reliability whatsoever, and furthermore are in some cases poorly written or developed. Some questions may be confusing in their wording,

---

12. Although the authors of the MIDSA expect to eventually develop a risk assessment component out of the scales, and the SAI-J is presently described by its authors as a risk assessment instrument.

and may result in the juvenile misunderstanding the question and accordingly giving an inaccurate answer. The same is true for self-report instruments that don't necessarily define their terms or questions, making it easy for respondent to either misunderstand or inaccurately answer questions. In other cases, the correct answers are fairly transparent, so the juvenile may know exactly how to answer a question in a way that is socially desirable.

In completing a comprehensive assessment of risk, then, many of these materials are of great value in providing useful supplementary information, but the evaluator must also remain aware that some of the available materials are not necessarily well developed and often add little more than useful, but not *defining*, information.

EXERCISING CAUTION IN THE USE OF NONCLINICAL SOURCES OF INFORMATION

For the reasons described above, information gathered through sources such as psychological, physiological, and other measures should be treated with caution. With particular respect to the use of psychological testing in risk assessment, Prentky and Burgess (2000) write:

> A vast array of different inventories, questionnaires, and scales are used by different clinicians to assess sexual offenders. By any rigorous psychometric standard, *very few* of the inventories and questionnaires should be used. To begin with, the psychometric properties . . . for most of these scales are unknown. . . . Additionally, very few of these instruments have been validated on sexual offender samples and very few have normative data from sexual offender samples. . . . In general, risk assessment studies that have included psychometric instruments, find that psychometric data are not particularly useful in predicting recidivism in sexual offenders. Since most psychometric instruments were never designed to assess reoffense risk, this finding is not surprising. (p. 85)

THE MENTAL STATUS EXAM

The mental status exam is a special variant of the clinical interview. Closely related to and always part of a mental health evaluation, the mental status exam may not be considered relevant to an evaluation of risk, and many such assessments will not include a mental status examination or its results. However, the mental status exam has great utility as it is aimed at revealing the mental underpinning of outward presentation, and thus the mental and cognitive capacity of the individual being assessed. Accordingly, whether administered as a separate interview entirely or woven into more general interviews with the juvenile, a mental status exam should be considered as part of the clinical interview process, and especially if the comprehensive assessment includes a mental health diagnosis.

A detailed description of the mental status exam is most definitely outside the scope of this book. However, it essentially involves an assessment of behavioral and cognitive aspects of mental status (Morrison, 1995), including general appearance, mood and affect, flow of thought, rate and rhythm of speech, content of thought and perception, cognition and awareness, attention and concentration, and insight and judgment. The mental status exam is useful, then, for understanding the mental status and capacity of the individual being interviewed.

For the most part, we can expect many juveniles to demonstrate a mental status within an expected and normative range. However, when mental status falls outside of the normative range, it tells us something about the individual diagnostically and additionally offers insight not only into the individual's current mental status, but also into factors that may have influenced his or her prior sexually abusive behaviors. Although an understanding of the mental status exam process should be developed through supervised practice, a simple mental status exam form is found in the Appendix.

CONCLUSION: PROVIDING STRUCTURE FOR THE PSYCHOSOCIAL ASSESSMENT

In describing the structure of the assessment process, O'Reilly and Carr (2004) frame the assessment in terms of four assessment sessions, one of which involves the youth and his or her primary caregivers, a second with the primary caregivers, and the third and fourth with the youth. Although O'Reilly and Carr describe a wide range of information to be gleaned through these sessions, their description is a grossly simplified, far understated, and limited description of the assessment process. Of course, assessment sessions—or interviews and meetings—are a central aspect of the assessment, but they constitute only one aspect of the overall process, and it is likely that more than two interviews with the juvenile will be necessary to fully understand the story, perspective, behavior, and character of the youth. In fact, the process is far more complex, multilayered, and comprehensive than O'Reilly and Carr's description, and is not a cut-and-dried process.

Assessments are individualized, and must be in terms of the number, types, and availability of informants; the number of interviews; the depth and nature of available records; and the use of nonclinical assessment measures. To be sure, the depth and breadth of the assessment will be delimited by the time frame within which the assessment must be completed, as well as the needs of the assessment referral source, the availability of records and informants, the time available to the evaluator given other responsibilities and tasks, and other factors that define each case. Nevertheless, even if we set clear parameters and have a well-defined method and framework by which to approach and administer assessments, there is no clear prescription by which every assessment will be completed. There is instead a framework by which we can understand and structure the assessment process, and thus work in an informed and organized manner. However, this framework is merely a shell waiting to be filled in with the particulars of individual assessments, including circumstances and needs unique to each case. It is these unique needs, circumstances, and particulars that will shape the actual assessment as it moves from model to application. Thus, although we can define and outline the steps and actions involved in the process of comprehensive assessment, description and guidelines are nevertheless not prescription.

That is, the map is not the territory, and although comprehensive assessment may follow a structure and format, it is nonetheless individualized. Nevertheless, the more prepared the evaluator, the more organized, the more focused from the outset on gathering the right information (some of which will be shared by every case, and some of which will be unique to each case), and the more tools at the evaluator's disposal, the more likely it is that the assessment process will move smoothly to produce an assessment that is comprehensive, well-informed, and solidly constructed.

CHAPTER 17

Conducting Interviews

O'REILLY AND CARR (2004) provide an exhaustive set of questions to be answered during the process of comprehensive risk assessment. In their model of the assessment process, they write that these questions should be posed directly to the youth and his or her parents, but they appear to assume that the questions will, or can be, answered through the process of youth and parent interviews.[1] In reality, however, although O'Reilly and Carr provide an excellent list of questions to be addressed by the evaluator, in most cases answers that are found will come from multiple sources, but not necessarily interviews alone. Reiterating this point, McConaughy (2005) has written that there is no "gold standard" for the child and adolescent assessment, and that comprehensive assessment requires data from multiple sources, in addition to interviews. In fact, for the most part the evaluator will piece together the answers to the questions posed by the assessment and weave these into the final assessment report.

Knowing what questions to ask is important, and these effectively represent the focus of the assessment process, as well as frame the content of the assessment report. The answers to these questions will be reflected in both the assessed level of risk and the narrative sections of the report, and eventually summed up and condensed in a case formulation. In practice, answers are most likely to be found and ascertained as best as possible through multiple sources and means, which, in part, is the whole point of a *comprehensive* assessment, and not solely through interviews with the

---

1. As previously noted, "parents" may also include adults who serve as primary parental figures or play the parental role, even if not a birth parent. In this chapter, the reader should thus consider the term parent to be inclusive of other adults who partially or completely fill this role for the youth, although their actual role and relationship must be explained in the assessment report.

juvenile or his or her parents. Nevertheless, interviews with the youth provide an opportunity to gain both answers and insight that can be gained from no other source, and over the course of several interviews not only widen the breadth of questions and answers, but deepen them as well. However, although answers are sometimes straightforward and readily given by the youth, this is not true for all questions asked or answers given. For the most part the answers to the most difficult and complex questions *emerge* from clinical interviews, rather than being directly given by the youth. In some cases, children and adolescents do not want to answer the question and for many good reasons (fear, for one, or perhaps embarrassment or even a hope that this will all go away, if only they wait long enough), and in other cases they may genuinely not know what prompted their behavior, how they felt at the time, or why they chose the choices they made. Of this, Lukas (1993) has written "the question to avoid is 'why.' First, and most obvious, the client may not know the answer" (p. 8).

For the most part, answers come piecemeal. Rather than being simply given by the youth (or other informants), answers emerge through the process of clinical interviewing, mediated by the skill of the evaluator in not only asking the right question but asking the right questions in the right order and at the right time, knowing how to ask the question, and subsequently knowing how to interpret and give meaning to what has been said (and hasn't).

This chapter, then, does not look at the questions to be answered or the content of the final assessment, which are addressed in Chapters 18 and 19. Instead, this chapter considers the interview itself, its focus and underlying structure, and its practice, and how to engage with informants. However, the current chapter addresses the interview processes in general, up to and including interviewing the parent, but does not tackle the process of interviewing the juvenile, which is addressed in Chapter 18.

GETTING ORGANIZED

In Chapter 16, I described the use of interview guides as a means by which interviews can be administered. To some degree, depending on their level of specificity and the degree to which the interviewer must strictly or loosely adhere to their questions and structure, interview guides can define the interview as more-or-less clinical in approach and application. However, even in the strictly clinical interview, which is the subject of this chapter, the evaluator is well advised to be prepared for interviews, deciding in advance the information that is wanted. To some degree, then, an interview guide provides a useful means by which to organize and plan for an interview, without the guide necessarily hijacking the clinical process.

For instance, an interview checklist will help evaluators ensure that they are organized and have, prior to the interview, considered the questions for which they want answers. It can be frustrating for the evaluator to later realize that he or she forgot to ask one or more specific questions, and it can also appear to the informant that the evaluator is poorly organized or, worse, unqualified. Organization makes all the difference in all forms of work, and evaluators who are organized in the interview process are likely to be both more efficient and more effective in their work; that is, they get the information they want the first time!

THE USE OF INTERVIEW GUIDES

In fact, interview guides can be very useful, minimally as reminders or "cheat sheets" of what to ask and perhaps when. In their more highly structured form, interview guides may provide not only a set list of questions, but also the language for the questions, a sequence in which to ask questions, and an algorithm that instructs the interviewer about the next question to ask. However, as noted, as the interview guide becomes more structured the interview itself becomes less clinical. One hallmark of a clinical assessment is the judgment and decision-making power of the evaluator as opposed to a process defined by a predetermined interview schedule that limits the freedom and flexibility of the clinician. In this regard, the more *nomothetic* the interview process, in which clear and universal rules are followed in every case, the more likely it is to be nonclinical in orientation. Conversely, the more the interview is *idiographic*, in which it is focused only on the case in hand and structured by and focused on the individual being interviewed, the more likely it is to be truly clinical in design, intention, and application.

Highly structured interviews not only strongly define the interview process and direct the clinician, but they are also often aimed at seeking particular kinds of information and sometimes have a scoring system that help point to the presence of a particular behavior or disorder. The CSI-PANNS,[2] for instance, is a structured clinical interview used specifically to interview schizophrenic patients about current symptoms of schizophrenia, providing a defined, sequential, and algorithmic set of questions and a scoring system to help the evaluator form a clinical

---

2. Structured Clinical Interview for Positive and Negative Syndrome Scale for Schizophrenia.

judgment and assess current psychiatric functioning. However, aside from highly structured interview schedules, it is possible to develop and use basic guidelines and checklists to ensure the consistency of questions and, perhaps equally to the point, thoroughness in completing interviews. As with all elements of the assessment, being prepared for interviews is key.

The Appendix includes a simple assessment question guide for interviews with parents, as well as a question guide for the assessment of youth. However, although these frame the questions you may want answered, they serve only as checklist guides for thinking about and gathering the range of desired information. They are not a means by which to simply and comprehensively complete the assessment process. Also in the Appendix is a simple outline for a genogram, another useful tool to help structure and capture interview information, in this case specifically about the family structure. The genogram offers an excellent example of a structured clinical tool that not only helps define the information to be gathered but also offers a means to capture, diagram, and easily show the information, which can be presented in both genogram form and integrated into the written narrative of the assessment. The genogram applies the same model of diagramming to all cases, but at the same time it is able to configure the diagram in each case to represent the unique characteristics of each individual family.

PRIMARY AND COLLATERAL INTERVIEWS

There are essentially two classes of interviewees. The first is of course the youth, who is the subject of the evaluation. All other interviews, however, are essentially collateral. These are aimed at gathering a complete picture of the juvenile's psychosocial development, functioning, and interactions, and understanding as much as possible about the child or adolescent, the family history and living environment, and the sexual offending and other related behaviors from the perspective of other individuals. Collateral interviewees thus include parents, probation officers, current and former therapists, teachers, social service workers, and so on.

In general, collateral interviews are less formal than interviews with the juvenile. They're more likely to have a collegial feel to them, even with parents, who are usually not expecting the evaluator to engage them in an interrogative style interview. Nevertheless, interviews with parents are likely to be more formal and more similar to interviews with the juvenile than interviews with other professionals.

Although collateral, these informants are nevertheless all important sources of information, and interview style and approach will vary with each. Obviously parents and other family members who are interviewed are usually intimately tied to the juvenile, and in many (if not most) cases they will be deeply affected by the youth's behavior and have a very different experience of and stake in the case than other informants. Accordingly, interviews with parents should be treated with great sensitivity and care, and will be very different in content, approach, and tone than interviews with objectively involved professionals not linked to the youth through family ties. Parent and other family interviews are additionally likely to be much longer than those held with other informants, and the parents may be involved throughout the assessment process in a way that is substantially different than professionals who serve as informants (who, in some cases, will not be involved again past an interview in which they provide information and perhaps their perspective about the youth).

THE INTERVIEW STRUCTURE

The evaluator must decide who will be interviewed, when, and how, as well as what information is to be gathered, from confirming information in the record to elaborating further upon that material and gathering fresh new information. However, although we can articulate guidelines and describe methods by which to conduct clinical interviews, there is no correct or set method that will be used in every case and under every circumstance. Similarly, there is no correct length for each interview or number of interviews required to gather the necessary information, although multiple interviews will typically be required only with the juvenile, although perhaps with family members as well.

The structure of and approach to clinical interviews with the youth is discussed in detail in the next chapter. However, these interviews are likely to involve three to five sessions if depth is sought, with each interview lasting 60–90 minutes (depending on the attention span, age, and cognitive capacity of the juvenile). Interviews with collateral informants will typically take far less time, often restricted to a single interview lasting anywhere from 5–15 minutes, and quite often conducted by phone. This is not the case with parents, and these interviews, which may be conducted in person or by phone, are more likely to take anywhere from 15–60 minutes, depending on the case and the involvement and participation of the parents; parent interviews may also require more than one session.

SELECTING COLLATERAL INFORMANTS

Collateral informants, at a minimum, should include one or both parents, depending on their marital status and involvement in the life of their child (i.e., the sexually abusive youth); the current primary caregiver, if not a parent; the referral source, such as a social service worker or probation officer; and, if the youth is placed outside of the home at the time of the evaluation, someone who can reasonably discuss and provide information about the youth in that placement. This may mean another family caregiver if the youth is placed with another family member, a foster parent if in foster care, or a clinician or administrator if the youth is placed in residential care or a locked correctional center. If assigned, the youth's attorney and guardian ad litem should also be contacted as collateral informants.

This list represents the minimum, however. In addition to these informants, a more complete list includes caregivers other than parents, other significant (usually adult) family members, current and former therapists, current or former educators or school guidance or adjustment counselors, clinicians or administration staff from former out-of-home or day treatment placements, mentors (from Big Brother/Big Sister-type programs), and others who will have a sense of the youth and his or her development and behavior over time and in various social settings, as well as information or a perspective about the youth's family. Obviously, there is a limit to how many informants are contacted, and this may be limited not only to the availability of informants but also the amount of time available to the evaluator. However, the evaluator should attempt to speak to as many informants that he or she considers important in developing a full and complete history of the youth, to the point where the evaluator considers that the necessary or adequate amount of information has been gathered, sufficient for the task of understanding the youth in his or her developmental and social context.

WHAT DO WE WANT TO KNOW?

Regarding the data-gathering phase of the assessment process in general, we wish to ask and answer the same questions regardless of the source of the information or the means for getting it. That is, the methods of record review, psychological testing, physiological examination, and interviews with the youth and collateral informants are all aimed toward gathering the same information from which we draw our conclusions and project risk for sexual recidivism. None of these information sources alone can provide the information sought, and in some cases the questions asked are quite narrow or limited. In psychological testing, for instance, we may be asking about personality traits, whereas in physiological examination we may be seeking information about sexual interests or deceitfulness. In interviewing a school adjustment counselor, we are hoping to learn about the juvenile's academic, social, and behavioral life in the school arena, and any related information the counselor may have about the youth outside of the school or the youth's family life. In other cases, the range of questions will cover multiple aspects of the youth's life, such as in a parent interview where we will also want to learn about the parents themselves and other family members, and assess the parent's response to the actual or alleged sexually abusive behavior.

All in all then, there is no single source from which to gather all the information necessary, but all the sources together can yield the information we seek. To a great degree this information is captured by the risk assessment instrument itself, which is an empty frame waiting to be populated with the necessary information, outlining many (or some) of the questions the evaluator will need to answer. The actuarial assessment instrument will be of the least use in this regard as it asks the least number of questions, whereas clinical assessment instruments more clearly define a wide range of questions to be asked and answered. The evaluator's choice of risk assessment instrument, then, will help define and frame the questions to ask, and the most comprehensive instruments include questions that range from sexual and nonsexual behavior to social interactions, prior treatment, personality characteristics, social interactions, and the family environment. The report format for the written assessment can also be a useful means for establishing the questions to be asked, (discussed in the Chapter 19), as can question guides that outline the information to be gathered.

In terms of the questions we want to answer, in Chapter 15 content was described in terms of 20 broad content areas. These each represent broad domains of information, each of which requires investigation, depth, and detail. Outlined again in Figure 17.1, these areas serve as a guide for the information to be gathered through multiple sources, including of course through the interview process described in this chapter, including primary interviews with the youth and collateral interviews with other informants.

A glance at the content areas makes it clear, however, that although some of the information will be available in the form of facts and other definite data, or may be readily available through records, much of the information is subjective and can be gathered only through the interview process, and in some cases from a single source only. The youth's description of his or

Broad Content Areas in Comprehensive Risk Assessment

- Relevant background and identifying information
- Cognitive functioning and intellectual capacity
- Social, developmental, and medical history
- Educational history
- Trauma history
- Mental health history/psychological functioning
- Personality characteristics
- Social relationships and social functioning
- Family history
- Current family functioning

- History of non-sexual problem behavior
- History of substance abuse
- Sexual development and sexual interests
- History of sexually abusive behavior
- Details of index and related sexual offenses
- Juvenile's description of sexually abusive behaviour
- Assessment of specific risk factors
- Environmental concerns
- Availability of environmental support
- Amenability to treatment

Figure 17.1   20 key content area for the comprehensive assessment of risk.

her sexually abusive behavior, for instance, can come only from the youth, and only through the youth can the evaluator assess his or her attitude towards that behavior or the victims of the behavior.

THE NATURE OF THE INTERVIEW

Although all interviews involve clinical skill, the term "clinical interview" is most typically reserved for interviews with the client, in this case the sexually abusive youth. However, the interview may just as well be called a conversation, meeting, discussion or, as O'Reilly and Carr (2004) call it, an "assessment session." This is as true in conversing with parents, former therapists, and other collateral informants as in meeting and talking with the youth. In fact, some of these informant contacts are more appropriately called meetings or conversations, given their tone, length, and often relative informality, such as a 10-minute phone call with a former teacher or clinician.

However, in conversation there is no clear or organizing theme, whereas there is a clear and central focus to the interview, and as opposed to the casual conversation in the interview the roles of the interviewer and interviewee are clearly defined. The flow and direction of the discussion is also clearly evident in the interview, in which the interviewer asks the questions and the interviewee answers (McConaughy, 2005). Thus, even if we experience some interviews as more conversational, the underlying construction and purpose is that of the interview, including its design and application as purposeful and intentional, and whereas conversation tends to be spontaneous the interview occurs under definite circumstances. Further, even if collegial and informal in feel, there really is nothing informal about the interview process other than perhaps its manner. Even if casual in tone, every interview, conversation, or meeting is part of a formal process aimed at gathering information that can help the evaluator develop a clear view of facts, allegations, developmental history, family history, events, and so forth in order to assess the youth and his or her risk for sexual recidivism.

Nevertheless, interviews will be experienced differently by informants at different levels in the assessment process and with different stakes in the outcome. There is thus a hierarchical structure to informants, from the most to the least knowledgeable, involved, and/or affected by outcome, ranging from the youth to parent (or parent figures, as noted), actively involved social service or court workers, current therapists, other family members, and so forth. These interviews will also be administered differently by the evaluator because of the different levels of information that can be provided by informants at each hierarchical level, and perhaps the nature of the relationship between the interviewer and interviewee. They will also vary in length, formality, the type of questions asked, and the amount and type of information that the evaluator thinks can be provided by the informant.

INTERVIEW CONTENT

Interviews with the youth are going to be the lengthiest and the most complex, will definitely involve face-to-face contact, and are also the most likely to involve multiple and sequential interviews, with at least two sessions and, for a thorough assessment, more like three to five. Parent contacts are not likely to be as lengthy or intense, although may also involve more than one assessment session, and may be held in person or by phone, and some information from parents may also be gathered through a written family history questionnaire.

Below this hierarchical level, interviews are increasingly likely to be brief, held by phone, and far less comprehensive in the range of questions. At the same time, they are likely to be far more focused on specific information relevant to each particular informant's sphere of knowledge about the youth or the youth's family. For instance, we may ask a parent about a vast range of information from the youth's birth and early developmental history to his or her treatment history, school functioning, behavioral and social development in late childhood and adolescence, and sexual development. We may also ask parents about their own history and the history of the immediate and extended family. However, we are not likely to ask other collateral informants this range of questions, and they are not likely to have the answers. We are, instead, going to ask these informants narrower questions that are related closely to their level of involvement with and knowledge of the youth and family, and the social domains in which their contact and knowledge developed.

THE SKILL OF THE INTERVIEWER

Knowing what questions to ask is a facet of the evaluator's preparation for the interview. However, the ability to make an informant feel comfortable so that he or she is best able or most willing to answer those questions, as opposed to feeling interrogated, for instance, comes down to the skill of the evaluator as a clinical interviewer. This involves the evaluator's ability to establish a tone, provide direction for the interview, and engage with informants in a manner that promotes their willingness to be responsive to the evaluator, and even form a relationship, albeit a brief one.

Furthermore, in addition to knowing *what* questions to ask (again a facet of preparation), the evaluator must know *how* and *when* to ask these questions, and sometimes when to not ask a particular question. This means that the evaluator must recognize and pay attention to the climate of the interview, and how the informant is responding, both emotionally and behaviorally, to the interview process and its content.

The evaluator may also need to clarify or further explain questions and answers as they emerge in the interview, and may sometimes draw attention to or make explicit content that might otherwise be unstated or unrecognized (Sattler, 1998). However, such clarification should serve only to move the interview process along and facilitate the discovery of more information. It is not the goal of the interview to openly address or evaluate content, although this is the evaluator's role in the final phase of the assessment and, of course, in the assessment report. The interview process is simply a means to gather the information that will be needed for the later evaluation. In a clinical interview, therefore, it is the interviewer's job to ask questions and prompt answers but not to evaluate or judge the information that emerges, other than as a means to build and ask further questions and seek depth and detail.

Beyond the questions that the evaluator planned to ask, he or she must also recognize new streams of questions that arise during the interview for which the evaluator had not previously planned. No matter how well prepared, there are bound to be times when one stream of questioning leads to another, previously unexpected stream. An interview, then, serves the process of discovery, as well as the further exploration of information and events already known. Related to this is the need for the evaluator to keep track of the interview and the information it addresses, deciding when to remain with one question stream and when to move to another, as well as when to return to a previous stream in order to further flesh out answers and information. Tracking in this context can be as simple as writing down not only the answers provided by the informant, but also other questions and topics to be addressed in the interview to which the evaluator may later return.

In general, we can identify nine key skill areas for the clinical interviewer.

1. *Preparing:* Knowing in advance of the interview what information will be sought from the informant and what questions will be asked.
2. *Timing:* Knowing when to ask particular questions during the interview.
3. *Sensitivity:* Recognizing the emotional state and experience of the informant, including which questions or topics should or should not be pursued at any given moment.
4. *Awareness of Cues and Nuance:* Related to both timing and sensitivity, this involves the evaluator's awareness of the climate of the interview, the informant's willingness or ability to answer questions, and the need or capacity to shift direction in the interview.
5. *Flexibility:* Also closely related to sensitivity, flexibility involves the evaluator's ability to recognize how the informant is responding or wants to respond, assess what questions may or may not be asked, and adjust the interview and its process accordingly; it effectively represents the evaluator's ability to go with the flow of the interview.
6. *Directing:* The evaluator is responsible for the flow and direction of the interview process, including how to move the interview forward, provide focus, and end the interview.
7. *Clarifying:* As part of the facilitation and exploration process, the evaluator must sometimes draw information, ideas, and content to the surface, making explicit and clear things that may otherwise remain invisible.
8. *Non-Evaluative:* Evaluation follows the gathering of information; one skill for the evaluator, then, is remaining nonjudgmental during the interviewing process.

9. *Tracking:* The evaluator must be able to keep track of the interview process, subject matter, and need to return to questions or open new question streams.

In presenting this set of essential interviewer skills, and in effect guidelines for interviews, it is worth noting Lambie and McCarthy's (2004) observation in reference to interviewing strategies: "the purpose is not to offer a one-size-fits-all approach, but rather to offer a range of effective techniques and practical strategies" (p. 121).

THE NATURE, STRUCTURE, AND GOALS OF THE CLINICAL INTERVIEW

Recognizing that interviews with collateral informants will be mostly information gathering, we understand that the concept of the clinical interview is most appropriately reserved for assessment sessions with the juvenile, and to a lesser degree his or her parents.

Morrison (1995) has described the clinical interview as "little more than helping people talk about themselves" (p. 1). However, he has also written that effective interviewers obtain a large amount of relevant information in the shortest period of time, while engaging with the interviewee in a manner consistent with creating and maintaining a good working relationship. McConaughy (2005) considers the essential purpose of the clinical interview as understanding the subject's perspective; observing the subject's behavior, affect, and interactional style; recognizing strengths and competencies in the subject; identifying potential treatment targets; and establishing rapport and mutual respect between the interviewer and subject, in which there is a bidirectional influence. Looking at the interviewer-subject relationship from a different perspective, Girón et al. (1998) observed that negative attitudes displayed by the interviewer towards the subject are likely to create distance and, therefore, inhibit the interviewee's communication and participation.

With respect to approaching the clinical interview, McConaughy (2005) observes that although differing from ordinary conversation, the interviewer may use strategies that make interviews seem more conversational and comfortable. Within the first moments of the interview, Morrison (1995) notes that the interviewer should describe both the purpose of the interview, including its length and the sort of questions that will be asked, and create a comfortable environment for the subject. Of particular importance to the forensic interview, Sattler (1998) noted that the interviewer maintains

confidentiality and discloses information in accordance with stated protocols or requirements; reiterated here, then, is that the actual or possible use
of information gathered during the assessment must be disclosed to the
juvenile and legal guardians prior to the interview process.

Returning to the relationship between interviewer and subject, like
Morrison and McConaughy, Lambie and McCarthy (2004), Long et al.
(1988), O'Reilly and Carr (2004), and Shea (1988) each describe the crucial
role of developing rapport, a positive environment, and a working
alliance. However, this is no mean task when interviewing a sexual
offender or, for that matter, anyone who has engaged in criminal activity
when the very process of assessment understandably may be threatening
to the individual being assessed. This doesn't negate the skills required of
the clinical interviewer or the necessity of the supportive and safe interview environment. On the contrary, it further stresses the need for the
evaluator to have and demonstrate strong interview skills and the ability
to build a positive environment and working relationship in order to
overcome the barriers established at the outset by the potentially threatening reason for the interview.

We can now make these simple observations about the clinical interview:

- It is a formal process with a specific purpose, even if casual and
  comfortable in application and format.
- Both the interviewer and interviewee have a specific role and
  relationship.
- The flow of the interview is established and directed by the
  interviewer.
- Topics for discussion and questions are introduced by the
  interviewer.
- The interviewer asks questions without forming judgments about the
  answers.
- It is built on a mutual and respectful relationship between interviewer
  and subject and the establishment of emotional comfort and rapport.
- The interviewer follows guidelines for confidentiality and disclosure
  of information.

THE INTERVIEW IN FORENSIC EVALUATION

As noted, in an assessment for sexual recidivism there is much at stake for
the juvenile and his or her family. Consequently, under such circumstances
there may be great reluctance to actively, honestly, or fully engage in the
interview process, which is, after all, the arena in which the youth and

family members have the most direct influence and play the strongest role. The evaluator should, therefore, not expect a full and open level of engagement by the juvenile or his or her parents, although this will, of course, vary widely from case to case and under different circumstances. Accordingly, when it comes to its role in risk assessment, clinical interviews are more rightly thought of as forensic interviews, and so the *clinical* evaluator must also assume the role of, and see and hear things through the eyes and ears of, the *forensic* evaluator.

Forensic evaluation involve the assessment of individuals facing legal consequences, the possible provision of court testimony as a witness, recommendations made to the court system or other authorities, and involvement in the outcomes of court proceedings (Barker & Branson, 2000). Accordingly, Grisso (1998) has described all evaluations as forensic if intended for direct use or to assist decision making in a legal environment, and advises that they require a different way of thinking than nonforensic evaluations. Grisso's comments are equally true of the clinical interview when it is used for forensic purposes, as is always the case in the comprehensive assessment of risk. Thus, although the principles and practices of clinical interviews may remain constant regardless of the setting in which they are conducted or their intended use, an awareness of how informants may respond to interviews should be clear in the mind of the interviewer. This principle applies not only to the youth being assessed but also to collateral informants, as they may well have formed opinions about the juvenile in one direction and share these in interviews.

With regard to interviews with the juvenile, however, or the juvenile's family, in the forensic role the interviewer must be aware that not every thing told to them will be an honest, accurate, or full representation of what occurred with regard to the sexually abusive behavior or the events leading to such behavior. If the clinical interviewer assumes that the juvenile or his or her parents will engage openly, honestly, and nondefensively in interviews, then the evaluator not only lacks familiarity with the client population but is additionally at risk for making significant mistakes in the assessment process, and the resulting level of assigned risk and recommendations for management and treatment. On the other hand, the evaluator must avoid the mistake of becoming mistrustful and suspicious of every juvenile sexual offender or family member, or assuming that they are never being honest in their manner, motivation, or presentation of information. As noted, Girón et al. (1998) observed that a negative mindset in the interviewer may significantly inhibit effective clinical interviews. Nevertheless, in the forensic setting, the interviewer is advised to assume the mindset of a forensic investigator as well as clinical evaluator.

With regard, however, to the relationship between the forensic mindset and the clinical skills of the evaluator, Lambert (Asay & Lambert, 1999; Lambert & Barley, 2002; Lambert & Bergin, 1993) has described the attitudes and beliefs of the client, including the client's pretreatment predisposition to change, as a significant contribution or obstacle to effective therapy. These client, or extra therapeutic, factors are equally at play in the development of a positive and facilitative interview relationship in which the skills of the clinical interviewer will play an important role in overcoming client factors that might otherwise inhibit the effectiveness of a clinical interview in the forensic setting.

Under any circumstances, Gudas and Sattler (2006) remind us that forensic assessments differ from clinical assessments in a number of ways, including in scope, content, and purpose. Most simply, whereas the clinical interview concerns the clinical and treatment needs of the individual being assessed, the forensic interview is focused on the concerns of the legal or juvenile justice system. Gudas and Sattler stress the importance of interviewers recognizing and understanding the nature of their role as forensic evaluators.[3]

INTERVIEWING THE PARENTS

Before addressing interviews with the juvenile in Chapter 18, we'll consider parent (or parent figure) interviews, recognizing how complex families can be in structure, dynamics, roles, and relationships. The evaluator must also be aware of the potentially sensitive nature of parent interviews, as well as the realities into which parents often find themselves thrust with regard to their child's behavior, often further exacerbated by the fact that another one of their children may be the victim of the sexually abusive behavior.

Given the varied combinations of families, in the event of sibling abuse it is possible that the juvenile sexual offender has sexually victimized a full sibling or a half- or step-sibling, which may further complicate already difficult parental relationships with the sexually abusive youth. Under such quite common circumstances, whereas one parent may be the full parent of either the offender alone or both the offender and victim(s), the other parent may have no blood relationship with the offending child but be the birth parent of the victim. Although this may be of greatest importance in the later

---

3. In their chapter in Sparta and Koocher's book on juvenile forensic mental health assessments (2006), Gudas and Sattler provide an excellent and detailed overview of the juvenile forensic interview.

treatment process, it is also a dynamic to be kept in mind during parent interviews, with regard to the state of mind of either parent and the relationship with and feelings toward the sexually abusive youth.

FORMING A COLLABORATIVE RELATIONSHIP

O'Reilly and Carr (2004) stress the goal of developing a collaborative relationship with the youth's parents and giving a message of support and understanding regarding the crisis and dilemmas they may presently now be experiencing. Calder (2001) similarly emphasizes support, and also stresses that parents should not be prejudged or assumed to be the problem or cause of the sexually abusive behavior. This once again reiterates the importance of ensuring that negative attitudes are not conveyed to the subjects of the interviews as this is only likely to influence a poor outcome and may further reinforce negative views already held by the evaluator and the parent as well. In meeting with and interviewing parents, evaluators must be sensitive to their situation, recognizing that it will be important to first establish a base and the beginning of a working relationship before simply opening up with a barrage of difficult questions. Again, bear in mind the goal of and opportunity for rapport and comfort in the interview relationship.

Thus, before asking the parents those questions you'd like to have answered, first recognize the situation they may be in and related emotions, confusion, and uncertainty. Both Calder (2001) and Lambie and McCarthy (2004) have identified useful pointers for the evaluator to consider in evaluating and working with parents, focusing on a sensitive, supportive, and go-slow approach.

These include acknowledging that parents may be feeling powerful emotions, such as shock, shame, or powerlessness, and allowing them to feel uncertain and vulnerable. If in denial, you may recognize this as a common response for parents, and through the provision of support encourage them to participate in the assessment process, help them recognize that they can be influential in treatment, and create opportunities for them to be more open and honest. You can also provide answers regarding sexually abusive behavior and help put it into perspective, as well as answering other questions that parents may have. Without minimizing the situation, help the parents recognize that their child's behavior can be treated but also prepare them for the possibility of further disclosure during the course of the assessment process and later treatment.

Before moving from initial contact to a deeper interview level, prepare the parent for open discussions of sexual behavior, while remaining sensitive to the possibility or likelihood that such discussion may be very difficult and awkward for the parent. Keep in mind also that a parent may deny allegations that his or her child engaged in sexually abusive behavior, even if the alleged victim was a sibling. The interview, however, is not the time to attempt to overcome or resolve such feelings and beliefs, or even significantly address them other than to collect information about and understand the parent's point of view. Nonetheless, denial is a factor to be dealt with in the interview so that it will not stand as an obstacle to both gathering important information and building a relationship with the parent. Remember that the assessment process is not aimed at the disclosure of the truth, even if this is the ideal state at which to arrive; it is instead aimed at information gathering, analysis, and formulation. Evaluation is the platform upon which treatment will stand, including arriving at the truth if possible, but itself is not treatment.

RECOGNIZING FAMILY DYNAMICS

In conducting the parent interview, the evaluator must not simply ask questions but, listening actively and attending to the process, watch for and recognize dynamic factors at work that may shape the parent's involvement or honesty in the interview. Some of these dynamics are specific to the presence of sexually abusive behavior within the family and include denial and minimization; blaming someone other than the sexually abusive youth; feelings of guilt or shame, stigmatization, or helplessness; or divided loyalties and splits within the family, and especially when the victim is also a family member or when parents are divorced or separated. Beyond these sexual abuse specific dynamics, however, other family dynamics are equally at play. These are shaped by what Minuchin (1974) described as the family structure, or the invisible set of demands and relationships by which families are organized and family members interact with one another and the outside world. At play in all family interactions, these dynamics are reflected in the roles played by individual family members, family relationships and interactions, explicit and implicit family norms, attitudes, and expectations, and in the manner in which family members communicate and interact with people outside of the family. It is these dynamics that, according to Minuchin, are imprinted upon each family member, and thus shape the behavior of family members within and outside of the family.

In interviewing parents, then, the evaluator not only seeks maximum information about the family and the developmental and behavior history of the sexually abusive youth, but is also actively seeking information that reveals information about the family structure and its operations. As

Calder (2001) emphasized, without blaming the family the evaluator seeks to understand how family dynamics and the family environment may have influenced or allowed the development of sexually abusive behavior.

REMAINING NONJUDGMENTAL

However, in recognizing that the families of troubled youth often have difficulties and experience dysfunction themselves, it is too easy for those who treat sexually abusive youth to look to the family as the source of the youth's trouble. It is important, then, that evaluators recognize that most parents want the best for their children. Even if family dynamics have contributed to the development of troubled behavior, and this is often the case, it is nevertheless important that the evaluator doesn't demonize the parents or assume the worst.

1. Don't negatively label families.
2. Don't create an environment that replicates a family's poor experience with the system.
3. Don't help parents feel incapable.
4. Don't become an adversary to the family.
5. Don't make unnecessary value judgments about families.
6. Don't become frustrated with parents.
7. Don't personalize your experiences with the family.
8. Don't display frustrations or hostility.
9. Don't treat the parents as idiots.
10. Don't assume you know best.

CONFIDENTIALITY

Revisiting confidentiality, it will also be important for the evaluator to explain the assessment process and ensure that parents understand limitations on confidentiality. It is also important that the evaluator explain mandatory reporting, as it sometimes becomes evident during the course of interviews that a further condition of neglect or abuse may exist for another child within the family environment, which must be reported.

A further variant on confidentiality involves circumstances in which parents describe situations that involve their own or another parent's confidentiality, such as a personal history of sexual victimization, infidelity, mental illness, or substance abuse. Here, unless the information provided by the parent involves a mandatory report or duty-to-warn situation, it will be important for the evaluator to either assure confidentiality or, if unable to do so, once again explain limitations on confidentiality. One way to ensure confidentiality, for instance in situations where the information is not critical to the assessment of the sexually abusive youth, is to either omit it from the final report or make only general references, or later ensure that such information is redacted from copies of the report that are distributed to outside parties.

INTERVIEWING THE JUVENILE

Interviewing skills are developed over time and apply to all forms of interviews. However, in interviewing the juvenile, who is, after all, the subject of the assessment, interviews and their requisite skills take on special meaning and require a fine focus. Because these interviews will involve difficult and personal questions, they are likely to be experienced by the youth as a high-risk proposition. The question, then, is how to engage with the youth in a process that he or she is not likely to seek out, experience as client friendly, or otherwise anticipate in a positive light.

In fact, there is much at stake for the youth, and many understandable reasons for him or her to avoid giving answers, give partial answers, lie by omission, give deceitful answers, deny knowledge, or provide answers that are just enough to meet the evaluator's expectations. The following chapter takes up where this chapter leaves off and describes the nature, complexities, and processes of juvenile forensic interviews and guidelines by which to approach and engage in such interviews.

CHAPTER 18

Interviewing the Youth

INTERVIEWING THE YOUTH lies at the heart of the assessment. It provides the opportunity, and the only opportunity, for the evaluator to meet and get to know the child or adolescent in a way that cannot be revealed through a record review or discussions with any number of other informants.

For evaluators who will continue to work with the youth after the evaluation is completed—for instance, if the youth is being evaluated after entering a residential or outpatient treatment program—the process of meeting with the juvenile for assessment interviews also serves to initiate the therapeutic relationship that will continue past evaluation and into the process of short- or long-term treatment. For evaluators whose sole role is the evaluation, as in a court-based or outpatient evaluation in which the clinician will not otherwise again meet the youth after the completion of the assessment, these meetings represent something quite different. In either case, however, under most circumstances the evaluator will not have met the juvenile prior to the assessment, and will get to know him or her through the evaluation process, through a review of the youth's records, through the eyes of collateral informants, including other providers, and perhaps through other forms of testing and evaluation.

How the evaluator approaches the youth, the questions he or she asks, and how the questions are framed and asked, how the evaluator reads, assimilates, and makes sense of other material regarding the youth, and even the expectations of the evaluator will have everything to do with how the youth is experienced and understood by the evaluator. Hence, the clinical interviews are critical, as is the way that the evaluator handles them. Thus, the preparation, approach, and clinical skills of the evaluator, described in Chapter 17, are brought to bear in clinical interviews with the juvenile. More specifically, Gudas and Sattler (2006) describe forensic interviews with juveniles as a task for clinicians trained and experienced in child and adolescent mental health, juvenile development, and forensic evaluation.

A FRAMEWORK FOR THE JUVENILE INTERVIEW

In applying these specialized skills, clinical interviews must also be geared toward each individual youth, with due consideration given to his or her age, gender, cognitive capacity, mental health, and other factors. Such considerations will, to a great degree, require differences in how the interviews are framed, how questions are asked, how long each interview lasts, and ultimately how the evaluator makes sense of the youth's answers and level of participation. However, given the importance of these interviews, it is unlikely that one interview, or even two, will yield enough detailed information about the juvenile—not simply what he or she did and why, but who the youth is and how he or she experiences and responds to the world.

Developing a full picture of the youth requires time and depth, and it is unlikely that anything less than three interviews can begin to paint a detailed or complete picture. These interviews will have a serial and sequential quality to them, and rather than being designed to simply gather information to cut-and-dried questions, they allow a relationship to develop between the evaluator and the youth and a picture of the youth to emerge. Typically, a single interview will last $1-1\frac{1}{2}$ hours, and typically 3–5 interviews are adequate to gather important data, including personal history, psychosexual development and behaviors, details of the sexual offense and the context in which it occurred, and the character and approach of the child or adolescent. Multiple interviews allow the evaluator to observe and experience changes in the juvenile's affect and willingness or ability to be honest and forthcoming with the evaluator. Multiple interviews also allow the youth the opportunity to reveal more information, provide more insights, and feel more comfortable in the relationship over the course of the interviews. In addition, multiple interviews allow the evaluator to switch gears in each interview, gathering different types of information, addressing different aspects of the assessment, and shifting the focus of the interviews over time.

Depending on the length of time allotted for the assessment and the schedule of the evaluator, interviews can be scheduled daily until completed, twice a week, or weekly. The appropriate frequency is up to the evaluator and will depend on the desired intensity of interviews (daily interviews constitute a more intense dose than weekly interviews), the method (connecting with the youth daily provides a potentially more effective means to build a clinical relationship and rapport), the setting in which the interviews are conducted (residential care, for instance, versus community based), and quite likely the timetable governing the assessment process.

APPROACHING THE JUVENILE INTERVIEW

With regard to the context of such evaluations, Grisso (2006) described two types of juvenile forensic evaluations: those of children and adolescents who have been harmed and whose safety and well-being are thus a prime concern ("those who are done to") and those of juveniles who have caused harm to others ("those who do unto others"), for whom the evaluation will shape decisions about how to best contain and treat the behavior of these juveniles (p. ix). It is clear that risk assessment interviews fall squarely into the latter type of forensic evaluation and, in fact, most people who engage in sexually abusive behavior do not seek out either assessment or treatment of their own volition, whether adult or adolescent and certainly not children. When caught engaging in such behavior, they often refuse or are afraid to honestly participate in the assessment process for many reasons, including shame, embarrassment, and understandable fear of the consequences.

In many cases, offenders may not outright refuse to engage in the process but engage only in the most minimal way, or perhaps make an effort to appear invested but actually engage only at the level they believe is required to avoid further discovery or consequences and in an effort to escape the situation as soon as possible. It is also common for the offender to attempt deception, providing some accurate information while also actively attempting to deceive and mislead the evaluator through active lies, lies of omission, claims of forgetfulness, or by providing only the information that the offender believes is already available to the evaluator. A goal for the offender in this case may be appearing invested and honest, while actually attempting to fool or manipulate the evaluator.

However, this does not mean that the offender's goal is to reoffend, and especially in the case of juvenile sexual offenders it is unlikely that this is their goal. It seems likely that many children and adolescents who have engaged in sexually abusive behavior and been caught will genuinely not want nor intend to engage in such behavior again, if only because of the consequences. The avoidance of open and complete honesty in assessment, then, for most juveniles is less likely aimed at the goal of getting away with it so that they can reoffend, but to avoid the pain of assessment, exposure, and consequences, all of which are now real possibilities for the juvenile. That is, deceit and lack of honest and open involvement are not likely due to the juvenile's plan to become a career sexual offender.

Of course, motivation to engage in assessment and the juvenile's real goals in assessment will vary from juvenile to juvenile. Like all things, their participation and engagement will be shaped and influenced by many factors, including their more general criminal versatility, their level of social skills and sophistication, how often they have been caught before for different criminal behaviors or prior sexually abusive behavior, the development of antisocial attitudes, the encouragement and attitude of important family members, and so on. Knowing, however, that for many different reasons juveniles entering assessment are not likely to openly or earnestly engage in the process, the evaluator is able to meet with the juvenile in a well-informed manner, eyes and ears wide open to the possibility, and even likelihood, of manipulation and dissimulation.

Perhaps obvious, in the assessment of sexually abusive behavior Medoff and Kinscherff (2006) point out that evaluators must feel comfortable discussing sexual behavior, including normal and deviant sexual behavior and fantasies. In addition to understanding the sexually abusive behavior, and the factors, events, and forces that contributed and led up to it, it is the goal of the assessment to also as fully as possible understand the child or adolescent who engaged in the behaviors and why. However, the goal is not necessarily to learn the truth of what occurred and why. In many cases, the full truth and extent of the sexually abusive behavior is unknown, and the juvenile being assessed is unlikely to reveal all of these details while being assessed, even if he or she discloses more during the evaluation. Rather than discovering the full truth, however, the assessment is more focused on learning about and understanding the history, thinking, relationships, and other behaviors that provide the context in which sexually abusive behavior occurred. It is this information, as well as the substantiated facts about the sexually abusive behavior, that can help us best determine the risk that the sexually abusive youth being assessed will reoffend and what treatment may be most appropriate in this case.

The approach of the forensic interviewer, then, is a sophisticated and well-informed one in which the interviews provide an opportunity to meet and get to know the child or adolescent. Rather than using the interviews to simply gather information, as though such information is black-and-white or the youth will truthfully provide answers to difficult questions, the interviews allow the evaluator to experience how the youth engages with others and also to listen to the youth's story and perspective. Over the course of several serial and sequential interviews, the evaluator also has the opportunity to build a relationship, address increasingly more detailed information, challenge the juvenile in a supportive manner that may not be possible during a first or second interview, and develop a deeper, more detailed, and more accurate view of the juvenile. Thus the evaluator's approach to and expectations of the interview are significant with respect to what might be gained or lost through the interview process.

THE FACILITATIVE INTERVIEW CLIMATE

In describing psychiatric interviewing, Shea (1988) describes the first interview as a creative act that can never be duplicated. It thus sets the stage not just for asking and answering questions, but for developing the bidirectional and supportive working relationship that will set the pace for the gathering of maximum information. Beginning with the initial meeting and proceeding through the following interviews, the clinical evaluator works toward the establishment and development of a safe and respectful environment. In this facilitative climate the juvenile increasingly feels able to share information, concerns, and problems, and experiences a relationship in which the evaluator is seen as genuine and supportive, and in which the evaluator "attempts to know what it would be like and what it is like to be the person sitting across from himself" (p. 50).

In accordance to our changing sensibilities and approach to work with sexually abusive youth in general (Rich, 2008), the clinical evaluator brings to the interview an approach that is supportive, warm, and empathic, as well as directive. This approach is very much in accordance to the attributes of clinicians described by Longo and Prescott (2006), who write that the use of hostile, confrontational, and harsh treatment styles are ineffective with sexually abusive youth. This change in sensibility and approach is evident in changing perspectives about work with adult sexual offenders as well, described by Marshall et al. (2003) and Marshall (2005, 2006), who note that the attributes and behaviors that therapists bring to treatment influence change in offenders more than technique, and recommend that clinicians adopt a relationally based and supportive approach to treatment. Similarly, Beech and Hamilton-Giachritsis (2005) note a change in treatment technique from a direct and confrontational style, which they write is likely to lead to increased resistance rather than change, to the development of a supportive and emotionally responsive treatment relationship.

In describing strategies for interviewing sexually abusive youth, Lambie and McCarthy (2004) stress the need for the evaluator to:

- Establish rapport
- Show respect
- Express concern
- Provide information
- Create a facilitative environment in which there are opportunities for honesty
- Establish credibility and control of the interview
- Ask open-ended questions
- Anticipate embarrassment
- Predict and challenge cognitive distortions
- Expect and work with denial
- Allow juveniles to tell their story
- Use reframing statements
- Allow face-saving maneuvers
- Take care in expressing personal emotions

Like Lambie and McCarthy, Morrison (1995) stresses the importance of establishing rapport, but describes the client's sense of being understood as a prerequisite. He describes the importance of "free speech" during interviews, in which the evaluator is established as someone who cares about and wants to hear the concerns of the client, and also provides the client with an opportunity for open self-expression. Such free self-expression also allows the evaluator the opportunity to learn what is on the juvenile's mind and provides insight into the juvenile's level of cognition and insight, as well as personality traits, which Morrison notes are more likely to emerge in a person who is speaking spontaneously. With respect to the evaluator's capacity to develop rapport and convey interest, Girón et al. (1998) have identified a number of behaviors associated with effective clinical interviews. These include making eye contact and ensuring a face-to-face posture, as well as asking relevant questions, asking open-ended questions, and ensuring few nonconstructive verbal interruptions, each of which they describe as active-listening behaviors. Gudas and Sattler (2006) have also described the need to establish rapport and create a safe and supportive interview climate, as well as the effect that the interviewer's attitude, tone, mannerism, phrasing of questions, and body language may have on the client, thus influencing and defining the process and outcome of the interview.

Morrison (1995) also describes the necessity for the evaluator to be aware of countertransference, or his or her own emotions and experiences during the interview, usually evoked by the juvenile. Like Girón et al. (1998), Morrison notes that the appearance of negative feelings or attitudes toward the client can have significant consequences for the working relationship and on interview outcomes. Calder (2001) similarly notes that negative evaluator attitudes, such as frustration and exasperation, may result in a nonsupportive and even punitive approach, and thus contribute to the juvenile's lack of engagement and desire to give up. It is important, then, that evaluators pay close attention to how they are expressing themselves to juveniles and how they may be conveying their thoughts and feelings. Gudas and Sattler (2006) similarly emphasize the importance of the evaluator's approach as neutral, objective, and detached, although they also note the importance of engaging with the juvenile in a supportive, accepting, and empathic stance when engaging in a clinical process.[1] Morrison further recommends that evaluators remain aware of the language they are using, making every attempt to talk in jargon-free language that is understandable to and sensitive to the needs and level of the client. Gudas and Sattler go further, describing an awareness of the juvenile's age, experience, linguistic and conceptual development, and emotional disturbance as cardinal to good interviews, and that "the wording of statements and vocabulary usage by the interviewer profoundly influence(s) the course and outcome of interviews" (p. 122). Here, Calder (2001) recommends not only the careful use of simple, concise, and concrete language, but also periodic checks to ensure that the juvenile understands what is being said and asked.

Boundaries must also be evident in the interview climate. These, in part, create a clear and emotionally safe environment in which roles and relationships are clearly defined and followed, and also to help ensure physical safety as the evaluator will most often be alone with the juvenile during the interview. As in therapy in general, then, the evaluator must establish clear boundaries and remain alert to subtle shifts and overstepping of boundaries in both directions. Although in part marked by the balance between the evaluator's responsiveness and detachment (Margison, 2002), boundaries essentially represent the distance between the juvenile and evaluator. They serve as the foundation that defines the structure of the working alliance, and upon which further structure is built. Here, where the working alliance

---

1. Gudas and Sattler distinguish between forensic and clinical evaluations, highlighting differences in not just purpose but approach as well. Despite this, they make it clear that the very elements of support and facilitation that they attach to the clinical interview are also very much at play in the development of a facilitative and effective forensic interview climate, despite the objective and neutral manner they ascribe to the forensic interviewer.

brings the evaluator and juvenile together in a relationship in which many sensitive and intimate issues are discussed, boundaries keep them apart and define their roles within this relationship.

Summing up these ideas, in order to facilitate engagement and openness in the environment in which the clinical interview occurs is characterized by the evaluator's:

- Awareness and anticipation of client distortions, denials, and lack of disclosure
- Use of careful and active listening skills
- Demonstration of concern, respect, and support for the juvenile
- Provision of information that can help the juvenile understand his or her situation
- Authentic presentation
- Effort to understand and see things through the eyes of the juvenile
- Awareness and careful control of evaluator self-expression
- Use of language geared to and understandable to the client
- Establishment of healthy and safe boundaries

The facilitative interview climate, then, is not a passive environment in which the evaluator simply asks questions and the interviewee responds or does not. It is, instead, an active environment in which two people, regardless of age or role, are engaged in a reciprocal relationship marked by clear boundaries. The outcomes of the interview and the goals of the evaluator are, in part, met not simply through the juvenile's honest responses, but through the evaluator's ability to develop, maintain, and further build the facilitative environment. That is, the interview environment is the medium, facilitated by the evaluator, through which effective interviews are created.

FRAMING QUESTIONS: ASKING THE RIGHT QUESTIONS

The Association for the Treatment of Sexual Abusers has defined the range of content areas and specific questions to be addressed during a comprehensive assessment of adult sexual offenders (2005), as has the American Psychological Association (1999), the National Task Force on Juvenile Sexual Offending (1993), the Colorado Department of Public Safety (2002), and individual authors such as Calder (2000, 2001), and O'Reilly and Carr (2004). Nevertheless, although in many cases the questions represent historical and developmental facts, regarding behavior, development, cognitive skill, education, previous treatment, and family history for instance, many of the content areas are more subjective and are pieced together through the investigative work of the psychosocial assessment. Describing the family history may be a fact-based task, but *understanding* that history and the role it may have played in shaping the behavior of the juvenile, including his or her sexually abusive behavior, is quite a different task and requires a different set of skills. Similarly, although we can learn about the child or adolescent's behavior through reading records and discussing his or her case with others, we are unlikely to learn about who the child *is* through these means. Understanding the juvenile, then, is a more complex task than simply gathering information and asking and answering questions. The whole (that is, the whole child) adds up to more than the sum of the parts.

The purpose of interviews with the youth is at least threefold. It is to gather information directly from the juvenile, it is to compare the information provided (or not provided) by the youth against information gathered from other sources, and it is to get to know the youth directly and in the flesh, so to speak. If the goal is merely actuarial assessment of risk, no interview is necessary. However, we have by now clearly established that comprehensive assessment of risk requires far more than the application of a statistical instrument.

Without further attempting to address here the sort of questions to be asked and information to be gathered during interviews with the juvenile,[2] let's first and foremost note that when it comes to questions about emotions, ideas, and motivation, including motivation to engage in sexually abusive behavior, in many cases, if not most, the child or adolescent may be able (if willing) to describe *what* happened, but not necessarily *why*. That is, he may be able to describe the events that led up to, occurred during, and followed the offense(s), but not necessarily his or her motivation for the behavior or the complex sequence and interaction of events, circumstances, emotions, cognitions, and behaviors that influenced and led to the sexually abusive behavior. Unlike other crimes or antisocial behaviors that may yield concrete outcomes and be less complex in motivation (such as shoplifting or bullying), juvenile sexual offending is often not motivated or prompted by any blatant reason(s) that youths can easily recognize or grasp themselves. Here, we return to Lukas' (1993) observation that the "why" question is to be avoided: "First, and most obvious, the client may not know the answer. Ask who, what, when, where, and how. Don't ask why" (p. 8).

---

2. Again, note that the Appendix contains an assessment question guideline that can help the evaluator identify questions to be addressed during interviews with the juvenile.

ASKING QUESTIONS THE RIGHT WAY

There are two basic structures to questions. Open-ended questions have no particular answer attached to them, other than that suggested by the question itself. For instance, *"tell me about yourself,"* or *"what brings you to this interview today?"* or *"what happened between you and your sister?"* are examples of open ended questions. *"Have you ever . . . ,"* *"What do you think of . . . ,"* and *"Why do you suppose . . . "* are also examples of open-ended questions.

In risk assessment interviews, questions like these allow open and free speech and can provide a great deal of information, although they also allow denial and minimization. Open-ended questions are often very general, as they don't imply a specific answer, and so answers may also be vague and general. Sometimes open-ended questions are too broad and vague and need to be narrowed down. *"What happened between you and your sister?"* can be narrowed down to *"Tell me what happened sexually between you and your sister?"* A question like this, although open ended, starts to move closer to the format of a close-ended question, which defines not just the type of answer but also often specifies and limits a choice of answer.

Close-ended questions often take the form of *"When did you . . . ,"* *"Why did you . . . ,"* *"When you first . . . ,"* *"How did you . . . ,"* and *"How many times have you . . . ?"* and thus are quite specific and narrow the range of answers. It's not that close-ended questions restrict denial, but there is a clear difference between the open-ended *"Did you ever sexually abuse your brother?"* and its close-ended counterparts, *"When did you first sexually abuse your brother?"* or *"How many times have you sexually abused your brother?"* In a survey or test, although an open-ended question may limit an answer (no more than 25 words, for example), it nevertheless leaves it up to survey or test takers to answer the question anyway they want. On the other hand, close-ended questions not only narrow the question but also restrict answers to a specific set of choices, as in multiple choice questions.

In a risk assessment, or any form of clinical interview, both types of questions are useful. Although both Morrison (1995) and Gudas and Sattler (2006) suggest that open-ended questions are more effective earlier in the interview or in earlier interviews, and more focused, close-ended questions are more to the point and more effective later, in the risk assessment interview your choice of open or close-ended questions will depend on what you want to know, as well as the responsiveness of the youth and his or her interactive style and participation. Nevertheless, it's clear that open-ended questions are less threatening, allow a great deal of leeway, and provide much room for self-expression and free speech. Close-ended questions are far more directive, restrictive, to the point, and demanding, allowing less self-expression and less room for denial and bias in how questions are answered. They are also potentially more threatening and can easily shut down an interview if asked at the wrong time and in the wrong way, such as forcing a particular answer, boxing the subject into a corner, or assuming guilt.

Gudas and Sattler (2006) state that the interview structure should help the juvenile speak openly and honestly, and that when children and adolescents are interviewed in a warm, supportive, and reinforcing manner they demonstrate improved participation and provide more accurate information. They note that the evaluator should remain aware of the influence of his or her verbal mannerism and body language on the client and the interview process and adopt a pleasant and non-judgmental tone, stating questions clearly and positively. They emphasize the role of the interviewer's tone and manner in influencing how the child or adolescent participates in and feels about the interview, including his or her willingness to provide information and answer questions openly and honestly. They also remind us that the evaluator's tone may signal to the youth the possibility of a positive or negative response to an answer, thus additionally influencing the answer given by the child or adolescent.

Gudas and Sattler recommend that, keeping in mind the cognitive and conceptual level of the child or adolescent, interviewers ask clear and concrete questions, and avoid "yes/no" questions, as well as double-barreled or compound questions (such as *"Why did you first do that, and what motivated you?"*), coercive questions, and sharp, offensive, or embarrassing questions. They also suggest that interviewers avoid asking leading questions (questions that lead the client towards a specific answer). However, close-ended questions often do just this, so the interviewer must be sensitive to and careful about the purpose and tone of the question. Is it a leading question or a question with a close-ended answer?

In addition to the type of questions asked, how questions are asked, and how interviewers present themselves when asking questions, Gudas and Sattler recommend the use of appropriate prompts and probes in the interview:

- *Elaboration* upon answers to gain further information.
- *Clarification* of answers that are not clear.
- *Repetition* of a question not fully answered, even if in different words or later in the interview.
- *Challenging*, confusing, contradictory, inconsistent, or omitted information.
- *Neutral phrases*, such as *"I see," "go on . . . ,"* and *"uh huh,"* to encourage the juvenile to talk.

- *Reflective statements* that summarize, paraphrase, or reflect back to the juvenile what he or she has said, or reflect upon the youth's unspoken body language such as crying, a clenched fist, or an upset facial expression; these may express both understanding and support, as well as encouraging the youth's further participation and self-expression.
- *Silence,* allowing the youth the opportunity to think about what is being asked or what he or she has said, or as means to create tension and opportunity for further expression and honesty while, at the same time, recognizing that silence may be experienced as coercive or anxiety provoking.

Medoff and Kinscherff (2006) also write that evaluators must recognize the need to challenge inconsistencies and probe for additional information. However, they additionally note that evaluators must avoid a confrontational style that may result in an angry, defensive, or non-participatory response from the youth that may then characterize the juvenile as in denial. "The evaluator will thus create an atmosphere that facilitates the juvenile's willingness to self-report accurately" (p. 350).

THIRTEEN SEXUAL QUESTIONS

Among the most important questions, of course, are those that directly or indirectly address the sexually abusive behavior itself, and Medoff and Kinscherff (2006) note that the discussion of the sexual offense must eventually include a number of specific elements. Although they describe only seven elements, building upon their work these can be expanded to include at least 13 questions that embrace the nature, circumstances, and events of the sexually abusive behavior.

However, although these are important questions to have answered, it is important that the evaluator bear in mind that not all information will be provided or questions answered by the youth, or even discovered by other means during the assessment period. The youth may not provide the desired information either because, for any number of reasons, he or she is unwilling to provide all of the information or because the youth may not have answers to some of the more complex questions. Nevertheless, these are the questions that figure prominently in the assessment and help reveal the nature, extent, and circumstances of the sexually abusive behavior, as well as contributory forces and risk factors.

1. Elements that may have predisposed or desensitized the youth to his or her sexually abusive behavior, thus to some extent preparing the

youth to engage in the behavior or to allow his or her behavior. These include mental rehearsal, sexual fantasies, use of pornography, or prior personal sexual victimization.

2. How and why victims were selected, and the number of victims.
3. How victims were induced to cooperate and comply, and how they were induced to not disclose the behavior to others.
4. Motivation for engaging in sexually abusive behavior, and the role and function it played for the sexually abusive youth.
5. The actual details of the sexually abusive behavior, including the nature and extent of the behavior itself and any progression in sexually abusive behavior over time.
6. The duration and frequency of the sexually abusive behavior, and the number of incidents.
7. The degree of planning or opportunity present in the steps leading up to the offense, both immediately and remotely.
8. The social circumstances of the offense, including the relationship between the offender and victim(s), and the social context in which the sexually abusive behavior occurred.
9. The presence or nature of deterrence factors, such as location and the presence of other people, including adults, and why these factors failed to deter the sexually abusive behavior.
10. The relationship between the sexually abusive behavior and a larger set of factors, such as more generally versatile conduct-disordered or criminal behavior, poor and inadequate social skills, substance abuse, or the presence of coexisting emotional or psychiatric disturbance.
11. The relationship between the sexually abusive behavior and recent or remote stressors, such as personal victimization or maltreatment, losses, rejections, or narcissistic injuries.
12. How the sexually abusive behavior was discovered, and the circumstances under which discovery occurred.
13. The likelihood that the sexually abusive behavior would have continued if undiscovered, progressed in severity or frequency (i.e., moving from molestation to rape, for instance, or occurring daily instead of weekly), or expanded to include additional victims.

TWENTY THREE INTERVIEW GUIDELINES

As noted, Morrison (1995) suggests that successful clinical interviewing is little more than helping people talk about themselves. In so doing, and in *how* we ask people to talk about themselves, Long, Higgins, and Brady (1988) write that the evaluator uses interpersonal skills to establish trust, define the role that he or she will play, allow the client an opportunity to voice fears and ask questions, and establish a positive environment in which the interview will be conducted.

However, there is no correct way to conduct a clinical interview or work with another individual, or method or technique by which to conduct the interview. We can provide only guidelines (and, ideally, training and supervision) at best. After all, even if it can be structured to some degree, clinical interviewing is clinical. Unlike psychometric testing procedures, which can be defined and must be followed, clinical interviews are not rigid processes that must be followed in a prescribed sequence or manner, even if they follow an interview schedule or protocol. Despite structure and preparation, including prepared questions to be asked and defined information to be gathered, each interview will take a different path, very much dependent upon the response, participation, and attitude of the interviewee, as well as the relationship that develops between interviewer and interviewee (and a relationship will develop, even if a bad one). Further, as there is likely to (and should) be more than a single interview with the juvenile in a risk assessment, ranging from at least two interviews to as many as five, the perspective and engagement of the interviewee may change over time, as well as the perspective, attitude, and style of the interviewer and, as a result, the nature and quality of the relationship between the interviewer and interviewee.

Therefore, like the comprehensive assessment of which it is a part, the clinical interview is not a static process, and especially when a single interview is simply one element of a larger process of multiple interviews. In the final analysis, the resulting interview interaction and environment itself will shape the style and approach adopted by the evaluator in each case, as well as the skill and experience of the evaluator. Nevertheless, guidelines can be developed, as shown below, to help direct the work of the evaluator in his or her approach to the interview process. Although the experienced evaluator will follow the path created during each individual interview process, he or she will bear in mind principles by which to conduct her or himself during the interview process. These 23 guidelines build upon and expand the 18 guidelines provided in Rich (2003).

1. *Be prepared.* Be prepared prior to beginning the interview process and have an already well-formed sense of information about the case. Carefully read the materials in the record.

2. *Recognize differences between clinical and forensic evaluations.* Both assessment and treatment of sexual offenders is quite different than similar work in the non-forensic environment, and both contain interventions and approaches that may conflict with other forms of evaluation

and treatment. For instance, there is limited confidentiality regarding sexually abusive behavior and related information, and clinical work with offenders is often more challenging and direct than with other client populations.

3. *Ensure limits on confidentiality are clear.* Ensure that the juvenile offender and his or her legal guardian are aware of his or her rights, as well as limitations on rights and confidentiality, informed of the general purposes of the evaluation, and informed that the results of the evaluation may or are likely to be shared with others, including authorities.

4. *Frame the assessment.* Ensure that the juvenile understands the assessment process, and any possible consequences of not participating honestly in the assessment.

5. *Work at the juvenile's level.* Be aware of the child's or adolescent's cognitive capacities, based upon both age and any cognitive impairments, and take into consideration cultural or ethnic factors that may influence participation and comprehension (including, of course, language barriers). Beyond this, ensure that you are addressing the youth at his or her level of comprehension, speaking in plain language, and expressing ideas and posing questions in a manner that recognizes how he or she can best understand what is being said and asked, and therefore best participate in the process. Talk the juvenile's language (figuratively, not literally) and in a manner aimed at the cognitive and emotional level of the youth.

6. *Be friendly and facilitative.* Assume an approach in which you are genuinely being friendly, supportive, and encouraging. This may change during an interview or series of interviews, and depending on the youth may be difficult to maintain, but is nonetheless a goal. Regardless of how the interview unfolds over time, this is certainly the starting point upon which to build the interview environment and a manner to display throughout the process.

7. *Build a relationship.* Treat the interview as therapeutic and not merely investigative. Even if forensic in purpose, a relationship fosters honesty, participation, and engagement with the interviewer. A relationship between client and clinician, or in this case clinical interviewee and clinical interviewer, is basic to any therapeutic relationship, including that of clinical assessment, and the development of the working alliance.

8. *Build safety.* Concentrate on building a safe environment for the child or adolescent. This is difficult because many of the steps taken and questions posed by the evaluator during the assessment are challenging and difficult for the juvenile. However, an important clinical skill involves the ability to make a difficult assessment environment as comfortable and safe as possible for the youthful offender.

9. *Don't increase stress or discomfort.* Sex offender assessment and treatment is difficult and often painful for the juvenile. It is a challenging environment for children and adolescents who are not, under the best of circumstances, able to handle difficult emotional situations or stress. By extension, this is equally true of the interview process, which explores difficult and frightening topics during a time of heightened uncertainty for the juvenile being interviewed. The goal is not to intentionally make the assessment environment uncomfortable, but to recognize that it is emotionally uncomfortable by nature. Conversely, recognizing that assessment and treatment is necessarily difficult, it is also not the job of the evaluator to make the environment less challenging or stressful. Instead, the task is to help the juvenile learn to deal and cope with the stress instead of trying to avoid it.

10. *Test for honesty.* Test the honesty, self-disclosure, and self-initiation of the juvenile. Facilitate an environment that will allow the youth to be honest and forthright, and provide opportunities for self-initiated and honest disclosure.

11. *Expect denial.* Expect denial and minimization of the offenses, ranging from complete denial to minimization of the frequency, duration, number, or type of offense(s), or the significance of the offending behavior. However, part of the assessment evaluates the level of the youth's honesty and self-disclosure.

12. *Seek detail.* Pursue details of the sexual offending behavior. The evaluator should gather more than just the facts. One goal is to understand the sexually abusive behavior as completely as possible, and usually it is only the juvenile who can answer questions that involve pre-, during, and post-offense details.

13. *Ask open- and close-ended questions.* Juvenile offenders are often evasive and will take the path of least resistance. Asking both types of questions will provide pathways for both open expression and answers that address narrow questions. There are times when it is most appropriate to ask leading and closed-ended questions, as well as indirect and open-ended questions. Both types of questions should be employed as appropriate.

14. *Expect attempts at manipulation and deceit.* Sexual offenders often provide minimal information that is sometimes based on what they think the evaluator already knows. In this way, the juvenile can appear to be participating openly. The evaluator should expect that in many cases youth will not freely or easily disclose or share information that they believe is not already known. It is consequently not a good idea to reveal to the youth what you already know, in order to help create conditions under which the

youth is more likely to reveal a broader range of information than he or she might otherwise.

15. *Reveal information only as necessary.* If information from the record or other informants is shared with the juvenile, use it primarily to help the juvenile piece together an accurate history and jog memory rather than providing information for the juvenile or as a prompt to be more open. Sharing information in this context recognizes the dynamic and interactive nature of the interview, the special needs of the interviewee, and the fact that the interview environment will shift during the course of both a single interview and certainly across multiple interviews.

16. *Look for and track inconsistency and gaps.* Stay tuned for differences in answers over time. In some cases this points to an increase in participation and honesty, whereas in others it reveals a trend towards dishonesty, evasiveness, or inauthentic participation and perhaps an attempt to manipulate the evaluator.

17. *Challenge and urge honesty.* Confront, in a facilitative manner, dishonesty and challenge misinformation, missing information, or contradictions. This may mean that the evaluator must disclose part of what is already known; consequently, this sort of intervention strategy may be more appropriate during the later stages of the assessment.

18. *Evaluate but don't judge.* Don't pass judgment. Although some of the tenets of traditional therapy are suspended in work with sexual offenders, the principals of acceptance, support, and nonjudgment are not. Others will, or already have, judged the youth. A safe environment means a nonjudgmental environment.

19. *Recognize and control countertransference.* Remain in emotional control. Some juveniles are easily able to arouse strong feelings in others, including anger.

20. *Stay in charge.* Stay in control of the process. If the juvenile refuses to work with the assessment or in some other way short cuts or sabotages the assessment, the evaluator must decide how to best remain in control of the process. This may mean allowing a refusal, insisting on meeting anyway, or assigning consequences for nonparticipation. The juvenile should be informed that lack of participation may be a factor in the assessment outcome.

21. *Maintain safe boundaries.* Interviews create an interpersonal environment between the evaluator and interviewee, and given the nature of many of the questions may also contribute towards a sexualized environment for some youths. Evaluators must establish clear boundaries through the manner in which they hold themselves and engage in the interview

process, as well as being aware of the location and time of day of interviews, as well as the location and availability of other persons.

22. *Seek more information as needed.* Seek additional clarification as needed from other sources, such as outside informants, previous records, or other current providers.

23. *Seek help.* If unclear, seek help, supervision, or consultation—discuss the assessment with a supervisor, other evaluators or clinicians, or other relevant providers. Don't go it alone if you don't have to. Even if you don't need help, talking the case out with someone else can help process a case, provide insight, and move the evaluator toward a greater understanding of the case.

TAKING CARE AND STAYING SAFE

As noted briefly in the interview guidelines, interviews present an environment in which a great many personal questions are asked and a great deal of sensitive information is provided. In the context of sexual abuse risk assessments this involves much sexual information in which the interviews, the questions, and the interview relationship may invoke sexual feelings in the offender, whether juvenile or adult. This constitutes a very personal and intimate environment.

Given the natural, and intended, therapeutic intimacy of this relationship, the transference and countertransference issues that are recognized by informed therapists, and the nature of the client as sexually inappropriate and sometimes aggressive, the intimacy of the interview environment requires that caution be exercised. In addition to the clear personal and physical boundaries that evaluators must establish in their interviews, caution extends to consideration of the location of interviews, the presence of other individuals, and the time of day when interviews are scheduled.

Aside from boundary confusion, the evaluator must never overlook the possibility of personal danger, including the possibility of physical or sexual assault, especially given the subject matter discussed in interviews and the nature of the interviewee as someone who has already crossed sexual boundaries and engaged in sexually abusive behavior.

CONCLUSION: BUILDING AND MAKING THE MOST OF INTERVIEWS

The most effective interviewers are real and authentic—that is, they are themselves. Feel free, therefore, and encouraged to use humor and warmth in interviews and be able to express support and encouragement for the youth, even at the same time you are pressing forward and challenging the youth (and perhaps his or her parents, as well) to be more honest, more engaged, and more forthcoming and self-initiating.

Use language that is understandable and responsive to the youth, as well as an approach that meets the juvenile half way (or more, if necessary). Recognize the importance of your timing and the pacing of the interview, but also that the most important elements combine your presentation, the questions you ask and the order in which you ask them, and the relationship you strive to build. Together, these create the environment in which interviews occur and out of which honesty and engagement (or conversely, dishonesty and disengagement) will emerge.

However, anticipate the possibility of dishonesty and lack of engagement and therefore don't get rattled, daunted, or frustrated by their appearance in the interview process. Expect and shoot for maximum information about the juvenile, his or her developmental experiences, and the sexually abusive behavior and its circumstances, but don't expect to necessarily get every thing you hope for from the interview process or the assessment process as a whole. You need get only enough by which to complete your assessment and form an estimate of risk, guided by a structured risk assessment instrument and process. For instance, experiencing a youth as unresponsive, dishonest, suspicious, or evasive during interviews is just as important and relevant as experiencing the youth as related, honest, trusting, and disclosive. Both experiences of the youth provide the evaluator with important data required to complete each individual assessment.

Accordingly, as long as the interview process is well understood and well administered, it will yield important results.

CHAPTER 19

The Assessment Report

WETTSTEIN (2005) RECENTLY noted the need to improve the quality of forensic evaluations. Among other barriers to quality improvement he described was the concern that practitioners are likely to be satisfied with the quality of their evaluations and believe that little improvement is needed, and as a result fail to undertake self-assessment or quality improvement unless externally mandated.

Clearly, one goal of this book is to provide support and guidance for well-informed assessment, and another is to help establish a basis for assessments of a high standard. However, regardless of the depth and breadth, and indeed quality, of the assessment process nowhere is that quality more clearly evident than in the written assessment report.

Such reports require a set of technical skills, including essential writing skills such as spelling, punctuation, and grammar, as well as a professional vocabulary. Beyond basic writing skills, the evaluator must have skills in expository writing in order to ensure that complex information and ideas are described and explained to the reader. To some degree, effective writing skills also include the capacity for creative writing, or the additional ability to write in an engaging and interesting manner. Together, these skills form the foundation for the ability to piece together and communicate complex and detailed information in a manner that makes that material accessible and understandable to the reader. Beyond basic and intermediate writing skills, an eye for detail and a focused approach is required in order to ensure not just comprehensive reports, but also reports that are coherent and internally consistent and move steadily toward their conclusion without providing contradictory or inconsistent information or failing to include important information.

Of course, a further discussion of essential writing skills and their development is far outside of the scope of this book. However, beyond Wettstein's argument that a lack of critical self-awareness is an impediment to quality assessments, on a very basic level so too is a lack of writing skills because ultimately good evaluations are reflected in the written report. It is not that the writers of evaluative reports need be Pulitzer Prize winners, but writing competency is nevertheless required of all clinicians and caseworkers who must write reports. Evaluators and clinicians who find themselves lacking these skills would be well advised to consider taking a course in basic writing skills and mastering the elementary skills of sentence structure, grammar, punctuation, and spelling, in addition to using the grammar and spelling checkers available in almost all word processing software.

In fact, the computer is an invaluable resource for any form of writing because it allows writers not just grammar- and spell-checking programs, but also the luxury of writing in any order and later reorganizing writing into a more coherent form by moving, cutting, and pasting text. Report writers are thus encouraged to also learn basic word-processing skills as an important aid to writing.

In addition to writing skills the evaluator must also have the capacity to both collect and organize large amounts of information, as well as being able to interpret and make sense of material pertinent to the case, and thus the skills of case formulation. However, as long as the information has been collected, the process of writing itself can help to organize and give meaning to the data, resulting in formulation. Hence, the writing process itself may become not merely a means to document the assessment process and outcomes and provide information to the reader, but also the means by which to organize, describe, and reflect upon the material.

Finally, the evaluator must recognize that people will read these reports. Every report should thus be written as though someone will read it. Better still, every report should be written as though someone is going to cross examine the evaluator in open court on what he or she has written and claimed. In fact, one of the very best ways for evaluators and clinicians to prepare for giving testimony is to ensure the quality, accuracy, and completeness of their reports.

CREATING A REPORT FORMAT

The idea of creating an outline for the report, or what has to be said and in what order, offers a useful means by which to organize reports and create a shell to later fill in with detailed information. Indeed, this is not very different than the structured clinical risk assessment instrument which, as described earlier, is itself a shell, an aide-mémoire, or an organized checklist. Therefore, the creation of an organized and structured report format, or template, is an invaluable tool to help writers both structure and sequence what they have to say and know what to say.

Beyond helping the evaluator to write any single report, an organized report format further ensures that all reports written by the evaluator are consistent from report to report, containing the same sort of information, presenting information in the same manner and order, and yielding outcomes and recommendation that follow the same pattern of presentation. Further, standard report formats ensure that evaluation reports written by different evaluators within the same agency are consistent with one another in terms of the information they contain, the inclusion of adequate information, and their quality. Of course, different evaluators and different agencies responsible for evaluations will create different reports, but standard report formats ensure that evaluators within the same practice or within the same organization follow the same practice and model in completing reports. Under such circumstances, the adoption of a standard report format ensures that all reports are similar in structure, content, and how they describe outcomes regardless of the writer.

Further, the sort of content that makes up the comprehensive assessment, as described in previous chapters, is captured and consolidated in the report format which, itself, is a mere reflection of such content. Hence, headings and subheadings that comprise the report and break it into sections into which detailed information later will be entered represents more than just the structure and sequence of the report. These headings themselves describe and embody the content of the comprehensive assessment. By following the structure outlined by the report format and adding the material defined and required by each section heading, the evaluator will find that the organization and content of the report will be taken care of and additionally be consistent in presentation from report to report.

COMPLETENESS OF AND INTERRELATIONSHIP AMONG REPORT SECTIONS

Each section of a report should be both complete and internally consistent, and additionally to some degree independent of other sections of the report. Consequently, each section, as defined by the section title or heading, focuses upon and fully captures one aspect of the content required by the overall report. Information contained within each section should both meet the content goals for that section and be consistent with other information contained within the same section. Further, each section should be capable of being read, to some degree, as a standalone section that can be read and understood independently of other sections that comprise the larger report.

At the same time, however, even if each section can be considered a complete and independent module, all sections relate to and are interrelated with every other section. Therefore, the report as a whole consists of the totality of information captured in individual sections. Information contained in any one section must therefore supplement, complement, and remain consistent with information in other sections. In many cases, the information contained in one section may relate directly to information in another part of the report, serving to enhance and further explain ideas and information. The result is a comprehensive report in which individual sections can be read independently of others but in which the full picture is revealed only through the interdependence of individual sections, and a report that is thus complete, consistent, and coherent.

This may mean that there is some redundancy built into the format, as different sections may contain shades of the same information. A family history section, for instance, is bound to contain details of the child's developmental environment, just as a section on the child's developmental history will necessarily include information about the child-rearing environment and therefore the family history. Redundancy is not necessarily to be avoided, however. Nevertheless, rather than simply repeating the same information over again, the writer can briefly describe the information and note that more detail has already been presented or will be later in the report. For example, "As previously described in the family history section of this report, Chris was raised in a chaotic family environment in which multiple geographic moves were a common feature, as was domestic violence between his parents, both of whom were active substance abusers," or "Chris was raised under difficult and unstable family conditions, including multiple moves, domestic violence, and parents who were active substance abusers, as described in the family history section found later in this report."

The solution to redundancy, then, is to briefly refer to similar material that has already been presented in a previous section or will be described in greater detail in a later section. One thing to avoid, however, is the wholesale repetition of the same information in different sections of the same report, although the cut-and-paste function makes it tempting to do this. This creates poor writing and tedious reading for the reader.

ORGANIZING THE REPORT AND ENSURING CLARITY

A structured report format will organize the overall report, in terms of both the required content and the sequence and interrelationship of report sections, each of which contains specific content. If the format is sufficiently detailed, it will also provide subheadings to be used within each section, thus further organizing and defining the report and describing required content in narrow detail.

However, the report format offers only a guide to content and a structure for written report organization, and not a means for bypassing the writing process. No matter how well organized, unless the format also provides for a report made up entirely of checklists or multiple-choice questions, the assessment report is, for the most part, composed of expository narrative. Therefore, no matter how organized or detailed the report structure, information and details are provided through the written narrative of the evaluator and must be organized by the writer.

COMPLETENESS

Ensuring a well-sequenced, consistent, and coherent narrative requires that the evaluator organize information and content within each section so that it is both complete and provided in the right order. Both are important. Thus, all necessary information must be provided to both document relevant details and help the reader understand the case, requiring the completeness of information provided. In this respect, there will be no gaps in information, such as describing the child's early life from ages 3–6, for instance, and then jumping to his or her life from age 9–14. Similarly, if information is given about the history of one parent, then it should also include information about the other parent. Family mental health history should provide details about the mental health and functioning of siblings, as well as parents, and perhaps other important extended family members as well.

In the event that information is missing from the record and therefore not available, the writer should highlight that information is missing and describe why it is missing so that is it clear that it is not simply the failure of the writer to include the information.

SEQUENCING

However, regardless of the thoroughness of the report, information must also be provided in a logical and well-paced manner, and thus in the right order. For readability and coherence, information and ideas must be presented in a sequence in which similar information is grouped together, within the same paragraph for instance, rather than providing important information in a hodgepodge manner that lacks organization.

As an illustration, the writer should finish describing the history of the mother before going on to describe the father's history. The writer should certainly not abruptly jump to the father's history and then come back and tell us something more about the mother; although there are exceptions of course. Using this example, the narrative (or the story telling) may require that additional information about the mother can only be understood after first providing information about the father, in which the father's history provides context for the additional information.

OUTLINING FOR ORGANIZATION

Word processing software allows the writer to write in any order and even jump around and get information into words and onto the page as ideas come to him or her and later reorganize the writing for clarity and coherence.

However, one way to organize the information required for each section, as well as its sequence, is to create and use bullet points as an organizing tool. Not only can bullet points serve as markers for more detailed information to be later added, but they can subsequently be moved into the right sequence, effectively creating an outline for each section in terms of both required content and sequence. Written narrative can then be added to each outlined point and the bullet points eventually removed so that the result is a paragraph and not simply a list of bulleted points.

BULLET POINTS AND CHECKLISTS

Aside from being used to organize and outline information that later will be converted into written narrative, bulleted points can also be used to summarize and quickly highlight complex information that has been presented, and therefore provide the reader with a quick overview of material. In some cases it may be entirely appropriate to provide information in a bulleted list form rather than a written paragraph, and in other cases it may be preferable to provide a brief bulleted list following a written paragraph in order to further and more simply highlight information.

Checklists, too, can serve a useful and summarizing function, quickly highlighting some aspect of the case before adding further written detail. The checklist may also serve as an organizing tool for the evaluator, ensuring that adequate and complete information is provided. For instance, a checklist may be used as an element of the child's behavioral history, following which details can be provided in the written narrative, as shown in this simple example: "Youth has a history of __outpatient care, __inpatient care, __ residential care, __ foster care, __other."

Providing Anchoring Dates and Ages

Reports become complex, and the reader cannot easily remember all of the details, even if the writer can. Accordingly, it is useful to provide the reader with reminders of certain items at strategic points throughout the report, such as the dates of certain events or the youth's age at key points during his or her life. Hence, rather than assuming the reader will know how old the juvenile was when he or she sexually abused another child because you told us the youth's date of birth on page 1 or described his or her age at the time of the offense on page 5, tell us again when relevant. Periodically describing the youth's age throughout the report also serves as an anchor point so the reader can get a sense of the unfolding sequence of events in the youth's life. This includes the youth's age at the time of treatment episodes, the occurrence of important family events, when psychological evaluations were administered, and so forth, as well as his or her age at the time of behavioral problems.

Periodically remind the reader of important events and circumstances that surrounded the youth's behavior, as well. Reminding us that the youth's parents had recently divorced, the family pet had just died, or the youth had been victimized just before his or her sexually abusive behaviors keeps the reader focused and allows the report to be read more easily with a clear sense of chronology.

ENSURING CONSISTENCY AND ACCURACY

Consistency is important. Reports should not, for instance, say that someone was age 5 at one point and later report he or she was age 6, or report that someone has a half-brother and later refer to the same brother as a step-brother. The same may be true for any number of things described in the report that are described differently at different points in the report, such as the location of an event, when an event occurred, or the frequency or duration of events. It is not uncommon to find inconsistencies like this in reports, and the only way to avoid them is either to have someone else proofread or edit the report or for the writer to be careful and double-check the report for consistency (and accuracy).

If you're not sure of an age, for instance, the best bet is to double-check or, if necessary, refer back to the original source of the information, even if this means an additional phone call. If information is reported differently in different reports available to the evaluator, it is the evaluator's responsibility to get the accurate information and not simply pass on an error or just ignore it, which takes us to accuracy in report writing. If, even after checking and double-checking, the evaluator is still not sure of the information, then this should be noted in the report itself: "It is not clear from the social service or police records exactly how many offenses occurred, but it appears to be between three and five. Unfortunately, there is no way to know the exact information at this time, as the only current sources of information are inconsistent."

In general this is true for all facts or other information that may be uncertain, regardless of the evaluator's attempts to gather adequate and accurate information. Here, the evaluator must state in the report, as in the example above, that it was not possible to gather certain information and why. This does not make the report stronger, but it does ensure that the reader recognizes and understands any weaknesses in the report that are outside of the evaluator's means. On the other hand, it is the evaluator's responsibility to do his or her best to gather and report information that the evaluator believes to be correct. Information that may be questionable, even if presented in a previous document or reported by an informant, should be double-checked.

In fact, although the evaluator cannot and should not check every fact, he or she should nevertheless not assume that information contained in prior records is accurate as it may not be, and often is not. Again, where there is doubt for any reason, and certainly inconsistency in previous records, the evaluator should take pains to ensure that he or she has the correct information. The evaluator otherwise risks simply passing along incorrect, inconsistent, or inadequate information, not only weakening the evaluation but actively adding to an inaccurate or inadequate record.

Taking Care to Safeguard and Ensure Accuracy

One of the unfortunate realities in assessment is that inaccurate, incorrect, incomplete, or otherwise faulty information does get passed on through reports and from report to report. However, in addition to clarity, consistency, and thoroughness, accuracy is a hallmark of a good evaluation.

The evaluator should refrain from using definitive statements in assessments and report writing, unless he or she definitively knows that the statement is an accurate representation of the facts as they happened.

Statements about what the youth did or did not do should only be made if the evaluator is reasonably sure that the behavior did or did not occur as described. This includes statements such as *"the adolescent did do such and such," "the child was told by his teacher,"* or *"the youth sexually assaulted three victims."* These each imply that the evaluator definitively knows that these behaviors did, in fact, occur. However, when the evaluator cannot verify or vouch for the accuracy or correctness of statements, or the certainty that a particular event took place as reported, terms should be used such as *"it is reported that . . . ," "it appears that . . . ," "the youth states that . . . ," "the offender reports that . . . ," "the victim alleges that . . . ," "the adolescent allegedly . . . ,"* and so on.

It is acceptable for the evaluator to make clinical speculations in the written report as long as the evaluator makes clear that this is his or her clinical opinion, based upon facts, details, circumstances, statements, and other factors. However, even under these circumstances, evaluators should avoid overly broad speculation and sweeping statements. It is critical that assessment and other professional reports do not overreport, assume, assign guilt or responsibility, or definitively make statements that are unproven or unverified. On a related note, it is the evaluator's job to gather and evaluate information, but not to pass judgment or conclude guilt or innocence. It is therefore important that the evaluator maintain a nonjudgmental and impartial style and present data both accurately and objectively.

It is also important for the evaluator to cite sources of information, using quotations if phrasing is taken directly from a previous report or describes what an informant actually said: "The youth stated that he didn't commit the alleged offense, and reported to me that 'It was my lawyer who told me to plead guilty.'" Additionally, when reports are cited, the actual report and its date, and perhaps author, should be given, certainly often enough to identify the source of information even if it's not each time the previous report is noted. For instance, "The Department of Social Services Family History Evaluation, dated 11/5/05, and the Psychological Evaluation completed by Paula Smith, Ph.D., dated 12/6/05, indicate that the family was especially troubled during this period."

GUIDELINES FOR ENSURING ACCURACY AND CLARITY

The evaluation report may be heavily scrutinized at a later point. As noted, the very best bet for the evaluator is to assume it will be heavily scrutinized. Accordingly, the evaluator is well advised to ensure the accuracy of the report and that due care was taken in stating fact, speculation, and case formulation, clearly distinguishing between fact and speculation.

- Ensure that the report is internally consistent and free from internal contradiction.
- Do not speculate without making clear that this is speculation.
- Provide evidence or support for speculative statements.
- Do not make definitive statements unless you know they are correct.
- Qualify uncertain statements.
- Cite the source of information.
- Use quotation marks to make clear that you are using the actual words of a particular informant.
- Use terms such as "alleged" and "reported" when you are reporting unsubstantiated facts.
- Avoid overly broad and sweeping statements.

PROTECTING CONFIDENTIAL AND SENSITIVE INFORMATION

It's clear that the youth's confidentiality is compromised by and through the assessment process. In all likelihood significant issues regarding his or her sexually abusive behavior will be disclosed to all relevant parties, including social service or court authorities, and perhaps legal authorities as well. Nevertheless, even within the forensic context the evaluator should remain sensitive to issues involving the youth's privacy and protect it whenever possible. Already noted is the need for informed consent to release information to external parties (Chapters 15 and 16), and the evaluator should be especially aware of the potential permanency of released records.

Also as noted, the right to confidentiality belongs to the client and not the clinician, and in the case of juveniles to the legal guardian. However, evaluators may want to caution the juvenile and legal guardian about when to exercise restraint regarding parties to whom information should or perhaps should not be sent, including a copy of the evaluation. For instance, if the evaluation or related clinical material is sent to the youth's local education authority, it will not only expose his or her case to the school system, but also may remain in the youth's permanent educational record for many years to come, and thus be available to anyone who has access to that record. Hence, the evaluator may want to consider stamping reports as confidential and not to be duplicated so that it will be obvious to the a reader if a report is later copied and distributed indirectly.

The evaluator should also remain cognizant of the fact that the report will also probably contain information about other persons that is equally confidential and sensitive. This will certainly include information and details about the victims of sexually abusive behavior. In order to best protect their privacy and anonymity, unless they are immediate or close extended family members whose identities will thus be clear anyway, the names of victims should not be disclosed, and initials or other identifying information used instead. However, reports may also include information about parents or other family members that is sensitive and not intended for dissemination, even through an informed consent process, or to be shared with the youth or other family members, including perhaps the other parent. Similarly, nonfamily informants, such as teachers, prior therapists, or social service workers may reveal information or share opinions that may be relevant to and included in the report that are not intended to be shared with the youth or the youth's family.

Therefore, in addition to stamping copies of disseminated reports as confidential, it may be important that, even when consent is given for dissemination or review, some information is redacted from copies of some distributed reports. In this case, the copy must be clearly marked as containing redacted information and explaining why (without, of course, explaining the actual content of the redacted material). It is simple enough in describing a redaction to note, "This copy of the evaluation report contains material that has been redacted in order to protect the confidentiality of informants and information provided by them." However, be aware that recipients of evaluation and other clinical reports are not always pleased to receive a redacted copy of a report.

ALTERNATIVE PRESENTATION AND WRITING STYLES

Frankly, although not flowing in the same way as expository writing, information in a written assessment report can be presented largely in bulleted, or outlined, form. This cannot be the case for the entire report, as sections will inevitably require narrative description, explanation, or elaboration. Nevertheless, although not as eloquent or elegant as expository narrative, there is no reason, other than style and readability, that facts about history, development, and behavior, for instance, cannot be presented in a bullet-point format. This is a choice for the writer and certainly an alternative both for evaluators who lack strong technical writing skills and those who do not wish to put the time into the writing process. Bulleted points:

- Quickly provide information and details
- Place information into a logical and relevant sequence

- Provide a simple overview by which readers can quickly scan information and see the big picture
- Require less writing time
- Require fewer technical writing skills
- Take up less space

As you can see from this example, bulleted points provide organized information and answers, but in a cursory fashion. A second alternative to more complex expository writing involves a *staccato* writing style, which is a step up from the bulleted point but involves less than carefully crafted sentences and paragraphs. Staccato writing involves short, rapid-fire sentences that lack any real connection to or conjunction with one another, other than in the sequence of sentences and in how information is thus ordered and presented. Such sentences often provide few words and short answers and lack depth in the information provided or an understanding of that information. Like the use of bulleted points, staccato writing requires fewer writing skills and less time spent in writing than does technically proficient expository writing.

Staccato writing is short and to the point. Less writing skills are required. Less writing time is required. Information is conveyed sparsely. However, relevant information is presented. It may be less readable. It does the job, though.

Providing information in a bulleted form or through a staccato writing style is not a preferred alternative to a more professional and standard form of writing. Although they require less from the writer and offer an alternative for those evaluators who have difficulty writing or lack time, neither is a recommended style for the presentation of written assessment reports.

WRITING STYLE AND VOICE

Aside from the alternative presentation styles described above (bullet point and staccato), write in the active voice and not the passive voice. Consider speaking directly to the reader, and feel comfortable using first-person pronouns such as "I" and "we" in the assessment. The idea that evaluators and clinicians must write in the third person, describing themselves as "this writer" or "this evaluator," is both a use of the passive voice and creates a barrier between the writer and reader. It is an antiquated style that was presumed to reflect a professional and sterile voice, but in reality adds nothing to the professional tone of a report.

Writing in the first person is a perfectly acceptable mode and is a stronger and more direct method for speaking to the reader. However, whether the first-person or third-person voice is adopted is a choice made by the writer or the organization that establishes writing style for each of its evaluators.

CONSIDERATIONS IN COMPLETING THE REPORT

The evaluation report should be complete and explain the process and purpose of the evaluation, identify sources of information, note any weaknesses in the evaluation, and take care to highlight important information. In the written evaluation, the evaluator should:

- State the purpose of the evaluation.
- Document all records reviewed and informants interviewed.
- Document unavailable records and informants not available for interview.
- Note any limitations on the assessment, including lack of collateral or supporting information that may affect the ability to make informed judgments about the juvenile, the reported offenses, or the risk for future sexual offending.
- Describe that consent was given for the evaluation, and that any limitations to confidentiality were explained to the juvenile and legal guardian.
- Ensure that nonfamily victims are not identified by name.
- Ensure a nonjudgmental and impartial style and that all data presented are both objective and accurate.
- Avoid making speculative statements, except when stating clinical formulations and when ample evidence exists to adequately support the hypotheses of the formulation.
- Be clear when expressing speculation rather than fact.
- Document any denial of offenses that the juvenile may make, as well as his or her explanation, if any, for false allegations.
- Form assessments of future risk only when adequate information is available upon which to base the risk assessment.

USING BOILERPLATE TEXT

Even though the report structure can be heavily organized and formatted, the actual report content is of course individualized and driven entirely by each case. However, sections of the report will remain standard from one report to the next, allowing the use of what is sometimes referred to as ''boilerplate'' material that will be included in every report.

Boilerplate text includes material that can be used in every report, independently of specific material that pertains to the case at hand. For instance, a description of the assessment process, how confidentiality issues were explained to participants, or the use of a risk assessment instrument may remain exactly the same in every report. In general boilerplate text need be developed only once and inserted into the structured and standardized report format, even though such text may need to be slightly modified to fit the particulars of each case. Some examples of boilerplate text are included in the Appendix.

CONTENT AND THE STRUCTURED REPORT FORMAT

Of course, there is no single or must have format for a written evaluation. Instead, the defined format is based on the preferences of each evaluator or agency that oversees evaluations. It will embody the content required by the assessment, not only providing structure for the report but also the detail to be included, but will also likely include explanatory boilerplate material that will remain standard in each report.

In addition to demonstrating an understanding of the sexually abusive behavior and sexual history in general, report content will also include and demonstrate a thorough understanding of the youth's functioning, development, family history, cognitive and emotional functioning, and comorbid psychiatric and/or substance abuse issues that may have influenced and shaped thinking, emotions, behavior, and social interactions in general.

Regardless of the amount of information outlined in the report format, the actual length of the report will depend entirely upon the depth and breadth of information provided by the evaluator as he or she fills in the shell provided by the format. However, depending on the range of material covered by the format, it is unlikely that a comprehensive written evaluation will be less than 12 pages in length, and for a thorough report that provides adequate detail, it is more than likely that the report will fall between 15–22 pages, with some material provided through boilerplate text.

The format for a comprehensive assessment report will include headings such as these (whether or not in this order), which not only provide structure but also define content.

- *Demographic/Identifying Information:* including the youth's date of birth, current age, evaluator name and credential, date of evaluation report, dates of evaluation period, and so on.

- *Purpose of Assessment:* describing the reason for the assessment.
- *Description of the Assessment Process:* explaining the use and process of the assessment, as well as noting that there is no way to fully ascertain future risk and that risk assessment is based upon a combination of current and past behaviors exhibited by the juvenile that place him or her at a particular level of risk.
- *Informed Consent/Matters Pertaining to Confidentiality:* documenting that the process and purpose of the assessment was described to the juvenile and legal guardians, that the limits of confidentiality were discussed, and consent was given for the assessment.
- *Informants to this Assessment:* identifying those individuals interviewed during the course of the assessment, including names, relationships, and titles and credentials where relevant.
- *Documents Reviewed:* noting documents reviewed for the assessment.
- *Identifying Information:* including information such as age, grade, race, religion, physical appearance, and other information that helps identity the juvenile or by which he or she identifies himself.
- *Legal Guardianship and Custody*
- *Legal Status and State Agency Involvement:* explaining current legal standing, custody and guardianship, pending charges, court dates, state agency involvement, probation or parole, current or pending charges or open court dates, and adjudication on sexual offender charges and sex offender board registration.
- *Reason for Referral:* explaining the specific reason the juvenile is being referred for assessment and usually providing a brief description of the sexual charges or allegations.
- *Presentation and Response to the Assessment Process:* explaining the juvenile's level of participation and engagement in the evaluation, and possibly including a mental status exam.
- *Placement and Treatment History:* including current or former placement such as home, foster care, or residential placement, and current or former treatment including outpatient, day treatment, inpatient, or residential treatment.
- *Family History:* which may include several subheadings, including family structure and relationships, current family environment and living arrangements, family trauma, family stability, significant history of other family members, family mental health history, family substance abuse history, and other important family dynamics.
- *Developmental History:* including birth, developmental milestones, early health issues, behaviors and interactions in infancy, preschool, and elementary school, and other early behaviors or difficulties.

- *School Functioning:* including current grade level and any grade retentions, general academic functioning, learning disabilities, history of special education and reasons, behaviors, and difficulties in school and the development of problem behaviors, excessive tardiness or absence, school disciplinary action, and so forth.
- *Social Functioning:* including peer and adult relationships outside of the school environment and social relationships and functioning in general.
- *Victimization or Trauma History:* including physical or sexual victimization or abuse, and/or trauma or life-transforming events experienced by the juvenile.
- *History of Problematic Nonsexual Behaviors:* providing a general overview of the development and history of non-sexual behavioral or emotional problems, including age of onset, extent and frequency of problems, and most recent occurrence of conduct disorder and oppositionality, violence and aggression, arrests and/or legal problems, school problems or difficulties, fire setting, cruelty to animals, running away, self-injurious behavior, and other significant behavioral concerns.
- *History of Substance Use:* including current or prior history of substance use/abuse, with special emphasis on whether alcohol or drugs were involved in problem behaviors or sexually abusive behavior.
- *Relevant Medical Information:* including significant or notable medical or health conditions, including enuresis and encopresis.
- *Psychiatric Medication History:* including dates and ages, and reasons for current medications.
- *Psychiatric Comorbidity and Diagnostic History:* including current or prior significant coexisting psychiatric conditions and mental health diagnoses.
- *Cognitive and Intellectual Functioning and Prior Evaluations/Testing:* including IQ score and history of prior or current psychological testing, dates, and general results.
- *Sexual Development and Nonoffending/Nonabusive Sexual Interests and Behaviors:* including all prior *nonoffending* sexual experiences and encounters, early interest in sexual activities, exposure to sexual activities (including personal sexual victimization), history of masturbation, sexual interests and fantasies, and use of pornography or other sexual materials.
- *History of Sexually Abusive Behavior:* including an objective description of actual or alleged sexually abusive behavior, forensic supporting evidence, the juvenile's description of and attitude toward his or

her sexually abusive behavior, and family attitude about and response to the sexually abusive behavior.

- *Sexual Offender Evaluation: Risk for Reoffending:* describing assessed risk level, the risk assessment instrument or process upon through which risk was assessed, description of significant risk factors, description of significant protective factors, and areas of greatest or special concerns about sexual interests, behaviors, or ideation.
- *Current Mental Health Diagnosis:* if relevant to the report and evaluation format.
- *Summary and Case Formulation:* summarizing the evaluation and providing a concise and condensed description of the youth's development and current behaviors, including sexually abusive behavior, and likely prognosis if things remain unchanged.
- *Recommendations:* regarding management needs, level and type of required treatment, and specific treatment goals and interventions.
- *Signatures and Dates:* including credentials and supervisor countersignature if supervisory oversight is provided for assessment.

A checklist version following this format is found in the Appendix. While providing evaluators with a quick view of required information, the checklist also serves as a means by which clinicians can ensure that they have gathered and reported upon the information required by the report.

THE INTERFACE WITH THE RISK ASSESSMENT INSTRUMENT

As noted, the comprehensive report includes the level of assigned risk for sexual reoffense and identifies the instrument used to assess and assign risk level. However, the risk instrument itself is a separate and stand-alone tool that will not be immediately available to the reader of the written report unless it is attached in some way. Accordingly, conclusions guided by the instrument will most typically be reported in, and therefore integrated into, the written psychosocial assessment report.

In terms of using the risk assessment instrument, conclusions based on its use are interjected into the written report only at the point where such information is necessary to, and therefore described in, the report. Obviously, this will be at different points in different reports, dictated by the structured report format. However, regardless of its location in the report, the risk assessment instrument need not be addressed, or even completed, until it has relevance to the written report. In fact, depending on how the evaluator works, it may not be possible to complete the risk assessment instrument until the point in the process where sufficient information is available by which to complete the instrument. As the information required to complete the risk assessment instrument is produced through the same process that provides the information required by the psychosocial assessment, it may make the most sense for the evaluator to take on the task of completing the risk assessment instrument only at the point where estimates of risk are required in order to continue and complete the written assessment report.

At that point, the evaluator may switch from writing the report to completing the risk assessment instrument, as there is now ample information by which to complete the tool and assess risk. Once the risk assessment instrument is completed and a risk level assigned, the evaluator may turn back to and continue the written report. At that point, the evaluator will describe the estimate of risk yielded through the use of the instrument, as well as relevant risk and protective factors, adding further explanation and description of estimated risk as necessary, including caveats and commentary. From that point on, assessed risk becomes part of and integrated into the body of the written report.

CASE FORMULATION: THE DEVELOPMENT OF INSIGHT

The clinical formulation represents the simple, concise, and condensed version of the evaluator's visualization of the case, and adds another level of richness to the assessment. Case formulation represents the process of reducing and synthesizing information into a more precise form. It reduces history, circumstances, and current functioning into a brief summary that conjectures causes, outlines current issues, provides meaning, and informs prognosis.

As described in Chapter 15, formulation provides a clinical theory about the case, offers explanatory information, identifies possible cause, and suggests meaning and future action. It thus allows the basis for both understanding the case and its likely trajectory, as well as treatment and management interventions. The formulation combines the detective work of the assessment process in which information is gathered and examined, the inventive work of piecing together information into a discernible whole, the development of hypotheses that suggest causes, and likely outcome if untreated, or prognosis. Case formulation thus helps evaluators and clinicians alike better understand the factors and motivations that shape and explain behavior, as well as prognosticate the further development or resolution of pathology.

In addition to summarizing the case, formulation should also describe:

- The motivations of the youth and hypothesized reasons behind the youth's behavior and thinking patterns.
- Past and present factors that influence and shape the youth's thinking, attitudes, behaviors, and interactions.
- Why the youth engaged in sexually abusive behavior in the first place.
- The prognosis if things go unchanged, including risk for sexual recidivism.
- Central issues or problems for the youth, and the treatment problem to be addressed and resolved.
- Interventions that might be useful or will be used to attack the problem and bring about change.

In addition to exploring the static and dynamic risk factors of the case, Medoff and Kinscherff (2006) describe individualized formulation as the third aspect and focus of the assessment, noting that simply knowing that a youth has sexually offended someone else does not provide much useful information. They write that forensic evaluations must instead integrate and effectively communicate the youth's developmental pathway, the dynamics and function of the sexually abusive behavior, and the juvenile's risk for continued sexually abusive behavior, defining this as the formulation that serves as the core of the forensic evaluation.

Formulation, then, implies the ability to recognize, add up, and put together the pieces. Without a formulation, the evaluator is working in the dark. Without explanation, we are merely predicting behavior without understanding it, and cannot possibly identify management and treatment interventions that can address change without understanding what led to the behavior in the first instance, or how all the factors fit together to produce the behavior. Although the assessment of risk is the point of the comprehensive risk assessment, the case formulation is the *pièce de résistance*. It represents that aspect of the assessment that ties it together, gives the assessment its unique character based on the individuality of the youth being assessed, and offers insight into and the basis for continued decision making and the development of intervention, management, and treatment strategies. Indeed, it is the case formulation that, in the final analysis, allows the assessment to embrace the ideas implicit in the risk, needs, and responsivity model, and the risk factors that must be recognized and addressed for each individual if treatment is to be individualized and geared toward the needs of each individual.

CONCLUSION: EVALUATION, NOT JUDGMENT

As noted in the opening of the chapter, people will read these reports. This is perhaps the best way to close the chapter as well. Not only will people form judgments about the youth being assessed, but in many instances they may also form opinions about the writer of the report or the agency responsible for the evaluation. Beyond this, however, there is a great deal at stake for the subject of the report. The youth's future may rotate in some way around the report, the information it includes, the conclusions it reaches, and the recommendations it may make. Further, although the report may have immediate impact on the juvenile, it may also continue to have an impact and effect well into the youth's future, remaining in his or her record and perhaps informing decision makers about the youth for years to come. Hence, the evaluator must recognize the powerful and sensitive nature of the assessment report, and thus exercise caution and sensitivity in undertaking and completing the report.

Finally, the written report represents the culmination of the comprehensive assessment of risk. Rather than simply predicting the likelihood of future behavior, the report should therefore capture and reflect a great deal of information that allows the evaluator and reader alike to understand the behavior itself, the motivators and influences that have and continue to drive the behavior, and the mind and person *behind* the behavior. Further, the report's conclusions should be transparent to the reader who must understand, through the process of reading the evaluation, how the evaluator arrived at his or her conclusions. Of great importance, then, is the evaluator's ability not simply to provide information but also to assume a neutral stance, reflected in a risk assessment that reports and concludes as objectively as possible. It is thus important for the evaluator to focus as much on protective factors, strengths, and assets as on risk factors, vulnerabilities, and deficits.

In part, the evaluator must thus come to see the youth through the youth's eyes and experiences and to understand the forces that have shaped and driven his or her behavior. Of equal importance is the evaluator's ability to assess the juvenile through his or her acts of sexually abusive and other troubled behavior, without writing a deficit-based report that focuses only on the youth's weaknesses and his or her potential to harm others. Accordingly, it is the job of the evaluator to evaluate but not judge, a task and goal reflected in assessment report.

CHAPTER 20

Risk in a Social World: Sexually Troubled Behavior in Context

U NLIKE PREVIOUS CHAPTERS, which have provided information, principles, guidelines, and methods by which to practice risk assessment, this current and almost final chapter offers a reflection on sexually abusive behavior and risk.

As you know, risk assessment is concerned only with risk for the *continuation* of behavior that may cause harm, rather than the etiology or prediction of first-time behavior. Nevertheless, without flinching from the task of assessing possibility, we must ask why so many adolescents, and possibly increasing numbers of preadolescent children, are gravitating toward sexual behavior, including sexually abusive behavior.

THE NORMALCY OF ADOLESCENT SEXUAL BEHAVIOR

Returning to the FBI and other arrest figures described in Chapter 5, in 2006 we saw a 4 percent reduction in general juvenile arrests, but only a 1 percent reduction in juvenile sexual arrests. The FBI report for 2005 (U.S. Department of Justice, 2006) showed a slight *increase* in juvenile sexual arrests over the preceding decade, and the Office for Juvenile Justice reported an increase of 12 percent in juvenile sexual arrests between 1996 and 2004 (Snyder, 2006). Putting aside the abusive nature of these sexual behaviors for one moment, we should put these figures, which are in some way a description of juvenile sexual behavior, into the context of general adolescent sexuality, which is quite commonplace, in the United States at least.

As described in Chapter 10, sexual behavior is common among adolescents in the United States (for example, Huston, Wartella, & Donnerstein, 1998). Sixty-five percent of all high school students have engaged in some form of intimate sexual activity, including either sexual intercourse or oral sex, or both (Hoff, Greene, & Davis, 2003), and Kirby (2001, May) reported that two-thirds of adolescents engage in sexual intercourse before graduating from high school. Further, Kann et al. (1998) reported that 7 percent of students engage in sexual intercourse before age 13, that boys are significantly more likely than girls to have initiated sexual intercourse before 13 years of age, and that 16 percent of U.S. students have had sexual intercourse with four or more partners.

Is it possible, then, to understand the nature of sexually abusive behavior without also recognizing the normalcy of nonabusive sexual behavior in general and sexual behavior as a desired commodity, at least among adolescents? The reality is that adolescent sexual behavior is not only normative, but also is typically depicted as both commonplace and expected by the media, and frankly actively promoted and encouraged. In addition to the actual sexual behaviors and practices of their peers, adolescents and sometimes children, just like adults in our society, are exposed to sexual ideas and portrayals on a regular, routine, and frequent basis.

PORTRAYALS OF SEXUAL BEHAVIOR IN THE SOCIAL ENVIRONMENT

Evidence that we live in a sexual world is perhaps no more clear than its presence and representation in our media. In movies and television there has been a steady and substantial increase in sexual messages and depictions over the past 25 years, the amount of explicit sexual content, and access to a much wider range of sexual information and depictions (Huston et al., 1998; Kunkel et al., 2001, 2005). The Mediascope Press (2001) reported 14,000 sexual references and innuendoes on television annually to which children and adolescents are exposed, and more recently the Kaiser Foundation (Kunkel et al., 2005) reported that 70 percent of all prime time television programming includes sexual content. The Center for Media and Public Affairs who reports on sexual imagery in popular entertainment (Lichter et al., 2000), who reported one scene of sexual material for every four minutes of programming on broadcast television in the 1998–1999 television season, with one scene involving hard-core sexual material (usually in talk, rather than action) every 10 minutes. The 2001 Kaiser report on television sexual content (Kunkel et al., 2001) also noted an increase in the number of teenagers depicted engaging in intercourse, from 3 percent of all teenage characters during the 1997 season to 9 percent during the 1999–2000 season.

The Kaiser Foundation has been studying the nature of sexuality on television since 1997 and has published four studies since that time, including analysis of over 4,700 television programs. Each report presents data drawn from the period covered by the specific report period, as well as describing an increasing database that incorporates accumulated information accrued since the initiation of the study and shifts and changes in trends. The most recent report covering the period 2002–2005 (Kunkel et al., 2005) concluded that the treatment and depiction of sexual behavior on television has expanded dramatically in recent years, and reported a 96 percent increase in television sexual content since the study began in 1997, including both discussions of sex as well as the portrayal of sexual behaviors.

The 2005 Kaiser report notes that 70 percent of more than 1,100 television programs studied contained some sexual content in the form of talk about sex and/or sexual behavior, in which 83 percent of the shows depicted two or more scenes with sexual themes or topics. Across all programs containing sexual content, there was an average of five scenes per hour involving sexual talk or behavior, making clear not only that sexual messages and behaviors are a common element of most television programming, but also that "most shows including sexual messages devote substantial attention to the topic" (p. 20). On average, the portrayals depicted moderate levels of sexual behavior, involving behaviors such as passionate kissing and intimate touching, and portrayals of sexual intercourse were depicted in about 11 percent of programs. Of television shows frequently watched by adolescents, 45 percent included some portrayal of sexual behavior, with an average of 2.1 scenes per hour. The study concludes that most viewers are likely to encounter televised portrayals of sexual intercourse on a regular basis.

Kunkel et al. (2005) report that the influence of television on social beliefs, attitudes, and behaviors is a gradual and cumulative process that develops with repeated and long-time exposure to frequent portrayals of social behavior and information. Indeed, as far back as 1982, Roberts wrote that the media plays an important role in the development of sexual knowledge, attitudes, and behaviors in children and adolescents, not simply due to the amount of exposure but also the realism with which sexual roles, relationships, and lifestyles are portrayed, and the overwhelming consistency of the messages about sexuality that are communicated to children and adolescents. In 2001, the American Academy of

Pediatrics (2001, November) described the media replacing the role of parents and teachers as "the primary source of information about the world and how one behaves in it" (p. 1223). More recently, Brown, Halpern, and L'Engle (2005) described the depth and amount of sexual information provided by the media, as well as increasingly frequent and explicit depictions of information and sexual behavior. Describing the media as a "super peer" in terms of its influence on the beliefs, attitudes and behavior of adolescents, they describe the possibility that media as "super peer" may be even more powerful for boys than girls. They recommend that researchers and practitioners interested in adolescent sexual behavior can benefit from paying more attention to juvenile sexual development in light of the social media.

Another variant regarding social messages about sexual behavior, of course, involves the personal experiences of individual juvenile sexual offenders. Unlike the pervasive influence of the media affecting all children, these experiences are part and parcel of developmental experiences unique to each child. Nevertheless, abundant studies tell us that the experiences of children who later engage in sexually troubled and abusive behavior commonly include both sexual victimization and exposure to the sexual behavior of others, either directly or through sexual imagery.

However, in his study of male adolescent sexual offenders, Loding's (2006) hypothesis that exposure to pornography prior to age 10 would help discriminate between juvenile sexual offenders and nonsexual juvenile offenders was not supported.[1] Nevertheless, Loding found that early exposure (prior to age 10) to pornography, actual sexual acts, and nudity was significantly higher among sexually abusive youth than nonsexual juvenile offenders, leading Loding to suggest that the world view of juvenile sexual offenders is more highly tuned into sexual aspects than other youth. He accordingly concluded that juvenile sexual offenders are more "tuned in" to sexual stimuli than other children and adolescents.

PORTRAYALS OF SEXUAL BEHAVIOR

Media portrayals of the normalcy of sexual behavior, including adolescent sexual behavior, no doubt contribute significantly to juvenile sexual ideas, attitudes, and behavior. It is also likely the case that the gap between media depictions of sexual relationships and real-life adolescent experiences

---

1. Loding's study of male adolescent sexual offenders also examined the relationship between the strength of parental attachment, early traumatic experiences, and exposure to both pornography and sexual behavior.

contributes to difficulties in understanding or making healthy sexual decisions (Brown & Keller, 2000). Sexual ideas and information and sexual depictions transmitted and disseminated by the media provide little to no support for an actual understanding of sexual feelings or help define responsible sexual behaviors, and such messages contribute to both confusing and contradictory beliefs and behavior in adolescents.

For instance, although attention is sometimes given to television portrayals of negative or risky sexual consequences, it is sparse. Lichter et al. (2000) reported that television shows and movies rarely show any negative consequences of sex. Ninety eight percent of 3,228 scenes studied showed no physical consequences at all, 85 percent showed no emotional consequences, and 96 percent of the scenes showed no moral judgment, and sexual activity was generally associated with positive portrayals. This, Lichter et al. describe as the glamorization of sex without consequences, or a view unbalanced by media messages about the dangers of unwanted and inappropriate sexual behavior, and Kunkel et al. (2005) reported that in the 2004–2005 television season negative consequences were represented in only 2 percent of television shows with sexual content. Similarly, ideas about or depictions of sexual abstinence or responsibility are equally limited. In the Kaiser 2005 study, scenes involving sexual patience (abstinence, virginity, or waiting until ready to assume the responsibilities of a sexual relationship) were present in only 1 percent of all scenes with sexual content. As was true in 1997, the Kaiser 2005 report found that only 4 percent of all television scenes associated with sexual behavior included some aspect of risk or responsibility, and even then "it is extraordinarily rare for any particular program to focus on sexual risk or responsibility concerns throughout an entire episode" (Kunkel et al., 2005, p. 41).

THE INFLUENCE OF THE SOCIAL MESSAGE

However, although the media no doubt serves as a significant social force, its power and influence is strengthened or weakened by personal and social differences in the lives of those who watch, read or listen to the media (Kunkel et al., 2001). In fact, it seems clear that in combination with social messages about sexual behavior, the personal vulnerabilities of juveniles and the social conditions under which they are raised further contribute to sexualized interests, ideas, and behaviors among juveniles. The American Academy of Pediatrics (2001, August), for instance, identified children at risk for early or coercive sexual behaviors as those who have been physically or sexually victimized or witnessed sexual or physical violence, and described children with social risk factors such as low IQ, learning problems, low academic attainment, social or emotional problems, patterns of substance abuse, and antisocial behavior. Also included as candidates for early sexual behaviors are children of low-income families and families in which marital discord and low levels of parental supervision are prevalent.

Emotional distress and sexual beliefs, attitudes, and social skills are factors that increase the likelihood of early sexual behavior (Huston et al., 1998; Kirby, 2001). However, Kirby (2001) also describes the role of social connections and attachment to social norms as important in the development of adolescent sexual values and behaviors, including both family values and attitudes toward sexuality and the perspectives, attitudes, and values of peers. In this vein, Huston et al. suggest that early onset of sexual intercourse is most likely for adolescents who have loose or loosening ties to their families, are in conflict with their families, and who are involved in peer groups with norms that support sexual activity.

Hence, the influence of social messages is mediated, partially at least, through individual differences, vulnerabilities, and social connections that make some individuals more susceptible to influences and events that may not significantly affect other individuals. However, as we consider why some juveniles exhibit sexually troubled behavior, it is important to not think solely in terms of individual and developmental characteristics and conditions, but also in terms of the developmental-learning environment in which sexual development occurs and sexually troubled behavior originates, is played out, and sometimes deepens and progresses. From this perspective, we recognize that children learn, grow, and develop through interactions with their environment and transactions with people in that environment. Through this process, to a great degree, children become the product of their environments in which individual psychology is shaped by social forces.

DEEPENING OUR UNDERSTANDING

In fact, the sophistication of our thinking about and understanding of sexual behavior in children and adolescents, including sexually abusive behavior, has deepened considerably over the past decade, and perhaps especially the past few years. Ideas about juvenile sexual offending have evolved beyond simplistic one-size-fits-all answers, and as a field we now more clearly recognize the complexity of both behavior and its influences, including sexually abusive behavior and its etiological path. Consequently, we have moved past the idea that all or most juvenile sexual offenders were themselves the victims of sexual abuse (even though we recognize that many sexually abusive youth have been sexually victimized). Similarly, ideas about motivation for sexually abusive behavior have progressed beyond a belief that "boys will be boys" or that all sexually abusive behavior is driven by the need for power and control and the domination of others. Although still holding currency, as general and overarching principles, these ideas have nonetheless been recognized as only single aspects of a far larger puzzle. Single-answer solutions have instead been replaced by more sophisticated multidimensional and multifactorial ideas about the different pathways that, for different juveniles and adults, lead to sexually abusive behavior.

Thus, it is not that these earlier ideas and beliefs about the development of and motivation for sexually abusive behavior have been dismissed; rather, they have been subsumed within larger ideas. For some children and adolescents it *is* about sexual experimentation gone wrong, for others about power and mastery, and for still others the recapitulation of their own sexual victimization. Beyond this, however, we recognize that, like all behaviors, the acquisition of the ideas, attitudes, and valences that form, motivate, propel, and maintain behavior is the result of a complex and multifaceted process, not single events or causes.

Without, of course, lessening either the nature of the behavior itself or its potential or actual impact on its victims, for many sexually abusive youth the sexually abusive behavior is socially deviant rather than sexually deviant. That is, there is no deviant sexual attraction involved in the sexually abusive behavior, such as arousal to children, animals, force, sadism, or control of others, even though these factors may sometimes figure prominently in the enactment of sexually abusive behavior. More often than not, the involvement of elements like these, with the exception of sadism, are *instrumental* rather than *expressive* means to get a need met. In this case, sexual behavior with a child or an animal, for instance, or the use of threats or force to engage in sexual behavior, is the instrument by which to achieve an end. Here, the end may involve the acquisition of sexual experience, a sense of social mastery, or a connection to someone, even if in a troubled and harmful manner. In these cases, engagement with a child, for example, is not the goal but may represent the only means available to the juvenile to meet his or her true purpose. On the other hand, when sexual engagement with a child or animal is the specific and desired goal, or the use of force is in itself desirable and pleasurable, the behaviors are expressive. In this case, the method for achieving the ends is not merely instrumental but expresses the actual goal. Hence, in the use of expressive behavior the means and ends are closely related and perhaps the same.

All this is by way of saying that for most juvenile sexual offenders the sexually abusive behaviors are often not sexually deviant, and the *content* of sexual ideation is therefore not a particular concern. Here, content is influenced by those very same messages about sexual behaviors already described that are so prevalent in the child's social environment, and in which sexual behavior is considered normal behavior and a desirable commodity. For many sexually abusive youth, containment of sexual ideation represents a greater concern than does sexually deviant content. For these youth, even if sexual ideation is completely normative (pleasurable sexual activity and engagement for both parties, or at least no intention or desire to harm anyone), the ability of the juvenile to contain these ideas to his or her mental realm is obviously a problem for those juveniles who act out sexually.

For many children and adolescents this lack of containment represents a failure to understand or recognize social norms or the needs and interests of the other party. Most typically it reflects poorly developed self-regulation, as well as an underdeveloped moral code, even for younger children or lower-functioning individuals who are nevertheless usually capable of distinguishing between right and wrong even at their developmental or cognitive level. In fact, even if sexual content is not a special concern, the idea that a child or adolescent can act sexually against another person is a concern with respect to socially deviant behavior. Even if the ends of sexual behavior are desirable (e.g., social mastery, connection, evidence of personal attractiveness, connection to a reference group), the idea that one can engage in the desired behavior by taking it, either inappropriately or without permission, represents socially deviant behavior.

SOCIAL DEVIANCE, SOCIAL GOALS, AND SOCIAL CONNECTION

If not sexually deviant, what, then, does it mean for the behavior to be socially deviant? In general, it means that the behaviors are outside of the norm and thus usually unacceptable to the larger society. However, from a sociological perspective socially deviant behavior represents an instrumental (but not expressive) means to achieve ends that are, in themselves, not deviant and, in fact, are often socially desirable. From the sociological perspective of strain theory,[2] some individuals who do not have the social or practical skills or means to otherwise achieve social goods valued by others, but who nevertheless want those same things, will resort to

---

2. Strain theory hypothesizes that behavioral deviance results from an inability to fulfill legitimate needs through conventional means, or conformity.

illegitimate means to acquire what Thakker, Ward, and Tidmarsh (2006) have described as legitimate "human goods." With specific respect to sexual behavior, ideas about such behavior as socially legitimate are, in part, influenced by those messages about sexual behaviors that are so prevalent in the child's social environment, and in which sexual behavior is considered and portrayed as both normal behavior and a desirable commodity.

Strain theory presupposes that individuals who have a limited sense of attachment to social norms and institutions lack the means to tolerate social pressure and perceived expectations, as well as the means to gain social goods. Further, Agnew and Passas (1997) write that changing and loosening, and especially a breakdown, in social norms creates pressure (or strain) on individuals to engage in deviant behaviors as a result of their inability to otherwise legitimately meet perceived social goals. Socially deviant behavior is thus required as the only means for some individuals to achieve socially desirable goals.

This is particularly relevant to the idea discussed in Chapter 5 that many juvenile sexual offenders are often and predominately socially isolated and experience a sense of social and masculine inadequacy (Daversa & Knight, 2007; Miner, 2004; Miner and Munns, 2005). Here, Passas' (1997) observation that increased rates of deviant behavior can be expected under conditions of weakened conventional social norms is especially pertinent in helping us to understand why some children and adolescents may turn toward sexually abusive behavior. Under circumstances of weakened norms and limited social attachment, Passas writes that people commit deviant acts not only in order to meet perceived needs, but also to feel connected to reference groups that help establish a sense of identity. In seeking connection with and social membership in nonmembership reference groups (or groups to which anyone can belong), he asks how the media affects and influences the adoption of such groups by young people. Returning to Brown et al.'s (2005) view of the media as "super peer" and the relationship between sexual development and the media, we can think of the media as representing a socially desirable reference group. We can thus better understand the development of and engagement in sexual behavior by juveniles as an illegitimate means by which to seek and gain a social goal perceived as legitimate and desirable.

Consequently, as we consider risk for continued sexually abusive behavior in sexually abusive youth, we must ask how much of their sexual drive and motivation reflects an internalized sexual deviancy and how much an acting out of social norms, messages, and expectations regarding sexual behavior. This is perhaps especially pertinent as we apply these ideas to children and adolescents who often exhibit a limited sense of secure attachment and connection to others, limited confidence in themselves, poorly developed self-regulation, arrested or limited moral development, and poor social skills in general. For such juveniles, where the fibers that connect us to one another are weak and poorly developed, we can consider sexually abusive behavior as a crime of *relationships* rather than a crime of *violence* (Rich, 2006).

Here, sexually abusive behavior offers a means, not only to meet a perceived social goal (i.e., being sexual or socially accomplished), but also to engage with someone in a social relationship or derive some perceived or imagined social benefit, regardless of how distorted or improper the means. Under such circumstances, despite the socially deviant behavior, the sexual abuse is intended to meet social needs that are themselves not necessarily deviant. Although this may be true for many adult sexual offenders, as Hudson and Ward (2000) conjecture, this idea may be especially relevant to our understanding of juvenile sexual offenders. Many of these youth are socially isolated, experience themselves as socially inadequate and low in masculine adequacy, and develop their sexual attitudes through early maltreatment, including abuse, and/or the conventional media and its usually attractive depictions of sexual behavior, as well as through depictions of sexual behavior available through easily accessible pornography.

SOCIAL SKILLS THROUGH SOCIAL CONNECTION

As we consider social and personal vulnerabilities and assets, or risks and resiliencies, we must also ask, or at least wonder, how people acquire social resources and personal strengths, and how these work. The converse question is how does a lack of resources, personal or social, contribute to or equal risk? These very issues were addressed in Chapter 8, albeit in a slightly different manner, in discussing the relationship between protective and risk factors and the sometimes inverse relationship between the two types of factors. In fact, for all intents and purposes, the acquisition of social skills, personal strengths, and a sense of social relatedness or attachment are protective factors, whereas deficits in each of these areas represent risk factors. It is probably more realistic to consider vulnerabilities in terms of deficits rather than an absence of assets, as it is unlikely that anyone is without some level of asset. Indeed, a strengths-based model is built upon the premise that we all have skills and resources in varying strengths, and that these can be built or rebuilt to be stronger and hence more effective.

Volumes have been written, of course, on the sort of strengths we require in order to successfully traverse and negotiate the social world, and how one acquires these resources. However, a quick review of the protective factors discussed in Chapter 8 (or an even quicker look at Figure 8.1) will show that, although some are genetic or biological in origin (IQ, for instance, and perhaps temperament), many of these resources (in fact, most) are acquired through the process of socialization and social learning. Hence, most protective factors are represented in both actual relationships with others or the self-perceived experience of relatedness, and in either case emotional bonding represents the root of such protective experiences and strengths. Indeed, Hirschi (2002) has written that the strength of the bond between individuals and their society figures prominently in theories about socially deviant behavior, in which the emotional bond is presumed to be a major deterrent to criminal acts and antisocial behavior.

A model of psychology derived from attachment theory offers a clear view of how such emotional bonds develop, and how individuals develop and act upon mental images that they hold of themselves and others in the world. From an attachment-informed perspective, the emotional bond is the product of the transactions and interactions between the individual and his or her social world. The bond is a reflection not just of the self or the other (i.e., society), but also of the relationship that exists between self and other, whether the connection is to other people, social institutions, or society as whole (or, presumably, all three levels of attached relationships). Through the eyes and ears of attachment theory we can recognize that many of the social skills required to be and feel effective are built upon an early sense of connection with and confidence in others, creating a matrix within which the critical social skills and personal resources are formed, come together, and are acted out in the social environment.

In this context, however, "social skills" don't simply refer to the etiquette of everyday relationships or the ability to make friends and do the socially appropriate things. The concept of social skills is instead directed toward the full range of skills required to maneuver through the social world. These include both the external skills of interpersonal interaction with others and the internal skills of intrapsychic self-regulation, self-awareness, and social comprehension, as well as the skills that bridge self to others, such as empathy and moral behavior. Fonagy (1999a, 1999b) describes the skills of "mentalization" as critical to effective social functioning, or the process of metacognition by which we are able to reflect upon, understand, and make sense of our own mental experiences and the mental experiences of others. Following Schank's (1999) description of our capacity to "say what we know and know what we think" (p. 254), our ability to be *self*-reflective influences our ability to reflect upon and understand the mind of others, resulting, in part, in what is often known as theory of mind.

Further, Fonagy proposes that crimes are committed by people with inadequate mentalizing capacities who instead engage in pathological attempts in order to adapt to a social environment in which mentalization is essential. He and his colleagues argue that those with limited reflective, or metacognitive, skills not only experience a poorly established sense of their own identity and mental states but also the needs and mental states of others. In turn, this may result in a failure to anticipate or care about the consequences of behavior to others and a subsequent devaluing of others. Fonagy further hypothesizes that poor mentalization results in a world view that both allows disengagement from prosocial behavior and also allows antisocial behavior to be experienced by the individual as appropriate, acceptable, and personally satisfying. Metacognition, involving awareness of the mental states of self and others, thus represents one of the essential social skills and is required in order to engage in effective social interactions. Without well-developed metacognition, behavior may be more reactive than reflective; conversely, the acquisition of metacognitive skills opens the door for the development and formation of other essential social skills. How, then, do people gain these other important social skills, and how do these relate to the development of sexually troubled or abusive behavior?

SOCIAL SKILLS AND MENTAL MODELS

The concept of mental models, or mental maps, involves the idea that we form mental representations of the real world (i.e., the external world outside of our head, in which we live).

The "map" is a small scale model of reality embedded within our minds, by which we mentally experiment with various alternatives, react to anticipated future situations, and use our knowledge of past events to deal with the present and future (Craik, 1952). This map, then, guides us through that world, preparing us for what we might face, helping us form decisions about how to respond to the world and its events and transactions, and negotiate our everyday lives without deep thought or planning. Built into this map, or mental model, are implicit assumptions and theories about the world (Drake, Ward, Nathan, & Lee, 2001; Ward & Hudson, 2000), resulting in cognitive, emotional, and behavioral responses that are fast, effortless, and almost intuitive, or the product of the automatic thinking that is usually the target of cognitive-behavioral therapy and the source of the cognitive distortions (thinking errors) that are often targets in sex offender specific treatment.

We understand the world and how to behave in it by constructing a working model of it in our minds (Johnson-Laird, 1983). However, of great importance, is that these mental maps are not mere reproductions of the actual world, or flawless copies of the world as it is. Instead, the model that is formed over time is colored by our perception and experience of the world, and the attitudes, beliefs, and storehouse of information that we collect and already hold about the world.

The world that we act upon is, in actuality, the world that we imagine based upon our experiences in it, not the world as it *is*. Hence, an individual with poor or suboptimal social experiences is likely to build a very different mental map than someone with positive, supportive, and optimal experiences in the world. Much of this optimal or suboptimal experience is, not surprisingly, gathered and built in early life.

In acting upon the world, we are not simply responding to that world that we find but also, in part, creating the world in which we live. Those with underdeveloped social skills and poor social experiences form impressions and build mental maps of the world that both limit their acquisition of necessary social skills and make it more difficult to develop those very same social skills. The very experience of being with others, including mutual recognition and attunement, quality of interaction, and reciprocal understanding, serves as one very important basis for our acquisition of skills, teaching us not only about others but also about ourselves and how to engage with others. These experiences are stored in our accumulating mental model of the world, which both stores our mental impressions of the world and forms the basis for our actions in the world. Bowlby (1973), the father of attachment theory, referred to the mental map as the internal working model and described two internal working models, one of which (the *organismic* model) contains representations of self, including behavioral skills and capacities, and the other (the *environmental* model) provides representations of the environment and the people in it. These two sets of representations, those of the inner world and those of the external, come together to form the basis for both our attitudes about, and our behavior in the world, mirroring the two primary domains in which risk factors are carried and operate and the interaction between the two.

EMPATHIC MORALITY THROUGH SOCIAL RELATEDNESS

Our acquisition of social skills is, of course, made more likely or limited by personal skills, such as temperament and cognitive capacity (IQ, for instance), and in extreme cases by biological conditions such as mental retardation or autism. However, the social realm is a primary source for learning, fostering, practicing, nurturing, and eventually fully acquiring social skills. As we consider the development of sexually abusive behavior and the risk for sexual reoffense, we must consider as significant the nature of the social environment and opportunities for the acquisition of social skills within that environment. In thinking about risk we must, then, understand the social environment in which the child or adolescent has developed and currently functions, as well as the role played by key social skills in the development and possible recurrence of sexually abusive behavior. These include the development of metacognition, already discussed, as well as empathy and moral behavior, each of which are developed in concert with one another and each of which, from an attachment-informed perspective, are mediated and influenced through early and ongoing experiences in the environment of social interaction and connection.

Much has been written about the role of empathy in the enactment of sexually abusive behavior and especially in adult sexual offenders. However, although often not considered a central risk factor in the assessment of adult sexual offenders, the presence and role of empathy is nevertheless key to theories about sexually abusive behavior such as those proposed by Knight and Sims-Knight (2003) and Malamuth (2003), and the development of empathy is frequently a central feature in the treatment of both adult and juvenile sexual offenders. Furthermore, displays of empathy by treatment staff are also considered central to treatment, described by Fernandez and Serran (2002) as integral to the therapeutic relationship. Similarly, Warner (1997) has written that the capacity of therapists to experience and display empathy for their clients is crucial when working with individuals who have experienced empathic failures in their early development and hence have poorly developed metacognitive and related critical social skills.

The capacity for empathic development is based, in part, on physical and cognitive developmental (Chapters 4 and 5). Nonetheless, Vetlesen (1994) describes empathy as the basic human emotional faculty that predisposes people to develop concern for others, always being other-directed rather than self-concerned, and Rogers (1980) describes empathy dissolving alienation, thus connecting the individual to others. Despite D'Orazio's (2002) conclusion that adolescents are generally less empathic than adults, we can nevertheless understand empathy as a sense of social understanding and social connection, as well as shared feelings. From this perspective, a lack of empathy reflects a lack of social relatedness rather than a lack of sympathy or concern for others.

Hoffman (2000) describes the cognitive dimension of empathy, or the ability to take the perspective and become aware of the experiences of others at an intellectual level.[3] He considers this cognitive layer to be the controller of the emotional experience of empathy, in which empathic concerns for others are translated into and become congruent with social moral codes and hence a basis for both social connection and moral development. Similarly, Vetlesen writes that empathy is a precondition for moral decision making, and that perceptions of morality are built on the experience of empathy for others. With this convergence of empathy and morality, in which moral development grows from and is an offshoot of empathy, morality becomes the attitudinal and behavioral equivalent of empathy.

Emotional and cognitive development, involving intertwined elements, thus come together to form Stilwell's domain of "conscience conceptualization." She and her colleagues (Stilwell, Galvin, Kopta, & Padgett, 1998) describe moral development incorporating social values and integrating emotional, cognitive, and behavioral systems into a dynamic mental model of conscience. This model largely involves the transformation of early attachment and social experiences into the values, attitudes, and beliefs that underlie relationships and behaviors, resulting in a moral conscience. With a focus on early attachment processes, Stilwell defines moral delay, arrest, and deviancy as developmental disruptions, interruptions, or derailments that result from disruptions in attachment, neglectful parenting, or trauma (Stilwell, Galvin, Kopta, & Norton, 1994) in which moral development is contingent upon the relational and social environment from which all experience is derived.

Indeed, Gilligan and Wiggins (1987) are critical of theories of moral development that overlook the implications of attachment, which they assert heavily influences the child's development of metacognition and mental models, or how the child comes to understand how to behave towards others and how others feel. They comment that it is through the process of attachment and subsequent socially connected relationships that the child develops an awareness of being affected by and in turn affecting others, thus recognizing and becoming attuned to moral relationships through social relatedness. Recognizing both empathy and morality as essential ingredients in the socialization of behavior, Kagan (1984) similarly considers the child's acquisition of standards to be facilitated by the recognition of feelings and thoughts in self and others (i.e., metacognition) mediated through the development of empathy. He thus makes moral development contingent upon the development of empathy, in which we again see morality as the ideational and behavioral counterpart of empathy, in which empathy is expressed through the effects of decisions and behaviors on others.

---

3. Again, keeping in mind age and cognitive/neural development.

The Commission on Children at Risk (2003) has described a crisis in American childhood based upon a lack of social connection, both to other people and to constructs such as morality and personal meaning, which the Commission considers the result of a breakdown in social institutions and norms. However, there is a circular relationship between the social environment and the attitudes and behaviors it produces, and in turn the impact of those attitudes and behaviors on the social environment. The larger social context, then, is not just an important backdrop to the development of or later re-engagement in sexually abusive behavior, but is itself an active ingredient in the acquisition or absence of the social skills that contribute to and drive prosocial or, conversely, antisocial behavior.

SOCIAL RELATEDNESS AND THE ACQUISITION OF SOCIAL SKILLS

Both strain theory and social control theory hypothesize that social deviance results from a desire for social goods and an impairment in social connectedness that otherwise prevents the expression of criminal behavior. In strain theory, the deficit is found in a lack of social connectedness and a resulting failure to acquire the social skills that allow one to legitimately achieve socially desirable goals. In social control theory, a lack of social connectedness fails to inhibit the commission of crimes and thus allows people to engage in self-indulgent behaviors that lack self-regulation. Both sociological theories presume that delinquent acts result from and are allowable due to a weak bond between the individual and society, following Durkheim's (1893, 1897) assertion that attachment to social values and norms provides the basis for prosocial behavior and engagement. In fact, rather than freeing the individual to engage in antisocial behavior, as social control theory asserts, Agnew and Passas (1997) write that the breakdown in social regulation creates pressure for individuals to engage in deviant behaviors as a result of their inability to meet their goals through legitimate means.

In exploring school performance, Libbey (2004) found that school success was often related to a sense of student-school bonding, involving belonging, having a voice, positive peer relationships, engagement in school activities, teacher support, and a sense of safety. Catalano, Haggerty, Oesterle, Fleming, and Hawkins (2004) similarly defined school bonding as close and affective attached relationships with peers and faculty, an investment in the school environment, and doing well socially and academically. Like Libbey, they concluded that school bonding contributes to academic performance and social competence. Once strongly established, Catalano et al. report that school bonding inhibits behavior that is inconsistent with the norms and values of the school and reduces problems with antisocial behavior.

Again, as we consider risk in the real world in which children and adolescents live, and not a separate and disjointed concept, we cannot fail to understand that both the development of sexually abusive behavior and the risk for recidivism are strongly influenced by the acquisition of social skills that are formed in the crucible of that social environment, and continue to form in their current social environment. These skills not only allow us to successfully negotiate the world in which we live and function, but provide the means to achieve socially desirable goals, the self-regulation required to cope with and manage frustrated desires, the empathy that ties us to others, the moral code that allows us to understand and act upon prosocial ideas, and the metacognition that is the basis for insight and judgment.

We can better understand the youth with whom we work, then, as well as the motivations for their behavior, by also understanding the sets of social skills required of each child, the degree to which each child develops and actually possesses such skills, and the social environment through which social connectedness is formed and social skills are acquired. In so doing, it is, of course, a mistake to lump all juvenile sexual offenders together as a single group, and assume they all suffer the same deficits and are motivated by the same factors (the subject of Chapter 5). Accordingly, we understand that in discussing risk in the real world our children are influenced by many different forces, are capable of many different sets of choices, and are simply not all the same. Nevertheless, recognizing heterogeneity doesn't mean blindly ignoring both common elements and common pathways.

Even for the most highly antisocial and criminalized adolescents who also commit sexual offenses,[4] juvenile sexual offenders are characterized by deficits in the social skills required for prosocial behavior: difficulty understanding or caring about others, demonstrating self-regulation under circumstances where self-regulation is required to maintain prosocial behavior, and buying into and adhering to social norms. However, if we break juvenile sexual offending into two strains, we will see that among the conduct disordered/juvenile delinquent group sexually abusive

---

4. These highly criminal youth represent a significant minority even among non-sexual delinquent adolescents. Forth et al. (2003) found that delinquents with the highest scores on the youth version of the Hare psychopathy checklist (PCL-YV) represented less than 20 percent of the most serious institutionalized delinquents, with less than 10 percent yielding the very highest scores.

behavior is more than likely aimed at peers and related to criminal versatility in general. The other strain involves a more socially isolated and socially inept group of sexually abusive youth, in which sexually troubled behavior is more clearly related to poor social skill development and poor group relatedness. Whereas, in this simplified (for illustrative purposes only) typology, the delinquent strain treats sexual behaviors as another form of taking what you want, this second group perhaps uses sexual behavior as means to connect with others, as well as feeling socially normal and part of a reference group, in which sexual experience is an imagined criteria for membership. In either case, however, juvenile sexual offenders are tied together by their lack of moral development, empathic experience, and intimacy, and a resulting poor social relatedness.

A simple path, then, from early experience to social relatedness can be seen passing through early attachment and bonding to the development of metacognition, the deepening of empathy, the acquisition of morality, and the sense of social connection and awareness reflected in the development of social conscience, or the moralization of attachment as Stilwell and colleagues describe it (Stilwell, Galvin, Kopta, Padgett, & Holt, 1997). As we understand risk, then, in a highly sexualized environment, we might think about the acquisition of normative social and sexual experiences in children who lack judgment, metacognition, moral development, and a sense of deep connection to others. This is of course all questionable, but it is certainly reasonable to believe that many of the children we see have difficulties with relatedness and often have early and ongoing histories of experiences that disrupt and damage deep and secure attachment.[5]

THE SEXUAL MESSAGE, THE SOCIAL ENVIRONMENT, AND THE INTERNALIZATION OF RISK

I don't mean to overplay a quote from Prendergast (1993), which I have used in previous writings. However, he speaks directly to juvenile development in the social environment when he writes that "society is preoccupied with sex and uses sex to prove everything, especially manhood. Both boys and girls are affected by this factor, especially as they enter adolescence. Boys develop the need to prove their manhood. What they see on television . . . portrays sex as the ultimate proof of reaching adulthood and being accepted as normal and healthy" (p. 6). This fits well with Miner's (2004) assertion that masculine attitudes may be tied to juvenile sexual

---

5. The Appendix contains three instruments that may be useful in assessing attachment-related experiences, behaviors, and relationships.

offending, and especially his reference to masculine inadequacy, when we consider the role that taking what you want sexually and living out a sexual dream may play in helping to dissolve and ameliorate social distress.

Returning, then, to the sexual messages embedded and contained in the social environment in which our children are raised and live, we cannot help but recognize and consider the impact of such messages and their influence on children and adolescents who otherwise lack the social skills required to make sense of and interact effectively in the world or perhaps experience satisfaction from their social environments. Like all of our children, these youth make sense of the world about them and behave in that world as best they can. However, for these youth the combination of social experiences, social connection, social comprehension, and personal development in a highly sexualized social environment sets off a series of behaviors that eventually lead to sexually abusive or otherwise troubled behavior, especially when catalyzed by myriad other forces that are too individualized for us to consider other than on a case-by-case basis.

Nevertheless, we can understand risk in the context of a world in which to a far greater degree than ever before sex is portrayed as a measure of normalcy, a socially desirable commodity, and a means for connection to and acceptance by others. For juveniles with inadequate social skill development and a lack of deep social and emotional connection, in the context of cognitive and emotional development, still developing judgment and identity, and the great influence of peer culture and values, we find the ingredients for poor choices. Here, then, we can see at least some of the elements that create risky conditions, and how risk begins to become internalized within the individual and not just in his or her environment. Understanding sexually abusive behavior from this social perspective seems important when understood within and against the backdrop of the real world in which children and adolescents live.

SEXUAL BEHAVIOR AND RISK IN ITS SOCIAL CONTEXT

As we consider how to best understand both risky sexual behavior and risk for sexually abusive behavior, without overlooking individual differences among juvenile sexual offenders, we must place both types of sexualized behavior in the social context. Here, we recognize that risk is both carried within the individual and the environment, but that the external environment provides the medium through which risk is transmitted.

The development of sexual behavior, including risky sexual and sexually abusive behavior, occurs in the context of the social environment, which both feeds and fuels ideas about sexual behavior and also disseminates them. This isn't to say that the social fabric itself is responsible for sexually troubled and abusive behavior, but it certainly contributes to the problem as it is, after all, the most widespread means through which ideas and attitudes are transmitted about sex and how it is used. When we think about sexually abusive behavior and risk for recidivism we have to understand it in light of our social environment. Indeed, in the public health approach to any problem, the primary target for action is the social environment, as it is the source for the spread or risk of contagion. In this approach, in a hierarchical fashion, the individual is merely a tertiary target. The public health approach, then, to sexually abusive behavior provides a focus on the larger community, and the environment through which social ideas are transmitted, and how, through the environment, sexually abusive behavior and its risk is spread and promulgated. This is no different than a model of how HIV, gun violence, measles, or teenage pregnancy is spread from one community and one individual to another, and in which the focus is on the macro, not the micro.

Indeed, the U.S. Surgeon General has already adopted a public health approach to sexual behavior problems in the United States (Office of the Surgeon General, 2001), describing "a serious public health challenge regarding the sexual health of our nation" (p. 16). The *Call to Action* report of the Surgeon General describes sexuality as an integral element of human life, helping to meet a number of personal and social needs, fostering intimacy, emotional bonding, and pleasurable relationships, in addition to merely filling reproductive needs. However, the report also identifies the risk of sexually transmitted disease, unintended pregnancy, and sexually abusive behavior as significant concerns.

As with all public health approaches, the model requires that we identify and understand the problem, recognize risk and protective factors, and develop and implement interventions. The model also recognizes that almost every source of risk and protection lies in the social environment outside of the individual. Recognizing biological factors, of course, as a potential source of risk and protection, the Surgeon General's office nevertheless identifies the primary sources of protection and risk (and also the targets for intervention) as parents and family members, schools, the community and its shared culture, the media, and religion, as well as health care professionals and the legal system.

When we act upon the individual alone, managing the problem through containment and other forms of social control, for instance, we may succeed in preventing that individual from further actions, and may even help that individual as well as preventing him or her from causing further harm to others. However, this will not affect the larger problem or its larger spread.

Further, although our interventions at the individual level may be effective at both helping the individual and curbing further harm, in the case of children and adolescents they may also have unintended consequences by restricting and impeding the normative behavioral and social development; in some cases they may even increase, rather than reduce, the very behaviors that we seek to curtail. But even if it is the case that individuals can be contained and their chances of causing harm limited, the individual approach fails completely to contain the larger spread. It's like trying to stamp out individual fires rather than having an understanding of and method for dealing with the root causes of the multiple smaller fires, thus ensuring that they don't develop in the first place.

FINDING COMPLEX ANSWERS

This book isn't about the management of adult or juvenile sexual offenders, treatment interventions, or how to recognize and tackle the issues that lead or contribute to sexually abusive and sexually troubled behavior. However, in understanding and evaluating risk for sexually abusive behavior, we must recognize that risk is embedded within the larger world in which it is acted out.

If we apply narrow thinking to social problems, we are likely to find only narrow solutions. When it comes to complex problems, however, more complex thinking and answers are required. Sexually abusive behavior represents one such complex question. It is a problem with many dimensions, requiring not only multidimensional answers, but also a multidimensional approach to understanding its etiology and assessing its chances for recurrence. To be knowledgeable about and understand juvenile sexual offending and its risk for recurrence, we must understand its context and circumstances and its development in the real world.

CHAPTER 21

Applying the Ideas

> A living thing is distinguished from a dead thing by the multiplicity of
> the changes at any moment taking place in it.
>
> — Herbert Spencer

T HE LAST CHAPTER always represents the end of a journey, an epilogue
of sorts. This journey has covered ideas about risk, ideas about how
to assess risk, models of risk assessment, risk assessment instruments and their design and methodology, and the idea that risk assessment
is part of a larger and more comprehensive psychosocial assessment.

I've touched also on the idea that the way we understand risk is
important, including how it develops and unfolds in the social environment, and that risk can be found in three domains. Risk factors that reside
within the individual and those found within the environment constitute
two of these domains, with the third represented by the harmonic interaction between the individual and his or her environment.

In this journey I've covered a lot of ground, starting with four
questions that essentially frame and give depth to risk assessment:
risk to whom, for what, when, and why? With respect to a rationale
for the practice of risk assessment, we can say that it provides a common
ground upon which to recognize, understand, and describe risk, by
which relevant concerns can be communicated to decision makers
regarding management and treatment, and by which we can best ensure
that interventions are matched to the risk, needs, and likely responsiveness of each assessed individual. This further leads to a definition of risk
assessment as the process by which the possibility of future harm is
estimated and an assigned level of risk expresses the potential for future
harmful behavior in an individual who has previously engaged in

similar behaviors. In turn, principles that can be extrapolated from this definition essentially frame a theory of risk assessment, which makes clear its elements and processes and lays the groundwork for still further exploration and depth. This includes an understanding of risk assessment as a static *or* dynamic process, in which *dynamic* risk assessment recognizes risk as a process involving a dynamic exchange and catalytic interaction between static and dynamic risk factors that reside within the individual and those that reside in the social environment.

In moving from the theoretical to the operational and practical, risk assessment has been amply described as a comprehensive process with both depth and breadth, in which the assessment of risk is a slice in a much larger and more complex psychosocial assessment process. Through this process, the risk for sexual recidivism in sexually abusive youth, and the sexually abusive youth him or herself, is examined and understood through a much larger lens than one that simply looks at factual or alleged information, and through which juvenile sexual offenders are seen as more than simply the sum of their parts. Assignments of risk are thus based on a broad understanding of the youth, the behavior, the circumstances, and the developmental trajectory, among other factors. I hope these ideas were furthered and made more accessible through the book's provision of discussions and guidelines by which to consider and frame risk assessment processes, as well as the Appendix which contains several forms, formats, and outlines that may be of further use in helping to understand, structure, and practice the risk assessment process.

Bumby, Carter, Talbot, and Gilligan (2007) have observed that "without a doubt, sex offender management has emerged as a highly specialized area within the criminal and juvenile justice fields" (p. 20). This is a specialized field in which we work, then, not just with regard to sex offender specific treatment as a whole but at the still more specialized level of our work with juvenile sexual offenders, including children and adolescents, boys and girls, and juveniles of average intelligence and those with intellectual disabilities. And within this field, the process of risk assessment is a still further specialty. I hope this book goes some way toward helping to build, shape, and define that specialization, as well as inform its practitioners. All in all, I hope the book has painted a landscape, and a fairly sweeping and detailed landscape, that captures the comprehensive nature, processes, and practices of risk assessment.

In fact, it's my hope, of course, that this book has provided much, if not all, of the information that you'll need to make decisions about risk assessment, no matter whether you choose an actuarial or clinical approach, and will help you apply an assessment model, as well as recognize and understand the difficulties and complexities inherent in such an endeavor. However, even if providing useful ideas, information, and guidelines, no book can answer the largest questions of all. Ultimately, as an evaluator how do you apply all of this information and these ideas about risk assessment and as accurately, sensitively, and meaningfully as possible assess risk for sexual recidivism, especially knowing the significant imperfections of risk assessment tools and the high stakes for the juvenile being assessed and the public-at-large?

In my own practice, there have been many times that I've despaired of being able to conduct or supervise assessments, or develop or find risk assessment instruments that I and others can count on to be fair, complete, or accurate representations of risk. Indeed, many skilled evaluators experience the same doubts some of the time, in which they might prefer not to make assessments of risk at all given the uncertainties of the process, and especially when they consider what's potentially at stake for the youth and his or her family, and indeed for the evaluator. I've tried to inject into this book a best practices model in light of the fact that risk assessment is such an uncertain and, no pun intended, risky process, partially as a means to buffer the evaluator against some of those uncertainties and anxieties. Frankly, however, I'd rather have a risk evaluator who is uncertain about the outcome because he or she recognizes the weaknesses and limitations of the risk assessment process, than one who is certain of the outcome based on the conviction that the process is flawless.

Nevertheless, the choice of risk assessment process goes a long way toward helping to guide, support, and buffer the evaluator. If you use an actuarial assessment, you essentially just fill in the data, add up the scores, and report risk. Nothing more is required from you. Just add water and mix. The other choice, of course, is a clinical risk assessment process where much more is required of and much more responsibility is placed upon the evaluator. Here you have the further choice of an unguided assessment process or a process guided by the use of a structured risk assessment instrument. I hope that, based on what I've said in this book, there's really no serious choice at all and the informed practitioner will always use the structured instrument, despite its weaknesses. Going further, that assessment instrument will be folded into the larger comprehensive psychosocial assessment through which an understanding and evaluation of risk will emerge. Indeed, it is the psychosocial assessment that provides the information required to complete the risk assessment instrument, and in turn the assessment of risk yielded by the instrument is understood in the context of the entire psychosocial assessment. A model like this is driven by a number of factors, but it is certainly informed by and meets the requirements of the risk, responsivity, and needs model described throughout the book.

The actuarial route is little more than a technical process, and thus removes the work from the realm of the clinician or clinical evaluator. Other than knowing how to use the instrument, it appears to remove all responsibility for the assignment of risk from the evaluator and shifts it entirely onto the developer of the instrument, and consequently depends entirely on the instrument's accuracy. On the other hand, the process of clinical assessment, even if it includes an actuarial assessment, requires the clinical judgment and experience of the evaluator, the very elements that many define as the essential and unavoidable weakness of the clinical evaluation. Indeed, as noted, in recent years there has been a clear preference for a model of actuarial over clinical assessment for these reasons, which has certainly become the dominant model in adult risk assessment.

However, at the conclusion of Chapter 2, I briefly described the dominant position to some degree defining the ideologies that drive models of treatments, and in this case models of risk assessment. Here, then, it is worth noting the view of Greenberg and Watson (2005) who have written that "the dominant group, believing the correctness of their views, claim superior understanding of the issues," in which "the dynamics of oppression lead to the marginalization of dissenting voices" (p. 112).

Regardless, only you or, if you work for an agency, your agency can decide which model to adopt and apply. In either case, in the larger environment your choice of a risk assessment model may be accepted or rejected by the larger system into which it fits, whether that be social services, the court system, or, for that matter the family or community systems from which the youth has emerged.

APPLYING THE IDEAS

I hope you've experienced a rich journey in which you've been exposed to or reminded of ideas and information about risk, what it is, where it resides, and how we can best understand and assess it. These are my ideas, of course, but they are drawn from and based upon a literature that addresses such ideas. As such, I have in many ways merely synthesized information and ideas, recast in light of my own experience and thoughts. I hope also that the book has both theoretical and practical application.

We finally reach a place where we see the conversion of risk to actual harm and risk as a complex process that is as much mediated by protective factors as it is amplified by risk factors. Most of all, however, we seek to discover and plot trajectory, not outcomes predetermined by history or even current risk factors, although we also recognize that trajectory becomes more and more difficult to alter or redirect as it canalizes and hardens over time. Nevertheless, in our work with sexually abusive youth we have every reason to believe that intervention helps change trajectory, including the process of risk assessment, which itself serves as a form of interaction and intervention with the youth.

This book is a guide, then, to what risk assessment is and how to think about and practice it. It is intended to be informative, but neither prescriptive nor rigidly didactic. It is your knowledge, experience, training, and skills that will bring risk assessment to life.

APPENDIX

Examples of Boilerplate Text

Purpose of Assessment

This assessment is for treatment planning purposes only. The assessment provides a summary of existing information on the youth's development, as well as the sexual abuses of record, in order to provide a baseline upon which an assessment of risk for continued sexually abusive behavior will be made, as well as the youth's treatment needs at this time. In some cases, the information disclosed in the assessment may be referred for review by the licensing agency in the state of record where the substantiated or alleged abuse occurred.

Informants to the Assessment

Data for this assessment are drawn from clinical (face-face) interviews with the youth and clinical observations, review of available prior records, and in-person or phone interviews with family members, state social or youth service agencies, community care providers, schools, probation officers, and other external parties relevant to this youth. Intake records include referral information provided by the youth's custodial agency, court documents and victim statements where applicable, past placement reports, and psychiatric and psychological evaluations where relevant and/or available.

Formulation and Assessment of Risk

The comprehensive psychosocial assessment integrates the youth's own perspective, the perspective(s) of other relevant parties, and information presented in reviewed case records into a consolidated view of the youth's personal, psychological, and behavioral development, with an emphasis on understanding the forces that shape, lead to, and/or maintain sexually abusive behavior.

The assessment of risk evaluates the risk of future sexually abusive behavior or otherwise inappropriate sexual behaviors if the youth remains untreated. Predictions of risk are not based upon any single factor or group of factors. Instead, prognosis is based upon a thorough review of not only the history of sexually abusive behavior, but personal and contextual factors that lend themselves to a more complete understanding of the juvenile and the circumstances that led or contributed to, or in some other way influenced, the sexually abusive behavior(s).

Informed Consent/Waiver of Confidentiality

Any and all relevant information pertaining to new, additional, or more detailed disclosures of sexually abusive behavior is subject to reporting by the evaluator to the appropriate social services, youth authorities, probation or parole, police, or other legal authorities. In addition, any disclosure of information that involves abuse or neglect to minor children or elder adults is required by law to be reported to social services authorities.

Absence of Confidentiality

The evaluation process and the purpose of the assessment is explained to the youth, and the absence of client/evaluator confidentiality in this process, and the youth and his legal guardian have signed a Waiver of Confidentiality form. This waiver notes that any information disclosed to an evaluator, interviewer, counselor, therapist (clinician), or other professional staff during the period of assessment, and information disclosed or discovered during the process is not privileged and may not be held confidential. The youth and legal guardian is aware that the evaluator will report to the appropriate authorities any occurrence or possible occurrence of a sexual offense or sexually abusive behavior, regardless of how the evaluator gains knowledge of such behavior or potential behavior, and that reports may be made to the relevant district attorney's office, state police, local police, social service, youth authority, or parole or probation agencies.

The youth was reminded of the lack of confidentiality prior to each interview in the assessment process, and was reminded that he or she has the right to refuse to answer any questions, or ask for the interview session to be ended at any time, although the youth was encouraged to be open, honest, and complete in the information he or she provides in order to participate to the fullest possible degree in the assessment and treatment process. The youth was told that written notes will be taken throughout interview sessions, and that these will be placed in his or her record, and that a written evaluation report will be written that describes and documents the assessment process, the youth's responses, and the details of the sexually abusive behavior, as well as other information relevant to the youth's behaviors and the process of assessment. The youth was asked if he or she understood the conditions of the assessment process and the lack of confidentiality, and to describe his or her understanding of this in his or her own words.

Specific Informants to this Assessment

For this assessment, information was gathered through review of records or through interviews with individual informants. Information was gathered directly through in-person or phone interviews with the following individuals: *(provide details)*.

Risk Assessment

A risk assessment is designed to assess the likelihood that an offender may re-offend at some point in the future. Risk for re-offense always involves future potential behavior and assessment attempts to assess the likelihood that such an offense will occur. Hence, risk assessment involves predictions of <u>low</u> risk, <u>moderate</u> risk, or <u>high</u> risk to re-offend. *It is extremely important to note that there is no certain way to determine whether or not a re-offense will occur, and it is <u>only</u> possible to assess the possibility or likelihood of re-offense based on history and information presented and collected during the course of the assessment.*

Predictions of risk are not based upon any single factor or group of factors. Instead, prognosis is based upon a thorough review of the history of sexually abusive behavior and personal and contextual factors that lend themselves to a more complete understanding of the juvenile and the circumstances that led or contributed to, or in some other way influenced, the sexually abusive behavior.

Explanation of Risk

<u>Risk</u> factors are factors and forces that increase the possibility of harm to self or others. In the case of sexually abusive or sexually inappropriate behavior, the presence of risk factors signals the possibility of continued sexually abusive and sexually inappropriate behavior in the future. Risk factors

not only serve a function in assessing risk, but they also become a prime target of treatment, in that a goal of treatment is to recognize and reduce or eliminate risk factors in order to reduce the risk for continued sexually abusive or inappropriate behavior.

Protective factors represent relationships, attitudes, beliefs, skills, and other factors at play in the life of the juvenile that may help mitigate the level of risk in any given domain, or the overall level of risk. These factors protect against risk, and also are a target of treatment, in that treatment attempts to recognize, develop, and build upon strengths and other factors that can protect the juvenile from risk.

Assessment Question Guide for Juveniles

This checklist guide provides general guidelines and ideas regarding questions to be posed and answered by the juvenile. It is neither intended to be comprehensive or exhaustive in the type and range of information sought and questions asked, or highly defined in construction or wording.

___ Referral question: Why are you here?
___ In all cases, where relevant, get age of youth at time of events and incidents.

Family History
___ Who is in your family?
___ Father, mother: names
___ Step-father, step-mother.
___ Current relationships with parents.
___ Current or most recent contact with parents.
___ Siblings (full, half, adopted, and step): names, ages, current location.
___ Current relationships with siblings.
___ Current or most recent contact with siblings.
___ Who is currently living with whom?
___ Role of important extended family members: grandparents, uncles, aunts, cousins, etc. *(maternal or paternal).*
___ Sexually or physically victimized by family member?
___ Witness to domestic violence.
___ Substance abuse in parents or siblings.
___ Mental health issues for parents or siblings.

Family Relationships
___ How do you feel about your parents?
___ How do your parents feel about you?
___ Are you close to your parents?
___ Who else are you close to in your family?
___ Current relationship and contact with parents.
___ Current relationship and contact with siblings.
___ Current relationship and contact with other important family members.

Personal History
___ Number of family or personal moves.
___ Important life shaping experiences or events.
___ Greatest problems.
___ History of physical victimization.
___ History of sexual victimization.
___ Traumatic experiences (as defined by youth).
___ Can you create a time line (by age and year) of important things that have happened in your life, including where you lived, what sort of things happened to you, what you've done, places you've been, and other things that can help us to understand how your life has developed and some of the important things that have happened in your life, and why they happened?
___ Any special anniversary dates that are important to the youth, and if so, when and why?

Strengths and Weaknesses
__ Strengths, favorite activities, interests: sports, music, art, acting, etc.
__ Favorite things to do.
__ Other strengths and interests.
__ Greatest difficulties.

Behavioral History
__ Ages and circumstances in all cases.
__ Special problems in the community.
__ Special problems in school.
__ Legal problems or arrests.
__ Theft, including shoplifting.
__ Aggression or violence to others.
__ Physical harm to others.
__ Property destruction.
__ Harm or cruelty to animals.
__ Fire setting.
__ Describe your best or proudest experience.
__ Describe your worst behavior, or the behavior you're most ashamed of.
__ Probation or parole.

Social Life
__ Friendships and ages.
__ Closeness to others, and who.
__ Time spent with others, with whom, and their ages.
__ Favorite things to do.
__ Isolated or connected to others.
__ Important adults or older persons.
__ Are you the sort of person that other peers want to know?
__ What would you like others to know about you that they might not already know?

School Experiences
__ School experiences.
__ Behaviors in school.
__ Behavioral problems in school.
__ Held back or pushed forward in grade.
__ Tardiness and absences.
__ Detentions, suspensions, or expulsions.
__ Academic strengths, favorites, and interests.
__ Academic difficulties or weaknesses.
__ Academic grades.
__ Sports and recreation strengths and interests.
__ Other special strengths, favorite activities, and interests.
__ Relationships with teachers.
__ Relationships with other youths.

Spiritual
__ Religious or spiritual beliefs.
__ Connected to a church or religious community.

Honesty
__ How honest are you, on a 1–10 scale?
__ When are you likely to be the most honest?
__ When are you likely to be the most dishonest?
__ What helps you to be honest?
__ What are your fears about being honest?

Treatment History
__ Previous experience in therapy.
__ Reason(s) for previous treatment.
__ Age when first in treatment.
__ Type of previous treatment: outpatient, day treatment, psychiatric hospitalization, group care, residential, and ages.
__ Other out of home placement location, and age.
__ Relationships with previous treatment providers.
__ Use of psychiatric medication, age, and reason.
__ Did you find treatment useful?
__ What was the best or most useful part of treatment?
__ What was worst or least useful part of treatment?

History of Substance Use
__ Use of alcohol or drugs.
__ Type of alcohol (beer, hard liquor, etc.).
__ Type of drugs (marijuana, hash, cocaine, crack cocaine, opiate such as heroin, amphetamine (methamphetamine), hallucinogenic, PCP, inhalants, sedatives, tranquilizers).
__ First use, by age.
__ Most recent use, by age.
__ Frequency of use.
__ Amount of substance used.
__ Increased use over time.
__ Isolated or social use.
__ Unsuccessful attempts to quit or cut back.
__ Previous treatment for substance abuse.
__ Attendance at AA, NA, etc.

Diagnostic History and Current Diagnostic Functioning
__ Affective disorders, including depression, dysthymia, and bipolar disorder.
__ Anxiety disorders, including anxiety, phobias, and PTSD.
__ Attention disorders, including attention deficit/hyperactivity disorder.
__ Compulsive disorders, including obsessive-compulsive disorder.
__ Developmental disorders, including mental retardation and borderline intellectual functioning.
__ Dissociative disorders.
__ Eating disorders, including anorexia and bulimia.
__ Elimination disorders, including encopresis and enuresis.
__ Impulse disorders, including explosive anger.
__ Pervasive developmental disorders, such as Asperger's disorder.
__ Psychotic disorders, including delusions, hallucinations, paranoia, and racing thoughts.
__ Stereotypic disorders, including facial or vocal tics.
__ Suicidal ideation and/or behaviors.
__ Self-injurious ideation and/or behaviors.

Sexual Development (Non-Offending)
__ Ever had a girlfriend or boyfriend.
__ Age at first sexual experience.
__ Nature of first sexual experience.
__ Range and extent of sexual experiences: touching, oral sex, masturbation of or by others, digital penetration, vaginal or anal penetration.
__ Nature and ages of sexual partners.
__ Use of phone sex lines or chat rooms.
__ Use of pornography, and type.
__ Age of first pornography use.
__ Frequency of pornography use.
__ Age of first masturbation.
__ Current frequency of masturbation.
__ Current masturbation fantasies.
__ Sexual behavior of other family members.

Sexual Victimization
__ History of being sexually abused.
__ Perpetrator(s), including name, age, and relationship.
__ Circumstances of sexual victimization.
__ Details of sexual victimization.
__ Prosecution of perpetrator.
__ How did youth feel about sexual victimization when it was occurring.
__ Did youth find the experience traumatizing (dystonic), pleasurable (syntonic), or neutral.
__ Effect of sexual victimization on youth's later sexual development.
__ Effect of sexual victimization on youth's later sexually abusive behavior.

Sexual Identity
__ Do you think of yourself as attractive or not attractive to others, in a sexual or a romantic way?
__ Sexual orientation: heterosexual, homosexual, bisexual, not sure.

Sexually Abusive Behavior
__ What happened, and with whom.
__ Age of youth at time of offense(s).
__ Name and age of victim(s).
__ Relationship to victim(s).
__ Number of victims.
__ Age at each offense.
__ Description of each offense: what, where, when, how, and why.

Sexual Interest and Arousal
__ Sexual interests: gender, age, appearance.
__ Sexual fantasies.
__ Masturbatory fantasies.

Victim Empathy and Awareness: *First spend time defining the concept of "victim"*
__ Do you think that you may have harmed the people you had sex with?
__ In what way(s) do you think you might have harmed your victim(s)?
__ Do you think about the victim(s) of your sexually abusive behavior?
__ Do you think your victim(s) need any help dealing with the effects of your sexual behavior with them?

__ How do you feel about what happened between you and your victim(s)?
__ Who do you think is responsible for what happened between you and your victim(s)?
__ Do you think that your victim(s) had any responsibility for what happened?
__ Do you think your victim(s) deserved what happened?
__ How important is what you did to your victim(s), from very important to not very important?
__ Can any of your own experiences help you to understand what your victim(s) may feel?
__ Do you feel sorry about what you did to your victim(s)?
__ Do you feel sorry for your victim(s)?

Presentation and Response to the Assessment Process: *Including Mental Status Exam*
__ Level of participation and cooperation provided by the youth during the assessment process.
__ Youth's behaviors, interactions, attitudes, etc. with the evaluator during the assessment process.
__ Youth's functional behaviors, interactions, attitudes, etc. in the community, treatment setting, and/or school during the assessment period.

Mental Status Exam
__ Appearance and Behavior. Assess age appropriate dress, grooming, and physical appearance; facial expression; motor behaviors such as slow, restless, or agitated; attitude; and unusual mannerisms, tics, etc.
__ Speech. Assess volume, rate, rhythm, spontaneity, impairments, word-finding problems, pressure, etc.
__ Mood and Affect. Assess subjective state of predominant emotional feeling, including range of emotions, flatness, blunted, normal, labile, and inappropriateness of affect to content. Note eating or sleeping problems.
__ Stream of Thought. Assess rate of thoughts, as slow or fast, and content as coherent, tangential, loose, or flight of ideas.
__ Thought Content. Assess for worry, preoccupation, fears, phobias, obsessions, compulsions, ideas of reference, persecutory or other delusions, grandiosity, jealousy, somatization, and auditory, visual, or other hallucinations.
__ Orientation and Concentration. Assess for orientation to person, place, and time, attention skills, and distractibility. Assess ability to do serial 7's or 3's, basic arithmetic skills, and spelling, such as "world" backwards.
__ Memory. Assess for immediate recall of digits, objects, and interviewer's name; recent memory for digits and three objects after five minutes; and remote memory for historical details like past presidents.
__ Judgement, Insight, and Abstraction. Assess based on information from interview, past decisions, and proposed social situations, assess for awareness of current problems, concreteness, and analysis of age appropriate metaphors or proverbs.
__ Suicidal Ideation. Assess current and previous thoughts and behaviors. If positive, assess for plan and intent to act on it.
__ Homicidal Ideation. Assess current and previous thoughts and behaviors. If positive, assess for plan and intent to act on it.

Assessment Question Guide for Parents/Caregivers

This checklist guide provides general guidelines and ideas regarding questions to be posed and answered by a parent or primary caregiver. It is neither intended to be comprehensive or exhaustive in the type and range of information sought and questions asked, or highly defined in construction or wording.

__ For all parents, birth, adopted, step, or "surrogate: first and last name."
__ For extended family members, including half-siblings, note maternal or paternal.

Youth Legal Guardianship
__ Legal guardianship of youth, and custodial parent

Personal Status
__ Current marital status.
__ Current age.
__ Current personal or family religious, spiritual, or lifestyle beliefs.
__ Employment/occupation.
__ High school/college.
__ Marriages and dates.
__ Divorce and separation dates.
__ Remarriages and dates.
__ Significant romantic relationships, dates, and status, including live-in.
__ Reason for parent separation/divorce.
__ Number of children, including birth, adopted, and step.
__ Age at birth of first child.

Family Status
__ Number of marriages/remarriages, other parental figures.
__ Current family living arrangements and locations. Who is currently living with whom?
__ Children, names and current ages.
__ Step-children, names and current ages.
__ Current location of children, including step-children.
__ Important family members, including extended maternal or paternal, in youth's life.

Personal and Family Mental Health and Substance Abuse History
__ Mental health and psycho-functional history: personal.
__ Mental health and psycho-functional history: children.
__ Mental health and psycho-functional history: family of origin.
__ Personal medication history, including current medication, name, and reason.
__ Substance abuse history: personal.
__ Substance abuse history: children.
__ Substance abuse history: family of origin.
__ History of sexual or physical victimization.
__ Significant other personal history/important life events.

Family Environment During Youth Development
__ Stable or chaotic family life.
__ Consistent or changing family environment.

__ Number of homes/moves.
__ Number of people in home, relationships, ages, etc.
__ Violence, substance abuse, criminality, mental health issues in home in parent figures.
__ Domestic violence.
__ Domestic arguments.
__ Violence, substance abuse, criminality, mental health issues in home in sibling figures.

Youth Developmental History
__ Course of pregnancy.
__ Use of alcohol, drugs, or tobacco during pregnancy.
__ Problems at birth.
__ Early milestone development: talking, walking, potty training.
__ Health during first 3 years.
__ Health age 3 on.
__ Significant illness, injury, or accidents.
__ Behaviors during first 3 years.
__ Behaviors ages 3 on.
__ Adjustment to school.
__ Traumatic experiences: sexual abuse, physical abuse, other.

Youth Behavioral Development
__ Age at onset of problem behaviors.
__ Changes in youth behavior over time, and when.
__ Changes in problem behaviors.
__ Type of behavioral problems.
__ Aggression to others.
__ Property destruction.
__ Fire setting.
__ Cruelty to animals.
__ Dishonesty.
__ Alcohol or drug use or problems.
__ Self-harming behaviors.
__ Legal problems, arrests, charges, adjudications.
__ Probation or parole.

Youth School History
__ Academic difficulties.
__ Academic strengths.
__ Learning difficulties or disabilities, including cognitive impairments such as mental retardation.
__ School behavioral problems.
__ School attendance.
__ Suspension, expulsions.
__ Held back or advanced in grade.
__ Grades.
__ Special education, and by what age and why.

Youth Social Development
__ Friendships.
__ Relationship to others.
__ Closeness of relationships.

__ Frequency of time in social relationships.
__ Age of friends.
__ Type of friends (antisocial, troubled, positive influence, etc.).
__ Relationship to adults.
__ Favorite activities, special interests, or strengths.

Youth Treatment History
__ Out of home placements, including other family members and foster care: reasons, locations, ages.
__ Prior treatment: outpatient, day treatment, psychiatric hospitalization, group home, residential, etc.
__ Reasons for and ages at time of prior treatment.
__ Prior family therapy.
__ Response to prior treatment.
__ Prior diagnoses.
__ Prior and current medications, ages, and reasons.

Youth Sexually Abusive Behavior
__ What is known to have occurred.
__ What else is alleged to have occurred.
__ What else is suspected to have occurred.
__ Who is the victim(s) of the sexually abusive behavior.
__ Relationship to the victim(s).
__ How old was the youth.
__ How old was the victim(s).
__ What is impact of sexually abusive behavior on the victim(s).
__ Is the victim(s) in treatment.
__ If the victim(s) is not in treatment, why not.
__ How does parent feel about the sexually abusive behavior.
__ What does the parent believe to be true about the sexually abusive behavior.

Psychosocial Assessment: Family Genogram

Youth: _____ Date of Birth: _____ Evaluation Date: _____

GENOGRAM KEY

Female · Male · Identified Patient · 23 Age · Deceased · Age at Death · Substance Abuser · Pregnancy · Still Birth · Abortion · Households

Married Couple · UnMarried Couple · Separated Couple · Divorced Couple · Biological Child · Adopted Child · Twins

Family Genogram

Guide to Content Areas and Detail for Comprehensive Assessment of Risk for Sexually Abusive Youth

This format serves only a general guide to content areas and detail. The specific content of an assessment report will vary depending upon the exact purpose and circumstances of the evaluation, and the nature and goals of the evaluation environment.

- **Demographic/Identifying Information** (Youth name, date of birth, current age, evaluator name and credential, date of evaluation report, dates of evaluation period [start and end dates], other information as needed or relevant).
- **Purpose of Assessment**
- **Description of the Assessment Process**
- **Informed Consent/Matters Pertaining to Confidentiality**
- **Informants to this Assessment** (including names, relationships, titles, and credentials as appropriate)
- **Documents Reviewed for Assessment**
- **Identifying Information** (age, school grade, race, IQ, religion, physical appearance, other important information that helps identify juvenile or by which he/she identifies him/herself or important family characteristics)
- **Legal Guardianship and Custody**
- **Legal Status and State Agency Involvement** (current legal issues; state social services, mental health, youth authorities, or other state agency involvement; adjudication on sexual offender charges, adjudication on other legal charges, sex offender registration, probation/parole, current or pending legal charges, guardian ad litem, attorney)
- **Reason for Referral** (immediate or index events and situation leading to evaluation)
- **Current Residence or Placement** (and reason for placement, if relevant)
- **Presentation and Response to the Assessment Process** (possibly including mental status exam)
- **Placement and Treatment History** (foster care, out of home placement, history of outpatient, residential, and inpatient treatment)
- **Family History**
  - Family structure, composition, and living arrangements
  - Parental history (marriages, divorces, etc., ages, relevant parent developmental history)
  - Sibling history (names, ages, birth order, full or half, adopted, step, etc.)
  - Other important family member history (if relevant)
  - History of family trauma, violence, significant loss
  - Family stability (stability of family, including criminality, domestic violence, significant geographic moves or other disruptions to family life, etc.)
  - Family mental health history
  - Family substance abuse history
- **Developmental History**
  - Pregnancy, birth, developmental milestones, and early health/medical issues
  - Infancy and preschool development, experiences, and behaviors (ages 0–4)

- Childhood experiences and behaviors, including school and social functioning (ages 5–12/13)
- Adolescent experiences and behaviors, including school and social functioning
- **Trauma History** (physical or sexual victimization or abuse, other trauma or life transforming events)
- **History of Problematic Non-Sexual Behaviors** (General overview of the development and history of non-sexual behavioral or emotional problems, including age of onset and extent and frequency: conduct disorder and oppositionality, violence and aggression, theft, arrests, school problems or difficulties, fire setting, cruelty to animals, running away.)
- **History of Substance Use**
- **Relevant Medical Information**
- **Psychiatric Medication History**
- **Psychiatric Co-Morbidity and Diagnostic History**
- **Cognitive and Intellectual Functioning and Prior Evaluations/Testing**
- **Sexual Development and Non-Offending/Non-Abusive Sexual Interests and Behaviors**
- **History of Sexually Abusive Behavior** (Description and details of sexually abusive behavior, forensic supporting evidence or reports, juvenile's description of and attitude towards sexually abusive behavior, family response to sexually abusive behavior)
- **Sexual Offender Evaluation: Risk for Re-Offending** (assessment instrument used, assigned risk level, description of significant risk factors, description of significant protective factors, areas of greatest or special concerns about sexual interests, behaviors, or ideation)
- **Supervision Requirements and Implications of Risk Level**
- **Current Diagnosis** (if relevant to evaluation model)
- **Summary and Case Formulation**
- **Recommendations**
- **Signatures and Dates**

Checklist for Completion of Comprehensive Risk Assessment Report

This checklist guide provides a general example of a format that can help evaluators complete a comprehensive assessment. However, this checklist is generic only as the specific content and format of a comprehensive assessment will vary from assessment to assessment, depending on the content and sequencing of the specific assessment format.

Youth: _____   Evaluator: _____

Specific Informants to this Assessment
__ *All relevant informants identified and contacted, or attempts made*
    __ *Parents*   __ *Social Service Case Worker*
    __ *Therapists*   __ *Prior Programs*
    __ *Probation/Parole*   __ *Home School Personnel*
    __ *Attorney, GAL, etc.*   __ *Other*
    Unsuccessful Contacts
    At least three attempts should be made to contact informants.
        __ *Unavailable informants listed by name and role, including:* __ *Method of contact* __ *Number of attempts at contact*

Documents Reviewed for this Assessment
__ *All Relevant Documents Reviewed or Requested*

    Unavailable Documents: __ *Unavailable documents identified*

Identifying Information
__ *Age*   __ *Current school grade*
__ *Race*   __ *IQ*
__ *Religion (if relevant)*   __ *Physical appearance (if relevant)*
__ *Other important information that helps identify youth, or by which he/she identifies him/herself*
__ *Any important family characteristics (brief) important as identifying features*

Legal Guardianship and Custody
__ ***Legal*** *Guardianship*   __ *Custodial Parent, Legal Guardian, or State Agency*

Legal Status and State Agency Involvement
__ *Current legal issues described*
__ *State social services, mental health, youth authorities, or other state agency involvement*
__ *Dates of first social services, etc. involvement*
__ *Adjudication on sexual offender charges*   __ *Adjudication on other legal charges*
__ *Sex offender registration*   __ *Probation or parole*
__ *Current or pending legal charges*   __ *Guardian ad litem assigned*
__ *Attorney*

Reason for Referral
__ *Described immediate events and situation leading to referral for evaluation or treatment*
__ *Brief explanation for referral*
__ *Brief description of sexual offense(s) related to referral for evaluation or treatment*
__ *Dates of the offenses*
__ *Ages and relationships of the victim(s)*
__ *Age of the youth at the time of the offense(s)*

Current Residence or Placement
If in an out-of-home placement describe:
__ *Name of placement*   __ *Type of program*
__ *Location*   __ *Dates*
__ *Reason for previous placement*

Presentation and Response to the Assessment Process (Including Mental Status Exam)
__ *Described level of participation and cooperation*
__ *Described behaviors, interactions, attitudes, etc. during the assessment process itself, and with the evaluator*
__ *Described behaviors, interactions, attitudes, etc. in the community, treatment setting, and/or school during the assessment period*
    __ *Brief mental status exam covering the period during which the evaluation took place*
    __ *Appearance and behavior*   __ *Speech*
    __ *Mood and affect*   __ *Stream of thought*
    __ *Thought content*   __ *Orientation and concentration*
    __ *Memory*   __ *Insight, and abstraction*
    __ *Suicidal ideation*   __ *Homicidal ideation*

Placement and Treatment History
__ Written narrative including foster care and other out of home placement
__ Dates and ages included

Family History
__ Begins with overview of current/most recent family living arrangements for youth and pertinent family members

Family Structure

Parents
__ Marriages, separations, divorces, re-marriages, and unmarried parental relationships and dates
__ Approximate age of youth when/if parents divorced or re-married
__ Names of parents and parent figures
__ Relationships of parent figures to youth (unless obvious, biological, adopted, step, etc.)

Siblings (note if none)
__ Names and current ages
__ Relationships to youth (biological, adopted, step, etc.)

Other Important Family Members (only note if relevant)
__ Relevant other parent relationships (e.g., romantic, sexual, live-in relationships, etc.)
__ Important grandparents, uncles, aunts, cousins, etc. (note if maternal or paternal)

Other Important Parent Dynamics (only note if relevant)
__ If relevant, number of parental (mother or father) romantic/sexual relationships, live-in or otherwise
__ If relevant, parents' sexual orientation

Current Family Arrangements, Environment, and Relationships
__ Present household arrangements (two parent, single parent, unmarried live-in, blended family, etc.)
__ Living arrangements in youth's immediate household (who lives with whom)
__ Current family relationships: positive, strained, negative, etc.
__ Current family environment: stable, chaotic, labile, etc.
__ Current family stressors: financial, legal, or medical issues, family disputes, significant disruptions, etc.
__ Physical/mental health of parents or other important family members (note if problematic or of concern)
__ Contact and communication with absent parents and/or siblings

Family Trauma/Life Transforming Experiences
__ Physical or sexual abuse among immediate or relevant extended family members
__ Deaths of important family members (dates and circumstances)
__ Significant illnesses of or injuries to important family members
__ Suicides or attempted suicides
__ History of significant violence within family
__ Fires, floods, and significant losses

Family Stability/Patterns/Environment
__ Criminality of parents, parent figures, siblings, or other relevant family members
__ Domestic or other violence
__ Significant geographic moves or other (current or past) disruptions to family life
__ Family environment in which youth was raised: stable, chaotic, labile, etc.

Family Mental Health History
__ Current and prior mental illness/problems, including diagnoses/names of mental illness
__ Biological, adopted, and step-parents
__ Grandparents (state which side: paternal or maternal)
__ Siblings
__ Uncles, aunts, cousins (state which side: paternal or maternal)
__ Prior treatment for family members, (known, including medications, hospitalizations, therapy, etc.)

Family Substance Abuse History
__ Current and prior substance abuse, and type of substance abuse
__ Biological, adopted, and step-parents
__ Grandparents (state which side: paternal or maternal)
__ Siblings
__ Uncles, aunts, cousins (state which side: paternal or maternal)
__ Prior treatment for family members, (known, including hospitalizations, therapy, etc.)

Developmental History

Pregnancy, Birth, Developmental Milestones, and Early Health/Medical Issues
__ Relevant details of pregnancy and delivery
__ Accomplishment, delay, or problems in early developmental steps, such as walking, talking, etc.
__ Early injuries or accidents
__ Substance use by mother during or at time of pregnancy or evidence of fetal alcohol syndrome at birth, if known
__ Other early or developmental problems, concerns, or items of note

Infancy and Preschool Development, Experiences, and Behaviors (ages 0-4)
__ *Early behaviors and milestones, with special focus on problem behaviors or events of concern in the youth's life during these years*

Childhood Experiences, and Behaviors, Including School and Social Functioning (ages 5–12/13)
__ *General written narrative describing early and middle childhood behaviors and milestones, with special focus on problem behaviors or events of concern in the youth's life during these years.*
__ *Ages and dates included, when relevant*
__ *Special life events, circumstances, or experiences*
__ *Includes sexually reactive behaviors as well, if relevant*

School Experiences and Functioning During Childhood
__ *General school functioning*
__ *Held back any grades*
__ *Academic functioning, learning disabilities, history of special education, including reason, dates begun, and services received*
__ *General behaviors, interactions, relationships, and difficulties in school*
__ *Suspensions, expulsions, other school disciplinary action*

Social Experiences During Childhood
__ *Relationships and behaviors in general*
__ *Summarize any sexually reactive/troubled behavior*
__ *Other early childhood behaviors or experiences that are notable or of special concern in the youth's life during these years*

Adolescent Experiences and Behaviors, Including School and Social Functioning
__ *General written narrative, include details of experiences and behaviors in early, middle, and later adolescence, as appropriate*
__ *Include ages and dates, when relevant*
__ *Special life events, circumstances, or experiences*
__ *Includes description of sexually abusive and sexually inappropriate behavior*

School Experiences and Functioning During Adolescence
__ *General school functioning*
__ *Current grade, held back any grades*
__ *Academic functioning, learning disabilities, current special education*
__ *General behaviors, interactions, relationships, and difficulties in school*
__ *Suspensions, expulsions, other school disciplinary action*

Social Experiences during Adolescence
__ *Relationships and behaviors in general*
__ *Summarize sexually abusive or inappropriate behavior*
__ *Other adolescent behaviors or experiences that are notable or of special concern in the youth's life during these years*

Problematic Non-Sexual Behaviors/Symptoms

General overview of the development and history of <u>non-sexual</u> behavioral or emotional problems, including:

__ *Age of onset*
__ *Most recent occurrence*
__ *Violence and aggression*
__ *School problems or difficulties*
__ *Running away*
__ *Trauma or life transforming events*

__ *Extent and frequency of problems*
__ *Conduct disorder and oppositionality*
__ *Theft, arrests, and /or legal problems*
__ *Fire setting*
__ *History of physical or sexual victimization or abuse, if any*

History of Substance Use

__ *Describe any current or prior history of substance use/abuse*
__ *Describe alcohol and/or other substances used*
__ *Approximate start date*
__ *Date of last use*
__ *Amounts used and frequency*
__ *Accompanying problems such as blackouts, passing out, and violence*
__ *Whether alcohol or drugs were involved in problem behaviors or sexual offending behaviors*
__ *Re-cap history of substance abuse in parents, immediate family, or extended family members*

Relevant Medical Information.

__ *Relevant medical information, conditions, history, or current concerns, including <u>allergies</u> and conditions such as asthma.*

Medications

__ *Past psychiatric medications.*
__ *Current <u>medical</u> medications, and reasons for medications*
__ *Current <u>psychiatric</u> medications, and reasons for medications*

Psychiatric Co-Morbidity and Diagnostic History
__ *Describe any current or prior significant co-morbid psychiatric conditions such as:*
    __ *Affective disorders, including depression, dysthymia, and bipolar disorder*
    __ *Anxiety disorders, including anxiety, phobias, and PTSD*
    __ *Attention disorders, including attention deficit/hyperactivity disorder*
    __ *Compulsive disorders, including obsessive-compulsive disorder*
    __ *Developmental disorders, including mental retardation and borderline intellectual functioning*
    __ *Dissociative disorders*
    __ *Eating disorders, including anorexia and bulimia*
    __ *Elimination disorders, including encopresis and enuresis*
    __ *Impulse disorders, including explosive anger*
    __ *Pervasive developmental disorders, such as Asperger's disorder*
    __ *Psychotic disorders, including delusions, hallucinations, paranoia, and racing thoughts*
    __ *Stereotypic disorders, including facial or vocal tics*
    __ *Suicidal ideation and/or behaviors*
    __ *Self-injurious ideation and/or behaviors*
__ *Re-cap history of mental illness/mental health in parents, immediate family, or extended family members*

Cognitive and Intellectual Functioning and Prior Evaluations/Testing
IQ
__ *Most recent IQ score, and subscales*
__ *Give test name, test date, and test evaluator*

Prior or Current Evaluations/Testing
__ *Describe history of psychological evaluations*
__ *History in chronological order (first to most recent)*

Sexual Development and Non-Offending/Non-Abusive Sexual Interests and Behaviors
__ *Prior non-offending sexual experiences, including* experiences, dates, ages, *and* frequency
__ *First interest in sexual activities, by age*
__ *History of non-sexually abusive and age appropriate sexual relationships*
__ *History of personal sexual victimization, including ages, circumstances, by whom, and outcomes*
__ *First sexual encounter (including sexual abusive behavior, if first sexual experience), including age*
__ *History of masturbation, including age started, frequency, and accompanying fantasies*
__ *Sexual interests and fantasies*
__ *Use of pornography or other sexual materials: magazines, video, television, internet, etc.*

History of Sexually Abusive Behavior
Description of Sexually Abusive Behavior/Sexual Offense(s)
__ *Approximate dates of offenses*   __ *Relationship to victims*
__ *Age of victims at the time of the offense*   __ *Age of youth at the time of the offense*
__ *Location and circumstances of the events*   __ *Description of offenses*
__ *Nature and severity of offenses*   __ *Offenses as planned or situational*
__ *Use of violence, force, threats, or weapons*   __ *Use of coercion*
__ *Use of alcohol or drugs*   __ *Use of pornography or other sexual materials*
__ *Means for keeping the sexually abusive behaviors secret*
__ *Were the behaviors clear offenses, or questionable sexual behaviors or inappropriate sexual behaviors*
__ *Description of circumstances surrounding and/or leading to offenses*
__ *Others engaged in the offenses*
__ *Other substantiated, reported, alleged, or suspected offenses*
__ *Describe availability of victim statements, witness reports, or other records that describe the offenses*
__ *How was the sexual behavior discovered?*

Forensic Supporting Evidence or Reports
__ *Description of forensic and other evidence used to describe or support allegations or substantiations of sexual offending*
__ *Overview of the value of the forensic evidence*
__ *Completeness and accuracy of forensic reports*
__ *Describe how the evidence supports or fails to support the case, or provides meaning, insight, and understanding*
__ *Review and describe inadequate, incomplete, or missing forensic evidence*

Youth Description of and Attitude Towards Sexually Abusive Behavior/Sexual Offense(s)
__ *Acknowledgment or denial of offenses*
__ *Perception and description of offenses*
__ *Agreement or disagreement with description of offenses*
__ *Explanation for offenses, motivations, goals, and intentions of sexual offending behavior*
__ *Honesty and self disclosure about offenses*
__ *Attitude towards victims: remorse or empathy demonstrated*
__ *Attitude towards sexual behaviors and offending*
__ *Was the offense syntonic (pleasurable) or dystonic (unpleasurable) for the youth*
__ *Capacity to distinguish right from wrong regarding sexual offending behaviors*

Family/Other Responses to Sexually Abusive Behavior/Sexual Offense(s)
__ Attitudes and expectations of family members, foster family, case workers, probation officers, etc., regarding offense(s)

Sexual Offender Evaluation: Risk for Re-Offending
__ Assessed Risk Level
__ Explanation of Risk
__ Instrument used to assess risk

Brief Summary and Description of Risk Factors Most Relevant to Assessed Risk Level
__ Description of most pertinent risk factors, based on assessment instrument used to assess risk

Protective Factors Contributing to Reduction or Lowering of Risk
__ Describe protective factors that help to reduce or mitigate risk for re-offense

Areas of Greatest or Special Concerns about Sexual Interests, Behaviors, or Fantasies
__ Highlighting any special concerns already noted under risk factors, or other concerns not previously noted

Supervision Requirements and Implications of Risk Level
__ Described

Current Diagnosis *(if relevant)*
__ Noted

Summary and Case Formulation
__ Summary of the youth and the development of his/her problems
__ Factors and dynamics that directly contribute, or may contribute, to his/her diagnosis, behaviors, and/or interactions
__ Description of etiology and contributing factors that may have led to or contributed to the sexually abusive behavior
__ Describe possible motivations for or factors that led to or maintained the sexually abusive behavior
__ Describe current prognosis

Recommendations
__ Described
__ Additional clarifying comments made, if necessary

Signatures and Dates
__ Signature and credential of evaluator and date of report
__ If applicable, counter-signature and credential of evaluation reviewer, and date

Mental Status Examination Format

Name: _____ Age: _____ Date: _____

Examiner: _____

1. **Appearance and Behavior** _____ **Within normal limits**

   Assess age appropriate dress, grooming, physical appearance, facial expression; motor behaviors such as slow, restless, agitated; attitude; and unusual mannerisms, tics, etc.

   Comment if unusual: _____

2. **Speech** _____ **Within normal limits**

   Assess volume, rate, rhythm, spontaneity, impairments, word-finding problems, pressure, etc.

   Comment if unusual: _____

3. **Mood and Affect** _____ **Within normal limits**

   Assess subjective state of predominant emotional feeling, including range of emotions, flatness, blunted, normal, labile, and inappropriateness of affect to content. Note eating or sleeping problems.

   Comment if unusual: _____

4. **Stream of Thought** _____ **Within normal limits**

   Assess rate of thoughts, as slow or fast, and content as coherent, tangential, loose, or flight of ideas.

   Comment if unusual: _____

5. **Thought Content** _____ **Within normal limits**

   Assess for worry, preoccupation, fears, phobias, obsessions, compulsions, ideas of reference, persecutory or other delusions, grandiosity, jealousy, and somatization, auditory, visual, or other hallucinations.

   Comment if unusual: _____

6. **Orientation and Concentration** _____ **Within normal limits**

   Assess for orientation to person, place, and time, attention skills, and distractibility. Assess ability to do serial 7's or 3's, basic arithmetic skills, and spelling, such as "world" backwards.

   Comment if unusual: _____

7. **Memory** _____ **Within normal limits**

   Assess for immediate recall of digits, objects, and interviewer's name, recent memory for digits and three objects after five minutes, and remote memory for historical details like past presidents.

   Comment if unusual: _____

8. **Judgement, Insight, and Abstraction** _____ **Within normal limits**

   Assess based on information from interview, past decisions, and proposed social situations, assess for awareness of current problems, concreteness, and analysis of age appropriate metaphors.

   Comment if unusual: _____

9. **Suicidal Ideation** _____ **Within normal limits**

   Assess current and previous thoughts and behaviors. If positive, assess for plan and intent to act on it.

   Comment if unusual: _____

10. **Homicidal Ideation** _____ **Within normal limits**

    Assess current and previous thoughts and behaviors. If positive, assess for plan and intent to act on it.

    Comment if unusual: _____

Sexual History Questionnaire

Name: _____ Date of Birth: _____ Current Age: ____

Evaluator: _____ Current Date: _____

1. Over the past six months have you had sexual thoughts or fantasies that concerned you?
   __ None   __ A Few   __ A Lot

2. Over the past six months have you felt an <u>urge</u> to act on sexual thoughts or fantasies that concerned you?
   __ No   __ A Little   __ A Lot

3. If you felt <u>urges</u> to act on sexual thoughts or fantasies that concerned you, did you:
   __ Control the urges and never acted on them   __ Occasionally acted on the urges   __ Often acted on the urges

4. Over the past six months have you <u>actually acted</u> on sexual thoughts or fantasies that you thought or knew were <u>wrong</u>?
   __ No   __ Yes

5. Over the past six months have you masturbated to sexual thoughts or fantasies that concerned you?
   __ No   __ Yes

6. If you have masturbated to sexual thoughts or fantasies that concerned you, how often?
   __ Never   __ Rarely   __ Occasionally   __ Frequently

7. Do your sexual thoughts or fantasies involve:
   __ I don't have sexual thoughts
   __ Children under the age of 13   __ Children under the age of 10   __ Children under the age of 6
   __ Children under the age of 3   __ Forcing someone to having sex with you   __ Hurting someone
   __ Seriously hurting or killing someone   __ Kidnaping someone   __ Tying someone up
   __ Gagging someone   __ Animals   __ Other

8. On an average day, how much time do you spend thinking about sex or having sexual fantasies?
   __ None
   __ Up to 15 minutes a day   __ Up to 30 minutes a day   __ Up to 1 hour a day
   __ Up to 2 hours a day   __ Up to 3 hours a day   __ More than 3 hours a day

9. On an average day, how many times do you masturbate?
   __ None   __ Once   __ Twice   __ Three   __ Four   __ More than Four

10. In an average week, how many times do you masturbate?
    __ Never   __ 1–2   __ 2–5   __ Daily or almost daily

11. Does thinking about sex or having sexual fantasies interfere with your ability to do other things?
    __ Yes   __ No   __ I'm not sure

12. Have your sexual thoughts or behaviors interfered with your school, work, or life performance?
    __ My sexual thoughts or activities haven't interfered with my life
    __ My sexual thoughts or activities have interfered with doing well in school
    __ My sexual thoughts or activities have interfered with doing well in work
    __ My sexual thoughts or activities have interfered with other parts of my life

13. How have your sexual thoughts, sexual fantasies, or sexual behaviors affected your relationships?
    __ They haven't affected my relationships   __ I don't know/I'm not sure   __ Difficult to keep a friendship
    __ Friends don't trust me   __ Family members don't trust me   __ Peers don't trust me
    __ Treatment staff don't trust me   __ I don't trust myself with strangers   __ I don't trust myself with friends
    __ I don't trust myself with family members   __ I don't trust myself with treatment staff

14. How have your sexual thoughts, sexual fantasies, or sexual behaviors affected your behaviors?

    __ I've gotten into trouble   __ I've lost the trust of people who are important to me

    __ I've been arrested   __ I've been embarrassed by my sexual thoughts or behaviors

    __ I've lied to people   __ I've stolen things to support my sexual thoughts or behaviors

    __ I've emotionally hurt people   __ I've spent a lot of money to support my sexual thoughts or behaviors

    __ I've physically hurt people   __ I haven't always been able to stop myself from doing sexual things

15. How have your sexual thoughts, sexual fantasies, or sexual behaviors affected other people you know?

    __ Some people have been physically hurt by me   __ Some people have been scared by me

    __ Some people have been emotionally harmed by me   __ Some people are scared of other people because of me

    __ Some people don't trust me anymore   __ Some people don't trust anyone anymore

    __ Some people don't know who to trust now   __ My family has been hurt because of my sexual behaviors

16. Have you had any psychological difficulties <u>because</u> of your sexual thoughts or behaviors?

    __ Difficulty concentrating   __ Difficulty falling asleep   __ Difficulty staying asleep

    __ Feeling suicidal or like hurting myself   __ Feeling out of control   __ Excessively worrying

    __ Excessively worrying about my future   __ Excessive guilt   __ Excessive shame

    __ Difficulty not thinking about sex   __ Not liking myself   __ Other

17. Before being admitted for evaluation or treatment, how much effort and time did you put into looking for or looking at pornography, sexual pictures, or sexual stories on the <u>*Internet*</u>?

    __ None   __ A Little   __ Moderate   __ A Lot

18. Before being admitted for evaluation or treatment, how much effort and time did you put into looking for or looking at pornography, sexual pictures, or sexual stories in <u>*videos*</u>?

    __ None   __ A Little   __ Moderate   __ A Lot

19. Before being admitted for evaluation or treatment, how much effort and time did you put into looking for or looking at pornography, sexual pictures, or sexual stories in <u>*magazines*</u>?

    __ None   __ A Little   __ Moderate   __ A Lot

20. Before being admitted for evaluation or treatment, how much effort and time did you put into looking for or participating in <u>*Internet sex chat rooms*</u>?

    __ None   __ A Little   __ Moderate   __ A Lot

21. Before being admitted for evaluation or treatment how much interest did you have in making <u>*phone calls to sex phone lines*</u>?

    __ None   __ A Little   __ Moderate   __ A Lot

22. Before being admitted for evaluation or treatment, how much interest did you have in looking at pornography, sexual pictures, or sexual stories?

    __ None   __ A Little   __ Moderate   __ A Lot

23. How much interest do you have in looking at pornography, sexual pictures, or sexual stories <u>*now*</u>?

    __ None   __ A Little   __ Moderate   __ A Lot

24. Before being admitted for evaluation or treatment did you ever steal, borrow, or use something that wasn't yours for sexual purposes?

    __ Never   __Rarely   __ Moderately   __ A Lot

25. Before being admitted for evaluation or treatment how much effort did you put into getting your sexual needs met or fulfilling your sexual ideas?

    __ None   __ A Little   __ Quite a Bit   __ A Lot

26. Who have you had sexual thoughts about?

    __ I don't want to answer this question   __ No one on this list

    __ Treatment Staff   __ Strangers

    __ Mother   __ Father

    __ Adopted mother   __ Adopted father

    __ Step mother   __ Step father

__ Foster mother	__ Foster father	
__ Aunt	__ Uncle	
__ Younger brother	__ Older brother	__ Twin brother
__ Younger half brother	__ Older half brother	__ Same age half brother
__ Younger adopted/step brother	__ Older adopted/step brother	__ Same age adopted/step brother
__ Younger foster brother	__ Older foster brother	__ Same age foster brother
__ Younger sister	__ Older sister	__ Twin sister
__ Younger half sister	__ Older half sister	__ Same age half sister
__ Younger adopted/step sister	__ Older adopted/step sister	__ Same age adopted/step sister
__ Younger foster sister	__ Older foster sister	__ Same age foster sister
__ Younger male cousin or nephew	__ Older male cousin or nephew	__ Same age male cousin or nephew
__ Younger female cousin or nephew	__ Older female cousin or nephew	__ Same age female cousin or nephew
__ Other family member, older	__ Other family member, same age	__ Other family member, younger

__ Older female friend, more than 2 years older   __ Older male friend, more than 2 years older

__ Same age female friend, within 2 years of your age   __ Younger female friend, more than 2 years younger

__ Younger female friend, more than 4 years younger   __ Younger female friend, more than 6 years younger

__ Same age male friend, within 2 years of your age   __ Younger male friend, more than 2 years younger

__ Younger male friend, more than 4 years younger   __ Younger male friend, more than 6 years younger

__ Older female friend, more than 2 years older   __ Older male friend, more than 2 years older

__ Same age peers in treatment, within 2 years of your age   __ Older peers in treatment more than 2 years older

__ Younger peers in treatment, more than 2 years younger   __ Younger peers in treatment, more than 4 years younger

__ Cat __ Dog __ Other animal

27. What sexual things have you done?

	Never	Once	Rarely	Moderately	A Lot
__ I exposed my penis to a stranger	__	__	__	__	__
__ I exposed my penis to a friend	__	__	__	__	__
__ I exposed my penis to a family member	__	__	__	__	__
__ I exposed myself in a public place	__	__	__	__	__
__ I watched someone undress or who was already naked without their knowledge	__	__	__	__	__
__ I watched someone having sex without their knowledge	__	__	__	__	__
__ I fondled someone without their permission	__	__	__	__	__
__ I penetrated someone's vagina with my penis, without their permission	__	__	__	__	__
__ I penetrated someone's anus with my penis, without their permission	__	__	__	__	__
__ I tried to penetrate someone's vagina or anus with my penis, without permission	__	__	__	__	__
__ I penetrated someone's vagina or anus with my finger, without permission	__	__	__	__	__
__ I tried to penetrate someone's vagina/anus with my finger, without permission	__	__	__	__	__
__ I penetrated someone's vagina/anus with an object, without their permission	__	__	__	__	__
__ I tried to penetrate someone's vagina/anus with an object, without permission	__	__	__	__	__
__ I performed oral sex to someone else, without their permission	__	__	__	__	__
__ I made someone perform oral sex on me, without their permission	__	__	__	__	__
__ I masturbated someone else, without their permission	__	__	__	__	__
__ I made someone else masturbate me, without their permission	__	__	__	__	__
__ I masturbated on someone else, without their permission	__	__	__	__	__
__ I masturbated in a public place	__	__	__	__	__
__ I used force or violence to make someone have sex with me	__	__	__	__	__
__ I used a weapon to force someone to have sex with me	__	__	__	__	__
__ I used threats to force someone to have sex with me	__	__	__	__	__
__ I coerced or manipulated someone into having sex with me	__	__	__	__	__
__ I used bribery or rewards to make someone have sex with me	__	__	__	__	__
__ I tied someone up so I could have sex with them	__	__	__	__	__
__ I gagged someone so I could have sex with them	__	__	__	__	__
__ I used alcohol or drugs to make someone have sex with me	__	__	__	__	__

__ I had sexual contact with a child 3–4 years younger . . . . __ __ __ __ __

__ I had sexual contact with a child 5 years or more younger . . . . __ __ __ __ __

__ I forced sexual contact with a same age peer (within 2 years of my age) . . . . __ __ __ __ __

__ I forced sexual contact with someone more than 2 years older than me . . . . __ __ __ __ __

__ I forced sexual contact with an adult over the age of 18 . . . . __ __ __ __ __

__ I stole clothing from someone for sexual purposes . . . . __ __ __ __ __

__ I shoplifted clothing for sexual purposes . . . . __ __ __ __ __

__ I dressed in female clothing for sexual purposes . . . . __ __ __ __ __

__ I made obscene phone calls . . . . __ __ __ __ __

__ I made phone calls to a sex line . . . . __ __ __ __ __

__ I watched pornography on the Internet . . . . __ __ __ __ __

__ I watched pornographic videos . . . . __ __ __ __ __

__ I looked at pornographic magazines . . . . __ __ __ __ __

__ I looked at pornographic photographs . . . . __ __ __ __ __

__ I read pornographic stories . . . . __ __ __ __ __

__ I gave or showed pornography to younger children . . . . __ __ __ __ __

__ I had sexual contact with an animal . . . . __ __ __ __ __

28. Who have you <u>actually</u> had <u>any</u> sexual contact with, including both consensual and abusive sex?

__ Treatment Staff	__ Strangers
__ Mother	__ Father
__ Adopted mother	__ Adopted father
__ Step mother	__ Step father
__ Foster mother	__ Foster father
__ Aunt	__ Uncle

__ Younger brother	__ Older brother	__ Twin brother
__ Younger half brother	__ Older half brother	__ Same age half brother
__ Younger adopted/step brother	__ Older adopted/step brother	__ Same age adopted/step brother
__ Younger foster brother	__ Older foster brother	__ Same age foster brother
__ Younger sister	__ Older sister	__ Twin sister
__ Younger half sister	__ Older half sister	__ Same age half sister
__ Younger adopted/step sister	__ Older adopted/step sister	__ Same age adopted/step sister
__ Younger foster sister	__ Older foster sister	__ Same age foster sister
__ Younger male cousin or nephew	__ Older male cousin or nephew	__ Same age male cousin or nephew
__ Younger female cousin or neice	__ Older female cousin or neice	__ Same age female cousin or neice
__ Other family member, older	__ Other family member, same age	__ Other family member, younger

__ Older female friend, more than 2 years older __ Older male friend, more than 2 years older

__ Same age female friend, within 2 years of your age __ Younger female friend, more than 2 years younger

__ Younger female friend, more than 4 years younger __ Younger female friend, more than 6 years younger

__ Same age male friend, within 2 years of your age __ Younger male friend, more than 2 years younger

__ Younger male friend, more than 4 years younger __ Younger male friend, more than 6 years younger

__ Older female friend, more than 2 years older __ Older male friend, more than 2 years older

__ Same age peers in treatment, within 2 years of your age __ Older peers in treatment more than 2 years older

__ Younger peers in treatment, more than 2 years younger __ Younger peers in treatment, more than 4 years younger

__ Cat __ Dog __ Other animal

29. Have you ever been sexually abused?

__ Yes __ No __ I'm not sure __ I don't want to answer this question

30. If you were ever sexually abused, by whom?
    __ I don't want to answer this question

Person: _____ Your Age: _____

Person: _____ Your Age: _____

Person: _____ Your Age: _____

Person: _____ Your Age: _____

Person: _____ Your Age: _____

Person: _____ Your Age: _____

Person: _____ Your Age: _____

Person: _____ Your Age: _____

Dimensions of Attachment Assessment Scale (DAAS)

1. Attachment Strength
Social Connection
(weak to strong, with pathological extremes)

Pathological Disconnected	Very Isolated	Somewhat Isolated	Cannot Assess	Somewhat Connected	Very Connected	Pathological Enmeshed
1	2	3	0	4	5	1

2. Attachment Security
Confidence in Relationships
(insecure to secure, with pathological extremes)

Pathological Paranoid	Very Uncertain	Somewhat Uncertain	Cannot Assess	Somewhat Confident	Very Confident	Pathological Grandiose
1	2	3	0	4	5	1

3. Attachment Experience
Subjective Experience in Relationships
(unsatisfying to satisfying, with pathological extremes)

Pathological Alienated	Very Unfulfilling	Somewhat Unfulfilling	Cannot Assess	Somewhat Fulfilling	Very Fulfilling	Pathological Unrestrained
1	2	3	0	4	5	1

4. Attachment Behaviors
Social Engagement
(distant to engaged, with pathological extremes)

Pathological Self-Serving	Very Self-Oriented	Somewhat Self-Oriented	Cannot Assess	Somewhat Mutually-Oriented	Very Mutually-Oriented	Pathological Preoccupied
1	2	3	0	4	5	1

5. Attachment Interest
Desire for Relationships
(disinterested to interested)

Pathological Schizoid	Very Unmotivated	Somewhat Unmotivated	Cannot Assess	Somewhat Motivated	Very Motivated	Pathological Expansive
1	2	3	0	4	5	1

Attachment Subscale Score	Overall Attachment Status	Consistency Across Attachment Subscales
__Strength	__Strong	__Consistent
__Security	__Moderate	__Variable
__Experience	__Weak	__Highly Variable
__Behaviors	__Pathological/Disturbed	
__Interest	__Cannot Assess	

Client: _____ Date Evaluated: _____

Evaluator: _____

Inventory for Attachment-Informed Analysis of Behaviors (IAAB)

1. Representation of Self . . . . .   *Sense of self, self image, self esteem, personal identity, etc.*
2. Self-Agency . . . .   *Sense of self as capable of acting upon the world and others.*
3. Self-Efficacy . . . .   *Sense of self as capable of satisfactorily accomplishing goals.*
4. Self-Regulation . . . .   *Capacity to contain and stabilize thoughts, emotions, and behaviors.*
5. Experienced Security . . . . . .   *Sense of security and trust in self and environment.*
6. Representation of Others . .   *Sense of others as reliable, trustworthy, caring, etc.*
7. Social Connectedness . . . . .   *Sense of belonging to social group larger than self.*
8. Parental Connectedness . . .   *Sense of connection to and relationship with parents.*
9. Parental Security/Model . . .   *Sense of parents as reliable, trustworthy, competent, caring, etc.*
10. Proximity Behaviors . . . .   *Organization of behaviors intended to maintain proximity to others.*
11. Signaling Behaviors . . . .   *Methods for expressing and communicating needs to others.*
12. Exploratory Behaviors . . . . .   *Level/type of risk taking behaviors when away from security figures.*
13. Capacity for Intimacy . . . . . .   *Ability to feel comfortable and engaged in intimate relationships.*
14. Empathic Connection . . . . .   *Vicarious understanding, concern, and support for others.*
15. Perspective Taking . . . .   *Ability to assume point of view of another person.*
16. Metacognition . . . .   *Capacity to recognize and reflect upon thoughts & feelings of self/others*
17. Goals of Behavior . . . .   *Purpose and drives behind sequences or patterns of behavior.*
18. Congruency of Social Norms   *Approval of/desire to conform with common social norms.*
19. Response to Social Norms .   *Capacity to meet social norms through legitimate means.*
20. Moral Decision Making . . . .   *Understanding and use of moral means to acquire goals.*

	Weak		Moderate		Strong
Representation of Self	1	2	3	4	5
Self-Agency	1	2	3	4	5
Self-Efficacy	1	2	3	4	5
Self-Regulation	1	2	3	4	5
Experienced Security	1	2	3	4	5
Representation of Others	1	2	3	4	5
Social Connectedness	1	2	3	4	5
Parental Connectedness	1	2	3	4	5
Parental Security/Model	1	2	3	4	5
Proximity Behaviors	1	2	3	4	5
Signaling Behaviors	1	2	3	4	5
Exploratory Behaviors	1	2	3	4	5
Capacity for Intimacy	1	2	3	4	5
Empathic Connection	1	2	3	4	5
Perspective Taking	1	2	3	4	5
Metacognition	1	2	3	4	5
Goals of Behavior	1	2	3	4	5
Congruency of Social Norms	1	2	3	4	5
Response to Social Norms	1	2	3	4	5
Moral Decision Making	1	2	3	4	5

Total Attachment-Related Behavior Score: _____
Weak = 20–46; Moderate = 47–73; Strong = 74–100

Client: _____   Date Evaluated:_____
Evaluator:_____

Attached Relationship Inventory (ARI)

1. Desire for Relationship	*Does the individual want or seek relationships with others?*
2. Importance of Relationships	*Does the individual see social relationships as important?*
3. Security in Relationships	*Do relationships enhance satisfaction and confidence rather than increase or produce anxiety or doubt?*
4. Security Through Relationships . . .	*Do relationships increase or enhance the individual's sense of self image and social connection?*
5. Confidence in Relationships.	*Does the individual believe that other parties in relationships can be trusted to and will care about and make his/her needs important?*
6. Confidence in Relationship-Building Skills	*Does the individual believe in his/her ability to form and maintain personal relationships?*
7. Perspective Taking.	*Does the individual have the capacity to recognize the needs, emotional states, attitudes, and thoughts of the other person in the relationship?*
8. Caring and Giving	*How giving is the individual with respect to recognizing and meeting the needs of other parties in the relationship?*
9. Reciprocal Mutuality	*Does the individual display mutuality and reciprocity in relationships (give and take), or just seek personal gratification (take and take)?*
10. Derived Satisfaction.	*Does the individual have insatiable relationship demands?*
11. Intimacy and Boundaries	*Is the individual capable of close and interdependent relationships without becoming possessive and incapable of separation?*
12. Relationship Independence	*Is the individual capable of close and interdependent without overdependence or enmeshment?*

	Minimal		*Moderate*		*Strong*
Desire for Relationship	1	2	3	4	5
Importance of Relationships	1	2	3	4	5
Security in Relationships	1	2	3	4	5
Security Through Relationships	1	2	3	4	5
Confidence in Relationships	1	2	3	4	5
Confidence in Relationship-Building Skills	1	2	3	4	5
Perspective Taking.	1	2	3	4	5
Caring and Giving	1	2	3	4	5
Reciprocal Mutuality	1	2	3	4	5
Derived Satisfaction.	1	2	3	4	5
Intimacy and Boundaries.	1	2	3	4	5
Relationship Independence.	1	2	3	4	5

Total Attachment Relationship Score: _____

Minimal = 12–27; Moderate = 28–44; Strong = 45–60

Client: _____ Date Evaluated: _____

Evaluator: _____

References

Abel, G. G., Jordan, A., Rouleau, J. L., Emerick, R., Barboza-Whitehead, S., & Osborn, C. (2004). Use of visual reaction time to assess male adolescents who molest children. *Sexual Abuse: A Journal of Research and Treatment, 16*, 255–265.

Ægisdóttir, S., White, M. J., Spengler, P. M., Maugherman, A. S., Anderson, L. A., Cook, R. S., et al. (2006). The meta-analysis of clinical judgment project: Fifty-six years of accumulated research on clinical versus statistical prediction. *The Counseling Psychologist, 34*, 341–382.

Agnew, R., & Passas, N. (1997). *The future of anomie theory.* Boston, MA: Northeastern University Press.

Alderson, P. (2004). Absence of evidence is not evidence of absence. *BMJ, 328*, 476–477.

Allan, M., Grace, R. C., Rutherford, B., & Hudson, S. M. (2007). Psychometric assessment of dynamic risk factors for child molesters. *Sexual Abuse: A Journal of Research and Treatment, 19*, 347–367.

Almond, L., & Canter, D. (2007). Youths who sexually harm: A multivariate model of behaviour. *Journal of Sexual Aggression, 13*, 217–233.

Almond, L., Canter, D., & Salfati, C. G. (2006). Youths who sexually harm: A multivariate model of characteristics. *Journal of Sexual Aggression, 12*, 97–114.

Altman, D. G., & Bland, J. M. (1995). Absence of evidence is not evidence of absence. *BMJ, 311*, 485.

American Academy of Child and Adolescent Psychiatry. (1999). Practice parameters for the assessment and treatment of children and adolescents who are sexually abusive of others. *Journal of the American Academy of Child and Adolescent Psychiatry, 38* (Suppl. December), 55S–76S.

American Academy of Pediatrics. (2001, August). Sexuality education for children and adolescents. *Pediatrics, 108*, 498–502.

American Academy of Pediatrics. (2001, November). Media violence. *Pediatrics, 108*, 1222–1226.

American Psychiatric Association. (1999). *Dangerous sex offenders: A Task Force Report of the American Psychiatric Association.* Washington, DC: Author.

American Psychiatric Association. (2000). *Diagnostic and statistical manual of mental disorders* (4th ed., Text Revision). Washington, DC: Author.

Andersen, S. L., Teicher, M. H. (2004). Delayed effects of early stress on hippocampal development. *Neuropsychopharmacology, 29*, 1988–1993.

442

Andersen, S. L., Tomoda, A., Vincow, E., Valenta, E., Polcari, A., & Teicher, M. (in press). Preliminary evidence for sensitive periods in the effect of childhood sexual abuse on regional brain development. *Journal of Neuropsychiatry and Clinical Neurosciences*.

Andrews, D. A., Bonta, J., & Hoge, R. D. (1990). Classification for effective rehabilitation: Rediscovering psychology. *Criminal Justice and Behavior, 17,* 19–52.

Andrews, D. A., Bonta, J., & Wormith, S. J. (2006). The recent past and near future of risk and/or need assessment. *Crime and Delinquency, 52,* 7–27.

Anthony, E. J. (1987). Risk, vulnerability, and resilience: An overview. In E. J. Anthony & B. J. Cohler (Eds.), *The invulnerable child* (pp. 3–48). New York: Guilford.

Araji, S. K. (2004). Preadolescents and adolescents: Evaluating normative and non-normative sexual behaviours and development. In G. O'Reilly, W. L. Marshall., A. Carr., & R. Beckett (Eds.), *The handbook of clinical intervention with young people who sexually abuse* (pp. 3–35). Hove, England: Brunner-Routledge.

Argyris, C., & Schön, D. A. (1974). *Theory in practice: developing professional effectiveness*. San Francisco: Jossey-Bass.

Asay, T. P., & Lambert, M. L. (1999). The empirical case for the common factors in therapy: Quantitative finding. In M. A. Hubble, B. L. Duncan, & S. D. Miller (Eds.), *The heart and soul of change: What works in therapy* (pp. 23–55). Washington, DC: American Psychological Association.

Association for the Treatment of Sexual Abusers. (1997). *Ethical standards and principles for the management of sexual abusers*. Beaverton, OR: Author.

Association for the Treatment of Sexual Abusers. (2000, March). *The effective legal management of juvenile sexual offenders*. (Position paper). Beaverton, OR: Author.

Association for the Treatment of Sexual Abusers. (2001). *Practice standards and guidelines for members of the Association for the Treatment of Sexual Abusers*. Beaverton, OR: Author.

Association for the Treatment of Sexual Abusers. (2005). *Practice standards and guidelines for members of the Association for the Treatment of Sexual Abusers for the evaluation, treatment, and management of adult male sexual abusers*. Beaverton, OR: Author.

Atkinson, L., & Goldberg, S. (2004). Applications of attachment: The integration of developmental and clinical traditions. In L. Atkinson & S. Goldberg (Eds.), *Attachment issues in psychopathology and intervention* (pp. 3–25). Mahwah, NJ: Erlbaum.

Baker, A. J. L., Tabacoff, R., Tornusciolo, G., & Eisenstadt, M. (2001). Calculating number of offenses and victims of juvenile sexual offending: The role of posttreatment disclosures. *Sexual Abuse: A Journal of Research and Treatment, 13,* 79–90.

Balbernie, R. (2001). Circuits and circumstances: The neurobiological consequences of early relationship experiences and how they shape behaviour. *Journal of Child Psychotherapy, 27,* 237–255.

Bancroft, J. (2006). Normal sexual development. In H. E. Barbaree, & W. L. Marshall (Eds.). *The juvenile sex offender* (2nd ed.; pp. 19–57). New York: Guilford.

Barker, R. L., & Branson, D. M. (2000). *Forensic social work: Legal aspects of professional practice* (2nd ed.). New York: Haworth Press.

Barr, R. G., Boyce, W. T., & Zeltzer, L. K. (1996). The stress-illness association in children: A perspective from the biobehavioral interface. In R. J. Haggerty, L. R. Sherrod, N. Garmezy, & M. Rutter (Eds.), *Stress, risk, and resilience in children and adolescents: Processes, mechanisms, and interventions* (pp. 182–224). Cambridge, England: Cambridge University Press.

Becker, J. V., & Harris, C. (2004). The psychophysiological assessment of juvenile offenders. In G. O'Reilly, W. L. Marshall, A. Carr, & R. Beckett (Eds.), *The handbook of clinical intervention with young people who sexually abuse* (pp. 191–202). Hove, England: Brunner-Routledge.

Beech, A., & Ward, T. (2004). The integration of etiology and risk in sexual offenders: A theoretical framework. *Aggression and Violent Behavior, 19,* 31–63.

Beech, A., & Ward, T. (2006, Summer). Risk assessment in the 21st Century: Towards an integrative model of risk. *The Forum, 18*(3), 1–13.

Beech, A. R., & Hamilton-Giachritsis, C. E. (2005). Relationship between therapeutic climate and treatment outcome in group-based sex offender treatment programs. *Sexual Abuse: A Journal of Research and Treatment, 17,* 127–140.

Behavior Data Systems. (1997). Sexual Adjustment Inventory SAI-Juvenile: Orientation and training manual. Phoenix, AZ: Author.

Belsky, J., & Nezworski, T. (1988). *Clinical implications of attachment.* Hillsdale, NJ: Erlbaum.

Berg, D. (2007, November). *Attachment style and isolation: Unique risk factors for adolescent child molesters.* Paper presented at the 26th Conference of the Association for the Treatment of Sexual Abusers, San Diego, CA.

Bjork, J. M., Knutson, B., Fong, G. W., Caggiano, D. M. Bennett, S. M. Hommer, D. W. (2004). Incentive-elicited brain activation in adolescents: Similarities and differences from young adults. *The Journal of Neuroscience, 24,* 1793–1802.

Bluglass, R. (1990). The scope of forensic psychiatry. *Journal of Forensic Psychiatry, 1,* 5–9.

Boer, D. P. (2006). Sexual offender risk assessment strategies: Is there a convergence of opinion yet? *Sexual Offender Treatment, 1*(2), 1–4.

Boer, D. P., Hart, S. D., Kropp, P. R., & Webster, C. D. (1997). *Manual for the Sexual Violence Risk-20.* Burnaby, British Columbia, Canada: The Mental Health, Law, & Policy Institute, Simon Fraser University.

Boer, D. P., McVilly, K. R., & Lambrick, F. (2007). Contextualizing risk in the assessment of intellectually disabled individuals. *Sexual Offender Treatment, 2*(2). Retrieved December 2007 from http://www.sexual-offender-treatment.org/index.php?id=59&type=123.

Bonner, B. L., Walker, C. E., & Berliner, L. (1999). *Children with sexual behavior problems: Assessment and treatment—final report.* (Grant No. 90-CA-1469).

Washington, DC: U.S. Department of Health and Human Services, National Center on Child Abuse and Neglect.

Bonta, J. (2002). Offender risk assessment: Guidelines for selection and use. *Criminal Justice and Behavior, 29*, 355–379.

Bonta, J., & Andrews, D. A. (2007). *Risk-Need-Responsivity model for offender assessment and rehabilitation.* (User Report No. 2007–06). Ottawa, Canada: Public Safety and Emergency Preparedness Canada.

Borum, R. (1996). Improving the clinical practice of violence risk assessment: Technology, guidelines, and training. *American Psychologist, 51*, 945–956.

Borum, R., Bartel, P. & Forth, A. (2002). *Manual for the Structured Assessment of Violence in Youth (SAVRY)*: Tampa, FL: Department of Mental Health Law & Policy, University of South Florida.

Bowlby, J. (1973). *Attachment and loss, Vol. 2: Separation: Anxiety and anger.* New York: Basic Books.

Bremer, J. (2006a). Building resilience: An ally in assessment and treatment. In D. S. Prescott (Ed.), *Risk assessment of youth who have sexually abused* (pp. 87–99). Oklahoma City, OK: Wood N' Barnes.

Bremer, J. (2006b). Protective Factors Scale: Determining the level of intervention for youth with harmful sexual behavior. In D. S. Prescott (Ed.), *Risk assessment of youth who have sexually abused* (pp. 195–221). Oklahoma City, OK: Wood N' Barnes.

Bronfenbrenner. U. (1979). *The ecology of human development: Experiments in human behavior.* Cambridge, MA: Harvard University Press.

Brown, J. D., Halpern, C. T., & L'Engle, C. L. (2005). Mass media as a sexual super peer for early maturing girls. *Journal of Adolescent Health, 36*, 420–427.

Brown, J. D., & Keller, S. N. (2000, September/October). Can the mass media be healthy sex educators? *Family Planning Perspectives, 32*, 255–256.

Bruner, J. (1996). *The culture of education.* Cambridge, MA: Harvard University Press.

Bumby, K., Carter, M., Talbot, T., & Gilligan, L. (2007, July). *The Comprehensive Assessment Protocol: A systemwide review of adult and juvenile sexual offender management strategies.* Silver Spring, MD: Center for Sex Offender Management.

Burton, D. L. (2000). Were adolescent sexual offenders children with sexual behavior problems? *Sexual Abuse: A Journal of Research and Treatment, 12*, 37–48.

Burton, D. L., & Smith-Darden, J. (2001). *North American Survey of Sexual Abuser Treatment Models: Summary Data 2000.* Brandon, VT: Safer Society Press.

Calder, M. C. (2000). The comprehensive assessment of juveniles who sexually abuse. In M. C. Calder (Ed.), *The complete guide to sexual abuse assessments* (pp. 73–88). Dorset, England: Russell House Publishing.

Calder, M. C. (2001). *Juveniles and children who sexually abuse: Frameworks for assessment* (2nd ed.). Dorset, England: Russell House Publishing.

Caldwell, M. F. (2002). What we do not know about juvenile sexual reoffense risk. *Child Maltreatment, 7*, 291–302.

Caldwell, M. F. (2007). Sexual offense adjudication and sexual recidivism among juvenile offenders. *Sexual Abuse: A Journal of Research and Treatment, 19*, 107–113.

California Department of Mental Health (2008, February). SARATSO (State Authorized Risk Assessment Tool for Sex Offenders) Review Committee Notification. Retrieved March 2008, from http://www.dmh.ca.gov/Services _and_Programs/Forensic_Services/Sex_Offender_Commitment_Program/ docs/SARATSO_Info_Notice_1.pdf.

Campbell, T. W. (2000). Sexual predator evaluations and phrenology: Considering issues of evidentiary reliability. *Behavioral Science and the Law, 18*, 111–130.

Campbell, T. W. (2004). *Assessing sex offenders: Problems and pitfalls.* Springfield, IL: Charles C. Thomas.

Cantwell, H. B. (1995). Sexually aggressive children and societal response. In M. Hunter (Ed.), *Child survivors and perpetrators of sexual abuse: Treatment innovations* (pp. 79–107). Thousand Oaks, CA: Sage.

Carpenter, D. R., Peed, S. F., & Eastman, B. (1995). Person characteristics of adolescent sexual offenders: A pilot study. *Sexual Abuse: A Journal of Research and Treatment, 7*, 195–203.

Carpentier, M. Y., Silovsky, J., & Chaffin, M. (2006a). Randomized trial of treatment for children with sexual behavior problems: Ten-year follow-up. *Journal of Consulting & Clinical Psychology, 72*, 482–488.

Carpentier, M., Silovsky, J., & Chaffin, M. (2006b, Fall). Treating children: Results from a 10-year follow-up. *The Forum, 18*(4), 2–18.

Catalano, R. F., Haggerty, K. P., Oesterle, S., Fleming, C. B., & Hawkins, J. D. (2004). The importance of bonding to school for healthy development: Findings from the Social Development Research Group. *Journal of School Health, 74*, 252–261.

Catchpole, E. H., & Gretton, H. M. (2003). The predictive validity of risk assessment with violent young offenders: A one-year examination of criminal outcome. *Criminal Justice and Behavior, 30*, 688–708.

Chaffin, M., Berliner, L., Block, R., Johnson, T. C., Friedrich, W., Louis, D., Lyon, T. D., Page, J., Prescott, D., & Silovsky, J. F. (2006). *Association for the Treatment of Sexual Abusers Task Force Report on Children with Sexual Behavior Problems.* Beaverton, OR: ATSA.

Chaffin, M., Letourneau, E., & Silovsky, J. F. (2002). Adults, adolescents, and children who sexually abuse children: A developmental perspective. In J. E. B. Myers & L. Berliner (Eds.), *APSAC handbook on child maltreatment* (2nd ed.; pp. 205–232). Thousand Oaks, CA: Sage.

Christodoulides, T. E., Richardson, G., Graham, F., Kennedy, P. J., & Kelly, T. P. (2005). Risk assessment with adolescent sexual offenders. *Journal of Sexual Aggression, 11*, 37–48.

Coffey, P. (2006). Forensic issues in evaluating juvenile sexual offenders. In D. S. Prescott (Ed.), *Risk assessment of youth who have sexually abused* (pp. 75–86). Oklahoma City, OK: Wood N' Barnes.

Colorado Department of Public Safety. (2002). *Colorado sex offender management board standards and guidelines for the evaluation, assessment, treatment and supervision of juveniles who have committed sexual offenses.* Denver, CO: Author.

Commission on Children at Risk. (2003). *Hardwired to connect.* New York: Institute for American Values.

Consortium on the School-based Promotion of Social Competence. (1996). The school-based promotion of social competence: Theory, research, practice, and policy. In R. J. Haggerty, L. R. Sherrod, N. Garmezy, & M. Rutter (Eds.), *Stress, risk, and resilience in children and adolescents: Processes, mechanisms, and interventions* (pp. 268–316). Cambridge, England: Cambridge University Press.

Courchesne, E., Chisum, H. J., Townsend, J., Cowles, A., Covington, J., Egaas, B., et al. (2000). Normal brain development and aging: Quantitative analysis at in vivo MR imaging in healthy volunteers. *Radiology 2000, 216,* 672–682.

Craig, L. A., Browne, K. D., Stringer, I., & Beech, A. (2004). Limitations in actuarial risk assessment of sexual offenders: A methodological note. *British Journal of Forensic Practice, 6,* 16–32.

Craig, L. A., Thornton, D., Beech, A., & Browne, K. D. (2007). The relationship of statistical and psychological risk markers to sexual reconviction in child molesters. *Criminal Justice and Behavior, 34,* 314–329.

Craig, R. A. (1998). The use of physiological measures to detect deception in juveniles: Possible cognitive developmental influences. *Dissertation Abstracts International: Section B: The Sciences and Engineering. 58*(10-B). (AAT No. 9812967).

Craik, K. J. W. (1952). *The nature of explanation.* Cambridge, England: Cambridge University Press.

Craissati, J., & Beech, A. (2003). A review of dynamic variables and their relationship to risk prediction in sex offenders. *Journal of Sexual Aggression, 9,* 41–55.

Cummings, G. F., & McGrath, R. J. (2005). *Supervision of the sex offender: Community management, risk assessment, and treatment* (2nd ed.). Brandon, VT: Safer Society Press.

Curwen, T. (2006). *Differentiating children with and without a history of repeated sexual behaviours following adult reprimand.* Unpublished doctoral dissertation. University of Toronto, Ontario.

Curwen, T. (2007, July). *Assessing risk for continued sexual behaviour problems by children.* Paper presented at the International Family Violence and Child Victimization Research Conference, Portsmouth, NH.

Curwen, T., & Costin, D. (2007). Toward assessing risk for repeated sexual behaviour by children with sexual behaviour problems: What we know and what we can do with this knowledge. In D. S. Prescott (Ed.), *Knowledge and practice: Challenges in the treatment and supervision of sexual abusers* (pp. 310–344). Oklahoma City, OK: Wood N' Barnes.

Daversa, M., & Knight, R. A. (2007). A structural examination of the predictors of sexual coercion against children in adolescent sexual offenders. *Criminal Justice and Behavior, 34,* 1313–1333.

D'Orazio, D. (2002). *A comparative analysis of empathy in sexually offending and non-offending juvenile and adult males.* Unpublished doctoral dissertation, California School of Professional Psychology at Alliant University, Fresno.

Doren, D. M. (2002). *Evaluating sex offenders: A manual for civil commitments and beyond.* Thousand Oaks, CA: Sage.

Douglas, K. S., Cox, D. N., Webster, C. D. (1999). Violence risk assessment: Science and practice. *Legal and Criminological Psychology, 4,* 149–184.

Drake, C. R., & Ward, T. (2003). Practical and theoretical roles for the formulation based treatment of sexual offenders. *International Journal of Forensic Psychology, 1,* 71–84.

Drake, C. R., Ward, T., Nathan, P., and Lee, J. K. P. (2001). Challenging the cognitive distortions of child molesters: An implicit theory approach. *The Journal of Sexual Aggression, 7,* 25–40.

Durkheim, E. (1893). *The division of labor in society.* New York: The Free Press.

Durkheim, E. (1897). *Suicide: A study in sociology.* New York: The Free Press.

Eaton, D. K., Kann, L., Kinchen, S., Ross, J., Hawkins, J., Harris, W. A., et al. (2006, June). Youth risk behavior surveillance – United States, 2005. *Morbidity and Mortality Weekly Report Surveillance Summaries 55, No. SS-5.* Atlanta, GA: Centers for Disease Control and Prevention.

Efta-Breitbach, J., & Freeman, K. A. (2004). Recidivism, resilience, and treatment effectiveness for youth who sexually offend. In R. Geffner, K. C. Franey, T. G. Arnold, & R. Falconer (Eds.), *Identifying and treating youth who sexually offend: Current approaches, techniques, and research* (pp. 257–279). Binghamton, NY: Haworth Press.

Elliot, D. S., Williams, K. R., & Hamburg, B. (1998). An integrated approach to violence prevention. In D. S. Elliot, B. A. Hamburg, & K. R. Williams (Eds.), *Violence in American schools: A new perspective* (pp. 379–386). Cambridge, England: Cambridge University Press.

Emerick, R. L., & Dutton, W. A. (1993). The effect of polygraphy on the self report of adolescent sex offenders: Implications for risk assessment. *Sexual Abuse: A Journal of Research and Treatment, 6,* 83–103.

Epperson, D. L. (2007, October). *Development, reliability, validity, and scoring of the JSORRAT-II.* Workshop presented at the 26th Annual Conference of the Association for the Treatment of Sexual Abusers, San Diego, CA.

Epperson, D. L., Ralston, C. A., Fowers, D., & DeWitt, J. (2004). *Juvenile sexual recidivism into adulthood: A long-term study of characteristics and predictors.* Workshop presented at the 24th Annual Conference of the Association for the Treatment of Sexual Abusers, Albuquerque, NM.

Epperson, D. L., Ralston, C. A., Fowers, D., DeWitt, J., & Gore, K. S. (2006). Actuarial risk assessment with juveniles who sexually offend: Development of the Juvenile Sexual Offense Recidivism Risk Assessment Tool-II (JSORRAT-II-II). In D. S. Prescott (Ed.), *Risk assessment of youth who have sexually abused* (pp. 118–169) Oklahoma City, OK: Wood N' Barnes.

Epps, K. J. (1997). Managing risk. In M. S. Hoghughi (Ed.), *Working with sexually abusive adolescents* (pp. 35–51). Thousand Oaks, CA: Sage.

Epstein, R. (2007). *The case of adolescence: Rediscovering the adult in every teen.* Sanger, CA: Quill Driver Books.

Fanniff, A. M., & Becker. J. V. (2006). Specialized assessment and treatment of adolescent sex offenders. *Aggression and Violent Behavior, 11*, 265–282.

Farrington, D. P. (1997). Early prediction of violent and nonviolent youthful offending. *European Journal on Criminal Policy and Research, 5*(2), 51–56.

Farrington, D. P. (2000). Explaining and preventing crime: The globalization of knowledge—The American Society of Criminology 1999 Presidential Address. *Criminology, 38*, 1–24.

Fernandez, Y. M., & Serran, G. (2002). Empathy training for therapists & clients. In Y. Fernandez (Ed.), *In their shoes* (pp. 110–131). Oklahoma City, OK: Wood N' Barnes Publishing.

Fonagy, P. (1999a). Male perpetrators of violence against women: An attachment theory perspective. *Journal of Applied Psychoanalytic Studies, 1*, 7–27.

Fonagy, P. (1999b). Psychoanalytic theory from the viewpoint of attachment theory and research. In J. Cassidy & P. R. Shaver (Eds.), *Handbook of attachment: Theory, research, and clinical application* (pp. 595–624). New York: Guilford Press.

Fonagy, P. (2004). The developmental roots of violence in the failure of mentalization. In F. Pfafflin & G. Adshead (Eds.), *A matter of security: The application of attachment theory to forensic psychiatry and psychotherapy* (pp. 13–56). London: Jessica Kingsley Publishers.

Ford, M. E., & Linney, J. A. (1995). Comparative analysis of juvenile sexual offenders, violent nonsexual offenders, and status offenders. *Journal of Interpersonal Violence, 10*, 56–70.

Forth, A. E., Kosson, D. S., & Hare, R. D. (2003). *Hare PCL: Youth Version. Techincal Manual.* North Tonawanda, NY: Multi-Health Systems (MHS).

Fortune, C., & Lambie, I. (2006). Sexually abusive youth: A review of recidivism studies and methodological issues for future research. *Clinical Psychology Review, 26*, 1078–1095.

France, K. & Hudson, S. M. (1993). The conduct disorders and the juvenile sexual offender. In H. E. Barbaree, W. L. Marshall, & S. M. Hudson (Eds.), *The juvenile sex offender* (pp. 225–234). New York: Guilford.

Frick, P. J. (2002). Juvenile psychopathy from a developmental perspective: Implications for construct development and use in forensic assessments. *Law and Human Behavior, 26*, 247–253.

Frick, P. J., Cornell, A. H., Barry, C. T., Bodin, S. D., & Dane, H. A. (2003a). Callous-unemotional traits and conduct problems in the prediction of conduct severity, aggression, and self-report of delinquency. *Journal of Abnormal Child Development, 31*, 457–470.

Frick, P. J., Cornell, A. H., Bodin, S. D., Dane, H. A., Barry, C. T., & Loney, B. R. (2003b). Callous-unemotional traits and developmental pathways to severe aggressive and antisocial behavior. *Developmental Psychology, 39*, 246–260.

Garmezy, N. (1987). Stress, competence, and development: Continuities in the study of schizophrenic adults, children vulnerable to psychopathology, and the search for stress-resistant children. *American Journal of Orthopsychiatry, 57,* 159–174.

Garmezy, N. (1990). A closing note: Reflections on the future. In J. Rolf, A. Masten, D. Cicchetti, K. Nuechterlein, & S. Weintraub (Eds.), *Risk and protective factors in the development of psychopathology* (pp. 527–534). New York: Cambridge University Press.

Garmezy, N. (1996). Reflections and commentary on risk, resilience, and development. In R. J. Haggerty, L. R. Sherrod, N. Garmezy, & M. Rutter (Eds.), *Stress, risk, and resilience in children and adolescents: Processes, mechanisms, and interventions* (pp. 1–18). Cambridge, England: Cambridge University Press.

Gendreau, P., Little, T., & Goggin, C. (1996). A meta-analysis of the predictors of adult offender recidivism: What works! *Criminology, 34,* 575–608.

Giedd J. N. (2002). *Inside the Teenage Brain.* Retrieved December 2004, from http://www.pbs.org/wgbh/pages/frontline/shows/teenbrain/interviews/

Giedd J. N. (2004). Structural magnetic resonance imaging of the adolescent brain. In R. E. Dahl & L. P. Spear (Eds.), *Adolescent brain development: Vulnerabilities and opportunities* (pp. 77–85). New York: Annals of the New York Academy of Sciences.

Gilgun, J. F. (1999). CASPARS: Clinical assessment instruments that measure strengths and weaknesses in children and families. In M. C. Calder (Ed.), *Working with young people who sexually abuse: New pieces of the jigsaw puzzle* (pp. 50–58). Dorset, England: Russell House Publishing.

Gilgun, J. F., Klein, C., & Pranis, K. (2000). The significance of resources in models of risk. *The Journal of Interpersonal Violence, 14,* 627–646.

Gilligan, C., & Wiggins, G. (1987). The origins of morality in early childhood relationships. In J. Kagan & S. Lamb (Eds.), *The emergence of morality in young children* (pp. 277–305). Chicago, IL: University of Chicago Press.

Girón, M., Manjón-Arce, P., Puerto-Barber, J., Sánchez-Garciá, E., & Gómez-Beneyto, M. (1998). Clinical interview skills and identification of emotional disorders in primary care. *American Journal of Psychiatry, 155,* 530–535.

Glasgow, D. (2003). *The Affinity 2.0 Manual.* Author: David@dvglasgow.wanadoo.co.uk.

Gore, S., & Eckenrode, J. (1996). Context and process in research on risk and resilience. In R. J. Haggerty, L. R. Sherrod, N. Garmezy, & M. Rutter (Eds.), *Stress, risk, and resilience in children and adolescents: Processes, mechanisms, and interventions* (pp. 19–63). Cambridge, England: Cambridge University Press.

Graham, F., Richardson G., & Bhate, S. (1997). Assessment. In M. S. Hoghughi (Ed.), *Working with sexually abusive adolescents* (pp. 52–91). Thousand Oaks, CA: Sage.

Greenberg, L. S., & Watson, J. C. (2005). What qualifies as research on which to base effective practice? In J. C. Norcross, L. E. Beutler, & R. E. Levant (Eds.), *Evidence-based practices in mental health: Debate and dialogue on the fundamental questions* (57–130). Washington, DC: American Psychological Association.

Greenberg, S. A., & Shuman, D. W. (1999). Irreconcilable conflict between therapeutic and forensic roles. In D. N. Bersoff (Ed.), *Ethical conflicts in psychology* (2nd ed.) (pp. 513–520). Washington, DC: American Psychological Association.

Grisso, T. (1998). *Forensic evaluation of juveniles.* Sarasota, FL: Professional Resource Press.

Grisso, T. (2000, March). Ethical issues in evaluations for sex offender re-offending. Invited address presented at Sinclair Seminars, Madison, WI.

Grisso, T. (2006). Foreword. In S. N. Sparta & G. P. Koocher (Eds.), *Forensic mental health assessment of children and adolescents* (pp. vii–x). New York: Oxford University Press.

Grove, W. M. (2005). Clinical versus statistical prediction: The contribution of Paul E. Meehl. *Journal of Clinical Psychology, 61,* 1233–1243.

Grove, W. M., & Lloyd, M. (2006). Meehl's contribution to clinical versus statistical prediction. *Journal of Abnormal Psychology, 115,* 192–194.

Grove, W. M., & Meehl, P. E. (1996). Comparative efficiency of informal (subjective, impressionistic) and formal (mechanical, algorithmic) prediction procedures: The clinical-statistical controversy. *Psychology, Public, Policy, and Law, 2,* 229–323.

Grove, W. M., Zald, D. H., Lebow, B. S., Snitz, B. E., & Nelson, C. (2000). Clinical versus mechanical prediction: A meta-analysis. *Psychological Assessment, 12,* 19–30.

Grubin, D. (1998). *Sex offending against children: Understanding the risk.* Police Research Series, Paper 99. Home Office Policing and Reducing Crime Unit Research, Development and Statistics Directorate.

Gudas, L. S., & Sattler, J. M. (2006). Forensic interviewing of children and adolescents. In S. N. Sparta & G. P. Koocher (Eds.), *Forensic mental health assessment of children and adolescents* (pp. 115–128). New York: Oxford University Press.

Guttmacher Institute. (2006, September). *U. S. teenage pregnancy statistics and state trends by race and ethnicity.* New York: Author.

Hagan, M. P., & Gust-Brey, K. L. (1999). A ten-year longitudinal study of adolescent rapists upon return to the community. *International Journal of Offender Therapy and Comparative Criminology, 43,* 448–458.

Hagan, M. P., Gust-Brey, K. L., Cho, M. E., & Dow, E. (2001). Eight-year comparative analyses of adolescent rapists, adolescent child molesters, other adolescent delinquents, and the general population. *International Journal of Offender Therapy and Comparative Criminology, 45,* 314–324.

Haggerty, R. J., & Sherrod, L. R. (1996). Preface. In R. J. Haggerty, L. R. Sherrod, N. Garmezy, & M. Rutter (Eds.), *Stress, risk, and resilience in children and adolescents: Processes, mechanisms, and interventions* (pp. xiii–xxi). Cambridge, England: Cambridge University Press.

Hall, D. K., Matthews, F., & Pearce, J. (1998). Factors associated with sexual behavior problems in young sexually abused children. *Child Abuse & Neglect, 22,* 1045–1063.

Hall, D. K., Matthews, F., & Pearce, J. (2002). Sexual behavior problems in sexually abused children: A preliminary typology. *Child Abuse & Neglect, 26,* 289–312.

Hamilton, B. E., Martin, J. A., & Ventura, S. J. (2007). Births: Preliminary data for 2006. *National Vital Statistics Reports 56* (7). Hyattsville, MD: National Center for Health Statistics.

Hannah-Moffat, K., & Maurutto, P. (2003, April). *Youth risk/need assessment: An overview of issues and practices.* Ottawa, Canada: Department of Justice Canada, Youth Justice Policy, Research and Statistics Division.

Hanson, R. K., (1997). *The development of a brief actuarial risk scale for sexual offense recidivism.* Ottawa, Canada: Department of the Solicitor General of Canada.

Hanson, R. K. (2000, January). *Risk assessment.* Beaverton, OR: Association for the Treatment of Sexual Abusers.

Hanson, R. K. (2002). Introduction to the special section on dynamic risk assessment with sex offenders. *Sexual Abuse: A Journal of Research and Treatment, 14,* 99–101.

Hanson, R. K., & Bussière, M. T. (1998). Predicting relapse: A meta-analysis of sexual offender recidivism studies. *Journal of Consulting and Clinical Psychology, 66*(2), 348–362.

Hanson, R. K., & Harris, A. (2000a). A. (User Report No. 2000–01). Ottawa, Canada: Department of the Solicitor General of Canada.

Hanson, R. K., & Harris, A. (2000b). Where should we intervene? Dynamic predictors of sexual offender recidivism. *Criminal Justice and Behavior, 27,* 6–35.

Hanson, R. K., & Morton-Bourgon, K. E. (2005). The characteristics of persistent sexual offenders: A meta-analysis of recidivism studies. *Journal of Consulting and Clinical Psychology, 6,* 1154–1163.

Hanson, R. K., & Morton-Bourgon, K. E. (2007). *The accuracy of recidivism risk assessments for sexual offenders: A meta-analysis.* (User Report 2007–01). Ottawa, Canada: Public Safety and Emergency Preparedness Canada.

Hanson, R. K., & Thornton, D. (1999). *Static 99: Improving actuarial risk assessment for sex offenders.* Ottawa, Canada: Department of the Solicitor General of Canada.

Hanson, R. K., & Thornton, D. (2000). Improving risk assessments for sex offenders: A comparison of three actuarial scales. *Law and Human Behavior, 24,* 119–136.

Hare, R. D. (1999). *Without conscience: The disturbing world of psychopaths among us.* New York: Guilford.

Harkins, L., & Beech, A. (2007a). A review of the factors that can influence the effectiveness of sexual offender treatment: Risk, need, responsivity, and process issues. *Aggression and Violent Behavior, 12,* 615–627.

Harkins, L., & Beech, A. (2007b). Measurement of the effectiveness of sex offender treatment. *Aggression and Violent Behavior, 12,* 36–44.

Harris, A., & Hanson, R. K. (2003, August). The dynamic supervision project: Improving community supervision of sexual offenders. *Corrections Today, 65*(5), 60–62.

Harris, A., & Hanson, R. K. (2007, Fall). STABLE-2007 & ACUTE-2007: Improving the assessment of dynamic risk potential. *The Forum, 19*(4), 4–7.

Harris, A., Phenix, A., Hanson, R. K., & Thornton D. (2003). *STATIC-99 Coding Rules: Revised - 2003*. Ottawa, Canada: Department of the Solicitor General of Canada.

Harris, G., & Rice, M. (2007). Characterizing the Value of Actuarial Violence Risk Assessments. *Criminal Justice and Behavior, 34*, 1638–1658.

Hart, S. D. (1998). The role of psychopathy in assessing risk for violence: Conceptual and methodological issues. *Legal and Criminological Psychology, 3*, 123–140.

Hart, S. D., Kropp. P. R., Laws, R. D., Klaver, J., Logan, C., & Watt, K. A. (2003). *The risk for sexual violence protocol (RSVP): Structured professional guidelines for assessing risk of sexual violence*. British Columbia, Canada: The Mental Health, Law, & Policy Institute, Simon Fraser University.

Hart, S. D., Michie, C., & Cooke, D. J. (2007). Precision of actuarial risk assessment instruments: Evaluating the "margins of error" of group v. individual predictions of violence. *British Journal of Psychiatry, 190 (suppl. 49)*, s60–s65.

Hart, S. D., Watt, K. A., & Vincent, G. M. (2002). Commentary on Seagrave and Grisso: Impressions of the state of the art. *Law and Human Behavior, 26*, 241–246.

Hawkins, J. D., Herrenkohl. T. I., Farrington, D. P., Brewer, D., Catalano, R. F., Harachi, T. W., et al. (2000, April). *OJJDP Juvenile Justice Bulletin: Predictors of Youth Violence*. Washington, DC: U.S. Department of Justice, Office of Justice Programs.

Hayslett-McCall, K. L., & Bernard, T. J. (2002). Attachment, masculinity, and self-control: A theory of male crime rates. *Theoretical Criminology, 6*, 5–33.

Henry, B., Caspi, A., Moffitt, T. E., & Silva. P. A. (1996). Temperamental and familial predictors of violent and nonviolent criminal convictions: Age 3 to age 18. *Developmental Psychology, 32*, 614–623.

Hilton, N. Z., Carter, A. M., Harris, G. T., & Sharpe, A. J. B. (2008). Does using nonnumerical terms to describe risk aid violence risk communication? Clinician agreement and decision-making. *Journal of Interpersonal Violence, 23*, 171–188.

Hirschi, T. (2002). *Causes of delinquency*. New Brunswick, NJ: Transaction Publishers.

Hiscox, S. P., Witt, P. H., & Haran, S. J., (2007). Juvenile Risk Assessment Scale (JRAS): A predictive validity study. *The Journal of Psychiatry & Law, 35*, 503–539.

Hoff, T., Greene, L., & Davis, J. (2003). *National survey of adolescents and young adults: Sexual health knowledge, attitudes and experiences*. Menblo Park, CA: Kaiser Family Foundation.

Hoffman, M. L. (2000). *Empathy and moral development: Implications for caring and justice*. Cambridge, England: Cambridge University Press.

Hoge, R. D. (2002). Standardized assessment instruments for assessing risk and need in youthful offenders. *Criminal Justice and Behavior, 29*, 380–396.

Hoge, R. D., & Andrews, D. A. (1996). *Assessing the youthful offender: Issues and techniques*. New York: Plenum Press.

Hoge, R. D., & Andrews, D. A. (2003). *Youth Level of Service/Case Management Inventory: User's manual*. North Tonawanda, NY: Multi-Health Systems.

Houston, J. (1998). *Making sense with offenders: Personal constructs, therapy and change*. Chicester, England: John Wiley.

Howell, D. (1995, May). *Guide for implementing the comprehensive strategy for serious, violent, and chronic juvenile offenders*. Washington, DC: U.S. Department of Justice Office for Juvenile Justice and Delinquency Prevention.

Hsu, L. K. G., & Starzynski, J. (1990). Adolescent rapist and adolescent child sexual assaulters. *International Journal of Offender Therapy and Comparative Criminology, 34*, 23–30.

Hudson, S. M., & Ward, T. (2000). Interpersonal competency in sex offenders. *Behavior Modification, 24*, 494–527.

Hudson, S. M., & Ward, T. (2001). Adolescent sexual offenders: Assessment and treatment. In C. R. Hollin (Ed.), *Handbook of offender assessment and treatment* (pp. 363–377). Chicester, England: John Wiley.

Hunter, J. A., (2000). Understanding juvenile offenders: Research findings & guidelines for effective management & treatment. *Juvenile Justice Fact Sheet*. Charlottesville, VA: Institute of Law, Psychiatry, & Public Policy, University of Virginia.

Hunter, J. A., Figueredo, A. J., Malamuth, N. M., & Becker, J. V. (2003). Juvenile sex offenders: Toward the development of a typology. *Sexual Abuse: A Journal of Research and Treatment, 15*, 27–48.

Hunter, J. A., Hazelwood, R. R., & Slesinger, D. (2000). Juvenile-perpetrated sex crimes: Patterns of offending and predictors of violence. *Journal of Family Violence, 15*, 81–93.

Hunter, J. A., & Lexier (1998). Ethical and legal treatment issues in the assessment and treatment of juvenile sexual offenders. *Child Maltreatment, 3*, 339–348.

Huston, A. C., Wartella, E., & Donnerstein, E. (1998, May). *Measuring the effects of sexual content in the media: A report to the Kaiser Family Foundation*. Menlo Park, CA: The Henry J. Kaiser Family Foundation.

Jacobs, W. L., Kennedy, W. A., & Meyer, J. B. (1997). Juvenile delinquents: A between-group comparison study of sexual and nonsexual offenders. *Sexual Abuse: A Journal of Research and Treatment, 9*, 201–217.

Jessor, R., Van Den Bos, J., Vanderryn, J., Costa, F. M., & Turbin, M. S. (1995). Protective factors in adolescent problem behavior: Moderator effects and developmental change. *Developmental Psychology, 31*, 923–933.

Johnson, T. C. (1999). *Understanding your child's sexual behavior: What's natural and healthy*. Oakland, CA: New Harbinger Publications.

Johnson, T. C. (2000, October/November). Sexualized children and children who molest. *Siecus Report, 29*(1), 35–39.

Johnson, T. C. (2001, August). Understanding the sexual behaviours of children— II. *CYC-Online, Issue 31*. Retrieved February 2008 from www.cyc-net.org/cyc-online/cycol-0801-toni2.html.

Johnson, T. C. (2002). Some considerations about sexual abuse and children with sexual behavior problems. *Journal of Trauma & Dissociation, 3*, 83–105.

Johnson-Laird, P. N. (1983). *Mental models: Towards a cognitive science of language, inference, and consciousness.* Harvard, MA: Harvard University Press.

Jung, S., & Rawana, E. P. (1999). Risk and need assessment of juvenile offenders. *Criminal Justice and Behavior, 26,* 69–89.

Kagan, J. (1984). *The nature of the child.* New York: Basic Books.

Kahn, T. J., & Chambers, H. J. (1991). Assessing reoffense risk with juvenile sexual offenders. *Child Welfare, 70,* 333–345.

Kann, L., Kinchen, S. A., Williams, B. I., Ross, J. G., Lowry, R., Hill, C. V., Grunbaum, J. A., Blumson, P. S., Collins, J. L., & Kolbe, L. J. (1998, August 14). Youth Risk Behavior Surveillance: United States, 1997. *CDC Surveillance Summaries, MMWR 1998;47 (No. SS-3),* 1–89.

Kemper, T. S., & Kistner, J. A. (2007). Offense history and recidivism in three victim-age-based groups of juvenile sex offenders. *Sexual Abuse: A Journal of Research and Treatment, 19,* 409–427.

Kirby, J. (2001, May). *Emerging answers: Research findings on programs to reduce teen pregnancy (summary).* Washington, DC: National Campaign to Prevent Teen Pregnancy.

Kirby, D. (2001, November/December) Understanding what works and what doesn't in reducing adolescent sexual risk-taking. *Family Planning Perspectives, 33,* 276–281.

Knight, R. A., & Sims-Knight, J. E. (2003). The developmental antecedents of sexual coercion against women: Testing alternative hypotheses with structural equation modeling. In R. A. Prentky, E. S. Janus, & M. C. Seto (Eds.), *Sexually coercive behavior: Understanding and management: Vol. 989. Annals of the New York Academy of Sciences* (pp. 72–85). New York: The New York Academy of Sciences.

Knight, R. A., & Sims-Knight, J. (2004). Testing an etiological model for male juvenile sexual offending against females. In R. Geffner, K. C. Franey, T. G. Arnold, & R. Falconer (Eds.), *Identifying and treating youth who sexually offend: Current approaches, techniques, and research* (pp. 33–55). Binghampton, NY: Haworth Press.

Kohlberg, L. (1976). Moral; stages and moralization: The cognitive-developmental approach. In T. Lickona (Ed.), *Moral development and behavior: Theory, research and social issues* (pp. 31–53). New York: Holt, Rinehart, and Winston.

Krueger, J. (2007, May). Research Bulletin: Sex *offender populations, recidivism and actuarial assessment.* New York State Division of Probation and Correctional Alternatives. Retrieved November 2007 from http://dpca.state.ny.us/pdfs/somgmtbulletinaugust2007.pdf.

Krueger, J. (2007, August). *Research Bulletin: Clinical and structured assessment of sexual offenders.* New York State Division of Probation and Correctional Alternatives. Retrieved November 2007 from http://dpca.state.ny.us/pdfs/somgmtbulletinmay2007.pdf.

Kunkel, D., Cope-Farrar, K., Biely, E., & Farinola, W. J. M., & Donnerstein, E. (2001, February). *Sex on TV (2): A biennial report to the Kaiser Family Foundation.* Menlo Park, CA: The Henry J. Kaiser Family Foundation.

Kunkel, D., Eyal, K., Finnerty, K., Biely, E., & Donnerstein, E. (2005, November). *Sex on TV (4): 2005: A Kaiser Family Foundation Report.* Menlo Park, CA: The Henry J. Kaiser Family Foundation.

Lahey, B. B., & Waldman, I. D. (2003). A developmental propensity model of the origins of conduct problems during childhood and adolescence. In B. B. Lahey, T. E. Moffit, & A. Caspi (Eds.), *Causes of conduct disorder and juvenile delinquency* (pp. 76–117). New York: Guilford.

Lambert, M. J., & Barley, D. E. (2002). Research summary on the therapeutic relationship and psychotherapy. In J. C. Norcross (Ed.), *Psychotherapy relationships that work: Therapist contributions and responsiveness to patients* (pp. 17–32). New York: Oxford University Press.

Lambert, M. J., & Bergin, A. E. (1993). The effectiveness of psychotherapy. In A. E. Bergin & S. L. Garfield (Eds.), *Handbook of psychotherapy & behavior change* (4th ed.; pp. 143–189). New York: John Wiley.

Lambie, I., & McCarthy, J. (2004). Interviewing strategies with sexually abusive youth. In R. Geffner, K. C. Franey, T. G. Arnold, & R. Falconer (Eds.), *Identifying and treating youth who sexually offend: Current approaches, techniques, and research* (pp. 107–123). Binghamton, NY: Haworth Press.

Langton, C. M., Barbaree, H. E., Harkins, L., Arenovich, T., McNamee, J., Peacock, E. J., et al. (2008). Denial and minimization among sexual offenders: Post-treatment presentation and association with sexual recidivism. *Criminal Justice and Behavior, 35,* 69–98.

Larsson, H., Viding, E., & Plomin, R. (2008). Callous-unemotional traits and antisocial behavior: Genetic, environmental, and early parenting characteristics. *Criminal Justice and Behavior, 35,* 197–211.

Laumann, E. O. (1996). *Early sexual experiences: How voluntary? How violent?* Menlo Park, CA: The Henry J. Kaiser Family Foundation.

LeDoux, J. (2002). *Synaptic self: How our brains become who we are.* New York: Penguin.

Lee, J. K. P., Jackson, H. J., Pattison, P., & Ward, T. (2002). Developmental risk factors for sexual offending. *Child Abuse & Neglect, 26,* 73–92.

Letourneau, E. J., (2003, Summer). Guilt-phase testimony and the ATSA Standards. *The Forum, 15*(3).

Letourneau, E. J. & Miner, M. H. (2005). Juvenile sex offenders: A case against the legal and clinical status quo. *Sexual Abuse: A Journal of Research and Treatment, 17,* 293–312.

Levenson. J. S., & Macgowan, M. J. (2004). Engagement, denial, and treatment progress among sex offenders in group therapy. *Sexual Abuse: A Journal of Research and Treatment, 16,* 49–63.

Lewis, D. O., Shankok, S. S., & Pincus, J. H. (1979). Juvenile male sexual assaulters. *American Journal of Psychiatry, 136,* 1194–1196.

Lewis, D. O., Shankok, S. S., & Pincus, J. H. (1981). Juvenile male sexual assaulters: Psychiatric, neurological, psychoeducational, and abuse factors. In D. O. Lewis (Ed.) *Vulnerabilities to delinquency* (pp. 89–105). Jamaica, NY: Spectrum.

Lewis, M. (1997). *Altering fate: Why the past does not predict the future.* New York: Guilford.

Libbey, H. P. (2004). Measuring student relationships to school: Attachment, binding, connectedness, and engagement. *Journal of School Health, 74,* 274–283.

Lichter, S. R., Lichter, L. S., & Amundson, D. R. (2000, March). *Sexual imagery in popular entertainment.* Washington, DC: Center for Media and Public Affairs.

Lindemann, H. (2005). Sex offender tests- SAI and SAI-Juvenile. In B. K. Schwatrz (Ed.), *The sex offender (Vol. V): Issues in assessment, treatment, and supervision of adult and juvenile populations* (pp. 7.1–7.29). Kingston, NJ: Civic Research Institute.

Lipsey, M. W., & Derzon, J. H. (1998). Predictors of violent and serious delinquency in adolescence and early adulthood: A synthesis of longitudinal research. In R. Loeber & D. P. Farrington (Eds.), *Serious and violent juvenile offenders: Risk factors and successful interventions* (pp. 86–105). Thousand Oaks, CA: Sage.

Litwack, T. R. (2001). Actuarial versus clinical assessments of dangerousness. *Psychology, Public Policy, and Law, 7,* 409–443.

Loding, B. V. (2006). *The relationship between attachment, trauma, and exposure to pornography in juvenile sexual offenders.* Unpublished doctoral dissertation, Clark University, Worcester, MA.

Loeber, R., Pardini, D., Homish, D. L., Wei, E. H., Crawford, A. M., Farrington, D. P., et al. (2005). The prediction of violence and homicide in young men. *Journal of Counseling and Clinical Psychology, 73,* 1074–1088.

Long, L. G., Higgins, P. G., & Brady, D. (1988). *Psychosocial assessment: A pocket guide for data collection.* Norwalk, CT: Appleton & Lange.

Longo, R. E., & Prescott, D. S. (2006). *Current perspectives: Working with sexually aggressive youth and youth with sexual behavior problems.* Holyoke, MA: NEARI Press.

Lukas, S. (1993). *Where to start and what to ask: An assessment handbook.* New York: W. W. Norton.

Lund, C. A. (2000). Predictors of sexual recidivism: Did meta-analysis clarify the role and relevance of denial? *Sexual Abuse: A Journal of Research and Treatment, 12,* 275–287.

Lundberg, G. A. (1941). Case-studies vs. statistical methods—an issue based on misunderstanding. *Sociometry, 4,* 379–383.

Luthar, S. S., Cicchetti, D., & Becker, B. (2000). The construct of resilience: A critical evaluation and guidelines for future work. *Child Development, 71,* 543–562.

Lynam, D. R. (2002). Fledgling psychopathy: A view from personality theory. *Law and Human Behavior, 26,* 255–259.

Lynam, D. R., Loeber, R., & Stouthamer-Loeber, M. (2008). The stability of psychopathy from adolescence into adulthood: The search for moderators. *Criminal Justice and Behavior, 35,* 228–243.

Malamuth, N. M. (2003). Criminal and noncriminal sexual aggressors: Integrating psychopathy into a hierarchical-mediational confluence model. In R. A.

Prentky, E. S. Janus, & M. C. Seto (Eds.), *Sexually coercive behavior: Understanding and management: Vol. 989. Annals of the New York Academy of Sciences* (pp. 33–58). New York: The New York Academy of Sciences.

Margison, F. (2002). Psychodynamic Interpersonal therapy. In J. Holmes & A. Bateman (Eds.), *Integration in psychotherapy: Models and methods* (pp. 107–124). Oxford, England: Oxford University Press.

Marques, J. K., Wiederanders, M., Day, D. M., Nelson, C., & van Ommeren, A. (2005). Effects of a relapse prevention program on sexual recidivism: Final results from California's Sex Offender Treatment and Evaluation Project (SOTEP). *Sexual Abuse: A Journal of Research and Treatment, 17*, 79–107.

Marshall, W. L. (2005). Therapist style in sexual offender treatment: Influence on indices of change. *Sexual Abuse: A Journal of Research and Treatment, 17*, 109–116.

Marshall, W. L. (2006, November). The random controlled trial: Is this the most appropriate approach to evaluating effectiveness in sexual offender treatment? *Nota News, 54*, 5–6.

Marshall, W. L., & Eccles, A. (1993). Pavlovian conditioning processes in adolescent sex offenders. In H. E. Barbaree, W. L. Marshall, & S. M. Hudson (Eds.), *The juvenile sex offender* (pp. 118–142). New York: Guilford.

Marshall, W. L., Serran, G. A., Fernandez, Y. M., Mulloy, R., Mann, R. E., & Thornton, D. (2003). Therapist characteristics in the treatment of sexual offenders: Tentative data on their relationship with indices of behaviour change. *Journal of Sexual Aggression, 9*, 25–30.

Martinez, R., Flores, J., & Rosenfeld, B. (2007). Validity of the Juvenile Sex Offender Assessment Protocol-II in a sample of urban minority youth. *Criminal Justice and Behavior. 34*, 1284–1295.

McCann, J. T. (1998). *Malingering and deception in adolescents: Assessing credibility in clinical and forensic settings.* Washington, DC: American Psychological Association.

McConaughy, S. H. (2005). *Clinical interviews for children and adolescents: Assessment to intervention.* New York: Guilford.

McGrath, R. J., Cummings, G. F., & Burchard, B. L. (2003). *Current practices and trends in sexual abuser management: The Safer Society 2002 nationwide survey.* Brandon, VT: Safer Society Press.

Mediascope Press. (2001). *Issue briefs: Teens, sex & the media.* Studio City, CA: Author.

Medoff, D., & Kinscherff, R. (2006). Forensic evaluation of juvenile sexual offenders. In S. N. Sparta & G. P. Koocher (Eds.), *Forensic mental health assessment of children and adolescents* (pp. 342–364). New York: Oxford University Press.

Meehl, P. E. (1954). *Clinical versus statistical prediction: A theoretical analysis and a review of the literature.* Minneapolis, MN: University of Minnesota Press.

Meehl, P. E. (1956). Symposium of clinical and statistical prediction: The tie that binds. *Journal of Counseling Psychology, 3*, 163–164.

Meehl, P. E. (1957). When shall we use our heads instead of the formula? *Journal of Counseling Psychology, 4*, 268–273.

Meehl, P. E. (1996). *Clinical versus statistical prediction: a theoretical analysis and a review of the literature.* Northvale, NJ: Jason Aronson.

Melton, G. B., Petrila, J., Poythress, N. G., & Slobogin, C. (1997). *Psychological evaluation for the courts* (2nd ed.). New York: Guilford.

Meyers, J. R., & Schmidt, F. (2008). Predictive validity of the Structured Assessment for Violence Risk in Youth (SAVRY) with juvenile sexual offenders. *Criminal Justice and Behavior, 53*, 344–355.

Miccio-Fonseca, L. C., & Rasmussen, L. A. (2006). Creating a new paradigm: Implementing MEGA, a new tool for assessing risk of concern for sexually abusive behavior in youth ages 19 and under. Retrieved February 2006 from California Coalition on Sexual Offending Web site: http://ccoso.org/newsletter/paradigmshift2006.pdf.

Miller, H. A. (2006). A dynamic assessment of offender risk, needs, and strengths in a pre-release sample of general offenders. *Behavioral Sciences and the Law, 24*, 767–782.

Milloy, C. D. (1998). Specialized treatment for juvenile sexual offenders: A closer look. *Journal of Interpersonal Violence, 13*, 653–656.

Mills, J. F. (2005). Advances in the assessment and prediction of interpersonal violence. *Journal of Interpersonal Violence, 20*, 236–241.

Miner, M., Berg, D., & Robinson, B. (2007, November). *Roots of sexual abuse: Results and implications of an application of attachment theory and the Confluence Model.* Presentation at the 26th Conference of the Association for the Treatment of Sexual Abusers, San Diego, CA.

Miner, M., Borduin, C., Prescott, D., Bovensmann, H., Schepklr, R., Du Bois, R., et al. (2006) Standards of care for juvenile sexual offenders of the International Association for the Treatment of Sexual Offenders. *Sexual Offender Treatment, 2*(2). Retrieved December 2007 from http://www.sexual-offender-treatment.org/index.php?id=59&type=123

Miner, M. H. (2004). *Risk for sexual abuse: A study of adolescent offenders.* Grant R49 CE000265 (project period, 8/1/04–7/31/07). Atlanta, GA: National Center for Injury Prevention and Control, Centers for Disease Control and Prevention.

Miner, M. H., & Crimmins, C. L. S. (1997). Adolescent sex offenders: Issues of etiology and risk factors. In B. K. Schwartz & H. R. Cellini (Eds.), *The sex offender (Vol. I): Corrections, treatment and legal practice* (pp. 9.1–9.15). Kingston, NJ: Civic Research Institute.

Miner, M. H., & Munns, R. (2005). Isolation and normlessness: Attitudinal comparisons of adolescent sex offenders, juvenile offenders, and non delinquents. *International Journal of Offender Therapy and Comparative Criminology, 49*, 491–504.

Miner, M. H., & Swinburne-Romine, J. (2004, October). *Understanding child molesting in adolescence: testing attachment-based hypotheses.* Presentation at the 8th International Conference of the International Association for the Treatment of Sexual Offenders, Athens, Greece.

Minuchin, S. (1974). *Families and family therapy*. Cambridge, MA: Harvard University Press.

Moffit. T. E. (2003). Life-course-persistent and adolescence-limited antisocial behavior: A 10-year research review and a research agenda. In B. B. Lahey, T. E. Moffit, & A. Caspi (Eds.), *Causes of conduct disorder and juvenile delinquency* (pp. 49–75). New York: Guilford.

Monahan, J. (1995). *The clinical prediction of violent behavior*. Northvale, NJ: Jason Aronson.

Monahan, J., Steadman, H. J., Appelbaum, P. S., Robbins, P. C., Mulvey, E. P., Silver, E., Roth, L. H., & Grisso. T. (2000). Developing a clinically useful actuarial tool for assessing violence risk. *British Journal of Psychiatry, 176,* 312–319.

Monahan, J., Steadman, H. J., Silver, E., Appelbaum, P. S., Robbins, P. C., Mulvey, E. P., Roth, L. H., Grisso. T., & Banks, S. (2001). *Rethinking risk assessment: The MacArthur study of mental disorder and violence*. New York: Oxford University Press.

Morrison, J. (1995). *The first interview*. New York: Guilford.

Mussack, S. E., & Carich, M. S. (2001). Sexual abuser evaluation. In M. S. Carich & S. E. Mussack (Eds.), *Handbook for sexual abuser assessment and treatment* (pp. 11–36). Brandon, VT: Safer Society Press.

National Task Force on Juvenile Sexual Offending. (1993). The Revised Report on Juvenile Sexual Offending, 1993 of the National Adolescent Perpetration Network. *Juvenile & Family Court Journal, 44,* 1–120.

Nettles, A. M., & Plack, J. H. (1996). Risk, resilience, and development: The multiple ecologies of black adolescents in the United States. In R. J. Haggerty, L. R. Sherrod, N. Garmezy, & M. Rutter (Eds.), *Stress, risk, and resilience in children and adolescents: Processes, mechanisms, and interventions* (pp. 147–181). Cambridge, England: Cambridge University Press.

Nisbett, I. A., Wilson, P. H., & Smallbone, S. W. (2004). A prospective longitudinal study of sexual recidivism among adolescent sex offenders. *Sexual Abuse: A Journal of Research and Treatment, 16,* 223–234.

Nunes, K. L., Hanson, R. K., Firestone, P., Moulden, H. M., Greenberg, D. M., & Bradford, J. M. (2007). Denial predicts recidivism for some sexual offenders. *Sexual Abuse: A Journal of Research and Treatment, 19,* 91–105.

O'Connor, T. G., & Rutter, M. (1996). Risk mechanisms in development: Some conceptual and methodological considerations. *Developmental Psychology, 32,* 787–795.

Office of the Surgeon General. (2001, July). *The Surgeon General's call to action to promote sexual health and responsible sexual behavior*. Rockville, MD: Author.

Olver, M. E., & Wong, S. C. P. (2006). Psychopathy, sexual deviance, and recidivism among sex offenders. *Sexual Abuse: A Journal of Research and Treatment, 18,* 65–82.

Oneal, B. J., Burns, G. L., Kahn, T. J., Rich, P., & Working, J. R. (2008). Initial psychometric properties of a treatment planning and progress inventory for adolescents who sexually abuse. *Sexual Abuse: A Journal of Research and Treatment, 20*, 161–187.

Onifade, E., Davidson, W., Campbell, C., Turke, G., Malinowski, J., & Turner, K. (2008). Predicting recidivism in probationer with the Youth Level of Service Case Management Inventory (YLS/CMI). *Criminal Justice and Behavior, 35*, 474–483.

O'Reilly, G., & Carr, A. (2004). The clinical assessment of young people with sexually abusive behavior. In G. O'Reilly, W. L. Marshall, A. Carr, & R. Beckett (Eds.), *The handbook of clinical intervention with young people who sexually abuse* (pp. 163–190). Hove, England: Brunner-Routledge.

O'Reilly, G., & Carr, A. (2006). Assessment and treatment of criminogenic needs. In H. E. Barbaree, W. L. Marshall (Eds.), *The juvenile sex offender* (2nd ed.; pp. 189–218). New York: Guilford.

Pardini, D. A., & Loeber, R. (2008). Interpersonal callousness trajectories across adolescence: Early social influence and adult outcomes. *Criminal Justice and Behavior, 35*, 173–196.

Parent, A., Teilmann, G., Juul, A. E., Skakkebaek, N. E., Toppari, J., & Bourguignon, J. (2003). The timing of normal puberty and the age limits of sexual precocity: Variations around the world, secular trends, and changes after migration. *Endocrine Reviews, 24*, 668–693.

Parks, G. A., & Bard, D. E. (2006). Risk factors for adolescent sexual offender recidivism: Evaluation of predictive factors and comparison of three groups based on victim type. *Sexual Abuse: A Journal of Research and Treatment, 18*, 319–342.

Passas, N. (1997). Anomie, reference groups, and relative deprivation. In N. Passas & R. Agnew (Eds.), *The future of anomie theory* (pp. 62–94). Boston, MA: Northeastern University Press.

Perry, G. P., & Orchard, J. (1992). *Assessment & treatment of adolescent sex offenders.* Sarasota, FL: Professional Resource Press.

Piaget, J. (1932). *The moral judgment of the child.* New York: Simon & Schuster.

Piaget, J. (1937). *The construction of reality in the child.* New York: Basic Books.

Pithers, W. D., Gray, A., Busconi, A., & Houchens, P. (1998). Children with sexual behavior problems: Identification of five distinct child types and related treatment considerations. *Child Maltreatment, 3*, 384–406.

Pless, I. B., & Stein, R. E. K. (1996). Intervention research: Lessons from research on children with chronic disorders. In R. J. Haggerty, L. R. Sherrod, N. Garmezy, & M. Rutter (Eds.), *Stress, risk, and resilience in children and adolescents: Processes, mechanisms, and interventions* (pp. 317–353). Cambridge, England: Cambridge University Press.

Polaschek, D. L. L., Ward, T., & Hudosn, S. M. (1997). Rape and rapists: Theory and treatment. *Clinical Psychology Review, 17*, 117–144.

Prendergast, W. E. (1993). *The merry-go-round of sexual abuse: identifying and treating survivors.* New York: Haworth Press.

Prentky, R., & Burgess, A. W. (2000). *Forensic management of sexual offenders.* New York: Kluwer Academic/Plenum Press.

Prentky, R., Harris, B., Frizzell, K., & Righthand, S. (2000). An actuarial procedure for assessing risk with juvenile sexual offenders. *Sexual Abuse, 12*, 71–93.

Prentky, R., & Righthand, S. (2003). *Juvenile Sex Offender Assessment Protocol-II: Manual* Office of Juvenile Justice and Delinquency Prevention, Washington, DC. Publication NCJ 202316.

Prentky, R. A. (2006, May). *Risk management of sexually abusive youth: A follow up study*. Washington, DC: U.S. Department of Justice, National Institute of Justice (NCJ 214261). Available at www.ncjrs.gov/pdffiles/nij/grants/214261/pdf.

Prentky, R. A., & Edmunds, S. B. (1997). *Assessing sexual abuse: A resource guide for practitioners*. Brandon, VT: Safer Society Press.

Prentky, R. A., Pimental, A., Cavanaugh, D. J., & Righthand, S. (in press). Predicting risk of sexual recidivism in juveniles: Predictive validity of the J-SOAP-II. In A. R. Beech, L. A. Craig, & K. D. Browne (Eds.), *Assessment and treatment of sexual offenders: A handbook*. Chichester, England: John Wiley.

Prescott, D. S. (2006). *Risk assessment: Theory, controversy, and emerging strategies*. Oklahoma City, OK: Wood N' Barnes.

Prescott, D. S. (2007). Adolescent risk assessment: Practice, policy, language, and ourselves. In M. C. Calder (Ed.), *Working with young children and people who sexually abuse: Taking the field forward* (pp. 134–147). Dorset, England: Russell House.

Print, B., Griffin, H., Beech, A., Quayle, J., Bradshaw, H., Henniker, J., et al. (2007, March). *The AIM2 Model of initial assessment: Guidance document*. (Available from the AIM Project, 14 Carolina Way, Salford M50 2ZY, England).

Proulx, J., Pellerin, B., Paradis, Y., McKibben, A., Aubut, J., & Ouimet, M. (1997). Static and dynamic predictors of recidivism in sexual aggressors. *Sexual Abuse: A Journal of Research and Treatment, 9*, 7–27.

Quinsey, V. L., Harris, G. T., Rice, M. E., & Cormier, C. A. (1998). *Violent offenders: Appraising and managing risk*. Washington, DC: American Psychological Association.

Quinsey, V. L., Harris, G. T., Rice, M. E., & Cormier, C. A. (2006). *Violent offenders: Appraising and managing risk* (2nd ed.). Washington, DC: American Psychological Association.

Rasmussen L. A. (2004). Differentiating youth who sexually abuse: Applying a multidimensional framework when assessing and treating subtypes. In R. Geffner, K. C. Franey, T. G. Arnold, & R. Falconer (Eds.), *Identifying and treating youth who sexually offend: Current approaches, techniques, and research* (pp. 57–82). Binghampton, NY: Haworth Press.

Rasmussen, L. A., & Miccio-Fonseca, L. C. (2007a). Empirically guided practice with young people who sexually abuse: A risk factors approach to assessment and evaluation. In M. C. Calder (Ed.), *Working with young children and people who sexually abuse: Taking the field forward* (pp. 177–200). Dorset, England: Russell House.

Rasmussen, L. A., & Miccio-Fonseca, L. C. (2007b). Paradigm shift: Implementing MEGA, a new tool proposed to define and assess sexually abusive dynamics in youth ages 19 and under. *Journal of Child Sexual Abuse, 16*, 85–106.

Reitzel, L. R., & Carbonell, J. L. (2006). The effectiveness of sexual offender treatment for juveniles as measured by recidivism: A meta-analysis. *Sexual Abuse: A Journal of Research and Treatment, 18*, 401–421.

Rich, P. (2003). *Understanding juvenile sexual offenders: Assessment, treatment, and rehabilitation.* Hoboken, NJ: John Wiley.

Rich, P. (2006). *Attachment and sexual offending: Understanding and applying attachment theory to the treatment of juvenile sexual offenders.* Chichester, England: John Wiley.

Rich, P. (2007a). The implications of attachment theory in the treatment of sexually abusive youth. In M. C. Calder (Ed.), *Working with young children and people who sexually abuse: Taking the field forward* (pp. 201–216). Dorset, England: Russell House.

Rich, P. (2007b). *The Juvenile Risk Assessment Tool.* Barre, MA: Stetson School. Retrieved from www.stetsonschool.org/clinical_materials/assessment_tools/ assessment_tools.html.

Rich, P. (2007c). *The Latency Age-Sexual Adjustment and Assessment Tool.* Barre, MA: Stetson School. Retrieved from www.stetsonschool.org/clinical_materials/ assessment_tools/assessment_tools.html.

Rich, P. (2008, Spring). Sense and sensibility: Our changing approach to the assessment and treatment of sexually abusive youth. *The Forum, 20*(2), 5–12.

Rich, P. (in press). The etiology and treatment of juvenile offending behavior: The complex task of understanding complexity in sexually abusive youth. In J. T. Andrade (Ed.), *Handbook of violence risk assessment and treatment for forensic social workers.* New York: Springer.

Richardson, G. (in press). Sharp practice: The Sexually Harmful Adolescent Risk Protocol. In M. C. Calder (Ed.), *The complete guide to sexual abuse assessments* (2nd ed.). Dorset, England: Russell House Publishing.

Richardson, G., Kelly, T. P., Bhate, S. R., & Graham, F. (1997). Group differences in abuser and abuse characteristics in a British sample of sexually abusive adolescents. *Sexual Abuse: A Journal of Research and Treatment, 9*, 239–257.

Righthand, S. (2005, November). *Juvenile Sex Offense Specific Treatment Needs & Progress Scale.* Retrieved March 2008 from http://www.csom.org/ref/ JSOProgressScale.pdf.

Righthand, S., Prentky, R., Knight, R., Carpenter, E., Hecker, J. E., & Nangle, D. (2005). Factor structure and validation of the Juvenile Sex Offender Assessment Protocol (J-SOAP). *Sexual Abuse: A Journal of Research and Treatment, 17*, 13–30.

Righthand S., & Welch, C. (2001, March). *Juveniles who have sexually offended: A review of the professional literature.* Washington, DC: Office of Juvenile Justice and Delinquency Prevention, U. S. Department of Justice.

Roberts, E. J. (1982). Television and sexual learning in childhood. In D. Pearl (Ed.), *Television and behavior: Ten years of scientific progress and implications for the 80s* (pp. 209–223). Washington, DC: U.S. Government Printing Office.

Rogers, C. R. (1980). *A way of being.* Boston, MA: Houghton Mifflin.

Rogers, R. (2000). The uncritical assessment of risk assessment in forensic practice. *Law and Human Behavior, 24,* 595–605.

Ronis, S. T. & Borduin, C. M. (2007). Individual, family, peer, and academic characteristics of male juvenile sexual offenders. *Journal of Abnormal Child Psychology, 35,* 153–163.

Rutter, M. (1987). Psychosocial resilience and protective mechanisms. *American Journal of Orthopsychiatry, 57,* 316–331.

Rutter, M. (1994). Family discord and conduct disorder: Cause, consequence, or correlate? *Journal of Family Psychology, 8,* 170–186.

Rutter, M. (1996). Stress research: Accomplishments and tasks ahead. In R. J. Haggerty, L. R. Sherrod, N. Garmezy, & M. Rutter (Eds.), *Stress, risk, and resilience in children and adolescents: Processes, mechanisms, and interventions* (pp. 354–385). Cambridge, England: Cambridge University Press.

Rutter, M. (1997). Nature-nurture integration: The example of antisocial behavior. *American Psychologist, 53,* 390–398.

Rutter, M. (2003). Crucial paths from risk to causal mechanisms. In B. B. Lahey, T. E. Moffitt, & A. Caspi (Eds.), *Causes of conduct disorder and juvenile delinquency* (pp. 3–24) New York: Guilford.

Rutter, M., Giller, H., & Hagell, A. (1998). *Antisocial behavior in young people.* Cambridge, England: Cambridge University Press.

Ryan, G. (1999). Treatment of sexually abusive youth: The evolving consensus. *Journal of Interpersonal Violence, 14,* 422–436.

Ryan, G. (2007). Static, stable and dynamic risks and assets relevant to the prevention and treatment of abusive behavior. In M. C. Calder (Ed.), *Working with young children and people who sexually abuse: Taking the field forward* (pp. 161–176). Dorset, England: Russell House.

Ryan, S., Franzetta, K., & Manlove, J. (2005, February). Hispanic teen pregnancy and birth rates: Looking behind the numbers. *Child Trends Research Brief* (publication #2005-01). Washington, DC: Child Trends.

Salekin, R. T., & Lochman, J. E. (2008). Child and, adolescent psychopathy: The search for protective factors. *Criminal Justice and Behavior, 35,* 159–172.

Sarbin, T. R. (1943). A contribution to the study of actuarial and individual methods of prediction. *American Journal of Sociology, 48,* 593–602.

Sarbin, T. R. (1944). The logic of prediction in psychology. *Psychological Review, 51,* 210–228.

Sattler, J. M. (1998). *Clinical and forensic interviewing of children and families: Guidelines for the mental health, education, pediatric, and child maltreatment fields.* La Mesa, CA: Jerome M. Sattler Publisher.

Schank, R. C. (1999). *Dynamic memory revisited.* Cambridge, England: Cambridge University Press.

Seager, J. A., Jellicoe, D., & Dhaliwal, G. K. (2004). Refusers, dropouts, and completers: Measuring sex offender treatment efficacy. *International Journal of Offender Therapy and Comparative Criminology, 49,* 600–612.

Seagrave, D., & Grisso, T. (2002). Adolescent development and the measurement of juvenile psychopathy. *Law and Human Behavior, 26,* 219–239.

Seto, M. C., & Lalumière, M. L. (2006). Conduct problems and juvenile sexual offending. In H. E. Barbaree & W. L. Marshall (Eds.), *The juvenile sex offender* (2nd ed.; pp. 166–188). New York: Guilford.

Seto, M. C., Lalumière, M. L., & Blanchard, R. (2000). The discriminative validity of a phallometric test for pedophilic interests among adolescent sex offenders against children. *Psychological Assessment, 12,* 319–327.

Shea, S. C. (1988). *Psychiatric interviewing: The art of understanding.* Philadelphia: W. B. Saunders.

Shonkoff, J. P., & Phillips, D. A. (2000). *From neurons to neighborhoods: The science of early childhood development.* Report of the Committee on Integrating the Science of Early Childhood Development. Washington, DC: National Academy Press.

Shweder, R. A., Mahapatra, M., & Miller, J. G. (1987). Culture and moral development. In J. Kagan & S. Lamb (Eds.), *The emergence of morality in young children* (pp. 1–83). Chicago, IL: University of Chicago Press.

Sjöstedt, G., & Grann, M. (2002). Risk assessment: What is being predicted by actuarial prediction instruments? *International Journal of Forensic Mental Health, 1,* 179–183.

Smallbone, S. W., Wheaton, J., & Hourigan, D. (2003). Trait empathy and criminal versatility in sexual offenders. *Sexual Abuse: A Journal of Research and Treatment, 15,* 49–60.

Smith, G., & Fischer, L. (1999). Assessment of juvenile sexual offenders: Reliability and validity of the Abel assessment for interest in paraphilias. *Sexual Abuse: A Journal of Research and Treatment, 11,* 207–216.

Smith, G. C. S., & Pell, J. P. (2003). Parachute use to prevent death and major trauma related to gravitational challenge: Systematic review of randomised controlled trials. *BMJ, 327,* 1459–1461.

Snyder, H. N. (2000, July). *Sexual assault of young children as reported to law enforcement: Victim, incident, and offender characteristics.* (NCJ 182990). Washington, DC: Bureau of Justice Statistics.

Snyder, H. N. (2006, December). *OJJDP Juvenile Justice Bulletin: Juvenile Arrests 2004.* Washington, DC: U.S. Department of Justice, Office of Justice Programs.

Snyder, H. N., & Sickmund, M. (2006). *Juvenile offenders and victims: 2006 National Report.* Washington, DC: Department of Justice, Office of Justice Programs, Office of Juvenile Justice and Delinquency.

Snyder, J., Reid, J., & Patterson, G. (2003). A social learning model of child and adolescent antisocial behavior. In B. B. Lahey, T. E. Moffitt, & A. Caspi (Eds.), *Causes of conduct disorder and juvenile delinquency* (pp. 27–48). New York: Guilford.

Sparta, S. N., & Koocher, G. P. (2006). *Forensic mental health assessment of children and adolescents.* New York: Oxford University Press.

Spear, L. P. (2000). The adolescent brain and age-related behavioral manifestations. *Neuroscience and Biobehavioral Reviews, 24,* 417–463.

Spear, L. P. (2003). *The psychobiology of adolescence.* (Working Paper 76–11). New York: Institute for American Values.

Sroufe, L. A., Egeland, B., Carlson, E. A., & Collins, W. A. (2005). *The development of the person: The Minnesota study of risk and adaptation from birth to adulthood.* New York: Guilford.

Steadman, H. J., Silver, E., Monahan J., Appelbaum, P. S., Robbins, P. C., Mulvey, E. P., Grisso, T., Roth, L. H., & Banks, S. (2000). A classification tree approach to the development of actuarial violence risk assessment tools. *Law and Human Behavior, 24,* 83–100.

Steinberg, L. (2003, April). *Less guilty by reason of adolescence: A developmental perspective on adolescence and the law.* Invited Master Lecture, biennial meetings of the Society for Research in Child, Development, Tampa, FL.

Steinberg, L., & Scott, E. S. (2003). Less guilty by reason of adolescence. *American Psychologist, 58,* 1009–1018.

Stilwell, B. M, Galvin, M. R., Kopta, S. M., & Norton, J. A. (1994). Moral-emotional responsiveness, a two factor domain of conscience functioning. *Journal of the American Academy of Child and Adolescent Psychiatry, 33,* 130–139.

Stilwell, B. M., Galvin, M. R., Kopta, S. M., & Padgett, R. J., (1998), Moral volition: the fifth and final domain leading to an integrated theory of conscience understanding. *Journal of the American Academy of Child and Adolescent Psychiatry, 37,* 202–210.

Stilwell, B. M., Galvin, M. R., Kopta, S. M., Padgett, J. R., & Holt, J. W. (1997). Moralization of attachment: A fourth domain of conscience functioning. *Journal of the American Academy of Child and Adolescent Psychiatry, 36,* 1140–1147.

Stouffer, S. A. (1941). Notes on the case-study and unique case. *Sociometry, 4,* 349–357.

Teicher, M. H., et al. (1997) Preliminary evidence for abnormal cortical development in physically and sexually abused children using EEG coherence and MRI. *Annals of the NY Academy of Sciences, 821,* 160–175.

Teicher, M. H., Tomoda, A., & Andersen, S. L. (2006). Neurobiological consequences of early stress and childhood maltreatment: Are results from human and animal studies comparable? *Annals of the NY Academy of Sciences, 1071,* 313–323.

Thakker, J., Ward, T., & Tidmarsh, R. (2006). A reevalaution of relapse prevention with adolescents who sexually offend: A Good-Lives model. In H. E. Barbaree & W. L. Marshall (Eds.), *The juvenile sexual offender* (2nd ed.; pp. 313–335). New York: Guilford.

Thomas, J., & Viar, C. W. (2001). Family treatment of adult sexual abusers. In M. S. Carich & S. E. Mussack (Eds.), *Handbook for sexual abuser assessment and treatment* (pp. 163–192). Brandon, VT: Safer Society Press.

Thornton, D. (2002). Constructing and testing a framework for dynamic risk assessment. *Sexual Abuse: A Journal of Research and Treatment, 14,* 139–153.

Thornton, D. (2006). Age and sexual recidivism: A variable connection. *Sexual Abuse: A Journal of Research and Treatment, 18,* 123–135.

Turner, S. M., DeMers, S. T., Fox, H. R., & Reed, G. M. (2001). APA's guidelines for test user qualifications: An executive summary. *American Psychologist, 56,* 1099–1113.

U.S. Department of Health and Human Services (2001). *Youth Violence: A report of the Surgeon General.* Rockville, MD: Author.

U.S. Department of Justice. (2006). *Crime in the United States 2005.* Washington, DC: Author.

U.S. Department of Justice. (2007). *Crime in the United States 2006.* Washington, DC: Author.

van Wijk, A., Vermeiren, R., Loeber, Hart-kerkhoffs, L., & Bullens, R. (2006). Juvenile sex offenders compared to non-sex offenders: A review of the literature 1995–2005. *Trauma, Violence, & Abuse, 7,* 227–243.

Varker, T., Devilly, G. J., Ward, T., & Beech, A. R. (2008). Empathy and adolescent sexual offenders: A review of the literature. *Aggression and Violent Behavior, 13,* 251–260.

Vetlesen, A. J. (1994). *Perception, empathy, and judgment: An inquiry into the preconditions of moral performance.* University Park: Pennsylvania University Press.

Viljoen, J. L., Scalora, M., Cuadra, L., Bader, S., Chávez, V., Ullman, D., et al. (2008). Assessing risk for violence in adolescents who have sexually offended: A comparison of the J-SOAP-II, JSORRAT-II, and SAVRY. *Criminal Justice and Behavior, 35,* 5–23.

Vitacco, M. J., Rogers, R., & Neumann, C. S. (2003), The Antisocial Process Screening Device: An examination of its construct and criterion-related validity. *Assessment, 10,* 143–150.

Von Bertalanffy, L. (1976). *General System Theory: Foundations, development, application* (revised ed.). New York: George Braziller.

Wachs, T. D. (1996). Known and potential processes underlying developmental trajectories in childhood and adolescence. *Developmental Psychology, 32,* 796–801.

Waite, D., Keller, A., McGarvey, E. L., Wieckowski, E., Pinkerton, R., & Brown, G. L. (2005). Juvenile sex offender re-arrest rates for sexual, violent nonsexual and property crimes: A 10-year follow-up. *Sexual Abuse: A Journal of Research and Treatment, 17,* 313–331.

Ward, T., Bickley, J., Webster, S. D., Fisher, D., Beech, A., & Eldridge, H. (2004). *The Self-Regulation Model of the Offense and Relapse Process: A Manual: Volume I: Assessment.* Victoria, BC: Pacific Psychological Assessment Corporation.

Ward, T., Gannon, T. A., & Birgden, A. (2007). Human rights and the assessment and treatment of sexual offenders. *Sexual Abuse: A Journal of Research and Treatment, 19,* 195–216.

Ward, T., & Hudson, S. M. (2000). Sexual offenders' implicit planning: A conceptual model. *Sexual Abuse: A Journal of Research and Treatment, 12,* 189–202.

Ward, T., Mann, R. E., & Gannon, T. A. (2007). The good lives model of offender rehabilitation: Clinical implications. *Aggression and Violent Behavior, 12,* 87–107.

Warner, M. S. (1997). Does empathy cure? A theoretical consideration of empathy, processing, and personal narrative. In A. C. Bohart & L. S. Greenberg (Eds.),

Empathy reconsidered: New directions in psychotherapy (pp. 125–140). Washington, DC: American Psychological Association.

Webster, S. D., Mann, R. E., Carter, A. J., Long, J., Milner, R. J., O'Brien, M. D., et al. (2006). Inter-rater reliability of dynamic risk assessment with sexual offenders. *Psychology, Crime & Law, 12,* 439–452.

Webster, C. D., Douglas, K. S., Eaves, D., & Hart, S. D. (1997). *HCR-20: Assessing risk for violence.* Burnaby, British Columbia, Canada: The Mental Health, Law, & Policy Institute, Simon Fraser University.

Weinrott, M. R. (1996, June). *Juvenile sexual aggression: A critical review* (Center Paper 005). Boulder, CO: University of Colorado, Center for the Study and Prevention of Violence.

Welldon, E. V. (1997). Forensic psychotherapy: The practical approach. In E. V. Welldon & C. VanVelsen (Eds.), *A practical guide to forensic psychotherapy* (13–19). London: Jessica Kingsley Publishers.

Werner, E. E., & Smith, R. S. (1992). *Overcoming the odds: High risk children from birth to adulthood.* Ithaca, NY: Cornell University Press.

Werner, E. E., & Smith, R. S. (2001). *Journeys from childhood to midlife: Risk, resilience, and recovery.* Ithaca, NY: Cornell University Press.

Wettstein, R. M. (2005). Quality and quality improvement in forensic mental health evaluations. *Journal of the American Academy of Psychiatry and the Law, 33,* 158–175.

Whitehead, P. R., Ward, T., & Collie, R. M. (2007). Time for a change: Applying the Good Lives Model of rehabilitation to a high-risk violent offender. *International Journal of Offender Therapy and Comparative Criminology, 51,* 578–598.

Wikström, P., & Sampson, R. J. (2003). Social mechanisms of community influences on crime and pathways in criminality. In B. B. Lahey, T. E. Moffitt, & A. Caspi (Eds.), *Causes of conduct disorder and juvenile delinquency* (pp. 118–148). New York: Guilford.

Will, D. (1999). Assessment issues. In M. Erooga & H. Masson (Eds.), *Children and young people who sexually abuse others: Challenges and responses* (pp. 86–103). London: Routledge.

Witt, P. H. (2000). A practitioner's view of risk assessment: The HCR-20 and the SVR-20. *Behavioral Sciences and the Law, 18,* 791–798.

World Health Organization. (2004). ICD-10: International Statistical Classification of Diseases and Related Health Problems (10th revision, 2nd ed.). Geneva, Switzerland: Author.

Worling, J. R. (2001). Personality-based typology of adolescent male sexual offenders: Difference in recidivism rates, victim-selection characteristics, and personal victimization histories. *Sexual Abuse: A Journal of Research and Treatment, 13,* 149–166.

Worling, J. R. (2004). The Estimate of Risk of Adolescent Sexual Offense Recidivism (ERASOR): Preliminary psychometric data. *Sexual Abuse: A Journal of Research and Treatment, 16,* 235–254.

Worling, J. R. (2006a). Assessing sexual arousal with adolescent males who have offended sexually: Self-report and unobtrusively measured viewing time. *Sexual Abuse: A Journal of Research and Treatment, 18,* 383–400.

Worling, J. R. (2006b). *Coding examples for the ERASOR*. Ontario, Canada: The Sexual Abuse Family Education & Treatment (SAFE-T) Program.

Worling, J. R., & Curwen, T. (2000). Adolescent sexual offender recidivism: Success of specialized treatment and implications for risk prediction. *Child Abuse & Neglect, 24,* 965–982.

Worling, J. R., & Curwen, T. (2001). Estimate of Risk of Adolescent Sexual Offense Recidivism. In M. C. Calder (Ed.), *Juveniles and children who sexually abuse: Frameworks for assessment* (pp. 372–397). Lyme Regis, U.K.: Russell House Publishing.

Worling, J. R., & Långström, N. (2003). Assessment of criminal recidivism risk with adolescents who have offended sexually. *Trauma, Violence, and Abuse, 4,* 341–362.

Worling, J. R., & Långström, N. (2006). Risk of sexual recidivism in adolescents who sexually offend. In H. E. Barbaree & W. L. Marshall (Eds.), *The Juvenile Sexual Offender* (2nd ed.; pp. 219–247). New York: Guilford.

Yurgelun-Todd, D. (2002). *Inside the Teenage Brain*. Retrieved December 2004 from http://www.pbs.org/wgbh/pages/frontline/shows/teenbrain/interviews/

Yurgelun-Todd, D. (2007). Emotional and cognitive changes during adolescence. *Current Opinion in Neurobiology, 17,* 251–257.

Zimring, F. E. (2004). *An American travesty: Legal responses to adolescent sexual offending*. Chicago, IL: University of Chicago Press.

Zolondek, S. C., Abel, G. G., Northey, W. F., & Jordan, A. D. (2001). The self-reported behaviors of juvenile sexual offenders. *Journal of Interpersonal Violence, 16,* 73–85.

AUTHOR INDEX

SUBJECT INDEX